Crime and the Media

Edited by
Richard V. Ericson
Green College, The University of British Columbia

Dartmouth
Aldershot · Brookfield USA · Singapore · Sydney

© Richard V. Ericson 1995. For copyright of individual articles please refer to the Acknowledgements.

All rights reserved. No part of this publication may be reproduced, stored in a retrieval system, or transmitted in any form or by any means, electronic, mechanical, photocopying, recording, or otherwise without the prior permission of Dartmouth Publishing Company Limited.

Published by
Dartmouth Publishing Company Limited
Gower House
Croft Road
Aldershot
Hants GU11 3HR
England

Dartmouth Publishing Company
Old Post Road
Brookfield
Vermont 05036
USA

British Library Cataloguing in Publication Data
Crime and the Media. – (International
Library of Criminology, Criminal Justice
& Penology)
I. Ericson, Richard V. II. Series
364.254

Library of Congress Cataloging-in-Publication Data
Crime and the media / edited by Richard V. Ericson.
    p. cm. — (International library of criminology, criminal justice and penology)
  Includes bibliographical references.
  ISBN 1-85521-433-4
  1. Crime in mass media. 2. Crime and the press. I. Ericson, Richard Victor. II. Series.
P96.C74C75 1995
364—dc20
                                                                                         94–39203
                                                                                           CIP

ISBN 1 85521 433 4

Printed and bound by Athenaeum Press, Ltd.,
Gateshead, Tyne & Wear.

Crime and the Media

The International Library of Criminology, Criminal Justice and Penology
Series Editors: Gerald Mars and David Nelken

Titles in the Series:

The Origins and Growth of Criminology
Piers Beirne

Comparative Criminology
Piers Beirne and David Nelken

The Psychology and Psychiatry of Crime
David Canter

Correctional Rehabilitation
Francis Cullen and Brandon K. Applegate

Crime and the Media
Richard V. Ericson

Psychological Explanations of Crime
David P. Farrington

Terrorism
Conor Gearty

Criminal Careers, Vols I & II
David F. Greenberg

Social Control: Aspects of Non-State Justice
Stuart Henry

Professional Criminals
Dick Hobbs

Crime, Deviance and the Computer
Richard Hollinger

Race, Crime and Justice
Barbara Hudson

Fraud: Organization, Motivation and Control
Michael Levi

Violence
Michael Levi

Street Crime
Mike Maguire

Occupational Crime
Gerald Mars

Theoretical Traditions in Criminology
Ross Matsueda

The Sociology of Punishment
Dario Melossi

Gender, Crime and Feminism
Ngaire Naffine

White-Collar Crime
David Nelken

Organized Crime
Nikos Passas

Criminal Statistics: Their Use and Abuse
Kenneth Pease

Police, Vols & II
Robert Reiner

Victimology
Paul Rock

Criminal Policy Making
Andrew Rutherford

Prosecution in Common Law Jurisdictions
Andrew Sanders

Drugs, Crime and Criminal Justice, Vols I & II
Nigel South

Youth Crime, Deviance and Delinquency, Vols I & II
Nigel South

Rape and the Criminal Justice System
Jenny Temkin

The Sentencing Process
Martin Wasik

Sex Crimes
Donald West

Contents

Acknowledgements	vii
Series Preface	ix
Introduction	xi

PART I MEDIA FORMATS AND FUN

1. Richard V. Ericson, Patricia M. Baranek and Janet B.L. Chan (1991), 'Media and Markets' in their *Representing Order: Crime, Law and Justice in the News Media*, Milton Keynes: Open University Press, pp. 20–49. — 3
2. Susan J. Drucker (1989), 'The Televised Mediated Trial: Formal and Substantive Characteristics', *Communication Quarterly*, **37**, pp. 305–18. — 33
3. Jack Katz (1987), 'What Makes Crime "News"?', *Media, Culture and Society*, **9**, pp. 47–75. — 47
4. Robert P. Snow (1994), 'Media and Social Order in Everyday Life', in Meryl Aldridge and Nicholas Hewitt (eds), *Controlling Broadcasting*, Manchester: University of Manchester Press, pp. 34–49. — 77

PART II INSTITUTIONAL RELATIONS AND FOLLY

5. Philip Schlesinger, Howard Tumber and Graham Murdock (1991), 'The Media Politics of Crime and Criminal Justice', *British Journal of Sociology*, **42**, pp. 397–420. — 95
6. Mark Fishman (1981), 'Police News: Constructing an Image of Crime', *Urban Life*, **9**, pp. 371–94. — 119
7. James D. Orcutt and J. Blake Turner (1993), 'Shocking Numbers and Graphic Accounts: Quantified Images of Drug Problems in the Print Media', *Social Problems*, **40**, pp. 190–206. — 143
8. Julian V. Roberts and Anthony N. Doob (1990), 'News Media Influences on Public Views of Sentencing', *Law and Human Behavior*, **14**, pp. 451–68. — 161
9. Shanto Iyengar (1991), 'Effects of Framing on Attributions of Responsibility for Crime and Terrorism', in his *Is Anyone Responsible? How Television Frames Political Issues*, Chicago: University of Chicago Press, pp. 26–46. — 179

PART III POPULAR DRAMA AND FEAR

10   Joel Best and Gerald T. Horiuchi (1985), 'The Razor Blade in the Apple: The Social Construction of Urban Legends', *Social Problems*, **32**, pp. 488–99.   203

11   Gray Cavender and Lisa Bond-Maupin (1993), 'Fear and Loathing on Reality Television: An Analysis of "America's Most Wanted" and "Unsolved Mysteries"', *Sociological Inquiry*, **63**, pp. 305–17.   215

12   Mica Nava (1988), 'Cleveland and the Press: Outrage and Anxiety in the Reporting of Child Sexual Abuse', *Feminist Review*, **28**, pp. 103–21.   229

13   Barrie Gunter (1987), 'Television and Perceptions of Crime: The British Experience', in his *Television and the Fear of Crime*, London: John Libbey, pp. 67–89.   249

14   Richard Sparks (1992), 'Television, Dramatization and the Fear of Crime', in his *Television and the Drama of Crime: Moral Tales and the Place of Crime in Public Life*, Milton Keynes: Open University Press, pp. 78–101.   273

PART IV POLITICAL SPECTACLE AND FAKE

15   David L. Altheide (1993), 'Electronic Media and State Control: The Case of Azscam', *The Sociological Quarterly*, **34**, pp. 53–69.   299

16   Joshua Meyrowitz (1994), 'The (Almost) Invisible Candidate: A Case Study in News Judgement as Political Censorship', in M. Aldridge and N. Hewitt (eds), *Controlling Broadcasting*, Manchester: University of Manchester Press, pp. 93–107.   317

17   Thomas Mathiesen (1987), 'The Eagle and the Sun: On Panoptical Systems and Mass Media in Modern Society' in J. Lowman, R. Menzies and T. Palys (eds), *Transcarceration: Essays in the Sociology of Social Control*, Aldershot: Gower, pp. 59–76.   333

18   Nicola A. Lisus and Richard V. Ericson (1995), 'Misplacing Memory: The Effect of Television Format on Holocaust Remembrance', *British Journal of Sociology*, **46**, pp. 1–19.   351

PART V BUSINESS COMMODIFICATION AND FETISH

19   Joseph R. Gusfield (1989), 'Constructing the Ownership of Social Problems: Fun and Profit in the Welfare State', *Social Problems*, **36**, pp. 431–41.   373

20   Steven Spitzer (1987), 'Security and Control in Capitalist Societies: The Fetishism of Security and the Secret Thereof', in J. Lowman, R. Menzies and T. Palys (eds), *Transcarceration: Essays in the Sociology of Social Control*, Aldershot: Gower, pp. 43–61.   385

21   Howard Tumber (1993), '"Selling Scandal": Business and the Media', *Media, Culture and Society*, **15**, pp. 345–61.   405

Name Index   423

Acknowledgements

The editor and publishers wish to thank the following for permission to use copyright material.

Avebury for the essays: Thomas Mathiesen (1987), 'The Eagle and the Sun: On Panoptical Systems and Mass Media in Modern Society', in J. Lowman, R. Menzies and T. Palys (eds), *Transcarceration: Essays in the Sociology of Social Control*, pp. 59–76; Steven Spitzer (1987), 'Security and Control in Capitalist Societies: The Fetishism of Security and the Secret Thereof', in J. Lowman, R. Menzies and T. Palys (eds), *Transcarceration: Essays in the Sociology of Social Control*, pp. 43–61.

British Journal of Sociology for the essay: Nicola A. Lisus and Richard V. Ericson (1995), 'Misplacing Memory: The Effect of Television Format on Holocaust Remembrance', *British Journal of Sociology*, **46**, pp. 1–19.

Eastern Communication Association for the essay: Susan J. Drucker (1989), 'The Televised Mediated Trial: Formal and Substantive Characteristics', *Communication Quarterly*, **37**, pp. 305–18.

Joshua Meyrowitz (1994), 'The (Almost) Invisible Candidate: A Case Study in News Judgement as Political Censorship', in Meryl Aldridge and Nicholas Hewitt (eds), *Controlling Broadcasting*, Manchester University Press, pp. 93–108. Copyright © 1994 Joshua Meyrowitz.

Mica Nava (1988), 'Cleveland and the Press: Outrage and Anxiety in the Reporting of Child Sexual Abuse', *Feminist Review*, **28**, pp. 103–21. Copyright © Mica Nava.

Midwest Sociological Society for the essay: David L. Altheide (1993), 'Electronic Media and State Control: The Case of Azscam', *The Sociological Quarterly*, **34**, pp. 53–69.

Open University Press for the essay: Richard Sparks (1992), 'Television, Dramatization and the Fear of Crime', in *Television and the Drama of Crime: Moral Tales and the Place of Crime in Public Life*, pp. 78–101.

Plenum Publishing Corporation for the essay: Julian V. Roberts and Anthony N. Doob (1990), 'News Media Influences on Public Views of Sentencing', *Law and Human Behavior*, **14**, pp. 451–68.

Routledge for the essay: Philip Schlesinger, Howard Tumber and Graham Murdock (1991), 'The Media Politics of Crime and Criminal Justice', *British Journal of Sociology*, **42**, pp. 397–420.

Sage Publications Limited UK for the essays: Jack Katz (1987), 'What Makes Crime "News"?', *Media, Culture and Society*, **9**, pp. 47–75. Copyright © 1987 Sage Publications Ltd. Howard Tumber (1993), '"Selling Scandal": Business and the Media', *Media, Culture and Society*, **15**, pp. 345–61. Copyright © 1993 Sage Publications Ltd.

Sage Publications US for the essay: Mark Fishman (1981), 'Police News: Constructing an Image of Crime', *Urban Life*, **9**, pp. 371–94.

Social Problems for the essays: James D. Orcutt and J. Blake Turner (1993), 'Shocking Numbers and Graphic Accounts: Quantified Images of Drug Problems in the Print Media', *Social Problems*, **40**, pp. 190–206; Joel Best and Gerald T. Horiuchi (1985), 'The Razor Blade in the Apple: The Social Construction of Urban Legends', *Social Problems*, **32**, pp. 488–99; Joseph R. Gusfield (1989), 'Constructing the Ownership of Social Problems: Fun and Profit in the Welfare State', *Social Problems*, **36**, pp. 431–41.

The University of Chicago Press for the essay: Shanto Iyengar (1991), 'Effects of Framing on Attributions of Responsibility for Crime and Terrorism', in *Is Anyone Responsible? How Television Frames Political Issues*, pp. 26–46. The University of Chicago Press.

The University of Texas Press for the essay: Gray Cavender and Lisa Bond-Maupin (1993), 'Fear and Loathing on Reality Television: An Analysis of "America's Most Wanted" and "Unsolved Mysteries"', *Sociological Inquiry*, **63**, pp. 305–17. By permission of the author and the University of Texas Press.

The University of Toronto Press, Canada and The Open University Press U.K. for the essay: Richard V. Ericson, Patricia M. Baranek and Janet B.L. Chan (1991), 'Media and Markets', in *Representing Order: Crime, Law and Justice in the News Media*, pp. 20–49. By permission of the University of Toronto Press, Toronto, Canada, and the Open University Press, Milton Keynes, U.K.

Every effort has been made to trace all the copyright holders, but if any have been inadvertently overlooked the publishers will be pleased to make the necessary arrangement at the first opportunity.

Series Preface

The International Library of Criminology, Criminal Justice and Penology, represents an important publishing initiative designed to bring together the most significant journal essays in contemporary criminology, criminal justice and penology. The series makes available to researchers, teachers and students an extensive range of essays which are indispensable for obtaining an overview of the latest theories and findings in this fast changing subject.

This series consists of volumes dealing with criminological schools and theories as well as with approaches to particular areas of crime, criminal justice and penology. Each volume is edited by a recognised authority who has selected twenty or so of the best journal articles in the field of their special competence and provided an informative introduction giving a summary of the field and the relevance of the articles chosen. The original pagination is retained for ease of reference.

The difficulties of keeping on top of the steadily growing literature in criminology are complicated by the many disciplines from which its theories and findings are drawn (sociology, law, sociology of law, psychology, psychiatry, philosophy and economics are the most obvious). The development of new specialisms with their own journals (policing, victimology, mediation) as well as the debates between rival schools of thought (feminist criminology, left realism, critical criminology, abolitionism etc.) make necessary overviews that offer syntheses of the state of the art. These problems are addressed by the INTERNATIONAL LIBRARY in making available for research and teaching the key essays from specialist journals.

GERALD MARS
Visiting Professor in Applied Anthropology, University of Bradford School of Management

DAVID NELKEN
Visiting Professor of Law (Criminology), University College London

Introduction

Cultures, Communications and Effects

Mass media consume our lives. Mass media consumption is not only the primary leisure activity of most people, it is part of the rhythms and rituals of everyday life.

A great deal of what is consumed and made integral to daily life are stories of crime, law and justice. The majority of news items focus on crime and other forms of human transgression (Graber 1980; Ericson, Baranek and Chan 1987, 1989, 1991). Crime and law enforcement are the main themes in one-third or more of television prime-time entertainment programming (Williams 1976; Dominick 1973; Graber 1980; Sparks 1992). In addition, crime and law enforcement activities occur regularly in programmes that are not primarily crime dramas.

The centrality of crime and law enforcement in the mass media results in an omnipresent public discourse about disorder and decline. Crime in the mass media becomes a metaphor for disorder and decline in society more generally, generating the urge for more order and security.

There is nothing new about crime and law enforcement being used in public culture to shape sensibilities about social order. Violence as entertainment preceded the advent of television by centuries (Elias 1978). There is a long history of using public dramas of punishment to constitute political authority (Erikson 1966; Hay 1975; Schattenburg 1981; Beattie 1986; Garland 1990). There is also a long history of using the public media to construct demons and enemies (Erikson 1966; Cohen 1972; Christie 1986; Edelman 1988) and to express 'respectable fears' (Pearson 1983) about them. The variation is in the media of public expression, not in the role of crime and punishment to give expression to sensibilities of disorder and decline. Today the dominant medium is television, augmented by radio, magazines, newspapers, novels and social science publications.

In the process of communicating this discourse of disorder and decline, the mass media become part of the discourse. That is, the mass media institution itself is seen as contributing to disorder and decline. In many instances – such as the work of moral campaigners like Mary Whitehouse or that of some media effects researchers (e.g. Berkowitz 1970; Liebert and Baron 1972; Tannenbaum and Zillman 1975; Parke et al. 1977) – the mass media are essentialized as *the* cause of disorder and decline. They are associated with the low culture and low life of crime and deviance, in contradistinction to an imagined high culture and better life.

In debates about crime in the mass media, both crime and the medium become a means of articulating moral sensibilities, tastes and distinctions (Bourdieu 1986). For example, while some find the depictions of violence in police crime dramas sordid and offensive, they have no similar qualms about the televised version of the Agatha Christie *Miss Marple* stories. These stories are unlikely to disturb moral sensibilities because they are mainly about the social sensibilities – the rituals, procedures and institutions – of the higher orders. As Williams (1989: 69–72) commented about such stories, it is 'never really the question of who done it. ... The effective and covert interest was in how it was done: a repertory of methods of killing which have been made to consort, very comfortably, with afternoon tea, residential villages, cricket and a classical education.'

Thus respectable fears about crime are coupled with respectable fears about the negative effects of mass media, especially of television, which is the dominant medium of our time. It is in this sense that one can speak of 'the crimes of mass media'. Crime is the predominant focus in mass media discourse on disorder and decline. But the mass media, and especially television, are also seen as a 'crime': as immoral, as upsetting rule-governed order, and as deconstructing hierarchy and authority. I am not referring to the criminogenic effects of the mass media in the narrow sense, which is the focus of public debate on the issue as well as most of the academic research literature (e.g. Rowland 1983; Gunter 1987). Rather, 'the crimes of mass media' become part of a more general concern about culture and communication. In this view, the disorder and decline potential of crime in the mass media is actually much more pervasive than simply leading some peculiar people to be more violent or to adopt a violent sensibility. Crime in the mass media articulates the most fundamental concern about the integrity and future of culture.

What are the 'crimes' of the mass media seen in these forms? First, there is the belief that the mass media and especially television are only able to provide *fun*. They entertain but do not educate: they dull the mind, induce laziness, foster political alienation and produce cultural dopes. In leading us to 'amuse ourselves to death' (Postman 1985), they are as harmful as other 'crimes' such as drug abuse. Second, there is the belief that the mass media are organized in such a way that they inevitably produce distorted knowledge or *folly*. For example, the politics of knowledge between journalists and their sources inevitably results in knowledge that is manipulated and self-interested, and therefore rarely a basis for rational action. A third 'crime' of the mass media is that its crime stories induce *fear*. This fear also leads to irrational action with major social consequences, for example distrust, social distance, privatized and individualized lifestyles, and lack of community. Fourth, mass media crime stories simulate reality in ways which make everything seem *fake*. Faking yields a sense of inauthenticity, lack of context or history, and a decline in hierarchical order. Fifth, the mass media commodify crime prevention and security products in the same way that they commodify toothpaste or a pop star, to the point of *fetish*. The result is that security products become as much a part of consumer style as any other product, with implications for social relations and individual identities. Fun, folly, fear, fake and fetish – these are the crimes of mass media.

How do mass media researchers explain each of these 'crimes' of the mass media? The explanations are largely focused on what aspects of culture and communication are highlighted by particular researchers, where culture is the contexts in which meaningful expressions are produced and received, and communication is the forms and technologies in which meaningful expressions are produced and received. As summarized in the table below, those who emphasize the effect of fun tend to focus on the culture of the particular formats of communication that are more entertaining than educational. Those who concern themselves with the effect of folly explain this in terms of the institutional arrangements of media operatives and their sources, and the peculiar communicative relations fostered by these arrangements. Researchers concerned with the effect of fear look primarily to the ways in which crime stories appeal to popular culture, and need for them to be dramatized to sustain their popular appeal.

Researchers who analyse how mass media representations of crime, law and justice are fake tend to focus on political culture and the need to display authority through spectacles. Finally, those who analyse fetishes about crime and security examine business culture and its penchant for commodification. Obviously, the relations among culture, communication and effect summarized in the table are simplified for heuristic purposes. In the everyday representation of crime, law and justice in the mass media, of course, all of these aspects of culture, communication and effect interact simultaneously.

Crimes of the Mass Media: A Model

Cultures	*Communications*	*Effects*
Media	Formats	Fun
Institutional	Relations	Folly
Popular	Drama	Fear
Political	Spectacle	Fake
Business	Commodification	Fetish

Media Formats and Fun

Communication media themselves constitute a culture because they provide contexts in which meaningful expressions are produced and received. A medium arranges, defines and communicates meaning. As such it has a significant bearing on formats or the logic of how subject matter is presented. Media formats establish grammatical rules regarding syntax (organization) and inflection (rhythm and tempo). Since these rules vary for newspapers, television and radio, each medium differs in how it selects and transmits knowledge. Each medium also differs in how it transcends time and space to make knowledge available, thereby creating a different social environment and context for thinking. Format differences thus produce variation in content and, ultimately, different consequences for the knowledge structure of society (Altheide 1985; Meyrowitz 1985; Crisell 1986; Ericson, Baranek and Chan 1991).

The reality of the content of each medium is a matter of *how* it presents knowledge in its established formats, rather than of *what* it presents. Content must always fit the format and therefore is always secondary to format. Moreover, reception of mass media subject matter is also governed by formats. 'Audience members claim to know instinctively when they see and hear something that can be defined as entertainment, news, historical documentary, and other frameworks, but they commonly explain these definitions as a function of content rather than form. Our position is just the opposite. People draw upon various forms to make sense of various kinds of experience. People interpret or make sense of phenomena through familiar forms. At that point context is established. It follows that our concern is to ascertain the various standardized features of these forms' (Altheide and Snow 1991: 18–19).

Media formats influence each other. Among contemporary news media, for example, television formats dominate and thus have fundamentally affected radio and newspaper formats. It is television in particular which drives all media in the direction of entertainment and fun.

In order to engage an audience at all – even regarding the *fait divers* of news – the subject matter must be presented in a dramatized, personalized, simplified, episodic, visually-appealing and jolt-like manner. Crime stories must be enjoyable, a diversion, fun. They must provide 'disreputable pleasures' (Hagan 1984).

The public and experts continually fret that we are 'amusing ourselves to death' (Postman 1985) on televised scenes of violence available around the clock. There is a concern that this fare inures people to human suffering, triggers crime, distorts social and political issues, trivializes serious problems and fosters a trained incapacity for any action beyond being a couch potato and consuming more. Fun is said to foster all of the other ill-effects attributed to crime in the mass media: folly, fear, fake and fetish are accentuated in a world of disreputable pleasures.

In Chapter 1, Ericson et al. initially specify the distinctive medium format differences among newspapers, radio and television and how these bear upon news of crime, law and justice. They then consider 'popular' and 'quality' market differences in format and their influence on news. 'Popular' media create a sense of being close to reality through an entertaining and lively presentation that includes iconic elements (e.g. television visuals, newspaper still pictures), brief items on simple themes, strongly opinionated items, colloquial expressions and parochial interests. 'Quality' media use more 'literary' and abstract means, such as longer items, features, continuing stories on complex issues, and close attention to language and to mechanisms for correcting errors that exude accuracy and authority. Newspapers are most able to sustain popular and quality alternatives, although the effect of television on newspaper formats is bringing the two closer together (Smith 1980). Radio also has a capacity to maintain popular/quality distinctions (Crisell 1986). On the other hand and in spite of the cable system move to 'narrowcasting', television is dominated by a 'popular' format because of its overwhelming visual, realistic, dramatic, entertaining and simplifying features. While newspapers and radio stations are able to maintain popular/quality distinctions to a degree and thereby engage competing parts of a market, television stations form the marketplace itself in the sense that competition is for a share of the total audience – people with their television sets on during a time segment – rather than for a share of a more specialized or narrow market.

The theme in Ericson et al.'s work is that 'crime' is something that is 'made' according to institutional classifications and communication formats. Hence, 'crime' looks different and means different things in popular and quality newspapers, radio and television (and in novels, law reports, films, social science journals, the book you are reading, etc.). When reporting on the same crime event, for example, each distinctive news medium and market format combination yields a distinctive account of the event. The interpretive process among sources, journalists and audience members is also different in each case.

In Chapter 2, Susan Drucker analyses the communication formats used in courtroom trials compared to televised trials and to trials that are dramatized as television entertainment programming. Each way of communicating the law has a distinctive format which yields different knowledge and effects. Compared to a trial confined to the 'live theatre' of the courtroom, the televised trial stresses personalities; extra-legal 'witnessing' and opinions; grammatical rules of media formats over legal rules of procedure, and public 'appearance' over legal evidence and burden of proof. Information about the trial is also interspersed with other information such as deodorant and condom commercials and news briefs.

Compared to the televised trial, dramatized trials as entertainment allow even further intervention by television formats. The courtroom becomes a stage designed to accommodate the needs of the camera (e.g. control over pacing, multi-shot techniques and shot variety). Without specific reporting purposes, dramatization can be intensified: the story is told on television time rather than on the legal system's time, and performers can offer embellishments not available to courtroom celebrities in actual cases who must fit their performances to legal discourse. Consistent with the view that format precedes content, Drucker's main point is that what trials are is inseparable from how they are mediated. Moreover, television mediation, driven by the need to be fun, has a number of potentially negative effects on the legal process including, for example, invasion of privacy of legal participants, prejudicing trials and producing 'public opinion verdicts'.

In 'What Makes Crime "News"?' Jack Katz asks 'What are the distinctive aspects of form or content that make daily news reports of crime continuously interesting to the modern public?' His search for an answer begins with the observation that crime news addresses four classic moral problematics: individual moral character (e.g. individual moral competence), community moral character (e.g. collective integrity), political morality (e.g. the criminalization of acts such as terrorism) and organizational morality (e.g. white-collar crime). It is these moral problematics which provide the fascination (fun) of crime stories, in addition to the specifics of how such stories are formatted in an interesting manner.

The fascination or fun combines with the moral puzzles on offer to yield sensibilities for everyday life. That is, crime news provides moral lessons that are useful in addressing the social pressures that people routinely confront in their own lives. People do not expect the representation of crime in the mass media to help them in their search for empirical truth about crime and criminal justice. Rather, they use it to make their own moral judgments regarding the story in question (the politician *is* corrupt, the victim *was* wronged, the criminal *deserved* a harsh sentence), and their own moral decisions regarding dilemmas they face in everyday life. Katz goes on to suggest that quality outlets have a greater tendency to leave moral execration to their audience, while popular outlets 'lead the chorus of invective'.

Katz concludes that people need news of crime and punishment as much as they need other basic necessities of daily life. While they experience mass media crime formats as fun, they take them as seriously as the other necessities of life they depend upon. 'Like vitamins useful in the body only for a day, like physical exercise whose value comes from its recurrent practice, crime news is experienced as interesting by readers because of its place in a daily moral routine. ... Although people often fear crime and criticize the news as too negative and disturbing, they apparently find it even more unsettling not to read. ... The reading of crime news appears to serve a purpose similar to the morning shower, routine physical exercise and shaving: ... sustaining faith in an ordered social world.'

In Chapter 4, Robert Snow pursues Katz's question of how people use the mass media to order their routine activities. Snow argues that people turn to their favourite media outlets because of the familiarity of the formats, not because they are looking for specific content or expressions of preferred ideology. It is the formats for presenting and interpreting crime that people absorb into their personal habits and routines and use to order their daily activities. Different media and formats are routine-specific. Thus the particular media outlet is selected for the routines it fits. An outlet may be selected because it provides a temporal element useful in scheduling daily routines. A particular format can also heighten or reduce the tempo and rhythm of the activities it accompanies. The mere presence of media in public places such as shopping malls, hospitals and airports adds to a sense of ontological security: 'The absence of media may also heighten self-consciousness, particularly when alone in public places and sensitivity to scrutiny from others becomes exaggerated. ... Here again, the content of the medium is secondary to its use as a form for para social interaction. ... Through the medium, the individual is immersed in a safer, albeit vicarious reality.'

Snow clearly takes a more positive view than other media analysts who overwhelmingly treat the media as a social problem. For example, contrary to the view of Postman (1985) that the disreputable pleasures of the media are a cultural opiate with deleterious consequences, Snow views the media as a major source of order and security in daily life. Far from disturbing our sense of order and security, crime in mass media formats helps people to routinize their daily activities. It gives them a sense of controlling their individual lives through familiar, usual and taken-for-granted formats.

Institutional Relations and Folly

A second culture of the mass media institution is that which arises at the level of production. In the news media, for example, journalists and their sources develop occupational cultures which significantly influence how their news communications are produced and received. News is a product of the communicative relations between journalists and their sources. Their strategies and tactics of secrecy and publicity have a strong bearing on what appears as news. Thus, 'the primary source of reality for news is not what is displayed or what happens in the real world. The reality of news is embedded in the nature and type of social relations that develop between journalists and their sources, and in the politics of knowledge that emerges on each specific newsbeat' (Ericson, Baranek and Chan 1989: 377).

The strategic institutional relations and politics of knowledge result in folly. Audience members are either 'kept in the dark' or made 'foolish' because relevant knowledge is erased (not communicated at all), distorted (selected) and manipulated (intentional deception). Knowledge is erased, distorted or manipulated because the primary purpose of news communication is to influence opinions, attitudes and actions by communicating only what is in the best interests of the communicators. In explaining folly, some analysts focus on the practices and interests of the news sources (e.g. Chapters 6 and 7), while others attribute self-interest to the news media (e.g. Chapters 8 and 9). In practice the interests of both journalists and their sources – filtered through their respective institutional relations and occupational cultures – appear in every instance of news production and contribute to folly (Ericson, Baranek and Chan 1987, 1989; Chapter 5; Schlesinger and Tumber 1994).

In Chapter 5, Schlesinger, Tumber and Murdock note that research has been media-centric, ignoring conflicts within and between institutions involved in crime newsmaking. They explain this lacuna in terms of the influence of the dominant ideology paradigm, exemplified by the work of Hall *et al.* (1978). This paradigm contends that politically and economically dominant sources frame news debates, ensuring the privileged reproduction of their discourse and even determining what is socially thinkable. Schlesinger *et al.* contend that adherence to this paradigm has blinded analysts to the importance of examining the communication process as a whole. It has also fostered a tendency to treat the media as homogenous, as *the* media, rather than as varying by media and markets.

Schlesinger *et al.* do not deny the importance of political economic considerations. Rather, their task is to show *how* these considerations are important in the context of 'the conflictual processes that lie behind the moment of definition both inside central social institutions and within the media themselves' (Chapter 5: 96–7). For example, in considering the criminal justice institution, they examine how news access is related to police resources for news production; how the police have adapted their public relations to commercial models, seeing their public as 'customers' to whom police activities have to be 'sold'; and how government has empowered voluntary-sector interest groups with publicity resources to challenge government agencies such as the police, courts and penal system. In a case study of *Crimewatch UK* and *Out of Court* (see also Schlesinger and Tumber 1993, 1994), the authors show how popular/quality market considerations of the media combine with criminal justice agency interests to yield significant variations in discourses about crime. These discourses each yield folly because they do not reflect the reality of crime and law enforcement as represented in criminology. Nevertheless, they do reflect the institutional relations and media and market format considerations of those who produce these shows.

In Chapter 6, Mark Fishman depicts the news media as being heavily dependent on the police for crime news. The news media are compelled to accept the institutional classifications and categories of the police and their resultant 'bureaucratic mode of story-telling' (Tuchman 1978). The police like to tell stories that support law-and-order themes; they therefore select crimes for news release that are serious, dramatic and raise public security concerns. Police stories must of course still fit the formats of news discourse. Hence, police investigators are always half-watching in terms of another show: they 'develop a journalist's eye for crime, viewing some incidents not only as "good busts" but also as good stories' (Chapter 6: 135). Moreover, their stories are most likely to receive substantial news play if they articulate with a news theme. For example, if a few major serious crimes can be linked to produce a theme – e.g. of crimes against the elderly (Fishman 1978), child abuse (Nelson 1984: chap. 4), or attacks on women (Voumvakis and Ericson 1984) – then many groups can ascend the public stage and engage in a prolonged socio-drama of law and order. 'Those who have the power to define what the police monitor [for news purposes] have the power to publicize new social problems. ... The specific ones [social problems] that emerge at a given time reflect the politics of newsmaking in a region, as particular interests vie for power in a community or particular police units seek to increase their importance within a law enforcement bureaucracy' (Chapter 6: 136–7).

In Chapter 7, Orcutt and Turner scrutinize the process by which social science data on drug abuse were crafted by journalists into graphic images of drug 'plagues'. They demonstrate the creative choices and skills used in fabricating distorted images of a drug epidemic. They also discovered that the process was not uniform, as different journalists varied systematically in how and how much they distorted the data. The authors indicate that organizational and competitive conditions among the various news outlets involved affected the process. Orcutt and Turner provide a classic case example of how a crime epidemic is actually a 'media epidemic' in which false statistical claims are used as political propaganda to support a law and order theme.

In Chapter 8, Roberts and Doob turn our attention to how newspapers contribute to the folly of their readers. They ask whether newspaper coverage of criminal sentencing leads to a preference for harsher penalties. They proceed to document the folly of news consumers, observing that 'misperceptions abound, and these inaccuracies can be directly traced to the mass media'. The public underestimates the severity of sentences, including maximum sentences, and the time served in prison before parole. It overestimates the number of offenders released on parole and the number of offenders who recidivate. Overall the public has a very negative view of sentencing outcomes, seeing them as being too lenient in the vast majority of cases.

Roberts and Doob designed three studies to show that this folly is attributable to the news media. In the first study, respondents were asked to rate the leniency of sentences reported in newspapers. They show that, through both the choice of cases reported and the formats for presentation, newspapers foster a view that sentences are too lenient. In the second study, respondents were asked to interpret stories from three different newspapers regarding the same sentencing decision. Most respondents viewed the sentence as too lenient, but there were significant differences depending on the newspaper format. The popular tabloid newspaper account elicited the greatest dissatisfaction both with the sentence and with the judge's reasoning. In the third study, one group of respondents was given three continuing stories about one case from a newspaper, while a second group was given excerpts from court documents about the case. Compared to the court document group, the newspaper group was much more likely to rate the sentence as too lenient, the judge as not having considered all appropriate factors, and the offender as worse than average. In the eyes of Roberts and Doob, the media do not provide accounts that are full or rational enough to allow news consumers to form rational opinions.

Chapter 9 by Shanto Iyengar is also a study of how the news media foster folly. In a series of field experiments on how television news accounts of crime and terrorism are interpreted by audiences, he shows that alternative news frames for the identical event induce shifts in how people understand that event and attribute responsibility for it.

Television news is presented within either episodic (specific event) or thematic (general issue) frames, which bear implications for accountability. It attributes accountability through the way it presents people with particular attributes (e.g. gender, race, age, socioeconomic standing) as being victims or perpetrators of social problems. For example, Iyengar found that when news focuses on white-collar crime, societal accountability is attributed most frequently, but when news focuses on violent black crime, individual accountability is emphasized. News also attributes accountability by adopting a particular focus, for example, how actions by responsible political authorities are meeting objectives or, alternatively, dwelling upon controversial decisions by authorities. For example, 'Thematic framing of terrorism that placed an airplane hijacking in the context of local political upheaval raised the prominence of societal causal attributions. When the same hijacking was framed in episodic terms, characteristics of individual terrorists were at the forefront of viewers' attributions' (p. 187).

Episodic framing, especially regarding security problems, dominates television news, and the public folly it yields has serious consequences for public policy. Episodic framing leads people to see accountability in individualistic terms (single problem, single issue, single individual responsibility, single immediate solution), rather than in terms of wider social forces and problems understood through a consistent ideological lens. For example, episodic framing of security problems intensifies attributions of individual responsibility and thus support for more punitive measures such as the death penalty and military retaliation against terrorism.

As such television news is pro-establishment; it desensitizes people to structural problems and the need for structural reform, and it relieves politicians of the need to take stronger reform action.

Popular Drama and Fear

A third culture of the mass media institution is the popular audience contexts in which mass communications are received and used. We live in a 'dramatical world' in which drama has become part of habitual experience (Williams 1989). In order to articulate with popular culture, all mass communications are dramatized. They are presented as 'staged' events, with lively and evocative language, sensational visuals, and attractive and appealing 'personalities'.

The need to dramatize is one of the reasons why crime, and especially violent crime, is so salient in the mass media (Sparks 1992). In addition to being fun, violence dramatizes disruptive forces in society and the process of restoring order. A hero/villain opposition, dramatized through violence, provides metaphors for political (power) struggles and their resolution. The evil of criminals is dramatized to the point of demonology (Cohen 1972; Pearson 1983; Christie 1986; Ericson, Baranek and Chan 1991: chap. 4). Their violence is presented as a shock, a threat and a sign of declining social order rather than as a perpetual and inevitable feature and an historical constant. In contrast, the violence of heroes such as the police is presented in cathected scenarios of rescue and 'saving the day'. The violence of such heroes is presented as resulting from noble motives and as necessary, although questionable within the rules of procedural propriety.

Violence is so central to dramatization in mass communication that news sources must sometimes use violence as a dramatic technique to gain news access (Holloran *et al.* 1970; Tumber 1982; Wagner-Pacifici 1986; Williams 1989; Ericson 1994). However, dramatization is by no means limited to violent episodes. In a world in which drama is built into the rhythms of life as habitual experience, even routine reactions to social problems are dramatized through news conferences, question time in the legislature, slick video packages and the like. For example, the news media routinely report law reform initiatives in dramatic fashion (Ericson, Baranek and Chan 1991: chap. 5). Law is presented as the happy ending to the political narrative; it becomes a central component of what is dramatized in consciousness and habitually experienced. It provides a didactic theatre of reform, instructing people about responsibility, accountability and moral ordering, and feeding back in the form of authoritative support for official institutions.

The dramatization of violence and other social problems is seen as the primary locus of popular fear. Fear has several dimensions. There is a fear for self that is temporary. Exposed to dangerous or threatening circumstances visualized on the mass media – graphic accounts of drug abuse, murderous incidents, police efforts to control riots, etc. – the viewer will variously and vicariously experience fright (agitation), terror (paralysis), horror (repugnance), panic (irrationality or folly) and alarm (shock). Indeed, these very terms are featured in newspaper headlines and broadcast news teases, especially in the popular media. They tell people at the outset that they should be shocked and appalled, and that they should take action accordingly.

There is also fear for the self that is more permanent. Exposed to the inevitable recurrence of shocking violence and apparently irresolvable social problems, a person may experience dread (feeling powerless to avoid a threat), dismay (apprehension that drains one of the capacity to act), consternation (being confounded) and trepidation (hesitancy).

Finally, there is fear of the medium itself. Television in particular has become a secular dread, an imputed source of 'crime', disorder and decline. Television perpetually disturbs our sense of propriety (Sparks 1992) and subverts our sense of place (Meyrowitz 1985). It is viewed as having a *felt relation* to social problems, as being literally part of the problems and of all the fearful emotions that go with them.

Social scientists who study the effects of popular dramas of crime on people's fears also buy into this 'evil causes evil' view. They are overwhelmingly concerned with the negative effects of violence and social problems discourse in the mass media. They see crime in the mass media as inevitably causing emotional upset and inducing folly and consequent irrational behaviour. But is fear inevitable and, if so, is it necessarily bad? Fear is a basic human emotion. People are drawn to the mass media because they like to be at least modestly frightened. People's fears stimulate them to take innovative or creative actions.

In Chapter 10, Best and Horiuchi argue that the news media dramatize fearful and threatening situations as a response to perceptions of threat and social strain in society. With the aid of a case study of news accounts of Hallowe'en sadism, the authors show how 'urban legends' are constructed by the news media to address fears about contemporary risks to safety and to express nostalgia about a lost past of tranquillity and tradition (see also Pearson 1983). That there was little or no danger to children in the incidents reported is almost beside the point. The point is that the news media are storytellers, and their legendary tales persist because they are linked to real fears – in the present case, to child abuse and to criminal victimization in general – and because they express highly salient features of contemporary life such as mistrust of strangers. Moreover, such stories have real effects in that people take action to better secure themselves. Thus, state legislatures have passed Hallowe'en sadism laws; schools have instituted special classes to train children how to detect candy tampering, communities and individual parents have banned trick-or-treating and hospitals have volunteered their radiology specialists to x-ray bags of treats.

Cavender and Bond-Maupin advance the concept of urban legends in Chapter 11. They employ content analysis to examine the new genre of reality programming that blends news and entertainment formats (see also Carriere and Ericson 1989; Schlesinger and Tumber 1993, 1994). They discover that while these programmes participate in the ongoing investigation of actual cases, they bear all of the conventional features of television crime drama, including urban legend storytelling about the insecurities of contemporary life. As the authors express it, 'Crime is an ideal idiom for expressing urban fear and a corresponding sense of danger'. Specifically, criminals are dangerous people beyond social control, motivated by greed and jealousy, or simply 'mindless' in their actions. Crime can occur at any time and in any place, in an evening at home with loved ones as easily as in the back alley of an urban ghetto. The feeling of insecurity is underscored by a strong emphasis on affective (emotive) dimensions (Carriere and Ericson 1989). These dimensions are evoked by cinematographic techniques (e.g. slow motion), a focus on vulnerable victims (e.g. children and the elderly), 'fear cues' (e.g. referencing spaces such as isolated rural roads where cries for help will go unheeded), and emphasis on lives tragically disrupted (e.g. the victim has just experienced a 'high point' in the life course such as graduation or marriage).

The unique aspect of this type of reality programme is that it enlists audience members as policing agents. Crime is a metaphor for a world out of control. The police and other authorities cannot themselves keep a lid on crime, in spite of all their heroic efforts. The only resource is to enlist citizens to conduct surveillance and provide information. The television audience as 'community' is *the* body that can help to fight crime and reduce fear. 'Participating in reality programs means the audience is part of that reality, making that reality almost indistinguishable from any other aspect of life.'

In Chapter 12, Nava explores how a child abuse panic in Cleveland (England) was dramatized in the national press, with political consequences. Controversy arose over a huge increase in the identification of child sexual abuse cases, and over a parallel increase in the taking of child victims into public care. Nava observes that expert opinion diverged with respect to the nature of the abuse and whether intervention was justified. Experts offered a wide range of competing and contradictory opinions, so that the narrative could not be advanced nor closure effected through reliance upon them. This left space for an alternative narrative of symbolic politics that followed a consistent, but narrow, line.

The child sexual abuse scandal in Cleveland was transformed into a socio-drama of non-traditional, feminist professional forces versus traditional, male working-class forces. On the one side was the physician who was the primary diagnostician. She became a symbol of feminism and anti-traditionalism: an Australian, middle-class, professional woman with a house-husband and five children, neither very English nor very feminine. On the other side was the local Member of Parliament. He became a symbol of male working-class culture and tradition: indigenous (northerner, local, son of a miner), salt-of-the-earth, populist, against left-wing progressive influences in local government and social services, both very English and very masculine. This political frame of fear about the erosion of tradition displaced the frame of fear over the best interest of the children (whether they were being exploited by sexual abuse or by abusive authorities who took them into care without proper grounds). Fears about children were transformed into fears about feminism as represented by the female physician. Against the template of working-class male authority and tradition, she became the deviant, the demon, the enemy. Once again 'respectable fears' (Pearson 1983) framed how crime was understood and reacted to.

In 'Television and Perceptions of Crime: The British Experience' (Chapter 13), Gunter provides a challenge to the 'cultivation' thesis of Gerbner and his associates that violence-laden crime drama leads television viewers to magnify the threat of crime, which in turn fosters distrust, fear of others and support for the politics of law and order. Employing a factor analysis, Gunter shows that fear of crime and other dangers may not be directly attributable to television crime drama viewing; rather, people who are already fearful and fatalistic about life in general are drawn to television crime drama. He then uses his research with Wakshlag to examine how 'selective exposure' to television crime drama relates to perceptions of risk of victimization. The volume of television viewing is significantly related to fear of crime. However, it is not clear whether television is the causal agent, or whether fearful people watch television because they find its justice and security resolutions comforting compared to venturing into the 'unsafe' world outside the home. Gunter concludes that there is circularity in the relationship: fear of crime in the social environment results in gravitation towards the 'electronic hearth' (Tichi 1991) where there is a perpetual supply of stories which both reinforce and relieve anxiety.

In Chapter 14, Richard Sparks takes issue with both the cultivation hypothesis of Gerbner and with selective exposure theory. The cultivation hypothesis does not inform us about how television production and reception are situated activities; it ignores issues of narrative and discourse; it fails to understand television as a technology of inscription and diffusion. The selective exposure view is more sensitive to differentiated audiences and to multiple interpretations and uses of crime drama. However, by simply inverting Gerbner's cultivation view to argue that crime drama has positive benefits, it suffers from many of the same deficiencies.

Sparks finds a solution by relying on Smith's (1986) work on how media information is used to address fears for personal safety and perceptions of risk in an immediate locality. The media provide 'improvised news' (Shibutani 1966), rumour and gossip that become part of the social experience of a locality and shape action. In the extreme, the ostensible criminal event topic of the rumour acts as a surrogate for other, more diffuse fears. That is, it both arouses and placates fears whose origins do not stem from the criminal event itself. Other political discourses – for example, concerning law and order, censorship and the need for surveillance – in turn become entwined with improvised news and have real effects on social relations. Sparks thereby indicates that fear is not a quantity but a mode of perception with emotional dimensions, used to construct identities and courses of action.

Political Spectacle and Fake

A fourth culture of the mass media institution is the public political sphere. The dramatization of crime, law enforcement and law and order creates a world of symbolic politics. Drama is the process of 'spectacularization': of staging, making symbols, constructing reality. Spectacle is the result of dramatization, a world in which symbols and images become the reality. The spectacularization of the politics of law and order results in law and order as a spectacle. Crime, criminals and law enforcers become signifiers of values, moral stances and ideologies which in turn create subjectivities (cf. Edelman 1988).

As political spectacle, the processes of crime, law and justice are fake. They seem to be not real, inauthentic, not genuine, a sham or even corrupt. They have this quality because mass media dramatization itself is characterized by faking (Ericson *et al.* 1987; Hartley 1992). The mass media visualization of crime, justice and order requires simulation devices and fictions that add unity and plausibility to storytelling. Mass media truths about crime are in fact the textual product of such faking devices (ibid), leaving audience members with a sense that they are fake. As such, the mass media institution 'has at this general structural level nothing to do with the reality or truth of pre-discursive events in themselves, but with the diegetic world imagined inside reporting; a world verified by constant and militant reference to the real, to be sure, but one in which the real is secondary to the vision, for it is the visualization of order/disorder that is authenticated by reference to actuality, not vice versa ... the vast populations it converts into contemplators of order must not associate truth with that which exists in fact, but with plausible stories, packed with diegetic visual verisimilitude [the simulation of truth]' (Hartley 1992: 141–2).

In Chapter 15, David Altheide shows that, while political spectacles of crime and law enforcement are fake, they are real in their consequences. Altheide provides a case study of how the police in Arizona used television formats to effect a 'trial by media' dismissal of corrupt state legislators. The police took the initiative to mount a 'sting' operation in which they had an operative pose as a lobbyist interested in the legalization of casinos and other forms of gambling. The operative arranged meetings with legislators in a hotel room equipped with a concealed television camera, and then offered them 'bribes' to support the legalization of gambling. The videos of eight legislators who accepted money were then packaged for the local evening newscasts; viewers were treated to the spectacle of having the corruption of each legislator released serially, to the news media, one segment at a time, one day at a time. Seven legislators resigned and were replaced with non-elected officials, without benefit of court proceedings, while one legislator opted for a trial. Those who contemplated a trial 'to put evocative pretrial images in a different context were stymied by the replaying of a barrage of "guilty-looking" visuals for more than a year. Jury selection became a major problem' (p. 300).

Altheide's analysis indicates that the police were sophisticated 'journalists', skilfully employing television news formats, dramatization, faking and political spectacle to secure their own instrumental goals. In using media logic to ferret out their political enemies, they had to 'fake' the crimes. They also created a 'fake' jury of millions of television viewers who saw the legislators as obviously guilty. The result was summary justice at every stage of the process: a 'trial' by media in which the legal trial defence of entrapment could be avoided; instant dispositions in the form of resignations, and shaming as punishment. The police operative became a media star, featured in a four-part newspaper series.

The police videos simulating 'crime' were highly successful in stimulating people to accept the police *modus operandi* of persecution without prosecution. Public opinion surveys following the sting revealed that legislators in general were held in very low esteem, while the police were regarded highly. Journalists were also very accommodating, supporting the contention of Altheide and Snow (1991) that we now live in a 'post-journalism' era in which sources are so sophisticated in mass media logics that journalists are largely redundant. Altheide did not uncover a single item in which a journalist reflected on the implications of this case for democratic processes and social justice. Mass media faking of crime and punishment has become part of good law enforcement.

Meyrowitz illustrates in Chapter 16 how news media work with other powerful political institutions to criminalize and exclude those who do not fit established institutional templates. Meyrowitz analyses how a politician seeking nomination as the US Democratic Party candidate for the 1992 presidential election was made into a 'political enemy' (Christie 1986) through routine news judgments. He observes that while blatant political censorship is common in explicitly totalitarian regimes, it is also routinely and systematically a part of political news judgment in America.

In spite of an illustrious education and previous careers, the aspiring presidential candidate was rapidly marginalized through a range of news faking devices. For example, a photograph of him with prominent political figures was eventually published in a newspaper, but with him cut out of the picture. He was similarly excluded from television appearances, with the criteria of exclusion varying as he tried to meet them. Political language was used to mark him as an outsider: he was described as a 'dark horse', a 'fringe candidate' and 'an obscure contender'. As his campaign became transformed into an act of social deviance, he was increasingly silenced. The politician eventually realized that he could achieve some visibility only by initiating his own spectacular techniques. For example, he stood up in a Democratic

Party forum (in which he was given no official status as a presidential candidate) and demanded an explanation as to why he was being excluded. The response of the Party was to hold the next forum in a high-security television studio with no audience. At a subsequent forum that was open, the politician again stood up to question his exclusion as an official debater. As Meyrowitz observes, 'For this crime, he was quickly tackled to the floor by plain clothes police, dragged down a flight of stairs head first, handcuffed, thrown into a police paddy wagon until the debate was over, and then kept in custody at a Bronx jail for four hours on charges of disorderly conduct, trespassing and resisting arrest. The TV cameras did not even turn away from the debate stage to focus on any of the drama.' The *New York Post* reported only that 'Two men were arrested inside the Lehman College auditorium when they started heckling candidates, according to police'.

Meyrowitz does not invoke conspiracy theory to explain what happened to the presidential candidate. Rather, he argues that routine news conventions, through which political spectacles are produced, systematically exclude all but the chosen few. It is only celebrity candidates and celebrity journalists, carefully pre-selected by elite party officials and news executives, who can make it onto the television-driven political stage. Those who try to upset this framework are quietly but efficiently silenced as 'unnewsworthy'. If they persist, their actions are framed as deviant and their efforts to participate in arenas of legitimacy are criminalized. It is little wonder that political spectacles such as election campaigns are increasingly experienced as fake.

In Chapter 18, Lisus and Ericson examine the construction of political spectacle and its fake effects in another context. They begin with the familiar observation that we live in a post-Gutenberg world in which television and other electronic media formats penetrate all arenas of social life. This influence extends to cultural institutions such as museums that try to preserve significant historical figures and events for cultural reflection. Whether the cultural institution's subject is cartoon characters, sports heroes or victims of violence, it must fit the formats of electronic media if it is to educate and communicate. Lisus and Ericson analyse this formatting and its effects in the case of a recently-built museum devoted to Holocaust remembrance.

At the Simon Wisenthal Center's Beit Hashoah Museum of Tolerance in Los Angeles, the designers use television formats to create a spectacle about the most horrific campaign of political violence in memory. Museum visitors are bombarded with media simulations as stimulation, on the assumption that they possess only Nintendo attention spans. It is evident that the television formatted spectacle cannot produce history; it can only yield effects that are entirely false.

The Museum is where Hollywood meets the Holocaust. It was officially opened by Arnold Schwarzenegger, the video-champion of violent summary justice. Lisus and Ericson observe that the designers put into storage some original Holocaust artifacts and documents left over from a previous unsuccessful museum, preferring instead multi-screen videos that *represent* those same artifacts and documents. This is an experiential museum where emotions and images, not objects, become the driving force. Indeed, in order to sustain their own unique narrative of the Holocaust in the context of other instances of intolerance, the Museum designers use signs and artifacts they know to be inauthentic. This type of faking is also used to sustain news narratives (Ericson *et al.* 1987; Hartley 1992). Other news media elements are incorporated: some of the material is produced by the MacNeal-Lehrer Newshour production team; familiar television news footage of famous cases of racial intolerance is used; familiar television personalities rather than actual Holocaust survivors voice-over visuals of life in concentration camps; in addition, a docent provides ongoing 'pointers' to the moral meaning of the exhibition in a manner paralleling the way in which journalists voice-over television news clips to point to preferred readings of the visuals. As the visitor proceeds through the Museum, she is gradually inducted as an 'extra' in the production. She enters into the docudrama set, interacts directly with it and literally *becomes* the format. This is hyper-television.

The Museum managers are putting the political spectacle formats of television to good use. Nevertheless, these formats arguably contain emotional experiences heightened to the point where there is no clear or direct translation into knowledge useful for genocide prevention. Moreover, these formats also circumscribe possible theoretical explanations of the Holocaust. There is an assumption that prejudicial, intolerant people rather than obedient functionaries of modern bureaucracies are responsible for genocide in general and the Holocaust in particular. This assumption, along with the belief that provoking emotions will help prevent genocide, is a limited and even dangerous fake effect. However, it may be the only assumption communicable within the political spectacle format of television.

In Chapter 17 'On Panoptical Systems and Mass Media in Modern Society', Mathiesen offers a change of focus. He observes that political spectacles in the mass media articulate with various facets of surveillance. In particular, they allow everyone to conduct surveillance on those political elites regularly in the news. Through mass media, the many are now able to engage in sustained surveillance of the few. This new surveillance has a democratic potential because it seems to make political elites more familiar and ordinary, and thus less distant from the rest of us (see also Meyrowitz 1985). However, Mathiesen contends that this democratic effect is more fake than real because the mass audience actually has little purchase on the agenda-setting capacity of political elites or the news media (see also Seaman 1992).

Mathiesen proceeds to argue that the main effect of mass-mediated political spectacles is the creation of beliefs which are conducive to the acceptance of surveillance in everyday life. In keeping with some of the ideas discussed in the earlier section on institutional relations and folly, Mathiesen suggests that the mass media give legitimacy to surveillance systems. Whether the object is dangerous criminals, threats to the environment or menacing nation-states, the mass media help legitimate the surveillance rationales for combatting enemies of the state. They create the belief that surveillance systems are efficient at both knowledge production and actual control; and, to the contrary, that surveillance systems are not efficient enough and therefore we need more of them. Both of these effects are real in their consequences. They simultaneously foster the unease, distrust and insecurity that characterize late modern society (Giddens 1990, 1991) as well as the proliferation of security commodities that offer fleeting relief from these anxieties (Spitzer 1987; Bauman 1992).

Business Commodification and Fetish

A fifth culture of the mass media institution arises at the level of ownership. With the partial exception of nationally owned broadcasting corporations such as the BBC, mass media outlets are business enterprises seeking audience market shares for profit. As a result, the instrumentalization and commodity logic of material production also governs cultural production (Schiller 1989; Featherstone 1991; Goldman 1992). Mass media products reflect exchange value more than 'higher' cultural values. The objects addressed by mass media – from crime and security to romance and progress – are symbolically transformed into different use values. That is, they are commodified in the process of mass communication.

Commodification involves abstraction, equivalence and reification (Goldman 1992). In abstraction, entities are transformed into purposes and subjectivities that are independent of any objective condition of existence. In equivalence, use-value becomes subordinated to exchange value, with objects being reduced to their comparable characteristics for exchange. In the process, individual identities and social relations are removed from their original specific context and placed in more universal and standardized formats. These formats result in human relations that are impersonal, objectified and more serial than social. In reification, one's self and relations are experienced as objects. One's body is made up of component parts, and one's social life is also compartmentalized. These parts – for example, beautiful legs in a body lotion commercial or beautiful friends in a beer commercial – are stylized and given a life of their own to the point where all desirable aspects of identity and social relations appear to require purchased objects. The objects themselves take on agency: the power to create a good night out, an enjoyable lifestyle, security and so on.

The totemism of re-valued objects becomes entwined with fetishism: an obsession with objects to the point of reverence. The good life is associated with the material life (Featherstone 1991) or, in the case of the electronic church (Hoover 1988), with spiritual life; in the case of lotteries (Clattfelter and Cook 1989), with a life of hope; in the case of fears about disorder and decline (Spitzer 1987), with a secure life. There is even fetish about fetish. Late modern rationality creates intolerance of all forms of life that are different. Thus, while commodification has the effect of fetish, fetishes themselves are a form of difference that, in the extreme, become defined as pathologies. Fearful of fetishes, people turn to expert products (e.g. medication) or professionals (e.g. psychiatrists and other counsellors) which of course are also packaged and sold as business commodities (Bauman 1992).

In Chapter 19, Gusfield addresses the link between mass media commodification of social problems and professional interests. He points out that crime and other social problems are increasingly brought into the public sphere as commodities that are then sold as being remediable by the 'troubled persons professions'. For example previously 'hidden' forms of crime, such as child abuse and other types of domestic assault, are made public by mass media operatives who also go on to manage debates about appropriate professional reform solutions. Gusfield urges more analysis of how the 'fun' industries of mass media entertain various professional solutions to social problems that 'profit' the professions concerned.

Gusfield makes the key analytical point that crime problems become 'owned' (commodified) by professions, which in turn must continually sell their enterprise through mass media in order to enhance the value of their services. The professional owners of solutions to crime problems are driven to advertise and to participate actively in news media debates about problems and their solution. 'To "own" a problem (Gusfield 1981) is to be obligated to claim recognition of a problem and to have information and ideas about it given a high degree of attention and credibility, to the exclusion of others. To "own" a social problem is to possess the authority to name the condition a "problem" and to suggest what might be done about it. It is the power to influence the marshalling of public facilities – laws, enforcement abilities, opinion, goods and services – to help resolve the problem' (p. 375).

In the process of problem commodification, deviants themselves become commodified. As Gusfield observes in Chapter 19, the political language of social problems in America is such that psychologistic explanations are especially strong. For example, 'substance abuse' locates the problem of drugs in the person, not the substance. Deviants are typically 'sick' or at least 'troublesome', appellations of personal deficiency which the mass media would not give to other public problems. For instance, they do not 'describe recession as the problem of sick businessmen, nor ... counsellors as "market therapists"; ... subsidies to the auto industry are not called "aid to dependent factories"' (p. 381).

In Chapter 20, Spitzer examines how fear of crime makes security products an object of desire. While many products are explicit security devices, almost everything has been invested with a security use value: the home in the 'good' neighbourhood, the car that is 'safer' than public transport or other cars, the food or medicinal product that has tamper-proof lids, and so on. Where fear meets desire, it is not just a matter of rational calculation, but also of abstraction, equivalence and reification as described earlier. That is, people will only be willing to participate in social relations if they feel assured about the security of the commodities that form part of these relations. The problem is that a large dose of faith is required because security products offer only faith, not certainty. Security is not a primary commodity form, but only a derivative which is defined symbolically and not directly available to the senses. As such 'security is one of those commodities which possesses an almost limitless ability to absorb signifiers' (p. 393).

The commodification of security creates the belief that there are simple solutions to the complex problem of crime; for instance, that you can buy a solution to the problem, either from an expert or in a technology. The daily mass media barrage of crime problems serves only as a reminder that one may not as yet have purchased the right security product. The problem of course is that the commodification process means that people will never feel that they have an adequate solution, that they are absolutely secure. 'Paradoxically, the more we enter into relationships to obtain the security commodity, the more insecure we feel; the more we depend on the commodity rather than each other to keep us safe and confident, the less safe and confident we feel; the more we divide the world into those who are able to enhance our security and those who threaten it, the less we are able to provide it for ourselves' (p. 392).

In Chapter 21, Tumber provides a valuable corrective to the conventional wisdom that business commodification is a top-down process in which media owners and advertisers dictate media content in their own interests. The prevailing political economy approach overlooks the politics of knowledge within and between business and mass media institutions. Businesses themselves are subject to imputations of deviance and efforts at control. For example, there is very substantial mass media coverage of corporate crime and business regulation. The increase in such coverage is a major reason why larger business enterprises have expanded their public relations units and accelerated advocacy and social responsibility advertising (see also Singer 1986; Ericson *et al.* 1989). It has also led to corporate surveillance of the mass media. For example, *Presswatch Quarterly* monitors and evaluates national newspaper reports on business enterprise in the UK, including as part of its service the weighting of the significance of the reports in terms of newspaper circulation and readership profiles.

Tumber observes that mass media audiences have become much more interested in business news because increasing numbers have a direct stake in business. Privatization of state business enterprises, expanded pension funds and the popularity of mutual funds as an alternative to property investment or low-interest bearing savings accounts have all combined to make more audience members concerned about business ethics and scandal. The dramatization of crime, sex and scandal in the popular media increasingly focuses on business enterprise simply because those media are pursuing their own commercial interest of audience-building for advertising revenue. As far as the mass media are concerned, if business crime sells as well as crime in other institutional contexts, then so be it. While they must be careful not to bite the hand that feeds, they can now exploit crime, sex and scandal for profit in the business sphere as much as in any other.

Conclusions

The five cultures, communications and effects of mass media outlined in this Introduction are explored in much greater depth in each of the sections that follow. In reading the following material it is important to bear in mind that, while each piece highlights a particular mass media culture, communication and effect, in practice all five cultures, communications and effects operate simultaneously. All mass media communications are the product of the media formats, institutional relations, popular dramas, political spectacles and business commodifications that are used in producing them. All mass media communications so produced have the simultaneous effects of fun, folly, fear, fake and fetish. Readers must not let the heuristic device of five discrete sections blind them to the fact that the mass media use the full combination of elements analysed here to engage their audiences.

Bibliography

Altheide, D. (1985), *Media Power*, Beverly Hills: Sage.
Altheide, D. and R. Snow (1991), *Media Worlds in the Postjournalism Era*, New York: Aldine de Gruyter.
Bauman, Z. (1992), 'Life-world and Expertise: Social Production of Dependency' in N. Stehr and R. Ericson (eds), *The Culture and Power of Knowledge*, Berlin and New York: de Gruyter, pp. 81–106.
Beattie, J. (1986), *Crime and the Courts in England 1660–1800*, Princeton: Princeton University Press.
Berkowitz, L. (1970), 'The Contagion of Violence: An S-R Mediational Analysis of Some Effects of Oberserved Aggression' in W. Arnold and M. Page (eds), *Nebraska Symposium on Motivation*, Lincoln: University of Nebraska Press.
Bourdieu, P. (1986), *Distinction: A Social Critique of the Judgment of Taste*, London: Routledge.
Carriere, K. and R. Ericson (1989), *Crime Stoppers: A Study in the Organization of Community Policing*, Toronto: Centre of Criminology, University of Toronto.
Christie, N. (1986), 'Suitable Enemies' in H. Bianchi and R. Van Swaaningen (eds), *Abolitionism – Towards a Non-Repressive Approach to Crime*, Amsterdam: Free University Press.
Clattfelter, C. and P. Cook (1989), *Selling Hope: State Lotteries in America*, Cambridge, MA: Harvard University Press.
Cohen, S. (1972), *Folk Devils and Moral Panics*, London: Paladin.
Crisell, A. (1986), *Understanding Radio*, London: Methuen.
Dominick, J. (1973), 'Crime and Law Enforcement on Prime-Time Television', *Public Opinion Quarterly*, 37, 241–50.
Edelman, M. (1988), *Constructing the Political Spectacle*, Chicago: University of Chicago Press.

Elias, N. (1978), *The Civilizing Process*, Oxford: Basil Blackwell.
Ericson, R. (1994), 'An Institutional Perspective on News Media Access and Control' in M. Aldridge and N. Hewitt (eds), *Controlling Broadcasting*, Manchester: Manchester University Press, pp. 108–33.
Ericson, R., P. Baranek and J. Chan (1987), *Visualizing Deviance: A Study of News Organization*, Toronto: University of Toronto Press; Milton Keynes: Open University Press.
Ericson, R., P. Baranek and J. Chan (1989), *Negotiating Control: A Study of News Sources*, Toronto: University of Toronto Press; Milton Keynes: Open University Press.
Ericson, R., P. Baranek and J. Chan (1991), *Representing Order: Crime, Law and Justice in the News Media*, Toronto: University of Toronto Press; Milton Keynes: Open University Press.
Erikson, K. (1966), *Wayward Puritans*, New York: Wiley.
Featherstone, M. (1991), *Consumer Culture and Postmodernism*, London: Sage.
Fishman, M. (1978), 'Crime Waves as Ideology', *Social Problems*, 25, 531–43.
Garland, D. (1990), *Punishment and Modern Society*, Oxford: Oxford University Press.
Giddens, A. (1990), *The Consequences of Modernity*, Cambridge: Polity.
Giddens, A. (1991), *Modernity and Self-Identity*, Cambridge: Polity.
Goldman, R. (1992), *Reading Ads Socially*, London: Routledge.
Graber, D. (1980), *Crime News and the Public*, New York: Praeger.
Gunter, B. (1987), *Television and the Fear of Crime*, London: John Libbey.
Gusfield, J. (1981), *The Culture of Public Problems: Drinking – Driving and the Symbolic Order*, Chicago: University of Chicago Press.
Hagan, J. (1984), *The Disreputable Pleasures*, Toronto: McGraw-Hill Ryerson.
Hall, S., C. Critcher, T. Jefferson, J. Clarke and B. Roberts (1978), *Policing the Crisis*, London: Macmillan.
Hartley, J. (1992), *The Politics of Pictures*, London: Routledge.
Hay, D. (1975), 'Property, Authority and the Criminal Law' in D. Hay et al. (eds), *Albion's Fatal Tree*, Harmondsworth: Penguin.
Holloran, J., P. Elliott and G. Murdock (1970), *Demonstrations and Communication*, Harmondsworth: Penguin.
Hoover, S. (1988), *Mass Media Religion: The Social Sources of the Electronic Church*, Beverly Hills: Sage.
Liebert, R. and R. Baron (1972), 'Some Immediate Effects of Televised Violence on Children's Behavior', *Developmental Psychology*, 6, 469–75.
Meyrowitz, J. (1985), *No Sense of Place: The Impact of Electronic Media on Social Behavior*, New York: Oxford University Press.
Nelson, B. (1984), *Making an Issue of Child Abuse*, Chicago: University of Chicago Press.
Parke, R., L. Berkowitz, J-P Leyens, S. West and R. Sebastian (1977), 'Some Effects of Violent and Non-Violent Movies on the Behavior of Juvenile Delinquents' in L. Berkowitz (ed.), *Advances in Experimental Social Psychology*, vol. 10, New York: Academic Press.
Pearson, G. (1983), *Hooligan: A History of Respectable Fears*, London: Macmillan.
Postman, N. (1985), *Amusing Ourselves to Death: Public Discourse in the Age of Show Business*, New York: Viking.
Rowland, W. (1983), *The Politics of TV Violence: Policy Uses of Communication Research*, Beverly Hills: Sage.
Schattenburg, G. (1981), 'Social Control Functions of Mass Media Depictions of Crime', *Sociological Inquiry*, 51, 71–7.
Schiller, H. (1989), *Culture Inc: The Corporate Takeover of Public Expression*, New York: Oxford University Press.
Schlesinger, P., H. Tumber and G. Murdock (1993), 'Fighting the War Against Crime: Television, Police, and Audience', *British Journal of Criminology*, 33, 19–32.
Schlesinger, P. and H. Tumber (1994), *Reporting Crime*, Oxford: Clarendon Press.
Seaman, W. (1992), 'Active Audience Theory: Pointless Populism', *Media, Culture and Society*, 14, 301–11.
Shibutani, T. (1966), *Improvised News*, Indianapolis: Bobbs-Merrill.
Singer, B. (1986), *Advertising and Society*, Don Mills: Addison-Wesley.

Smith, A. (1980), *Goodbye Gutenberg: The Newspaper Revolution in the 1980s*, New York: Oxford University Press.
Smith, S. (1986), *Crime, Space and Society*, Cambridge: Cambridge University Press.
Sparks, R. (1992), *Television and the Drama of Crime: Moral Tales and the Place of Crime in Public Life*, Buckingham: Open University Press.
Spitzer, S. (1987), 'Security and Control in Capitalist Societies: The Fetishism of Security and the Secret Thereof' in J. Lowman, R. Menzies and T. Palys (eds), *Transcarceration: Essays in the Sociology of Social Control*, Aldershot: Gower, pp. 43–58.
Tannenbaum, P. and D. Zillman (1975), 'Emotional Arousal and the Facilitation of Aggression through Communication' in L. Berkowitz (ed.), *Advances in Experimental Social Psychology*, New York: Academic Press.
Tichi, C. (1991), *Electronic Hearth: Creating an American Television Culture*, New York: Oxford University Press.
Tuchman, G. (1978), *Making News*, New York: Free Press.
Tumber, H. (1982), *Television and the Riots*, London: British Film Institute.
Voumvakis, S. and R. Ericson (1984), *News Accounts of Attacks on Women*, Toronto: Centre of Criminology, University of Toronto.
Wagner-Pacifici, R. (1986), *The Moro Morality Play: Terrorism as Social Drama*, Chicago: University of Chicago Press.
Williams, R. (1976), *Communications*, 3rd ed., Harmondsworth: Penguin.
Williams, R. (1989), *Raymond Williams on Television*, Toronto: Between-the-Lines.

Part I
Media Formats and Fun

Media and Markets

Medium Differences

In the news process, reality is not a solid but a fluid. All knowledge is mediated by a medium, whether print, television, or radio. The medium does not stand apart from the work as a technological apparatus through which news operatives simply transmit their messages. Rather, the medium is 'any process, technique or technology that produces something visible from something invisible ... Media provide a means to visualize, identify, and locate meaning. Although media rely on symbols for communications, they also do something more: media arrange, define, and communicate meaning' (Altheide 1985: 39). As such, the particular medium the news operative uses is integral to his or her work, and he or she helps to constitute its meanings and uses. While the medium constrains the formats in which knowledge can be presented, it is also a means of discovery, creativity, and innovation. While the medium frames discourse, it also accomplishes it.

In this section we contemplate how the newspaper, television, and radio news media each have a distinctive influence on news discourse. We consider how each medium influences the use of particular news formats, sources, knowledge, and topics. This consideration provides the necessary analytical framework for our empirical inquiry into how news of crime, law, and justice varies by medium.

FORMATS

How something is communicated precedes what is communicated. Newspapers, television, and radio have distinct formats. Each medium has different procedures for the selection, transmission, and reception of knowledge. Each medium differs in how it transcends the limits of time and space to make news available, and thereby creates a different social environment and context for thinking. Format differences yield variation in content, and ultimately, different consequences for the knowledge structure of society (Altheide 1985; Meyrowitz 1985; Crisell 1986). Thus how communications are mediated by formats has an importance beyond particular expressions of economic and political power in news accounts. This is the importance of 'media power' (Altheide 1985).

The news reality of each medium is a matter of *how* it presents knowledge in its established formats, rather than of *what* it presents. Aspects of format fundamentally delimit and shape the news product: for example, the time available for a broadcast-news bulletin and the space available in a newspaper; the sequencing of broadcast-news items and the layout of a newspaper; the technologies associated with the medium; and the beats available as routine rounds for acquiring preselected material from sources that is itself formatted for the purposes of the reporter's medium. The format requirements are paramount. Content must always fit the format, and it is therefore always secondary to the format.

> Any medium's first commitment is to itself as a legitimate format for the definition, recognition, and communication of meaning ... Whatever defines a particular medium, e.g. sound for radio and visuals for TV, will essentially define and shape how the event's temporal and spatial features will be translated into those of the listener or viewer. Furthermore, whatever content is produced, e.g. people, places, things, will be subservient to and largely a result of these format considerations. And, whatever elements of format are deemed the most important will weigh disproportionately on the resulting messages. (Altheide 1985: 40, 56)

A fuller appreciation of media and formats can be derived from a detailed comparison of the capacities and limitations of newspaper, television, and radio formats as summarized in table 2.1.

A basic point of comparison, from which several other points follow, is that the newspaper is a visual medium, television both visual and audio, and radio audio. The fact that radio has no visual capacity and is therefore 'a *blind* medium' (Crisell 1986: 3) is fundamental. Television can transmit printed material: some cable-television stations present nothing but news in print, and newscasts use printed vistas to identify sources and to highlight key points in a story. Newspapers can use still photographs, graphics, and visually 'catchy' headlines, captions, and layouts. While television and

22   Representing Order

TABLE 2.1
A comparison of newspapers, television, and radio news formats

Newspaper	Television	Radio
Visual	Visual and audio	Audio
Weak validation of context	Strong validation of context	Some validation of context
Least redundancy/simplification	Considerable redundancy/simplification	Most redundancy/simplification
Considerable imaginative work	Least imaginative work	Most imaginative work
Narrative/symbolic/abstraction	Most dramatization/entertaining/concrete	Considerable abstraction dramatization/entertaining/concrete
Least personalization	Most personalization	Considerable personalization
Structure with space	Structure with time	Structure with time
Least immediacy/past tense	Considerable immediacy/present tense	Most immediacy/present tense
Largest number of items	Intermediate number of items	Least number of items
Longest items	Intermediate length of items	Shortest items
Linear/sequential	Mosaic/episodic	Mosaic/episodic
Static	Dynamic/continuous	Dynamic/continuous
Consistent/permanent/a record	Ephemeral/evanescent	Ephemeral/evanescent
Self-pacing	Imposes own pace	Imposes own pace
Individual/primary activity	More social/secondary activity	Most social/secondary activity

newspaper words and visuals can gloss a lot, radio words gloss everything because there is no opportunity for visual interpretation of individual character and interactional contexts.

As their medium lacks a visual capacity, radio journalists are more limited in their ability to convey connotative meanings. There is, of course, a great deal of connotative potential in the use of words alone. As Monaco (1981: 131) observes, 'If denotation were the only measure of the power of a language, for example, then English – which has a vocabulary of a million or so words and is the largest language in history – would be over three times more powerful than French – which has only 300,000 or so words. But French makes up for its "limited" vocabulary with a noticeably greater use of connotation.' A particular skill required of the radio announcer is to keep the audience engaged by dropping in witty and entertaining connotations as he or she talks (Goffman 1981: chap. 5; Crisell 1986). Nevertheless, radio talk, and especially radio-news talk, must be presented within a very limited, simple, 'perfected' form, not only to be engaged and understood, but also so as not to connote meanings that might give offence to some segment of the audience (Goffman 1981: chap. 5). While music and other background sounds can be used in radio news (Crisell 1986), they are not used often.

Language use in newspapers is similarly restricted, but the restrictions are not as great. The newspaper has considerable latitude in arriving at connotative meanings by contrasting and juxtaposing pictures, headlines, and stories in its page layouts. 'In both television and the newspapers – especially the popular tabloids – there is as much attention given to, and signification in, the spatial composition as the sequence of verbal/written signs. The composition within the TV screen puts different iconic signs together so that they modify or reinforce each other's signification. The same is true of the combination of headline and picture and story in newspapers. We read them simultaneously, and this is where a picture can indeed be worth a thousand ideological words' (Hartley 1982: 31).

The film and video technologies of television greatly enhance its connotative capacity. The television journalist can use camera angles, lighting, and background staging 'props,' and editing to connote meaning. The television journalist can also combine visuals with sound – words, music, background noise – to connote ideologically (Fiske and Hartley 1978, chap. 3; Ericson, Baranek, and Chan 1987: chaps. 7 and 8).

The visual capacity of television allows it to bind its messages to the context in which they were produced. Through the use of sounds from the context of production, radio also has some capacity in this regard. 'Quotes in a newspaper may have nothing to do with the place in which the words were spoken, but a recording of a speech also captures aspects of the physical environment in which the speech was made' (Meyrowitz 1985: 122). Newspapers are limited to the use of still photographs, and these provide a relatively weak means of tying messages to context.

The greater the capacity to bind messages to context, the greater the validation powers of the medium. Television appears most valid because statements made by its sources can be contextualized in the real places in which they were made. As politicians who preen themselves for television interviews know best (Ericson, Baranek, and Chan 1989: chap. 4), television can capture not only the offices and assembly rooms where important decisions are made, but also the source's dress, demeanour, and direct reaction to questions, from which readings of character are made. Television's capacity to bind messages to context and thereby validate its messages accounts for the fact that survey research in Canada, Britain, and the United States consistently shows that readers find television news more believable, fair, and influential than radio news or newspapers (Glasgow University Media Group [GUMG] 1976: 1ff; Royal Commission on Newspapers [RCN] 1981b: 35; Robinson and Levy 1986; Fiske 1987).

Radio, too, has some power of validation, although extra effort is required to accomplish it. The radio journalist must establish context by describing the environment in which events are occurring, and by using surrounding messages, source clips, and news items. Background sounds associated with the context in which statements are made also provide validity, although these are used indexically rather than iconically. Radio sounds require 'textual pointing – support from the dialogue or narrative' (Crisell 1986: 51). The context of all radio sounds is provided by the script, just as the context of all television sounds and visuals is 'anchored' by the script (Barthes 1977: 39). While radio and television are validated through the ability to use 'actualities,' it is the written text that directs one to the meaning of those actualities and anchors them in a framework.

Newspaper journalists have a limited ability to do the same thing, for example, by writing pointed captions for still photographs. A still photograph of a demolished car wrapped around a tree, with the caption 'Drunk driving tragedy,' can serve as a poignant reminder about the 'terror' of impaired driving. Without the caption, the picture would be polysemous and serve as a reminder of the 'terror' of uncertain signs. Outside the use of still photographs, which is limited (see chapter 7), newspapers must rely upon the visual aspects of their layout (juxtaposing stories, using bold-type headlines, etc.) to magnify the contexts of their stories and to give them force and validity. Popular newspapers in particular use layouts in this way, while quality newspapers rely more upon the authority of their sources to validate what it is they have to say and to lend authority to the newspaper itself.

Compared to most other cultural products, news is quite redundant and simplified. Newspapers are the least redundant and simplified because they have the capacity to present long and complex items in a literate mode. They present detailed features either singly or in a series. They also present stories on a continuing basis, using a wide range of sources (characters) in detailed and subtle narratives. Whether in features or in complex continuing stories, newspapers are more capable of introducing experts and their specialist knowledge than is television or radio news.

Television news is much more simplified and redundant than that in newspapers. It tends towards the concrete and dramatic and has great difficulty in being subtle. Its representations are sometimes 'cartoon stick-figure like' (Gitlin 1980). While television can use its visual capacity to establish context and to present written materials on the screen, this is of little help when it comes to detail and expert knowledge. It is difficult to watch and listen to detailed, specialized knowledge being conveyed because the television-audience member, unlike the newspaper reader, has no chance for retrieval, for introducing his or her own redundancy, unless he or she goes to the trouble and expense of recording the material and playing it over. While specialist knowledge is conveyed on television, it is revealing that 'ideas' programs – such as 'Realities' on TVOntario and 'Ideas' on CBC Radio – provide follow-up printed transcripts of what was said so that the reader can introduce his or her own redundancy at leisure. It is also revealing that in televised distance-education programs, such as those offered by the Open University and the BBC in Britain, the written textual materials are paramount and the broadcast materials are secondary. 'Paulu has pointed out that students of the Open University are expected to spend 65 per cent of their time reading and only 10 per cent of their time listening or viewing (1981: 270); more recently Bates has conceded that broadcasting is a relatively minor component of its teaching system (1984: 139)' (Crisell 1986: 114).

Lacking television's visual capacity, radio is forced to be even more simplified and redundant. 'Radio is the art of communicating meaning at first hearing' (Crisell 1986, quoting Lawrence Gillian of BBC Radio). Communicating meaning at first hearing is difficult because our ears are not terribly 'intelligent.' We tend to miss a lot and forget even more when what we hear is not augmented by something seen. Hence radio talk is reduced to being, as far as possible, simple, redundant, and without the errors typical in natural conversation. Radio is a kind of 'perfect speech machine' (Goffman 1981: chap. 5).

> It is a general truth that much language is written down precisely because its meaning is too complex to be assimilated by ear ... And it is certainly the case that radio language will not be easily followed unless it is syntactically fairly simple or else fairly concrete in subject-matter ...·[when] ideas and arguments become more abstract and their expression is premeditated, or when they require sustained explanation or specialist knowledge, the radio medium is less effective (McWhinnie 1959: 49–50). The BBC's Audience Research Department once tested a group of people on how much they could understand of a talk intended for the 'average' Light Programme listener: the average listener in the group could correctly answer only 28 per cent of the questions which were asked about the talk after it was broadcast (Silvey 1974: 141). Indeed it has been observed that the importance of the radio interviewer is not only as the poser of questions but as the interpreter of answers, the 'plain man' who in brief paraphrases renders the complex or

26   Representing Order

specialist responses of the expert into language intelligible to the lay public (Cardiff 1980: 38). (Crisell 1986: 62; see also Goffman 1981: esp. 241)

The radio listener must make up for being blind by using his or her imagination. The visualization function of imagination is to an extent provided for by the visual capacities of television and newspapers. In relation to radio, however, the listener must supply the visualization, that is, making something visible to the mind because it is not visible to the eye. This includes imagining the setting, the characters, and even the facts of the matter. The listener must interpret the words as symbols of what they represent, and the voice (accent, stress) as an index of the character who is speaking. In radio, 'speech must be regarded as both typographic and photographic, as equivalent not only of the newspaper text but in many cases of its photographs' (Crisell 1986: 88). As Crisell (ibid: 116) also observes, radio 'is the only medium in which reality is in some sense directly presented yet must *at the same time* be imagined.'

While the visual capacity of television means that the television viewer has to do less imaginative work, there is still a considerable amount of visualization required (Fiske 1987: chap. 5). While television news *seems* to present reality more or less directly, it is nevertheless a highly mediated product that is produced out of considerable imaginative work by journalists and sources, and requires considerable imaginative work by its audience members. The following observation of Monaco (1981: 136–7) regarding the imaginative work required of the cinema viewer is equally applicable to the role of the television-audience member.

> Just as, in general, our sense of cinema's connotation depends on understood comparisons of the image with images that were not chosen (paradigmatic) and images that came before and after (syntagmatic), so our sense of the cultural connotations depend on understood comparisons of the part with the whole (synecdoche) and associated details with ideas (metonymy). Cinema is an art and a medium of extensions and indexes. Much of its meaning comes not from what we see (or hear) but from what we don't see or, more accurately, from an ongoing process of comparison of what we see with what we don't see. This is ironic, considering that cinema at first glance seems to be an art that is all too evident, one that is often criticized for 'leaving nothing to the imagination.' Quite the contrary is true.

Newspapers invite some conceptualization and abstraction, whereas radio and especially television must deal with the concrete and do so in a dramatic and entertaining way. Newspapers can be somewhat discursive, while radio and television tend to be more expressive and 'presentational' (Meyrowitz 1985: 93ff), providing 'experience' and tertiary understanding.

Television in particular is rich in its expressive dimensions, allowing a reading of people and how they answer that is unavailable to the other media, especially newspapers. As Meyrowitz (ibid: 103, 108) observes, it is therefore acceptable for a politician to appear on television reading a speech everyone knows was prepared by someone else, but it would not be acceptable for that someone else to appear on television reading a speech everyone knows was prepared by the politician. Moreover, television allows certain charismatic characters – such as the Polish Solidarity leader Lech Walesa – to become *powerful* communicators expressively, even though they are rather inarticulate discursively.

Newspapers try to convey reality by being 'realistic' in discursive terms, while radio and especially television try to convey reality by 'realism' in dramatic terms. Radio (Pietropaolo 1982) and television (Fiske and Hartley 1978; Fiske 1987) therefore are much more attuned to entertaining presentations. Television producers are directed to treat news as theatre and to keep the entertaining features uppermost (Epstein 1974; Cayley 1982). While snippets of information are dropped in along the way, and form the basis for doing the story in the first place, an entertaining angle and visuals provide the frame (Ericson, Baranek, and Chan 1987). Even serious matters must be treated in this way, 'lightened' more than 'enlightening,' 'livened' more than 'enlivening.' This is why, in Postman's (1985) view, television is contributing to the Huxleian nightmare that we are 'amusing ourselves to death.'

Personalization is part of the entertainment formula, especially in broadcast media. People tune in to radio and television to spend time with their favourite personalities, whether they be soap-opera stars, news anchorpersons, sports heroes, or regular news sources. In the broadcast-news media, there is also the tendency to simplify stories by personalizing them through the eyes of people involved. While newspapers also personalize to a considerable degree – for example, people like to read a regular column by their favourite opinionated columnist, and they like to read about their favourite television personalities in the newspaper – they arguably do so less often because the medium does not have the same expressive and dramatic dimensions of tertiary understanding available to radio and especially to television.

Television and radio use time as the major structuring agent, whereas newspapers use space. The auditory codes of television and radio exist in time, and give the sense that they are dealing in the 'here and now.' They are 'present-tense,' seeming 'to be an account of what *is* happening rather than a record of what *has* happened' (Crisell 1986).

Some of the differences among media in this regard relate to the practicalities of production. Newspaper production – even with the aid of electronic media such as word processors and computer-assisted editing and printing techniques – is still relatively cumbersome and slow. As a result, newspapers cannot compete in terms of immediacy. The very latest news has the least chance of making it into the newspaper ahead of broadcast media. While it has been argued that television is much more immediate than is the newspaper (e.g., RCN 1981b: 105), television journalists are encumbered by the need to obtain visuals and to edit them as scripted. To achieve a predictable supply, most of what television journalists cover is prescheduled and pre-scripted, and a lot of what they broadcast is prepackaged and days old (Epstein 1974; Schlesinger 1978; Ericson, Baranek, and Chan 1987).

Radio is most instantaneous and spontaneous. Radio can link an event and listeners very quickly. For example, radio can report a traffic jam quickly so that the knowledge is very helpful to listeners; by the time television and newspaper journalists are able to report it, the problem is likely to be over and therefore the knowledge is unhelpful. Moreover, radio listeners are often in a better position to receive the knowledge, since radio can be attended to in a greater variety of settings (e.g., while driving an automobile, while working) than can newspapers or television. Radio also has a 'rotating feature' (Altheide 1985: 54) whereby key items are repeated in frequent newscasts or special bulletins so that they are unlikely to be missed by anyone who is tuned into the station even for a relatively short time. Nevertheless, radio news is often less immediate than it seems. In face of limited budgets, radio journalists also do a lot of prescheduling and pre-scripting in a narrow range of preselected beats. While radio provides the illusion of 'fresh talk' (Goffman 1981: 172), the reality is usually scripted talk that narrows the speaker into the redundant grooves and recurrent paths of story themes and language.

The need to structure in time, and to hold audience attention through successive items, means that television and radio journalists are limited to a few items per newscast, and to brief items. In comparison, newspaper journalists have scope for a much larger number of items and for longer items, knowing that their readers will pick and choose among them. In a given day's news output, newspapers have a substantial number of items, television considerably less, and radio less still. Television and radio make up for this through other 'information programming' formats, including documentaries, talk shows, and investigative features. However, within the news genre itself broadcast media tend to limit themselves to a few items. For example, a ten-minute radio newscast, at 160–180 words per minute, is equivalent in words to only one and one-half columns of a newspaper (Crisell 1986: 71). The main evening television-news show typically contains fewer words than a single page of a broadsheet quality newspaper. While it is contentious as to whether more words provide more knowledge, it is clear that the brevity of broadcast-news shows and items indicates how limited they are in discursive potential.

The newspaper page layout allows for a mosaic-like, creative juxtaposition on a given page, although the overall presentation in print is linear and sequential, especially within the story. In contrast, television and radio are much more mosaic-like in their presentation as well as between items. They make a collage of very brief (ten- to fifteen-second) clips from sources and journalists to capture a sense of what has gone on and who the key players seem to be. While several items are sometimes combined into a 'wrap' with a theme, the presentation is still episodic and sometimes even strobe-like in effect. Reduced to the condition of advertising, and even overlapping with it (Fiske and Hartley 1978; Postman 1985), broadcast news paints an abstract mosaic of the world even while appearing to be closest to reality and to involve little imaginative work.

Television and radio have the related feature of presenting their picture of the world in motion. Their clips and items are presented continuously and therefore have a dynamic quality, in contrast to the newspaper, which is relatively static. This feature relates also to the element of immediacy raised earlier. In motion, television and radio seem to be very much in the present tense. Static, newspapers seem to be very much in the past tense. As Williams (1989) observed, while you can 'read all about it' in newspapers, the newspaper statement that 'a man was shot' has a less immediate and realistic quality than television-news pictures of a man *being* shot.

Researchers of broadcast news have shown that a lot can be read into it if only one takes the time to record it, stop its motion, and keep it still. When broadcast news is not captured in this way, it imposes its own pace, and people experience it as ephemeral and evanescent. All television-news sources have had the experience of having a friend say, 'I saw you on television last night but I can't remember what you said. What was it about?' The image lingers, but most of the details have evaporated. In contrast, newspapers are characterized by self-pacing. Readers can repeatedly review a permanent *record* that is consistent in presentation and tone. As a record, the newspaper functions not only as a reference work of the activities of contemporary élites (RCN 1981g; Ericson, Baranek, and Chan 1989), but also a rich source for social historians. Crisell (1986: 72–4) ably summarizes comparative dimensions of these elements.

> The language of newspapers is permanent: the reader sets her own pace and can reread what she has missed or cannot understand. This means that the press is capable of considerable linguistic variety. It can therefore divide the heterogeneous audience with which every mass medium is confronted into different intellectual levels by providing different kinds of newspapers for different kinds of reader ... The language of radio is evanescent. The radio newsreader sets an arbitrary pace and his words dissolve into thin air ... This means that however complex the material – and complexity is especially

30   Representing Order

> likely in news, documentary and educational programmes – it must be expressed in language which is fairly simple and straightforward in style and diction. Since radio lacks the linguistic range of newspapers we would expect it to be less capable of providing different levels of output for different kinds of listeners and to remain confronted with a largely heterogeneous audience. This certainly seems to be the case with television, whose language code is also evanescent ... In both television and radio the heterogeneous nature of the viewers imposes constraints and restraints on the referential power of the message, but the nature of the contact makes a prior, even more basic imposition for it requires that the message should be relatively simple: and it must be even simpler in the case of radio since it is unassisted by visual codes and must therefore be apprehensible through ear alone.

The newspaper is read more as a primary activity and individually. While it may be read while doing other things – talking on the telephone, chatting to one's husband, listening to the radio, hectoring one's children, watching television – it is often read in isolation from all other social activities. In contrast, television and especially radio are typically used as secondary activities while doing something else, and this frequently includes being in the presence of other people. Most radios, and some television sets, are portable and can be used while driving, working, lying on the beach, etc. They accompany the flow of the day, providing a 'presence' and an 'aural environment' (Monaco 1981: 375) or 'sound' whose function goes beyond particular content. Meyrowitz's (1985: 90) observations on television in this regard are also applicable to radio.

> A great part of the social significance of television ... may be less in what is *on* television than in the very existence of television as a shared arena. Television provides the largest simultaneous perception of a message that humanity has ever experienced ... Recognition of television's role as a new public arena solves a number of mysteries surrounding television viewing, including: why people complain so bitterly about television content but continue to watch so much of it, why many Americans say they turn to television for 'most' of their news even though – by any objective standard – there is remarkably little news on television, and why people who purchase video tape machines often discover they have little interest in creating 'libraries' of their favourite television programs.

SOURCES

We have already considered how media format requirements influence journalists in their selection and use of sources (pp. 16–17; Altheide 1985;

Ericson, Baranek, and Chan 1987). Media format requirements also influence sources in their selection and use of journalists (Ericson, Baranek, and Chan 1989; Schlesinger 1988, 1989). Through their procedures for controlling knowledge, different sources create different media environments, more suitable to one medium than others. For example, we found that, because of the nature of legal discourse, the fact that electronic media were excluded from the courtroom, and the ways in which reporters were effectively excluded from back regions where case settlements were negotiated, the court beat was primarily print-oriented (Ericson, Baranek, and Chan 1989). In contrast, on the police beat, the major-occurrence news releases, with updates on crimes and investigations, were especially attuned to the hourly update requirements of radio stations and therefore radio reporters were at the core of the reporters' subculture on the police beat (ibid). A further contrast was provided on the legislature beat, where politicians and their officials favoured television because of the assumed size and breadth of television's audience and the impact of its images (ibid). While radio reporters had a leading place on the police beat, they were referred to as mere 'spit collectors' at the legislature, indicating the fact that they picked up only residual material from interviews and questions framed by reporters working in other media. Different news requirements of different sources *vis-à-vis* medium format capabilities lead them to favour a particular medium, and variation in content across media is the result.

Each medium offers sources different formats for expressing their authority. Meyrowitz (1985) argues that a print-oriented society is supportive of hierarchy based on specialized and compartmentalized knowledge, whereas electronic media, especially television, tend to undermine claims to authority based on specialized knowledge and thereby foster a levelling and democratic effect.

> In a print society, the graded complexity of print data and the highly compartmentalized nature of print audiences leads to high esteem for 'experts' (the 'top' in the field) and 'specialists' (people whose knowledge is focused in one tiny cluster of information about a particular subject) ... [In the electronic society] messages from all bodies of knowledge are more equally accessible to all people. While such messages, especially as presented on radio and television, often offer more 'awareness' than 'understanding,' the new communication pattern works to undermine the stature of authorities whose knowledge and skills are based on isolated communication networks. (ibid: 326–7)

Meyrowitz's observations help explain the fact that while politicians and other members of the élite gravitate towards television to express their authority, they turn to the newspaper as a source of authority. When it comes

32 Representing Order

to actually using knowledge available in the news in the course of their activities, members of élites who are regular news sources favour the quality newspaper. For example, in a survey of 602 élite decision-makers, 55 per cent said they relied on daily newspapers, especially the *Globe and Mail*, while only 22 per cent expressed a preference for television, 13 per cent for radio (mainly the CBC), and 10 per cent for periodicals (RCN 1981b).

KNOWLEDGE

The format requirements of a medium create an affinity with particular types of knowledge. Newspapers, television, and radio vary in the degree to which they each rely on knowledge that is primary (factual, asking 'What happened?'), secondary (explanatory, asking 'Why did it happen?'), tertiary (emotional, empathetic, asking 'What was it like to be involved in what happened?'), and evaluative (moral, asking 'Was what happened good or bad?'), and involves recommendations (asking 'What should be done about what happened?').

The distinction among these types of knowledge in any given news item is a matter of context, not syntax (Runciman 1983: 38). The journalist, like the novelist, uses various source clips, including his or her own, as part of a spoken dialogue to sustain a narrative. 'Whatever an individual character may say, its meaning will be determined not by his or her intentions or situation, but by placing of the interview in the overall context of the story. The terms he or she uses may be taken approvingly, or be contradicted and appear to be cynical, short-sighted, or bloody-minded ... All the individual voices, like individual notes in a musical score, are then orchestrated together with the overall news story. The effect of this on the narrative is to provide it with authenticity, the *reality effect*' (Hartley 1982: 109–10).

While the intended effect of the news story is to make consumers believe that they are witnesses to reality, reality is always inferential. What appears as iconic is actually the result of a process in which journalists and sources have necessarily gone beyond the knowledge apprehended by them, reconstructing it in ways that displace the observed world. The reality is that the news is embedded in the criteria of rational acceptability of news practice, and as such it is not mind- or discourse-independent. News discourse is not about objects; it constitutes objects. News reality depends on how the comments of journalists and sources have been contextualized in the narrative, and ultimately on how this contextualization is visualized by the consumer.

This context-dependency means that it is not a straightforward matter to specify what is a fact, explanation, empathetic understanding, evaluation, or recommendation. For example, depending on the context, the word 'inconsiderate' can be used as part of a statement of fact, explanation, evaluation, or prediction (Putnam 1981: 138–9; see also Dworkin 1986). The same can be said for many words that appear regularly in news discourse, including words taken from the discourses of professions that deal with social problems. For example, the psychiatrist's use of 'psychotic' and the sociologist's use of 'exploitation' vary in their knowledge-use, depending on their context within the text. Thus the term 'psychotic' can involve a mere report, an explanation, a prediction, and/or an evaluation (Runciman 1983: 38). As Putnam (1981: 139) observes, 'When we think of facts and values as independent we typically think of "facts" as stated in some physicalistic or bureaucratic jargon, and the "values" as being stated in the most abstract value terms, e.g., "good," "bad." The independence of value from fact is harder to maintain when the facts themselves are of the order of "inconsiderate," "thinks only about himself," "would do anything for money."'

These considerations indicate that even primary (factual) understanding can be polysemous. Reformulation of the factual depends on the methods people use to attribute meaning to the world, including especially the medium formats and language they use for what they observe. A fact cannot be photographed. In examining a photograph, we select certain features and express them in the forms and linguistic terms available to us. All factual empirical statements are entwined with interpretation (in the case of science, see Ryle 1949; Mulkay 1979; Brannigan 1981). In accomplishing primary understanding, the journalist does not simply reproduce the interpretations of his or her sources, he or she gives them a 'constructive interpretation' (Dworkin 1986: esp. chap. 4). That is, his or her interpretations contest and pass judgment on the interpretations of his or her sources. Similarly news consumers engage in 'constructive interpretation,' reading in an interpretation that contests and passes judgment on the interpretations of journalists. We know things only in terms of their significance to us. We always have to propound the world in which our description makes sense (Geertz 1983). Even the simplest facts are differentially interpreted in different contexts (Monaco 1981: 122; Fiske 1987: chap. 5). The reading or interpretation of facts gives them a fictive character, yet such fictions are essential to making sense of a communication and its context. As Crisell (1986: 124) observes with respect to radio, 'however factual the events which the commentator describes, they must be "created" in the listener's mind, very probably in a form which is in many respects different from the reality itself, and are in that sense a "fiction."'

Consider that statements that are descriptive on one level may also be read as evaluative. This is so because the very language we use to describe the world depends on our values (Putnam 1981). Thus descriptive terms may also bear evaluations and yet be assessed as 'fair comment' by journalists. As Hartley (1982: 27) observes, 'the sign *moderate* may be used to denote a politician or union leader, but it also connotes approval of their status and therefore of that individual. Much of the media's attention is devoted to giving people labels that denote their job or status, but these also connote the attitude or value they attach to it. The trick is to make multi-accentual connotation look like uni-accentual denotation.'

Another reason why factual or descriptive statements are read evaluatively is because the facts that people construct are related to the moral conclusions they draw (Midgley 1982). The use of facts in making moral judgments best explains why sources take the news so seriously even though they are very sceptical about its factual accuracy (Ericson, Baranek, and Chan 1989). Sources are sensitive to 'the cultural significance of mass communication for assessment of one's moral qualities by others. In this sense all media reports are sanctionable as public documents and thereby call for an accounting (Scott and Lyman 1968)' (Altheide 1985: 192). The news is taken seriously because of its moral power, not because it is the best available source of primary facts.

The news media frequently value the facts through tertiary (emotional, empathetic) understanding, addressing the question, 'What is it like to be involved in what happened?' Sources provide 'emotional exhibitions' (Wagner-Pacifici 1986: 95) as part of the performance of their authority and how they wish others to value the facts of what happened. Television and radio have greater scope in this regard, including the use of emotive music on radio and emotive music and visuals on television (Epstein 1974: 242; Crisell 1986; Carriere and Ericson 1989: chap. 3). In the extreme, tertiary knowledge is a synthetic creation of sources and journalists that can intrude on or even extinguish other knowledge potentially available in the news item. When this occurs the news consumer is left with the feeling that 'we had the experience but missed the meaning' (T.S. Eliot, quoted by Gitlin 1980: 233).

The valuing of facts is also a matter of medium. News accounts involve technologically mediated metaphorical reconstructions that emphasize particular emotions and social and political realities. For example, on television 'an apparently direct or iconic representation of reality is more accurately a metaphorical reconstitution of that reality in the terms of the television medium. The similarity we perceive between signifier and signified should be thought of as a *constructed equivalence*; the metaphoric real world shown on television does not *display* the real world but *displaces* it' (Fiske and Hartley 1978: 48).

In contributing to the valuing of facts, each medium thus bears ideological functions (Elliott 1979; Altheide 1985; Meyrowitz 1985). 'For example, TV news information has a certain look and rhythm to it. As long as this is associated with news and the contexts of these special effects are not exploited, then it looks fine, complete, good enough, even true ... [It] can be regarded as a feature of rational ideology in its own right, and, therefore, is far more persuasive and consequential than run-of-the-mill political preferences' (Altheide 1985: 234). The medium itself takes on a familiar, credible, authoritative character that makes the knowledge it presents seem acceptable, as if what it offers is all that one needs to know. This ideological power of a medium can transcend political and economic power in framing how people see events and in influencing actions taken in relation to those events (ibid: 71ff; Meyrowitz 1985; Ericson, Baranek, and Chan 1987, 1989).

Market Differences

News formats, sources, and knowledge also vary in accordance with the market orientation of media organizations. Newspapers in particular pursue distinct markets. 'Popular' newspapers seek acceptance through seeming to be close to reality. Their formats thus incorporate iconic elements, including pictures, brief items on simple themes, strongly opinionated columns on simple themes, colloquial expressions, and parochial interests. These elements are combined in an entertaining and lively manner. The presentation of material in an entertaining manner does not contradict the sense of being close to reality, but rather underpins it. Playing on the heart, and on lower regions of the anatomy, popular newspapers are able to effect a sense of what it is 'really' like to be involved in a situation. Material that is lively also seems 'alive,' and thus real.

'Quality' newspapers, by contrast, seek acceptance through more 'literary' and symbolic means. Their formats include longer items, features, and continuing stories on complex matters affecting business and political élites on a national and international scale. There is a concern with being a source of record both at the moment and historically, resulting in close attention to language and to mechanisms for correcting errors that exhume accuracy and authority.

There are also newspapers that try to encompass both ends of the spectrum, to be all things to all people. For example, in Toronto, while the *Sun* is explicitly a popular newspaper and the *Globe and Mail* is explicitly a quality newspaper, the *Star* is a mass newspaper that includes elements of both and is read *in addition to* the others (RCN 1981c: 70–1). Instead of finding a particular limited niche in the market, the mass newspaper tries to be the market itself.

36 Representing Order

An appeal to the mass market is more characteristic of broadcast media, especially television, because of their medium formats. There is particular pressure on broadcast outlets to appear popular when advertising revenue is a consideration. For reasons we shall outline shortly, and document in substantive chapters that follow, television news is least able to offer distinct popular and quality products. However, as Crisell (1986: 48–9) has shown, there is scope within radio to make news distinctly popular or quality in character.

FORMATS

The need to sell markets leads to particular news formats. News that is relatively discursive, and unadorned with sensational and dramatic constructions, fails to hold readers and therefore fails to sell goods (Seaton 1980: 96–7). Hence news, like the advertising system that supports it, moves in the direction of non-discursive, entertaining formats of presentation. Fifty years ago the Gallup organization discovered that 'more people read comic strips than the news,' and this 'led advertisers to exploit emotional symbols and techniques' (Draper 1986: 15). The success of this exploitation in advertising has had a recursive influence on news producers who use the techniques of advertising to hold their readers for advertising. For example, the news focus on sensational crimes is in part explained by their entertainment value. A survey of newspapers in Ontario found that the greater the advertising space in the newspaper the greater the emphasis on crime news (Dussuyer 1979: 100). A television news producer informed us that 'news must be packaged in a glittering way so that viewers who have just finished watching Carol Burnett will stay tuned for the news. In noting that the 'Newshour' rating had gone up to 24 per cent of the audience in the previous eighteen months, this producer observed that Kellogg's does not spend most of its money on cornflakes, but rather on the cornflakes box' (Ericson, Baranek, and Chan 1987: 86).

Advertising offers no opportunity for assessing products on the basis of truth claims. Its claims are neither true nor false, just more interesting or less interesting, more imaginative or less imaginative, more beautiful or less beautiful. Television news in particular takes on these characteristics of advertising. It offers brief clips that show people making claims to authority, knowledge, and doing good, but this is largely presentational and non-discursive and as such does not allow for judgments of truth (Meyrowitz 1985; Postman 1985). Viewed this way, news is indeed a 'social hallucinogen' for a commercial culture in which the 'boundaries between news, entertainment, public relations and advertising, always fluid historically, are now becoming almost invisible' (D. Schiller 1986: 36, 21).

Advertising affects news organizations in other ways. In at least one newspaper chain in Canada, favourable news treatment for advertisers has been reinforced by promoting advertising managers to the publisher's chair and to other senior and influential positions that affect editorial content (RCN 1981b: 69; RCN 1981c: 100). People in the news business, of course, appreciate that news and advertising are entwined. For example, in commenting on a newspaper's decision to refuse two advertisements, the Ontario Press Council declared, 'Advertising is a form of news and the paper has a responsibility to publish advertising news whether it agrees with it or not' (RCN 1981b: 77). Ask an academic colleague why he bought a copy of the local popular newspaper and he will tell you that it has the best selection of advertisements for stereo equipment.

Distinctive quality and popular news products, and the organizational differences associated with them, may be more applicable to radio news, and especially to newspapers, than to television news. Research has shown repeatedly that television news production and products are similar. Epstein (1974) reported no substantial differences in the approach and coverage of the three national television networks in the United States, and the Glasgow University Group (1976) reported similarities in industrial news coverage among the BBC1, BBC2, and ITN channels in Britain. A study of television news comparing Ireland, Sweden, and Nigeria (Golding and Elliott 1979) concluded that there was a 'broad similarity of news production practices and of the news values embodied in the output of these three quite diverse societies, despite the distinctive relationships of broadcasting to the state in each case. The study presented broadcast news as an "international genre" with significant national variations, and argued for an understanding of news as ideology, in its emphasis upon consensus, in its alignment with the assumptions and preoccupations of the powerful, and on its inherent inability to provide "a portrayal of social change" or to reveal "the operation of power within and between societies"' (Golding, Murdock, and Schlesinger 1986: 4–5). These findings suggest that the format requirements of the television medium may predominate in limiting the range of what it is possible to present (Altheide 1985).

The format limitations of the television medium are a major reason why television news is directed at a mass audience. A newspaper can build its readership by appealing to an aggregate of minorities, each of whom will select and read only particular sections and items from the total volume available in the newspaper. Television must do the selecting of items for its audience and hold its attention through the newscast. Therefore television includes material that is attractive to the widest possible range of people, which means an appeal to the lowest-common-denominator mass audience. 'Whereas individual newspapers are assumed to be the competing parts of the market, individual broadcasters are assumed to be the market-place itself' (Epstein 1974: 64). Competition is for a share of the total audience – people with their television sets on during a time segment – rather than for a share of a more specialized or narrow market. Television has the greatest capacity for this popular appeal because of its pictorial strength, sense of realism, and simple language. Television news is accessible to virtually everyone, including young children (Meyrowitz 1985: chap. 13). The popular formula of dramatic, entertaining, simple, and short items is adopted by television journalists to fulfil the competitive requirements for audience share, and form takes precedence over content (Elliott 1978, 1979). Hence television journalists converge on similar topics, sources and story angles, and the popular/quality distinction is blurred.

Some of the format requirements of radio create a popular tendency in its newscasts. Like their counterparts in television, radio journalists must select items for their listeners, and hold their attention through the newscast with limited language and dramatic structuring. This means that radio news shows are relatively short and each item is brief; that coverage focuses on dramatic events and conflict; and that such techniques as alternating voices and sound actualities are used to strengthen the auditory appeal. These components combine to enhance the listener's ability to visualize what is being said, to make the radio news story as 'photographic' as it can be without the actual capacity to present a visual.

In spite of these tendencies, the radio medium does not preclude a quality orientation. Radio cannot be like the quality press. Its language is not that of the quality London *Times* or Toronto *Globe and Mail*. Because it is auditory, radio news must use a more limited vocabulary and a less complicated syntax than the *Times* or *Globe and Mail*. But neither is radio language that of the popular English *Sun* or Toronto *Sun*. Radio news has a greater need for a more objective, and a less individualistic, emotive, and opinionated tone than popular newspapers exhibit.

Crisell's (1986: chap. 4) detailed comparison of a popular newscast and a quality newscast, both emanating from the BBC radio network, shows clearly that the popular/quality distinction holds for radio. In language, presentation, content, and some aspects of format, popular and quality radio newscasts are very different. 'For all the linguistic compression which the medium imposes, its inability to editorialize and its need to use its voices not only for reportage but also as actuality, radio news does succeed to a remarkable extent in paralleling and evoking the differences between the popular and quality newspapers' (ibid: 99). For example, Crisell's analysis shows that in the popular radio outlet he studied, the newscast is presented as an enclave within an existing entertainment (pop music) show. It therefore tends to assimilate news to the wider broadcasting context of its entertainment programming. This assimilation is indicated, for example, by the title for the show – 'Newsbeat' – and by the fact that the show frequently ends with an item on pop music, such as an interview with a pop star. This packaging is based on the assumption that people listen to the station for the music, not the news, and so the news is in essence made part of a 'newsic' formula. In contrast the quality radio outlet studied by Crisell has a more discrete, self-contained, and much longer news show. The news show is therefore a program in its own right, rather than, in effect, an extended news summary. It is presented with greater detail and complexity on the assumption that people tune in because they want news, that they are seeking knowledge and detail rather than merely the station's 'sound.'

The format of newspapers allows their journalists to focus on various special interests, and thereby to increase circulation through the aggregate of interest groups who buy it for their particular purposes. Alternatively, newspapers can tailor their coverage to the interests of a single narrow or specialized group, who can be sold to advertisers whose products and services are of special interest to the group. These possibilities exist in particular because the newspaper is capable of linguistic variety, has a permanency to its language, and provides the self-pacing such permanency allows. The basic distinction is between the popular newspaper which is simple in structure and colloquial in its use of vocabulary, and gives more emphasis to emotive or tertiary understanding, and the quality newspaper, which tends towards great complexity in structure, 'literary' use of vocabulary, and primary and secondary (explanatory) understanding presented in an 'objective' tone.

While newspapers retain these flexible features of their format, there have been encroachments on the autonomy of their formats from the broadcast media, especially from television. All newspaper journalists have been affected by how television formats dominate particular beats, such as the legislature (RCN 1981b: 135; Meyrowitz 1985; Ericson, Baranek, and Chan 1989). They have also been affected by the peculiar conception of objectivity fostered in broadcast news, where an allegation is quoted from one source, a counterpoint is made by a spokesperson for the organization subject to the allegation, and truth is held to reside somewhere in between (Epstein 1974; Tuchman 1978; Ericson, Baranek, and Chan 1987). This approach has increased the expectation of impartiality in all media and has made the bias of newspapers appear increasingly improper (A. Smith 1980: 179).

Popular newspapers in particular have changed in tune with television formats. They are explicitly formatted in terms of television, and serve as a complement to television. The Toronto *Sun* has been described as the closest thing to television in print. Various executives in popular newspaper organizations have acknowledged the impact of television. 'John Hamilton, publisher of the Calgary *Albertan* at the time it was converted into a tabloid in 1977, said "Our format of tight editing rules related to young people brought up on television. They're used to brief presentation of news." Pierre Péladeau, whose two daily tabs have half Canada's tabloid circulation and enjoyed the fast growth of any Canadian newspaper in the 1970s, sees them as a complement to television' (RCN 1981b: 82). Entwined with this influence of television on newspaper formats is television's impact on newspaper marketing. The growth of life-style, entertainment, and sports sections of newspapers is associated with the spread of television, as is the 'zoning' of special supplements within a newspaper to different market areas. More fundamentally, television has become predominant in framing and demarcating the market that newspapers must feed into. 'The modern newspaper is essentially reaching out towards the *television* audience, a demographically defined audience, paid for by advertisers, which requires the kind of detail that turns into spectacle or reveals the panorama of events lying behind the reports that have already reached the audience in aural and/or visual terms' (A. Smith 1980: 241).

SOURCES

Market considerations, blended with media format requirements, have a substantial influence on the selection and use of sources.

Given their tendency towards non-discursive, entertaining, and simple accounts of events, outlets oriented to the popular market are likely to use fewer sources. They are also likely to rely more heavily on particular types of sources offering particular types of knowledge: officials who provide them with primary facts already formatted for their medium/market, and individual citizens who offer tertiary understanding that fits their 'vox pop' format.

The subtleties and nuances of source selection and use vary with the local market environment. In large urban markets with dozens of news outlets, there is sometimes a condition of 'overproduction.' This condition leads news outlets to pursue more unique stories with unofficial or minority-status sources in an effort to capture at least some of the market seeming to be different.

Advertising is a major factor in source selection. Those who advertise regularly are often given favourable treatment in news items and features about the wonders of their company and its products. This is especially the case with smaller, local newspapers and radio stations, and with feature sections of large newspapers such as those dealing with entertainment, travel, and real estate (RCN 1981b: 69; RCN 1981c: 100). Private-sector sources themselves treat the news accordingly, seeing access primarily in terms of their own marketing needs (Ericson, Baranek, and Chan 1989).

Sources in government are also oriented to their own marketing needs, blending news with advertising in the hope that the public will remain faithful to the belief that they are good public servants. However, with sources in government there is not a crude exchange of advertising revenue for news space that serves marketing functions, but rather a tit-for-tat subtle favouritism with particular outlets because their formats best fit the source's needs (Ericson, Baranek, and Chan 1989). For example, the police favour popular news outlets because these outlets offer a format suitable for communication of the primary facts of major occurrences at the core of police-defined newsworthiness (Ericson 1989; Wheeler 1986; Fishman 1981; Chibnall 1977). The police shy away from quality outlets because these outlets largely eschew the reporting of crime incidents in favour of a focus on police mismanagement and procedural propriety. Moreover, quality outlets, especially quality newspapers, search out a greater number of sources and a more diverse range of source types, and present them more discursively to make innuendo about police deviance. The police therefore perceive quality news outlets as a threat rather than as an ally, and erect different physical, social, and cultural barriers to the access of journalists from quality outlets than is accorded to journalists from popular outlets (Ericson 1989). The different needs of news sources and news organizations in terms of media/market format considerations are clearly reflected in content.

KNOWLEDGE

The news media have always been criticized for pandering to their readership to create and sustain a market share. John Stuart Mill described journalism as 'the vilest and most degrading of all trades because more of affection and hypocrisy and more subservience to the basic feelings of others are necessary for carrying it on, than for any other trade, from that of a brothel-keeper up.' In recent times there are complaints that journalism is done by market survey (RCN 1981b): deciphering what news readers want to fit with their 'life-styles,' which can in turn be linked to 'life-style' advertising. While reporters have little detailed knowledge of their readership (Schlesinger 1978; D. Clarke 1981; Ericson, Baranek, and Chan 1987), editors' expectations are framed by market considerations and they assign and edit accordingly (Seaton 1980). Hence news outlets with the same market orientation are likely to cover the same events, to talk to the same most influential sources involved in those events, and to formulate stories in similar terms. The result is pack journalism and convergence in news content.

These forces of convergence can also foster divergence. For example, the ascendancy of broadcast media has been accompanied by an advertising-driven need to appeal to a mass audience. In face of this need some newspapers try to appeal to a more limited readership that is attractive to particular advertisers. For example, quality newspapers take up an investigative and adversarial style that articulates with the institutional concerns of upscale readers who in turn are a market for upscale advertisers. The *Globe and Mail* has evolved to such a place within the Toronto news-media market. While finding a market niche in these terms leads to divergence in topics and sources on one level, on another level the product may not be different from more popular renditions of news. The popular news outlet continues its traditional formula identified by Mill, using salacious gossip, titillation, and sensationalism to allow its readers to be vicarious voyeurs, and then denouncing the very people and activities it preys upon (Roshier 1973). The quality news outlet does the same thing, only its targets are those prostituting themselves for the high life in established institutions (political corruption) more than those engaged in the low life of illicit prostitutions (vice and 'normal crime').

Ultimately the market orientation a news outlet tries to find for itself combines with its medium-format consideration to yield a distinct process of knowledge flow, system of knowledge, and type of knowledge. The popular format is characteristic of all television outlets because of medium considerations, and is chosen by particular radio and newspaper outlets for marketing purposes. It features particular knowledge: factual updating (largely bureaucratic constructs), evaluation and tertiary understanding (largely from the people as 'vox pop'), both of which are personalized and dramatized. Enclosed in these terms, the popular format is preferred by particular sources, especially the police, politicians, and others whose primary interest is helpful news and positive images (Ericson, Baranek, and Chan 1989). The quality format suits particular newspapers and radio outlets, but is available to television in a more limited way because of medium constraints. The quality news outlet features a more discursive presentation of knowledge: multiple institutional sources who offer greater depth in the form of explanation of events as well as evaluations and recommendations pertaining to legal change and political reform. Relatively more open in these terms, the quality format is preferred by particular sources, especially those who can benefit from particular instances of adversarial-style journalism to bring about the legal changes and political reforms they desire.

The market orientation a news outlet finds for itself also combines with its medium-format considerations to lead it in particular ideological directions. Popular news outlets tend towards strong ideological positions that are stated explicitly. For example, in their everyday crime reporting, they are strongly pro-police and pro–law and order; in their everyday international reporting they are strongly nationalistic and anti-communist. Quality news outlets offer their ideologies more gently. They appear more liberal, offering a greater number and wider range of sources and opinions, arriving at a particular ideological position only after a managed dialogue and debate.

Sources of Convergence

Our emphasis in this chapter has been on differences in media and market orientation of news outlets as these differences have a bearing on news formats, sources, knowledge, and topics. The emphasis on differences has provided an analytical starting-point for our empirical inquiry into how news of crime, law, and justice varies by medium and markets. However, we would be remiss if we failed to give weight to the many influences on news production that may yield similar news content across media and markets. We have already indicated some sources of convergence, including the important point that some factors that precipitate differences can also serve in contradictory ways to produce convergence. At this point it is worthwhile to make the sources of convergence more evident as they inform the empirical investigation that follows.

> We have the greatest, most sophisticated system for mass communication of any society that we know about, yet somehow mass communication becomes more and more synonymous with less communication ... We have the mistaken, conduit-metaphor influenced view that the more signals we can create, and the more signals we can preserve, the more ideas we 'transfer' and 'store.' We neglect the crucial human ability to reconstruct thought patterns on the basis of signals and this ability founders ... The conduit metaphor is leading us down a technological and social blind alley. That blind alley is mass communications systems coupled with mass neglect of the internal, human systems responsible for nine-tenths of the work in communicating. We think we are 'capturing ideas in words,' and funnelling them out to the greatest public in the history of the world. But if there are no ideas 'within' this endless flood of words then all we are doing is replaying the myth of Babel – centering it, this time, around a broadcasting tower. (Reddy 1979: 310)

44   Representing Order

Reddy articulates a pervasive sentiment that more media outlets have not brought better knowledge, and may be narrowing and trivializing public discourse (see also Postman 1985). In spite of the capabilities of each medium, and the competitive quest of news outlets for a different product that will secure a niche in the market-place, if anything the proliferation of news outlets may offer less diversity, not more. Why does the large urban news market-place – like the beer market-place or the automobile market-place – offer such a rich variety of brand names and yet end up being so bland?

One answer lies in monopoly capitalism and its relation to markets. In the case of newspapers, chains have become increasingly dominant, at least in the North American context (A. Smith 1980: 45–6; RCN 1981b: 9). The effect of the advertising-based chain monopolies has been to encourage journalism's peculiar version of objectivity, neutrality, and fairness, where overt and diverse opinion is reduced and blandness is produced. 'The professional code of the editor, and journalists as a whole, has been profoundly influenced by the evolution of the distribution methods of newspapers and their successive delineations of appropriate markets' (A. Smith 1979: 193). While 'narrowcasting' has expanded in recent years, the attitude in broadcasting is still " 'Least Objectionable Programming" (LOP). That is, the key is to design a program that is least likely to be turned *off*, rather than a program viewers will activity seek out' (Meyrowitz 1985: 73). Even the Public Broadcasting System in the United States is dependent on corporate donors and therefore tends towards programming that will not offend and that is lacking in political relevance. It is difficult to show a direct link between advertising and particular features of news content. However, it is revealing that readers perceive the news as having been influenced by news organizations catering to advertisers. In survey research conducted for the Royal Commission on Newspapers (1981b: 36–7), 72 per cent of respondents said they believed newspapers play down facts in news items that might offend advertisers.

News outlets operating with different market orientations but within the same medium may converge in their coverage because of medium-format requirements. As addressed earlier (pp. 37–8), the format requirements of television make television-news production and products very similar, not only between outlets within a local market, but also between national networks and even in international comparisons. Television outlets compete head-on for a share of the total audience rather than dividing up into more narrow or specialized markets, and this inevitably leads all outlets into the popular formula of dramatic, entertaining, short, and simple items which are, in any event, most suited to the medium.

The impact of one medium upon another medium is also a source of convergence. As considered previously (pp. 39–40), television has had a major impact on newspapers. Some popular newspapers are explicitly formatted as the closest thing to television in print. They emphasize the visual, with display headlines, still photographs, and captions in bold type taking up more space in a story than the written narrative. More broadly, television has had a fundamental impact on newspaper marketing, essentially framing and demarcating the market that newspapers feed into.

Practices in news production also foster convergence. The knowledgeability of journalists – the norms, values, and precedents of the craft – leads them to focus on similar topics, sources, and angles regardless of the medium or market orientation of their news organization (Schlesinger 1978; Tuchman 1978; Ericson, Baranek, and Chan 1987). The journalist's 'nose' for news seems to be the same, even if the details of what is required for each medium and market vary. It is the shared knowledgeability of journalists that leads to 'pack journalism': reporters covering news conferences, public hearings such as court cases or legislative proceedings, and continuing stories such as election campaigns, tend to focus on similar angles, use the same sources, and even reproduce the same 'quotable quotes.' It is as if journalists sometimes do no more than reflect a reality that is self-evident, at least to them. It is as if all that is required is to send one reporter to scoop up the facts, while the rest can simply polish them off and turn them into the symbolic gems required by their particular medium and market.

Pack journalism is compounded by the fact that journalists view existing news stories as their primary source of knowledge about newsworthiness (ibid). Broadcast journalists in particular rely on newspaper stories for their own ideas and assignments, with the result that 'newspapers are more of a source than a competitor' (Schlesinger 1978: 85). At some nth-level removed from what they are reporting on, broadcast journalists use newspaper reports verbatim, as background detail that they cite without attribution, for matching stories suitable to their medium, and as second-day leads that seek to further the story through a different angle, or at least a different twist. 'Newsmen come to see the print media as purveyors of *original* material while radio and TV extend or recirculate information, in the form of current affairs discussion or follow-up interviews. So newsmen turn to print media for information, and strengthen the pattern of dependence' (RCN 1981a: 2). As far as journalists are concerned, it is as if all one really needs to know is contained in the news, and one's only job is to repackage it in the different containers available in one's medium and market to make it appear new.

These journalistic practices are related to resources. The fewer the resources of a news outlet, the more it is dependent on a predictable supply

46 Representing Order

of material from source bureaucracies and from other news outlets, and the greater the number of steps it is removed from the events reported on. Among the news media, radio stations tend to have the least journalistic resources and therefore are most dependent in this regard. Television stations are in an intermediate position, while newspapers have the most journalistic resources. Thus radio, with least resources, produces fewer items, shorter items, and more simple items that reproduce the bare essentials of stories as framed by sources and/or by previous newspaper stories. However, the limited aspects of radio news are not only a matter of resources. The radio medium is restrictive to the point where it may not be worthwhile for a radio organization to multiply the resources of its news division. Increased resources might not enhance its product greatly, and may even have a negative impact; for example, long items with multiple sources on complex matters might lead people to switch off mentally or literally.

A limited budget and therefore circumscribed content are characteristic of popular news outlets more than of quality news outlets. However, this is not a straightforward matter. For example, in our observation of the court beat in Toronto, we discovered that a popular newspaper and a quality newspaper each devoted limited resources to the beat, especially in comparison to a mass-market newspaper. As a result, the reporter for the quality newspaper and the reporters for the popular newspaper helped each other routinely, exchanging cases to cover, story angles and ideas, quotations from sources, and basic factual details. There was no similar exchange with reporters from the mass-market newspaper. The exchanges resulted in a convergence in coverage between the popular and quality newspapers (Ericson, Baranek, and Chan 1989: chap. 2).

Sources are another point of convergence (ibid). By restricting reporters to particular times and places, and by enclosing on knowledge, sources can effectively circumscribe news stories to a narrow range so that 'pack journalism' is the only possible outcome. While particular sources may favour particular media and markets on particular occasions, on other occasions they may offer a news release to all outlets, so that the only choice for those outlets is to report what everyone else has or not report at all.

In summary, there is a large number of medium and market considerations that yield both convergence and divergence in news coverage. We keep these considerations in mind as we embark upon our empirical investigation into how news formats, sources, topics, and knowledge vary across different media and markets. In this chapter, we have raised many of the relevant issues through an overview of the current state of knowledge. In the next chapter, we crystallize this overview into questions for research, and then describe the research project we designed to address them.

References

Altheide, D. 1985. *Media Power*. Beverly Hills: Sage
Barthes, R. 1977. *Image - Music - Text*, trans. S. Heath. Glasgow: Fontana
Bates, A. 1984. *Broadcasting in Education*. London: Constable
Brannigan, A. 1981. *The Social Basis of Scientific Discoveries*. Cambridge: Cambridge University Press
Cardiff, D. 1980. 'The Serious and the Popular: Aspects of the Evolution of Style in Radio Talk, 1928-1939,' *Media, Culture and Society 2*.
Carriere, K., and R. Ericson. 1989. *Crime Stoppers: A Study in the Organization of Community Policing*. Toronto: Centre of Criminology, University of Toronto
Cayley, D. 1982. 'Making Sense of the News,' *Sources*, Spring: 126-8, 130-3, 136-7
Chibnall, S. 1977. *Law-and-Order News*. London: Tavistock
Clarke, D. 1981. 'Second-Hand News: Production and Reproduction at a Major Ontario Television Station,' in L. Salter, ed., *Communication Studies in Canada*, pp. 20-51. Toronto: Butterworths
Crisell, A. 1986. *Understanding Radio*. London: Methuen
Draper, R. 1986. 'The Faithless Shepherd,' *New York Review of Books*, 26 June, pp. 14-18
Dussuyer, I. 1979. *Crime News: A Study of 40 Ontario Newspapers*. Toronto: Centre of Criminology, University of Toronto
Dworkin, R. 1986. *Law's Empire*. Cambridge, Mass: Harvard University Press
Elliott, P. 1979. 'Media Organizations and Occupations: An Overview,' in J. Curran, ed., *Mass Communication and Society*, pp. 142-73. Beverly Hills: Sage
Epstein, E. 1974. News from Nowhere. New York: Vintage
Ericson, R. 1989. 'Patrolling the Facts: Secrecy and Publicity in Police Work,' *British Journal of Sociology* 40: 205-26
Ericson, R., P. Baranek, and J. Chan. 1987. *Visualizing Deviance: A Study of News Organization*. Toronto: University of Toronto Press; Milton Keynes: Open University Press
– 1989. *Negotiating Control: A Study of News Sources*. Toronto: Univeristy of Toronto Press; Milton Keynes: Open University Press
Fishman, M. 1981. 'Police News: Constructing an Image of Crime,' *Urban Life* 9: 371-94
Fiske, J. 1987. *Television Culture*. London: Methuen
Fiske, J., and J. Hartley. 1978. *Reading Television*. London: Methuen
Geertz, C. 1983. Local Knowledge. New York: Basic Books
Gitlin, T. 1980. *The Whole World Is Watching*. Berkeley: University of California Press
Glasgow University Media Group. 1976. *Bad News*. London: Routledge
Goffman, E. 1981. *Forms of Talk*. Philadelphia: University of Pennsylvania Press
Golding, P., and P. Elliott. 1979. *Making the News*. London: Longman
Golding, P., G. Murdock, and P. Schlesinger. 1986. *Communicating Politics: Mass Communications and the Political Process*. Leicester: University of Leicester Press
Hartley, J. 1982. *Understanding News*. London: Methuen
McWhinnie, D. 1959. *The Art of Radio*. London: Faber and Faber
Meyrowitz, J. 1985. *No Sense of Place: The Impact of Electronic Media on Social Behavior*. New York: Oxford University Press
Midgley, M. 1982. 'Moral Melodrama,' *Times Higher Education Supplement*, 16 April, p. 10

Monaco, J. 1981. *How to Read a Film: The Art, Technology, Langauage, History and Theory of Film and Media.* Oxford: Oxford Univeristy Press

Mulkay, M. 1979. *Science and the Sociology of Knowledge.* London: Allen and Unwin

Pietropaolo, D. 1982. 'Structuring "Truth": The Uses of Drama in "Information" Radio,' *Canadian Theatre Review* 36: 52-6

Postman, N. 1985. *Amusing Ourselves to Death: Public Discourse in the Age of Show Business.* New York: Viking

Putnam, H. 1981. *Reason, Truth, and History.* Cambridge: Cambridge University Press

Reddy, M. 1979. 'The Conduit Metaphor - A Case of Frame Conflict in Our Language about Language,' in A. Ortony, ed., *Metaphor and Thought,* pp. 284-310. Cambridge: Cambridge University Press

Robinson, J., and M. Levy. 1986. *The Main Source: Learning from Television News.* Beverly Hills: Sage

Roshier, B. 1973. 'The Selection of Crime News by the Press,' in S. Cohen and J. Young, eds., *The Manufacture of News,* pp 28-39. London: Constable

Royal Commission on Newspapers. 1981a. *Canadian News Sources.* Ottawa: Research Studies on the Newspaper Industry, Supply and Services Canada
1981b. *Final Report.* Ottawa: Supply and Services Canada
1981c. *The Journalists.* Ottawa: Research Studies on the Newspaper Industry, Supply and Services Canada
1981g. *Newspapers and Their Readers.* Ottawa: Research Studies on the Newspaper Industry, Supply and Services Canada

Runciman, W.G. 1983. *A Treatise on Social Theory.* Vol. 1: *The Methodology of Social Theory.* Cambridge: Cambridge University Press

Ryle, G. 1949. *The Concept of Mind.* London: Hutchinson

Schiller, D. 1986. 'Transformations of News in the U.S. Information Market,' in P. Golding, G. Murdock, and P. Schlesinger, eds., *Communicating Politics,* pp. 19-36. Leicester: Leicester University Press

Schlesinger, P. 1978. *Putting Reality Together*: BBC News: London: Constable
1988. 'Rethinking the Sociology of Journalism: Source Strategies and the Limits of Media Centrism.' Paper to the Economic and Social Research Council Workshop on Classic Issues of Mass Communication Research, Madingley Hall, Cambridge
1989. 'Crime and Mass Media: Theoretical Issues.' Paper to the British Criminology Conference, Bristol

Scott, M., and S. Lyman. 1968. 'Accounts,' *American Sociological Review* 33: 46-62

Seaton, J. 1980. 'Politics and Television,' *Economy and Society* 9: 90-107

Silvey, R. 1974. *Who's Listening?* London: Allen and Unwin

Smith, A. 1979. 'Technology and Control: The Interactive Dimensions of Jornalism,' in J. Curran et al., eds., *Mass Communication and Society,* pp. 174-94. Beverly Hills: Sage
1980. *Goodbye Gutenberg: The Newspaper Revolution of the 1980s.* New York: Oxford University Press

Tuchman, G. 1978. *Making News.* New York: Free Press

Wagner-Pacifici, R. 1986. *The Moro Morality Play: Terrorism as Social Drama.* Chicago: University of Chicago Press

Wheeler, G. 1986. 'Reporting Crime: The News Release as Textual Mediator of Police/Media Relations,' MA thesis, Centre of Criminology, University of Toronto

Williams, R. 1989. *Raymond Williams on Television: Selected Writings.* Toronto: Between the Lines

[2]

The Televised Mediated Trial: Formal and Substantive Characteristics

Susan J. Drucker
(Based on a Case Study Done with Dr. Janice Platt Hunold)

Mediated trials are distinct from trials observed in person. The author argues that trials observed face-to-face are distinct from televised mediated trials. Because television "reformats" the events it covers, the medium affects what viewers ultimately understand the legal process to be. The authors posit that televised trials should be approached as a media event that represents a discrete genre of television programming, the televised mediated trial. Generic features of face-to-face trials and televised mediated trials affect what is communicated to an audience. Implications for public knowledge of the legal system are then discussed.

SUSAN J. DRUCKER is an Assistant Professor in the Department of Speech Arts & Sciences, Hofstra University. The author wishes to express her appreciation to Professor James W. Chesebro for his suggestions and editorial advice.

Television cameras are being admitted to an ever increasing number of courtrooms throughout the country. These televised trials may provide viewers with more information about the legal system and the societal conflicts they seek to adjudicate. Yet, insofar as television "reformats" the events it covers, the medium of television itself may dramatically affect what viewers ultimately understand the legal process to be. This essay examines the production conventions of the televised trial, the entertainment environment into which mediated trials are placed, and how they are processed by the audience.

Our central contention is that the decision to televise an event transforms what that event communicates to viewers. Specifically, we posit that televised trials should initially be approached as a media event distinct from the understanding derived from directly observing a trial within a courtroom. Ultimately, we suggest here that televised trials constitute a distinct genre, *the televised mediated trial,* possessing unique substantive and stylistic features which can be distinguished from other kinds of trials and other types of televised programming.

The communications discipline is not short of concepts and yet another concept should be introduced judiciously. The *televised mediated trial* is worthy of inclusion for three reasons:

It is the *televised mediated trial* that redefines the legal process in terms of mass understanding. Such understanding of trials had previously been defined through in-court observation or print coverage.

It is the *televised mediated trial* that has blurred the distinction between media news coverage of the legal system and entertainment and influenced both. This has resulted in a recasting of legal procedures into that which is entertaining to the lay audience, dramatically altering what the legal system is believed to be.

It is the *televised mediated trial* which provides an application of the media perspective. The medium employed to convey content affects the way in which the content is understood.

We are dealing with the interaction between the legal system and a media system. The terminology of the legal system and terminology of communication literature dealing with media coverage of trials are inadequate. They fail to explain the public's perception of trials. We therefore introduce the new term *televised mediated trial.*

The retrial of Claus von Bulow has been selected to illustrate this contention by examining a trial which was a face-to-face communicative event in a courtroom in which television cameras were permitted. The television coverage provided a distinct *televised mediated trial* for the viewing audience. We analyze this trial as both a face-to-face trial, and as a mediated communicative event or *televised mediated trial.* The concept of *televised mediated trial* presumes media coverage on both an internal and external level. Television coverage of face-to-face trials represents the internal level. The external level is provided by the interfacing of print and electronic media coverage which is always present when a face-to-face trial is televised. Trials are thus televised in a context of media intertextuality. We likewise use the *televised mediated trial* as a vehicle for the comparison with other television forms and identify the formal features and discrete boundaries of the genre of *televised mediated trial.* This essay concludes with a discussion of implications of the *televised mediated trial* on perceptions of the legal system and constitutionally guaranteed rights to a fair trial.

Face-to Face Trials vs. Televised Mediated Trials

In classical rhetorical conceptions, law is one of the primary modes of communication. Indeed, trials are said to be as old as *homo sapiens,* or at least to date back to the time when human beings began to live with others (Aymar & Sagarin, 1985). In this view, trials provide a means of informing the populace that the legal system is a fair, orderly, truth-seeking opportunity for the just resolution of conflicts. Trials themselves thus become concrete expressions of significant moral relations which are not adequately understood by analyzing them solely in terms of their consequences (Doret, 1974).

Television news cameras have received increasing acceptance in state courts. Concerns surrounding decorum in the courtroom and potential influence on trial participants had resulted in an almost total ban on cameras dating from the mid 1930's. By the mid 1970's a number of states experimented with cameras in courts (Barber, 1986). A pilot program in Florida led to a test of whether states would be allowed to authorize news cameras in courtrooms. The United States Supreme Court voted to allow states to continue experimenting with cameras as this did not violate the Sixth Amendment right to a fair trial (Chandler v. Florida, 1980). The Chandler decision worked in conjunction with technical advances to encourage state legislatures to vote for introduction of cameras into selected trials and or appellate courts. As cameras move into courtrooms, conceptions of trials may need reconsideration. As for the majority of the populace, televised court procedures become the only practical way of observing the legal system.

Both face-to-face trials—observable by those inside a courtroom—and *televised mediated trials*—observable by those beyond courtroom walls—are social constructions of reality. A trial is a competitive narrative or story-telling reality.[2] Indeed, the capacity for narrative rationality enables juries to be composed of lay people (Fisher, 1984).

The *televised mediated trial* is the mediated counterpart of this social construction. Media systems affect audience understanding of the trial. Face-to-face trials become *televised mediated trials* whenever print and electronic media become the vehicle by which the proceedings of a face-to-face trial are received. One of the trials most thoroughly covered by print and electronic media in recent years was the retrial of Claus von Bulow accused of attempting to murder his heiress wife Sunny. The live gavel-to-gavel television coverage provided by Cable News Network (CNN) was the result of Rhode Island joining the growing majority of state jurisdictions permitting electronic and photographic coverage of courts (Summary of Cameras in the State Courts, 1985).

These two categories of trials share common features but differ in at least five significant different ways. The concepts of *participants, trial site, rules, degree of evidence required to sustain proof,* and *purpose* provide a foundation for these comparisons.

Participants vs. Persona

There are three ways in which the participants in face-to-face trials differ from those who populate the *televised mediated trial*. First, in the face-to-face trial, courtroom participants are highly socialized to the trial's events and to each other, and they function to perform highly specialized roles and circumscribed activities (Taylor, Buchanan & Strawn, 1984). Jurors are instructed as to how they may use what they hear inside the courtroom and what they may read, hear and view outside the courtroom. Witness testimony is strictly regulated by the rules of evidence. Rules of decorum mandate near silence by courtroom spectators. We may readily identify the judge, the lawyers, the bailiff, and the court stenographer. The participants are defined predominantly by role and function rather than personality.

In the *televised mediated trial,* the focus is on character and image of courtroom participants. *Persona* is the key. *Persona* is an image concept, emphasizing factors external to the individual, perceived by others and used to determine motives and values. Television personalizes whenever it can by attaching concepts to individuals. " 'Good television' is television that embodies and articulates a world of 'personalities' who thoroughly penetrate and organize its viewing agendas, or enter television by being on those agendas" (Langer, 1981). Characters in the televised trials are created and transcend the courtroom walls. For example, in the von Bulow trial, the defendant, who never took the witness stand, told Barbara Walters on ABC's nationally televised *20/20* that he "loved his wife" (Walters, 1985). The stepchildren, Alex and Ala, appeared on *60 Minutes* to label von Bulow a "liar" (Dershowitz, 1986). Magazines reported titillating insights which were not part of the evidence of the face-to-face trial. "Von Bulow . . . said any number of times that they would have divorced if what happened had not happened" (Dunne, 1985, p. 48). The cover of *People Magazine* called it "A Shattered Family" (Ryan, 1985, p. 108). The more dramatic *Vanity Fair* featured Claus von Bulow's "Fatal Charm" (Dunne, 1985, p. 41). The press reported overheard conversations such as "It's those awful drugged-out children who have brought all this on and framed him" (Dunne, p. 47).

The second distinction is that the characters in the *televised mediated trial* need not be actual participants in the face-to-face trial itself. Cosima von Bulow, born to Claus and Sunny, was neither a witness nor a courtroom observer and did not play any formal role in the face-to-face trial. Her portrayal in the media was that of a daughter loyal to her father, believing in his innocence, whose loyalty resulted in the revocation of a $25 million inheritance from her maternal grandmother (Dunne, 1985). The defendant's relationship with his daughter and his desire to protect her by keeping her from observing daily courtroom events were the focus of media attention. In addition, Andrea Reynolds, Claus von Bulow's love interest and constant companion during the second trial, was another non-courtroom participant who was a critical part of the *televised mediated trial.* Her flamboyancy, her move into Sunny's Fifth Avenue apartment, her efforts to mastermind trial strategy and press relations all affected public perception of von Bulow. Thus, in the *televised mediated trial,* Claus von Bulow was not merely a person accused of criminal activity, he was the man whose wife lay in an irreversible coma while he and his mistress posed for magazine covers in matching leather outfits (Dunne, 1985). Non-courtroom participants played a significant role in defining the *televised mediated trial.*

Third, unlike the distance created between spectators and other participants in a face-to-face trial, the *televised mediated trial* creates an illusion of intimacy about the mediated trial participants. The form of the programming promotes the illusion of intimacy. Television suggests a reduction of distance between itself and the viewer, television personalities and viewers share a common universe and experience (Langer, 1981). The extensive television coverage brought Claus rather than "the defendant" into homes each day. The stepchildren remained remote figures throughout most of the second trial appearing on television interviews and press conferences occasionally (Dunne, 1985). Von Bulow appeared on screen everyday; the central *persona* of the program. "The Claus von Bulow Retrial" was the name of the program; the title took its name from the leading character.

> Television appears to have benefited Von Bulow in [a] . . . subtle way. It is much easier to impute heinous crimes to anonymous names in the newspapers than to people known personally. To an extent, someone seen regularly on television becomes "known." This would be particularly true of one seen—not glowering for a mug shot or dashing into court with a coat over his head—but turning up calmly in court each day, reserved, well dressed. (Wright, 1983, p. 326).

Sunny von Bulow would normally be characterized as the victim, the anticipated recipient of public sympathy. Her children characterized her as a non-person because she was lying in a deep coma (Dunne, 1985), but Sunny von Bulow became a non-person for the viewing audience when she did not appear on screen "live from Providence on the Claus von Bulow Retrial." Through testimony we came to know the Sunny that no longer existed, the Sunny who lived on was described as a vegetable surviving in a distant, antiseptic hospital room (CNN, 1985). Claus, familiar through his constant presence on the small screen garnered sympathy. We all saw "his eyes darting again and again to the door from which the jury would emerge . . tears . . . real emotion" (Live At Five, 1985). This aristocrat "we know." Lawyers with difficult murder cases often invoke the old principle of trying the victim. Von Bulow's defense before the Rhode Island jury made use of this strategy (Burton, 1985). The television presentation may have furthered this appeal to the viewing audience; a peculiar shift in sympathy.

Situs vs. Scene of the Trial

In the face-to-face trial, there is a *situs,* a place where a thing is considered with reference to jurisdiction over it. Jurisdiction is the authority by which courts and judicial officers take cognizance of and decide cases (*Black's Law Dictionary,* 1979). The jurisdictional power is exercised within the physical boundaries of a courtroom in which the actual proceedings of a trial take place. Trials are closed systems with fixed boundaries which permit no interaction with the environment (Brock et al., 1973). The amount of information introduced at trial is therefore limited to admissible evidence. The result of the closed system is that the structure, function and behavior of the system are relatively stable (Brock et al., 1973). A carefully regulated inspection of premises relevant to the trial may be authorized for the judge or jury (Prince, 1973) or conference in chambers, but basically it is the walled courtroom that is the *situs.*

The *televised mediated trial* takes place in a "courtroom without walls," a larger perceptual field which provides more information to an audience, but which blurs the distinction between what is relevant to a legal decision as to guilt or innocence. It alters an understanding of the circumstances affecting judgments of right and wrong. The *televised mediated trial* scene encompasses "testimony" given on the courthouse steps, in the corridor outside the physical courtroom, and in television studios. The "location" of the *televised mediated trial* can range from demonstrations about the legal controversy to any site of a reporter's research. A *televised mediated trial* would thus function as an alternative, extra-legal, forum for the adjudication of the case.

Thus, *situs* of von Bulow's face-to-face trial was a courtroom in Providence, Rhode Island. This *situs* carefully regulated all that could be considered in rendering a verdict. In contrast, the scene of the *televised mediated trial* included the courtroom, but it also extended to Clarendon Court in Newport, Rhode Island, the mansion in which comatose Sunny was found. It extended to Sunny's exclusive Manhattan apartment and the campus of Brown University where student Cosima was photographed lunching with her father. Reporters on the streets of New York City, Newport, and Providence further stretched the scene of the retrial. The only courtroom in which von Bulow testified in his own behalf was that presided over by Barbara Walters in his own living room (Walters, 1985).

Rules of Procedure vs. Rules of Coverage

Both face-to-face and *televised mediated trials* are constrained by rules. The face-to-face trial is bound by testimony given under oath or an affirmation to tell the truth. Courts and legislatures have developed rules of evidence that prohibit or limit the introduction of certain forms of evidence. One of the most important of these exclusionary rules is the exclusion of hearsay, defined as any statement made out of court and offered to prove the truth of the matter stated. The types of questions that may be asked and the elicited responses are also highly regulated. The basic rule concerning admissibility of evidence is that it must be relevant and competent (Prince, 1973). A state court is required to exclude evidence obtained by an unreasonable and hence unconstitutional or warrantless search and seizure by a state officer (Mapp v. Ohio, 1961).

There are rules which govern *televised mediated trials,* but these differ dramatically from face-to-face trials. In the *televised mediated trial,* there are no rules limiting testimony and evidence to be presented to the audience. Testimony of the interview variety is not given under oath. There are no constraints on the introduction of evidence and hearsay testimony. This type of trial is ruled by deadlines, budgets, judicial gag orders, limitations on access to face-to-face courtrooms and by restrictions on what may be photographed and broadcast.

In the von Bulow retrial, even as newspapers reported on the defendant's possible $14 million motive for murder, evidence of finances were ruled irrelevant to the case in the face-to-face trial (Breton, 1985). A judicial ruling prevented the prosecution and defense teams from utilizing videotape of testimony given at von Bulow's first trial on these charges in 1982. The *mediated trial* had no such restrictions. Witnesses from the first trial were brought into *mediated retrial* via videotape. A butler who testified for the state in 1982 and died before the retrial, a reluctant former mistress and other testimony ruled inadmissible in the face-to-face trial were freely injected into CNN's coverage of the retrial (CNN Coverage, 1985). The retrial was the result of a ruling that police should have obtained a warrant before a state toxicologist tested some of the drugs turned over to police by von Bulow's stepson Alexander von Auersperg. Evidence obtained by state police without a warrant was only inadmissible in the face-to-face trial. Von Bulow only answered questions in the *televised mediated trial,* not under oath or subject to cross examination (Dershowitz, 1986).

Degree of Evidence Required to Sustain the Burden of Proof vs. Appearance

In a face-to-face trial, the burden of proof rests upon one of the parties to an action to persuade the trier of the facts that the asserted proposition is true. In a civil case, the party with the burden of proof is required to prove a contention by "a fair preponderance of the evidence" or proof by a "clear and convincing evidence" (Prince, 1973). In a criminal trial, a defendant may not validly be convicted unless the evidence established beyond a reasonable doubt every element of the offense charged and the defendant's commission. The United States Supreme Court has defined a "reasonable doubt" as including an actual doubt of which a jury member is conscious. This is the highest degree of proof required in order to find against a defendant.

Mere *appearance* is the degree of evidence required to sustain proof in the *televised mediated trial.* Circumstances may indicate guilt and produce a verdict. The audience is not instructed to make its verdict conform to degrees of proof and questions of doubt. An opinion may be rendered before all of the evidence is heard. A previous criminal record or unsatisfactory social behavior may provide the impression of guilt in the *televised mediated trial.*

Claus von Bulow was acquitted by a sworn jury in Providence, Rhode Island on June 10, 1985 ("June 11 Daily News," 1985). The defense created reasonable doubt by asserting insulin was not the cause of Sunny's coma. Any link between the defendant and the alleged weapon which was a little black bag with an insulin encrusted syringe became irrelevant. The *mediated trial* resulted in a hung jury. Post trial interviews indicated that public opinion was mixed (CBS Evening News, June 10, 1985).

Judicial Resolution vs. Judicial Information

In the face-to-face trial, the entire process whereby controversies are adjudicated is assumed to conform to the goal of justice as a societal good. The entire trial system may be seen as a mechanism to achieve justice. The pragmatic goal of the trial system is to provide the opportunity for justice. A trial is an adversarial process which is an important forum for the discovery of truth (Barber, 1983). Truth is the ultimate goal of a trial and the end result is the verdict, the very derivation of which is from the Latin "veredictum"—a true declaration (*Black's Law Dictionary,* 1979). A principal function of a trial is to resolve conflict and effectuate a definitive solution. Enforcement of judgment is a key moment in the test of this mechanism for dispute resolution (McKinney, 1981). The face-to-face trial therefore has several purposes.

The *televised mediated trial* has two distinct purposes and functions which when fulfilled, alter the way trials are understood.

First, media access to face-to-face trials is desirable as a means of enhancing public understanding of the administration of justice. Education of the public and the role of the media in fulfilling the public's right to know about judicial proceedings have been used to justify a First Amendment right of the public and press to attend judicial proceedings (Richmond Newspapers v. Virginia, 1980). The fundamental principles of freedom of the press to comment on public affairs and to provide information of public concern support the selection of trials as newsworthy events.

A second function of the *televised mediated trial* is entertainment. "Audiences have come to expect the media technology will produce entertainment, and every type of medium has done exactly that" (Altheide & Snow, 1979). A trial is inherently dramatic; it is filled with the tension produced when adversaries meet. When a trial is mediated it no longer operates within the restraints imposed by the law governing face-to-face trials alone. When a trial is mediated the restraints imposed by the technology of the medium shapes the presentation and imposes the entertainment value upon the audience. Audiences see television in particular as primarily a form of entertainment; they process as entertainment coverage of reports of the real world. It is now generally agreed that even the presentation of reality on television has taken on certain properties of television's entertainment format and style (Bogart, 1980). Television creates its own reality for all of the programs it presents to the viewing audience. The expectations of entertainment can easily account for a popular desire to gain increased information about the trial process. We hold that the way in which audiences process the *televised mediated trial* is affected by the entertainment environment connected with televising the event.

Courtroom spectators at the courtroom trial may seek entertainment, but that entertainment is derived after sitting through long recesses and side bar conferences between attorneys and the judge. The action takes a long time to unfold. The home viewing audience of the *televised mediated trial* merely tunes in for information and entertainment. The program they see is interrupted by commercials, news briefs and voice-overs explaining delays in the action. The level of attention required for the lay person to make sense of the trial and enjoy the dramatic tension of the conflict varies from the non-mediated to the mediated context.

Five formal features distinguish the genre of face-to-face trials and genre of the *televised mediated trials.* Each of these generic features potentially affects that which is communicated to and therefore understood by an audience.

With the increased televising of trials, many in their entirety, the *televised mediated trial* is emerging. The *televised mediated trial* is a multi-media event which incorporates televised coverage of face-to-face trial action as well as media constructions of the trial. The act of televising face-to-face trials modifies the reality shown and creates a different reality for the viewing audience. That new reality is the *televised mediated trial.* Trials as television are therefore distinct from trials as observed in person. In order to determine how the public's understanding of the legal process and trials may be affected by *televised mediated trials* it is useful to understand the rhetorical form it takes.

The Televised Mediated Trial and Televised Trial Dramatizations

Rhetorical forms establish genre and a genre analysis involves isolating stylistic and substantive responses to perceived (situational) demands (Campbell & Jamieson).

In order to delineate the specific characteristics of the *televised mediated trial,* the stylistic and substantive generic characteristics of the CNN satellite coverage of the von Bulow retrial are compared to televised trial dramatizations.[3] There are many televised trial dramatizations. Dramatized trials appear in programs such as "L.A. Law," "Perry Mason," "Matlock," and "You are the Jury." The courtroom action in these programs is placed within the larger framework of a television drama which focuses on character development, relationships and the investigations and tensions that precede the trial. The televised trials selected for comparison are those dramatized trials and trials presented primarily for television in which action takes place almost solely within the confines of the courtroom. "People's Court," "Divorce Court," "Superior Court," and "The Judge" are typical of this category of the televised trial dramatization.

The five features which distinguish the *televised mediated trial* from the televised trial dramatization turn on the ways in which the scene, production techniques, purpose, story construction, and the participants are portrayed.

Reel Courtroom vs. Real Courtroom

The sound stage is the location for televised trial dramatization. Television cameras are placed to achieve the best television production. Directors make this decision. Theatrical courtrooms are designed to accommodate the needs of the camera. Real courtrooms, the locales for shooting the *televised mediated trial,* are designed to accommodate the needs of the legal system rather than the camera. Cameras may be limited to one area where they will not interfere with traffic in the courtroom. Many states limit the number of cameras and proscribe natural lighting (Summary of Cameras in State Courts, 1985). Sound quality may be affected by judicial limitations on audio equipment and acoustics of real courtrooms. The coverage of the von Bulow retrial was marked by natural lighting, natural sound (with voice-over play-by-play). On many occasions the camera placement prevented clear shots of portions of the courtroom. The sound quality was particularly poor with many extraneous noises. While content and locations of televised trial dramatizations are designed for televising, the courtroom does not provide the same freedom or aesthetic quality as does the sound stage.

Production Techniques vs. Production of Courtroom Coverage

All television programming share structural or formal features of television production which influence information processing (Huston et al., 1981). Formal features of television include shot size (variations of the three basic shots: close up, medium shot, and long shot); shot transitional devices (cut, dissolve, fade, wipe); and camera movement (pan, tilt, zoom, dolly, truck, arc).

Televised trial dramatizations use multi-camera techniques, large shot variety with moderate pacing; the tension is high. There is a variety of shot sizes making particular use of two-shots and chest shots. Cuts are the predominant shot transitional device. Programs are generally scripted so coverage of the action is smooth, objections are covered and appropriate reaction shots are gone to quickly. If a trial is not scripted, such as "People's Court," multiple cameras allow for greater shot variety and presenting more complete video of courtroom action. Programs are edited, resulting in a professional looking television program.[4]

The major structural features of the von Bulow retrial were found to include shot sizes which ranged from extreme close ups to medium long shots. Shot transitions were made through camera zooms which were quick and limited in number. The *televised mediated trial* coverage was characterized by slow pacing, and low tension. The axis movement of "characters" across the screen was predominantly from side-to-side creating low depth or visual interest. The use of a single camera inhibited the camera operator's choices for shot sizes and lack of transitional devices dictated the structure. The technological provisions for coverage resulted in a program with a rather amateurish appearance. The von Bulow footage resembled a home movie more than a professional television program.

In many instances, the coverage of the retrial differed dramatically from televised trial dramatizations. Structure of *televised mediated trial* programming is influenced by the restraints on the production technology imposed by the legal system. *The televised mediated trial* provides coverage of an event and transforms that face-to-face trial into a media event. Coverage adapts to the conventions of production of the television medium. Televised trial dramatization is the result of the creation of a television production tailored to the constraints and requirements of television production.

Dramatization vs. Reporting Purposes

Televised trial dramatizations stem from televised drama formats. Drama is a composition involving conflict or contrast of character, especially intended to be acted on the stage (*Random House Dictionary,* 1967). Dramatic shows were an early and popular television format (Primeau, 1979). It is common practice to take ... stories possessing potential dramatic life and breathe into them the necessary ingredients for dramatic existence (Busfield, 1958). Televised trial dramatization programs are made into theatric material or dramas with an audience in mind.

The televised mediated trial grows out of the news and documentary format. Reporting or journalistic technique is used to explore an existing problem (Bryski, 1986) such as the issues of a face-to-face trial. Recording life directly without apparent rearrangement or staging provides the illusion that manipulation has been minimized.

Claus von Bulow was tried by the state of Rhode Island for the purpose of enforcing criminal laws. The face-to-face trial selected for televising was viewed as a "bona fide" news event. Televising generated a different "pseudo-event" through the way in which the "real event" was covered. The von Bulow *televised mediated trial* had to adapt to the conventions of the television medium and the organizations producing the end product. The televised trial is affected by the production environment connected with televising the event. The institutional position of stations carrying trials is that they seek to produce "good television." The production staff and crew may work on news, sporting events, soap operas and game shows. Staffing decisions are based on availability of crew members rather than a philosophical view of the event being televised. The coverage of the von Bulow retrial emanating from cameras placed in courtrooms was forced by the sheer power of conventions of television to become not a drama but another type of television program.

Story Construction in Reel Time vs. Story Telling in Real Time

The story of televised trial dramatization is told in television time. This alters and compacts time. Delays of routine interaction are edited and action flows to avoid boredom. Tempo of a program is a significant defining characteristic of a program (Altheide & Snow, 1979). These programs provide the audience a beginning, middle and end; there is dramatic resolution of a trial, usually in one sitting. Legal conflicts are adjudicated in thirty minutes minus commercials.

The televised mediated trial of Claus von Bulow was told in real time. CNN did cut away for news updates and commercials during many breaks in the action. However, bench conferences, delays, routine activities of court personnel moving exhibits, witnesses moving to and from the witness stand were included in natural flow of time presented by CNN's coverage. The story followed a linear progression of time keeping pace with time through the day. Many viewers said this was boring (Drucker & Platt Hunold, 1986). This was a continuing story with simultaneous plots distinct from other televised courtroom action.

Performers vs. Celebrity Courtroom Participants

The set of the televised trial dramatization is populated by professional actors or "real litigants" who actually have what happened to them discussed on the screen (Pollan, 1987). There is a sense of presentation; a willingness to voluntarily inject oneself into the homes of the viewing audience. There is a blurring of the distinctions between programs which involve actual cases, litigants, attorneys, witnesses and fictional ones. Dr. Joyce Brothers has "played" an expert witness on "Divorce Court" (Pollan) while actual practicing attorneys have appeared for client actors playing roles (Galante, 1985). Court personnel, reporters or MC's, and judges are the recurring cast members. Retired jurists presiding over syndicated courtroom dramas such as Judge Joseph A. Wapner of "People's Court," Judge William B. Keene of "Divorce Court," and Judge William D. Burns of "Superior Court" are stars with fan clubs of their own (Pollan, 1987). Only the regular cast members working on the "right" side of the law have achieved celebrity status from these programs.

One of the functions of the *televised mediated trial* is to transform many participants including defendants into media celebrities. This is yet another generic characteristic of the televised trial. The heroes of a culture are a function of cultural priorities and values (Cawalti, 1985; Strate, 1985). The media celebrity has replaced traditional American heroes, much to the detriment of societal values (Boorstin, 1961). The celebrity is a person who is known for being well known. This person does not have to be great or even good. The media creates the celebrity who is a contemporary figure who becomes a celebrity through the agency of publicity (Boorstin, 1961). The characters in *televised mediated trials* like that of von Bulow become celebrities in this sense with media coverage. It is the filmic/electronic media that creates and maintains the celebrity of today. "All von Bulow has to do is walk past the line of trial watchers and the hallway crackles with excitement. He is tall as a lodgepole pine and just as stately... With such style, no wonder von Bulow has cultivated a coterie that is absolutely convinced of his innocence..." (Goldstein, 1985 p. 3). The electronic media celebrity has become the functional alternative to the action and intellectual hero of the past. There has been a shift from hero to celebrity which is related to the form of information made available through the dominant medium of communication (Drucker & Cathcart, 1986). This relationship is distinguished from that of hero/worshiper. It is not simply the amount of detailed information brought to the audience that "deheroizes," but the entire context of additional scientific and economic information on all levels which may affect the notion of hero. The defendant's deeds may not be viewed as being aspirational goals of society, but the audience may identify with this celebrity defendant. Von Bulow's deed may not have been heroic but his well-knowness fostered a new celebrity/fan relationship with viewers. Von Bulow "groupies" emerged (Goldstein, 1985, p. 3). Many different participants of a *televised mediated trial* may become celebrities.

Televised mediated trials have a generic resilience; they evidence a distinct genre. Typical elements found within diverse extant genre are brought together to form a new and unique grouping of recurring elements—a new genre. Apparently, this new genre is restrained chiefly by technological rather than aesthetic or structural considerations. The specific characteristics of the televised von Bulow retrial aid in clearly establishing the discrete boundaries and features of this distinct emerging genre.

Implications

Public knowledge of the trial process has been augmented by *televised mediated trials*. What trials are for most Americans has become inseparable from how trials are mediated. The public's understanding of trials is altered by the additional information about face-to-face trials that is provided by media coverage. Moreover, there is distinct information provided by *televised mediated trials*. There is not merely more information available, there is different information available.

The discrete features of *televised mediated trials* (*persona,* scene, rules of coverage, proof by appearance, judicial information for public edification and entertainment) provide a body of information which changes what trials communicate to an audience. Public knowledge achieved by observing face-to-face trials is devoid of the ramifications of this type of information. The *televised mediated trial's* greater degree of latitude in what is considered "relevant" and "admissible" to a case expands issues the public may consider in evaluating the operation of the trial process in resolving a case. *Persona* of parties, and nuances gleaned from enlarged settings for action, provide a unique and more humanistic type of information.

The communicative ability of a television narrative (such as the *televised mediated trial*) is, in large part, a function of the production techniques utilized in its creation (Barker, 1985). Video grammar has been documented as an influence on information processing (Huston & Wright, 1983). The production of televised trials functions to create a different trial reality for the viewing audience. Within the larger schema of televising, the trial is placed among other television programming which are seen primarily as forms of entertainment. The entertainment value is imposed upon the audience which may process coverage of trials as entertainment.

The American trial process operates under the presumption of openness whereby the public's presence will insure fairness and due process in the proceedings. The very notion of "public" trial may now be changing as different types of public trials providing radically different kinds of information become available. The nature of the audience or "public" presence is altered as receivers of information vary from those in the face-to-face courtroom to include those in the viewing audience of *televised mediated trials*. Each public is in a slightly different position as it fulfills the intended role of the "public presence" at trials. Each "public" has a peculiar perspective on violations of due process as a result of divergent views of a trial.

Courtroom spectators, and audiences for *televised mediated trials* develop differing expectations about the trial process. Future participants in face-to-face trials may be unprepared for the long delays associated with trials taking place in real time. When observing or participating in one of the altered trial situations, a cognitive imbalance may result.

Awareness of the effects of the mediation process on trials and information processing provide grounds for redefining the traditional fair trial/free press debate surrounding press coverage of trials. Conflict has centered around issues of the right to administer justice without undue interference and concern for a criminal defendant's constitutionally guaranteed right to a fair trial by an impartial jury. These interests confront freedom of the press and the public's right to know about governmental and judicial affairs (Devol, 1982). The conflict may now be extended to include greater concern for public opinion verdicts which are the products of different types of information provided by *televised mediated trials*.

Privacy rights of litigants, witnesses and jurors are implicated in a legal system which generates celebrities of all kinds. The notion of "impartial jury" may be changed as jurors selected to hear a retrial (such as von Bulow's) may have viewed a prior trial in whole or in part. The *form* (mediation) as well as the content of press coverage should be examined in determining invasion of privacy, impartiality of jurors and the effects of prejudicial pre-trial publicity.

What trials communicate to the public is dependent upon generic features of mediated presentation. Understanding how trials communicate provides a more realistic and comprehensive approach to the long standing concern about public participation and knowledge of the legal system.

NOTES

[1] As of the end of 1987, news cameras were being admitted in to courts in 43 states on either a permanent or experimental basis (Engels & Landa, 1987). The issue of access for photographic and electronic equipment has been a controversial issue often traced to the 1935 coverage of the Bruno Hauptmann kidnapping trial. The American Bar Association recommended banning cameras in courtrooms as early as 1937 with Canon 35 of the ABA's Canons of Professional and Judicial Ethics. Cameras have been viewed as a threat to the dignity and decorum of court proceedings as well as a distraction and source of pressure on court participants. After the Chandler decision of 1980, ABA revised its position to remove the suggested ban. Federal courts still ban cameras (Federal. R. Crim. P. 53).

[2] Fisher (1984) suggests the narrative paradigm in which man is essentially a story-telling animal. Human communication is viewed as "stories competing with other stories constituted by reasons, as being rational when they satisfy the demands of narrative probability and narrative fidelity, as inevitably moral inducements" (Fisher, 1984, p. 2) Fisher further indicates that because persons have the capacity of narrative rationality it is reasonable to have juries of lay persons (Fisher). Narrative rationality may be extended to trial spectators. Bennett and Feldman (1981) have identified narrative or story-telling as the form applied to the communicative event of the criminal trial. Story-telling is the implicit framework of social judgment that untrained participants bring into the courtroom to make sense of trials. It is the device that simplifies an event, selects information and organizes it so that adjudicators can interpret the event and judge its validity within the context created by the story. Bennett and Feldman posit strategic options for presenting a criminal defense; a reconstruction strategy of structuring a complete story, a challenge strategy to contradict points in the prosecutor's discrete story or a redefinition strategy which reinterprets elements of the prosecutor's story.

The von Bulow retrial may be viewed as an example of competitive narrative reality. The jury and audience heard contradictory versions of the same story. The prosecution argued that von Bulow committed a cold-blooded, premeditated act. He injected his wife with insulin to rid himself of her without ridding himself of her fortune. Doctors called by the prosecution testified that cause of the first coma was hypoxia or a lack of oxygen to the brain. A redefinition strategy was employed when the defense relied on contradicting medical evidence offered by the state. Doctors for the defense testified that hypoxia and not insulin was the cause of Mrs. von Bulow's comas (Breton, 1985). The defense maintained that while von Bulow may have been unfaithful to his wife, the charge of attempted murder was a fabrication by hostile step-children and was fueled by a devoted servant and a scorned mistress. The defense redefined the significance of the alleged weapon, a little black bag with an insulin encrusted syringe, asserting that insulin was not the cause of the coma. By removing the weapon, the defense removed the link between von Bulow and the comas.

[3]The method used to study the television coverage of the von Bulow retrial involved observation of the "video transcript" of the trial from the CNN satellite coverage for the week of May 13, 1985.

[4]Major features appearing in current television programming were derived from suggestions of Ronald Primeau in *The Rhetoric of Television* (1979). The authors had approximately 35 undergraduate students view several hours of representative samples of each genre. This produced an exhaustive analysis of not only courtroom programming but situation comedy; nightly news programs; dramatic prime time programs; daytime soap operas; game shows; and talk shows.

REFERENCES

Altheide, D., & Snow, R. (1979). *Media logic*. Beverly Hills: Sage.
Aymar, B., & Sagarin, E. (1985). *A pictorial history of the world's great trials from Socrates to Jean Harris*. New York: Bonanza Books.
Barber, S. (1986). *News cameras in the courtroom*. Norwood, New Jersey: Ablex.
Barber, S. (1983). The problem of prejudice: a new approach to assessing the impact of courtroom cameras. *Judicature, 66,* (6), p. 248–255.
Barker, D. (1985). Television production techniques as communication. *Critical Studies in Mass Communication, 2,* p. 234–246.
Bennett, W. L. & Feldman, M. S. (1981). *Reconstructing reality in the courtroom*. New Brunswick, New Jersey: Rutgers University Press.
Black's law dictionary, (5th ed.). (1979). St. Paul, Minn.: West Publishing.
Bogart, L. (1980). Television news as entertainment. In Percy H. Tannenbaum (Ed.), *The entertainment function of television*. Hillsdale, New Jersey: Lawrence Erlbaum Associates.
Boorstin, D. J. (1961). *The Image: A guide to pseudo-events in America*. New York: Atheneum.
Breton, T. (1985, June 24). Von Bulow's victory. *The National Law Journal,* p. 24.
Brock, B., Chesebro, J., Cragan, J. F., & Klump, J. F. (1973). *Public policy decision-making: Systems analysis and comparative advantages debate*. New York: Harper & Row.
Bryski, B. (1986). *On genres of television documentaries: Videotaped segments*. Unpublished manuscript.
Burton, T. (1985, May 30). Puccio: The Guilt Rests With Sunny. *Daily News,* p. 2.
Busfield, R. M. Jr. (1958). *The playwrights's art*. New York: Harper & Brothers.
Campbell, K. K. & Jamieson, K. H. (no date). *Form and genre: shaping rhetorical action*. Annandale, VA: SCA Publications.
Cawalti, J. G. (1985). With the benefit of hindsight: Popular culture criticism. *Critical Studies in Mass Communication, 2,* 363–379.
Chandler v. Florida, 449 U.S. 568.
CBS Evening News, (1985, June 10).
CNN Coverage, (1985, May 30).
Daily News, 11 June 1985 40.
Dershowitz, A. (1986). *Reversal of fortune: Inside the Von Bulow Case*. New York: Random House.
Devol, K. S. (1982). *Mass media and the Supreme Court* (3rd ed.). New York: Hastings House.

Doret, D. (1974). Trial by videotape—Can justice be seen to be done? *Temple Law Quarterly, 47,* 228-268.

Drucker, S. & Cathcart, R. (1986, December). Media Relationships: The celebrity and the fan. Paper presented at the Speech Communication Association of Puerto Rico conference, San Juan, Puerto Rico.

Drucker, S. & Platt Hunold, J. (1986, May). Lights, Camera, Justice: The Claus von Bulow retrial. Paper presented at the International Communication Association convention, Chicago, Illinois.

Dunne, D. (1985). Fatal Charm the social web of Claus Von Bulow. *Vanity Fair, 48,* 40-56, 106-109.

Engels, M. & Landa, R. (1987, Dec. 2). Justice gets its eyes back. *Daily News,* p. 8.

Federal rules of criminal procedure 53.

Fisher, W. R. (1984). Narration as a human communication paradigm: The case of public moral argument. *Communication Monographs, 51,* 1-22.

Galante, M. A. (1985, Sept. 29). An L. A. lawyer finds fame in Divorce Court. *National Law Journal.* p. 39.

Goldstein, M. (1985, June 5). Hottest ticket in town. *Newsday,* II, p. 3.

Huston, A. C., Wright, J. C., Wartella, E., Rice, M. L., Watkins, B. A., Campbell, T., & Potts, R. (1981). Communicating more than content: Formal features of children's television programs. *Journal of Communication, 31,* 32-47.

Huston, A. C., & Wright, J. C. (1983). Children's processing of television: The informative functions of formal features. In Bryant & D. R. Anderson (Eds.), *Children's understanding of television* (p. 33-68). New York: Academic Press.

Langer, J. (1981). Television's "personality system'. *Media, Culture and Society, 4,* 351-365.

Live at Five, (1985, June 10).

Mapp v. Ohio, 367 U.S. 643 (1961).

McKinney's New York civil practice and rules. (1981). St. Paul, Minn.: West Publishing.

Pollan, M. (1987). Reality shows: The syndicated bench. *Channels, July/August,* 52-54.

Primeau, R. (1979). *The rhetoric of television.* New York: Longman.

Prince, J. (1973). *Richardson on evidence.* Brooklyn, New York: Brooklyn Law School.

Richmond Newspapers, Inc. v. Commonwealth of Va., 448 U.S. 555 (1980).

Ryan, M. (1985, June, 17). A shattered family. *People Magazine,* p. 108.

Strate, L. (1985). Heroes, fame and the media. *Et Cetera,* p. 44.

Summary of cameras in state courts (January 15, 1985). Compiled by the Research and Information Service, National Center for State Courts, Williamsburg, VA.

Taylor, K., Buchanen, R., & Strawn, D. U. (1984). *Communication strategies for trial attorneys.* Glenview, Illinois: Scott, Foresman and Co.

The Random House dictionary of the English language. (1967). New York: Random House.

Walters, B. (1985, June 13). (Interview With Claus von Bulow). *20/20.*

Wright, W. (1983). *The Von Bulow affair.* New York: Dell Publishing.

[3]

What makes crime 'news'?

Jack Katz
UNIVERSITY OF CALIFORNIA, LOS ANGELES

How do news readers sustain an appetite for journalistic reports of crime? From day to day, many news stories on crime differ only in details about time, place and the identities of victim and defendant. How do daily readers come to take interest in today's report of murder or robbery, given that the story they read yesterday was substantially similar? For reliable information on crime, newspaper readers could turn to sociological studies. For entertainment they could, and indeed many do, read detective novels. What are the distinctive aspects of form or content that make daily news reports of crime continuously interesting to the modern public?

The sociological study of news is burgeoning, but one of its fundamental questions, the explanation of 'the appetite for news' (Carey, 1982; cf. the conceptualization of the problem in 'gratifications' research: Katz, Blumler and Gurevitch, 1973), remains very open. The need is to account for the significance to readers of the structure as well as the substance of news. In the case of crime news, how can we explain not only the relative importance of this category of news, but also: the emphasis on reporting crime as it enters the criminal justice process?; the differentiation of types of crime stories?; the daily recurrence of the reading appetite?; the way in which crime news is shaped to make it appear 'recent'; the dispersal of crime stories throughout the paper?

A coherent theoretical answer can be developed by addressing a number of themes previously marginal to the sociological studies both of news and of social problems. First I will offer an analysis of the content of daily news stories on crime. Sociologists have become increasingly sophisticated in examining the social organization of the news production process for biases which affect whether and how particular stories are reported (e.g. Fishman, 1980). But despite the contingencies affecting whether a particular item will be published, in fact all crime news stories that are published fit one or more of four classic forms of moral problematics. These categories should be understood as necessary but not sufficient conditions for publication. The argument is that candidate crime stories for publication in daily newspapers must be shaped along one or more of these four lines before they will be treated as newsworthy.

The substantive analysis was developed and tested until it exhausted sets of news stories drawn from New York and Los Angeles daily newspapers running over seven years. The first section below describes the samples and, with illustrations of the most novel, borderline cases, in effect reproduces the coding book used to analyse the news articles.

In the second section, I argue that, whatever the influences on news organizations that affect their selection and rejection of particular stories, daily news readers have an independently generated fascination with the stories that are published. This fascination is not primarily with learning about crime itself: daily news readers do not sustain an interest in crime stories either to do folk sociological theorizing about causes, or to become better prepared to cope with the realities of crime in society

In the final section, I attempt to comprehend the patterns revealed by the current data sets and the research literature with a theory of the quotidian reconstruction of news readers' appetites for stories of crime. My thesis is that crime is made 'news' by a modern public searching for resources to work out sensibilities routinely made problematic in everyday modern urban life.

Moral boundaries in crime news

I first became curious about the recurrent content of crime news while studying the federal criminal prosecution office for the Eastern District of New York (hereafter, EDNY). The leadership of the office was highly sensitive to publicity and had instituted a clerical routine for clipping local stories that made mention of the office. Working with the eight volumes of clipped stories covering the office from mid-1974 through 1978, I developed definitions of several types of crime news items and I employed six undergraduate students to code the stories from the *New York Times* and from *Newsday*. The resulting data set included approximately 550 stories on about 200 separate crimes. The definitions in the coding book were continuously revised to resolve ambiguities revealed in review sessions and to assure that each story would fit at least one category.

This data set had obvious weaknesses but it also had a subtle strength. The jurisdiction of a federal prosecutor's office only covers the major 'street' crimes (robbery, rape, assault, murder) in a relatively minor and incidental manner as compared to state-level prosecution offices. As a result, those federal crimes which make the news tend to show idiosyncratic wrinkles or exceptions to the typical crime news story. For the purpose of discovering the fundamental dimensions of newsworthiness, apparently exceptional or idiosyncratic cases have special value. In this study the research objective was to articulate, via the logic of analytic induction, the essential or universal basis of crime newsworthiness; or the necessary contents which a story on crime must be given before it will appear as news. The relative frequency with which stories of different types appeared was not the central concern.

The New York data had the further limitation of a possible bias in the selection criteria of the prosecution office. (We did check the *New York Times* index against two of the eight volumes of clippings collected by the prosecution office and found a handful of additional cases but none of a qualitatively novel type.) In order to increase the reach of the analysis, I employed two other students to code all crimes, state and federal, covered on the front page and on the first page of the Metro section of the *Los Angeles Times* published in 1981, 1982 and 1983. For each year, each Saturday, Sunday and Monday edition was examined; for the other weekdays, a different day's edition was examined for each week, on a rotating basis. This coding operation eventually selected 1,384 stories. Again the coding categories were revised continuously in the style of analytic induction, in order to define categories capable of identifying the newsworthy feature or features of all cases.[1]

An initial lead into 'the factors associated with newsworthiness' was provided by Bob Roshier (1973: 34) in his analysis of crime coverage by British dailies. He found that 'whimsical circumstances' — 'flower people' stealing flowers from a cemetery, the theft of a detective's car, a bank tricked by a 10-year-old — loomed large: 'This category, perhaps surprisingly, seemed to be probably the most important in relation to crime reporting in general.' Another important category was the involvement of an important person, as defendant, victim, or bystander. Roshier's study suggests the hypothesis that crimes do not become newsworthy because of what they tell about crime, but because crimes may be especially telling about other things of interest to readers.

Despite the rich variety of crimes in the news, we eventually found that a small number of recurrent themes could encompass all the data. In order to be made newsworthy, we concluded, crimes must be depicted in one or more of four ways. Each appears to call into question a moral boundary recurrently defined by adults in everyday modern life.

Personal competence and sensibility

In this category we placed the most numerous single type of crime story: accounts of ingenious, vicious, and audacious crimes — of deceptions that trick the close scrutiny of diligent customs inspectors, of the most bloody murders, of big heists in broad daylight. Such stories instruct readers on the nature and limits of personal competence and sensibility. Because of the general implications of the news they generate, artful dodgers and cool killers have often provoked a public interest bordering on affection. In a tradition extending back at least to Durkheim's time, crimes and criminals have been prized for what they say about the ingenuity and audacity that readers can reasonably expect not so much from criminals but from their civil fellows and of themselves.

One sub-category contained stories dramatizing exceptions to presumed demographic patterns of personal competence and moral sensibility. Reports of armed robberies by children (in 1982 there was a highly publicized case in Manhattan) or by the flamboyantly homosexual (the facts on which the film *A Dog Day's Afternoon* was based), by women, and by the elderly challenge our stereotypes not simply about crime but about the capabilities associated with those age and sex statuses. A story about a 10-year-old bank robber shows a surprising intentionality or seriousness of purpose and carries implications that run not only to juveniles charged with crime, but to aggressive acts performed by one's children against each other as well as to demands by children for adult privileges. If one's 10-year-old is seen as a potential bank robber, it might appear silly to insist that he go to bed at nine o'clock or eat his peas.

Containing Kennedy Airport, the EDNY federal criminal jurisdiction regularly produces stories illustrating the competence of daring ingenuity. Contraband dealers, especially those who must take their goods across inspection points, contribute an endless series of examples proving the possibilities of ingenuity. Long Island and New York City news readers may read one day about gems or high technology machine parts smuggled in toothpaste tubes, the next day about amazingly large quantities of heroin unsuccessfully stashed within vaginas and anuses.

Crime news stories illustrating the dimensions of human competence and moral sensibility include not only those that portray criminals as exceptionally insensitive or exceptionally daring, but also those that indicate the limits of criminal insensitivity. Illustrative of the latter was a NY *Daily News* story (15 June 1977) about a 21-year-old ex-convict who jumped out of a tenth-floor Brooklyn Criminal Court building moments after he was convicted of armed robbery. By noting that the fellow 'had been in trouble with the law since he was 15', the story made the point that even apparently hardened criminals may not be totally insensitive to social pain. Although this particular tenet of journalistic social philosophy may be unusual, it is routine for crime news to imply some sort of teaching about the contemporary state of moral character. Thus despite its reputation as sensational, the *Daily News* does not in fact routinely report either suicides or armed robberies. To be made newsworthy, a provocative theme about personal moral competence will typically be built into the story.

Collective integrity

A second type of news story on crime addresses the moral integrity of the community. Large baggage thefts at Kennedy Airport and thefts at the Grumman Company, 'Long Island's single largest private employer', will be covered by *Newsday* and the *New York Times*, while equally large 'takes' pulled off at establishments less central to the collective identity of the region will be ignored by the local press. Virtually all thefts deemed newsworthy are depicted as events endangering one or another foundation of collective identity. Thus the illegal taking of small clams by commercial fishermen on Long Island became newsworthy because the 'pirates' were depicted as so cruel as to take 'baby' clams, but also because their activity was said to threaten 'the hard clam resource of the Great South Bay'.

Hijackings of shipments will be more likely to make the news if the shipments by chance are headed for institutions deemed integral to the moral character of the community, for example a prominent church or any public school district. Prosecutions of students for smoking pot are not usually worth news attention, but they are if the students attend Long Island's Merchant Marine Academy. Such stories have an unspoken melodramatic quality: they implicitly tap folk ideas about the vulnerability of collective identity, suggesting that the crime threatens to rip society in some essential part or symbolizes the presence in the community of forces so malevolent as to threaten the metaphorical social fabric.

On the federal level, counterfeiting is a venerable candidate for news of crime cast as a danger to community institutions. Counterfeiting has the symbolic distinction of representing a challenge to the integrity of the entire economy. *Sub voce* it cries the fear: 'What if we can't trust our money! How could commerce proceed?'

Threats to collective integrity are also represented by crimes occurring in contemporary centres of goodness, places symbolizing the American conception of the good life: sneak thefts from collection plates in churches, robberies at Disneyland, murders at Bob's Big Boy or McDonald's. These stories raise the spectre that 'the centre does not hold', that no place is safely sacred. A related set of stories denotes places and personnel trusted to be healthy for the soul and the body, and describes events which undermine the faith that draws the public to them. Examples include reports of torture or sexual abuse occurring at child care centres and while under anaesthesia in dentists' offices.

The personal identity of the victim may also make the crime a symbolic challenge to collective identity. Thus the 1982 street murder of ex-Senator Ribicoff's niece in Venice (Los Angeles) generated enormous publicity. Crimes become newsworthy when they victimize the elite, as was the case in a *Newsday* story about the theft of several twenty-to-thirty-foot cabin cruisers, but also when they merely come within the charismatic penumbra of elites. In Los Angeles, one may read of burglaries that occurred just in the neighbourhood, not in the house, of famous movie stars; in Washington one may read of drug dealing in the shadows of the Capitol; throughout the country one may read of petty criminality by distant relatives of the president. Crime news of this sort tracks the people and places that have come to be regarded as central to collective identity. Indeed, crime news provides the sociologist with a handy, detailed map to trace the institutional geography of the sacred in modern society.

Implicitly recognizing the importance to the public of this form of crime, some federal statutes directly define attacks on certain symbols of national character as criminal. New York newspapers have covered criminal prosecutions of pathetic individuals who, in so obvious and amateurish a manner as not to be really threatening, have sent threatening notes to the president; and the case of a seemingly nice young man who somehow managed to find an American Eagle to shoot on Long Island.

Also in the category of crimes portrayed as threats to the character of the community are the large number of stories on organized crime. Organized crime, depicted as emanating from an 'underworld', has become a powerful and versatile imagery for evil in the United States. Secretly organized, dark ('swarthy') in complexion, threatening always to taint or contaminate good people, organized crime is a contemporary metaphor structured along ancient images of infectious disease and satanic danger. Once labelled a 'member' of organized crime, an individual's misfortunes (e.g., an auto accident) may generate a news story containing no reference at all to a crime or to a victim.

Similarly, stories lacking allegations about offenders may be newsworthy if they document the existence of other forms of vast, uncontrolled, anti-social forces. Thus we read periodically of discoveries of large caches of arms, seizures of huge stores of narcotics, and realizations that national security information has been accessed by some otherwise innocent savant skilled in manipulating computers.

Moralized political conflicts

The third category of crime news that conveys general messages about moral character is exemplified by reports of weapons offences by a local organization sympathetic to the PLO or the IRA; bank robberies by members of the Black Liberation Army; and extortionate demands by Puerto Rican independence groups. The audiences for such stories are constituted as interested parties before the crime occurs. Far from surprise being an essential condition for reader interest, many of the most avid readers will be those who are predisposed in opposition to the targeted group. For them, the offenders may now be pointed out to be, not only politically undesirable or substantively wrong-headed but so beyond the boundaries of respectable moral sensibilities as not to merit a hearing for their political claims: 'They are really (basically, essentially, after all the niceties of debate are said and done) bad people, nothing but criminals.' Most obviously with this category of news, crime becomes newsworthy not as a source of information about crime but as a morally charged message about other issues of interest to the readership. These crime stories feed dimensions of moral character into political conflicts.

The relationship between political conflict and the newsworthiness of crime is complex. Intense political conflict raises to the level of the newsworthy, crimes that otherwise would not be deemed of general interest. Conversely, audacious crime makes newsworthy political conflicts that had been ignored by the news media and the general public. An example from the late 1970s was the hijacking by Croatian nationalists of an airplane over Long Island, and the related death of a policeman attempting to disarm a bomb. Before reading of this crime, many New Yorkers were unaware of the historic grievance of Croatians against the Yugoslav state. In recent history, the ironic strategy of terrorists frequently has been successful: the seriousness of harm to victims has often been taken, not (or not only) as grounds for damning the cruelty of the offenders but as a stimulus for recognizing the seriousness of their concerns: 'They are so upset, they would even do this!'

White-collar crime

White-collar crime comprises a fourth category of items deemed newsworthy because they provide moral instruction about matters of pressing concern for readers quite apart from crime. White-collar crimes sometimes appear to be newsworthy because of the size of the booty involved. But it is the magnitude of the defendant's legitimate power or wealth, not the measure of the ill-gotten gain, that is distinctively newsworthy. The ABSCAM cases, which convicted one senator, several congressmen, and numerous local officials for taking bribes, made more news than have many bank robberies in which the take has been greater than the amounts the congressmen received. Frequently, white-collar crimes will not involve any discernible monetary amount. Thus prosecutors may cite as the gravamen of the offence, false statements made on documents submitted to the government or perjury before a grand jury. In addition to ABSCAM, the most publicized EDNY cases in the last few years involved relatively small amounts of money. The successful prosecution of Joseph Margiotta, the Republican boss of Nassau County, asserted only $5,000 as a personal bribe; a case against Bedford-Stuyvesant Democratic boss Sam Wright alleged a bribe of the same amount. In another highly publicized matter, the prosecutors investigated (but ultimately did not bring) charges that Kenneth Axelrod, a senior executive in the J. C. Penney Company and a nominee by the Carter Administration to a high position in the Treasury Department, corruptly received about $5,000 of free work on his Manhattan apartment from a contractor. The status of the person rather than the structure of the crime accounts for the newsworthiness of these cases.

Multiple boundaries and the extent of newsworthiness

Depending on the analyst's purpose, the four categories of crime news could be collapsed into two or perhaps one.[2] White-collar crimes, which involve charges of criminality against people invested with a form of sacred trust, might be lumped into the second category, threats against centres of collective integrity, which category already includes crimes victimizing elites. In some sense, all crimes fit the second category, as they point to weaknesses in the undergirding of social order. There are, however, at least two important reasons for distinguishing the four categories.

First the distinctions enable us to see how crimes become particularly newsworthy. Other things equal, the more categories that can be filled by a given crime, the bigger the news story. Thus the Lindbergh kidnapping case (see Hughes, 1936), once touted as 'the crime of the century', was initially the kidnapping of a baby, and therefore predictably newsworthy as a crime illustrating extraordinary insensitivity to a distinctively vulnerable victim; as well as an attack on a national hero, and therefore additionally newsworthy as an assault on a sacred centre of society. Later, after a German-American, Bruno Hauptmann, had been made a criminal suspect, the story became a vehicle for moralizing the growing political tension between America and Germany. Still later, as questions were raised about the state's falsification of evidence against Hauptmann, it became a story suggesting white-collar crime in the form of official corruption.

The Patty Hearst story also contained elements placing it within each of the four categories: the famous photograph — Hearst with a machine gun apparently standing guard during a robbery — dramatically depicted audacity; the demands by the Symbionese Liberation Army and the political history of the Hearst family made the event a moral tale on the political conflicts of the 1960s; and the wealth and prestige of Patty Hearst's family gave her alleged complicity the character of white-collar crime.

The stories linked under the rubric 'Watergate' also show the relevance of the four categories. Initially reported as an attempted burglary whose intended victim happened to be the Democratic Party, it was at first depicted as an attack against a centre of authority in American society. Watergate then became a moral debate over the reasonableness of possibly biased partisan suspicions, and thus a testing ground for morally weighing the major political divisions in the country. It became a flooding stream of stories about white-collar crime as various forms of elite immorality, from falsified personal tax returns to corporate international bribery, became implicated in the investigation. And finally the fascination with Watergate turned into an inquiry into the personal competence and moral sensibilities of Richard Nixon. A burglary newsworthy at the start only because of the sacred stature of the intended victim, Watergate became an extraordinarily transparent and therefore extraordinarily brazen criminal cover-up.

The second, and for present purposes the more relevant reason for distinguishing the four categories of crime news is that each points to different aspects of an explanation of the social generation of the appetite for news. Each of the four categories highlights a different social pressure which readers routinely confront in their own lives, quite apart from their personal experience with crime. The fourfold distinction helps us investigate the larger sociological question of how the social lives of readers lend crime a newsworthy character.

But before we take up this question, we must address an intermediate concern. Even assuming that crime news fits the delimited categories described above, a content analysis alone does not warrant the further assumption that there are corresponding lines of interest among readers. The research literature on public knowledge about crime and patterns of news reading provides some support for the inevitably difficult jump from the analysis of news content to assertions about reader experience.

Crime news, crime statistics and reader interest

As an initial point, it is clear that the meaning of crime news, whatever it may be, is important to news readers. Crime news has been continually present in the metropolitan daily for about 150 years. It might be argued that if this long record ever did indicate a strong interest among readers, it no longer does. Perhaps today's more educated (and presumably more sophisticated) readers ignore crime news or read with only superficial interest, failing to absorb content. The evidence is otherwise. Graber (1980: 50–1) asked a panel of Chicago-area news readers to recite details of news stories on a variety of topics. She found their recall of stories on crime exceeded their recall of stories on many other matters, including education, congressional activities, conflicts in the Middle East, and state government. Recall of news about crime was at about the same, relatively high, level as recall of news about accidents and political gossip. On an average day, stories on crime and justice comprise about 15 percent of the topics actually read.[3]

The fact that readers find crime news spontaneously involving does not mean that news organizations are not biasing the public appearance of crime in the news. Indeed there are systematic biases in the reporting of crime news, at least in the respect that crime as presented in the daily news differs consistently from crime as described in official police statistics. In order to home in on what it is that readers find so interesting in crime news, we should clarify the nature of this 'bias.'

Comparisons of crime news and crime statistics have produced consistent findings. In study after study, the content of crime news has been found to diverge widely from the patterns available in official statistics. The relationship does not appear to be random or incoherent: in many respects, the picture one obtains about crime from reading the newspapers inverts the picture about crime one gets from reading police statistics. In a recent study of thirty years of front-page crime news in each of nine cities, Jacob (1980) found that violent crime made up about 70 percent of crime news and about 20 percent of the official crime rate. Sherizen (1978: 215) computed the percentages of crimes known to the police (FBI Schedule 1 types) that were reported in four Chicago newspapers in 1975: 70 percent of homicide cases were reported, five percent of the rapes, one percent of larceny/thefts. He concluded: 'the more prevalent the crime, the less...reported'. This systematic 'over-representation' of violent crime in the news is also characteristic of black community newspapers (Ammons et al., 1982). And in a study of British newspapers, Roshier (1973) similarly found that crimes against the person were consistently over-represented in contrast to official criminal statistics. (See also Jones, 1976, on St. Louis; and the review in Garofalo, 1981: 323)

News reporting of white-collar and common crimes has also been found to reverse the relationship found in official statistics. In our set of federal crime news stories published in New York between 1974 and 1978, about 66 percent concerned white-collar crimes and 21 percent, common crimes. In a separate study, we counted the types of cases which, according to federal court records, were actually prosecuted during these years in the local jurisdictions. Court records showed the inverse of news reports: about 22 percent of filed criminal cases charged white-collar crimes, 70 percent, common crimes. This over-representation of white-collar crime has been documented in studies of newspaper coverage of all crimes, state and federal. Roshier (1973: 34), on British papers, and Graber (1980: 38, 40) on Chicago papers, also found an over-representation of higher social class offenders: the *Chicago Tribune* identified about 70 percent of the criminals as white and about 75 percent as from middle or upper socioeconomic statuses.[4]

For our purposes, these patterns of over-representation of violent and white-collar crimes might suggest that news organizations have gravely distorted readers' understandings of crime. If so, the moral tales isolated by our content analysis of crime news — in which violent and white- collar crimes loom large — should not be taken as leads to special sources of reader interest. That is what they read, one might say, because that is what they have been lead to believe crime is! Readers are interested in these moral tales because they believe that, through them, they are learning about crime in society.

It has often been suggested that readers' perceptions of crime in society more closely reflect crime as described in the news than crime as described in official statistics. But on closer inspection, the supposed power of the news to shape readers' perceptions of crime in society has not been clearly established by research. Perhaps the most famous study in this area, F. James Davis's 30-year-old study of crime news in Colorado newspapers (1952), presented narrow evidence of a lack of 'consistent relationship' between crime news and the FBI's compilation of local police reports. Davis found that a community's perception of a crime wave was generated by an increase in news coverage that was not justified by changes in official crime rates. But Davis cautioned that he found no clear evidence that public perceptions of crime generally follow the news more closely than the Uniform Crime Rates (UCR).

Outside the context of a 'crime wave', the news does not appear to dominate public perceptions of crime. There is evidence that the public is aware of the different images of crime portrayed by police statistics and journalistic descriptions of crime, and thus reads the two for different purposes. Stinchcombe et al. (1980) compared the coverage of crime in magazines published between 1932 and 1975, with periodic surveys asking the public whether crime was a major problem. There was almost random change in the level of magazine crime coverage, but the public's opinion about crime as a major problem changed in a clear pattern, jumping in 1969 and remaining high to 1974. Between 1970 and 1974, violent crime increased dramatically on official statistics, as did the public's fear of crime, while the attention given to crime in the periodical literature decreased. The authors conclude (at pp. 36–7):

> The weight of the evidence is that people pay more attention to the true crime rate than to the level of media coverage. As far as one can tell from recent developments in fear of crime, the radical increase in the crime rate observed by the police (and reported in FBI Uniform Crime Reports) is also observed by the people, and it frightens them.[5]

These data are complemented by those found by Herbert Jacob (1980). Jacob did not report on public attitudes but, unlike Stinchcombe et al., he did study newspaper crime reports. For the period 1948 to 1978, he found little increase in front-page crime news, even while, for the nine cities studied, UCR statistics increased by 300 percent. (Front-page crime news increased from two to four percent.) Thus the increase in the fear of crime reported by Stinchcombe et al. again appears to be related much more closely to official police statistics than to newspaper coverage.

Synchronic as well as historical evidence shows a public

understanding of crime in society that more closely tracks official than media descriptions of crime. Graber (1980: 49) compared characteristics of offenders and victims in the news and in interviewees' perceptions: 'The press does not depict criminals and victims largely as non-whites, poor, and lower class, but the panelists do.' In her study, the *Chicago Tribune* identified about 70 percent of the criminals as white, about two-thirds of the victims as female, and about 75 percent of the criminals as of middle or upper socioeconomic status. The panelists interviewed by Graber, on the other hand, estimated the race, sex, and socioeconomic status of criminals and victims almost inversely to the picture given in the *Tribune*.[6]

A recent study conducted in New Orleans (Sheley and Ashkins, 1981) compared the rank order of FBI Index crimes in police statistics and in a telephone sample of community residents. The public ranked homicide the fourth most common type of crime; police statistics showed it to be in seventh place. The public ranked burglary as the second most common type of crime, the same ranking found in police statistics. Robbery was in first place according to the public but in third place according to police statistics. As in other cities, a resident of New Orleans who received information on crime solely from the local news media would rank murder and robbery at the top of the list and burglary at the bottom. Roshier (1973: 37) used a similar methodology with British readers and concluded: 'Public perceptions do not seem to be influenced by the biases in their newspapers but, in fact, are surprisingly close to the official picture.'

The public does not appear to read crime news in a naive search for the empirical truth about crime. Other concerns appear to sustain the readers' interests. This is suggested by comparing crime as represented in the news and in entertainment media. The most common, serious (FBI Part One, 'index') crimes according to police statistics, larcenies and burglaries, are rarely the focus of either news stories, TV shows (Dominick, 1973: 245) or the silver screen; murders and rapes, among the least frequent crimes in FBI statistics, are among the most frequent crime subjects on both news and entertainment shows. (See Garofalo, 1981: 326, on the 'similarities in the characteristics of crimes, offenders, and victims conveyed by the news media and by television drama.') And there is a marked parallel between crime in the news and in fiction: 'the author of one of the first British stories of crime detection, "Clement Lorimer; or the Book with Iron Clasps" (1848), turns out to be a newspaper crime reporter... Throughout their history the genres of crime fiction writing and crime newsreporting have gone hand in hand and even today are occasionally hard to distinguish from each other' (Chibnall, 1980: 209–10). It is less plausible to assume that the public takes cinematic, novelistic, and press depictions of crime as evidence about crime than to suggest that, in approaching both news and entertainment media, the public is not essentially trying to learn about crime.

Is there not a disparaging assumption of public naïvety underneath the view that people generally read crime news to understand crime? If crime experts can read crime news on a daily basis while remaining sceptical of the material as criminological data, perhaps the lay reader is no more foolish. Within the culture created by law enforcement personnel, the crimes that make everyday occupational 'news', or are subjects of informal conversation, appear substantially similar to those that make it into the newspaper. According to Sudnow's (1965) study of interactions between local public defenders and prosecutors, the cases that generate the most informal commentary among these criminal justice professionals are not those which most accurately represent the statistically typical crimes they handle. Personal and situational idiosyncrasies, not 'normal' crimes, distinctively generate their folk news. In the federal prosecutors' office in which I did observational research, several of the cases receiving the most informal commentary were also those that became big news stories and major Hollywood movies (*A Dog Day's Afternoon*, *The French Connection*, *Prince of the City*). The same 'common sense' appears to govern law enforcement officers when they gossip about their cases and both lay and expert readers of news reports of crime. Why should reporters and editors not follow the same 'common sense' in selecting crime news? As Park long ago noted (1940: xiii-xiv), reporters are disciplined to be atheoretical in determining what is newsworthy and to put themselves in the perspective of the average reader responding emotionally to events.

The social generation of the appetite for crime news

We have already in effect rejected one hypothetical explanation of reader interest, the utilitarian theory that crime news, by depicting unexpected events, enables readers to reduce their practical problems with crime through reshaping knowledge about crime toward greater empirical accuracy. Readers appear to be so well aware of the atypicality of crime as covered by the news that their reading seems to be a search for 'the unexpected'. But 'the unexpected' provides only the beginnings of an adequate theory. We must still specify in just what sense newsworthy crime is 'unexpected'.

Ambiguities of 'the unexpected' in crime news

Consider the theoretical implications of the pattern of 'recency' in newsworthy crimes. As almost all sociologists of the news have noted, there is an urgency with which a story must be published lest it lose its character as 'news'. (Tuchman, 1978: 51, on 'hard' versus 'soft' news; Hughes, 1940: 67, on 'big' versus 'little' news; and Roshco, 1975: 10–12, on the 'recency', 'immediacy' and 'currency' of the news.) But if in the reporting of crime it is taken for granted that something newsworthy should have happened in the immediate past, the necessary something is in fact only rarely the crime itself. Of the 200 crimes reported in the previously described sample of New York area newspapers, about 100 were common crimes and seventy white-collar crimes. Only 6 percent of the initial reports of white-collar crimes clearly described the crimes as occurring within six months of the date of publication, in part because the criminality indicated was typically a pattern of fraud or corruption that did not appear to begin or end on any particular date. But even for common crimes, such as robberies, thefts from post offices or at airports, and contraband sales, only 30 percent were described as occurring within six months of the first article on the given offence.

A similar indication appeared in our examination of about 1,400 crime articles appearing in the *Los Angeles Times* in 1981, 1982 and 1983. Incidents and cases were coded separately: crimes were coded as cases if they had been processed to the point of arrest or beyond (indictment, trial, sentence, post-prison release, etc.). Of these news articles on crime, only 45 percent reported criminal incidents, or crimes that had not been officially processed to the point of arrest. If the newsworthiness of crime could be explained by expectations violated by crimes themselves — the *victim's* experience of the unexpected in the form of surprise, or the shock waves set off in public consciousness when the crime was committed, we should find an overwhelming predominance of recent criminal incidents in crime news.

While the news emphasizes yesterday's events, the crimes covered in daily newspapers did not necessarily happen yesterday nor even in the recent past. Some feature of the story signals a currency that makes the crime newsworthy, but the current element is less often and less clearly the incidence of the crime than a feature of the criminal case, a subsequent event affecting the victim, or a vicissitude of the alleged criminal's life. If a violation of 'the unexpected' somehow must qualify crime to be newsworthy, the necessary element of surprise is a matter neither of the victim's experience nor of the reader's empathic shock that something so awful might also happen to him.

More directly, we should question whether surprise is a common, much less essential, feature in the experience of reading crime news. Here I would ask the reader to review his or her own experience for evidence that the most avid readers of stories on particular crimes may be those who are least surprised. During Watergate, it was not necessarily Republican readers who were the most religious followers; many left-wing Americans rejoiced in the daily unfolding of what they regarded as more proof for what they had long believed.

Especially newsworthy crimes do not appear to be especially unexpected, either to victims or to readers. According to highly publicized opinion polls, Americans believe that a substantial proportion of unindicted congressmen are corrupt. Yet a new official charge of corruption against a congressman will always generate news coverage. Banks are robbed more than many other types of commercial establishment, yet they remain distinctively newsworthy sites of crime.

In short, if crime news inevitably carries a sense of the unexpected, just what that sense is, is not obvious. Perhaps, following Durkheim, we should turn the explanation around and consider whether crime is newsworthy for its symbolic value in articulating the normatively expected.

The historical limitations of the Durkheimian view

Durkheim (1958: 67; 1964: 108) argued that in violating social order, deviants may actually promote collective consensus — normative cohesion, the moral integration of society, a widespread sense of order in society — by providing occasions for mass reactions against deviance. Crime news may be the best contemporary example of what Durkheim had in mind. The reading of crime news is a collective, ritual experience. Read daily by a large portion of the population, crime news generates emotional experiences in individual readers, experiences which each reader can assume are shared by many others. Although each may read in isolation, phenomenologically the experience may be a collective, emotional 'effervescence' of moral indignation. But the application of the Durkheimian perspective to crime news requires a tortured reasoning.

There is a fundamental, historical difference between the social meanings of contemporary crime news and those of the public ceremonies of labelling deviants that Durkheim had in mind and that Kai Erikson (1966) documented in his celebrated book on seventeenth-century Puritans. Contemporary news stories on crime focus on stages in the criminal justice process before punishment. In our data set of crime news stories published in New York area newspapers between 1974 and 1979, the perspective of official authority, as represented by a description of an action or comment by a law enforcement agent, was present in less than half of the articles. About 65 percent of the articles appeared before disposition, when the outcome of official investigation and allegation was still unclear. Less than 12 percent of the cases first appeared in the news at or after the stage of sentencing. On the surface, the contemporary reading of crime news disconcerts rather than reassures.

The previously noted study of the *Los Angeles Times* provides additional support. About 45 percent of the articles for 1981, 1982 and 1983 ($n = 1,384$) were on incidents or criminal events as distinguished from crime cases or crimes reported as officially processed to the point of arrest or beyond. There are thus a variety of indicators that crime news raises perhaps as many questions about collective integrity as it resolves; its structure seems as likely to increase doubts about social order, by publicizing crimes that are still open criminal cases, as to strengthen a sense of collective order by celebrating a triumph of collective will over deviants and disorder.[7]

In a long historical perspective, the modern newspaper appears as a distinctive social structure for collectively observing deviance, a structure dramatically different from that existing before the nineteenth century. Shortly before a mass Sunday newspaper was created in England in the 1830s, crime news was circulated on broadsheets. One of the last and most successful broadsheets was widely disseminated in the 1820s; the 'Last Dying Speech and Confession' of the murderer of Maria Marten sold more than 1,100,000 copies (Williams, 1978: 43). Before the nineteenth century, in western and in primitive societies, among Erikson's Puritans and among the primitives Durkheim examined in his book on religion (1965), deviance was made a mass public symbol most emphatically, through exemplary forms of punishment and subsequent gossip, after doubt about criminal responsibility was resolved. Broadsheets were written to detail the behaviour of the condemned on the scaffold: 'The best sellers were the literature of the gallows. These were the last dying confessions of murderers and an account of their execution' (Hughes, 1940: 140). The wayward Puritan was put on trial, then in stocks on public display and made the subject of sermonizing, primarily after punishment was decided upon and delivered by officials symbolizing the collective identity of the society. Witchcraft trials in the American colonies and throughout medieval Europe were means of dramatizing the execution of collective will, not processes in which a problematic outcome was subject to adversary skill (see Currie, 1968).

In western societies, mass media for disseminating news about crime at first threatened confidence in collective order, then with the rise of print media came to serve the official interest in order, and then with the advent of the daily newspaper once again took on an unsettling role. Chibnall (1980: 180) notes that in Great Britain in the middle ages, before the advent of printed media for conveying crime news, ballads often disserved a social control function by dramatizing the heroic defiance of outlaws. Then, in the late seventeenth century, when pamphlets and broadsheets emerged to give a written form to crime news, they emphasized 'dying speeches' in which official authority, often through the quoted (or invented) words of the condemned, displayed the terrible costs of crime and praised the path of virtue. But the twentieth-century newspaper offers a much less moralistic format for news about crime. In many respects it more clearly celebrates than excoriates criminals.[8]

As Foucault (1979) has analysed historical change in the social meaning of deviance, in pre-Enlightenment society adjudication was private (as symbolized by 'star chamber' proceedings) and punishment was public (as exemplified by elaborate torture and execution ceremonies); in post-Enlightenment society, trials became the public drama of criminal justice, while punishment retreated to the privacy of prisons, emerging into publicity only rarely and then in shame. Before the nineteenth century, public viewing of deviance may have had a morally integrative effect on the community; but to make the same analysis of today's crime news is to ignore its distinctive contemporary social organization. Metropolitan daily news stories on victimization and arrest are routine and are only in the exceptional case followed up by stories on conviction and punishment.

A social class sub-pattern is notable in this context. The higher the educational and economic level of a newspaper's readers, the more it appears to employ a form that provokes rather than resolves its readers' moral anxieties. Comparing New York's *Times* and *Daily News*, studies have found the latter to be more sensational in that it contains a higher proportion of crime news (Deutschmann, 1959). But comparing the crime stories published in the two papers, there is little difference in reported fact. Both papers draw on essentially the same police sources and records. The difference lies in the language used to describe the crime.

The *Daily News* moralizes while the *Times* uses what are conventionally regarded as emotionally neutral, technical terms, in particular the formally non-prejudicial, officially constrained language of courts and lawyers (Meyer, 1975). Thus the *Daily News* reports the illegal harvesting of undersized clams as clams that were 'copped', while the *Times* refers to a 'theft'. The *Times*, under a headline of moderate size, describes an arrangement by which GTE-Sylvania officials paid money to public transit officials in order to ensure acceptance of bulbs not meeting specifications, as a bribery; while the *News* runs a large front-page title: 'Subway Bulb Gyp'. The difference, which becomes even more pronounced if one compares contemporary daily US newspapers with those published sixty years ago, is that newspapers with readers of a higher social class level leave moral execration to readers, at least as a matter of form; while newspapers with relatively lower-class readers lead the chorus of invective. Thus it appears that the more modern the newspaper, or the more formally educated the readership, the more that crime news is styled to provoke rather than resolve doubt.[9]

Daily crime news reading as a ritual moral exercise

Although the frequency of news stories on homicides, violent robberies and rapes might seem evidence of a 'lowbrow' insensitivity in the modern public, an opposite interpretation is more revealing and more consistent with the overall patterns in crime news. The interest is less morbid than inspirational. If portrayals of violent crime show in the extreme the lack of sensibility with which members of our society may treat each other, readers' appetites for such stories suggest that they are not so coarse as to take for granted destructive personal insensitivity. The fact that assaults on property are far less newsworthy than assaults on the person indicates that readers' fundamental concerns are more humanistic than material. Or rather, by picking up the paper to read about yet another brutal crime, readers can attempt to sustain their conviction that their own moral sensibility has not yet been brutalized into a jaded indifference. The predominance of stories on violent crime in contemporary newspapers can be understood as serving readers' interests in re-creating daily their moral sensibilities through shock and impulses of outrage.

Instead of the empirically ambiguous idea that crime becomes interesting to the extent that it is 'unexpected', and in place of a simple invocation of Durkheim's ideas, I would argue that crime news is taken as interesting in a process through which adults in contemporary society work out individual perspectives on moral questions of a quite general yet eminently personal relevance.

Each of the categories of crime news relates to a type of non-criminal, moral question that adults confront daily. First, crime stories with implications about personal competence and sensibility are taken as interesting because readers sense that they must deal with analogous questions in everyday life. In routine interactions with others, we must make assumptions about their essential qualities, assumptions about the age competencies of the young or old, about qualities related to gender, or about qualities like intelligence (which today are less politically controversial but no more visible than the competencies supposedly associated with age and sex). If children can hold up banks, should we take as serious the statement by our 7-year-old that he would like to kill his younger brother? If there is a 'Grandma Mafia', should we be concerned that the elderly woman behind us in the supermarket line may have a lethal intent as she rams her cart into our rear?

We must also make assumptions constantly about our own essential competencies and sensibilities. The question of audacity is faced not only by criminals. How daring, how ingenious, can I be? Would it be admirably daring; just reasonably cautious; or really, recklessly foolish to submit a paper for publication in its current draft? Crime news is of widespread interest because it speaks dramatically to issues that are of direct relevance to readers' existential challenges, whether or not readers are preoccupied with the possible personal misfortune of becoming victims to crime.

Similarly, the second group of crime news stories, those that depict threats to sacred centres of society, are deemed interesting because readers understand that they themselves must work, day after day, to define moral perspectives on questions about elusive collective entities. The interest in such stories comes not just from the practical necessity of evaluating the physical safety of different places, but from inescapable encounters with enigmas of collective identity. In contemporary bourgeois life, questions of physical safety are of minor relevance compared to questions about collective moral character — mundane, recurrent questions such as: What's a 'nice' (morally clean) place to take the family to dinner?

The question raised by this type of crime news — is society holding together? — is the global form of questions asked more narrowly by readers in their daily routines. In everyday, concrete work settings, do you sense the collective identity of the university in which you are employed? If so, your behaviour will have a significance otherwise lacking: you will shape your behaviour somehow to fit into or against the character of the whole. Sociologists have long argued that social facts are real, that there is a reality to collective identity that transcends individual experience. The debate about the reality of collective identity is bothersome not only to sociological theorists, but to laymen as well as sociologists in their everyday, practical action.

The forms of the issue, as it appears in the lives of each member of society, are extremely diverse. Some worry about the level of 'strength' or 'health' of 'the economy' (or 'the military', or their 'family'). In this anxiety, 'the economy' is addressed as a whole, a thing that presumably exists objectively, not only as a convenient metaphoric shorthand for summarizing some arbitrary aggregation of individual economic events. But the objective measure of 'its' identity is always in dispute. 'The economy' is recurrently experienced as a precarious collective entity whose integrity may be threatened by hidden forces, an entity which goes up and down in response to pressures that no one has been able to locate precisely. Many news readers shape their everyday emotional mood as well as their consumption and investment decisions upon a sense of optimism or pessimism about the fate of 'the economy'.

As members of society continuously confront issues of personal and collective competence, they develop an appetite for crime news. Worrying about miscalculating their own and others' personal abilities, people find interesting the questioning of personal moral competence that is often intensely dramatized in crime stories. Repeatedly assessing whether, how, and how effectively certain people, organizations and places represent collective identity, members of society consume tales about the vulnerable integrity of personages, institutions, and sites.

As to the third category of crime news, stories reflecting pre-existing tensions among groups, people in persistent political conflict often hunger for moral charges to use against the character of their opponents. They find satisfying morsels in crime news.

Finally, what process of daily stimulation might be behind the widespread taste for news of white-collar crime? I would suggest that the newsworthiness of white-collar crime is constructed in a dialectical relationship to the moral routines of everyday life. The crimes of people in high white-collar occupations are especially newsworthy, not because they are shocking or surprising — not because such people are presumed to be more conforming, decent, respectable or trustworthy than blue-collar workers or the unemployed; but because *they have to be treated as if they are.*

It is certainly inadequate to attribute the newsworthiness of white-collar crime to shocked expressions of honour. News readers maintain appetites for stories of white-collar crime, day after day — another congressman caught taking bribes!; another multinational corporation caught corrupting foreign governments! — while common crimes committed by poor, young, minority males continue in their redundant, typically non-newsworthy procession, because every day, in infinite ways, news readers only feel forced to enact trust in and deference towards the former. However cynical a person's view of the morality of business, political, and civic institutional leaders, he or she lives surrounded by symbols of their superior status: their towering offices, their advertised qualities on subway or bus placards or on TV commercials, their names on hospitals. Readers of a news story about white-collar crime recall that they have made many payments to that firm; that they were moved around by that airplane or bus company; that they have had their neighbourhood or recreational environment defined by those politicians or lay leaders; that each day at work they must defer to a person in that type of superior status. The newsworthiness of white-collar crime owes much to the routine moral character of the division of labour. (On the 'moral division of labour', see Hughes, 1971).

I have argued that crime news takes its interest from routinely encountered dilemmas, not from concerns focused on crime. The reading of crime news is not a process of idle moral reflection on past life; it is an eminently practical, future-oriented activity. In reading crime news, people recognize and use the moral tale within the story to orient themselves towards existential dilemmas they cannot help but confront. What level of competence should I impute to that 10-year-old? Is the economy strengthening or weakening? Should the political arguments of the PLO be heard with respect? Am I wise to defer to the boss in earnest, or should I balance apparent fealty with self-respecting cynicism?

The content of crime news provides no solutions, not even advice on how the reader should resolve the dilemmas he will confront. Instead, crime news provides material for a literal working out of the moral perspectives that must be applied to dilemmas of everyday life. Crime is in today's newspaper, not because it contradicts the beliefs readers had yesterday, but because readers seek opportunities to shape-up moral attitudes they will have to use today.

The idea that crime news serves readers' interests in performing a daily moral workout explains not only the content but several features of the structure of crime news. Crime news features details on the identities of victim and offender, and on time and place. As such, it encourages readers to see the event as potentially within his or her own experience. Its form serves to mobilize the reader's response by providing a shock or inviting outrage; it is a type of 'hot news' (Hughes, 1940: 234), specifically provoking an emotional experience, inducing a response of the 'whole organism' (Park, 1940: 670). The focus of crime news on the early criminal justice stages, stages before formal adjudication and punishment, when questions of guilt have been raised but not resolved, also provokes readers' emotions by challenging them to react against the face of uncertainty.

As several studies have documented (Graber, 1980: 49; Sherizen, 1978), crime news focuses on criminals much more than on victims.

In our New York area data set from the mid-1970s, a comment by the victim or a representative of the victim was reported in only twenty-one of 527 articles, compared to 162 comments from the defence side and 185 comments by the prosecutor. A focus on victims would have substantial practical relevance for readers, were they concerned with learning how to avoid the costs of crime. Some neighbourhood 'throwaway' papers respond directly to these concerns. Unlike the major metropolitan dailies, the neighbourhood newspapers often present crime news under the by-line of a local policeman who begins the story from the victim's perspective (e.g. 'When driving back to her house at 11 p.m. on September 5, a resident of the 600 block of Lucerne noticed an unfamiliar car in her driveway. As she exited her car...') and concludes with annotated advice on what the victim might have done to avoid vulnerability. The same readers, picking up the metropolitan daily and inspecting its crime news, are no less pragmatic in their perspectives on crime news, but their practical concerns appear to be different — larger and more pervasively relevant.

The emphasis of the city papers on the criminal rather than the victim is understandable if we understand the reader's concerns as less with avoiding victimization than in working out moral positions on which his own behaviour will be based. If the victim's behaviour is often as important as the criminal's for understanding the causality of victimization, a focus on the criminal's behaviour stimulates moral sensitivities with which the reader may wish to identify. Each day in myriad ways the metropolitan news reader must work out his position on dimensions of moral callousness, personal audacity and faith in collective enterprises, and these are the very matters which the news depicts criminals as testing.

This perspective on interest in crime news makes understandable the apparent contradiction of substantive redundancy and constantly sustained reader interest. Laid side by side, stories about violent crime published over a sequence of days may appear quite similar. But they are experienced as new, as 'new-s', because the questions they tap re-emerge daily in readers' social lives.

The experience of reading crime news induces the reader into a perspective useful for taking a stand on existential moral dilemmas. The dilemmas of imputing personal competence and sustaining one's own moral sensibility, of honouring sacred centres of collective being, of morally crediting and discrediting political opponents, and of deferring to the moral superiority of elites, cannot be resolved by deduction from rational discourse. In these moral areas, a measure of faith — of understanding a position or making a commitment that underlies the reasons that can be given for one's beliefs — is an essential part of everyday social life. Crime news accordingly moves the reader through emotions rather than discursive logic, triggering anger and fear rather than argumentation.

Like vitamins useful in the body only for a day, like physical exercise whose value comes from its recurrent practice, crime news is experienced as interesting by readers because of its place in a daily moral routine. The very location of crime stories in the newspaper indicates that editors and readers understand this. Although minor local crime stories have a regular place in 'Metro' sections, crime stories may be scattered in unpredictable places throughout the general news sections; they are not as neatly confined to a substantial, specialized section as are sports and financial news. The structural location of crime news re-creates the unpredictable character of the phenomenon, and transfers to the reader a measure of responsibility to organize its place in his life.

Modern newspapers appear to emphasize this role. The more modern or sophisticated the newspaper, the less it moralizes in style; the more it imposes responsibility for moral reaction on the reader as a matter of form. Another modern feature of crime news, its focus on the early stages of the criminal justice system, places the responsibility for 'conviction', in both its narrow, criminal justice sense and in its broader, existential sense of commitment through faith, on the reader.

This responsibility is not necessarily one desired by readers, yet it appears to be one they acknowledge they cannot ignore or escape. Although people often fear crime and criticize the news as too negative and disturbing, they apparently find it even more unsettling not to read. To understand what makes crime 'news', one must explain the voluntary affliction of disturbing emotional experience on the self, on a mass level, day after day, throughout modern society. The reading of crime news appears to serve a purpose similar to the morning shower, routine physical exercise, and shaving (cf. Douglas, 1966): the ritual, non-rational value of experience that is, to a degree, shocking, uncomfortable, and self-destructive, and that is voluntarily taken up by adults in acknowledgment of their personal burden for sustaining faith in an ordered social world.

Notes

This paper stems from a programme of research at Yale Law School which was guided by Stanton Wheeler and supported by LEAA Grant 78 NIAX 0017. Points of view or opinions stated are those of the author and do not necessarily represent the official position or policies of US Department of Justice. Additional support came from the Academic Senate of UCLA. Elizabeth Sammis provided extensive bibliographic research assistance and, with William Shipley, she coded the Los Angeles newspapers. I wish to thank David G. Trager for his gracious assistance in providing the New York data.

1. Unlike the traditional examples of analytic induction, I sought to define necessary but not sufficient causal conditions. The fact that I present four alternative paths to newsworthiness is not inconsistent with this methodology; I note later on how, depending on the research purpose, the four paths can be folded into three, two or one. The key advantage of analytic induction was in driving the analysis to a deeper level than could be obtained by initially fixing coding categories and applying them to produce quantitative results. On the distinctive implications of analytic inductions for the traditional questions of methodology in social research, see generally Katz (1982).

2. Our set of 1,384 *Los Angeles Times* articles was distributed as follows: 'personal competence', which included stories on crimes of violence that did not otherwise fit any of the other categories, made up about 50 percent of all articles; 'collective integrity' held 33 percent; 'moralized political conflict', 8 percent; 'white-collar crime', 10 percent.

3. Other studies are supportive (Dominick, 1978: 110). Schramm (1949: 264) found no patterned difference in the reading of 'immediate reward news', a category which included the comics, crime news, sports and society news, although economic status was significantly (and directly) related to reading of public affairs news.

4 Dominick (1978) studied crimes reported on the front pages of the *New York Times* and the *Los Angeles Times* in 1950, 1960 and 1969. Although he found that violent crime was covered at three times the rate of white-collar crime, these figures, when compared to statistics on prosecution, still indicate an over-representation of white-collar crime. State district attorneys file more than ten times as many cases as do federal district attorneys, and white-collar criminal cases are so rare as to be virtually invisible in state court statistics. See the literature review in Davis (1982: 32). Gans (1980: 141), examining the news on TV and in weekly magazines, found about equal coverage of 'knowns' and 'unknowns' in trouble with the law, a pattern of equality which again, when compared to statistics on official action, shows a strong bias towards the coverage of people of higher social status.

5. Cf. Jones (1976: 240), comparing periodically reported FBI statistics and daily news articles: 'one suspects that readers are more likely to rely on the much more common day-to-day stimuli in forming their impressions about trends in the amount and distribution of crime'.

6. Graber's panel also saw 'street crime' as occurring less often than many rarely reported crimes: drug offences, drunk driving, fencing stolen goods, weapons violations, prostitution, welfare cheating, consumer fraud, and parole violations.

7. See also Garofalo (1981): 'the press gives very little attention to the postdispositional processes of the criminal justice system', citing three studies. But cf. Roshier (1973: 33), on British papers: 'all the newspapers gave an exaggerated

impression of the chances of getting caught and, when caught, of getting a serious punishment'.

8. Crimes in the entertainment media, however, may follow the Durkheimian pattern. On TV, but not in the news, the audience learns that 'evil is always punished in the end'. See Schattenberg (1981).

9. Cf. Schudson (1978: 119): 'Perhaps...the *Times* established itself as the "higher journalism" because it adapted to the life experience of persons whose position in the social structure gave them the most control over their own lives.'

References

Ammons, L., Dimmick, J. and Pilotta, J. (1982) 'Crime News Reporting in a Black Weekly', *Journalism Quarterly*, 59: 310–13.
Carey, J. (1982) 'The Discovery of Objectivity', *American Journal of Sociology*, 87: 1182–8.
Chibnall, S. (1975) 'The Crime Reporter: A Study in the Production of Commercial Knowledge', *Sociology*, 9: 49–66.
Chibnall, S. (1980) 'Chronicles of the Gallows: The Social History of Crime Reporting', pp. 179–217 in H. Christian (ed.), *The Sociology of Journalism and the Press* (Sociological Review Monograph 29). Stoke-on-Trent: J.H. Brookes.
Currie, E. (1968) 'Crimes Without Criminals: Witchcraft and its Control in Renaissance Europe', *Law & Society Review*, 3: 7–32.
Davis, F.J. (1952) 'Crime News in Colorado Newspapers', *American Journal of Sociology*, 57: 325–30.
Davis, J.R. (1982) *The Sentencing Dispositions of New York City Lower Court Criminal Judges*. Washington, DC: University Press of America.
Deutschmann, P.J. (1959) *News Page Content of Twelve Metropolitan Dailies*. Cincinnati: Scripps-Howard Research Center.
Dominick, J.R. (1973) 'Crime and Law Enforcement on Prime-Time Television', *Public Opinion Quarterly*, 37: 241–50.
Dominick, J.R. (1978) 'Crime and Law Enforcement in the Mass Media', pp. 105–28 in C. Winick (ed.), *Deviance and Mass Media*. Beverly Hills: Sage.
Douglas, M. (1966) *Purity and Danger*. London: Routledge & Kegan Paul.
Durkheim, E. (1958) *The Rules of Sociological Method*. Glencoe, Illinois: Free Press.
Durkheim, E. (1964) *The Division of Labor in Society*. New York: Free Press.
Durkheim, E. (1965) *The Elementary Forms of the Religious Life*. New York: Free Press.
Erikson, K.T. (1966) *Wayward Puritans*. New York: Wiley.
Fishman, M. (1980) *Manufacturing the News*. Austin: University of Texas Press.
Foucault, M. (1979) *Discipline and Punishment*. New York: Vintage Books.
Gans, H. (1980) *Deciding What's News*. New York: Vintage Books.
Garofalo, J. (1981) 'Crime and the Mass Media: A Selective Review of Research', *Journal of Research in Crime and Delinquency*, 18: 319–49.
Graber, D. (1980) *Crime News and the Public*. New York: Praeger.
Hughes, E.C. (1971) 'The Study of Occupations', pp. 283–97 in E.C. Hughes, *The Sociological Eye*, Vol. 1. Chicago: Aldine-Atherton.
Hughes, H.M. (1936) 'The Lindbergh Case', *American Journal of Sociology*, 42: 32–54.

Hughes, H.M. (1940) *News and the Human Interest Story*. Chicago: University of Chicago Press.
Jacob, H. (1980) 'Police and Newspaper Presentations of Crime: An Examination of Nine Cities, 1948–78'. Unpublished manuscript, Department of Political Science, Northwestern University, Evanston, Illinois.
Jones, E.T. (1976) 'The Press as Metropolitan Monitor', *Public Opinion Quarterly*, 40: 239–44.
Katz, E., Blumler, J.G. and Gurevitch, M. (1973) 'Uses and Gratifications Research', *Public Opinion Quarterly*, 37: 509–23.
Katz, J. (1982) 'A Theory of Qualitative Methodology', pp. 197–218 in J. Katz, *Poor People's Lawyers in Transition*. New Brunswick: Rutgers University Press.
Meyer, J. (1975) 'Newspaper Reporting of Crime and Justice', *Journalism Quarterly*, 52: 731–4.
Park, R.E. (1940) 'Introduction' to H.M. Hughes, *News and the Human Interest Story*. Chicago: University of Chicago Press.
Roshco, B. (1975) *Newsmaking*. Chicago: University of Chicago Press.
Roshier, B. (1973) 'The Selection of Crime News by the Press', pp. 28–39 in S. Cohen and J. Young (eds), *The Manufacture of News*. Beverly Hills: Sage.
Roshier, B. (1973) 'The Selection of Crime News by the Press', pp. 28–39 in S. Cohen and J. Young (eds.), *The Manufacture of News*. Beverly Hills: Sage.
Schattenberg, G. (1981) 'Social Control Functions of Mass Media Depictions of Crime', *Sociological Inquiry*, 51: 71–7.
Schramm, W. (1949) 'The Nature of News', *Journalism Quarterly*, 26: 259–69.
Schudson, M. (1978) *Discovering the News*, New York: Basic.
Sheley, J.F. and Ashkins, C.D. (1981) 'Crime, Crime News, and Crime Views', *Public Opinion Quarterly*, 45: 492–506.
Sherizen, S. (1978) 'Social Creation of Crime News', pp. 203–24 in C. Winick (ed.), *Deviance and Mass Media*. Beverly Hills: Sage.
Stinchcombe, A.L., Adams, R., Heimer, C.A., Scheppele, K.L., Smith, T.W. and Taylor, D.G. (1980) *Crime and Punishment — Changing Attitudes in America*. San Francisco: Jossey-Bass.
Sudnow, D. (1965) 'Normal Crimes', *Social Problems*, 12: 255–75.
Tuchman, G. (1978) *Making News*. New York: Free Press.
Williams, R. (1978) 'The Press and Popular Culture: An Historical Perspective', pp. 41–50 in G. Boyce, J. Curran and P. Wingate (eds), *Newspaper History*. London: Constable.

[4]

[3]

Media and social order in everyday life

ROBERT P. SNOW

This chapter differs from others in the volume in several respects. It is not directly concerned with access to or control of media or audiences. Rather, it focuses on how people use media in a matter-of-fact manner without regard to specific media content or ideological concerns. Instead of suggesting how media may affect audience beliefs, attitudes, or various aspects of social class, this chapter examines how media may be used to establish and maintain social order in a mundane fashion. In addition the author emphasises that claims are based on an American media experience.

There are two aims. One is to further the argument stated most clearly and elegantly by Anthony Giddens (1984) that the 'seeming fixity' of social order and structure resides in the development and maintenance of routine everyday life activity. The other is to demonstrate the significance of media in this process. The perspective that informs this discussion follows, in part, from Simmel (1971), and is based on the assumption that media should be understood and analysed primarily as a social form. As social form, media consist of standardised procedural strategies (formats) for presenting and interpreting cultural content, as well as protocols for interaction among media professionals and between media and audience. The focus here will be on those format characteristics, such as top-forty radio, television entertainment, or newspaper comics that are used as grammatical devices to accompany and aid in ordering the ordinary activity of everyday life.

For nearly two centuries, sociology has offered a Comtean promise for social order – namely that social order results from social structure and normative patterns of authority and power. As outlined in classical works from Spencer through Parsons, it has been held that people are socialised into the norms and values of status and roles in a manner that produces an internalised collective consciousness that insures stability in social affairs.

The role of media in this 'mainstream' sociological approach has always been considered secondary or extraneous to the core institutions of the family, religion, economic structure, government and so on. And yet, media have received significant attention whenever establishment values and norms seem to have broken down. Dramatic examples include the issue of television violence (Eron 1992), the false reality of media (Parenti 1991), the destructive impact of media on taste and high culture (Twitchell 1992), and the trivialisation of intellect (Dorfman 1983). Even when media are accorded some potency, such as in the hegemony thesis, media are cast more as an ideological tool (Gitlin 1987). But for most sociologists, the road to understanding media is through other institutions, namely economics and politics.

An example of the problems that emerge through this secondary analysis approach can be seen in content analysis research. Typically, this methodology tends to decontextualise media content from its format characteristics – more accurately it ignores format – and grounds content in ideological or commercial concerns. This should be considered a classic case of putting the cart before the horse. The problem is compounded when the analysis is placed within a framework of evaluating how media function in support or destruction of the norms and values of the so-called dominant institutions. With few exceptions this has led to a decidedly negative assessment of the media's role in society. Over the years, this view has gained such legitimacy that media are generally thought of as a necessary evil. Clearly this is an underlying tone in Semiotics (Fiske 1987; Carey 1987), and 'agenda-setting' (Shaw and McCombs 1977; Gitlin 1987). The problem in all this is the deterrent toward recognising potentially positive consequences in media use. To overcome that deterrent, consider examining the social form properties of media rather than media content. And, consider examining media as an individual habit or routine that aids in ordering a person's ordinary life. The question is: 'Are media used to establish a sense of social order and control in an ordinary practical consciousness without a requisite concern for value or ideology?'

In defining social order, this essay proceeds from the assumption in chaos theory (Briggs and Peat 1990; Gleick 1987) that stability or order is not the central, inherent, or normal state in physical, biological, or social realms. Rather, each of these realms is in continual movement in and out of order and chaos – neither state constituting a normative condition. Consequently, structure and order in the social world are fragile, and everyone is continually involved in their construction, or as Giddens prefers – 'structuration' (1984). As this view of social life

36 Controlling broadcasting

gathers momentum in sociology, its practitioners return to Georg Simmel's question 'How is society possible?' As implied in works by Goffman (1963), a sense of social order results from the repetitive character of episodic encounters, particularly in public places. Giddens (1984), reworks Goffman's highly systematic and rich descriptions into the notion of routinised day-to-day activity that 'binds the fleeting encounter to social reproduction, and thus to the seeming fixity of institutions' (1984, p. 72).

Whereas Goffman's and Giddens' work seems to apply primarily to routine social encounters, it is useful to extend this reasoning to ordinary personal routines that occur in public and private. Reference here is to the daily activity thought of as necessary drudgery and usually of secondary or trivial importance in the structuration of institutional order that Giddens describes. The significance of this so-called drudgery is masked by the often-heard complaint that everyday life routines are the stuff of boredom – that if anything, routine life is too ordered. But, therein lies its importance, particularly for social order and stability. As Giddens states:

> Whatever is done habitually is a basic element of day-to-day social activity.... The repetitiveness of activities which are undertaken in like manner day after day is the material grounding of what I call the recursive nature of social life ... [and this] routinisation is vital to the psychological mechanisms whereby a sense of trust or ontological security is sustained in the daily activities of social life (1984 p. xxiii).

Typically, the daily activity schedule for a working adult in modern urban society consists of waking up, personal grooming, eating, pet care, morning small talk, commuting to work, job routines (including lunch), the homebound commute, meal preparation, the evening meal, clean-up, playing with children, pets or both, evening entertainment, and preparing for bed. Periodic additions include supporting routines for any or all of the previously-mentioned activities, such as stopping to talk with a neighbour while retrieving the morning newspaper, or taking a favourite parking space or seat on mass transit. Other periodic routines include shopping, physical fitness, cleaning and maintenance, hobbies, interpersonal contacts, administration (paying the bills), recreation, waiting, and sleep itself. Although these activities are common to nearly everyone, and of little apparent consequence in the so-called big picture, there is a growing popular interest in the types of mundane activity that people share. Trade books, such as *Inside America*, by pollster Lou Harris (1987), *100% American* by Patrick McDonnell

(1988), and *Do's and Taboos Around the World* (Axtell 1985) are a few good sellers that normalise what may seem to be idiosyncratic routines, and indicate that perhaps urbanites today recognise a mutual bond in this commonality.

Casual observation demonstrates that much daily activity is routinised through repetitive actions, standardised sequence, and a temporal pattern of rhythm and tempo. The few situations of a typical day that are not routinised certainly stand out by contrast. Their unplanned, perhaps spontaneous character may seem fun or serious, fleeting or exhausting, and memorable as hallmarks or even lessons in life. But it is routine life that makes up the majority of social actions that provide a sense of plodding continuity and 'ontological security'. Support for this contention may rest on as trivial an illustration as one's own reaction to the disruption of a morning routine, such as the newspaper that does not arrive 'on time', a lack of hot water for a morning shower, the absence of a cup of coffee or tea, an unexpected detour or wait in the morning commute, or a pet that suddenly does the unexpected. Voluntarily, we are creatures of habit, and those habits instill order and continuity in an otherwise problematic world.

As routinised strategies render daily life durable, life flows in an orderly and stable manner. And, as the psychologist Csikszentmihaly (1990) claims, 'flow' in personal life may be the most important factor in achieving a sense of well-being. In this sense, social order in a broader sense may be abstracted and projected from an ordered personal life. What is essential to this strategy is both continuity or standardisation over time, and the desire to facilitate continuation. How then is continuity achieved? According to Giddens: 'Routinized character of paths along which individuals move in the reversible line of daily life does not just happen. It is made to happen through reflexive monitoring of action which individuals sustain in circumstances of co-presence' (1984, p. 64).

Giddens builds on this to include motivation as a consequence of reflexive activity (an idea based on G. H. Mead's discussion of the philosophy of the act). While reflexivity is central to social action in a Meadian framework, and the reciprocity required in meeting commitments underlies anticipation in social affairs, it has been assumed that these conceptions account for sustained action in the absence of co-presence or in anonymous encounters where interaction appears to be with a 'generalised other'. Without delving into the conceptual problems in 'socialisation' 'internalised norms', 'roles', and so on, it is suggested

38 Controlling broadcasting

that 'momentum' as a temporal factor aids in understanding how routine behaviour may be sustained.

To date, sports provides the most acceptable explanation of the nature and utility of momentum. Peter Adler (1981) points out in his ethnography of college basketball that achieving and losing momentum is often the single most important factor in accounting for wins and losses. And, what is critical for momentum is not the rationality of means-ends action. Teams coasting to apparent victory suddenly lose momentum and end up losers. Weaker teams upset Goliaths with a magical momentum that players and coaches can't explain, at least not rationally. In fact, momentum is the antithesis of rationality, as it implies a force that pulls rather than causes. In these terms, it is a temporal phenomenon of rhythm and tempo rather than a spatial pattern or strategy of positioning. How then is momentum established?

One readily available source of rhythm and tempo, and a potential source of momentum, is media. Figure 3.1 represents a fairly typical utilisation of media in everyday routines. Not only are media used extensively throughout the day, they are almost always available to modern urbanites in these situations. In fact, most people would agree that media use in daily routines is essential. Evidence includes the fact that stereo AM/FM receivers are standard equipment in American automobiles, teenagers and young adults are rarely without a headset close at hand, most older mass transit riders carry reading material, the typical American home has a radio or television or both in nearly every room, and recorded music is standard background in shopping situations, waiting areas, bars, and eating establishments. Figure 3.1 covers only the most common routines for typical urbanites in Western society, and most people could add to this list a number of personally unique routines that underscore individuality. Despite the limits of this list, it demonstrates the degree to which daily activity can be routinised, and the likelihood that routines will be accompanied by mass media.

In examining the situations in figure 3.1, a somewhat hidden observation is that most of the routines call for particular media and particular formats. Here format refers to the grammatical (syntax and inflection) rules used to present various kinds of subject matter, such as top–40 format for popular music, TV entertainment (info-tainment) for the newspaper *USA TODAY*, and one-liner stand-up comedy for TV sitcoms. To illustrate, morning wake-up radio is not only set to a particular station, but given the precision of most radio formats (adult contemporary, talk, news, and so on), knowledgeable listeners know how the content (news, weather, type of music), is organised (sequence)

Routines	Media use
Domestic	
wake-up	radio alarm
personal grooming	radio/recorded music/newspaper
exercise regimen	audio headset/print media
pet regimen	audio headset
morning meal	radio/TV/newspaper
evening meal preparation	radio/recorded music/TV
evening meal	specific TV programmes/music
bedtime	radio/specific TV programmes
indoor cleaning	radio/TV/music
outdoor cleaning	audio headset
routine shopping	background music
Work related	
job commute	radio/headset/print
work	background music
homebound commute	radio/headset/print
Routine waiting	
medical	print/background music
traffic	phone and almost anything
telephone hold	programmed music or radio
shopping queues	print
repairs	print/TV
Scheduled media use	
evening entertainment	scheduled TV
Sunday morning	newspaper
children's use	after school TV
	Saturday morning TV cartoons
	weekend TV music
Leisure time	
parties	recorded music
hobby activity	radio/TV
relaxation (beach)	radio/headset/read

Figure 3.1 Typical media use in daily routines

and accented within segments of a broadcast. These listeners can easily use radio format as a clock to monitor as well as 'time' their progress and determine whether they are 'on schedule' in their routines. Morning newspapers must arrive at a specific time, and they are read according to a particular sequence, which in turn may be integrated with

40 Controlling broadcasting

particular routines or segments of routines. Anyone who routinely reads a morning newspaper will readily admit to such behaviour. On it goes throughout the day, with particular media and formats becoming routine specific.

A closer look at the association of type of medium, the format, and the type of routine suggests that the format features of the medium may be at least as important, if not more important than the content. The weather report may be obtained from any one of several media, and the choice may initially rest on convenience. However, once the choice is routinised, it becomes an integral part of the routine, and change to another medium for needed information may momentarily destroy the flow of the routine. More to the point, a change in medium, or specifically a change in format, alters the rhythm and tempo of the action, and any momentum may be lost.

Three decades ago, Marshall McLuhan (1964) proposed that fundamental technological differences among the media affected the way in which a message would be interpreted. In other words, 'The medium is the message'. At the time, most students of media thought this idea was absurd. Today, many feel that McLuhan was on the right track. We know that people vary in their familiarity and comfort with various media, and we know that people selectively tune in and out based on these preferences. But, in contrast to McLuhan's position, the variations from one medium to the next are not a direct result of the technological character of the medium. Rather, as David Altheide and I have argued elsewhere (1979; 1991), variation in media selection is due to formats, or how the technology is used to present the content. A vivid example is the application of visual television grammar to rock music in the form or format of music video, and similarly to newspaper journalism in *USA TODAY*. This illustrates the independence of form or format from content, as well as preference among the audience for one format over others. As such, McLuhan's dictum is rephrased to 'The format is the message'. Further evidence of the ability to transfer formats is found in the recent history of commercial radio in America. During the late fifties rock'n'roll music of youth culture found its home on the little used and short broadcast radius of the FM band frequencies. While middle-aged, middle-class parents listened to AM middle-of-the-road radio, the baby boom generation developed highly specialised alternative formats on FM stations. As the 'boomers' grew older many of these FM stations quite naturally attempted to increase their ratings by aiming for broader popular appeal, and tailored the format of the old middle-of-the-road radio to rock music. Currently this can be heard as 'Lite Rock', 'Adult Contemporary', and 'Eclectic'. As might be expected, esoteric alternative formats are now found on the AM band.

While technology is certainly an important factor in explaining the popularity of various media, understanding what people pay attention to rests on the grammatical structure and logic of format. This lesson was learned by the designers of the Reagan and Bush presidential election campaigns, who knew that the primary format for an American audience is prime-time entertainment television. They also knew that as a general format, entertainment television could be used in any medium from billboards and newspapers to network television news. The so-called 'sound bite' is essentially a situation comedy one-liner, and along with simple and dramatic visuals, they were used effectively to help elect Reagan twice and Bush once. The losers, Mondale and Dukakis, followed a traditional campaign strategy of hard news issues combined with long-winded rhetoric which made for boring television. Observation of the 1992 Democratic Party convention indicates that the Democrats may have learned their lesson. Similar success and failure stories are found in advertising campaigns, sports programmes, religion, education, and others. Format won't guarantee success, but there is little success without the right format.

The utilisation of media as an integral feature of everyday life routines is primarily a matter of using formats as organisational features of routines. Among the most important features are the temporal elements of rhythm and tempo. As beat or cadence, rhythm is the accent or inflection achieved through action and pause which marks emphasis as well as progression. To engage oneself rhythmically is to lean into the future through anticipation, and to sustain momentum. As such, rhythm is fundamental rather than extraneous to establishing and maintaining order. At the macro level, Condon (1978), Leonard (1978), Hall (1983) and others, claim that the key to understanding any culture lies in identifying its rhythmic character and sources. For micro-analysis order is synonymous with entrainment, or the sychronisation of self with others in social affairs. By contrast, arrhythmia may occur when core rhythms are lost or rendered monotonous and boring (Brissett and Snow 1993). Nowhere is the threat of this arrhythmia more evident than in everyday life activity, and everyone has strategies designed to meet this threat. When boredom threatens, typical strategies include increasing the tempo and altering the rhythm (the latter being the most successful). Abundant examples are found where the potential for boredom is high, such as travel and captive audience situations. In these

42 Controlling broadcasting

and similar situations, media can be a sufficient antidote. Specifically, in the absence of co-presence, media used as a metronome may provide the entrainment necessary to establish momentum, although the more common feeling is simply a wish to sustain a constant rhythm for the situation. One playful example is the practice among youth of constantly changing the car radio station as a strategy for sustaining or changing rhythm.

Every media format has a discernible rhythm, which consists of the inflection or accent features of the format. Those accents or places of emphasis form a cadence of beat and pause that provide progression to an otherwise continuous blur of activity. These rhythms may be identified by reducing the number of cues that are normally used in a particular medium. For example, to capture the rhythm of a particular newspaper begin by looking at a foreign-language paper and glance through the layout. Note the position of photographs to written copy, headlines to copy, long to short paragraphs, column lengths, graphics, colour schemes, and so on. Each type of format from tabloids to finance papers has a distinct rhythmic pattern that may become integrated into particular daily routines, such as headlines, comics and human interest for breakfast, more serious material or the crossword puzzle for the mass transit commute, and the classified section for coffee breaks. With television, the identification of rhythm may be more difficult. As McLuhan (1964) pointed out, television involves all the senses, and has the appearance of a fuzzy mosaic. To reduce the interference, limit the TV experience to either sound or visuals. The most dramatic observations are made with music video, although soap operas, sitcoms, and game shows work well also. Compare different TV formats, such as soaps to sitcoms, and different time periods, such as *circa* 1950s black and white to the 1980s. In the latter comparison it should become apparent that the dominant rhythm today is visual, whereas during the early TV era auditory rhythm tended to lead the visual material. A similar comparison can be made with Hollywood film. In fact today, the dominant rhythmic pattern for most media is visual. Subtle variations in rhythm are found in different film genre, as well as cultural differences, such as the temporal differences between British and American comedy or mystery, and subculture and regional differences in music and talk. Simply reading through academic papers such as this one, illustrates a fairly standard rhythm of 'threes' when an author presents examples. With commercial media, the rhythms can become complex through simultaneously layering two or more sources, such as talk over music, and both over sound effects. To the untrained ear this may be irritating, but to others it demonstrates the degree to which we can be attuned to inflection characteristics in format.

In relating rhythm to a routine activity, it is suggested that maintaining a sequence of routine actions is facilitated by the rhythm or rhythms embedded in media format. Formatted or designed rhythm sustains momentum through the anticipation that occurs in the progression of accent, pause, accent. Restated, activity that might otherwise be experienced as tedious is infused with zest through the subtle ambiguity of anticipating the next act or beat. Given the history of work songs, it seems reasonable to suggest that rhythms in contemporary media formats help us through those unpleasant or potentially boring routines, such as rush-hour traffic, cleaning jobs, grocery shopping, the routine medical visit, and perhaps physical exercise. In more mundane routines the rhythmic accent may be more subtle, but none the less significant as background for the activity. Reading the Sunday newspaper helps establish the routine of 'down time', and classical music may accompany an evening meal.

Whereas rhythm provides the cadence for anticipation and momentum, tempo adds fervour or induces calm. A person can ease into the day or hit the floor running, eat a meal calmly or gobble fast food on the move, race or ease through the rush-hour, and fall into bed exhausted or relaxed. At the extremes, a very slow or very hurried tempo may distort the sense of momentum and result in a feeling of separation from the mundane world. This may be at the root of the hurried or frenzied society, as critiqued by Rifkin (1987) and others. Perhaps most important, tempo enables a person to pace a routine in order to keep it within desired time parameters. To keep a routine manageable, we may admonish ourselves to 'get it in gear, or slow it down a bit'. Although changing tempo can be accomplished without media, in today's urban Western world most people would agree that media are an excellent means of establishing tempo. A common example is the use of radio to keep a driver awake and alert at the wheel, especially at night. At bedtime the procedure is reversed by reading ones self to sleep. In these situations, the tempo in media format becomes a means for controlling the pace of orderly progression. Since we know intuitively that increasing or decreasing tempo too much can destroy rhythm, media may be called upon to check runaway pace or increase the pace when tedium threatens.

Conceptualising rhythm and tempo as temporal ecology may serve to expand our understanding of the importance of temporality in everyday life. A significant step toward defining this concept may be found

44 Controlling broadcasting

in Edward Hall's *The Dance of Life* (1983). Hall observes that every culture has well-established temporal rhythms that function as a language for experiencing the everyday world. Following this logic, temporal ecology becomes core culture, and serves to integrate like-minded members in entrained social action, as well as to identify and exclude outsiders. His classification of cultural time rests on a distinction between monochronic (one thing at a time) and polychronic (multiple tasks occurring simultaneously), and his comparisons afford interesting insights into cultural differences, particularly for economic activity. What is needed to further his seminal beginning is identification of the features of culture that directly and indirectly establish a temporal ecology. In today's world media certainly are one, if not the most important element in a temporal ecology, and the power in this element is format.

Whereas format contains what becomes an essential temporal structure for routine activity, continued use of particular formats in specific routines become part of the overall appearance of familiarity and normality. Familiar pictures include a newspaper and morning coffee, cars and their sound systems, television and children after school, Sunday evening and television, Saturday evening and video rentals, waiting-rooms and well-worn magazines, and the list goes on. Each of these situations becomes incomplete and awkward without the appropriate medium or media. A broken car radio makes the morning commute unnerving. A pre-empted television programme at mealtime sends individuals searching for a substitute that will probably be unsatisfactory.

One explanation for these familiar scenes is that the medium is an essential part of the *gestalt* or unity of the event. Side-stepping the gestalt assumption, one could simply say that a missing piece of the picture introduces a degree of ambiguity and corresponding emotional change that at the very least is uncomfortable and at worst intolerable. Extreme cases are those routines which can't be rescheduled and where no alternative media are available. Examples include traffic grid-lock without a phone or radio, meal preparation in the company of guests who can't stand the cook's choice of music or television, or the breakdown in one routine that fouls successive routines so that the media must be abandoned. In such cases we may seek out media that are normally ignored, or we create it internally.

The absence of media may also heighten self-consciousness, particularly when alone in public places and sensitivity to scrutiny from others becomes exaggerated. Waiting at a bus stop, riding the underground, eating alone in a cafeteria, or waiting in an airline terminal are situations of potential discomfort through feeling awkward or vulnerable. In these situations media may be used to divert one's attention from unwanted attention by strangers, to an engagement with a medium as a surrogate other. Here again, the content of the medium is secondary to its use as a form for para-social interaction. Familiar examples include the newspaper, magazines, paperbacks, audio headset, and the infamous 'boombox', which may also serve as a weapon to keep others at a distance. Most important, the medium in these situations enables the individual to avoid or diminish contemplating impressions of 'looking-glass self'. Through the medium the individual is immersed in a safer, albeit vicarious, reality.

Finally, establishing a sense of normality through the use of familiar media formats can be useful for maintaining the proper sequence and temporal order of routines. One of the problems in the video-taping of programmes is with programmes that are normally watched along with particular daily routines. People who go to sleep with a particular programme find it difficult if not impossible to watch that programme in the morning. Doing so may even induce sleep. Similarly, reading the morning newspaper in the evening may feel strange if it is routinely read in the morning. In fact, it may be necessary to replicate the morning routine (coffee or a drink of some kind), in order to read it with comfort. The problem compounds when other routines are expected to follow in sequence. For example, when television programmes are associated with the temporal progression of the work week, shifting a Thursday evening programme to Monday or Tuesday may reduce its enjoyment, as the programme may formerly have been associated with the beginning of the weekend. More dramatic perhaps, is missing a particular evening TV news programme, particularly if that programme is used as a culminating routine for the day.

Just as media routines aid in establishing a feeling of normality for a particular routine, or more accurately the absence of media make some routines awkward and non-normal, a traumatic non-routine situation may be imbued with a sense of normality by using familiar media in the background. Examples include the medical waiting rooms, surgery preparation areas in hospitals, dental offices, airline boarding areas and on-board flight preparation and flight, and even the mildly ambiguous situation of the grocery check-out queue, where we can read outrageous and bizarre tabloid headlines. When standard media sources, such as radio or television are unavailable or become tedious, alternative media, such as billboards, bumper stickers, T-shirts, and business signs may be substituted. In sterile environments, such as temporary confinements,

46 Controlling broadcasting

people will go to great lengths to stimulate mental activity. Under such conditions any medium may be better than none at all.

Non-routine situations in which media is often used as supplementary background also deserves brief mention. These include social events, such as parties, and establishing private moods, such as romance or solitary quiet times. Since the primary concern in these situations is to establish an appropriate rhythm and tempo, background media, especially music, can act as a subtle or perhaps dramatic metronome to establishing and maintaining flow. In turn, the most likely potential problem in these situations is the awkward pause that can destroy the flow. Background media can not only fill the pause, it may serve as a topic for a small talk to maintain momentum in the affairs. Moreover, music background is usually an impression management strategy to convey social class and personality characteristics about the host in the situation, which in turn imply certain future possibilities for the encounter. In short, media background may stimulate anticipation among participants in both a temporal fashion and for particular actions and meanings.

The importance of media as background has long been overlooked in staging and enacting social affairs. In fact, the term background is a misnomer to the extent that it implies extraneous status among the factors that comprise a situation. Close observation of any situation in which media seems or are claimed to serve as background usually reveals that its absence leaves a noticeable void and discomfort. Its importance in maintaining momentum or flow, and consequently control (Csikszentmihaly 1990) is obvious to media users. In fact, in some situations such as driving, coming home to an empty place of residence, reading, eating, exercising, and so on, the main activity cannot begin until the media are operating. To ensure immediate media operation, common practices include leaving the car radio power switch left in the 'on' position, connecting the home stereo to a light switch near the front door or to a remote-control device, and making sure reading material is close at hand in dining areas, patios, bedrooms, and bathrooms. In these and similar situations, the medium is integral to the overall activity.

As a means for establishing order and control, the previous discussion has focused on the use of media format as a temporal structure for rhythm and pace in everyday life. These temporal features of media format may also serve as a means for ordering and controlling the space needed to carry out and complete a routine. A familiar example is the newspaper which may be used as a protective barrier against physical and social encroachment while riding mass transit. In a study of subway riders some years ago (Levine *et al.* 1973), the newspaper was also seen as a means for maintaining civility through civil inattention, or as an act of posing no threat to other travellers. Here the physical form of media technology is recognised as a legitimate part of the process of establishing and maintaining social order. Today, stereo headsets, cellular phones, the paperback novel, magazines, and the lap-top computer may serve the same function. While these technologies may also foster an extreme privatisation in public social arenas, the result is still order and control.

Despite the fact that media pervade almost every corner of modern society, people should view the claims made here with some scepticism. Certainly large numbers of people use media sparingly, and these people most likely do not use media to support daily routines. But statistics on the average number of hours a television is turned on each day, average number of radios per household, newspaper circulation, video rental figures, and so on, support the claim that heavy media use is commonplace in Western urban society, and there is no sign of its decline. Indeed, the question of 'why media use is so great?' is seldom heard today.

Media critics, such as Neil Postman (1984), would have us believe that our fascination with media is primarily an ever-increasing demand for entertainment. In the early days of television the fear was that there was something sinister and addictive about 'the tube'. Today we're back to the addiction notion, but this time it's entertainment – we just can't get enough. Clearly almost everything on television, including news and sports, is presented through entertainment formats. As television formats became the preferred media format among audiences throughout America, other media, such as newspapers, magazines, radio, and movies, joined the strategy and reformulated their formats to conform to television. On the surface it appears that every medium presents almost everything through entertainment, which has prompted Postman to suggest that we're 'amusing ourselves to death'. Perhaps. But an alternative explanation is that in many situations, a reason for using a mass medium is to develop and sustain a temporal ecology (a time order) and the appearance of familiarity, particularly in daily affairs.

Today, temporal ecology in Western urban society is established and maintained largely through electronic media formats. While it may appear to the uninvolved observer that media is content-specific, and driven by market strategies, politics, currents in education, sports, and

48 Controlling broadcasting

economic realities of daily life, the most common use of media is primarily as support for other activities. In fact, it seems quite plausible that media as form may be one of the more powerful factors in constructing and maintaining social order and control in everyday life. The order and control referred to here is not understood as a consciousness of collectivity, nor is it informed through ideology. Rather, it refers to order in the sense of maintaining individual life as familiar – as usual. It is the orderly arrangement of ordinary activity, task, space, and time. As sociologist Carl Couch claims, 'Temporal structures are an absolute necessity for the production of orderly human action' (1989, p. 29) It is this order that fosters synchronisation or entrainment in those social affairs that are essential to the smooth flow of daily activity. As argued by Csikszentmihaly (1990), this what is well-being is all about.

And yet Jeremy Rifkin argues in *Time Wars* (1987) that we are in the throes of a crisis in temporality. By abandoning the rhythms and tempo of nature and embracing a new temporal order imposed through cybernetics and the computer chip, Western society has developed a temporality based almost entirely on artificial dimensions of time. In the process, Rifkin argues, community and self-assurance are sacrificed for power and control. However, he feels that this control is an illusion, and we must 'seek a new temporal orientation based on an empathetic union with the biological and physical clocks of nature' (p. 194). On the other hand, perhaps we have gained a sense of order and comfort through mass-mediated daily routines. In today's world of apparent complexity, rapid change, and uncertainty, this may constitute the realm where people feel some control over life. That media provide a useful tool in this control ought to be taken seriously.

Bibliography

Adler, P. (1981), *Momentum: a Theory of Social Action,* Beverly Hills, Sage.
Axtell, R. E. (1985), *Do's and Taboos Around the World,* New York, John Wiley & Sons.
Briggs, J. and Peat F. D. (1990), *The Turbulent Mirror: an Illustrated Guide to Chaos Theory and the Science of Wholeness,* New York, Harper and Row.
Brissett, D. and Snow, R. P. (1993), 'Boredom: where the future isn't', *Symbolic Interaction,* 16, 3, pp. 237-256.
Carey, J. (ed.) (1987), *Media Myths and Narratives,* Newbury Park CA, Sage.
Condon, W. S. (1978), 'An analysis of behavioral organization', *Sign Language Studies,* 13, pp. 285-318.
Couch Jr., C. (1989), *Social Processes and Relationships: a Formal Approach,* Dix Hills, NY, General Hall Inc.
Csikszentmihaly, M. (1990), *Flow: the Psychology of Optimal Experience,* New York Harper & Row.
Dorfman, A. (1983), *The Empire's Old Clothes,* New York, New Pantheon.
Eron, L. (1992), *Report of the American Psychological Association Commission on Violence and Youth.*
Fiske, J. (1987), *Television Culture,* New York, Methuen.
Giddens, A. (1984), *The Constitution of Society,* Cambridge, Polity Press.
Gitlin, T. (1987), 'Prime-time ideology; the hegemonic process in television entertainment', in Newcomb, H. (ed.) *Television: the Critical Review,* New York, Oxford University Press.
Goffman, E. (1963), *Behavior in Public Places,* New York, The Free Press.
Hall, E. (1983), *The Dance of Life,* Garden City, Anchor/Doubleday.
Harris, L. (1987), *Inside America,* New York, Vantage.
Levine, J., *et al* (1973), 'Subway behavior', in, Birenbaum, A. and Sagarin E. (eds), *People in Places,* New York, Praeger.
Leonard, G. (1978), *The Silent Pulse,* New York, E. P. Dutton.
McDonnell, P. (1988), *100% American,* New York, Posiedon.
McLuhan, M. (1964), *Understanding Media: the Extensions of Man,* New York, McGraw-Hill.
Parenti, M. (1991), *Make Believe Media:the Politics of Entertainment,* New York, St Martin's Press.
Postman, N. (1984), *Amusing Ourselves to Death,* New York, Viking.
Rifkin, J. (1987), *Time Wars,* New York, Henry Holt and Company.
Shaw, D. L. and McCombs, M .E. (1977), *The Emergence of American Political Issues: the Agenda-Setting Function of the Press,* St Paul's, Minn., West Publishing.
Simmel, G. (1971), *On Individuality and Social Forms,* (ed. D.N. Levine), Chicago, University of Chicago Press.
Twitchell, J .B. (1992), *Carnival Culture: the Trashing of Taste in America,* New York, Columbia University Press.

Part II
Institutional Relations and Folly

Part II

Inspiring Recovery and Unity

Philip Schlesinger, Howard Tumber and Graham Murdock

The media politics of crime and criminal justice

ABSTRACT

This paper is concerned with the treatment of crime and criminal justice in the British national news media. It begins by proposing a break with 'media-centric' approaches to the study of relations between news sources and the media which have tended to ignore the conflicts within and between social institutions. It moves on to illustrate the argument by examining the media strategies pursued by sources in the crime and criminal justice fields, drawing attention to the relevance for these activities of such factors as the relative institutionalization of social actors and their use of available resources. Recent developments in crime, legal affairs and home affairs reporting are the background to a discussion of the specialist organization of press journalism and television coverage. Some illustrative discussion of media content is presented that highlights pertinent differences within and between television broadcasting and the press. Brief observations are also made concerning the relations between patterns of media consumption and fear of crime in sections of the television audience. The paper concludes by arguing for more connections to be made between bodies of existing work in media sociology, political science and criminology.

INTRODUCTION

The relationship between crime and the media has long been a matter of recurrent controversy. Social scientific research on this topic dates from the early part of this century, and one notable theme has been the press coverage of crime.

Such work grew out of a broader concern with the role of the mass media in liberal democracies, prompted by the rapid growth of a popular daily press. Many commentators perceived there to be a growing tension between the press's idealised political role and the proprietor's audience-building strategies. The popular press was seen as busily abandoning its political responsibilities as a source of disinterested and accurate information and forum for rational debate, instead becoming an arm of the burgeoning entertainment industry by using the techniques of melodrama to capture and hold its readers. The coverage of crime and justice could hardly avoid being debated from the outset, since it exemplified the new 'sensationalism' and also concerned an increasingly central area of state activity, with far-reaching implications for public policy.

Alongside worries that coverage of crime might encourage or incite criminal activity by means of an 'imitation effect', there was a persistent anxiety that inaccurate or sensationalist reporting might create unnecessary public fear, leading to pressure for tough and immediate responses to given situations that pre-empted more considered initiatives, possibly with counter-productive results.

These fears were given added credence by an early study of how the press in Cleveland had 'manufactured' a 'crime wave', in January 1919. Although the actual number of offences reported to the police had increased only marginally, newspapers massively increased coverage of crime during the second half of the month. By generating demands for summary action and quick 'results', and by thus putting pressure on public officials to rate popularity above adherence to due process, it was held that such reporting seriously damaged the policy debate.[1]

Of course, this kind of press campaign is but one of the ways in which the mass media mediate between the discourses and strategies employed by the various agencies concerned with the field of crime and justice and the discourses and understandings of audiences. This article takes up the traditional concern with content analysis, but also goes substantially beyond this, to explore how crime and criminal justice are handled in the communication process as a whole, from production and content to audience reception. The empirical material in the sections that follow is based upon research conducted in 1986–88 which focused on the London-based national television channels and daily and Sunday press.

Much recent media research has been based upon a 'dominant ideology thesis'.[2] Using either a neo-Gramscian theory of hegemony[3] or a 'propaganda model',[4] it has been argued that the power of politically and economically dominant groups in the society defines the parameters of debate, ensures the privileged reproduction of their discourse, and by extension, largely determines the contours of the dominant ideology – of what is socially thinkable.

Whether culturalist or political-economic in emphasis, such work has paid inadequate attention to the communication process as a whole. Specifically, it has neglected the conflictual processes that lie behind the moment of definition both inside central social institutions and within the media themselves. Furthermore, such work has been characterised by a tendency to treat media as homogeneous, as *the* media. This largely ignores the distinctiveness of particular media (say, the press or television) and the ways in which such media are internally differentiated (e.g., the 'popular' vs the 'quality' press).

In recent years, sociological arguments about communication have developed against the backdrop of wider theoretical disputes between Marxists and pluralists. At the heart of the matter is whether the workings and output of the media are seen (more or less sophisticatedly) as subject to the control of the ruling class in capitalist societies or alternatively, whether they are seen as enjoying substantial autonomy vis à vis contending forces and interests.[5] The resultant tendency has been to pose either 'Marxist' or 'pluralist' questions for research.

Such inflexibility has its shortcomings, for it is necessary to consider questions of both structure and agency. For instance, whilst recognising structured inequalities of access to the media, one should not ignore the competitive strategies for media attention employed by news sources.

Virtually all research to date on this question has been media-centric: that is, it has failed to focus on the relations between news sources and news media from the standpoint of the *sources* themselves. Thus, in Stuart Hall's well-known formulation, official sources' access to the media is presented as essentially guaranteed by their structural positions within the political and economic system and as therefore affording them a 'primary defining' role.[6] One effect of this standpoint is that the sociological question of how sources might organise *media strategies* and compete with one another is entirely neglected. 'Primary definition', which ought to be an empirically ascertainable outcome, is taken instead to be an a priori effect of the privileged access of the powerful. For its part, the empirical sociology of journalism, whilst more sensitive to the existence of source competition (which unquestionably takes place on unequal terms) has still remained largely trapped within methodological frameworks that preclude the direct investigation of source strategies.[7]

This article sets out to demonstrate some of the complexities of how the definitional struggle is organised in the field of crime and criminal justice. It also indicates some of the consequences that this may have upon the ways in which the news is constructed.

Discourse about crime and criminal justice is produced in a social space in which the contending social actors range from government departments through to pressure groups. They pursue their communicative goals in what Jürgen Habermas calls the 'public sphere', namely a realm in which 'something approaching public opinion can be formed' and where, ideally, access, 'is guaranteed to all citizens'.[8]

But the normative ideal hardly matches contemporary conditions. As Habermas himself notes, organized groups rather than individual citizens prevail in what is essentially 'a field for the competition of interests'.[9] Indeed, others have observed that the contemporary public sphere is under threat from the concentration of media ownership and control, the weakening of public service goals in broadcasting and the internationalising tendencies of media production and distribution.[10] Moreover, in Britain, recent legislation and overt political intervention have tended to reinforce both state secrecy and a climate of journalistic caution.

For present purposes, this highly pressured public sphere of capitalist democracies may usefully be seen as divided into numerous discursive fields that are subject to symbolic struggle. Such ideological conflict involves an incessant mobilization of resources by social actors in pursuit of their strategies and tactics, during the course of which they manipulate what Pierre Bourdieu[11] terms their 'cultural capital' in an effort to impose an orthodoxy of interpretation upon public attitudes and judgments about matters in dispute.

Discursive competition in the public sphere requires social actors to seek contexts for their messages that may enable them to shape the public agenda. As there is a scarcity of public spaces relative to the number of views competing for recognition, what Hilgartner and Bosk[12] call the 'carrying capacity of public institutions – amongst which the media are of major importance – acts as an important constraint upon access.

Richard Ericson and his colleagues[13] have amply demonstrated in a cognate study of Canadian media and the criminal justice process that the state and its agencies must be at the centre of any analysis of competition for media attention. However, at the same time, as they also show, it is essential to recognize that other organised forces may also have the capacity to intervene with varying effect in the public domain.

THE CRIME AND CRIMINAL JUSTICE FIELDS

In the sections that follow, we present a number of cases and illustrations from our empirical research. During 1986–88, full-length interviews were conducted with a range of news sources in the crime and criminal justice fields in order to investigate how news sources might pursue strategies towards the media. In the course of our study, we have also examined the social organization of specialist reporting and programme-making in detail. Furthermore, based upon a sample of two weeks' national press and prime time television coverage, our content analysis has explored patterns of coverage across the national media. Finally, in a limited way, we have attempted to investigate patterns of audience consumption for different types of television programme dealing with crime and criminal justice.

The media politics of crime and criminal justice

So far as news sources are concerned, apart from considering the organization and media strategies of state institutions, our study has focused upon pressure groups such as those dealing with prison and penal reform, civil liberties, and police accountability. Thus, the aim has been to investigate what John Kingdon[14] terms the 'policy community', namely those with specialised interests in the areas of crime and criminal justice.

The role played by resources is fundamental. First, there is the extent to which any given source is institutionalized. The most advantageous locations within the field are occupied by the apparatuses of the state such as the Home Office and the Metropolitan Police. These are locuses of permanent activity for which the routine dissemination of official information is important. In competition for space in the media, but relatively disadvantaged by comparison, are long-standing pressure groups such as the National Council for Civil Liberties (NCCL, which in May 1990 renamed itself Liberty) and the Howard League for Penal Reform. At the other end of the continuum are the least institutionalized actors, consisting of *ad hoc* issue-oriented groups or bodies such as police monitoring groups, whose base of public support is narrow and weak.

Second, the investment in media and public relations by a given actor is extremely important. As the development of media strategies has become increasingly common, the impact of symbolic media-oriented action has more and more become a crucial criterion of effectiveness. However, this can pose problems, even for the best resourced: for instance, where the Home Office and the police have invested in media monitoring and public relations, this has come up against internal budgetary limitations and has required explicit thinking about goals that might justify substantial expansion. Criteria of success in publicity are not as clear-cut as a rational-utilitarian set of assumptions might predict. Ensuring the attention desired is not just a matter of filling space and time but of achieving an impact, which is very difficult to assess.

Social actors' information management activities (and specifically their media strategies) are not solely intended to influence the policy agenda, that is those 'items which decision makers have formally accepted for serious consideration'.[15] Other reasons and motives may be discerned. For example, organizational imperatives such as the need to increase resources, to aid recruitment, and particularly in the case of professional associations and trade unions, to boost membership morale. For voluntary and pressure groups media coverage can also enhance feelings of solidarity, dissipate isolationist tendencies and give a fillip to staff confidence.

There has been a developing process of news source sophistication. For instance, in the case of pressure groups the Child Poverty Action Group's effective media strategy has been seen as an example to be followed and applied in the criminal justice area. Groups may go in for competitive profiling: for example, HM Customs and Excise have consciously competed for image space with the police, and the Prison Officers have self-consciously changed their profile by learning from others' mistakes. A further instance of such reflexivity concerns the incorporation of the anticipated strategies of others into ongoing media strategies: the Home Office, for instance engages in second-guessing NCCL. Linked to this is the way in which responses to others' interventions in the field are part of some source strategies, with attempted control over timing being particularly important. Nor is it necessarily the case that all communicative action is aimed at the wider public.

HM Customs and Excise, for instance, has raised its profile considerably in recent years because of concern about its public image. Due to past actions over Value Added Tax they felt that they had acquired an image of jackbooted men who visited during the night and kicked down the door. Secondly, even though the Customs were scoring major drug-busting successes as a result of their investigations, their efforts were going largely unnoticed by both government and public because they did not have a very active public relations and press policy.

By attempting to increase public support through the media and by public relations activities the Customs have aimed especially to influence the government, believing that their case was not in the forefront of ministers' minds and that in the competition for resources with other departments they had become overlooked. In fact, the department suffered quite savage cuts in manpower as part of the government's review of Civil Service staffing. Having managed to achieve a higher publicity profile, our informants thought it no accident that the flow of resources had increased, allowing more staff time to be devoted to both tax collection and drug enforcement.

The Home Office has operated similarly to secure extra resources. According to one pressure group, towards the end of the 1970s the Home Office wanted to embark upon a new programme of prison construction. One way to obtain resources was to pressure the Treasury by opening up the prisons and showing just how decrepit they were. Hence the invitation to a film-maker, Rex Bloomstein, to make a television series on Strangeways gaol. This was part of a new strategy of approaching journalists and pointing out the difficult situation in the prisons. Previously, the Home Office had always discouraged journalists, keeping them out of the establishments and rarely telling them anything either on, or off, the record.

The police, too, have developed on these lines, by considerably reorganizing their information departments. These changes have taken place mainly in the large metropolitan forces where, with one notable exception, a more open and pro-active policy has replaced a closed and reactive one. Although during the Thatcher years there has been a heavy emphasis upon state secrecy, the police's desire (and need) for an improved image has steadily gathered momentum, requiring a semblance of openness. This image change, whilst initially involving a process of organizational adjustment, later also called for dissemination through the media. Journalists, although welcoming this more open policy, have remained sceptical of some of its aspects.

For the police, it has been the crisis of confidence both inside the force and amongst the general public that has led them to redevelop their press and public relations operations. In fact, the 1980s were not a very good time for the police in Britain. Their handling of the inner-city riots of the early years of the decade came in for heavy criticism in some quarters. Violent confrontations during the course of industrial relations disputes were also at the forefront of political debate. The most important such instances were the coal miners' strike in 1984-85 and the print workers' disputes with newspaper proprietor Eddie Shah at his Warrington plant in 1983, and the subsequent much more serious confrontations with News International's Rupert Murdoch at his new Wapping plant in 1987. The shooting of innocent citizens in the course of police operations also caused great public concern, as did allegations of corruption and accusations of beatings to obtain confessions. All of these contributed to a widespread shaking of public confidence and a diminution of support.

It is not surprising, therefore, that some large forces, such as the West Midlands police, have invested considerable time and energy searching for a suitable model on which to base their PR operations. This search has spread as far as the United States, as well as involving the seeking out of 'best practice' in the British forces.

In a recent move aimed at boosting support, the current Commissioner of the Metropolitan Police, Sir Peter Imbert, hired one of the best-known design consultancies and corporate image specialists, Wolff Olins, to make an audit of internal and external attitudes towards 'the Met'. The designers' belief is that a change in image will produce more favourable public opinion with the eventual outcome of a changed impression of police effectiveness (whether genuine or not).

Design is a currently fashionable aspect of marketing. Many government departments have adopted high street images to sell their services. After the General Election of 1987, the Department of Trade and Industry under Lord Young led the way in sales techniques. With the contemporary emphasis on business and entrepreneurship, public sector organisations have adapted their public relations to commercial models in order to provide themselves with a more acceptable image. And the police have not been slow to follow suit, seeing citizens as customers to whom their activities have to be 'sold'.

Such image-building has characterized many of the social actors involved in the crime and criminal justice field. It is a version of the mobilization model used by political leaderships to gain support for their objectives which has spread to those on the outer rim of the policy-making circle.

Unions such as the National Association of Probation Officers (NAPO) have completely revamped their communications both internally and externally. In 1985 they appointed an assistant general secretary to organize and run their communications and a working party was set up to examine in detail and substantially improve their external and internal channels of communication. Amongst the recommendations put forward were 'the re-organization of NAPO's publications and "house-style" to present it as a vital organization central to criminal justice issues', and also the appointment of an information manager to provide expertise in information collection and storage, and communications systems. External relations with the media changed rapidly. The new assistant general secretary produced press releases, gave briefings and wrote articles for journals and magazines as well as appearing on television and radio.

Returning to the question of the policy agenda, we found that while some groups were targetting the wider public in order to arouse attention, many concentrated their efforts on influencing the political elites or liberal elements in the establishment in order to achieve their objectives. The Prison Reform Trust is an example of a group that attempts to do both. They accept, however, that because most of their contact with the media is with the quality press and with television current affairs and documentary teams, this inevitably means that their audience is relatively restricted. This is not seen as a problem, however, since like many pressure groups, their prime objective is to influence people in the Home Office and in Parliament, and to inform policy and opinion makers amongst the readers of the quality press. Getting the message across to the wider public is achieved either through occasionally being mentioned in the tabloids or through popular television fiction.

At first glance, the actions of this group, and others that behave similarly, suggests that policy initiatives or changes are purely a top-down phenomenon. However, our research has shown that the situation is much more complex. Oppositional and alternative entry into the policy agenda process does take place, and raises questions about a conception of 'primary definition' that tends to assume a largely closed circle of definers. The influential analysis of Hall *et al.* failed to examine the multifold processes whereby the definitions of the powerful were themselves at times partially shaped by negotiations with those outside official circles. For example, even though we found that many of the radical groups were treated as marginal, some of their ideas were adopted by the more reformist groups, who in turn treated with state agencies. The question of where 'primary definitions' originate and the ultimate 'authorship' of policy discourse may therefore be less obvious than would appear from studying media content alone.

To say this is by no means to deny that there is inequality of entry to the media agenda and that different actors have different abilities to exert influence based on their various endowments of resources – whether this be financial capital, cultural capital, organizational capacities or public relations skills.

Some of the more radical groups, such as Women in Prison, whilst refusing funding from the Home Office, do nevertheless have contact with it over specific cases under the spotlight and sometimes this has led to changes in prison policy. In some instances, the threat of publicity (and possible ministerial embarrassment) can be an effective tactic for a group if it requires some action by the Home Office.

On other occasions, pressure or voluntary groups will desist on tactical grounds from resorting to the media. The principal reason for this lies in their relationship with the Home Office, and their concern that too much publicity might result in a case being treated unfavourably, because the issue comes to be seen as a political battle to be won outright. Much of the time, therefore, pressure groups, even the more radical, will negotiate directly with the Home Office, avoiding publicity altogether.

At times a voluntary or pressure group's media tactics can be orchestrated by the Home Office, not in an underhand way but with the tacit approval of those concerned. For instance, a particular group may be used to put over a position on an issue or change in policy which, for political reasons, the Home Office is either unable or unwilling to undertake, usually because it is itself in conflict with another arm of the state apparatus.

The National Association for the Care and Resettlement of Offenders (NACRO) provides a pertinent example. On one occasion, pressure was being exerted on the government by the judiciary to be given the power to impose suspended sentences on young offenders. The Home Office believed that the measure would do more harm than good. But because of political pressure from the Lord Chief Justice and the judiciary the Home Office had to show willing and included it in the White Paper preceding the 1988 Criminal Justice Bill. Unofficially, however, the Home Office, made its own position clear to bodies such as NACRO, and indicated that adverse comments from them would be extremely helpful to its cause.

The general shift against the public sector in favour of the voluntary sector during the Thatcher years has meant that groups such as NACRO, and more recently victim support schemes, have received increased publicity with the active encouragement of government departments. The emphasis on voluntary groups and charities as ways of relieving the burden on the state was a hallmark of Conservative thinking in the 1980s. In 1989/90, for instance, the National Association for Victim Support Schemes was receiving £4 million in funding for its local schemes from the Home Office, which is extremely anxious for such ventures to operate successfully. In fact, the Home Office was very keen for NVASS to promote its image more actively with a view to attracting more resources from the private sector.

In this instance, the Home Office needed to demonstrate its contribution to the 'fight against crime'. However, setting up this kind of structure can have other consequences, two of which merit comment. First, groups such as NACRO and others that are funded by the state do criticize government policy and obtain media coverage for their efforts. Secondly, and more speculatively, this raises the more general question of whether coverage by the media of a particular group or government department's activities may have effects on the general viewer or reader quite different from the intended impact on the specific target audience. Does increased coverage of the victims of crime enhance a sense of insecurity and fear of crime amongst given sectors of the public?

THE MEDIA

Changes in the numbers and types of social actors in the crime and criminal justice field, and the development of media strategies by news sources have contributed to changes in the nature of reporting during recent years. Consequently, we have investigated the current organization of specialist coverage, both in the press and in television.

Journalists covering crime and criminal justice fall under the rubrics of 'Crime', 'Home Affairs' and 'Legal Affairs'. Although these three categories encompass the whole field, not all national newspapers have separate correspondents covering each area as there are variations in the designations of personnel. The five UK national 'quality' daily newspapers (The *Daily Telegraph*, The *Financial Times*, The *Guardian*, The *Independent*, and *The Times*) all have legal affairs correspondents, who together with their BBC counterpart constitute a fairly cohesive group.

There were four main reasons for the growth in coverage of this specialism in the 1980s. First, in the wake of its 'law and order' campaigns, the Conservative government introduced several major pieces of legislation, such as the Police and Criminal Evidence Act and the Criminal Justice Act. Second, proposed changes in the legal system (for instance, giving solicitors the right of appearance) served to focus the spotlight on this area. Third, the major prosecutions of Sarah Tisdall, Clive Ponting, and Peter Wright over official secrets meant that newspapers required specialists to handle these stories' legal ramifications and could not rely solely upon home affairs or general reporters to cover them. Fourth, with the launch of The *Independent*, competition amongst the 'up-market' quality newspapers intensified, with battle joined for an audience that included solicitors, barristers and others working in the legal profession.

The brief of home affairs correspondents is not as easily defined as those of legal affairs or crime correspondents as they cover a wide area shaped mainly by the remits of the Home Office, which is divided into a number of departments. Some home affairs correspondents cover all of these, others concentrate upon just one or two areas. For example, broadcasting is now predominantly covered by media correspondents, particularly in the quality press, whereas previously it was a subject for the home affairs correspondent. The scope of home affairs varies across the press and can at times depend on the news editor's definition of the story, with the previous experience and contacts of the individual correspondent also playing a part in defining the brief.

Crime is one of the biggest and most competitive areas in journalism. Newspapers differ in the number of specialist crime correspondents and reporters they employ. The majority have one, although some have three. The nature of coverage has altered considerably over the years and the type of journalist has also changed. Twenty-five years ago, crime coverage mainly concerned murder, jewel thefts and petty crime. It now encompasses drugs, terrorism, child abuse, rape, mugging and policy matters. As a result, rather than attempting to cover the whole area, some crime correspondents specialize in particular sub-fields. The relationship with the main source of information – the police – has altered: there is now less drinking in the pubs together, for instance.[16] The overall orientation of the crime correspondent is also changing. The new breed are thought to be more critical of the police, more analytical and less cohesive as a group.

Routine press and television coverage is structured in terms of the organization of specialist and non-specialist reporting. In response to the growing prominence of crime and criminal justice issues, and recognizing that audiences can be built for such programming, television has developed a number of specialised vehicles with diverse approaches, two of which we studied in depth.

Crimewatch UK is a sometimes controversial instance of popular action-oriented television, focusing on crime and aiming at the mobilization of the audience in order to catch criminals. Despite its factual, documentary features slot, it has many of the characteristics of entertainment, and its great drawing power is underlined by a capacity to attract an average audience on the BBC's main channel, BBC1, of 11.5 million. This is higher than some of the less popular soap operas, and much greater than that of the national main nightly news, whether on the BBC or ITV. It is broadcast monthly, apart from during the summer break, and attains high audience appreciation ratings.

By contrast, although *Out of Court* comes from the same 'stable' in BBC Television as *Crimewatch*, it is consumer-orientated and addresses the workings of the criminal justice system, often critically. A weekly factual programme dealing with legal affairs, the programme concept follows a BBC tradition of providing a 'live', half-hour magazine and attracts approximately two million viewers. There is no great pressure to achieve a larger audience because this could be interpreted as a loss of seriousness. The two programmes, then, represent quite distinct sectors of the crime and criminal justice field.

Crimewatch UK is perhaps best interpreted as chiming in with the mood of law and order politics and fear of crime that characterized the 1980s in Britain. It also fits in with the new wave of 'participative' television which has taken the form, for instance, of successive charity-seeking *Telethons* and, in the case of social concern about child abuse, of *Childline*. *Crimewatch*, a forty-minute programme, has been adapted to British conditions from a similarly successful West German model of more than twenty years' vintage. In the British context, the only precursor has been ITV's *Police Five*, a five-minute news bulletin style of production (itself some twenty-five years old) which obviously has a much more limited scope. Latterly, thirty-second and one-minute appeals on ITV for information about given crimes have become part of the televisual scene under the label of *Crimestoppers*. In North America, as Carriere and Ericson[17] have shown, there has been a considerable investment in programming of this kind – under the identical label of *Crimestoppers* – by what they call the 'deviancy defining elite', involving collaboration between the police, news media and private corporations. There are indications that a similar self-conscious social control movement is beginning to develop in the UK.

Although intended to mobilize audiences to help the police solve crimes, *Crimewatch* entertains to hold its viewers. In doing so, apart from the use of reconstructions (which raise interesting questions about the relation of the documentary dramatization of a crime to actuality) the programme team select their crime stories from the popular end of the market, with murder, armed robbery with violence, and sexual crime as the staple items of coverage. Corporate crime, which is seen as difficult to visualize, and political crime, which is seen as too sensitive (especially in the case of Northern Ireland), do not figure in *Crimewatch's* menu. The style is fast-moving and visually varied.

The importance of news source-media relations and the ways in which these might vary has already been noted. *Crimewatch* is based upon a close exchange relation between the various police forces that provide access to the details of the crimes covered, and the BBC production team. The programme is premised upon an identification with the fight against crime, without raising awkward questions about police effectiveness or the methods used in achieving results. Although the programme team insist upon their editorial independence, they obviously have to maintain exceptionally good relations with the police, who are *the* source for their major stories. The police have a right of veto (never used to date) over the broadcasting of material put together in the programme's characteristic 'reconstructions', whereas the broadcasters have full access to the known facts about a given case on a confidential basis, to safeguard them from being used to 'fit up' suspected criminals. For the broadcasters, it is essential that their programme be seen as independent of police control, an objective also shared by the police themselves.

Before agreeing to collaborate with the programme in 1983, a great deal of discussion took place in the Association of Chief Police Officers. Ever since Sir Robert Mark's policy of 'openness' in the mid-1970s, a new style of information management has gradually become diffused amongst police forces and consequently the more sophisticated chief constables were very aware of the potential public relations benefits of the programme, as well as the marginal contribution it might make to the solution of particular cases by encouraging a flow of information from the public. On the basis of our own research, we would concur with Carriere and Ericson's view that the legitimation of the system of social control is an important objective of the police in supporting the creation of such programming. When speaking candidly with us, police officers tended to see the programme's appeal as lying in its entertainment value but were appreciative of its national reach. So far as the programme team were concerned, justificatory rhetorics of public service and social control comingled with a recognition of the televisual imperatives that had to be accepted for the programme to remain successful. Of particular importance is the need to have a 'clear-up rate' as a measure of its social value or effectiveness. This functions both as self-validation and as a defence against those critics who accuse it of a sensationalism and gratuitous violence that provoke public fear of crime.

For its part, *Out of Court* has been running for ten years on the BBC's minority channel, BBC2, and usually appears for only twenty-six weeks of the year. This is quite usual for programmes of this type, but as a result it suffers from a lack of continuity. By contrast, law magazines do not stop publishing in the middle of the year and newspapers do not stop printing legal stories. Television scheduling, though, works differently.

The programme, which generally consists of two films and two studio-based items, often adopts a critical stance towards aspects of the legal system by basing stories on particular victimized individuals. The sources for the issues covered are newspapers, legal magazines, pressure groups, government and Parliament. The focus on the law offers a point of departure for the programme to consider how justice works in British society. Since *Out of Court* is critical of lawyers and government departments, it often produces reactions in the form of letters directed to the programme team or complaints to the Director-General and Chairman of the BBC. Occasionally, a contentious item is taken up by the national press, and in general, the programme-makers also have to be careful because of the potential embarrassment of making legal errors.

Out of Court likes to adopt a campaigning stance and a participatory role on certain issues: if the law is subsequently changed the programme can claim some small part of the credit. In reality, however, with a small budget and team it is difficult for the programme to become too deeply involved in a campaign unless there is already some momentum. Unlike a high audience consumer programme such as *That's Life* (which can organize letter-writing campaigns and use the personal influence of its presenter) *Out of Court* can only make a marginal impact.

SOME FEATURES OF MEDIA CONTENT

Media representations are a key moment in the process whereby public discourses concerning crime and justice are made available for general consumption. They are the end result of the strategies and practices deployed by sources and media personnel outlined earlier and one of the means whereby audiences make sense of this domain. Consequently, we have aimed to provide an account of patterns of coverage in the two major mass media, the national press and television. We were particularly interested in charting the similarities and divergencies in coverage *within* and *between* these two media. Did tabloid, mid-market and quality newspapers differ significantly in their patterns of attention and exclusion and in the ways in which they presented material? Did broadcast television 'hold the middle ground'?

Our content analysis has built upon (but also goes beyond) previous British studies of crime and criminal justice, as for the first time we have sampled both national newspapers and national broadcasting. The study reported here included all national newspapers (both dailies and Sundays) and television programmes on all four terrestrial channels broadcast between 5.45 p.m. and close-down.[18] A full account of the findings is beyond the scope of the present article, in which we limit ourselves to presenting some basic results relating to differences within and between the national press and the television channels.

The study of news content, as pointed out above, can be traced back to the very beginnings of social scientific interest in the media coverage of crime and justice. Some investigators set about deepening and systematizing the casual and anecdotal observations of general commentators by undertaking detailed studies of how particular cases were being handled in the press.[19] Others employed systematic sampling and column inch counts to describe the general pattern of newspaper coverage,[20] and some years later, began to use official crime statistics as a point of comparison with the situation on the ground.[21]

This approach became standard after World War Two. From James Davis' pioneering study of Colorado papers onwards,[22] a succession of American studies covering a wide variety of newspaper markets has shown that interpersonal crimes, particularly those involving violence, are consistently over-reported in relation to the official statistics, whereas routine property crimes are under-reported. Ditton and Duffy's analysis of Scottish newspapers – the closest British equivalent to the US work, most of which deals with regional markets – reaches the same basic conclusion.[23]

Surprisingly, given its centrality as a source of public knowledge, there are virtually no British studies of national press coverage of crime. A rare exception is Roshier's study of the *Daily Mirror*, *Daily Express*, and *Daily Telegraph*, which found the expected over-reporting of crimes against the person (particularly murder) but also made two other important points.[24] First, up to one third of the stories analysed concerned a variety of trivial offences. This suggests that instead of talking about 'crime news' as though it were a unitary category, it is necessary to distinguish between two types of story. On the one hand, there are 'sensational' stories which are given extended treatment, often on the front page and with accompanying pictures. On the other hand, there are the short, terse, 'mundane' items which are tucked away on the inside pages.[25] Roshier's second suggestive finding is the over-reporting of fraud, indicating that although white collar crimes receive less attention than interpersonal violence, they are by no means neglected.

A similar pattern emerged from Doris Graber's study of local and network television news in Chicago in the late 1970s in which official corruption accounted for between 20 and 24 per cent of all crimes mentioned.[26] Her argument that this was a product of the sensitizing effects of the Watergate scandal is certainly part of the explanation, but it may also be that covering the 'crimes of the powerful' taps into and articulates a strong streak of populism in the audience. There was a parallel instance during the sample period of our own study when the Guinness share scandal and other instances of 'insider dealing' attracted a great deal of coverage.

Turning now to our own results, as Tables I and II show, between 18 and 29 per cent of all crime-related items recorded for the national daily press and national television news mentioned offences against

TABLE I: *Percentage of crime-related items in national daily newspapers mentioning various types of offence*

Type of offence	Quality	Mid-market	Tabloid
Non-sexual violence against the person	24.7%	38.8%	45.9%
Sexual offences	7.2%	9.3%	11.3%
Non-violent offences against the person	3.7%	5.1%	4.4%
Drug offences	3.1%	5.4%	6.4%
Offences against animals	0.4%	0.2%	0.3%
Property offences	25.7%	23.2%	18.8%
Corporate offences	5.6%	2.9%	2.1%
Public order offences	5.3%	5.9%	4.1%
Offences against the justice system	1.9%	2.4%	2.3%
Offences against the state	5.0%	4.6%	2.8%
Number of items	835	410	388

Notes: (1) More than one type of offence could be recorded for each item.
(2) Only items dealing with the UK are represented in these figures.

property, and more detailed analysis revealed that most of these were related to City scandals rather than to more routine property offences such as burglary and theft.

Recent American studies of prime-time fiction and entertainment programming also show a strong bias towards the misdeeds of the powerful with the majority of offenders being white males aged between 20 and 50 in white collar jobs. Conversely, blacks, young people and members of the working class are under-represented.[27] We need to be cautious in applying this argument directly to British television however, since it takes no account of the mediating effects of genre.[28]

Also noteworthy is the distribution of attention to different kinds of discourse in the print media. This is somewhat crudely indicated by variations in the space allocated to the views of different groups and individuals. As Table III shows, there are important differences between the top and bottom ends of the newspaper market, particularly amongst daily titles. Whilst the quality dailies are focused upon Parliament and government, and offer space to the views of experts, elites and pressure groups, tabloid newspapers give far greater play to the opinions and perspectives offered by the victims of crime and their relatives and by those suspected or convicted of crimes. They are more oriented, that is, to 'common sense' thinking and discourse, and less to professionalized debate and the evaluation of policy. These variations throw light upon the complexity of the process of 'secondary definition' through the media, as they suggest that the distribution

The media politics of crime and criminal justice 413

TABLE II: *Percentage of crime-related television news items mentioning various types of offence*

Type of offence	News items on National bulletins	News items on Local bulletins	National news bulletins on ITV	National news bulletins on BBC1	National news bulletins on Channel 4
Non-sexual violence against the person	40.0%	63.2%	43.5%	42.3%	18.2%
Sexual offences	5.5%	8.8%	8.7%	–	9.1%
Non-violent offences against the person	8.3%	8.8%	10.1%	5.8%	9.1%
Drug offences	4.8%	1.8%	5.8%	3.8%	4.5%
Offences against animals	0.7%	5.3%	–	1.9%	–
Property offences	23.4%	12.3%	20.3%	26.9%	27.3%
Corporate offences	2.1%	1.8%	2.9%	1.9%	–
Public order offences	18.6%	5.3%	14.5%	23.1%	18.2%
Offences against the justice system	7.6%	7.0%	10.1%	7.7%	–
Offences against the state	6.2%	–	4.3%	9.6%	4.5%
Number of items	145	57	69	52	22

Notes: (1) More than one type of offence could be recorded for each item.
(2) Only items dealing with the UK are represented in these figures.
(3) This table refers solely to news bulletins and excludes daily current affairs programmes. Consequently, BBC2, which does not carry a nightly bulletin, has not been included in the channel columns. However, two news flashes on BBC are included in the item total for all national bulletins.

TABLE III: *Percentage of crime-related items in national daily newspapers containing the views or comments of selected groups*

Group	Quality	Mid-market	Tabloid
Members of the Government and Conservative MPs	15.7%	8.0%	5.7%
MPs from Opposition parties	11.9%	8.0%	3.6%
Local government officials and local politicians	3.8%	3.4%	1.0%
Judges, lawyers and court officials	19.9%	17.6%	18.8%
Police and law enforcement sources	12.2%	15.1%	16.2%
Probation and prison workers	1.3%	1.0%	1.8%
Experts/elites/members of lobby and pressure group	21.7%	17.3%	11.3%
Victims, suspects' relatives and criminals	13.4%	22.9%	24.2%
Vox pops, members of general public	3.0%	4.4%	7.0%
Number of items	835	410	388

Notes: (1) More than one type of offence could be recorded for each item.
(2) Only items dealing with the UK are represented in these figures.

TABLE IV: *Percentage of crime-related items on the front pages of national daily newspapers mentioning various types of offence*

Type of offence	Quality	Mid-market	Tabloid
Non-sexual violence	22.0%	45.0%	45.5%
Sexual offences	2.8%	20.0%	22.7%
Non-violent offences against the person	5.5%	10.0%	22.7%
Drug offences	–	5.0%	4.5%
Property offences	35.8%	40.0%	27.3%
Corporate offences	6.4%	–	–
Public order offences	6.4%	5.0%	–
Offences against the justice system	0.9%	–	13.6%
Offences against the state	8.3%	10.0%	–
Number of items	109	20	22

Notes: (1) More than one type of offence could be recorded for each item.
(2) Only items dealing with the UK are represented in these figures.

and hierarchy of discourses between different types of daily newspaper may vary significantly in relation to different readerships.

The second major set of differences concerns variations in the general pattern of attention to crime within the national press. As Table I shows, the overall distribution confirms the commonsense distinctions made between quality, mid-market and tabloid newspapers. Whereas almost half (46 per cent) of crime-related items in the daily tabloids mention violent crimes against the person, the corresponding figure for the quality dailies is only 25 per cent, with mid-market papers falling almost exactly in between. A similar, though far less dramatic pattern emerges in the coverage of sexual offences and offences involving drugs.

As Table IV shows, these differences are also evident in variations in the prominence given to stories featuring different kinds of crime. Although their smaller page size results in mid-market and tabloid dailies carrying far fewer crime-related items on their front pages than the quality titles, those that do appear are twice as likely to feature violent crimes against the person (45 per cent as against 22 per cent). Tabloids and mid-market papers are also far more likely to feature sexual offences on the front page than are quality papers. In other words, the world of front-page crime in the 'popular' press (both tabloid and mid-market) is primarily oriented towards personalised crime affecting identifiable individuals, with a strong emphasis on interpersonal violence.

Turning now to some of the findings for television news (shown in Table II), several points are worth noting. First, the overall pattern of attention to different kinds of violent crimes against the person, drug offences, and property offences in national television news approximates to the pattern established for the mid-market dailies, lending weight to the argument that in certain key areas television news seeks the 'middle ground'. However, as Table II also shows, this pattern is by no means consistent across all categories of offence. Compared to all types of national daily paper, television news pays rather more attention to offences relating to public order, to the justice system and to the state.

Second, compared to the national bulletins, local news gives markedly more attention to violent crimes against the person, which perhaps suggests a heavy reliance on the police and courts (and the local press) as sources of news items. Third, there are some important differences between channels, with violent crimes against the person attracting many more mentions on the two 'popular' channels, BBC1 and ITV, than on the more 'upmarket' Channel 4. Indeed, the pattern for ITV more closely approximates to the pattern displayed by the tabloid dailies – particularly in the areas of interpersonal violence, sexual crimes, and drug offences.

These different patterns of emphasis in coverage have important implications for our understanding of audience perceptions, since they suggest that differences in newspaper readership and television viewing may regulate access to significant variations in discourses about crime.

SOME ASPECTS OF THE TELEVISION AUDIENCE

Although there was no provision for a study of public perceptions of media coverage in the research budget, we were fortunate to be offered co-operation by the Special Projects Group of the BBC's Research Department, who allowed us to insert a limited number of questions into one of their regular Omnibus Surveys, which covered a stratified national sample. Although this was a very limited exercise, it did allow us to gather relevant information on one central area of current debate – the fear of crime.

The questionnaire responses revealed consistent relations between patterns of media consumption and respondents' fear of becoming a victim of crime. Tabloid readers, heavy TV viewers and those preferring to watch ITV were more likely to say that they worried about becoming victims, and these relations were particularly strong for fear of being 'mugged' or physically attacked. It is possible that high consumption of 'popular' media – with an emphasis on violent crimes against the person – may contribute independently to feelings of fear and insecurity, as well as reinforcing given social groups' experiences and life-situations. In order to explore the possible dynamics of this process in more detail, it would be necessary to combine the insights gained from research on fear conducted within criminology and victimology with some of the lines of enquiry opened up by recent media research. At the moment there would appear to be two extensive but separate literatures on fear of crime, one of which hardly mentions the possible role of the media[29] and another that scarcely mentions anything else.[30] This is clearly an unproductive situation.

Paying careful attention to distinctive patterns of media consumption is a necessary step towards developing a more complex model of the dynamics involved not only in fear of victimization but also in the generation of attitudes towards the police and towards the criminal justice system more generally. Asking respondents how often they watched named programmes revealed some noteworthy variations in viewing. *Crimewatch UK*, for example, was more likely to be watched by tabloid and mid-market newspaper readers and by those with a preference for ITV, suggesting that its entertainment orientation (and its emphasis on serious crimes, particularly murder and rape) might resonate with and partially reinforce the world of crime as presented in the 'popular' press.

There were differences too in patterns of viewing for the two main UK police fictions listed. *The Bill* is a fast-paced, action-oriented series set in inner London, whereas *Juliet Bravo* is centred on a female officer in charge of a police station in a small Yorkshire town, is slower in pace and features more mundane crimes. The audience for both dramas follows the normal pattern for popular programmes at peak-time on the main channels in being skewed towards tabloid readers, ITV viewers and heavy television viewers generally. However, viewers of *The Bill* are markedly younger, more male-dominated, and more heavily concentrated in inner city areas. Conversely, *Juliet Bravo* finds its audience more securely centred in women, people over 55, and those living in small towns or suburbs. Again, these patterns suggest a possible resonance and perhaps reinforcement between the world as portrayed on the screen and the world as experienced. How exactly these resonances work, how they interact with situational factors and knowledge, and what role they play in helping to construct popular attitudes in the area of crime and criminal justice are questions that deserve more attention than they have had to date.

CONCLUDING REMARKS

This paper has offered some synoptic accounts of our current research into the coverage of crime and criminal justice in which the central concern has been to examine media production and content and, to a much lesser extent, audience reception. These are the usual touchstones of media sociology, though still more often dealt with independently of one another than in combination. Within this established framework of concerns, we have deliberately cast our net more widely than usual, particularly by comparing the press with television (at a time when the press continues to be largely neglected) and by going beyond a concern with crime reporting alone to take in the wider field of criminal justice.

A further objective has been to go beyond the media-centrism of most recent communications research and to investigate some of the ways in which state agencies and pressure and interest groups develop their symbolic politics in order to affect media coverage. Despite the occasional foray into these issues (notably the work of Ericson et al.[31]), this theme is still largely unexplored territory.

Contemporary media sociology has tended to be singularly incurious about the inner workings of political institutions and organizations. This lack of interest has been reciprocated by mainstream political sociology and political science, which, in turn, have been unaccountably neglectful of the media. There is room for much more exploration of media strategies and the generally uncharted field of political public relations, along lines which we have begun to develop here. In similar vein, there are also connections to be developed between criminology and media research, especially in the area of fear of crime, where mutual ignorance seems to be prevalent. These offer two potentially productive lines of departure for the sociology of the media.

(Date accepted: March 1990)

Philip Schlesinger
Department of Film and Media Studies
University of Stirling

Howard Tumber
Department of Social Studies
The City University

and

Graham Murdock
Department of Social Sciences
University of Loughborough

ACKNOWLEDGEMENTS

The present article derives from a project on 'Crime, Law and Justice in the Media: Production and Content' funded by the Economic and Social Research Council (UK), reference number: E 625 0013, in its 'Crime and Criminal Justice System' Research Initiative. The authors gratefully acknowledge the ESRC's support and thank Alison Love

418   *Philip Schlesinger, Howard Tumber and Graham Murdock*

(now Anderson) for her research assistance with the content analysis. We have much appreciated the detailed critical comments made by Russell Dobash. This paper was first presented at the Crime and Media Workshop at the British Criminology Conference, held at Bristol Polytechnic in July 1989, where many helpful observations were made.

NOTES

1. F. Frankfurter and R. Pound, *Criminal Justice in Cleveland*, Cleveland Ohio, The Cleveland Foundation, 1922, ch. 4.

2. N. Abercrombie, S. Hill, and B. S. Turner, *The Dominant Ideology Thesis*, London: George Allen and Unwin, 1980, and *ibid., Sovereign Individuals of Capitalism*, London, Allen and Unwin, 1986.

3. S. Hall, C. Critcher, T. Jefferson, J. Clarke, and B. Roberts, *Policing the Crisis: Mugging, the State and Law and Order*, London, MacMillan, 1978.

4. E. H. Herman and N. Chomsky, *Manufacturing Consent: The Political Economy of the Mass Media*, New York, Pantheon Books, 1988.

5. J. Curran, M. Gurevitch and J. Woollacott, 'The study of the media: theoretical approaches' in M. Gurevitch, T. Bennett, J. Curran, and J. Woollacott, (eds), *Culture, Society and the Media*, London and New York, Methuen, 1982, pp. 11–29.

6. Cf. Hall *et al.*, 1978, *op. cit.* and S. Hall, 'Media power and class power', in J. Curran, J. Ecclestone, G. Oakley and A. Richardson (eds), *Bending Reality: The State of the Media*, London, Pluto Press, 1986, pp. 5–14.

7. For fuller criticisms both of Hall's and Herman and Chomsky's positions (amongst others), cf. P. Schlesinger, 'From production to propaganda?', *Media, Culture and Society*, vol. 11, no. 3, July 1989, pp. 283–306, and *ibid.*, 'Rethinking the sociology of journalism: source strategies and the limits of media-centrism', in M. Ferguson (ed.), *Public Communication: The New Imperatives*, London, Sage, 1989, pp. 61–83.

8. J. Habermas, 'The public sphere', in A. Mattelart and S. Siegelaub (eds), *Communication and Class Struggle*, vol. 1, New York, International General, 1979, p. 198.

9. *Ibid.*, p. 200.

10. Cf. P. Elliott, 'Intellectuals, the "information society" and the disappearance of the public sphere', *Media, Culture and Society*, vol. 4, no. 3, July 1982, pp. 243–53; N. Garnham, 'The media and the public sphere', in P. Golding, G. Murdock and P. Schlesinger (eds) *Communicating Politics: Mass Communications and the Political Process*, Leicester University Press, 1986, pp. 37–53; and P. Scannell, 'Public service broadcasting and modern public life', *Media, Culture and Society*, vol. 11, no. 2, April 1989, pp. 135–66.

11. Cf. P. Bourdieu, *Distinction: A Social Critique of the Judgement of Taste*, London and New York, Routledge and Kegan Paul, 1986. The concept of 'strategy' has become increasingly important in contemporary sociological analysis across a wide range of social actors. G. Crow, 'The use of the concept of "strategy" in recent sociological literature', *Sociology*, vol. 23, no. 1, pp. 1–24 points out rightly that the use of strategic analysis has become somewhat over-extended, and that many of the problems of how it relates to institutional analysis remain unresolved. Nevertheless, in the present study we believe that there is demonstrable utility in applying strategic analysis to the inter-relations between media and news sources in the crime and criminal justice fields.

12. S. Hilgartner and C. L. Bosk, 'The rise and fall of social problems: a public arenas model', *American Journal of Sociology*, vol. 94, 1988, pp. 53–78.

13. R. V. Ericson, P. M. Baranek and J. L. Chan, *Negotiating Control: A Study of News Sources*, Toronto, Buffalo, London, University of Toronto Press, 1989.

14. J. Kingdon, *Agendas, Alternatives and Public Policies*, Boston, Toronto, Little Brown and Co., 1984.

15. R. W. Cobb, J-K. Ross and M. H. Ross, 'Agenda-building as a comparative political process', *American Political Science Review*, vol. 70, no. 1, 1976, p. 126.

16. S. Chibnall, *Law-and-Order News: An Analysis of Crime Reporting in the British Press*, London, Tavistock, 1977.

17. K. D. Carriere and R. V. Ericson, *Crime-Stoppers: A Study in the Organization of Community Policing*, University of Toronto, Centre of Criminology, 1989.

18. The sample covered two full weeks of seven days each spread over a total period lasting from 11 January to 21 March 1987, made up of one continuous seven day period and a further seven days sampled at intervals. Constructing the sample in this way allowed for a systematic overview of coverage in the two major national media over a sufficiently long time period to compensate for any special circumstances during the initial week. It worked well for forms of output with a daily cycle, such as news, but had the disadvantage of yielding comparatively few examples of relevant current affairs, documentary and fictional programmes.

The sample included all programmes or newspaper items which mentioned or featured any aspect of crime, policing, the legal system and the treatment of offenders. All relevant dimensions of all items were coded. For example, a report of a court case could be coded under courts and policing (if police evidence was featured) as well as under crime. In order to ensure that the analysis was as comprehensive as possible, up to four separate crimes could be recorded for each news item featuring crime.

19. J. L. Holmes, 'Crime and the press', *Journal of Criminal Law*, vol. 20, 1929, pp. 246–93.

20. F. Fenton, *The Influence of Newspaper Presentations upon the Growth of Crime and Other Anti-Social Activity*, The University of Chicago Press, 1911.

21. F. Harris, *Presentation of Crime in Newspapers*, Hanover, New Hampshire, The Sociological Press, 1932.

22. F. J. Davis, 'Crime news in Colorado newspapers', *American Journal of Sociology*, vol. 57, 1951, pp. 325–30.

23. J. Ditton and J. Duffy, 'Bias in newspaper reporting of crime news', *British Journal of Criminology*, vol. 23, 1983, pp. 159–65.

24. B. Roshier, 'The selection of crime news by the press, in S. Cohen and J. Young (eds), *The Manufacture of News: Deviance, Social Problems and the Mass Media*, London, Constable, 1973, pp. 28–39.

25. P. Dahlgren, 'Crime news: the fascination of the mundane', *European Journal of Communication*, vol. 3, no. 2, 1988, pp. 189–206.

26. D. Graber, *Crime News and the Public*, New York, Praeger, 1980.

27. L. S. Lichter and S. R. Lichter, *Prime Time Crime: Criminals and Law Enforcers in TV Entertainment*, Washington DC, The Media Institute, 1983.

28. Crime is shown in a greater variety of contexts on this side of the Atlantic because the system supports a wider range of programme formats – from the street-level inner city policing of *The Bill*, through the complexly contextualised offences in *EastEnders*, to the boardroom struggles of *Howard's Way*. Different formats organise discourse and imagery diversely though their patterns of exclusion and emphasis and their construction of varying points of view of the actions presented. In soap operas such as *Brookside* or *EastEnders*, routine crimes emerge out of well-established situations and milieux and are committed by characters the audience knows well. In contrast, the action in *The Bill* (which shares many of the basic features of a soap opera) is viewed through the eyes of the police. We see only the incident or its aftermath. It is something to be dealt with. The motivations involved often remain obscure. These variations suggest a possible link between differences in patterns of media consumption and differences in public perceptions and attitudes.

29. M. Mafield, *Explaining Fear of Crime: Evidence from the 1984 British Crime Survey, Research and Planning Unit Paper No. 43*, London, Home Office, 1988; S. Box, C. Hale and G. Andrews, 'Explaining fear of crime', *British Journal of*

Criminology, vol. 28, no. 3, 1988, pp. 340–56.

30. B. Gunter, *Television and Fear of Crime*, London, John Libby/Independent Broadcasting Authority, 1987.

31. Ericson *et al.*, 1989, *op. cit.*

[6]

POLICE NEWS
Constructing an Image of Crime

MARK FISHMAN

NEWS ORGANIZATIONS KNOW OF THE WORLD they report almost exclusively through legitimated institutions (Fishman, 1980; Tuchman, 1978; Roshco, 1975; Sigal, 1973). A good deal of what we see in the news is the result not only of what journalists do, but also of accounts which other agencies produce in the course of enforcing laws, rescuing survivors, negotiating treaties, investigating corruption, and trading stocks. The possibilities of news are set by some as yet unanalyzed "bureaucratic mode of story-telling" (Tuchman, 1976). While a growing literature on newsmaking has shown the considerable extent to which media accounts are first formed outside news organizations, that literature has not tackled the question of how routine sources construct accounts for the press. This article is an attempt to help fill that gap in media research by addressing the issue of how one legitimated institution, the police, produces accounts which become the journalist's raw materials for news.

AUTHOR'S NOTE: This is a revised version of a paper presented at the 1979 Annual Meeting of the Society for the Study of Social Problems. I wish to acknowledge Antonio Valderrama and Israel Rios for their invaluable research assistance, and Pamela Fishman for her help in formulating several points in this article.

EDITOR'S NOTE: Mark Fishman examines the processes within a major urban police department that determine the possibilities of crime news in the press. The

As *the* routine source of crime news (Gordon, 1979; Sherizen, 1978: 210-211; Fishman, 1978: 538; Chibnall, 1977, 1975), law enforcement agencies formulate for journalists what is "out there" and what can be said about it. News organizations may choose what crimes to report, but the pool of occurrences from which they draw is preselected and preformed within police departments. Thus in this study, the issue of how the police make news for the press does not mean analyzing the relationship of individual crime reporters and police sources,[1] but examining how these sources get *their* accounts. To study this is to examine the organized ways a law enforcement bureaucracy keeps tabs on itself by continually monitoring what its officers are dealing with moment by moment in a community. This article reports research on such a monitoring system in the New York Police Department. It will be shown that the police crime-reporting apparatus systematically exposes the media to incidents which perpetuate prevailing law-and-order themes in crime news. It will also be shown how the monitoring system is vulnerable to news promoters (Molotch and Lester, 1974) who attempt to publicly formulate new social problems.

THE POLICE CRIME REPORTING SYSTEM

For the most part, crime news is news of individual occurences. Thus, almost anywhere one finds crime news, one finds police departments supplying news organizations with an assortment of crime incidents every day. In towns

---

media's report is based on information the police provide, which in turn, is based on a system for monitoring "unusual occurrences." This system is sensitive to incidents that disrupt order in public places as well as relations between strangers. It tends to ignore crimes in the public sphere. Public order disturbances are judged as unusual on the basis of three considerations: an incident's frequency, its seriousness, and its newsworthiness.

Fishman then examines the history of a "crime wave," and he concludes that the police reporting system reiterates old law-and-order themes until moral entrepreneurs promote new types of incidents in the news. The police reporting system then can amplify coverage of new "problems."

and small cities this assortment often consists of all crimes known to the police in a 24-hour period. But in large urban areas journalists must rely on the police for a "summary" of daily incidents.[2]

In New York City this daily summary is known as the "press wire."[3] Each of the city's major media has a newsroom teletype which receives crime dispatches from the NYPD. This press wire types out from 12 to 25 messages per day. It is the main means by which news organizations first learn of crime in the city.

To determine the origin of the press wire and the nature of the decisions made in selecting information for it, in-depth interviews were conducted with twenty-two police officers at two levels of the NYPD. Fifteen were patrol and supervisory personnel in three different precincts. Seven officers were connected with the sections of headquarters that control the press wire. In addition, NYPD crime figures, the records of one precinct, and participant observation data from an earlier study of a New York City television newsroom (Fishman, 1978) were analyzed to examine the role of the police in the construction of a crime wave.

The press wire originates from a unit in the police department known as the Operations Section. In essence, this is the NYPD's central command post which surveys what is happening throughout the city, moment by moment. Reports of incidents are funneled into the operations room from two major sources: an "incident log" and "the field." The press wire is made up in the process of monitoring these two sources.

The incident log is a teletype which continuously prints brief summaries of emergency phone calls from citizens who have dialed "911" for police assistance. Because it produces an enormous volume of messages (about 6000 every day), this source is very quickly scanned for only a few types of incidents: certain "serious crimes" (mainly homicides) and emergencies that either require rapid mobilization of large numbers of police, e.g., looting, plane crashes, or require notification of other city agencies, e.g., power failures, delays in subway service. However, the main source of incidents for the press wire are reports received from "the field."

The NYPD requires officers to report any "unusual occurrences." Thus, the field consists of precinct police who, in the course of their work, look for events that the Operations Section would want to know about. A telephone call, later followed by a written report,[4] would be made from a precinct to the office of its local area commander, who in turn, would pass on the news to the Operations Section in headquarters.[5] If the Operations Section has any doubts about reporting an occurrence to the press, they would contact the Office of Public Information, which has the final say in such matters.

Although the police department issues official guidelines as to what constitutes an unusual occurrence, the police acknowledge that these are too vague to be of use in actually deciding whether any given happening is unusual or not. Instead, both precinct police and officers in the Operations Section use a set of informal criteria for identifying unusual incidents and thus, for deciding what occurrences to transmit to the news media. Before discussing these criteria, a few things first must be said about routine police work. It is within an environment of "ordinary occurrences" that police officers perceive unusual happenings.

ON POLICING THE CITY

In large urban areas like New York, crime is perceived as a monolithic problem. It is seen as an enduring blight that resists every effort to reduce or control it. "Crime control" is a term little used by veteran officers, because they see their efforts as having little effect on the overall situation. As one put it:

> We could double our arrests and it probably wouldn't solve the problem in New York. I think a lot of our leaders in this job realize that. Therefore, the amount of arrests really

doesn't count. All they do is cost the city more in terms of manpower and money.

And when law enforcement officers speak about policing the city, they do not talk in terms of enforcing the law when they see it broken. If conceived in this way, their job would overwhelm them:

> [At our precinct] we could make arrests practically anywhere we turned every night of the week, if we chose to. But we don't. You have to use discretion.

In this context, the use of discretion when making arrests does not mean deciding on a case-by-case basis whether to make an arrest. It means deciding where, in the first place, to look for trouble.[6]

The police want to save their limited resources for intervening in what they view as the worst cases (LaFave, 1965: 5). And worst cases almost always mean threats to public order, i.e., troubles in public places and crime between strangers.[7] For precinct police, such cases typically include muggings, bank robberies, stickups of small businesses, auto theft, burglaries, homicides, and gang fights. At the level of police headquarters, where crisis management is the explicit concern of the department's top commanders, officers in the Operations Section scan their sources of information looking for even larger disruptions of public order than precinct police ordinarily see. These include bombings, looting, riots, demonstrations, attacks on the police, and all civil disasters (large fires and floods, train and plane crashes, storage tank explosions, and the like).

In contrast, the police would rather not be bothered with incidents which they view as not endangering relations in public. These typically include troubles between intimates, friends, acquaintances, and neighbors, as well as the so-called victimless crimes: drug use, numbers running, prostitution, bookmaking, most rapes, and all family violence falling short of homicide or hospitalization. At the Operations Section of headquarters, reports of these matters would be ignored unless they appeared to involve murder. At the precinct level, police officers view these matters (particularly family violence and rapes) as essentially private or interpersonal troubles which only incidentally involve law-breaking. Police in precincts do not seek out these situations, and when called into them, they prefer not to pinpoint a wrongdoer and make an arrest (Walker, 1979: 26, 64, 206-210; Brownmiller, 1975: 364-368; Shearing, 1974: 84). Speaking about family violence, one officer said:

> Historically, in my 16 years in the department, we've always really stayed away from family disputes. At least we try to. . . . When called into a dispute, we try to handle the situation by asking one party to leave—and not necessarily the male, either—for a cooling-off period. . . . And these things tend to blow over. I think very rarely is a complaint ever taken. . . . [The police] realize these things tend to iron themselves out, and to take a complaint where a detective will call three days later when it's a dead issue—it might just further aggravate the situation.

In the police view, disturbances in the private sphere are best left alone to work themselves out, while crimes in the public sphere are seen to require police intervention (see Reiss and Bordua, 1967: 29-31). It is important to note, though, that disturbances in the public sphere exclude such matters as price-fixing, political bribery and corruption, environmental pollution, tax evasion, and unsafe food, drugs, housing, and work conditions. The police generally are not concerned with these because other agencies are responsible for their enforcement. From the outset, these kinds of crime are excluded from consideration as candidates for the press wire.

Whether in a precinct or at headquarters, the police are geared to look for disruptions in the flow of business as usual in the city. It is with reference to this conception of social order that the police see unusual happenings and report them to the news media. This means that public-order crimes will be considered as either usual or unusual instances of their type. But disturbances in the private sphere fall outside such evaluations. The police will consider whether any given robbery is unusual, but the question will not even arise for family disputes, unless homicide is at issue.

DECIDING WHAT'S UNUSUAL

Public-order crimes were evaluated as unusual on the basis of three considerations: the frequency with which the police encountered a type of incident, their estimation of its seriousness, and their anticipation of its newsworthiness.

FREQUENCY

Police officers did not keep count of how many suicides they had seen, how many muggings they had dealt with, and so on.[8] But they did show a general concern with the frequency of particular types of incidents, by using such phrases as: "This kind of thing happens every day of the week," or "We see these things by the dozens." As one might expect, it is with reference to this sense of "normal crimes" (Sudnow, 1965) that officers noted unusual incidents.

The perception of unusualness (in the sense of the frequency of occurrence) varied from area to area. The commander of a Brooklyn precinct pointed out:

> What's unusual in one place is not unusual in another. For instance, if you go out to the 75th precinct [one of the highest crime areas of the city] a stickup is not unusual. In Parkville [a low crime area], if you get the same stickup there, they want an unusual.

Despite this variation among precincts, something can be said about what kinds of troubles in the public sphere generally were reported to headquarters as unusual.

Some types of incidents were considered uncommon no matter where they occurred. Homicides,[9] bombings, bank robberies, hostage situations, looting, and race riots did not happen every day in any one precinct. Thus, if an incident could be seen as one of these types, it would be telephoned to the Operations Section simply *because* it was one of these types, and they, in turn, would place the incident on the press wire.[10] The process was virtually automatic.

Other types of incidents were considered common in most precincts as well as in the Operations Section. These included muggings, robberies of businesses, burglaries, vandalism, larcenies, arson, auto theft, rape, and other nonfatal assaults. To be seen as an instance of one of these types was not enough to ensure the incident would be reported as unusual to headquarters and placed on the press wire. Bombings did not happen every day; muggings did. There had to be something special about the mugging for it to be unusual.

SERIOUSNESS

Among other things, this "something special" involved the police officer's sense of the seriousness of an incident. In most precincts, only muggings with extensive injuries would be serious enough to warrant an unusual report. Similarly, only robberies and burglaries involving large sums of money and other valuables would be reported as unusual. In contrast, a bombing would be reported as unusual whether or not there were injuries or extensive damage. Generally, the police sense of seriousness was based on the most visible or quantifiable consequences of an incident: the number of deaths, the extent of injuries, the dollar amount stolen, the number of alarms for a fire, the size of an area flooded, and so on.

NEWSWORTHINESS

Interestingly, I found it difficult to get police to give even ballpark estimates of how much money stolen made a theft unusual, or how extensive the injuries had to be for a mugging to be considered unusual. The police would not or could not give such estimates because they could think of too many exceptions whenever they proposed an answer. One reason for this was that many officers knew that the delineation of seriousness varied from precinct to precinct, just as frequency varied. But another reason was that unusualness did not simply depend on the measurable consequences of an incident. Newsworthiness was also involved. For example:

> PO: In our precinct, a typical unusual would be a serious assault or a major robbery.
>
> MF: Major in terms of dollar amount taken or extent of injuries?
>
> PO: Yeah.
>
> MF: Is there roughly a dollar amount? If there's a robbery in a supermarket, and you're getting up into eight, ten, twelve thousand dollars. . . .
>
> PO: I'd say if it was in a supermarket, you'd probably have an unusual. Then again, probably politics enters into it. I've never really given it much consideration. If your Walbaums is knocked over, there'll probably be an unusual—probably, not always. I don't know. It also is discretionary on the part of the sergeant who responds; does he think it's unusual.
>
> MF: What is he thinking when he's thinking, "Is this unusual?"
>
> PO: More than likely, if the borough [commander] doesn't know about it and the newspapers pick it up, then, will there be static for them not to have done the unusual?
>
> MF: You also said serious assaults would be unusual. Does serious injury mean hospitalization or that the injury would look serious enough for hospital treatment? Is that the dividing line?
>
> PO: Ahhh [sighing and thinking] serious injury. You could have a stabbing on Jerome Street in the 75th precinct, where the perpetrator is known, and there'd be no unusual on it. Let's say it's two friends, drinking beer, hot summer night. You know. Typical. The department considers it nothing newsworthy. It's normal and routine for that area.

Any incident which the police anticipated the news media might want to report was considered unusual regardless of whether the incident met the other criteria of frequency or seriousness. As long as the occurrence looked like the kind of thing the media might pick up, precinct police felt it imperative that headquarters be notified immediately, even if they also felt that the incident was fairly common in their area or that it was not very serious. Thus, newsworthiness had priority over other criteria for judging the unusualness of an incident.

The police anticipation of media interest was based mainly on their reading of newspapers and viewing of television. Like any other news consumers, the police inferred that the press was interested in any bizarre or ironic incident, as when a man intending to commit suicide jumped off a 12-story building into an open automobile, killing another man who was riding in the funeral procession of a friend. Similarly, the police inferred that any crime involving a celebrity was of interest to the press, as was apparent when the New York *Daily News* featured on its front page the arrest of John F. Kennedy's brother-in-law for refusing to pay a 60-cent cab fare.

Most of the time, however, the police provided the media with newsworthy incidents of a different sort. All officers were aware of current themes in criminality and law enforcement being covered in the print and broadcast media. For instance, as examples of unusual incidents several officers indicated types of crime that were receiving moderate and heavy publicity at the time of the interviews: crime in the subways, robberies of taxicabs and diamond merchants, and crimes against the elderly. Incidents which could be seen as instances of these types of crime were placed on the press wire by the police in the Operations Section. Before discussing the consequences of this, let us first examine why the police attach such importance to the possible news value of the incidents they deal with.

The police motivation for identifying unusual occurrences on the basis of what the media seemed to want was not intended in quite the spirit of charity that it might appear. If an unusual report were not made for an incident which had already come to the attention of journalists, then a wave of unanswered questions could sweep through the NYPD's chain of command. Reporters would call the Office of Public Information with questions. If this office knew nothing of the incident, a public information officer would telephone the Operations Section. If Operations was unaware of the event, an officer in that unit would call the office of the relevant area commander, who in turn would call the relevant precinct commander, who then would contact the sergeant in charge of patrol, who finally would talk to the offending patrol officer. No subordinate wanted to be in a position of not knowing what his superior would hold him accountable for knowing, and—even worse—not being able to find it out from subordinates.

The system of unusual reports is meant to obviate this problem by anticipating those matters about which the police might get inquiries. Moreover, the system supplies headquarters with a pool of incidents that could be given to the press before journalists even knew of any specific happenings. If journalists then call for more information about an incident they had seen on the press wire, the police already would have an available account (based on the unusual report). Thus, the system of unusual reports allows the police department both to define for news organizations the set of possibly interesting crimes of the day and to formulate for reporters "what happened" in any one of these incidents. This gives the police considerable control over their own image in the press. Not only could the department publicize examples of "good police work" to the media, but they would be prepared with explanations of potentially embarrassing incidents.

From the individual officer's standpoint, unusual reports offer some protection from potential troubles. More importantly, from an institutional standpoint, unusual reports not only maintain the police department's image as a competent bureaucracy, but also strengthen the dependence of media organizations on the police for accounts of crime. In general, the system of unusual reports is the way an urban police department cements its relations with the media and maintains its position as a routine source for news.

CONTROLLING CHANGES IN THE IMAGE OF CRIME

The anticipation of newsworthiness as a criterion for transmitting incidents to the press has a curious effect on the overall crime-reporting system. On the one hand, a police officer explained the perception of unusualness in these terms:

> An unusual [report] is predicated on what the media itself feels is newsworthy. So I guess *they* really determine what to us is unusual.

On the other hand, in the television newsroom I observed, the selection of crime news was predicated on the assumption that the police supplied the press with only the most important crimes of the day. Without this assumption, journalists would not have taken the press wire seriously enough to make it their main source for crime stories.

Thus, the press selection of crime news is based on what the police make available to them. And what the police make available is, in large part, based on what the press reports. Crime news recreates itself.[12] This circularity of the reporting system keeps the same sorts of crime in the news.

One might be tempted to conclude that the sorts of incidents available to the press do not change, and therefore crime news continually reproduces the same image of crime. But crime news does change, within limits. New kinds of crime appear briefly in the media, and, periodically, new categories of incidents receive continuous and heavy publicity. That is, crime waves occur which impress upon the public's new social problems and which insure the existence of new categories of crime for years to come. To see how this occurs, let us look at the history of a recent crime wave.

CRIMES AGAINST THE ELDERLY

From October to December 1976, New York City experienced a major crime wave. For seven weeks all the city's media were filled with reports of crimes against its elderly citizens. News stories formulated a new kind of crime with typical victims (poor elderly whites who had not yet fled neighborhoods in transition) and typical offenders (black and Hispanic youths with long juvenile records). The crimes involved were largely homicide, robbery, and purse snatching.

Interestingly, the police department's figures for crimes against the elderly do not indicate that a surge of violence aimed at senior citizens was taking place. Homicides against the elderly for 1976 were down 21% over the previous year (and down 2.5% for the whole population). Even more detailed figures for robberies and purse snatchings reveal that the wave of publicity was occurring in the midst of a general decrease in the reported rates of crimes against the elderly. (See Appendix A. See also Hoyer, 1979: 9; Braungart et al., 1979: 24.)[13] What, then, accounts for the crime wave in the media?

PROMOTING A CRIME WAVE

This crime wave can be traced back to October 24, 1976, when a series of feature articles on crimes against the elderly appeared in the New York *Daily News*. The reporter who wrote this series told me that he received "considerable help" from the Senior Citizens Robbery Unit (SCRU), a newly formed police squad specializing in robberies and assaults on the elderly. On October 7 the reporter first wrote a story on two crimes with elderly victims, which had appeared over the press wire the same day. At that time an editor thought it would be a good idea to do a series of feature stories on "this kind of crime." (Other news organizations had done such features in the past.)

While researching these stories, the reporter was in frequent contact with SCRU. This police unit let him know it felt beleaguered, understaffed, and that it was fighting a battle that deserved more attention. After he finished the feature stories, the reporter was able to follow up the series with several reports of specific incidents because SCRU officers were calling him whenever they knew of the mugging or murder of an elderly person. This kept the issue alive in the *Daily News,* and soon the theme of crime agianst the elderly began to catch on in other news organizations.

One incident in particular brought all the city's media into covering the theme. Police from SCRU, in a phone conversation with the *Daily News* reporter, complained that the courts were releasing juvenile offenders almost as fast as they were apprehended. The reporter replied that to write about this problem he needed to know of a specific incident. The police told him about a recent case of a black youth who was released on $500 bail after being charged with beating an 82-year-old woman. This story was published. Upon reading it in the *News,* a state legislator (who sat on a juvenile justice subcommittee) obtained access to the youth's record of prior offenses and found that one of these was a homicide. The legislator telephoned several of the city's media, who then publicized this latest development. Seeing the kind of coverage his case was receiving, the youth promptly jumped bail. That event quickly made headlines throughout the city. At this point, the mayor called a press conference and "declared war" on crimes against the elderly. He denounced the juvenile justice system, advocated harsher punishment for young offenders, and allocated more money and manpower to the Senior Citizens Robbery Unit. (This, too, was heavily covered in all media.)

In these early days of the crime wave several things occurred which underlay its growth. The most obvious of these was the active promotion of a new social problem by parties with interests in it: the state legislator on the juvenile justice subcommittee, the mayor (just beginning to run for reelection), and the Senior Citizens Robbery Unit (established only months before and concerned about budget cuts in the police department). All strategically used their power to make news (Molotch and Lester, 1974) as a way of formulating the problem and discerning what could be done about it. Thus, some actual occurrences of crimes against the elderly plus the statements and actions of local newsmakers generated enough stories to begin a "crime wave dynamic" in New York's community of news organizations.

CONSTRUCTING A CRIME WAVE IN NEWSROOMS

My observations in a television newsroom at the time of "crimes against the elderly" indicated that a crime wave is little more than a *theme* in the news which is heavily and continuously reported. Editors use news themes not only to give their program or newspaper a presentational order, but also to sort through and select a few stories from the masses of news copy they receive every day. Moreover, journalists depend on other news organizations for a sense of "what's news today," i.e., which themes to look for in raw materials for news. This means that judgments as to what is a current news theme can spread quickly throughout a community of news organizations all watching each other. Within the space of a week, a crime theme (such as "crimes against the elderly") can become so "hot," so entrenched in the news community, that even journalists skeptical of the crime wave cannot ignore reporting each new incident that comes along.

But no matter how much journalists expect to see a certain theme in the news, they cannot continue to cover it without a steady supply of fresh incidents. In part, local news promoters served this function. But the NYPD's press wire apparently provided the bulk of incidents which made the crime wave possible after it arose in the last week of October.

Unfortunately, no record of the press wire for the period of time in question could be obtained for analysis. But there is enough indirect evidence to confirm that when the wave of publicity had just begun, the press wire suddenly started to report incidents of the new problem in far greater numbers than it ever had. Journalists interviewed after the crime wave recalled suddenly seeing "a run of crimes against the elderly" on the press wire. And the police in the Operations Section and Public Information Office remembered that more of these types of incidents than usual were placed on the press wire "because the media was interested in them."

Even more significant was the fact that when the mayor "declared war" on crimes against the elderly, an unpublicized part of his "battle plan" included a policy directive which affected the system by which the police monitored unusual occurrences. Operations Order 96/76, issued on November 4, required precinct police to make unusual reports for the new category of crimes against the elderly, and it told officers in the Operations Section to place instances of these crimes on the press wire. But the order was just temporary. It specified that all precincts were to specially monitor crimes against the elderly only from November 1976 to January 1977.

As it turned out, the crime wave died down in mid-December. Thus, it does not appear that the expiration of the police order was directly responsible for the end of the crime wave. But it does appear that, in conjunction with the early news coverage of crimes against the elderly, the departmental directive led police suddenly to see a new kind of crime as unusual in greater numbers than they had, and thus increase the flow of incidents over the press wire. The records of one precinct show that when the policy order was in effect, the number of unusual reports on crimes against the elderly suddenly increased even though the amount of crimes known to that precinct did not (see Appendix B). Therefore, the mayor and police officials not only promoted the new social problem directly to the media through their public statements, but in a far more powerful way, they indirectly nurtured the growing crime wave by institutionalizing a new category of unusual incident. Their seemingly innocuous act of "keeping better track of this new kind of crime" led to a flood of news stories for weeks to come.

SUMMARY AND CONCLUSIONS

The system by which the police report incidents to the news media reflects two concerns: managing order in public and managing the image of the police department. Incidents that satisfy these concerns become the journalist's raw materials for news.[14]

The department's concern with containing crime's "worst cases" results in a system which is fixed on monitoring troubles in the public sphere: crime in public places, crime between strangers, and disruptions of the flow of business as usual in the city. Thus, the system of unusual reports provides media newsrooms with a steady diet of the most extreme examples of street crime (large gang fights, brutal muggings, and the like) punctuated every now and then by even larger disturbances of public order, such as bombings and violent demonstrations. Because they rely on the police for raw materials, journalists convey an image of crime wholly in accord with the police department's notion of serious crime and social disorder.[15]

But just as journalists implicitly adopt a police perspective on crime, so do the police adopt a journalistic perspective. The department's concern with managing its image and remaining the media's routine source for crime news results in the use of "newsworthiness" as a means for deciding which incidents are unusual. Police officers develop a journalist's eye for crime, viewing some incidents not only as "good busts," but also as good stories. Because their criteria for newsworthiness are inferred from media coverage, the police continue to provide the press with the same types of incidents that have been reported in the past.

Thus, contrary to the assumptions of previous research (Sherizen, 1978; Roshier, 1973; Antunes and Hurley, n.d.), the selection of crime news is not located exclusively in media organizations, nor are judgments about the newsworthiness of crime strictly a function of the conventions of journalism. Rather, crime news is mutually determined by journalists, whose image of crime is shaped by police concerns, and by police, whose concerns with crime are influenced by media practices.

During periods when new crime issues are not being promoted in the press, the police reporting system on its own continues to provide the media with incidents that reiterate old law-and-order themes. But when moral entrepreneurs begin to promote a new type of crime, the crime-reporting system can amplify coverage of the issue. Entrepreneurs who have the power to make news can promote coverage of a new social problem by calling press conferences, issuing news releases, leaking information, and arranging dramatic coverage for TV film crews. In the case of New York's "crime wave," favored news sources (like the mayor, the state legislator, and SCRU) increased the number of stories about crimes against the elderly by exploiting their routine access to the press. This kind of news promotion has been noted by other researchers not only in crime reporting (Chibnall, 1977; Tillman, 1976), but in all forms of news (Tuchman, 1978; Schudson, 1978; Roshco, 1975; Molotch and Lester, 1974; Sigal, 1973; Boorstin, 1961).

But this study has shown that another, less-recognized form of news promotion can occur in crime reporting. The power to construct social reality rests not only with those who promote their public statements as news, but also with those who can control the media's raw materials for news. A police department's system for monitoring unusual occurrences can be altered so that it reveals new kinds of crime to the media. Once police start keeping track of a new category of crime, as long as there are some occurrences every day that can be seen as instances of the category, then a previously invisible form of crime suddenly will appear as a crime wave to journalists. Those who have the power to define what the police monitor have the power to publicize new social problems.

The number of such problems that await discovery in this fashion are vast because there are an indefinite number of conceivable types of existing public order disturbances, e.g., muggings of tourists, crime in buses, schoolyard crime. The specific ones that emerge at a given time reflect the politics of newsmaking in a region, as particular interests vie for power in a community or particular police units seek to increase their importance within a law enforcement bureaucracy.

But the police crime-reporting apparatus will not sustain any social problem that makes its way into the news. As long as the routine sources for crime news are police departments, whose enforcement net is fixed on troubles in the public sphere, the press reinforces a climate of opinion that keeps the police concerned with "crime in the streets." Particular social problems may come and go, but law-and-order news is here to stay.

APPENDIX A
Crimes Against the Elderly as a Percentage of Crimes Against the Total Population
(Robberies and Purse Snatchings Only)

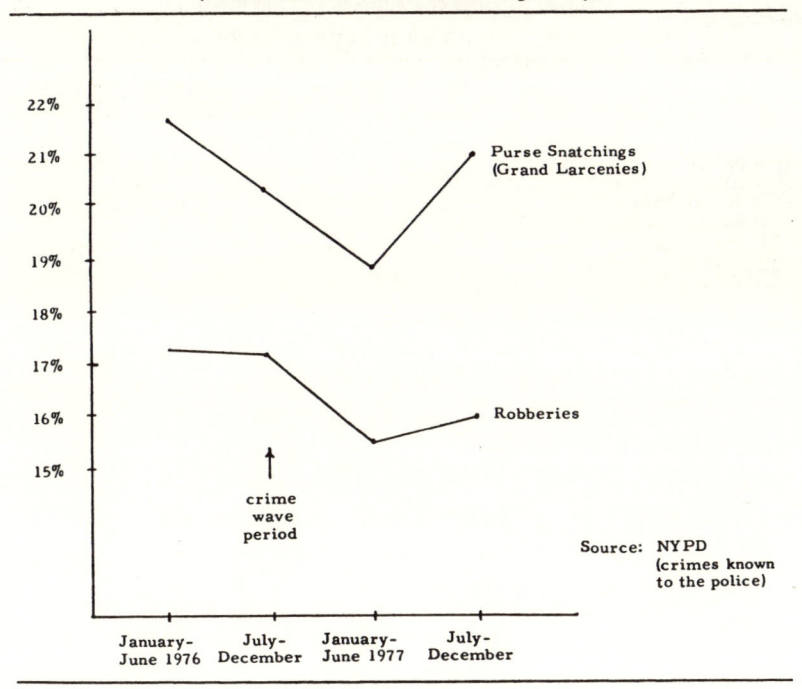

Source: NYPD (crimes known to the police)

APPENDIX B

As a way of testing whether the publicity on crimes against the elderly and the departmental directive concerning these crimes affected the system for reporting unusual occurrences, the records of one police precinct were analyzed.[16] The number of unusual reports for crimes against the elderly were compared with the number of crimes against the elderly known to the police (as indicated by complaint forms) from February 1976 to September 1977. Because there were so few unusual reports involving elderly victims in this precinct, frequencies were tabulated for four-month blocks of time. October 1976 to January 1977 was the crucial period which included the crime wave and the NYPD policy order.

TABLE B
Crimes Against the Elderly in One Precinct:
Crimes Known to the Police and Crimes Reported as Unusual

	Unusual Reports	Crimes Known to the Police	Percent of Unusuals Out of Crimes Known
February-May (1976)	1	43	2.33
June-September (1976)	1	30	3.33
October-January (1976-77)	3	36	8.33
February-May (1977)	2	27	7.40
June-September (1977)	1	45	2.22

The small number of unusual reports involving elderly victims in this precinct makes any conclusions highly tentative. Nevertheless, the figures do indicate that the police increased their unusual reports for crimes against the elderly in just the period we would expect. The table also shows that the variation in the number of elderly victimizations known to the police would not account for the increase in unusual reports.

NOTES

1. For studies of police beat reporters and their relationship to the law enforcement bureaucracies they cover, see Fishman (1980), Sherizen (1978: 209-213), Chibnall (1977, 1975), and Tillman (1976).

2. Even in communities where there are few enough incidents for journalists to know of all crimes known to the police in one day, newsworkers still depend on someone in a police department (usually a press officer) to provide some kind of summary of the "most important" crimes of the day. Not only does this method simplify the newsgathering process for reporters, but also these sources often have more recent information and can provide more details about a case.

3. Journalists refer to this teletype as the "police wire" and call its messages "squeals." Police refer to it as the "press wire" and call its messages "principal cases." Although I used the journalist's terminology for the teletype in an earlier study (Fishman, 1978), I shall follow the policeman's terms here because the focus of this article is on the police department.

4. Unlike other official forms which the police fill out in the course of taking complaints, doing investigations, and making arrests, the "Unusual Occurrence Report" has no legal status and plays no role in the processing of a case in the criminal justice system. As one precinct commander put it, unusual reports are "strictly informational, for internal department use only."

5. The office of an area commander would not screen unusual reports. All would be passed on to headquarters. Apparently, precincts do not directly call the Operations Section because area commanders expect their precincts to keep them informed of all unusual happenings.

6. The sense I am interested in police discretion here differs from most discussions of the issue which usually focus on the individual officer as a decision maker (Skolnick, 1975: 71-90; Bittner, 1970: 107-113; LaFave, 1965; Piliavin and Briar, 1964; but see also Cicourel, 1968; Reiss and Bordua, 1967). Instead, I am concerned with discretion as an organizational phenomenon wherein priorities of enforcement are initially set by the distribution of manpower, the specialization of subunits in a department, the known policy of superiors, and the like. For example, if it is informal department policy "not to go out of one's way" to arrest customers of prostitutes, or if manpower is deployed in a way that makes such arrests unlikely, then we can speak of discretion being exercised at an organizational level.

7. I say "almost always" here because there is one notable exception: homicide. Any suspicious death (or assault likely to result in death) was considered a "worst case" whether it occurred in public or private and whether it involved strangers, acquaintances, friends, or intimates.

8. See Sudnow (1967: 36-42) for a discussion of the significance of counting occurrences and the conditions under which professionals will keep count of the matters with which they deal, e.g., nurses counting deaths witnessed in a hospital.

9. There is some question that this is true of homicides. One officer maintained that homicides happened "every day of the week" in a precinct in the South

Bronx where he had worked, and claimed that not every murder would be considered as unusual and reported to headquarters. Nevertheless, officers in the Operations Section considered all homicides unusual, and because they monitored the 911 emergency phone calls to the police, they were likely to know of murders even if local precincts did not bother to report them as unusual.

10. Often the Operations Section would already know of these occurrences before a precinct called to report them because this unit monitored 911 phone calls.

11. Incidents would not immediately be reported to the press in the event that (a) the police were in doubt about the authenticity of the incident as an instance of its type, e.g., discovering a bomb was fake, or (b) the police felt that publicity might hamper their operations or escalate the incident e.g., encourage more looting. In both cases the Office of Public Information was contacted and they decided what to do.

12. For a detailed discussion of the circularity of all types of news, see Rock (1973).

13. The police data is offered here only to point up the problematic character of what was happening "on the streets." In fact, NYPD crime data is not a reliable indicator of actual amounts of crime and thus, should not be taken as proof that there really was not a "behavioral crime wave" (see Fishman, 1980: 157-158).

Actually, a case could be made—albeit a weak one—for the existence of more crimes against the elderly at the time of the heavy publicity. If one measures the crime rate in terms of victimizations per 1000 elderly, one finds a moderate increase (3.4%) in the robbery rate over the previous six months. (However, one also finds a 4.9% increase in reported robberies for the general population. And one still finds decreases in the rates of homicide and purse snatching for both the elderly and the general population.)

The point here is that no one at the time of the publicity knew—or still knows—if there was a sudden increase in victimization of the elderly. Given this state of indeterminacy—typical of social problems in their early stages—I am raising the question of how a crime wave was formulated in the press.

14. It is important to note that the generality of the findings of this research are at present an open question. This is so not only because this study deals with a single police department, but also because smaller law enforcement agencies may employ somewhat different mechanisms for monitoring "what is happening" in their communities. Even if this is the case, it is possible that the NYPD crime-reporting apparatus represents one of the most bureaucratically developed systems toward which smaller law enforcement agencies may be moving as they expand their public information functions and formalize the reporting of unusual occurrences.

Research on the routines of crime reporting in small cities (Fishman, 1980: 38-46; Tillman, 1976: 61-63) indicates that police beat reporters to a large extent rely on official "summaries" of daily incidents provided by headquarters through a variety of means: the comments of a public information officer or other centrally located person, e.g., a dispatcher or desk sergeant; a clipboard, blackboard, or other crime blotter in the dispatcher's room; and a telephone "newsline" with a prerecorded message on the few "most important" crimes of the day. It seems likely that some kind of system similar to New York's for defining "unusual occurrences" underlies these devices.

15. In discussing the content of news from television networks and newsmagazines, Gans (1979: 57-58) notes: "The frequent appearance of disorder stories suggests that order is an important value in the news, but order is a meaningless term unless one specifies what order and whose order is being valued. For one thing, there are different types of order; a society can have violence in the streets and a stable family life at home, or public peace and a high rate of family instability. . . . Social disorder [in the news] is generally defined as disorder in the public areas of society."

16. This one precinct was chosen because its records were accessible. (The NYPD does not centrally compile statistics for unusual reports and, in general, the police do not make such records available to the public.) There is good reason to think that the precinct studied was fairly typical in the amount of crimes against the elderly that most precincts would have dealt with. It ranked close to the median precinct in the amount of elderly victimization reported by all precincts for 1977.

REFERENCES

ANTUNES, G. and P. HURLEY (n.d.) "The representation of criminal events in the metropolitan press." Univ. of Houston. (unpublished)

BITTNER, E. (1970) The Functions of the Police in Modern Society. Rockville, MD: National Institute of Mental Health.

BOORSTIN, D. (1961) The Image: A Guide to Pseudo-Events in America. New York: Harper & Row.

BRAUNGART, M., W. HOYER, and R. BRAUNGART (1979) "Fear of crime and the elderly," pp. 15-29 in A. Goldstein et al. (eds.) Police and the Elderly. New York: Pergamon.

BROWNMILLER, S. (1975) Against Our Will: Men, Women, and Rape. New York: Simon & Schuster.

CHIBNALL, S. (1977) Law-and-Order News: An Analysis of Crime Reporting in the British Press. London: Tavistock.

——— (1975) "The crime reporter: a study in the production of commercial knowledge." Sociology 9 (January): 49-66.

CICOUREL, A. (1968) The Social Organization of Juvenile Justice. New York: John Wiley.

FISHMAN, M. (1980) Manufacturing the News. Austin: Univ. of Texas Press.

——— (1978) "Crime waves as ideology." Social Problems 25 (June): 531-543.

GANS, H. (1979) Deciding What's News. New York: Pantheon.

GORDON, M. (1979) "Some costs of easy news." Presented at the annual meetings of the Society for the Study of Social Problems, Boston, August.

HOYER, W. (1979) "The elderly: who are they?" pp. 1-14 in A. Goldstein et al. (eds.) Police and the Elderly. New York: Pergamon.

LaFAVE, W. (1965) Arrest: The Decision to Take a Suspect Into Custody. Boston: Little, Brown.

MOLOTCH, H. and M. LESTER (1974) "News as purposive behavior: the strategic use of routine events, accidents, and scandals." Amer. Soc. Rev. 39: 101-112.

PILIAVIN, I. and S. BRIAR (1964) "Police encounters with juveniles." Amer. J. of Sociology 70 (September): 206-214.
REISS, A. and D. BORDUA (1967) "Environment and Organization: a perspective on the police," pp. 25-55 in D. Bordua (ed.) The Police: Six Sociological Essays. New York: John Wiley.
ROCK, P. (1973) "News as eternal recurrence," pp. 73-80 in S. Cohen and J. Young (eds.) The Manufacture of News. Beverly Hills: Sage.
ROSHCO, B. (1975) Newsmaking. Chicago: Univ. of Chicago Press.
ROSHIER, B. (1973) "The selection of crime news in the press," pp. 28-39 in S. Cohen and J. Young (eds.) The Manufacture of News. Beverly Hills: Sage.
SCHUDSON, M. (1978) Discovering the News. New York: Basic Books.
SHEARING, C. (1974) "Dial-a-cop: a study of police mobilization," pp. 77-88 in R. L. Akers and E. Sagarin (eds.) Crime Prevention and Social Control. New York: Praeger.
SHERIZEN, S. (1978) "Social creation of crime news: all the news fitted to print," pp. 203-224 in C. Winick (ed.) Deviance and Mass Media. Beverly Hills: Sage.
SIGAL, L. (1973) Reporters and Officials. Lexington, MA: D. C. Heath.
SKOLNIK, J. (1975) Justice Without Trial. New York: John Wiley.
SUDNOW, D. (1967) Passing On: The Social Organization of Dying. Englewood Cliffs, NJ: Prentice-Hall.
——— (1965) "Normal crimes: sociological features of the penal code in a public defender office." Social Problems 12 (Winter): 255-276.
TILLMAN, R. H. (1976) "The police reporter: a study in strategic interaction." M.A. thesis, Univ. of Oklahoma.
TUCHMAN, G. (1978) Making News. New York: Free Press.
——— (1976) "Telling stories." J. of Communication 26 (August): 93-97.
WALKER, L. (1979) The Battered Woman. New York: Harper & Row.

MARK FISHMAN is Assistant Professor of Sociology at Brooklyn College, City University of New York. His recent book, Manufacturing the News *(Austin: University of Texas Press, 1980), is an ethnography of news reporting. For the past six years he has been unearthing the massive bureaucratic apparatus which constructs ideological knowledge for publics.*

Shocking Numbers and Graphic Accounts: Quantified Images of Drug Problems in the Print Media*

JAMES D. ORCUTT, *Florida State University*

J. BLAKE TURNER, *Florida State University*

> *This paper examines how journalists and graphic artists in the national print media used statistical results from annual surveys of student drug use to construct quantified claims about a cocaine epidemic and other drug problems in 1986 and in subsequent years. Editorial and creative decisions entailed in transforming modest yearly changes in time-series data into a dramatic graphic image of "a coke plague" early in 1986 are reconstructed. The changing character of quantified images in the print media during the summer and fall of 1986 provides additional insights into how the rise and decline of a media "feeding frenzy" altered the claims-making activity of media workers. Finally, a recent case of the construction of a "new" drug problem on the eroding foundation of the cocaine epidemic is presented. The paper concludes with a discussion of how competitive conditions in the journalistic arena affect the production and distortion of quantified images of drug problems.*

Since 1975, the Monitoring the Future project at the University of Michigan Institute for Social Research (ISR) has been conducting annual surveys of drug use and attitudes in representative samples of high school seniors in the United States (Johnston, O'Malley, and Bachman 1991). Reports released from this project in 1986, which presented time-series data from 1975 to 1985, received extensive coverage in the mass media. Much of this publicity focused on the "disturbing finding that *cocaine* use increased among seniors in 1985" (Johnston, O'Malley, and Bachman 1986:13) following a period of little or no change in sample estimates of prevalence from 1979 to 1984.

Our purpose here is to show how media workers used this and other findings from the ISR surveys of high school seniors and older cohorts to construct quantified images of a "drug crisis" in 1986. We examine some of the products of journalistic and artistic work—statistical and graphic representations of drug problems which appeared in national print media—to gain insight into the labor process through which raw materials from the ISR reports were crafted into "plagues" and other icons of antidrug crusades. Our constructionist analysis of this historical episode departs from earlier efforts to adjudicate the "objective reality" of the 1986 drug crisis (see Goode 1989; Jensen, Gerber, and Babcock 1991; Reinarman and Levine 1989). Instead, we focus on the empirically verifiable correspondence between numbers contained in the ISR reports—sample estimates of points and trends in the prevalence of drug use—and reproductions of those numbers in the mass media. This strategy allows us to move beyond Best's (1989) analysis and refutation of baseless "statistical claims" about missing children. Given the known statistical properties of the survey data reported by Johnston, O'Malley, and Bachman (1986), we can use quantitative criteria such as tests of significance and measures of distortion to assess the shocking numbers and graphic accounts that media workers constructed from the ISR estimates.

---

* This is a revised version of a paper presented at the 1992 annual meeting of the Society for the Study of Social Problems, Pittsburgh. We are grateful to John Galliher, Larry Hazelrigg, and the anonymous *Social Problems* reviewers for their helpful comments. Correspondence to: Orcutt, Department of Sociology, Florida State University, Tallahassee, FL 32306-2011.

The Media Epidemic of 1986

Media coverage of drug problems generally, and cocaine use specifically, reached epidemic proportions in 1986. Although similar in some ways to earlier "drug crises" (Musto 1987), an unprecedented and well-documented "feeding frenzy" of drug coverage emerged by the middle of 1986, an election year, as the electronic and print media, the president and Congress, and other claims makers competed for audiences, voters, and ownership of this issue (Diamond, Accosta, and Thornton 1987; Kerr 1986b; Shoemaker 1989).

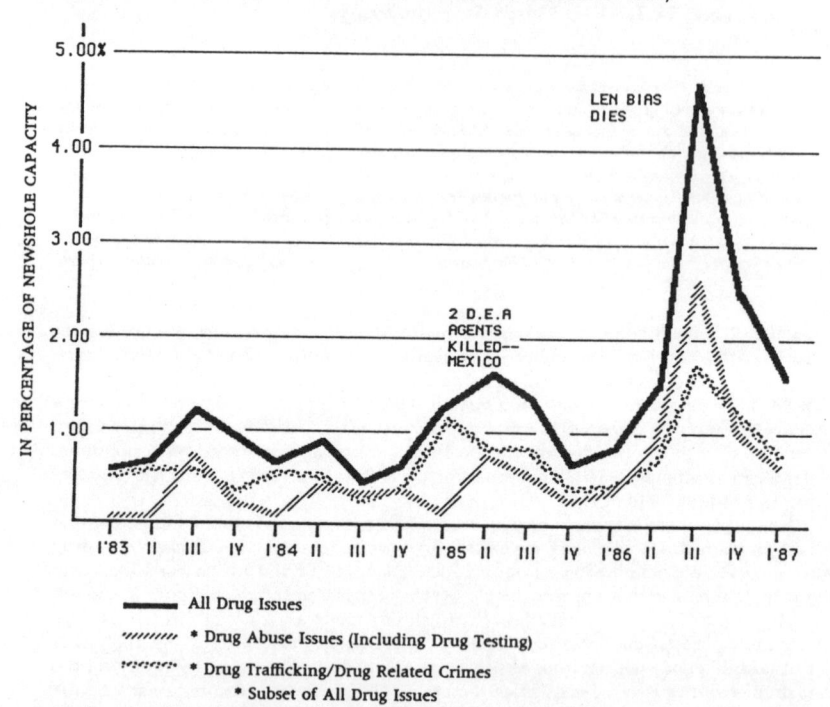

Figure 1 • *Media Coverage of Drug Issues, 1983-1987*

Source:
Merriam 1989:23. Reprinted by permission of Lawrence Erlbaum Associates. Copyright 1987 by The Conference on Issues & Media, Inc.

Merriam (1989:23) provides an especially clear picture of this media epidemic in his descriptive analysis of the National Media Index. Figure 1 shows his plot of the proportion of space and time devoted to drug issues by television network news, weekly news magazines, and five major newspapers from 1983 to 1987. Until 1985, coverage of drug issues rarely exceeded 1 percent of the total space and time in the news media. Drug stories, mainly concerned with trafficking and crime, received a greater share of total coverage in 1985; but, as Merriam points out, this was merely a "foothill for the mountain of drug coverage that was to come" (1989:24). Starting from less than 1 percent of total coverage in the first quarter of

1986, coverage of all drug issues eventually consumed nearly 5 percent of the space and time in the national media during July, August, and September. As noted in Merriam's graph, the peak of the media epidemic immediately followed a classic drug "horror story" (Johnson 1989): the death of basketball star Len Bias on 19 June, which was attributed to cocaine ingestion. More specifically, four weeks after Bias's death, coverage of drug abuse issues (apart from trafficking and crime) accounted for 3.2 percent of total space and time in the national media (Merriam 1989). By the final quarter of 1986, the media epidemic subsided somewhat, but attention to all drug issues still amounted to 2.4 percent of news coverage by network television, news magazines, and major newspapers.

Based on an extensive search of several media data bases, Reese and Danielian (1989) found important differences in the timing and relative contributions of various national news media to coverage of cocaine issues during the 1986 "drug crisis." In contrast to coverage of cocaine issues by network television and the *New York Times*, which peaked during the summer months of 1986, the number of pages in *Newsweek* and *Time* on cocaine and "crack" reached its highest level in March. A large share of this early news magazine coverage came from a seven page cover story in the 17 March issue of *Newsweek*, "Kids and Cocaine: An Epidemic Strikes Middle America." Kerr links this important, precedent-setting article to the concern of Richard M. Smith, the editor-in-chief of *Newsweek*, about the growing "drug crisis" and his feeling of responsibility "as an editor ... to put the drug problem in a larger context than we had in the past" (1986b:B6).

Following Smith's editorial design, the team of correspondents, feature writers, photographers, and graphic artists who worked on the 17 March issue produced a dramatic account of a frightening epidemic: "In cities and suburbs all across the nation, a generation of American children [is] increasingly at risk to the nightmare of cocaine addiction" (Newsweek 1986a:58). For the most part, this story was assembled with conventional journalistic material on the personal troubles of individuals, such as vignettes ("A Cheerleader's Fall—and Rise") and photographs of teenage victims. It cited expert testimony on the psychopharmacological powers of crack cocaine ("almost instantaneous addiction") and pessimistic reports from the front-line of the drug war (" 'We have lost the cocaine battle,' Los Angeles police detective Frank Goldberg says flatly" [1986a:60]). However, to lend authority and substance to their epidemiological rendition of the "larger context" of the cocaine problem, senior writer Tom Morganthau, graphic artist Christoph Blumrich, and their co-workers turned to the research of Johnston and his associates at the ISR.

The ISR Time Series, 1975-85

The 1986 annual report of the ISR surveys of high school seniors from 1975 through 1985 was not released until July (Halloran 1986). *Newsweek* "scooped" the other national media with results from this time series and an interview with Johnston in the 17 March article. As the final ISR report would show (and *Newsweek* noted in passing), prevalence estimates for most illicit drugs had steadily declined since the late 1970s—although Johnston, O'Malley, and Bachman (1986:13) pointed out that the downward trend in overall drug use "appears to have halted" in 1985. Nevertheless, the staff of *Newsweek* saw the potential for a "plague" in the ISR estimates of cocaine use.

In Figure 2 we use the simple line graph preferred by Johnston, O'Malley, and Bachman (cf. 1986:58) to present the ISR trend results for three measures of cocaine prevalence among high school seniors from 1975 to 1985. First, all measures of prevalence reflected "a dramatic and accelerating increase in popularity" of cocaine from 1976 to 1979—followed by a period of "little or no change in any prevalence statistics" from 1979 to 1984 (1986:48). However, from 1984 to 1985, Johnston and his colleagues noted statistically significant and "disturbing"

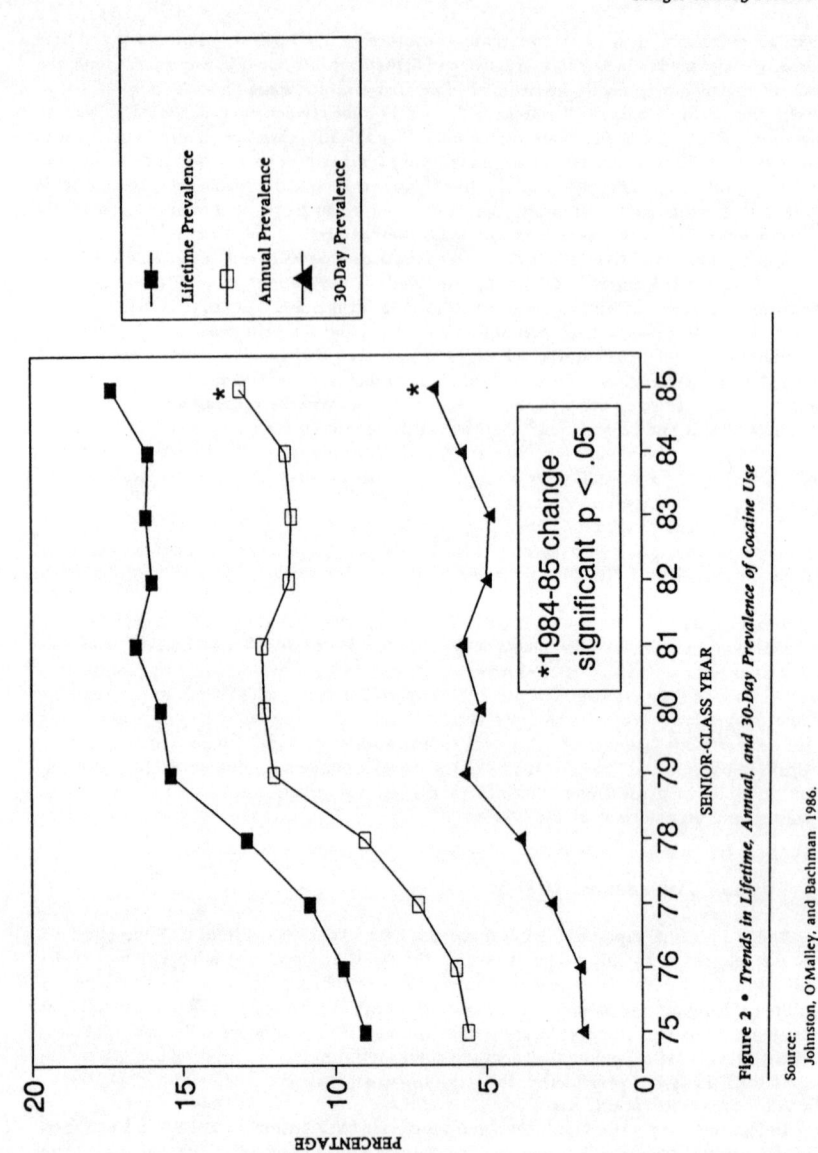

Figure 2 • *Trends in Lifetime, Annual, and 30-Day Prevalence of Cocaine Use*

Source: Johnston, O'Malley, and Bachman 1986.

increases in their estimates of 30-day (used in the last 30 days) and annual prevalence (used in the last 12 months). On the other hand, their most inclusive estimate of cocaine use—lifetime prevalence (ever used)—did not show a significant change in 1985, remaining essentially stable since 1979.

The *Newsweek* "Coke Plague"

To align the ISR time series with the master metaphor of the 17 March issue—the national "epidemic" of cocaine use—the media workers at *Newsweek* faced two major dilemmas. First, as Best points out, claims makers and the media "tend to use big numbers when estimating the scope of a social problem" (1989:21). Yet, the statistically significant change in 30-day prevalence or "current use" that Johnston, O'Malley, and Bachman (1986:13) highlighted in their report provided a relatively "little" number: 6.7 percent of high school seniors in 1985. Although the figures for lifetime prevalence offered the biggest numbers, this particular estimate did not yield a statistically significant change from 1984 to 1985. Setting aside this technical difficulty, *Newsweek* followed the claims maker's rule of thumb—"big numbers are better than little numbers" (Best 1989:32)—and focused on lifetime prevalence in the 17 March issue and subsequent articles on the "drug crisis" (Newsweek 1986b; Smith 1986).

Second, whereas Johnston, O'Malley, and Bachman documented a dramatic increase in cocaine use from 1976 to 1979, this in itself was hardly newsworthy seven years later. In fact, these early changes dwarfed the yearly fluctuations in prevalence estimates from 1980 to 1985. The staff of *Newsweek* grasped both horns of this dilemma by incorporating the shocking numbers from the 1970s into the text of the 17 March article while using graphic techniques to highlight the threat of more recent changes in lifetime prevalence. Figure 3 shows the final product of this work: *Newsweek's* graphic account of "A Coke Plague."

The text immediately adjacent to this graph in the *Newsweek* "Kids and Coke" feature story reads as follows:

> There is simply no question that cocaine in all its forms is seeping into the nation's schools. An annual survey conducted by the Institute of [sic] Social Research at the University of Michigan shows the percentage of high-school seniors who have ever tried cocaine has nearly doubled in the past 10 years, from 9 percent to 17.3 percent (chart) (1986a:63).

The quantified image of "doubling" in the text, where the referent to the full 1975-85 time series is left implicit, reinforces the visual impact of the recent, upturned spike in the "plague." Note also the textual forecast within the graph which projects this spike toward an even bigger number in the near future: "Within the next two years, more than 20 percent of high-school seniors may have tried cocaine." Even the label, "cocaine usage," is put to work, transforming lifetime prevalence into a more active, ongoing condition.

In Figure 4 we reconstruct the "Coke Plague" by tracing the creative steps of Blumrich, *Newsweek's* graphic artist. Panel A displays the original construction site—the 1975-85 ISR time series for lifetime prevalence of cocaine use. In Panel B we show the heavy "editorial deletions" that Blumrich had to make to prepare the foundation for his graphic account. First, he obliterated the historic increase in lifetime prevalence during the 1970s by censoring the first half of the ISR time series from 1975 to 1980. Then, he cut away over four-fifths of the original foundation for the remaining portion of the time series by trucating the 1980-85 data at the lofty level of 15 percent. In effect, these initial stages of construction removed over 95 percent of the information from the ISR time series on lifetime prevalence.

Panel C illustrates an intermediate stage of construction which increased the intensity of the "Coke Plague." By setting the Y-axis to a finer scale and focusing closely on the residue of his editorial deletions, Blumrich transformed statistically nonsignificant fluctuations in the ISR estimates of lifetime prevalence from 1980 to 1985 into striking peaks and valleys.

A Coke Plague

Within the next two years, more than 20 percent of high-school seniors may have tried cocaine.

Cocaine Usage
HIGH-SCHOOL SENIORS IN PERCENT

1980 — 81 — 82 — 83 — 84 — 85
17 — 16 — 15

SOURCE: THE UNIVERSITY OF MICHIGAN, INSTITUTE FOR SOCIAL RESEARCH   CHRISTOPH BLUMRICH—NEWSWEEK

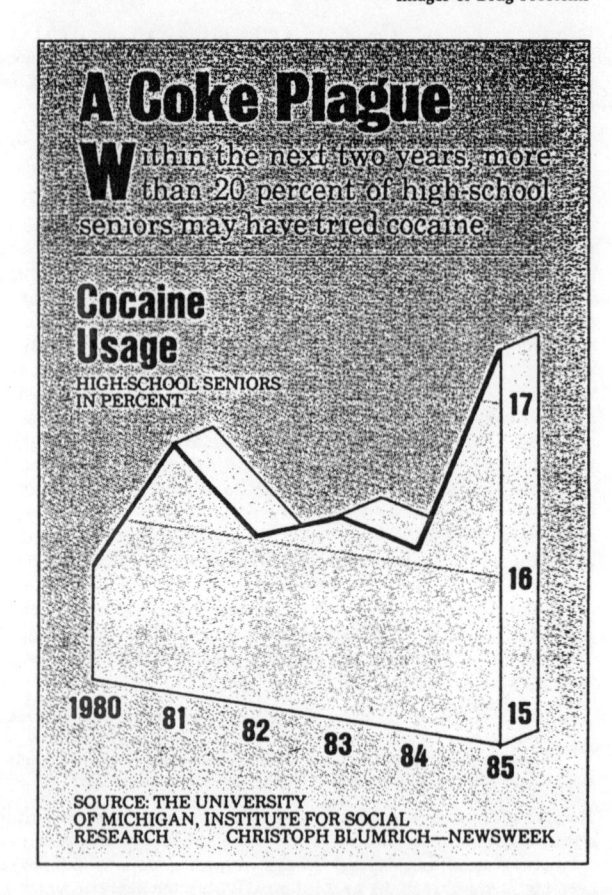

Figure 3

Source:
  Newsweek 1986a:63, Christoph Blumrich. Reprinted by permission.

We reconstruct some of the final stages of Blumrich's creative labor in Panel D. With the addition of color, the illusion of depth, and the name of an ancient terror, he completed his job of transfiguring a series of six numbers into a tangible and threatening social fact. Through Blumrich's compelling graphic account, *Newsweek* readers could literally *see* the menacing, three-dimensional entity that was "seeping into the nation's schools."

Editor-in-chief Smith (1986:15) drew upon this image for the title of a special editorial in the 16 June issue of *Newsweek*, "The Plague Among Us," in which he expressed his pride with the "Kids and Cocaine" issue and his concern with a drug "that 1 of every 6 of our teenage youngsters will have sampled before senior-prom night in high school." This editorial also marked the debut of a thematic logo, "The Drug Crisis," which highlighted coverage of this putative epidemic for several years as *Newsweek* implemented Smith's plan "to cover it as a

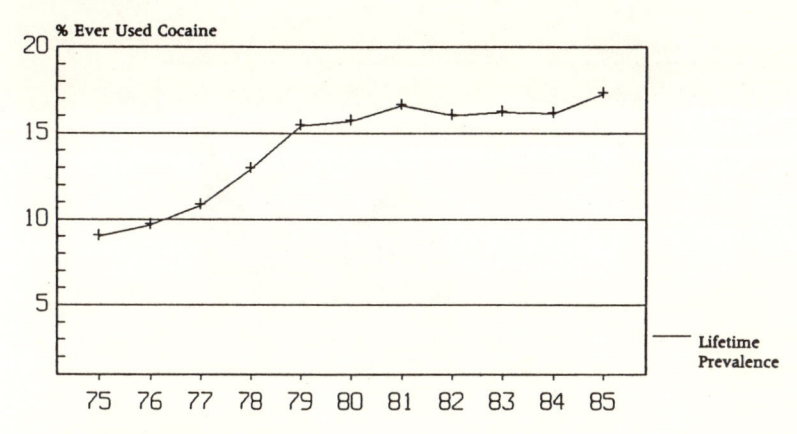

A. ISR Time Series for Lifetime Prevalence of Cocaine Use

B. Newsweek Editorial Deletions

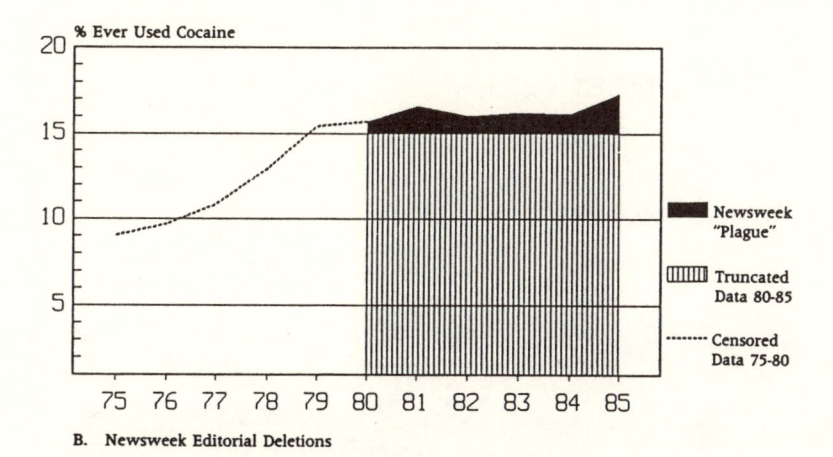

Figure 4 • *Reconstruction of "A Coke Plague"*

crisis, reporting it as aggressively . . . as we did the struggle for civil rights, the war in Vietnam and the fall of the Nixon presidency" (1986:15).

Other Images of the ISR Time Series

We searched 1986 issues of *Newsweek, Time,* and *U.S. News & World Report* as well as the *New York Times, Washington Post,* and *Chronicle of Higher Education* for other quantified images of drug problems constructed from the ISR time series. The final 1986 report, which Johnston and his associates released on 7 July at the peak of the media epidemic, included for the first

% Ever Used Cocaine

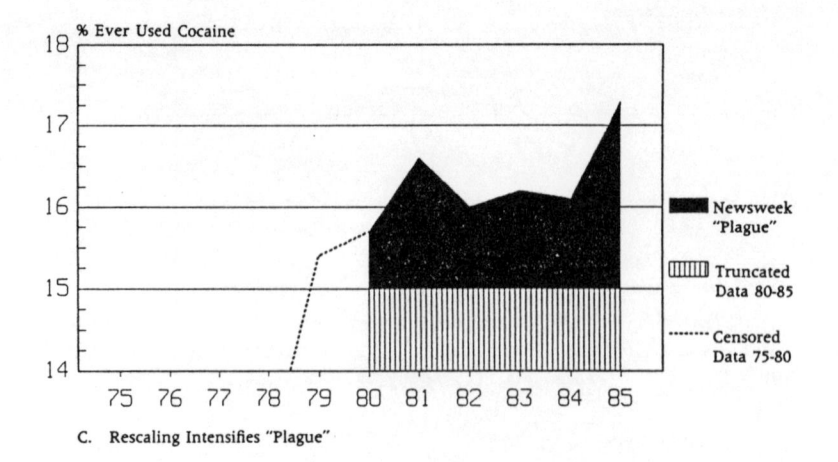

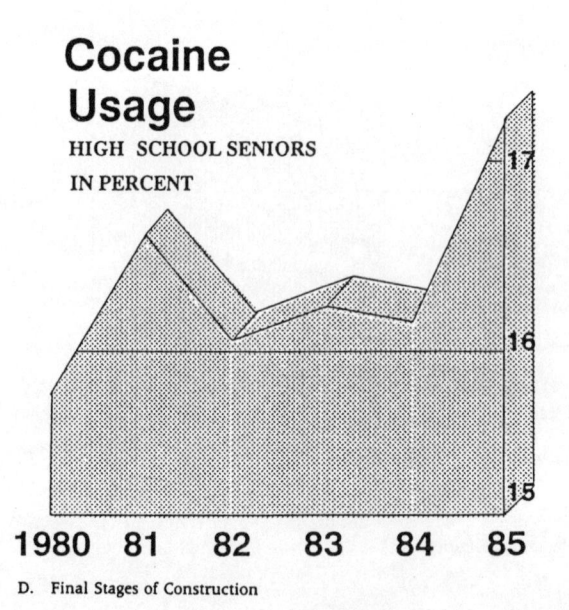

- Newsweek "Plague"
- Truncated Data 80-85
- Censored Data 75-80

C. Rescaling Intensifies "Plague"

Cocaine Usage
HIGH SCHOOL SENIORS
IN PERCENT

D. Final Stages of Construction

Figure 4 • *Reconstruction of "A Coke Plague" (Continued)*

Source:
Johnston, O'Malley, and Bachman 1986; Newsweek 1986a:63.

time follow-up data from panels of college students and other young adults. The print media devoted extensive coverage to a limited set of findings contained in an ISR press release, whose headline read: "U-M study indicates cocaine use remains high on American college campuses, while other drug frequency is down" (University of Michigan 1986). To document these trends, the press release presented one table from the 1986 report (Johnston, O'Malley, and Bachman 1986:182) showing 1980-85 estimates of annual prevalence for a variety of drugs from the college panel data. A reasonably faithful reproduction of this table in a 8 July *New York Times* article (Halloran 1986) included an essentially stable series of percentages for the annual prevalence of cocaine use:

1980	1981	1982	1983	1984	1985
17%	16%	17%	17%	16%	17%

Yet, the eye-catching headline over Halloran's article offered a more dynamic interpretation of this flat line of numbers than did the ISR press release: "Student Use of Cocaine Is Up as Use of Most Other Drugs Drops."

Similar versions of the annual prevalence table appeared in the *Washington Post* (Russell 1986) and *Chronicle of Higher Education* (Meyer 1986), but the headlines over these articles highlighted a shocking estimate of lifetime prevalence reported in the 7 July press release: "By the end of their fourth year of college, roughly 30 percent of all students will have tried cocaine" (University of Michigan 1986). This lifetime estimate was rounded up to "One-Third of College Students" in the 8 July *Washington Post* headline and "1 in 3 College Students" above the 16 July *Chronicle of Higher Education* story, and it was mentioned at some point during July or August in virtually all of the print media we examined (Halloran 1986; Newsweek 1986b; U.S. News & World Report 1986a). In contrast, only one of these articles (Russell 1986) cited the relatively low figure for 30-day prevalence of cocaine use among college students—"one in 14 (7 percent)"—which also appeared in the ISR press release (University of Michigan 1986). Despite the prominence of the shocking number of "1 in 3 College Students" in media coverage during the summer of 1986, Johnston, O'Malley, and Bachman did not include separate estimates of lifetime prevalence of cocaine use among college students in their final report (1986:201-232)—only 30-day and annual prevalence.

The surge of shocking numbers during the summer of 1986 reached an apex in August when Kerr incorporated the following claim into his *New York Times* account of the "Rising Concern on Drugs":

> A continuing survey by the University of Michigan Institute for Social Research found that 10 percent of the high school seniors who graduated in 1975 had used cocaine. In 1985, *40 percent of the graduating seniors* had at least tried the drug (italics added, 1986a: A28).

The 7 July ISR press release did state that "nearly 40 percent of all high school graduates have tried [cocaine] by age 26 or 27" (University of Michigan 1986:1), a finding based on follow-up data from young adults who had graduated in 1976 (cf. Johnston, O'Malley, and Bachman 1986:150). We do not know if Kerr simply misread this statement while preparing his story, but we can be sure that his inference of a ten-year quadrupling of cocaine use among high school seniors created rising concern among many readers of the *New York Times*.

Although the media epidemic continued through September, there were clear signs of change in the nature of this coverage and the quality of quantified images of drug problems. A shift toward a more reflective and occasionally critical posture was signalled by William Safire's 11 September essay in the *New York Times* (1986) on "The Drug Bandwagon," in which he observed that "news magazines have been conducting a circulation-building war on drugs for months." Less than a week later, the cover of *Time* (15 September 1986) featured a special report on "Drugs: The Enemy Within" with a lead article on "America's Crusade." This piece raised the possibility that the "press and politicians may be guilty of hyping the drug crisis" and used Musto's (1987) historical work to show that "the U.S. periodically launches antidrug crusades" (Time 1986:61). More to the point of our analysis, the article noted that since 1978 the "percentage of high school seniors [who] smoked marijuana every day . . . has dropped by half" and that "even cocaine use has evened out" (Time 1986:62). Finally, we see some revealing differences between the *Newsweek* "Coke Plague" and the graph that Joe Lertola prepared for this issue of *Time* from the ISR time series (Figure 5).

HIGH SCHOOL HABITS
% of seniors who are current users (within past 30 days)

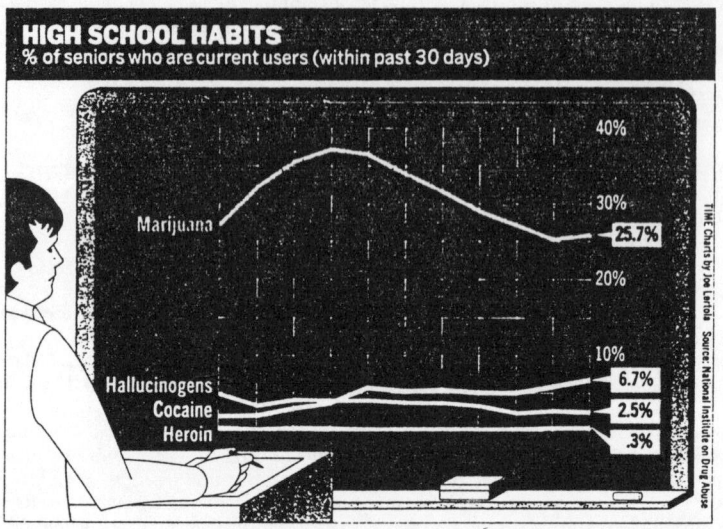

Marijuana — 25.7%
Hallucinogens — 6.7%
Cocaine — 2.5%
Heroin — .3%

TIME Charts by Joe Lertola Source: National Institute on Drug Abuse

Figure 5

Source:
Time 1986:64, Joe Lertola. Copyright 1986 Time Inc. Reprinted by permission.

Although it is certainly arguable whether figures on 30-day prevalence can sustain the title image of "High School Habits," it is noteworthy that this graph neither censors nor truncates the ISR percentage estimates from 1975 to 1985. Lertola's inclusion of marijuana prevalence in this graph not only calls attention to the long-term decline in ISR estimates for this drug, but it also provides a distinct contrast to the much lower and flatter trends for cocaine, hallucinogens, and heroin. Most interesting, perhaps, is Lertola's use of embellishments or "chart junk" (Tufte 1983): The academic scene of a student reading from the flat surface of a blackboard invites us to reflect on *our* act of reading and reminds us that these are "only numbers."

A very similar graph titled "Shifting Habits" appeared just two weeks later in a *U.S. News & World Report* article which raised the question, "War on drugs: More than a 'short-term high'?" (29 September 1986). Using annual prevalence figures from 1975 to 1985, an anonymous graphic artist contrasted incremental changes in cocaine, tranquilizer, and heroin use with a much higher, parabolic trend-line for marijuana use that literally goes "off the chart" in 1979. In addition, the text of this article drove home the following point about the "drug crisis":

The antidrug frenzy in Washington notwithstanding, there is little evidence to support alarmist claims. Indeed, reliable data show some forms of drug use declining, while others have remained flat. Only cocaine use . . . is up [but] it's barely a blip on the statistical screen (1986b:28).

In little more than half a year, the quantified image of a "Coke Plague" had shrunk to a mere "Statistical Blip."

Back to the Future: *Newsweek's* Recycled Crisis

As we noted earlier, the media epidemic declined precipitously during the last three months of 1986, with drug stories virtually disappearing from the major news magazines by the end of that year (Reese and Danielian 1989). Reinarman and Levine (1989:120-21) have already commented on a brief spate of "skewed reporting" in February 1987, when figures from the 1986 ISR high school survey were released to the press. While the familiar estimates of lifetime, annual, and 30-day prevalence of cocaine use all showed slight decreases, the *New York Times* (Kerr 1987) highlighted a similarly slight increase in daily prevalence (i.e., used on 20 or more occasions in the preceding 30 days). Interestingly, in his own commentary on "American's Drug Problem in the Media," Johnston (1989) cites this same prevalence estimate—which entailed only 0.4 percent of approximately 15,200 seniors in the 1986 sample—as evidence of a "real cocaine crisis" during that year.

However, toward the end of 1987, even *Newsweek* seemed ready to make a grudging withdrawal from its aggressive campaign on the "drug crisis" in a brief story written by Mark Miller, "Drug Use: Down, But Not in the Ghetto" (23 November 1987). Miller portrayed the long-term declines in ISR estimates of marijuana prevalence as "preliminary . . . signs of progress among middle-class teens" (1987:33). More importantly, his account of the recent ISR estimates for cocaine provided only a faint echo of the "Coke Plague" and a substantial revision of its two-year forecast of a growing epidemic:

> Cocaine use by high-school seniors rose to 17.3 percent in 1985, a U.S. record, and dropped only slightly in 1986. . . . Lloyd Johnston, a Michigan survey researcher, predicts that the 1987 high-school survey will chart a growing disenchantment in cocaine use (1987:33).

Having touched on this "good news," in which the ISR probability sample is narrowly framed as "middle-class teens," Miller devoted most of his article to the "bad news . . . that crack . . . is now deeply entrenched in the ghetto" (1987:33).

As the "good news" of decreasing cocaine prevalence, including "crack," flowed unrelentingly from the ISR surveys through the late 1980s (e.g., Berke 1989), the print media generally turned to more reliable sources of shocking numbers such as the Drug Abuse Warning Network (DAWN) reports of medical room emergencies or State Department estimates of worldwide cocaine production (e.g., Newsweek 1988; New York Times 1989; Sciolino 1989, 1990). However, the media's growing disenchantment with the cocaine problem was epitomized by contributing editor Larry Martz's article in the 19 February 1990 issue of *Newsweek*: "A Dirty Drug Secret: Hyping Instant Addiction Doesn't Help." Although Martz did not mention any specific cases, his disclosure of the "dirty little secret about crack" struck close to home:

> As with most other drugs, a lot of people use it without getting addicted. In their zeal to shield young people from the plague of drugs, the media and many drug educators have hyped the very real dangers of crack into a myth of instant and total addiction (1990:74).

Martz also turned the "big number" strategy against the image of a national epidemic by pointing to a steep decline of "50 percent, from 5.8 million to 2.9 million" in the National Institute on Drug Abuse's household survey estimates of monthly users of cocaine in 1985 and 1988 (NIDA 1989). Even though the editorial staff of *Newsweek* segregated Martz's "Ideas" piece from hard news and buried it in the back pages, it still read like an epitaph for the "Coke Plague" and other spawn of the media epidemic.

Yet, just two years later, *Newsweek* came back with an especially stunning illustration of how the "good news" of declining prevalence estimates can be recycled as "bad news" of a new "drug crisis." The 3 February 1992 issue included a report on "The New Age of Aquarius," whose headline proclaimed that "LSD . . . is turning on a new generation of American teenagers." Lead writer Jean Seligmann reinforced this theme with statistical observations from the ISR surveys:

> Though far more teenagers still resort to liquor or marijuana, the use of LSD is *rising alarmingly*. In 1990 and 1991, for the first time since 1976, annual surveys by the University of Michigan and the National Institute on Drug Abuse found more high-school seniors had used LSD than cocaine in the previous 12 months (italics added, Newsweek 1992:65).

Seligmann's quantified image of a recent and "alarming rise" in LSD relative to the well-known cocaine problem leaves it to the reader's imagination to fill in the missing data from 1976 to 1990. In Figure 6, we offer a more explicit and uncensored account of the trends in annual prevalence that link the original "Age of Aquarius" with the 1990s.

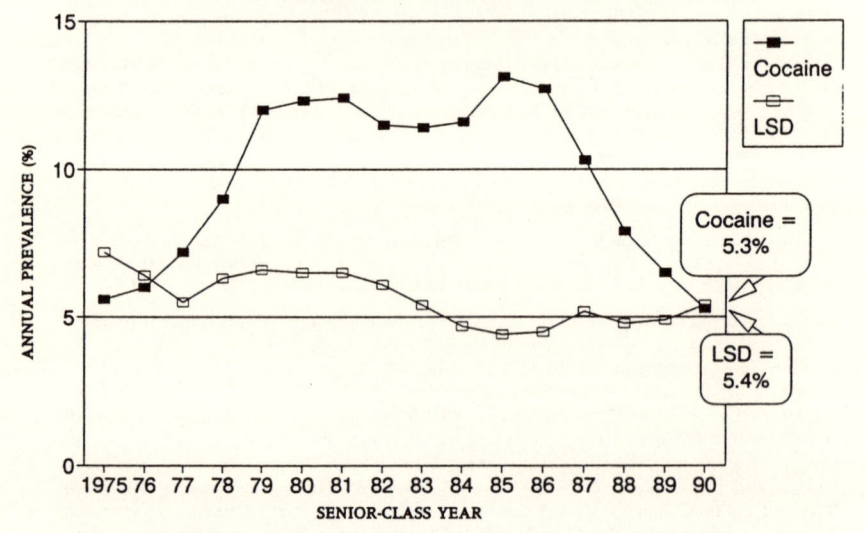

Figure 6 • *Percentage of High School Seniors Who Used Cocaine or LSD within the Last 12 Months*

Source:
Johnston, O'Malley, and Bachman 1991.

The critical implications of our graphic account of how *Newsweek* recycled a dying epidemic should be clear. It seems almost gratuitous to add that the decrease from 1989 (6.5 percent) to 1990 (5.3 percent) in the annual prevalence of cocaine use among high school seniors was statistically significant ($p < .01$), whereas the corresponding increase for LSD from 4.9 percent to 5.4 percent was within the range of sampling error. In his 16 June 1986 editorial, Smith had noted that *Newsweek's* very first cover story on drugs "dealt with LSD, then the drug of choice of flower children" (1986:15). And so, in fabricating this fantastic image of an emerging "drug crisis," his current staff truly "jumped back to the future."

Discussion and Conclusion

Consistent with Spector and Kitsuse's (1977:75) occupational approach to the study of claims-making activity, we have examined the journalistic and artistic products of "people who work in . . . the process of creating" drug problems. This exhibition of numerical and graphic reproductions of the ISR time series displays, at least indirectly, the skills, choices, and routine practices of the media workers who constructed these quantified images. In particular, our own archeological reconstruction of the *Newsweek* "Coke Plague" demonstrates the potential complexity and transformative power of this creative process.

Again, our purpose here is not to enter the arena of claims making and the familiar debate over the "reality" of the 1986 "drug crisis"—e.g., "Social construction or objective threat?" (Goode 1989); "Is it real or is it Memorex?" (Johnston 1989). That is, we are not concerned about population parameters estimated by Johnston, O'Malley, and Bachman, but with uses of the ISR statistical estimates per se by media workers. From this standpoint, we might consider another question: Did journalists and graphic artists "lie" about those statistics? Even though Tufte (1983:54) argues that preoccupation with the question of statistical and graphical integrity has stifled intellectual progress in the study of data graphics, this question bears on some broader issues in our study of the claims-making activities of media workers.

We can start with the *Newsweek* "Coke Plague." In truncating the ISR time series at the 15 percent level and rescaling the Y-axis to intensify yearly changes, Blumrich followed the classic blueprint for a "Gee-Whiz Graph" in Huff's *How to Lie with Statistics* (cf. 1954:65). Tufte (1983:56-57) provides a more formal way of assessing how much distortion—how big a "lie"—resulted from these operations in his first principle of graphical integrity and his measure of its violation:

> The representation of numbers, as physically measured on the surface of the graphic itself, should be directly proportional to the numerical quantities represented. . . . Violations of the first principle constitute one form of graphic misrepresentation, measured by the

$$\text{Lie Factor} = \frac{\text{size of effect shown in graphic}}{\text{size of effect in data}}$$

Let us use the crucial (albeit nonsignificant) increase from 16.1 percent in 1984 to 17.3 percent in 1985 to calculate Tufte's Lie Factor for the "Coke Plague." First, when this annual increase of 1.2 percent is divided by the actual 1984 baseline of 16.1 percent, the size of the effect in the ISR data stands at a relatively modest 7.4 percent change. However, the scale in the graph is truncated at the level of 15 percent. Thus, the 1984 baseline shown in the "Coke Plague" is *not* 16.1 percent but, rather, a much smaller 1.1 percent. In relation to this truncated baseline, an increase of 1.2 percent amounts to a 109.1 percent change from 1984 to 1985. The Lie Factor is simply the ratio of the effect in the graph over the effect in the data:

$$\text{Lie Factor} = \frac{\text{effect in "Coke Plague"}}{\text{effect in ISR data}} = \frac{109.1\% \text{ change}}{7.4\% \text{ change}} = 14.7$$

This result is intriguing because it is virtually identical to the degree of distortion in a *New York Times* graph that Tufte (1983:57-58) selected as an "extreme example" of graphic misrepresentation (Lie Factor = 14.8).

The "Coke Plague" also violates Tufte's second, qualitative principle of graphical integrity: "Clear, detailed, and thorough labeling should be used to defeat graphical distortion and ambiguity" (1983:56). Far from defeating distortion, labels within the graph and the ambiguous reference to "doubling" in the text add conceptual energy to the ominous image of a growing epidemic. Judged against Tufte's principles for "telling the truth about the data," it is evident that Blumrich and his co-workers told the readers of Newsweek a story which stretched the "true" numbers in the ISR report considerably.

Yet, if Blumrich's "Coke Plague" lacked graphical integrity, it made a vital contribution to the thematic integrity of Newsweek's coverage of "Kids and Cocaine" with its concrete, visual representation of the social facticity of this national epidemic. As the graphic artist for this major project, Blumrich's job was neither to report—nor to distort—the findings of the ISR surveys, but to make the hard reality behind "abstract statistics" (Smith 1986) more accessible to the readers of Newsweek. The numbers from the ISR survey authenticated his work of art; he could in truth say, "I'm not making this up." But, along with the reporters, writers, and photographers who worked on this issue, Blumrich had to edit, polish, and interpret his source material to get at the real story of a growing epidemic. In form and content, his graphic account of "A Coke Plague" was ultimately faithful to this journalistic design.

The "Kids and Cocaine" issue was a well-coordinated and highly successful venture into the journalistic arena of social problem definition (Hilgartner and Bosk 1988). Editor-in-chief Smith's early decision to put the cocaine "problem in a larger context" with a thematic issue on a "national epidemic" was influential in setting the agenda for subsequent coverage of this story in Newsweek and among its competitors (Kerr 1986b:B6; Reese and Danielian 1989). From his own account of this project, it appears that Smith (1986) took an unusually strong and active role in the planning and execution of work on the cocaine problem. Although Gans notes that journalists often describe news organizations as "militaristic," he points out that news magazine executives at the level of editor-in-chief rarely exercise their potential control over the story selection and production process (1979:84-85). Yet, Smith's (1986) editorial statement reflected his personal command of drug statistics and of Newsweek's mission to cover "The Plague Among Us"—a title which acknowledged the editor-in-chief's special pride in Blumrich's skillful contribution to this operation. In introducing a distinctive graphic trademark, "The Drug Crisis," Smith staked his organization's proprietary claim to the discovery of an "epidemic . . . as pervasive and as dangerous in its way as the plagues of medieval times" (1986:15).

As other news organizations rushed to cover the epidemic, their fevered pursuit of this story through the summer of 1986 retraced the outline of Blumrich's plague (cf. Figures 1 and 3) and reproduced on a much grander scale the competitive dynamics which Fishman (1978) found in his analysis of a local media "crime wave." Blumer's (1971) characterization of social problems as collective behavior provides an apt description of the labor process among media workers during this period of focused competition over the drug crisis. As he noted, knowledge about putative conditions—such as the ISR estimates of drug prevalence—"may be ignored, distorted, or smothered by other considerations . . . in the process of collective definition which determines the fate of social problems" (1971:305). Indeed, "other considerations" seemed to prevail during the media "feeding frenzy," and we found ample evidence of media workers snatching at shocking numbers from an ISR press release, smothering reports of stable or decreasing use under more ominous headlines, and distorting the cocaine problem to epidemic proportions as high as 40 percent of high school seniors. In contrast to the more deliberate, thematically integrated quality of Blumrich's work, the heavy-handed and sometimes shoddy images during the summer of 1986 reflect a labor process that was itself distorted by competitive pressures in the journalistic arena.

Our comparison of college panel data contained in the 7 July ISR press release (University of Michigan 1986) with those that Johnston and his associates (1986) chose to include in their final report indicates that these researchers delivered a special order of lifetime prevalence estimates to meet the heavy demand for "big numbers" in the media marketplace. Just as Fishman (1978) observed that media crime waves depend on the supply of thematically relevant incidents from law enforcement agencies, the construction of shocking headlines about "1 in 3 College Students" during the summer of 1986 depended on the provision of numbers that could be used as instances of an "epidemic." It is important to note that media workers largely ignored smaller numbers from the college data that appeared in both the ISR press release and the final report—the annual and 30-day prevalence estimates that Johnston, O'Malley, and Bachman treat as indicators of "active use" (1986:16). Thus, the production of quantified claims at the peak of the media epidemic depended both on a supply of suitable materials by the ISR researchers and on an internal labor process through which the highest estimates were extracted and refined into shocking numbers.

The media epidemic of the "cocaine summer" became the story in September. Taking a new tack, *Time*, *U.S. News & World Report*, and some newspaper columnists seemed to grant *Newsweek's* claim to the "drug crisis," and then to show how this claim had been abused through "hype" and political misappropriation. Working under this condition of counterissue competition, graphic artists created images of the ISR time series that conformed fairly well to Tufte's (1983) standards for graphical integrity. But, here too, we should not lose sight of Blumer's (1971) point that the uses and representations of such knowledge are always contingent on other considerations in the process of collective definition. The "honest" design of the graphs of drug "habits" in September 1986 issues of *Time* and *U.S. News & World Report* reinforced textual claims that the cocaine epidemic was only a "statistical blip" and that the "real story" behind the crisis was yet another U.S. crusade against drugs.

In the meantime, Smith and his staff were clearly reluctant to relinquish their claim to the "drug crisis." Miller's (1987) article placed the declines in the ISR time series within a middle-class ghetto, and directed attention to the plague that was still roaming freely in the streets of the inner city. Even Martz's (1990) belated entry into the counterissue market had less to say about the role of the media in "hyping" the cocaine problem than about limitations in the survey data that had betrayed predictions of a growing epidemic. Above all, the recent image of an "alarming rise" in LSD which was erected on the eroding foundation of the "Coke Plague" shows that the prospectors at *Newsweek* are still at work. We suspect that Seligmann and her colleagues were put on the trail of the "New Age of Aquarius" by advance information of a flat trend that was announced in a 27 January 1992 press release from the ISR (University of Michigan 1992). After commenting on dramatic declines in prevalence estimates for cocaine and other drugs, Johnston noted that "one drug which bears watching is LSD, since use of it has not declined among seniors since the early 1980s" (University of Michigan 1992:4). Rather than waiting and watching, the staff of *Newsweek* went to work on the numbers and, in virtually no time at all, produced a new and "alarming" drug problem.

Media distortion of research findings may not be fresh news in the field of social problems. However, we question whether analysts who dispose of this material by debunking statistical claims or reducing media coverage to political propaganda have fully explored its sociological potential. We find ample grounds for the claim that media workers "lie"; but we have also tried to understand the creative choices and skills that are entailed in the fabrication of these distorted images of drug problems. Moreover, by attending to systematic variations in the nature and degree of distortion in media workers' products, we have attempted to gain insight into organizational and competitive conditions that affect this labor process. Although our work sheds no light on what "really" happened to drug use in 1986, we think it offers a sociologically pertinent account of how media workers used drug data to construct the social reality of a national epidemic.

References

Berke, Richard L.
    1989   "Student survey detects decline in use of crack." New York Times 1 March: A16.

Best, Joel
    1989   "Dark figures and child victims: Statistical claims about missing children." In Images of Issues: Typifying Contemporary Social Problems, ed. Joel Best, 21-37. New York: Aldine de Gruyter.

Blumer, Herbert
    1971   "Social problems as collective behavior." Social Problems 18:298-306.

Diamond, Edwin, Frank Accosta, and Leslie-Jean Thornton
    1987   "Is TV news hyping America's cocaine problem?" TV Guide 7 February: 4-10.

Fishman, Mark
    1978   "Crime waves as ideology." Social Problems 25:531-543.

Gans, Herbert J.
    1979   Deciding What's News. New York: Pantheon.

Goode, Erich
    1989   "The American drug panic of the 1980s: Social construction or objective threat?" Violence, Aggression and Terrorism 3:327-348.

Halloran, Richard
    1986   "Student use of cocaine is up as use of most other drugs drops." New York Times 8 July: A12.

Hilgartner, Stephen, and Charles L. Bosk
    1988   "The rise and fall of social problems: A public arenas model." American Journal of Sociology 94:53-78.

Huff, Darrell
    1954   How to Lie with Statistics. New York: W.W. Norton.

Jensen, Erich L., Jerg Gerber, and Ginna M. Babcock
    1991   "The new war on drugs: Grassroots movement or political construction?" Journal of Drug Issues 21:651-667.

Johnson, John M.
    1989   "Horror stories and the construction of child abuse." In Images of Issues: Typifying Contemporary Social Problems, ed. Joel Best, 5-19. New York: Aldine de Gruyter.

Johnston, Lloyd D.
    1989   "America's drug problem in the media: Is it real or is it Memorex?" In Communication Campaigns About Drugs: Government, Media, and the Public, ed. Pamela J. Shoemaker, 97-111. Hillsdale, N.J.: Lawrence Erlbaum.

Johnston, Lloyd D., Patrick M. O'Malley, and Jerald G. Bachman
    1986   Drug Use Among American High School Students, College Students, and Other Young Adults: National Trends through 1985. Rockville, Md.: National Institute on Drug Abuse.
    1991   Drug Use Among American High School Seniors, College Students and Young Adults, 1975-1990. Volume I: High School Seniors. Rockville, Md.: National Institute on Drug Abuse.

Kerr, Peter
    1986a   "Rising concern on drugs stirs public to activism." New York Times 10 August: A1, 28.
    1986b   "Anatomy of the drug issue: How, after years, it erupted." New York Times 17 November: A1, B6.
    1987   "High-school marijuana use still declining, U.S. survey shows." New York Times 24 February: A21.

Martz, Larry
    1990   "A dirty drug secret: Hyping instant addiction doesn't help." Newsweek 19 February: 74-77.

Merriam, John E.
    1989   "National media coverage of drug issues, 1983-1987." In Communication Campaigns About Drugs: Government, Media, and the Public, ed. Pamela J. Shoemaker, 21-28. Hillsdale, N.J.: Lawrence Erlbaum.

Meyer, Thomas J.
   1986   "1 in 3 college students tries cocaine, study finds." The Chronicle of Higher Education 16 July: 1, 30.

Miller, Mark
   1987   "Drug use: Down, but not in the ghetto." Newsweek 23 November: 33.

Musto, David F.
   1987   The American Disease: Origins of Narcotic Control. Expanded Edition. New York: Oxford University Press.

National Institute on Drug Abuse (NIDA)
   1989   National Household Survey on Drug Abuse: Population Estimates 1988. Rockville, Md.: National Institute on Drug Abuse.

Newsweek
   1986a   "Kids and cocaine." 17 March: 58-65.
   1986b   "Trying to say 'no'." 11 August: 14-19.
   1988   "Crack, hour by hour." 28 November: 64-75.
   1992   "The new age of Aquarius." 3 February: 65-67.

New York Times
   1989   "Crack: A disaster of historic dimension, still growing." 28 May: E14.

Reese, Stephen D., and Lucig H. Danielian
   1989   "Intermedia influence on the drug issue: Converging on cocaine." In Communication Campaigns About Drugs: Government, Media, and the Public, ed. Pamela J. Shoemaker, 29-45. Hillsdale, N.J.: Lawrence Erlbaum.

Reinarman, Craig, and Harry G. Levine
   1989   "The crack attack: Politics and media in America's latest drug scare." In Images of Issues: Typifying Contemporary Social Problems, ed. Joel Best, 115-37. New York: Aldine de Gruyter.

Russell, Cristine
   1986   "One-third of college students try cocaine, survey finds." Washington Post 8 July: A3.

Safire, William
   1986   "The drug bandwagon." New York Times 11 September: A27.

Sciolino, Elaine
   1989   "Drug production rising worldwide, State Dept. says." New York Times 2 March: A1, 12.
   1990   "World drug crop up sharply in 1989 despite U.S. effort." New York Times 2 March: A1-2.

Shoemaker, Pamela J., ed.
   1989   Communication Campaigns About Drugs: Government, Media, and the Public. Hillsdale, N.J.: Lawrence Erlbaum.

Smith, Richard M.
   1986   "The plague among us." Newsweek 16 June: 15.

Spector, Malcolm, and John I. Kitsuse
   1977   Constructing Social Problems. Menlo Park, Calif.: Cummings.

Tufte, Edward R.
   1983   The Visual Display of Quantitative Information. Cheshire, Conn.: Graphics Press.

Time
   1986   "America's crusade." 15 September: 60-68.

University of Michigan
   1986   "U-M study indicates cocaine use remains high on American college campuses, while other drug frequency is down." Press Release, 7 July. Ann Arbor: News and Information Services.
   1992   "Most forms of drug use decline among American high school and college students, U-M survey reports." Press Release, 25 January. Ann Arbor: News and Information Services.

U.S. News & World Report
   1986a   "America on drugs." 28 July: 48-54.
   1986b   "War on drugs: More than a 'short-term high'?" 29 September: 28-29.

News Media Influences on Public Views of Sentencing

Julian V. Roberts† and Anthony N. Doob‡

Opinion polls in Canada, the United States, Great Britain, Australia, and elsewhere suggest that most members of the public would like their criminal courts to be harsher. Does media coverage of criminal sentencing contribute to a preference for harsher sentencing? Most people derive their information about sentencing from the news media, and content analyses of news stories in Canada and the United States demonstrate that crimes of violence and sentences of imprisonment are overrepresented. Moreover, the news media provide little systematic information about the sentencing process or its underlying principles. This article reports the results of three studies examining the effects of media coverage on public opinion about sentencing. Subjects who read actual newspaper stories about sentencing that appeared in Canadian newspapers rated most reported sentences as too lenient. However, the specific account they read influenced their leniency judgments. Furthermore, in one experiment, participants assigned to read a newspaper account of a sentencing decision supported harsher sentences than participants who read a summary of actual court documents from the sentencing hearing.

---

* The authors gratefully acknowledge the assistance of Valerie Hans and two anonymous reviewers for their comments on an earlier draft of this paper. The research reported in this article was carried out under contract with the Department of Justice, Canada, in some instances, and as part of the research program of the Canadian Sentencing Commission in others. Some of this research is derived from material contained in Doob and Roberts, 1982, 1983, 1984, and 1988, and the Report of the Canadian Sentencing Commission (1987). The writing of this article was supported by the Contributions Programme of the Solicitor General, Canada, to the Canadian criminology centers—specifically the Centre of Criminology, University of Toronto and the Department of Criminology, University of Ottawa. The views expressed in this article do not necessarily reflect the views of any government department or commission. We wish to thank Patricia Parker for running Study 2, and Brian Greenspan for providing the materials for Study 3. We would also like to thank the administration of the Ontario Science Centre for generously giving us access to facilities and visitors. Copies of the research materials used in any of the studies described here are available from the authors. Correspondence should be directed to: J. V. Roberts, Department of Criminology, University of Ottawa, 1 Stewart Street, Ottawa, Ontario, Canada K1N 6N5.
† Department of Criminology, University of Ottawa.
‡ Centre of Criminology, University of Toronto.

It has been clear for some time now that the news media play a pivotal role in the formation and transformation of public attitudes towards crime, criminals, and the criminal justice system. Most recently, researchers have focused their attention upon media coverage of sentencing and its effect on public understanding of and attitudes toward the sentencing process. The reason for this increased interest in sentencing and the news media should be apparent: Sentencing reform is currently a priority in many countries. In the United States, the U.S. Sentencing Guidelines Commission has recently introduced sentencing guidelines for federal offenders (U.S. Sentencing Commission, 1987). In Canada, the reform of the sentencing process appears imminent following the release of two major reports. A federal commission (Canadian Sentencing Commission, 1987) produced one report following two years of study and consultation, and a Parliamentary committee (Standing Committee on Justice and Solicitor General, 1988) wrote a second document. Both reports contain heavy criticism of the current system as well as prescriptions for reform. In addition, reforms have recently been proposed or implemented in both the United Kingdom (1990) and Australia (Law Reform Commission—Australia, 1988).

At this critical point in the history of criminal law reform, it is clearly important to understand the views of the public. We shall argue that this is possible only if we first understand the impact of the news media on public views of sentencing. Recent polls in Canada made it clear that members of the public are dependent almost exclusively upon the news media for information on sentencing. A nationwide survey conducted by the Canadian Sentencing Commission in 1986 asked respondents where they got "most of their information about the sentencing of offenders." Almost all respondents (95%) cited the news media. What then do we know about news media coverage of this vital component of the criminal justice process?

News Media Coverage of Crime and Punishment

News media treatment of sentencing must be seen in the context of media coverage of crime. The media overrepresent crimes of violence. For example, in one content analysis of news reports (Graber, 1980), murder accounted for 25% of crime stories, although it constitutes less than 1% of all reported crimes. Likewise, Doob (1985) found that over half the newspaper stories about crime in a sample of Canadian newspapers described crimes of violence, also an overrepresentation. Gordon and Heath (1981) examined news media in the United States and found that one in five front-page news stories involved a serious crime of violence (see also Dussuyer, 1979; Surette, 1984). After reviewing the literature, the Canadian Sentencing Commission concluded that "the public . . . is forced to build its view of sentencing on a data-base which does not reflect reality, where fewer than 6% of all crimes involve violence" (pp. 95–96).

Just as the crimes that appear in the news media are unrepresentative of crimes committed (or even crimes reported to the police), the sentencing stories reported in the news media do not reflect reality. A recent content analysis (Canadian Sentencing Commission, 1988) of all the sentencing stories appearing in major Canadian newspapers for a one-year period found that over half were sentences imposed upon offenders convicted of crimes involving violence.

The distorted view of sentencing is not restricted to the nature of offenses selected for transmission to the public. The sentences reported by newspapers are equally atypical of actual practice. In fully 70% of the stories, the sentence reported was a period of imprisonment. Fines appeared in fewer than 10% of the stories. In reality, sentences of custody are relatively rarely imposed in Canada, whereas fines are handed down in approximately half of all convictions (Department of Justice, Canada, 1983). In the United States, it has been estimated that fines comprise three quarters of all sentences for criminal offenses (Verdun-Jones & Mitchell-Banks, 1988). Alternative community-based sanctions, such as community service orders or restitution, almost never appeared in the sample of newspaper stories examined in this study (Canadian Sentencing Commission, 1988). In short, the news media present crime as being predominantly violent and sentences as being largely periods of custody.

It is therefore worthwhile to look at the way in which stories about sentencing actually appear in the media. To return to the newspaper content analysis conducted by the Canadian Sentencing Commission, perhaps the most notable aspect of the stories was that they were short and provided little information about the offense or the offender. As well, little explanation of the judicial reasoning behind the sentence was provided: In 70% of the sentencing stories, no reason for the sentence was given; in 20% of the stories only one reason was mentioned.

What does the public do with this kind of information? If people were professionally trained in statistics, they would discount much of what they read because of its unrepresentativeness. However, many studies (e.g., Hamill, Wilson, & Nisbett, 1980; Tversky & Kahneman, 1973) have shown that people are overly influenced by single-case information. Hence, when forming an opinion about the appropriateness of sentences, a person will give undue weight to a single sentence. If the sentences that are reported actually represented typical cases, then this would not be so bad; however, if the sentences reported appear to be unduly lenient, then people may falsely generalize that leniency characterizes the entire sentencing process. Public views of sentencing, then, may be based upon inadequate information.

Public Opinion of Sentencing

In light of the above, it is perhaps not surprising that the public knows little about the actual structure of the sentencing process or sentencing trends. Moreover, misperceptions abound, and these inaccuracies can be directly traced to the news media. For example, the Canadian public underestimates the severity of sentences, the amount of time offenders spend in prison before being released on parole, and the severity of maximum penalties (Canadian Sentencing Commission, 1988). As well, they overestimate the number of offenders released on parole and the number of offenders who will commit fresh offenses (Roberts & White, 1986). Most importantly, the public has a highly negative view of sentencing outcomes. Surveys in Canada (Canadian Sentencing Commission, 1988), the United States (Flanagan, McGarrell, & Brown, 1985), Australia (Broadhurst & Indermaur, 1982), Great Britain, and elsewhere (Hough & Moxon, 1985; Walker & Hough, 1988) reveal that most people view sentences as being too lenient. It is highly likely that this ubiquitous perception of judicial leniency is derived from incomplete news media coverage of sentencing hearings. The purpose of this research was to explore the role of the news media in shaping negative attitudes about sentencing.

Public Opinion and Sentencing Policy

It is important to understand both public opinion and the role of the news media, for two reasons: First, the apparent public desire for harsher sentences is frequently cited by policy makers as a reason to oppose reform initiatives. The public, we are told, will not tolerate changes that may result in more lenient dispositions (see Doob & Roberts, 1988). Second, judges are not immune to the force of public opinion—or what they perceive public opinion to be. As Walker and Hough (1988) note, "The sentencer who is trying—as most do—to strike a balance between [various approaches to sentencing] cannot altogether disregard public opinion." They further suggest that "there are signs that at a political level, at any rate, greater importance is now being attached to the congruence of public opinion and sentencing practice" (p. 1). Before the practice of the courts can be reconciled with the views of the public, we need to know precisely what those views are and where they come from. We need to know if the public really does have views of sentencing that are discrepant with the practice of the courts, or whether the public is responding to biased news media accounts of sentencing. The studies described below address this question.

STUDY 1: EVALUATING SENTENCES REPORTED IN NEWS STORIES

The first study examined public reactions to the sentences appearing in a sample of stories from Toronto newspapers. The aim was to present the public with an array of common stories, rather than selected high-profile stories. The hypothesis tested was that perceptions of sentencing leniency are created and confirmed by what the public reads in the newspapers.

Method

Subjects

Throughout this article we shall be describing two kinds of data. Some data derive from small samples of members of the general public who participated in experimental research; other data come from recent representative surveys of the Canadian public. Experimental subjects were members of the general public visiting the Ontario Science Centre, a science museum in Toronto. This facility was chosen in order to reach a more ecologically valid sample than college undergraduates participating for money or course credit. Though the Science Centre attracts a relatively heterogeneous sample of people, the subjects cannot be regarded as a representative or random sample of the general population. They are, in all probability, better educated than the average Canadian. However, in the experimental studies, our intention was not to make *general* statements about public opinion, but rather to compare reactions of randomly created groups of subjects. In Study 1, the responses of the Centre sample were compared to data derived from a representative survey of adult Canadians conducted at about the same time. These comparative data are drawn from a systematic comparison of the two populations, described in Doob and Roberts (1983). The distributions of the responses to 13 questions related to sentencing from the two samples were very similar, and in some cases identical. For example, when asked for their general view of sentencing (i.e., "Are sentences too harsh, about right, or not severe enough?") the responses from the experimental and survey samples were quite similar. Seventy-nine percent of the experimental subjects endorsed the view that sentences are too lenient compared to 80% of the respondents from the nationwide survey. These data suggest that the reactions of our subjects resemble those derived from a more representative sample.

Demographic Variables

Of the 99 participants, 62 were Canadian residents. The remainder came largely from the United States. All subjects were over 18; 38 were male, 62 female. No significant differences emerged as a function of respondent's gender or country of residence.

Stimulus Materials

The aim of this study was to provide subjects with an array of recent sentencing stories. Accordingly, all the stories concerning sentencing by Canadian courts that appeared in any Toronto daily newspaper for the week preceding the data collection were photocopied. Sixteen stories appeared, but because two newspapers covered one sentencing hearing, there were 15 independent sentences reported. These 16 stories were divided randomly into four groups of four stories. (A typical story appears in Appendix A.) Consistent with the findings of other systematic analyses of sentencing stories, referred to in the introduction, the stories were all rather short. They varied in length from 2.5 to 18 column inches and from 68 to 488 words. The average length of the 16 stories was 215 words.

Each story was accompanied by two dependent measures. One addressed subjects' perceptions of the appropriateness of the sentence: "What do you think of the sentence given the offender in this article?" Responses were rated on a 7-point Likert scale, which ranged from "much too harsh" to "much too lenient." The second dependent measure assessed confidence: "How confident are you of your opinion about the appropriateness of the sentence in this article?" Subjects responded on a 3-point scale: very confident, somewhat confident, and not at all confident. In addition, subjects were asked whether they thought sentences in general were too lenient.

Procedure

Subjects were recruited inside the museum by means of a sign requesting volunteers for a study in criminal justice. The topic of sentencing was not explicitly mentioned. Subjects were randomly assigned to receive one of the four packages containing four sentencing stories. Each individual subject received a booklet that included instructions, four sentencing stories, and dependent measures for each story. The study was conducted in a secluded laboratory provided by the authorities at the Ontario Science Centre. It took approximately 25 min to complete. Following completion of the ratings of the final story, subjects were thanked and provided with a complete description of the aims of the research.

Results

Evaluations of the Sentences

Because we are not concerned with ratings of any particular story but rather with reactions to the stimulus array as a whole, we aggregated ratings of the individual stories. Table 1 presents a breakdown of these ratings. For the purposes of this table, the seven dependent variable options have been collapsed to three. This table makes it clear that the modal reaction to these stories was to regard the criminal sentences reported in them as too lenient. In 13 of the 16 stories, the sentence was seen on average as too lenient. Generally speaking then, the sentences reported by the newspapers during the week confirmed the a priori view held by most respondents that sentences are generally too lenient. There was a significant correlation, $r(98) = .31$, $p < .01$, between average ratings of the reported sentences for an individual and that individual's response to the question of whether sentences in general were too lenient. Subjects who thought sentences

TABLE 1. Study 1: Ratings of Sentences Reported in Newspapers

Evaluation of sentence[a]	N[b]	Percent
Too harsh[c]	61	16
About right	130	33
Too lenient[d]	200	51
	391	100

[a] Seven-point scale: 7 = *much too harsh;* 6 = *too harsh;* 5 = *slightly harsher than it should have been;* 4 = *about right;* 3 = *slightly more lenient than it should have been;* 2 = *too lenient;* 1 = *much too lenient.*
[b] N = 99, each subject provided four ratings. In five instances a response was omitted.
[c] Includes subjects selecting options 7, 6, or 5.
[d] Includes subjects selecting options 1, 2, or 3.

in general were too lenient were more likely to rate the individual sentences as being too lenient.

Confidence Ratings

Interestingly, in 58% of the ratings, subjects indicated that they were "very confident" of their evaluations. In an additional 35%, subjects indicated they were "somewhat" confident. In only 7% were subjects "not at all confident." These results are surprising given the length of the stories: Little information was conveyed on which to base a reasoned evaluation of the appropriateness of the sentence.

Moreover, there was a significant correlation across the stories (Spearman's rho = .50, $p < .05$) between the percentage of respondents rating the story as too lenient and the percentage indicating they were very confident about their sentence. Those sentences perceived as being too lenient were evaluated with a greater degree of confidence. When the particular sentence being rated was consistent with subjects' general view of sentencing (i.e., too lenient) people were more confident of their evaluations.

Discussion

We have demonstrated that (a) people are willing to evaluate a sentence on the basis of a brief newspaper article, and (b) they generally provide these evaluations with confidence. Could demand cues or evaluation apprehension have produced these results? It might be argued that by asking subjects to provide ratings we are eliciting evaluations that people would not otherwise generate. This seems to us unlikely; our experience with public reactions to sentencing stories has been that people react quickly and with a high degree of confidence even to headlines of sentences in the news media (Doob & Roberts, 1983).

The construct of evaluation apprehension suggests an explanation for the pattern of results on confidence ratings. According to this perspective, subjects feel uneasy about acknowledging that they are anything but confident of their judgments. In the present research, this alternative explanation is refuted by the pattern of data: Evaluation apprehension should cause inflated confidence ratings for *all* judgments; for some sentences, however, subjects in our study did rate themselves as being very unsure of their evaluations. This implies that the confidence ratings were not simply the product of an experimental artifact.

In short, while these possible influences of demand cues and evaluation apprehension are important to consider, the naturalistic experimental task of reading newspaper articles, the ecologically valid subject population, and the overall pattern of results argue against an artifactual explanation of our findings.

The results of this study support several conclusions. First, the sentences people read about tend to be ones they would regard as too lenient. (We assume when making this statement that there was nothing atypical about the week preceding data collection. There are no grounds to believe that a rash of lenient dispositions arose during this particular week.) Either by the choice of cases reported or by the way in which the cases were described, the newspapers in our sample contribute to the view that sentences are too lenient. As well, notwithstanding the paucity of information contained in these stories, members of the public appear quite confident in their evaluations. This study also suggests that people's general beliefs about sentencing leniency may well influence their reactions to individual cases.

The information about sentencing conveyed by the newspapers supports the widespread public perception of judicial leniency. This suggests that if newspaper readers had more, or at least better, information at their disposal, they might have different views about sentencing. A serendipitous finding from Study 1 lends support to this argument. Two of the stories were different news accounts of the same sentencing hearing. Yet, although readers had been randomly assigned to read one or the other, readers of the tabloid newspaper's account of the case were significantly more likely than readers of the broadsheet account to rate the sentence as being too lenient, $\chi^2(2, N = 49) = 13.97, p < .05$. Thus the specific style and content of a news report of a sentencing hearing can shape perceptions of the sentence's leniency. In the next study, we describe an experiment in which this hypothesis is tested.

STUDY 2: EXPERIMENTAL COMPARISONS OF DIFFERENT STORIES

In this study, subjects were randomly assigned to read one of three different newspaper accounts of the same sentencing hearing. The aim was to evaluate the extent to which different news media accounts of criminal justice events affect public reactions. Two competing models of public opinion suggest themselves. One is that the public is concerned only with the relation between the sentence and the offense, and that additional material (such as would emerge in a sentencing hearing) is not relevant. This theory would suggest that knowing simply the sentence and the offense would suffice. The opposing theory suggests that the public, not unlike judges, maintains a complicated view of sentencing that takes numerous factors into account. According to this latter theory, different accounts of the same set of facts will have different impacts upon the readers. In this study (and in Study 3), we gave subjects different accounts of a sentencing hearing from different newspapers.

Method

Subjects

The subjects were visitors to the Ontario Science Centre. Of the 157 participants, 97 were male, 60 female. Once again, the majority (71%) were Canadian, but no significant differences emerged as a function of country of residence or gender.

Stimulus Materials

The case used was the sentencing of an offender convicted of the manslaughter of his wife. All three Toronto newspapers covered the sentencing hearing, and the actual newspaper articles were photocopied. The lengths of the stories from the three newspapers were 400, 410, and 750 words. The dependent variables were ratings of the appropriateness of the sentence in the case and also of sentences in general. Subjects were asked if they thought the judge had given proper weight to all relevant factors and to rate the importance of several sentencing purposes (viz., rehabilitation, general and individual deterrence, punishment and incapacitation). Definitions of each sentencing purpose were provided.

Procedure

Subjects were recruited in the same manner and participated in the same location as in the previous study. Subjects were randomly assigned to read one of the three versions of the case. After reading one account, subjects completed the questionnaire containing the dependent variables. The experiment took about 20 min to complete.

Results and Discussion

Consistent with the reactions to the sentencing stories in Study 1, most subjects in this study saw the sentence as being too lenient. On a 5-point scale (1 = *much too harsh;* 5 = *much too lenient*), the average rating collapsed across conditions was 4.28. More importantly, however, significant differences emerged in ratings of the appropriateness of the sentence as a function of the account read. The means for the three conditions were 4.12, 4.21, and 4.52, $F(2,153) = 5.29$, $p < .01$. Once again, the tabloid newspaper's story elicited greatest dissatisfaction with the sentence.

Given this last finding, it is not surprising that subjects assigned to read the tabloid newspaper's version were significantly more likely to think that the judge had *not* given weight to all relevant factors (means: 3.13; 3.36; 3.81), $F(2,153) = 5.34$, $p < .01$. There was also a significant effect on the question of whether sentences in general are appropriate (means: 3.76; 4.02; 4.08), $F(2,148)$[1] = 3.66, $p < .05$. With one exception,[2] there were no significant differences on the sentencing purpose questions. This result is in keeping with recent research suggesting that importance ratings of sentencing aims are unaffected by transitory manipulations such as exposure to a brief newspaper article (Roberts & Edwards, 1989).

The results of this study make it clear that the context is critical in determin-

---

[1] The reader will note occasional minor variations in the degrees of freedom associated with the statistical tests reported in this article. One of the costs of using members of the public rather than more meticulous college students as subjects is that they sometimes omit a dependent variable.

[2] There was a marginally significant ($p < .05$) result to the effect that readers of two newspapers provided higher importance ratings for incapacitation.

ing public reactions to sentences. The account of the hearing affects the evaluation that readers give the sentence. Readers appear to respond to much more than simply the offense and the few facts common to all three newspaper accounts. Second, the nature of the account also influences readers' evaluations of the judge. Finally, this experiment also produced evidence of a *generalizing* effect: The nature of the account of a single sentencing hearing affected the view that sentences in general are too lenient.

These findings raise several new questions. If reactions differ significantly from one news account to another, how would these subjects have reacted to the sentence if they had had more complete information at their disposal? What would have been their reaction to the sentence and the sentencer if they had been present in court throughout the entire sentencing hearing? In the third and final study reported here, we compared reactions to a media account of a sentencing hearing and reactions to a summary of actual court documents.

STUDY 3: COMPARISONS BETWEEN MEDIA VERSIONS AND OFFICIAL DOCUMENTS

Ideally, in order to effect a comparison between reactions to news media accounts and reactions to events as they unfold in the court, one would randomly assign people to either attend an actual sentencing hearing, or to read a newspaper account of the same hearing. This is somewhat impractical. Instead, in Study 3, subjects were randomly assigned to read either a news story or a summary of relevant court documents.

By using the mundane stories appearing in a typical week (Study 1), we failed to employ those few cases that draw more extensive media coverage. Apologists for the news media can argue that there is insufficient space or time for detailed coverage of garden-variety sentences. But when circumstances warrant greater attention, the news media can and do report the case in more detail. Accordingly, in this experiment we used a case that attracted a substantial degree of newspaper coverage. We also expanded the range of dependent variables to include ratings of the offender and the offense.

Method

Subjects

Subjects were 115 visitors to the Ontario Science Centre, 63 males and 52 females.

Stimulus Materials

The case selected for this experiment involved an offender convicted of assault causing bodily harm in London, Ontario. He had been sentenced to 21 months in prison. The selection of the case in a study of this nature is critical. If we employed a case in which an offender received an extremely lenient sentence, it would be unsurprising if readers of the newspaper version adopted this view. However, this was not the case with this particular sentence. In relation to Canadian sentencing practices for this crime, a sentence of 21 months is relatively severe. Statistics covering the time of the incident indicate that 90% of the custodial sentences for assault causing bodily harm were less than a year (Department of Justice, 1983).

The sentence was discussed in three lengthy articles in the London Free Press, totaling about 2,700 words. As with the previous study, the newspaper articles were reproduced to constitute the media version. London, Ontario, has only one daily newspaper; accordingly, comparisons between different publications were not possible.

In Study 3, we compared a single news media version and a summary of information from court documents. Materials for the court documents condition were a challenge to compile. First, a transcript of the sentencing hearing was obtained from the counsel for the accused. However, simply reproducing this document would have provided subjects with a confusing dialogue between the judge and counsel; much information from the trial proceedings was assumed by both sides in the exchanges. In addition, although the judge and crown and defense counsel had a copy of the offender's criminal record (and made references to it), the record had not been directly entered into the transcript. The same was true for the presentence report: References were made to it and all the parties had copies, but readers of the transcript would have little accurate idea of its contents. Finally, of course, although they were often alluded to, the details of the offense were also absent from the hearing transcript.

In order to provide the subjects with all the relevant information, a summary of the case was constructed, largely from quotes or paraphrases of actual documents. The offender's previous convictions were listed along with a brief description of the offense, the defense and crown arguments on sentencing, a summary of the presentence reports, and the final comments of the judge. The maximum penalty for the offense was noted. In order to prevent direct anchoring effects, this was accompanied by the following statement: "The courts have indicated that the maximum sentence should be reserved for the worst possible offender convicted of the worst possible example of the offense in question." This summary of court documents then comprised the stimulus materials for the second condition, the experimental analogue to actually attending the sentencing hearing. (Hereafter this condition will be referred to as the court documents condition.)

The questionnaire containing the account of the case also included four dependent variables. Subjects were asked to evaluate the *sentence* (the same questions as in previous studies), the *judge* (whether he had considered all the relevant factors), the *offender* (whether he was worse than the average offender), and the *offense* (whether it was a more or less serious case than the average assault causing bodily harm).

Procedure

Volunteer subjects were randomly assigned to read one of the two descriptions of the case. When they had finished reading, they were asked to complete the questionnaire containing the dependent measures. They were then thanked and debriefed. The study took approximately 30 min.

Results and Discussion

Analysis of the ratings showed systematically different perceptions of the same case between subjects who had read the media version and subjects who read the version based on court documents. For example, whereas 63% of the media condition subjects rated the sentence as being too lenient, only 19% of the court documents group shared this view, $\chi^2(2, N = 115) = 28.11, p < .001$. Results on the evaluation of the judge were similar: 46% of the media subjects thought he had not considered all the appropriate factors, compared to 24% of the court documents group, $\chi^2(2, N = 115) = 11.26, p < .001$. Significant differences also emerged on ratings of the relative seriousness of the offense and the offender: media condition subjects had more negative views of the offender (76% said he was worse than average compared to 36% in the court documents condition, $\chi^2(2, N = 115) = 19.20, p < .001$, and the offense, $\chi^2(2, N = 115) = 7.35, p < .01$. The results and the exact questions are presented in Table 2. Even when a newspaper presents a great deal of information about a particular sentencing hearing, people reading the news account are likely to receive a very different picture of all aspects of the case than they would have received had they read actual court documents.[3]

Replications of the Effect

Although the effects emerging from this experiment were in statistical terms very strong, they obviously derive from a single sentencing hearing. Using a single case raises questions of external validity; there may have been something atypical about this sentence. For instance, if this offender had received a very lenient sentence, this might explain the media/transcript differences without the necessity of a more general explanation that we favor. We have noted above that the sentence in this case was far from lenient, but it is possible that some other explanation exists to set this sentence apart. In any case, similar results emerged from two other studies (see Doob & Roberts, 1983) in which responses from subjects reading a transcript of the judge's reasons for sentencing were compared to responses from other subjects reading newspaper versions of the same case. For example, in one case involving a white-collar crime (and using 140 subjects) the following pattern of means emerged using a 5-point sentence evaluation scale (where 1 = *too harsh;* 5 = *too lenient*): transcript = 2.85; Newspaper A = 2.83; Newspaper B = 3.40, $F(2,139) = 8.52, p < .001$. (In this case, the significant

---

[3] The offender in this case launched a successful appeal against his sentence. The decision of the Ontario Court of Appeal was to reduce the sentence from 21 months to one year. Readers of the newspaper account of the original sentence were probably outraged at what they would perceive to be further leniency by the courts. This might be taken as further evidence of the gap between courts and public except that the Court of Appeal decision is clearly in step with public opinion *based upon court documents.*

TABLE 2. Study 3: Ratings of Sentence, Judge, Offender, and Offense by Experimental Condition[a]

Experimental condition[b]				
	Evaluation of sentence[c]			
	Too harsh	About right	Too lenient	Total
Court documents	52	29	19	100%
Newspaper	13	24	63	100%
	Did judge consider all factors?[d]			
	Yes	Cannot say	No	Total
Court documents	59	17	24	100%
Newspaper	29	25	46	100%
	Evaluation of offender[e]			
	Better than average	Average	Worse than average	Total
Court documents	22	42	36	100%
Newspaper	7	17	76	100%
	Evaluation of offense[f]			
	Less serious than average	Average	More serious than average	Total
Court documents	30	46	24	100%
Newspaper	20	32	48	100%

[a] All chi-squares $p < .01$
[b] $n = 115$.
[c] Question: "What do you think of the sentence (21 months in prison) given to [offender's name] for the offense of assault causing bodily harm?"
[d] Question: "Do you think the judge considered and gave proper weight to all of the appropriate factors in deciding the sentence?"
[e] Question: "Compared to other people sentenced for criminal offenses, how bad a criminal do you think [offender's name] was at the time of his sentencing?"
[f] Question: "Compared to other cases where people are found guilty of assault causing bodily harm, how serious do you feel the actual sentence was?"

difference arose between the transcript and one newspaper on the one hand and a second newspaper on the other.) Thus the experimental effect uncovered in Experiment 3 would not appear to be restricted to the assault causing bodily harm case. Finally, the first author has conducted two unreported replications using the same stimulus materials from Study 3 with college students as subjects. On both occasions the same media/transcript differences emerged on all dependent measures.

Members of the public, it would appear, are often getting information about the sentences of the court that leads them to believe that sentences are too lenient. These same people, when given access to more extensive accounts of sentences, are more content with the judges' decisions. Public opinion about sentencing is more likely to be shaped indirectly by the news media than directly by events as they occur in courts. In short, people appear to be reacting not only to the actual sentence (which in these experiments was constant across different accounts) but also to the context in which the sentence is placed.

SUMMARY AND GENERAL DISCUSSION

This series of studies examined the role of the news media in promoting the perception that the courts are insufficiently harsh towards convicted offenders. In the first study, subjects received accounts of sentencing hearings that appeared, during one week, in Toronto newspapers. These stories were generally short and provided little information about the offense, the offender, or the judicial reasoning underlying the sentence. Ratings of the stories indicated that subjects were generally confident about making judgments of the reported sentences, the majority of which were rated as being too lenient. Subsequent experiments demonstrated the importance of the context in which sentences are placed. In Study 2, accounts of the same sentencing hearing by different newspapers had variable effects upon subjects' ratings of the sentence. Finally, in our third study, comparisons of ratings by subjects who read a transcript summary with the reactions of others who read news media accounts of the same sentence revealed that those who read the news media account had more negative views of the judge, the offense, the offender, and the sentence. This effect was replicated with different offenses and other subject populations.

The Impact of Media Misinformation

We have noted that people get most of their information about sentencing from the news media and that the majority of the public in Canada, the United States, and elsewhere endorse the view that sentences are too lenient. Now we may speculate as to the consequences—upon public opinion, and ultimately sentencing policy—of the generally poor news media coverage of sentencing.

First, however, it is important to locate the perception of leniency in the context of public perceptions of other criminal justice issues. The fact that most people want harsher sentences does not necessarily mean that they are punitive in all respects. When people respond to a question about sentences in general, they are usually thinking of violent offenders. The reason for this is apparent: When people think about crime, they think about the violent crimes they have learned about from the mass media. Some recent opinion poll data make this clear. In 1986, a representative sample of Canadian adults was asked what type of offender they had in mind when evaluating sentences (Canadian Sentencing Commission, 1987). Table 3 presents a cross-tabulation of responses to this question with responses to the question about sentencing severity. This table shows that violent offenders, who in fact constitute only a small minority of all offenders sentenced in Canada, are most salient for respondents. Consistent with this view is the

PUBLIC ATTITUDES, MEDIA, AND SENTENCING

Table 3. Type of Offender Subject Was Thinking of and View of Sentences Generally[a]

View of sentences[c]	Type of offender[b]				Total[e]
	Violent	Repeat	Various	All[d]	
About right or too harsh	21	10	29	39	100%
Too lenient	45	18	6	31	100%

[a] χ^2 (3, N = 1008) = 103, p < .01. Data obtained from a nationwide Gallup poll (see Doob & Roberts, 1983).
[b] Exact question: "What type of criminal were you thinking of when you answered this last question?"
[c] Exact question: "In general, would you say that the sentences handed down by the courts are too severe, about right, or not severe enough?"
[d] Includes juveniles, first offenders, and property offenders.
[e] Excludes 5% who did not respond.

finding that when asked to recall an offense resulting in a lenient sentence, 42% of respondents to the same poll recalled a homicide, 23% a sexual assault, and 9% a nonsexual assault—all high-frequency crimes in terms of media reporting. It is also the case that Canadians substantially overestimate the recidivism rates of both property offenders and offenders convicted of crimes of violence (Doob & Roberts, 1983; Roberts & White, 1986).

All these findings suggest that the public may not necessarily favor a sentencing policy that is universally more punitive. To interpret opinion polls as connoting this would be to adopt an erroneous interpretation. When Canadians were asked their opinions about the most effective way to control crime, the most popular crime prevention strategy—even among respondents who believed sentences to be too lenient—was to reduce unemployment. In addition, a comparison of the types of sentences members of the public say they want for specific offenses with the types of sentences actually handed down reveals that they do not differ dramatically (Roberts & Doob, 1989). Other research coming at these issues from a somewhat different perspective leads to a similar conclusion. Diamond (1989) found that members of the public (in her case, people who had been called for jury duty) recommended sentences for hypothetical defendants that were very similar to those sentences recommended by practicing judges who responded to the same material.

Findings such as these could be used to support recommendations such as those made recently by Morris and Tonry (1990). They note that quite independently of the *overall* level of severity of sentences, the types of sentences assigned in particular cases may be inappropriate. Morris and Tonry suggest that in many jurisdictions there should be an increased use of intermediate punishments—punishments less severe than imprisonment, but more punishing than simple probation. But policy makers may be reluctant to endorse or adopt such recommendations for fear that they would lead to even greater public dissatisfaction with sentencing decisions because of the apparent reduction in severity of some sentences.

As we have noted, intermediate punishments are rarely reported in the news media. Hence one cannot expect members of the public to consider them when thinking about what would be an appropriate sentence in a particular case. However, we have discovered that when these intermediate punishments are made salient, the desire to imprison diminishes significantly (Doob & Roberts, 1983, 1988). Furthermore, the Canadian public appears to prefer to invest in the increased use of intermediate punishments rather than to invest in the building of new prisons (Doob & Roberts, 1988).

How then are policy makers in the area of sentencing to interpret public opinion in light of our findings and those of others regarding the news media? If asked simple questions about sentences currently being imposed, Canadians and residents of several other countries indicate that they think that sentences are too lenient. Policy makers should realize that this view reflects the selection and quality of information the public receives from the news media. The policy maker who blindly follows superficially expressed responses to a single poll's questions would advocate an increase in the severity of sentences. However, the overall pattern of our findings suggests that much current public dissatisfaction with sentencing is based upon media misinformation about general and specific sentencing practices.

The news media are the public's main source of information about sentencing. An examination of crime-related and sentencing-specific information in our news media makes it clear that sentences as described in our news media do not give an adequate picture of sentences as handed down in court. Interestingly enough, the Canadian public appears to be aware of this fact. In 1986, a majority of a national sample of Canadians answered no to the question "Are the news media, in your view, providing the public with adequate information about sentencing?" (Doob & Roberts, 1988).

In many jurisdictions, sentencing policy and practice have been evaluated carefully. One uniform conclusion from all of these studies is that sentencing is a complex phenomenon in need of careful analysis. The mass media, in reporting individual sentences handed down in individual cases as if the issues involved were very simple, do not appear to present sentences in a manner that allows members of the public to draw reasonable conclusions about sentencing. It is the naive, dishonest, or cynical policy maker, then, who recommends increased harshness in overall sentencing policy on the basis of simple assertions about sentencing made in response to simple questions.

APPENDIX A

An example of the newspaper stories used in Study 1: Of the 25 subjects rating this story, 1% stated that the sentence was too harsh, 4% rated it as about right, and 95% rated it as too lenient.

MAN SENT UP FOR ASSAULT ON GIRL, 9

A Toronto man who sexually assaulted a nine-year girl he lured from a schoolyard has been sent to prison for five years.

Douglas Gerald Trache, 25, of Blake St., pleaded not guilty to buggery in the Oct. 4 incident but was found guilty by an Ontario Supreme Court jury.

Trache did not testify at his trial.

The girl, now 10, was waiting for a friend at Blake Public School when Trache approached her and identified himself as an undercover policeman.

He showed her a card with his picture on it and said he had to get her out of the area. They walked to the Rosedale ravine behind Castle Frank Cres. where she was attacked. He threatened to strangle her if she told what had happened.

"It's every parent's nightmare," Crown prosecutor Jim Ramsay told Mr. Justice John Osler. "He brutally robbed her of her childhood."

The assault was "painful and revolting," the judge said, adding "no one can tell what lasting damage may have been done."

REFERENCES

Broadhurst, R., & Indermaur, D. (1982). Crime seriousness ratings: The relationship of information accuracy and general attitudes in Western Australia. *Australia and New Zealand Journal of Criminology, 15*, 219–234.

Canadian Sentencing Commission (1987). *Sentencing reform: A Canadian approach*. Ottawa: Canadian Government Publishing Centre.

Canadian Sentencing Commission (1988). *Sentencing in the media: A content analysis of English-language newspapers in Canada*. Research reports of the Canadian Sentencing Commission. Ottawa: Department of Justice, Canada.

Department of Justice, Canada (1983). *Sentencing practices and trends in Canada: A summary of statistical information*. Ottawa: Department Justice, Canada.

Diamond, S. S. (1989) Using psychology to control law: From deceptive advertising to criminal sentencing. *Law and Human Behavior, 13*, 239–252.

Doob, A. N. (1985). *The many realities of crime*. In A. N. Doob & E. L. Greenspan (Eds)., *Perspectives in criminal law*. Aurora, Ontario: Canada Law Book.

Doob, A. N., & Roberts, J. V. (1982). *Crime: Some views of the Canadian public*. Ottawa: Department of Justice, Canada.

Doob, A. N., & Roberts, J. V. (1983). *An analysis of the public's view of sentencing*. Ottawa: Department of Justice, Canada.

Doob, A. N., & Roberts, J. V. (1984). Social psychology, social attitudes, and attitudes toward sentencing. *Canadian Journal of Behavioural Science, 16*, 269–280.

Doob, A. N., & Roberts, J. V. (1988). Public punitiveness and public knowledge of the facts: Some Canadian surveys. In N. Walker and M. Hough (Eds.), *Public attitudes to sentencing: Surveys from five countries*. Aldershot, England: Gower.

Dussuyer, I. (1979). *Crime news: A study of 40 Ontario newspapers*. Toronto: Centre of Criminology, University of Toronto.

Flanagan, T. J., McGarrell, E. F., & Brown, E. J. (1985). Public perceptions of the criminal courts: The role of demographic and related attitudinal variables. *Journal of Research in Crime and Delinquency, 22*, 66–82.

Gordon, J. T., & Heath, L. (1981). The news business, crime and fear. In D. A. Lewis (Ed.), *Reactions to crime*. Beverly Hills, CA: Sage.

Graber, D. A. (1980) *Crime news and the public*. New York: Praeger.

Hamill, R., Wilson, T. D., & Nisbett, R. E. (1980). Insensitivity to sample bias: Generalizing from atypical cases. *Journal of Personality and Social Psychology, 39*, 578–589.

Hough, M., & Moxon, D. (1985). Dealing with offenders: Public opinion and the views of victims—Findings from the British crime survey. *Howard Journal of Criminal Justice, 24*, 160–175.

Indermaur, D. (1987). Public perception of sentencing in Perth, Western Australia. *Australian and New Zealand Journal of Criminology, 20*, 163–183.

Law Reform Commission—Australia (1988). *Sentencing* (Report No. 44). Canberra: Australian Government Publishing Service.

Morris, N., & Tonry, M. (1990). *Between prison and probation: Intermediate punishments in a rational sentencing system*. New York: Oxford.

Roberts, J. V., & Doob, A. N. (1989). Sentencing and public opinion: Taking false shadows for true substances. *Osgoode Hall Law Journal, 27*, 491–515.

Roberts, J. V., & Edwards, D. (1989). Contextual effects in judgements of crimes, criminals and the purposes of sentencing. *Journal of Applied Social Psychology, 19*, 902–917.

Roberts, J. V., & White, N. R. (1986). Public estimates of recidivism rates: Consequences of a criminal stereotype. *Canadian Journal of Criminology, 28*, 229–241.

Standing Committee on Justice and Solicitor General (1988). *Taking responsibility: Report of the Standing Committee on Justice and Solicitor General on its review of sentencing, conditional release and related aspects of corrections.* Ottawa: House of Commons.

Surette, R. (1984). *Justice and the media.* Springfield, IL: C. C. Thomas.

Tversky, A., & Kahneman, D. (1973). Availability: A heuristic for judging frequency and probability. *Cognitive Psychology, 5*, 207–232.

Verdun-Jones, S., & Mitchell-Banks, T. (1988). *The fine as a sentencing option in Canada.* Research Reports of The Canadian Sentencing Commission. Ottawa: Department of Justice, Canada.

Walker, N., & Hough, M. (1988). *Public attitudes to sentencing: Surveys from five countries.* Cambridge Studies in Criminology, LIX. Aldershot, England: Gower.

United Kingdom (1990). *Crime, justice and protecting the public: The government's proposal for legislation.* London: HMSO.

U.S. Sentencing Commission (1987). *Manual: Sentencing guidelines.* Washington, DC: U.S. Sentencing Commission.

FOUR
Effects of Framing on Attributions of Responsibility for Crime and Terrorism

On the surface, crime and terrorism appear to be similar political issues because both entail threats to public security. Crime, however, is the more immediate danger and, for many, is a matter of intense personal experience, providing a dramatic connection between everyday life and the affairs of society at large. The threat posed by terrorism is generally distant and remote. Indeed, terrorism is the prototypical mediated issue, public awareness is limited to scenes of aircraft hijackings, hostage situations, bombings, and similar dramas played out in the mass media. Though spectacular, these events are of little direct personal relevance.

Differences in the relative obtrusiveness of the two issues has important implications for the framing hypothesis. Because crime is a real personal threat, citizens were expected to have more intimate familiarity with the issue, and attributions of responsibility for crime were expected to be less responsive to contextual cues such as framing. In contrast, because terrorism is associated with poorly understood disputes in distant locales and with ideological conflicts, attributions of responsibility for terrorism were expected to be highly responsive to framing. In short, media influence on attribution was expected to be more powerful for terrorism than for crime.

How Television News Frames Crime and Terrorism

Crime and terrorism, especially the latter, were at the forefront of the networks' issue agenda in the 1980s. Some eleven hundred news re-

Responsibility for Crime and Terrorism

ports on crime and more than two thousand reports on terrorism were aired by ABC, CBS, and NBC between 1981 and 1986. The average of eleven stories on terrorism per month for each network represented an unusually intense degree of coverage. Between 1981 and 1986, more stories were broadcast on terrorism than on poverty, unemployment, racial inequality, and crime combined. Hijackings, hostage situations, and similar events have been emblazoned on the public consciousness.

The networks framed crime and terrorism almost exclusively in episodic terms (see figure 4.1). Eight-nine percent of all news stories on crime fell into this "police-blotter" format.[1] Within both the thematic and episodic categories, the news tended to focus on violent crime. Thus, the focus of the typical news report was a specific individual (perpetrator or victim) and a violent criminal act.

Although news coverage of terrorism was slightly more thematic than coverage for crime, episodic reports still outnumbered thematic reports by a ratio of three to one: 74 percent of all news stories on terrorism consisted of live reports of some specific terrorist act, group, victim, or event, while 26 percent consisted of reports that discussed terrorism as a general political problem (see appendix A). These results are consistent with prior content analyses performed by others, which identified a strong "event" bias in network treatment of terrorism.[2] These researchers have speculated that the event bias and the concomitant inattention to general, background information occurs because of the dramatic qualities of news stories on terrorist acts. As Altheide argues:

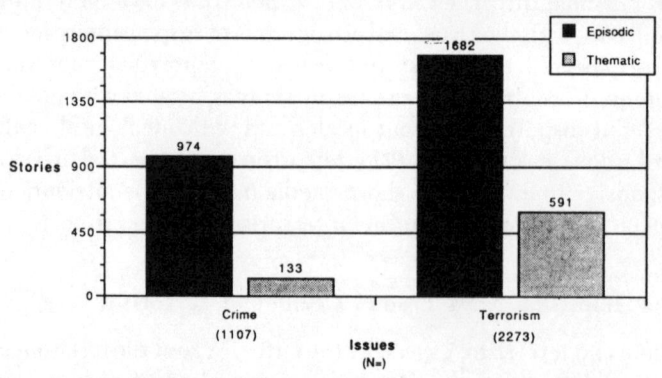

Fig. 4.1 Episodic and Thematic Coverage of Crime and Terrorism, 1981–86

Chapter Four

> Television reports that rely on visuals of an event will be more entertaining to an audience, yet provide little useful narrative interpretation to understand the broader issue. As long as more dramatic visuals are associated with the tactics and aftermath of terrorism, these aspects will be stressed over the larger issues of history, goals, and rationale.[3]

Episodic and thematic treatments of terrorism were examined within specific subject matter categories. Episodic reports were classified by the nationality of the subject individual(s), group(s), or organization(s). Third-world nationals accounted for 51 percent of episodic stories; within this group, Middle Easterners received the most attention, followed by Central Americans. Western terrorists were also the subject of extensive coverage, accounting for 34 percent of episodic stories.

Thirty-three percent of the thematic news reports focused on the U.S. government's counter-terrorist efforts. The remaining thematic stories were widely scattered in subject matter focus.

Who Is Responsible?

Crime elicited the highest average number of causal and treatment attributions of responsibility (2.7 and 2.1 per respondent, respectively) of any of the issues examined (see figure 4.2). Presumably, people had more to say about crime because crime is more of a "doorstep" issue than terrorism, poverty, unemployment, or racial inequality.

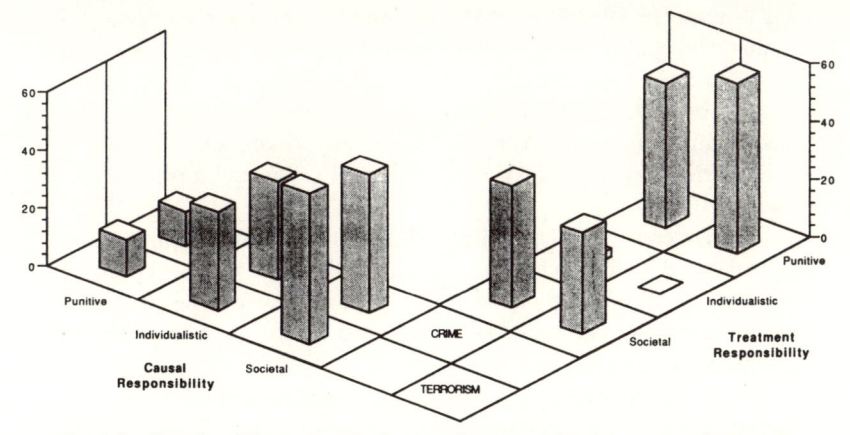

Fig. 4.2 Causal and Treatment Attribution of Responsibility for Crime and Terrorism

28

Responsibility for Crime and Terrorism

Causal responsibility for both crime and terrorism was assigned to the individuals who commit criminal or terrorist acts, to a variety of societal conditions, and to a lack of adequate punitive policies.[4] Individualistic attributions for crime consisted of two causal themes—character deficiencies (such as greed, personality disorders, and the desire to avoid working) and inadequate education and employment skills. Individualistic attributions for terrorism consisted exclusively of character references, primarily political fanaticism and associated personality traits, such as lack of concern for human life and a craving for power. The level of individualistic attributions of causal responsibility was virtually identical for crime and terrorism (38 and 34 percent, respectively).

References to society in causal attributions for crime and terrorism consisted of two opposing themes. Participants either referred to a variety of social, economic, or political conditions that fostered crime and terrorism or to society's failure to punish adequately those who engage in criminal or terrorist acts. The former category was labelled societal causal responsibility, and the latter punitive causal responsibility.

Attributions of societal causal responsibility for crime included references to economic conditions, discrimination, racial inequality, poverty, and cultural institutions. The category of cultural institutions was reserved for responses that cited the role of the mass media and the entertainment industry in glamorizing crime and legitimizing the use of violence. Societal causes of terrorism included economic and political oppression, the actions and policies of the U.S. government (including support for Israel, insufficient economic aid to underprivileged nations, siding with repressive leaders, and realpolitik), global politics (such as meddling by the superpowers and other nations, most notably, Libya), and local political turmoil (including breakdown of institutions, political strife, and lack of strong leadership). Societal attributions represented 48 and 52 percent of all attributions of causal responsibility for crime and terrorism, respectively.

Punitive causal responsibility—the argument that people engage in crime and terrorism because they are able to avoid severe punishment—was infrequently mentioned. Approximately 10 percent of all causal responses for both issues referred to the lack of adequate punitive measures.

Respondents assigned treatment responsibility for both crime and terrorism almost exclusively to society in general. Very few responses

Chapter Four

implied that self-improvement was an appropriate treatment, indicating that apparently individuals do not view criminals and terrorists as able or willing to mend their ways. Thus, the prescription for crime and terrorism was almost exclusively improvements in the underlying socioeconomic and political order (societal treatment responsibility), or the imposition of stricter and more certain punishment (punitive treatment responsibility).

Societal treatments suggested for crime included reductions in poverty and inequality, rehabilitative and educational programs, and an improved economy. Respondents also cited heightened public awareness ("form neighborhood crime-prevention groups"; "educate people on ways to avoid being a victim") as a potential treatment. These four categories made up 42 percent of all crime treatments mentioned. In the case of terrorism, suggested societal treatments included resolution of terrorists' political grievances, putting an end to oppression, the use of more responsive methods of negotiating with terrorists, and greater public awareness (for example, "provide tourists with information regarding political conditions"). Societal responsibility accounted for 35 percent of the treatment responses directed at terrorism.

The dominant prescription for both issues (both in terms of content and frequency) called for the imposition of more severe retaliation or punishment against terrorists and criminals (punitive treatment responsibility). This category accounted for nearly 66 percent of all treatment responses for terrorism and 50 percent of all treatment responses directed at crime.

The degree to which causal and treatment responses corresponded within each issue was also examined by constructing dichotomized "net" causal and treatment responsibility scores. In the case of causal responsibility, low scores indicate a tendency to cite individual characteristics or inadequate punishment as causes; high scores indicate a tendency to assign causal responsibility to prevailing societal conditions. In the case of treatment responsibility, low scores represent a preference for attributions of punitive responsibility, while high scores represent a preference for attributions of societal responsibility (see appendix B).

By combining the causal and treatment responsibility scores, a four-fold typology was identified, as follows:

1. Deterrence model: individual tendencies and insufficient pun-

Responsibility for Crime and Terrorism

ishment cause crime and terrorism; stronger punishment of criminals and terrorists is the treatment.
2. Societal model: inadequate societal conditions cause crime and terrorism; improvements in societal conditions are the treatment.
3. Guardianship model: individual tendencies and insufficient punishment are the primary causal factors; improvements in societal conditions are the treatment.
4. Punitive model: inadequate societal conditions cause crime and terrorism; stronger punishment is the appropriate treatment.

Figure 4.3 shows the number and percentage of participants falling within each of the above models. For both issues, the deterrence model was applied most frequently and, in the case of crime, attracted close to 50 percent of the sample. The societal and guardianship models were applied to terrorism more frequently (by small margins) than to crime. The punitive model of responsibility attracted less than 20 percent of the sample for both issues. Overall, the pattern of causal and treatment responsibility for crime and terrorism was similar.[5]

Experimental Tests of Framing

Terrorism Experiment 1

This study was essentially an exploratory probe of individuals' causal attributions. The experimental manipulation focused on a specific terrorist event—the hijacking of TWA Flight 847 and the ensuing hostage situation in Beirut.[6] Following the release of the hostages, all three networks broadcast detailed recapitulations of the

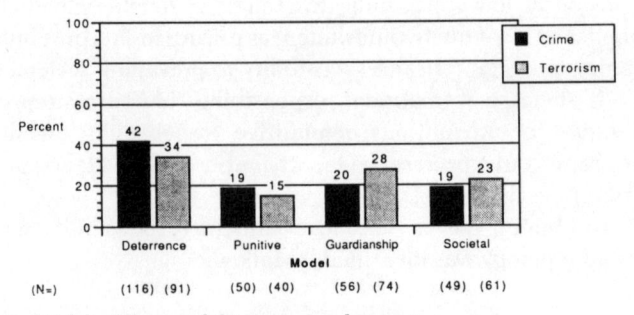

Fig. 4.3 Models of Responsibility: Crime and Terrorism

Chapter Four

crisis. The ABC report was edited into three very different versions. Two of the reports embodied a thematic frame, while the third represented the more frequently encountered episodic frame.

The first thematic framing condition, "U.S. Foreign Policy," interpreted the hijacking incident as an act of political protest against U.S. foreign policy. The report commented on the role of the United States as a traditional ally of Israel and the hijackers' demands that Israel release Lebanese citizens held as political prisoners. President Reagan was then shown declaring that the United States would never negotiate with terrorists.

The second thematic-framing condition, "Local Turmoil," examined the incident exclusively within the context of Lebanese political strife. The report discussed the breakdown of governmental authority and the rise of various Lebanese paramilitary organizations, including Amal, the Shiite organization holding the hostages. The group's ideology was described, and its growing influence noted. This condition made no reference to the United States, to Israel, or to the broader Middle East conflict.

The third condition was designed as a noninterpretive, episodic frame—"Hostages Released." The report merely announced the release of the hostages. Individual hostages were seen greeting each other prior to departing from Beirut. Some of the former hostages commented on their health and their treatment in captivity. This condition provided no particular perspective on the hijacking incident beyond describing the eventual outcome.

Finally, a fourth, "control" condition was added to the design. Individuals assigned to this condition saw no news of the TWA hijacking. In place of the hijacking, they watched a story describing recent developments in the U.S. space program.

The major objective of this study was to examine the possibility that alternative news frames for the identical act of terrorism might induce shifts in attributions of responsibility. First, it was expected that thematic framing would induce viewers to attribute responsibility for terrorism to societal factors while episodic framing was expected to contribute to higher levels of individual or punitive responsibility. In addition, it was anticipated that viewers in the control condition would seize upon individual responsibility in their explanations of terrorism—the terrorist's fanaticism, evil intent, amorality, and other related traits. This prediction was derived from attribution theory, which suggests that people typically exaggerate the role of in-

32

Responsibility for Crime and Terrorism

dividuals' motives and intentions and simultaneously discount the role of contextual factors when attributing responsibility for individuals' actions, a tendency that psychologists have dubbed "the fundamental attribution error."[7]

In order to examine framing effects on attributions of causal responsibility for terrorism, indices of societal, punitive, and individualistic responsibility were computed corresponding to the number of responses that referred to these themes divided by the total number of responses (fig. 4.4). In the case of societal causal responsibility, for example, the index was the percentage of causal attributions citing political oppression or other societal factors (see appendix B). The use of such a standardized indicator of attribution served to neutralize possible differences in respondents' writing ability, locquacity, political interest, and related skills.

The degree to which attributions of causal responsibility for terrorism were affected by the particular news frame is shown in figure 4.4. As expected, societal attributions were least prominent when the hijacking was framed in episodic terms, and the episodic condition differed significantly from the thematic Local Turmoil condition (see

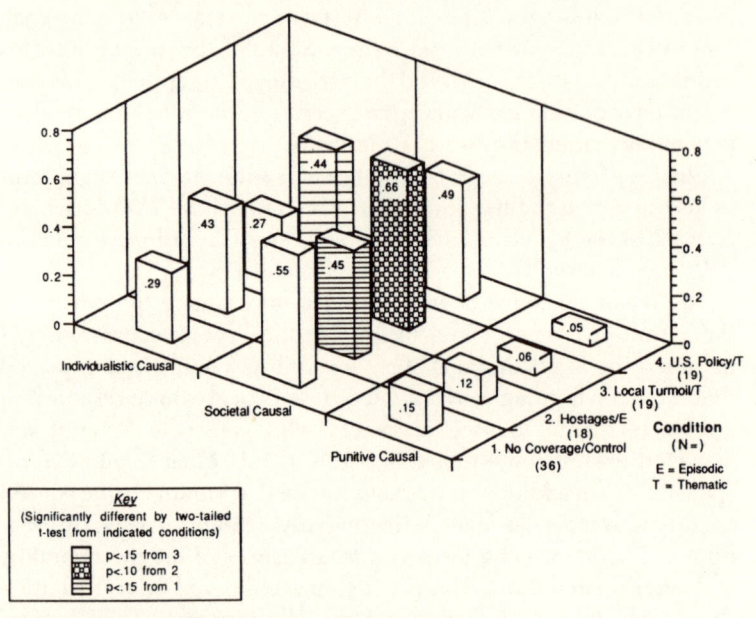

Fig. 4.4 Framing Effects: Terrorism Experiment 1

Chapter Four

appendix B). Contrary to expectations, however, the two thematic conditions did not elicit an equivalent pattern of responses. The frequency of individualistic attributions was highest in the thematic U.S. Foreign Policy condition and lowest in the thematic Local Turmoil condition. As a result, the two thematic conditions differed significantly in the level of individualistic attributions.[8]

Another surprising result was that individuals in the control condition attributed causal responsibility to society rather than to the individual terrorist. Rather than making the "fundamental attribution error," individuals who were given no information about terrorism tended to think of the issue as a product of social or political problems.

Finally, there were no differences between the four conditions in the proportion of viewers citing punitive responsibility. The level of punitive treatment responsibility did not exceed 15 percent in any of the experimental conditions.

Thus the results from the initial study are at least suggestive of network framing. Thematic framing of terrorism that placed an airplane hijacking in the context of local political upheaval raised the prominence of societal causal attributions. When the same hijacking was framed in episodic terms, characteristics of individual terrorists were at the forefront of viewers' attributions.

Terrorism Experiment 2

The second terrorism study was designed as a broader replication of the initial results. Seven conditions were established, three of which represented thematic framing and four episodic. All three thematic framing conditions were directed, in varying degrees and contexts, at U.S. governmental policies. Three of the four episodic framing conditions focused on terrorist acts in the Third World, while the fourth described a terrorist bombing in Great Britain.

The first thematic framing condition, "U.S. Counter-Terrorism Policy," described President Reagan's recently announced "war on terrorism." The report covered several policy options under consideration, ranging from economic sanctions against governments aiding terrorists to military reprisals. The reporter noted that a "tough" stance on terrorism had bipartisan congressional support. President Reagan was shown on screen declaring that he was "determined to fight this new barbarism."

Responsibility for Crime and Terrorism

The two other thematic framing conditions dealt with two particular regional hotbeds of terrorist activity. In the "Middle East–Thematic" condition, the anchor began by reporting an Israeli bombing raid against Lebanese villages said (by the Israelis) to be terrorist havens. The report then discussed the increasing internal strife in Lebanon following the Israeli invasion of that country. An Israeli government spokesman was asked questions concerning the policy of military retaliation and emphatically declared that Israel's actions were consistent with U.S. objectives in the region.

In the third thematic condition, "Central America–Thematic," the anchor began with the disclosure that the U.S.-backed Contra forces had distributed a "terrorism manual" to their units that had been allegedly prepared with Central Intelligence Agency collaboration. The report then surveyed the state of the Nicaraguan civil war, noting the high level of noncombatant casualties inflicted by both sides. A Contra spokesman denied charges that the Contras had made attacks against civilians. A prominent congressman reacted to the charges by noting that U.S. support for terrorist activity in Central America would be a foreign policy "disaster."

Three of the four episodic conditions focused on Third World participants. In the first such condition, "Arab Hijacker," the report described the hijacking of an Egypt Air plane and the subsequent assault on the aircraft by Egyptian commandoes, resulting in the deaths of sixty passengers, including several Americans. Two survivors described their ordeal. The reporter stated that the alleged hijacker was "Arab" and that a Libyan-backed splinter group of the Palestine Liberation Organization had claimed responsibility for the hijacking.

The second episodic-coverage condition, "Sikh Saboteurs," described the crash of a Air India Boeing 747 under mysterious circumstances, prompting widespread suspicion that a bomb had been placed on board by Sikh extremists. The two principal suspects, both active in the Sikh separatist movement, were described. The report ended with film of militant Sikhs demonstrating in New Delhi against the Indian government.

The third episodic condition, "Central American Insurgents," described the killing of six Americans, including three off-duty marines by "The Front for National Liberation" in San Salvador. Witnesses described the attack, the bodies of the victims were shown on screen, and the reporter noted the increasing frequency of such terrorist attacks in El Salvador.

35

Chapter Four

Finally, the fourth episodic condition, "IRA Bombers," consisted of a report on an Irish Republican Army plot to kill Prime Minister Thatcher and several members of her cabinet. A Scotland Yard official announced the discovery of several sophisticated explosive devices at the site of the annual Conservative Party conference and described efforts to trace the IRA members involved. A cabinet member commented on the increasing dangers of holding public office in Great Britain.

In summary, the design of the second terrorism study was faithful to the major undercurrents of network news coverage—U.S. policy toward terrorism in the case of thematic framing and the Middle East, Central America, and Western Europe, as the principal arenas of terrorist activity in the case of episodic framing. The results of this study are shown in figure 4.5.

The three thematic conditions yielded similar and generally low levels of individualistic causal attributions but differed among themselves in the level of societal attributions. The Middle East–Thematic condition elicited the highest level of societal causal at-

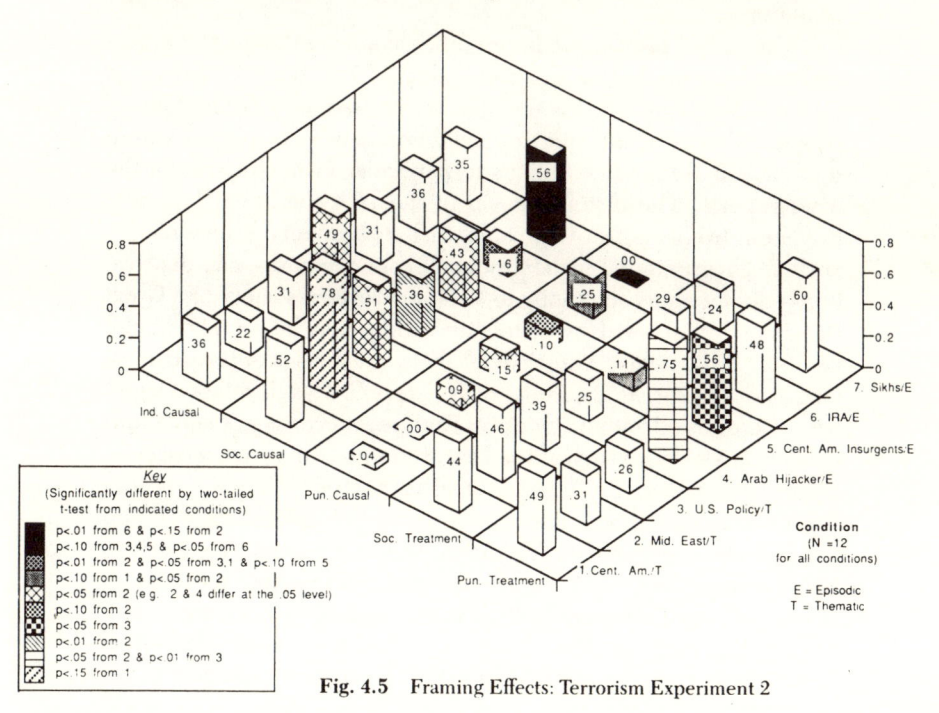

Fig. 4.5 Framing Effects: Terrorism Experiment 2

Responsibility for Crime and Terrorism

tributions (78 percent) and differed significantly from both other thematic conditions. The Middle East–Thematic condition also elicited significantly fewer references to punitive causal responsibility than the U.S. Counter-Terrorism Policy thematic condition. The three thematic conditions elicited a uniform pattern of responses for attributions of treatment responsibility. Thematic framing tended to polarize treatment responses; in all three thematic conditions, the ratio of punitive to societal treatment responses was roughly equal.

The episodic conditions proved diverse in their effects on causal attributions but were homogeneous in their effects on treatment attributions. The IRA Bombers condition elicited a distinctively high proportion (25 percent) of punitive causal attributions and a correspondingly low proportion of societal causal attributions. The Sikh Saboteurs condition had precisely the opposite effect, drawing extensive attributions of societal causal responsibility and, despite the large number of people killed, no reference whatsoever to inadequate punitive measures. In this latter respect, the Sikh Saboteurs condition differed significantly from the three remaining episodic conditions.

Because the episodic conditions differed among themselves in several respects (including the nationality of the terrorist group or individual(s), depicted, the terrorist tactic used, and the number of people killed), it is difficult to trace differences in responses within the episodic framing conditions to particular characteristics of the news reports. The distinctiveness of the IRA condition, however, may stem from the fact that contextual antecedents of terrorism—such as governmental instability and economic and social deprivation—do not apply so readily to a stable Western society like Great Britain. In other words, societal attributions may be prominent elements of individuals' "knowledge" about the causes of terrorism so long as the terrorists are from non-Western or less-developed countries. Confronted with instances of European terrorism, people turn to alternative causes such as the lack of adequate punitive measures.

Notwithstanding the preceding idiosyncratic differences within the episodic conditions, the overall pattern of differences between the episodic and thematic conditions provided strong evidence in support of framing. All four episodic conditions elicited lower levels of societal causal attributions than at least one of the thematic conditions, and all four episodic conditions pulled higher levels of punitive causal attributions than at least one of the thematic conditions. In the

Chapter Four

case of treatment responsibility, the Arab Hijacker condition induced a significantly higher level of punitive responsibility than two of the three thematic framing conditions. In addition, the Central American Insurgents condition elicited significantly fewer societal attributions than two of the thematic conditions and significantly more punitive attributions than the U.S. Counter-Terrorism Policy thematic condition. All told, differences between the episodic and thematic framing conditions far outnumbered differences within either category. There were seventeen statistically significant "inter-frame" differences, compared with only eight significant "intra-frame" differences. Figure 4.6 shows the effects of framing in this study by comparing the aggregated data from the thematic conditions with the aggregated data from the episodic conditions.

Collectively, the episodic and thematic framing conditions made for sharply diverging patterns of causal and treatment attributions. Causal attributions were primarily individualistic and punitive when the networks framed terrorism as a specific terrorist act; they were primarily societal when the networks framed terrorism as a general problem. Attributions of treatment responsibility were also strongly influenced by framing. Episodic framing elicited a much more one-sided distribution (in the direction of punitive responsibility) of responses than did thematic framing; the ratio of punitive to societal

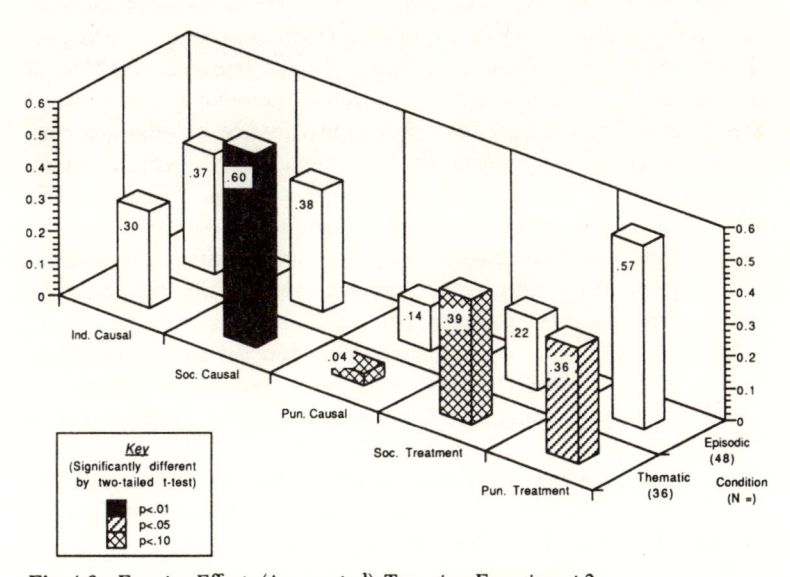

Fig. 4.6 Framing Effects (Aggregated): Terrorism Experiment 2

Responsibility for Crime and Terrorism

treatment attributions was nearly three to one under episodic framing but only one to one following thematic framing.

Finally, it is revealing to compare differences in the particular combinations of causal and treatment responsibility expressed following thematic and episodic framing of terrorism. Under conditions of episodic framing, 64 percent of viewers were found to fit the deterrence model of responsibility (individual causes coupled with punitive treatments) compared with only 33 percent of viewers in the thematic conditions. The discrepancy was even greater in the case of the societal model (societal causal and treatment responsibility). While this model attracted 25 percent of the participants in the thematic conditions, it accounted for only 5 percent of the sample in the episodic conditions.

Taken together, the two experiments on terrorism indicate that attributions of responsibility differ substantially depending upon episodic or thematic framing of the issue. When terrorism is depicted as a general outcome, viewers gravitate toward societal attributions. On the other hand, when terrorism is framed as a specific act or event, viewers gravitate toward individualistic and punitive attributions.

Crime Experiment 1

This experiment was designed to reflect the sheer dominance of violent crime in network news. Violent crime was depicted using either thematic or episodic framing. Thematic framing consisted of information about crime and victimization rates for the country or particular areas, elements of the criminal justice process, governmental or community responses to crime, and so forth. Episodic framing depicted a specific instance of violent crime. The thematic and episodic framing conditions were then further divided according to race, focusing alternatively on black or white crime. The distinction between black and white crime was based on the individuals or groups depicted as the perpetrators of criminal activity.

In the "Black Crime-Thematic" condition a feature report on "Crime in Black America" described the increasing rate of violent crime and the increasing number of crime victims in predominantly black inner-city areas of Chicago, Houston, Los Angeles, and New York. The reporter traced the economic decline of these areas since the 1960s, and a black civic leader commented that people living in the inner city faced conditions of "desperation."

In the "Black Crime–Episodic" condition, the news story de-

Chapter Four

scribed a violent confrontation between two black youth gangs in Los Angeles that resulted in seven deaths. Individual gang members were shown in police custody. The police chief of Los Angeles denounced the gangs, and the mother of one of the victims expressed her grief.

News coverage of white violent crime was also presented in thematic and episodic terms. In the "White Crime–Thematic" condition, the news report detailed the growing economic power of organized crime and identified some of the major groups involved in the struggle for control of the underworld. The assassinations of several prominent organized crime figures were cited as evidence of growing factional conflict. An FBI official speculated about the origins of the conflict and noted that governmental electronic surveillance of organized crime groups had been intensified.

In the "White Crime–Episodic" condition, the focus of the news report was directed at a well-known shooting in the New York City subway by a passenger, Bernhard Goetz. The reporter briefly summarized the incident, a clip of Bernhard Goetz's videotaped confession was shown, and Goetz stated in an interview that he would repeat his actions if placed in a similar situation. (Goetz shot a group of four unarmed black youths—injuring two of them seriously—who approached him in a "menacing" manner on the subway.)

Although violent crime was the major component of the study design, two additional categories of news stories on crime were incorporated—"Illegal Drugs" and "Criminal Justice Process." Stories about drugs were included simply because no other aspect of crime has commanded as much public (and media) attention in recent years. Coverage of the criminal justice process was included because prior research indicated that beliefs about the effectiveness of the criminal justice system influence individuals' attributions of responsibility.[9]

News coverage of illegal drugs and the criminal justice process were also framed in both thematic and episodic terms. The "Illegal Drugs–Thematic" condition consisted of a news report that described the significant increase in the consumption of heroin and cocaine-based substances nationwide. The reporter cited figures indicating the lucrativeness of the drug trade and interviewed a Justice Department official who noted that a significant portion of the drug trade was controlled by international crime organizations and that the Reagan administration's "War on Drugs" featured cooperative multi-government efforts to fight the problem.

Responsibility for Crime and Terrorism

The "Illegal Drugs–Episodic" condition consisted of a report on "Crack" that began with the anchor's lead-in statement concerning the growing number of Americans using this drug. The story then proceeded to describe two addicts—a black male New Yorker and a white female Midwesterner—and their unsuccessful efforts to break their drug dependence.

The "Criminal Justice Process–Thematic" condition was adapted from a "Special Segment" news report on "Crime in America" in which the U.S. crime rate was contrasted with that of other industrialized nations. The report highlighted the congestion in the courts, the high proportion of plea bargains, and the low percentage of criminals who are jailed. The reporter concluded that, given adequate legal counsel, crime "pays" in America.

The "Criminal Justice Process–Episodic" condition consisted of a report that described the outcome of two criminal cases in which well-known and wealthy defendants (former Louisiana Governor Edwin Edwards and boxing promoter Don King) were acquitted of felony charges. The report summarized the charges brought against Edwards (a white) and King (a black). The reporter interviewed a Justice Department official (concerning the outcome of the trials) who denied charges of leniency and lax prosecution.

In sum, the experimental manipulation consisted of four subject matter manipulations corresponding to news coverage of white violent crime, black violent crime, illegal drugs, and the criminal justice process. In all four manipulations, crime was framed either with thematic or episodic news reports. This design enabled investigation of several hypotheses going beyond the basic framing notion. The racial comparison, for instance, was designed to address the question of whether viewers would assign responsibility for crime differently depending on the race of the individual(s) seen engaging in criminal activity. The general expectation was that, while news coverage of black crime would tend to elicit a relatively lower level of societal responsibility, coverage of white crime would direct the predominantly white audience to attribute responsibility to society. This was a particularly strong expectation in the episodic framing comparison since Bernhard Goetz's actions were widely heralded in the local media as courageous and taken in self-defense.[10]

In addition to racial cuing in coverage of violent crime, news coverage of illegal drugs and the criminal justice process were expected to differ in their effects on attributions of responsibility. It is difficult to think about the problem of illegal drugs without considering indi-

Chapter Four

viduals who use drugs, and coverage of drugs was therefore expected to highlight individual causal responsibility. News about the criminal justice process was expected to draw attention to procedural factors that enable law breakers to evade prosecution; therefore, it was expected that these reports would increase references to punitive causal and treatment responsibility.

Indices of individual, societal, and punitive causal responsibility were constructed in order to assess the impact of the subject matter and framing manipulations. Treatment responsibility was analyzed in terms of societal and punitive attributions (see appendix B). The observed differences among the four subject matter manipulations on the various measures of responsibility are shown in figure 4.7.

Societal attributions of causal responsibility were cited most frequently when the news focused on white violent crime. Societal attributions also appeared frequently when news coverage was directed at the criminal justice process. In contrast, societal attributions were mentioned least frequently when the news focused on black violent crime. The mean societal responsibility score of 29 percent in this condition differed significantly from all other subject matter conditions. News coverage of black crime not only diverted

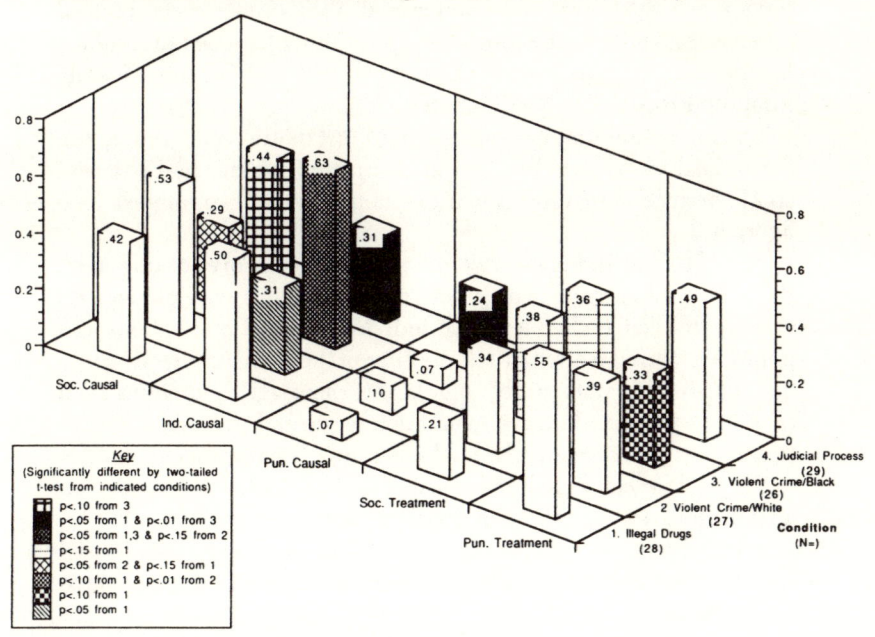

Fig. 4.7 Subject Matter Effects: Crime Experiment 1

42

Responsibility for Crime and Terrorism

attention from societal responsibility, but also attracted attention to individual responsibility. More than 60 percent of all causal attributions were directed at individuals when the news reported on black violent crime. This was *double* the comparable percentage in the White Crime condition. Once again, the Black Crime condition differed significantly from all other subject matter conditions.

News coverage of illegal drugs and the judicial process also affected causal attributions for crime. As expected, individualistic attributions of responsibility were more prominent following news coverage of illegal drugs. This condition differed significantly from both the Criminal Justice Process and White Crime conditions, where references to individual responsibility made up less than 33 percent of all causal attributions. The proportion of causal attributions citing inadequate punishment in the Criminal Justice Process condition was more than double the proportion in the remaining conditions.

The effects of variations in the subject matter of the news on attributions of treatment responsibility for crime were most visible in the Illegal Drugs condition. While societal responsibility accounted for only 20 percent of all treatment attributions in the Illegal Drugs condition, it accounted for nearly 40 percent of all treatment attributions when the news report concerned black crime or the judicial process. In addition, the Illegal Drugs condition induced the highest level of punitive treatment attributions and differed significantly from the Black Crime condition ($p < .10$).

Turning to the combined effects of subject matter and framing, the five indicators of responsibility were subjected to a four-by-two analysis of variance (four subject matter categories and two frames). (See figure 4.8.)

The effects of framing were erratic and generally overshadowed by the effects of subject matter coverage. Although episodic reports tended to elicit higher levels of individual causal attributions and punitive treatment attributions, neither of these "main effects" could be considered statistically significant; however, individual and punitive causal attributions, in addition to societal treatment attributions, were interactively affected by framing. Interaction effects refer to the joint, or combined, influence of subject matter and framing on attributions. In the case of individual causal responsibility, the interaction effect was significant; for punitive causal responsibility and societal treatment responsibility, the interaction effect approached statistical significance.

Thus, the effects of framing on individualistic causal attributions

Chapter Four

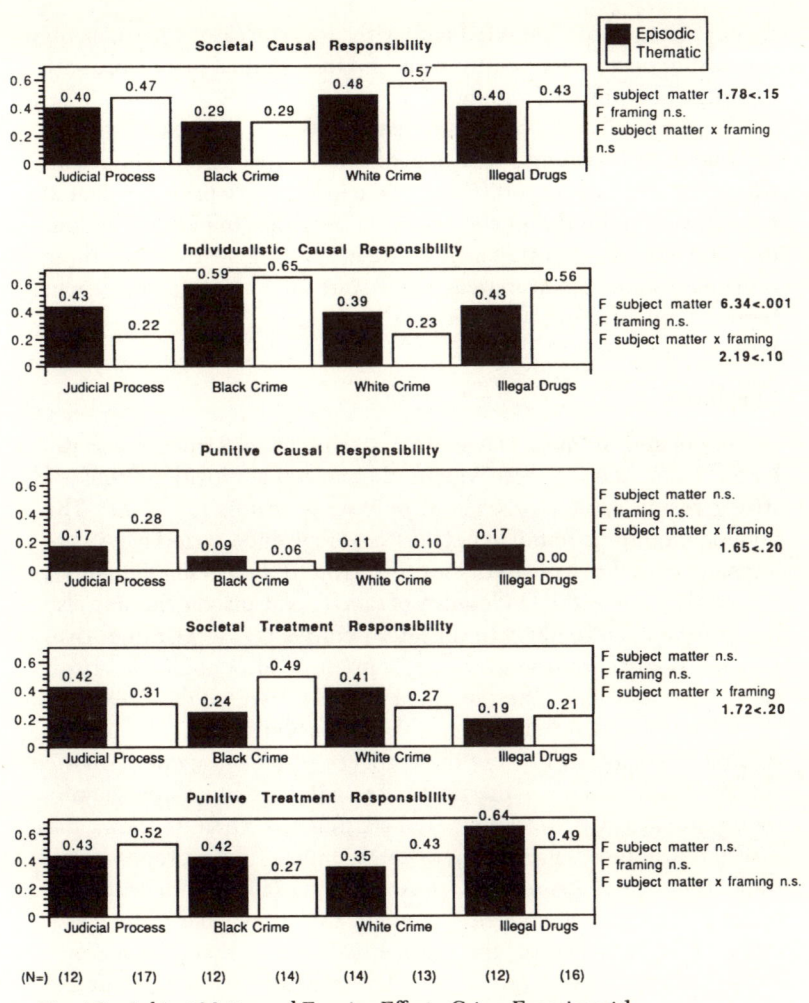

Fig. 4.8 Subject Matter and Framing Effects: Crime Experiment 1

depended upon the particular subject matter focus of the news. Episodic framing of white crime and the judicial process elicited significantly higher levels of individual responsibility than thematic framing, but framing effects were absent in the areas of black crime and illegal drugs. This inconsistency can be traced to the already dominant status of individual responsibility in the Black Crime and Illegal Drugs conditions. Where references to individual responsibil-

Responsibility for Crime and Terrorism

ity were not so prominent to begin with (as in the case of participants exposed to news about white crime and the criminal justice process) framing effects proved significant.

The marginally significant interaction effect in the case of societal treatment responsibility was traced to the Black Crime condition, where the thematic report (rising crime in black urban areas) elicited more than double the percentage of societal treatment attributions than the episodic report (gang warfare in Los Angeles). For the three remaining subject matter areas, there were no noticeable differences between episodic and thematic conditions.

Conclusion

As anticipated, framing was more powerful when terrorism was the target issue; the episodic versus thematic manipulations yielded strong results for terrorism, but only weak results for crime. The dominant episodic frame in network coverage encouraged viewers to attribute causal responsibility for terrorism to the personal qualities of terrorists and to the inadequacy of sanctions. Episodic framing also made viewers more likely to consider punitive measures rather than social or political reform as the appropriate treatment for terrorism. In the case of crime, the dominant episodic frame did increase attributions of individualistic causal responsibility and of punitive treatment responsibility, but these effects were contingent upon the subject matter focus of the news. Episodic framing made viewers more individualistic in their causal attributions when the news was directed at either white crime or the criminal justice process. Episodic framing of crime also dramatically reduced references to societal treatment responsibility when the news focused on black crime. All told, however, the distinction between thematic and episodic framing proved less substantial than the particular subject matter focus of news reports in shaping attribution of responsibility for crime. Given that crime is both a highly threatening and emotionally charged issue (34 percent of the participants in this study spontaneously named crime as among the most important problems facing the country), it is remarkable that relatively modest amounts of exposure to news about illegal drugs, white or black crime, and the criminal justice process proved sufficient to induce significant shifts in viewers' attributions.

Endnotes

1. For similar findings based on a content analysis of newspapers, see Graber 1980. The extent to which the networks presented episodic reports on crime fluctuated, but episodic framing accounted for at least 75 percent of coverage of crime in every year.

2. See especially Paletz, Ayanian, and Fozzard 1982; Altheide 1987.

3. Altheide 1987, p. 174.

4. A similar breakdown of causal attributions for crime was obtained by Carroll et al. 1987 with a battery of closed-ended questions and a sample of "expert" attributors, namely, parole-board members and probation officers.

5. This aggregate-level similarity should not, however, be taken to imply that any given individual assigned responsibility for the two issues consistently. As the results in chapter 9 demonstrate, individual-level consistency in causal and treatment attributions for both issues was weak.

6. In every methodological respect except one this study was identical to all others. The exception was the use of a control group that watched no news report dealing with terrorism. This study was carried out in September 1985, shortly after the hijacking occurred.

7. See, for instance, Ross 1977; Jones 1979.

8. A plausible post hoc explanation for the high level of individualistic attributions for terrorism in the thematic U.S. Foreign Policy condition concerns affect. Because this report presented the hijacking as an expression of political opposition to the United States, and because President Reagan angrily condemned the terrorists, the story may have prompted a stronger "outgroup" stereotype (i.e., higher negative affect toward the hijackers) thus strengthening participants' inclination to cite terrorists' personal deficiencies as causal factors. The posttest questionnaire included a set of questions asking viewers whether the story on the hijacking had "made them feel" a variety of emotions, including "disgust," "anger," and "fear." These responses were summed to form a summary measure of negative affect. Participants in the U.S. Foreign Policy condition were significantly ($p < .05$) more aroused by the news report than were subjects in all remaining conditions. Moreover, across all conditions, the greater the arousal of negative affect, the greater the proportion of individual causes cited. In short, the presentation in the U.S. Foreign Policy condition unintentionally raised viewers' hostility toward the hijackers, thereby inducing individualistic attributions.

9. See, for example, Graber 1980.

10. Under these circumstances, there is an obvious risk of confounding the race of the perpetrator and the degree of "justifiability" of the criminal acts portrayed in the black and white episodic conditions. The Goetz case was included in the design because its high level of newsworthiness in the New York area made this incident highly representative of episodic news coverage of crime at the time of the study.

46

References

Altheide, David L. 1987. Format and symbol in television coverage of terrorism in the United States and Great Britain. *International Studies Quarterly* 31: 161-76.
Carroll, John S., William T. Perkowitz, Arthur J. Lurigio, and Frances M. Weaver. 1987. Sentencing goals, causal attributions, ideology, and personality. *Journal of Personality and Social Psychology* 52: 107-18.
Graber, Doris A. 1980. *Crime news and the public.* New York: Praeger.
Paletz, David, J. Ayanian, and P. Fozzard. 1982. Terrorism on television news: The IRA, the FALN, and the Red Brigades. In William Adams (ed.), *Television coverage of international affairs.* Norwood, N.J.:Ablex.
Ross, Lee. 1977. The intuitive psychologist and his shortcomings. In Leonard Berkowitz (ed.), *Advances in experimental social psychology,* vol. 10. New York: Academic press.

Part III
Popular Drama and Fear

THE RAZOR BLADE IN THE APPLE:
THE SOCIAL CONSTRUCTION OF URBAN LEGENDS*

JOEL BEST
GERALD T. HORIUCHI
California State University, Fresno

> This paper examines the widespread belief that anonymous sadists give children dangerous treats on Halloween. A review of news stories about Halloween sadism from 1958 to 1983 suggests that the threat has been greatly exaggerated. Halloween sadism can be viewed as an urban legend, which emerged during the early 1970s to give expression to growing fears about the safety of children, the danger of crime, and other sources of social strain. Urban legends, like collective behavior and social problems construction, are responses to social strain, shaped by the perception of the threat and social organization.

The 1970s witnessed the discovery of a frightening new deviant—the Halloween sadist, who gave dangerous, adulterated treats to children. Each year, Halloween's approach brought warnings to parents:

> ... that plump red apple that Junior gets from a kindly old woman down the block ... may have a razor blade hidden inside (*New York Times*, 1970).

> If this year's Halloween follows form, a few children will return home with something more than an upset tummy: in recent years, several children have died and hundreds have narrowly escaped injury from razor blades, sewing needles and shards of glass purposefully put into their goodies by adults (*Newsweek*, 1975).

> It's Halloween again and time to remind you that.... [s]omebody's child will become violently ill or die after eating poisoned candy or an apple containing a razor blade (Van Buren, 1983).

Various authorities responded to the threat: legislatures in California (1971) and New Jersey (1982) passed laws against Halloween sadism; schools trained children to inspect their treats for signs of tampering; and some communities tried to ban trick-or-treating (Trubo, 1974). According to press reports, many parents restricted their children's trick-or-treating, examined their treats, or arranged parties or other indoor celebrations (*New York Times*, 1972; *Los Angeles Times*, 1982). By 1984, the threat of Halloween sadists was apparently taken for granted. Doubts about the threat's reality rarely appeared in print. Several Oregon third graders wrote letters to a newspaper: "I wish people wouldn't put poison in our Halloween treats" (*Times*, 1984). Adults questioned for an Illinois newspaper's "Sidewalk Interview" column (*DeKalb Daily Chronicle*, 1984) expressed concern: " ... part of it is checking to make sure you know your neighbors and checking the candy. I think it's terrible that people are doing this and I guess people's morals have to be examined." "Dear Abby" printed a letter describing a North Carolina hospital's program to X-ray treats (Van Buren, 1984); radiologists at a Hanford, California hospital checked 500 bags of treats (*Fresno Bee*, 1984). In 1985, 327 students at California State University, Fresno wrote essays for an upper-division writing examination, advocating the abolition of some holiday. Nearly a third (105 students) wrote about Halloween, and 90 percent of those essays mentioned the threat of Halloween sadism.

Halloween sadism is thought to involve random, vicious, unprovoked attacks against small children. The attacks seem irrational, and the attackers are routinely described as disturbed or insane.

---

* An earlier version of this paper was presented at the 1983 meeting of the Pacific Sociological Association. We want to thank Gary Alan Fine, Joseph F. Jones, and David F. Luckenbill for their helpful comments. Correspondence to: Best, Department of Sociology, California State University, Fresno, CA 93740.

These "child-haters" are theorized to "have had a really deprived childhood" having been "abused as children," they are now "frustrated and filled with resentment against the world in general" (Isaacs and Royeton, 1982:69; *New York Times*, 1970; Trubo, 1974:28). Law enforcement officials and the media reaffirm that the threat is real, urging parents to protect their children against sadistic attacks.

Although Halloween sadism is widely regarded as a serious threat, it has received little scholarly attention. In this paper, we examine the phenomenon from a sociological perspective, addressing three issues. First, we try to assess the incidence of Halloween sadism in order to demonstrate that the threat has been greatly exaggerated. Second, we draw upon a concept from folklore studies to argue that the belief in Halloween sadism is best viewed as an "urban legend." Finally, we suggest that urban legends can be understood as unconstructed social problems. Like collective hysteria and organized claims-making efforts, urban legends are a product of social strain and of the social organization of the response to that strain.

A HOLIDAY FOR SADISTS?

There are no reliable official statistics on Halloween sadism. Minor incidents, particularly those that do not involve injuries, may never be reported to the police. Cases that are reported may be classified under a wide range of offenses, and there is no centralized effort to compile cases from different jurisdictions. Moreover, the circumstances of the crime—the young victim, the unfamiliar assailant, the difficulty in remembering which treats came from which houses—make it unlikely that offenders will be arrested.

While the true incidence of Halloween sadism cannot be measured, newspaper reports reveal changes in public reaction to the threat. Therefore, we examined the coverage of Halloween sadism in four daily newspapers between 1959 and 1984. For the *New York Times*, we checked all entries under "Halloween" in the paper's annual indexes for information about Halloween sadism. The *New York Times Index* proved to be unusually complete, listing even short items of a sentence or two.[1] The published indexes for two other major regional newspapers, the *Chicago Tribune* and the *Los Angeles Times*, were less thorough, so for each year, we read both papers' issues for the first three days in November. Finally, we examined all Halloween stories in the files of the *Fresno Bee*. Our search found stories about 76 alleged incidents of Halloween sadism, which included at least the community where the incident occurred and the nature of the attack.[2] Table 1 shows the number of incidents reported in each year.

Obviously, the 76 incidents identified through this procedure do not form a complete list of cases of Halloween sadism. However, there are several reasons why it is unlikely that many serious incidents—involving deaths or serious injuries—were overlooked. First, the papers' coverage was national. The 76 reported incidents came from 15 states and two Canadian provinces; while each of the four newspapers concentrated on incidents in its own region, all reported cases from other regions. All four included at least one case from the South—the only major region without a newspaper in the sample. Second, the 76 reported cases were generally not serious. Injuries were reported in only 20 cases, and only two of these involved deaths. It seems unlikely that newspapers would choose to print accounts of minor incidents, while ignoring more serious crimes. This impression is bolstered further by the frequent appearance of stories—often from different states—about other Halloween tragedies: children struck by cars and other accidental deaths; people murdered when

---

1. On the reliability of this index, see Troyer and Markle (1983:141-42).
2. In addition, all entries under "Halloween" in the *Reader's Guide to Periodical Literature* and MEDLINE—the computerized medical data base—were checked. Neither popular magazines nor the medical literature described any additional cases of Halloween sadism. Every case was included if the news report treated it as an instance of Halloween sadism. As noted below, some of the cases included were of questionable authenticity.

TABLE 1
Reported Incidents of Halloween Sadism, 1958–84

Year	Number of Incidents	Year	Number of Incidents
1958	0	1972	1
1959	1	1973	4
1960	0	1974	1
1961	0	1975	2
1962	1	1976	2
1963	1	1977	0
1964	3	1978	0
1965	1	1979	3
1966	5	1980	0
1967	4	1981	0
1968	3	1982	12
1969	7	1983	1
1970	10	1984	0
1971	14		

they opened their doors, expecting trick-or-treaters; racial disturbances; vandalism; and so on. At least two of the newspapers carried reports on each of the two deaths attributed to Halloween sadists. It is therefore unlikely that the list of 76 incidents excludes any fatal instances of Halloween sadism.

Table 1 reveals two peaks in the pattern of reporting. Thirty-one of the 76 incidents occurred in the three years from 1969 to 1971. This wave of reports encouraged recognition of Halloween sadism as a threat. As a holiday when millions of children venture out at night, Halloween has a long history of tragic accidents. Routinely, newspapers and magazines print lists of safety tips, warning parents against flammable costumes, masks that obscure the wearer's vision, and the like. A systematic review of such lists found no mention of the danger posed by sadists before 1972; but, from that year on, lists of safety tips almost invariably warned parents to inspect their children's treats for signs of tampering. At the same time that these warnings spread, reports of Halloween sadism fell to a few per year until 1982, when there was a dramatic increase. Of course, this reflected the fear caused by the Tylenol murders. A month before Halloween, seven people died after swallowing poisoned Extra-Strength Tylenol capsules. In the weeks that followed, there were hundreds of reports of "copycats" adulterating food, over-the-counter medications, and other household products. As Halloween approached, the media repeatedly warned parents that trick-or-treaters would be in danger. After raising the specter of Halloween sadism, the press naturally covered the incidents that were reported. A year later, however, coverage fell to pre-Tylenol levels.

Examining the reports of the 76 incidents leads to three conclusions. First, the threat of Halloween sadism has been greatly exaggerated. There is simply no basis for *Newsweek*'s (1975) claim that "several children have died." The newspapers attributed only two deaths to Halloween sadists, and neither case fit the image of a maniacal killer randomly attacking children. In 1970, five-year-old Kevin Toston died after eating heroin supposedly hidden in his Halloween candy. While this story received considerable publicity, newspapers gave less coverage to the follow-up report that Kevin had found the heroin in his uncle's home, not his treats (*San Fransisco Chronicle*, 1970). The second death is more notorious. In 1974, eight-year-old Timothy O'Bryan died after eating Halloween candy contaminated with cyanide. Investigators concluded that his father had contaminated the treat (Grider, 1982). Thus, both boys' deaths were caused by family members, rather than by anonymous sadists.[3]

---

3. The particulars of these cases are sometimes forgotten, so that the deaths continue to be used as proof that Halloween sadists pose a real threat. Trubo (1974:28) describes Toston as "the victim of a sadistic prankster." Similarly, an anonymous reviewer of an earlier draft of this paper recalled the O'Bryan case but did not mention that it was the boy's father who was convicted.

Similarly, while the newspaper reports rarely gave detailed information about the remaining 18 cases in which injuries were reported, most of the victims were not seriously hurt. Several incidents involved minor cuts and puncture wounds; what was apparently the most serious wound required 11 stitches. In short, there were no reports where an anonymous sadist caused death or a life-threatening injury; there is no justification for the claim that Halloween sadism stands as a major threat to U.S. children.[4]

A second conclusion is that many, if not most, reports of Halloween sadism are of questionable authenticity. Children who go trick-or-treating know about Halloween sadism; they have been warned by their parents, teachers, and friends. A child who "discovers" an adulterated treat stands to be rewarded with the concerned attention of parents and, perhaps, police officers and reporters. Such a hoax is consistent with Halloween traditions of trickery, just as the fear of sadists resembles the more traditional dread of ghosts and witches (Santino, 1983). The 76 reported incidents included two cases that were identified as hoaxes at the time, and it seems likely that other cases involved undiscovered fraud. After all, it is remarkable that three-quarters of the children who reported receiving contaminated treats had no injuries. Efforts to systematically follow up reports of Halloween sadism have concluded that the vast majority were fabrications. After Halloween 1972, *Editor and Publisher* (1973) — the trade magazine of the newspaper industry — examined several papers' efforts to trace all local reports of Halloween sadism; it concluded that virtually all the reports were hoaxes. Ten years later, in the wake of the Tylenol scare, the confectionary industry tried to reassure potential customers in a "white paper" on Halloween candy tampering in 1982 (National Confectioners Association et al., n.d.) The report noted that "more than 95 percent of the 270 potential Halloween 1982 candy adulterations analyzed by the Food and Drug Administration have shown no tampering, which has led one FDA official to characterize the period as one of 'psychosomatic mass hysteria.'" Further, a confectionary industry survey of police departments in "24 of the nation's largest cities, as well as smaller towns in which highly-publicized incidents were alleged to have occurred, found two reports of injuries — neither requiring medical treatment — from among the hundreds of claims of candy tampering."[5] Thus, not only does a survey of press coverage reveal fewer reports of Halloween sadism than might be expected, but there is good reason to suspect that many of the reports are unfounded.

Third, the press should not be held responsible for the widespread belief that Halloween sadism poses a serious threat. While the news media can manufacture "crime waves" by suddenly focusing on previously ignored offenses (Fishman, 1978), the press has given Halloween sadism relatively little publicity. Many of the 76 reported incidents received minimal coverage, in news stories of only two or three sentences. Often the reports were embedded in larger stories, such as a wire service summary of Halloween news from around the country. Nor did popular magazines highlight Halloween sadism; before 1982, only two short articles focused on the problem. The absence of

---

4. Certainly other elements of everyday life, while not receiving as much attention, are far more hazardous. In 1980-81, according to the U.S. Consumer Product Safety Commission (1982), 60 children under age five died in "product associated deaths" involving nursery equipment and supplies; another 13 deaths involved toys.
5. In one apparent hoax:

> ... a youth claimed to have ingested an insecticide-saturated candy bar. ... Testing showed no traces of any chemicals in the youth's blood. ... although there was insecticide on one end of the bar, the side of the candy bar that had been bitten into was insecticide-free. (National Confectioners Association et al., n.d.)

Similarly, over 80% of the reports of so-called "copycat" poisonings that followed the Tylenol deaths were apparently fabricated (*Time*, 1982). Some were anonymous pranks, but others involved publicity-seekers or schemes to collect insurance settlements from manufacturers. As in the case of Halloween sadism, the threat was exaggerated: Congressional hearings denounced "a new kind of thug that is stalking the American communities" (U.S. Congress: House of Representatives, 1982:2), while psychiatrists speculated that "copycat criminals may have weak ego structures and 'have difficulty running their lives'" (*New York Times*, 1982).

authentic cases of serious injuries caused by Halloween sadism undoubtedly explains this limited coverage. While the publication of annual warnings to parents to inspect their children's treats, as well as occasional short items reporting minor incidents, may help keep the fear of Halloween sadism alive, the media do not seem to be the principal channel by which people learn of the danger. Rather, knowledge of Halloween sadism apparently spreads by word of mouth.

ROOTS OF AN URBAN LEGEND

The belief in Halloween sadism as a serious threat can be understood using a concept developed by folklorists: Halloween sadism is an *urban legend* (Grider, 1982). Urban legends are contemporary, orally transmitted tales that "often depict a clash between modern conditions and some aspect of a traditional life-style" (Brunvand, 1981:189). Whereas traditional legends often feature supernatural themes, most urban legends "are grounded in human baseness . . ." (Fine, 1980:227). They describe criminal attacks, contaminated consumer goods, and other risks of modern life.[6] Halloween sadism combines two themes found in several other urban legends: danger to children (e.g., the babysitter who cooks an infant in a microwave oven; the child kidnapped from a department store or an amusement park); and contamination of food (e.g., the mouse in the soft-drink bottle; the Kentucky Fried Rat) (Brunvand, 1981, 1984; Fine, 1979, 1980, 1985). These legends, like that of the Halloween sadist, are typically told as true stories. They "gratify our desire to know about and to try to understand bizarre, frightening, and potentially dangerous or embarrassing events that *may* have happened" (Brunvand, 1981:12) Urban legends may even have a factual basis; soft-drink manufacturers have been sued by people claiming to have found mice in their drinks (Fine, 1979). Whether a legend begins with a real incident or as a fictional tale, it is told and retold, often evolving as it spreads. On occasion, urban legends appear in newspaper stories, reinforcing the tale's credibility (Brunvand, 1981, 1984). The belief in Halloween sadism is maintained through orally transmitted warnings about the dangers contemporary society poses for the traditional custom of trick-or-treating. These warnings, which greatly exaggerate the threat, are an urban legend. That some incidents of Halloween sadism have occurred, and that the media have reported such incidents, does not disqualify the warnings as legends.

Viewing Halloween sadism as an urban legend helps explain why the belief became widespread when it did. News reports of Halloween sadism are not new (cf., *New York Times*, 1950).[7] But the general perception that Halloween sadism is a serious threat can be dated to the early 1970s. This was the period when the press began reporting more incidents and warning parents to inspect treats, and legislatures began passing laws against Halloween sadism. In general, urban legends are products of social tension or strain. They express fears that the complexities of modern society threaten the traditional social order (Fine, 1980, 1985). Urban life requires contact with strangers who—the legends suggest—may be homicidal maniacs, unscrupulous merchants, voyeurs, or otherwise threatening. By repeating urban legends, people can respond to social strain, expressing their doubts about the modern world.

While it is obviously impossible to establish a causal link between particular social tensions and the spread of a particular urban legend, folklorists typically examine a legend's elements for clues

---

6. The term "urban legend" is generally used by folklorists to distinguish modern folk tales from those told in traditional societies; it ignores the differences between contemporary urban and rural communities. Some familiar urban legends include: "The Hook"—a maniac who terrorizes a couple parked in a lover's lane; the black widow spider that nests in a beehive hairdo; the deep-fried rat sold at a fried-chicken franchise; and "The Choking Doberman," that swallows a burglar's fingers. Brunvand's (1981, 1984) books present several dozen such tales.

7. This case involved giving children pennies heated on a skillet. Apparently this was an early image of Halloween sadism; Grider (1982) recalls a heated pennies legend circulating among Texas children in the 1940s. Of course, the fear of Halloween sadism also seems linked to traditional warnings about accepting candy from strangers.

about its roots (Brunvand, 1981, 1984; Fine, 1980). Some legends feature a transparent message, but others are more difficult to interpret. In the case of Halloween sadism, a plausible argument can be made that the legend's flowering in the early 1970s was tied to the heightened social strains of that period. The late 1960s and early 1970s were years of unparalleled divisiveness in post-World War II America (Carroll, 1982; O'Neill, 1971). The media exposed several serious crises to the public, including an increasingly unpopular war, ghetto riots, student demonstrations, and increased drug use. It was a period of intense social strain. Three forms of strain that emerged or grew during these years seem related to the growing fear of Halloween sadism.

Threats to Children

The form of strain that seems most clearly linked to a belief in Halloween sadism was the growing sense that children were no longer safe in the United States. During the 1960s and early 1970s, physicians and social workers promoted child abuse as a major social problem; the popular press responded with dozens of dramatic stories about children who had been cruelly treated by their parents (Pfohl, 1977). The rhetoric of this campaign emphasized that all children were potential victims, that child abuse occurred in all sectors of society. But even parents who remained confident that their children would never be abused could worry about losing their children to other threats. Older children adopted radical political views and experimented with illegal drugs.[8] Other parents found their grown children facing a less symbolic threat—death in Vietnam. The social conflicts that marked America during these years must have left many parents wondering if their hopes for the next generation would be fulfilled.

Since the emergence of the belief in Halloween sadism, the generation gap seems to have narrowed, but threats to children remain visible. The movement against child abuse continues to spread, receiving still more publicity. And, during the late 1970s and early 1980s, emerging campaigns against incest, child pornography, child molesting, and abortion may have contributed to a larger sense of children in jeopardy. Perhaps the clearest link between threats to children and the fear of Halloween sadism appeared during the series of murders of Atlanta schoolchildren. In 1980, STOP, an organization of the victims' parents, argued that "the city should organize Halloween night events that will minimize dangers to the children" (*New York Times*, 1980).[9]

Fear of Crime

Other forms of strain involved more general threats. Survey data reveal that the fear of crime grew substantially between the mid-1960s and the early 1970s (Erskine, 1974; Stinchcombe et al., 1980). Although violent crimes often involve offenders and victims who are acquainted, the fear

---

8. The possibility that their children might adopt disapproved values may have suggested betrayal to some parents, creating another source of strain—ambivalence toward one's children. This ambivalence is nicely revealed in a popular cultural genre which regained popularity during the late 1960s and early 1970s. In popular novels and films (e.g., *The Exorcist* and *Rosemay's Baby*), the horror tale—traditionally associated with Halloween—took on a new emphasis: stories about children with demonic powers.

The concern with growing drug use may have been especially important in fostering the initial fear of Halloween sadism. Although only one of the 76 newspaper reports involved "hippies" giving drugs to children, early oral versions of contaminated-treat tales often took this form. (On a related, early 1970s legend—that LSD was being distributed on pictures of Mickey Mouse, which children might mistake for a lick-on tatoo—see Brunvand, 1984:162–69.) Only later did the razor blade in the apple become the standard image for Halloween sadism. Six on the 12 incidents reported before 1967 involved over-the-counter or prescription drugs; only one involved a sharp object. In contrast, 49 of the 64 reports after 1966 involved razors or other sharp objects, while only four involved drugs. Of course, razor blades, pins, and so on are readily available equipment, which would make it easy to carry out hoaxes.

9. Similarly, the Tylenol poisonings raised the prospect of attacks via product contamination. Like the Atlanta murders, these real crimes by an anonymous sadist led to warnings about Halloween sadists.

of crime focuses on the threat of an anonymous attacker.[10] The threat of an unpredictable, unprovoked criminal attack parallels the Halloween sadist menace.

Mistrust of Others

Survey data also reveal rising expressions of general mistrust during the early 1970s. The proportion of Americans who agreed that ". . . you can't be too careful in dealing with people" rose from 45.6 percent in 1966, to 50.0 percent in 1971, to 54.3 percent in 1973 (Converse et al., 1980:28). Studies of urban dwellers in the 1970s found high levels of mistrust for strangers (Fischer, 1982; Merry, 1981; Suttles, 1972). While warnings about the collapse of the neighborhood in the anonymous modern city have proven exaggerated, the belief that people now live in greater isolation remains widespread. The social conflicts of the 1960s and early 1970s may have encouraged doubts about the trustworthiness of other people. Such doubts provided another form of strain during the period when the belief in Halloween sadism spread.

These sources of strain—threats to children, fear of crime, and mistrust of others—provided a context within which the concern about Halloween sadism could flourish. The Halloween sadist emerged as a symbolic expression of this strain: the sadist, like other dangers, attacks children—society's most vulnerable members; the sadist, like the stereotypical criminal, is an anonymous, unprovoked assailant; and the sadist, like other strangers, must be met by doubt, rather than trust.[11] Placed in the context of the late 1960s and early 1970s, the spread of Halloween sadism is easily understood.

If these sources of strain account for the belief's spread, what explains its persistence? The extraordinary social conflicts of the early 1970s have moderated, yet the belief in Halloween sadism remains. Why? First, some of the same sources of strain continue to exist: the media still publicize threats to children (e.g., child abuse), and the fear of crime and strangers remains high.

Second, and more important, Halloween sadism is an established urban legend; it can remain as a taken-for-granted, if dormant, part of American culture. The survey of newspaper stories found only five reports of Halloween sadism from 1976 to 1981—less than one per year.[12] However, warnings about sadists continued to appear during these years and, of course, the Tylenol poisonings in 1982 led to both predictions and reports of Halloween sadism.

Third, folklorists have traced the evolution of some legends over centuries (Brunvand, 1984). Legends seem most likely to persist when they have a general, underlying message (for instance, warnings about trusting outsiders) which can be tailored to fit new situations. Thus, the dangers of eating commercially prepared food were detailed in nineteenth-century stories about cat meat in baked pies and, more recently, in tales about rats sold at fried-chicken franchises (Fine, 1980; Simpson, 1983). Like other urban legends about homicidal maniacs, the Halloween sadist legend expresses fears about criminal attacks. Given the general nature of this threat, the legend may persist as long as the custom of trick-or-treating.

URBAN LEGENDS AS UNCONSTRUCTED SOCIAL PROBLEMS

Where do urban legends fit within the broader framework of sociological theory? The case of

---

10. This fear also found expression in a popular culture horror genre—the "mad slasher" films in which a maniac stalks and kills a series of high school or college students. Interestingly, the first of these films was *Halloween* (1979).
11. Grider (1982:6) agrees: "The Razor Blades Syndrome expresses a deep-rooted fear of strangers, a distrust of old customs and traditions, an acknowledgment of child abuse and infanticide, and an ambivalence toward random, wanton violence."
12. Presumably, incidents continued to be reported during this period. The decline in press coverage may have reflected journalists' doubts about the authenticity of the reports (*Editor and Publisher*, 1973), as well as their recognition that the reported incidents were minor and, given the well-established nature of the legend, no longer newsworthy.

Halloween sadism suggests (1) that urban legends may be viewed as a form of unconstructed social problem, (2) that collective hysteria, urban legends, and social problems construction offer alternative responses to social strain, and (3) that the emergence of a particular response to strain reflects social organization.

At first glance, the fear of Halloween sadists resembles some of the instances of collective hysteria in the collective behavior literature. The Halloween sadist can stand beside the "phantom anesthetist" of Mattoon (Johnson, 1945), the "phantom slasher" of Taipei (Jacobs, 1965), the "June bug epidemic" in a Southern textile plant (Kerckhoff and Back, 1968), and the windshield pitting in Seattle (Medalia and Larsen, 1958) as a focus of exaggerated fears. Studies of collective hysteria usually account for the emergence of hysterical beliefs as a response to social strain: the Mattoon episode occurred during wartime; the workers in the textile plant were putting in heavy overtime, and so on. In response to this strain, there emerges a belief in some threat, "an ambiguous element in the environment with a generalized power to threaten or destroy" (Smelser, 1962:82). This threat is credible, frightening, and difficult to protect oneself against:

> Instead of simply having a feeling that something is awry, the belief in a tangible threat makes it possible to *explain* and *justify* one's sense of discomfort—instead of anxiety, one experiences fear, and it is then possible to act in some meaningful way with respect to this tangible threat rather than just feeling frustrated and anxious. (Kerckhoff and Back, 1968:160-61—emphasis in original)

However, some of this model's key features do not fit the emergence of the belief in Halloween sadism and other urban legends. Collective hysteria is bounded in time and space. Hysterical beliefs are short-lived; they typically emerge, spread, and die within the space of a few days or weeks. Further, they are typically confined to a restricted locality—a single region, town, or facility (Lofland, 1981). In contrast, the belief in Halloween sadists appears to have spread more slowly, over a period of years, and to have become an established, taken-for-granted part of the culture. Nor has the belief observed the normal geographic limits of collective hysteria—reports of Halloween sadism have come from throughout the country, suggesting that the belief is nationwide. If the Halloween sadist resembles the threats identified in instances of collective hysteria, the dynamics of the belief's spread do not fit the hysterical pattern.

The process of social problems construction offers an alternative perspective for understanding the fear of Halloween sadism. Blumer (1971) and Spector and Kitsuse (1973, 1977) defined social problems as products of claims-making activities, in which people call others' attention to social conditions. Thus, the emergence of a social problem is a political process: ". . . recognition by a society of its social problems is a highly selective process, with many harmful social conditions and arrangements not even making a bid for attention and with others falling by the wayside in what is frequently a fierce competitive struggle" (Blumer, 1971:302). Case studies of claims-making focus on the role of social movements (Tierney, 1982), professionals (Pfohl, 1977), the press (Schoenfeld et al., 1979), and other interested parties in constructing social problems. While these studies demonstrate how some claims-making campaigns succeeded, they do not explain why other social conditions, with the potential to be defined as social problems, never reach this status. Emergent or unconstructed social problems are less often studied (Troyer and Markle, 1983, 1984). Urban legends, such as the Halloween sadist, may be seen in these terms.

While the belief in Halloween sadism is widespread, it has not led to effective claims-making activities. Halloween sadism has, for brief occasions, occupied the attention of legislators, city officials, journalists, and PTA associations, but the belief spread largely outside institutionalized channels.[13] The press never reported more than a handful of incidents in a given year, and most

---

13. Medical professionals, for instance, paid minimal attention to Halloween sadism. MEDLINE listed no articles on the subject from 1966 to 1983.

of these reports were very short; the belief spread informally, by word-of-mouth. Similarly, there was no especially visible response to the threat. By the mid-1970s, the press reported a few organized attempts to thwart sadists — hospitals offering to X-ray treats, communities organizing alternative celebrations, and municipalities passing ordinances against trick-or-treating.[14] But most of these efforts remained localized; they received little publicity and did not lead to a broader, organized response to Halloween sadism. (Similarly, organized campaigns by the confectionary industry to expose fabricated reports of Halloween sadism also failed to attract widespread recognition [*Editor and Publisher*, 1973; National Confectioners Association et al., n.d.].) While it is possible to trace the claims-making activities by which many social problems are constructed, this is not true for Halloween sadism. Although the belief spread widely, it moved largely through informal channels, and the principal reaction — parents restricting their children's trick-or-treating — was equally informal.

This analysis suggests that collective hysteria, urban legends, and social problems construction are alternative responses to social strain, alternatives in which strain is translated into different forms of threat that are spread through different forms of social organization. Strain — discomfort caused by existing social conditions — is made manifest in a perceived threat to the collectivity.[15] This threat may be genuine or false. Commonly, genuine threats identify the source of social strain (e.g., pollution endangers the quality of life), while false threats are a more symbolic expression of strain (e.g., a "June bug" attacks people under a heavy work load). The identification of genuine threats often suggests a solution — something that can be done to reduce or eliminate the threat — while false threats are frequently amorphous and difficult or impossible to manage. In general, collective hysteria and urban legends respond to strain through the identification of false threats, while social problems construction deals with genuine threats. Social organization affects the spread of perceptions of threat. In compact, homogeneous collectivities, collective hysteria can spread quickly. In larger, more diffuse collectivities, it takes longer to attract attention to the threat and to mobilize concerned individuals. Typically, in social problems construction, some individuals take the lead in organizing claims-making activities, while urban legends spread through informal contacts.

The example of Halloween sadism suggests some specific factors that may affect the response to social strain. The reports of Halloween sadism did not lead to collective hysteria for two reasons. First, the belief spread throughout the country, rather than within a compact collectivity. Second, this spread could occur relatively slowly, given the limited nature of the threat. Reports of sadistic incidents posed no threat to other children for another year. There was no urgency to the news; the tale could be disseminated slowly, through informal channels. Although a few organizations began claims-making activities directed at Halloween sadism, little came of their efforts. In part, this may have been caused by the absence of serious, documented sadistic incidents; without genuine atrocities to demonstrate the need for action, claims-makers had trouble making a convincing case. Further, potential social movements aimed at Halloween sadism lacked a well-organized natural constituency; while no one approved of Halloween sadism, no group found it in its interest to mount a sustained campaign against the threat. Again, the fact that the danger was limited to one evening a year may have inhibited the construction of Halloween sadism as a social problem. Nor was it clear how collective action might stop Halloween sadism; parents who worried about the threat found the best protection in individually curtailing their children's trick-or-treating or inspecting

---

14. While the press routinely interpreted these actions as responses to Halloween sadism, many attempts to restrict trick-or-treating were, in fact, prompted by more traditional Halloween problems, e.g., vandalism or children struck by cars (cf. Trubo, 1974).

15. Social constructionist theorists attack the notion that strain or other objective social conditions offer a sufficient explanation for social problems; they argue that claims-making activities must occur (Blumer, 1971; Spector and Kitsuse, 1977). Troyer and Markle (1983), however, suggest that strain usually, if not always, precedes claims-making.

their treats. Thus, the diffuse collectivity, the infrequency of the reported attacks, the absence of convincing evidence, the lack of interested individuals willing to commit extensive time to the cause, and the difficulty of devising solutions meant that Halloween sadism became the focus of neither collective hysteria nor successful claims-making. Yet, retaining considerable symbolic power as an expression of social strain, Halloween sadism endured as an urban legend.

IMPLICATIONS: "HALLOWEEN AND THE MASS CHILD" REVISITED

Holiday celebrations reflect the larger culture. The events celebrated, as well as the customary ways of celebrating, reveal the society's values and structure. And, as society changes, its holidays often take on new meanings, consistent with the altered culture. Where earlier American celebrations were communal, ceremonial, and often religious or patriotic, contemporary observances tend to be individualistic, materialistic, secular occasions, marked largely by unstructured leisure time (Caplow, 1982; Caplow and Williamson, 1980; Hatch, 1978).[16]

Gregory P. Stone's (1959) "Halloween and the Mass Child" developed this thesis. Stone traced the evolution of Halloween activities in his lifetime, from the elaborate pranks of adolescents in the 1930s, to the playful trick-or-treating of young children in the 1950s. He found the 1950s children did not understand the extortionate premise of "trick or treat;" for them, Halloween was merely an occasion to receive candy. Stone interpreted this shift as consistent with the changes in American values described in Reisman's (1950) *The Lonely Crowd*:

> ... Reisman's character type of "other-direction" may, indeed, be a *prototype* of American character and not some strange mutation in the northeast. Consumption, tolerance, and conformity were recognizable in the Halloween masquerade of a near-southern town. Production, indignation, and autonomy were not. (Stone, 1959:378—emphasis in original)

Twenty-five years after Stone's analysis, the fear of Halloween sadism has further altered the meaning of Halloween. While Stone saw trick-or-treating as a part of the emerging culture of consumption, folklorists view Halloween as among the least commercialized of modern holidays (Grider, 1982; Santino, 1983). But this informality has been labeled dangerous by those who warn against Halloween sadists. Children are urged to refuse homemade treats and accept only coupons or mass-produced candy with intact wrappings, as though commercialism offers protection.[17] Long celebrated through vandalism and extortion, Halloween has been a symbolic expression of disorder. Today, the Halloween sadist has become an annual reminder of the fragility of the social bond—an expression of growing doubts about the safety of children, the trustworthiness of strangers, and the strength of the modern urban community.

Examining the fear of Halloween sadists reveals topics that deserve further sociological attention. First, urban legends merit more analysis as expressions of social strain. Second, theories of social problems construction need to address the processes by which topics become the focus of claims-making activities. Most existing case studies describe relatively successful claims-making efforts, taking for granted the appropriateness of those efforts. But a complete theory of social problems construction would also examine the earliest stages in the process, asking why some social conditions fail to become the focus for claims-making, how strain, social organization, and other social conditions generate claims-making, and why some strain is translated into collective hysteria or urban legends, rather than claims-making. To define social problems in terms of claims-making without identifying the roots of that process begs the question of why some phenomena become social problems.

---

16. When they are inconsistent with modern practices, earlier forms of celebrating may be forgotten. On the drunken, riotous Christmas customs of the nineteenth-century working class, see Davis (1982).

17. The intense reaction to the Tylenol murders reflected consumers' dependence on mass-produced food and medications. "The revolt of the product is the ultimate nightmare for a society like ours" (Spiro, 1982:11). However, new standards for tamper-resistant packaging apparently reestablished confidence in product safety.

REFERENCES

Blumer, Herbert
   1971 "Social problems as collective behavior." Social Problems 18:298-306.
Brunvand, Jan Harold
   1981 The Vanishing Hitchhiker. New York: Norton.
   1984 The Choking Doberman. New York: Norton.
Caplow, Theodore
   1982 "Christmas gifts and kin networks." American Sociological Review 47:383-92.
Caplow, Theodore and Margaret Holmes Williamson
   1980 "Decoding Middletown's Easter Bunny." Semiotica 32:221-32.
Carroll, Peter N.
   1982 It Seemed Like Nothing Happened. New York: Holt, Rinehart, & Winston.
Converse, Philip E., Jean D. Dotson, Wendy J. Hoag and William H. McGee III
   1980 American Social Attitudes Data Sourcebook. Cambridge: Harvard University Press.
Davis, Susan G.
   1982 "'Making the night hideous.'" American Quarterly 34:185-99.
DeKalb Daily Chronicle
   1984 "Sidewalk interview." October 28:10.
Editor and Publisher
   1973 "Press finds Halloween sadism rare but warns of danger." 106 (March 3):22.
Erskine, Hazel
   1974 "The polls: fear of crime and violence." Public Opinion Quarterly 38:131-45.
Fine, Gary Alan
   1979 "Cokelore and coke law." Journal of American Folklore 92:477-82.
   1980 "The Kentucky fried rat." Journal of the Folklore Institute 17:222-43.
   1985 "The Goliath effect." Journal of American Folklore 98:63-84.
Fischer, Claude S.
   1982 To Dwell Among Friends. Chicago: University of Chicago Press.
Fishman, Mark
   1978 "Crime waves as ideology." Social Problems 25:531-43.
Fresno Bee
   1984 "No tricks found in Fresno treats." November 1:B1.
Grider, Sylvia
   1982 "The razor blades in the apples syndrome." Unpublished paper.
Hatch, Jane M. (ed.)
   1978 The American Book of Days. Third edition. New York: Wilson.
Isaacs, Susan and Robert Royeton
   1982 "Witches, goblins, ghosts." Parents Magazine 57 (October):66-9.
Jacobs, Norman
   1965 "The phantom slasher of Taipei." Social Problems 12:318-28.
Johnson, Donald M.
   1945 "The 'phantom anesthetist' of Mattoon." Journal of Abnormal and Social Psychology 40:175-86.
Kerckhoff, Alan C. and Kurt W. Back
   1968 The June Bug. New York: Appleton-Century-Crofts.
Lofland, John
   1981 "Collective behavior." Pp. 411-46 in Morris Rosenberg and Ralph H. Turner (eds.), Social Psychology. New York: Basic Books.
Los Angeles Times
   1982 "Trick or treat subdued amid poisoning scares." November 1:1,28.
Medalia, Nahum Z. and Otto N. Larsen
   1958 "Diffusion and belief in a collective delusion." American Sociological Review 23:180-86.
Merry, Sally Engle
   1981 Urban Danger. Philadelphia: Temple University Press.
National Confectioners Association, Chocolate Manufacturers Association, and National Candy Wholesalers Association
   n.d. "Halloween/1982: an overview." Unpublished paper.
New York Times
   1950 "Punish Halloween 'witch,' angry parents demand." November 3:52.
   1970 "Those treats may be tricks." October 28:56.
   1972 "Trick-or-treating till stroke of 7." November 1:30.
   1980 "Atlanta and Miami curbing Halloween." October 31:A14.
   1982 "Experts theorize about 'copycat syndrome.'" October 30:6.
Newsweek
   1975 "The goblins will getcha. . . ." 86 (November 3):28.

O'Neill, William L.
  1971 Coming Apart. Chicago: Quadrangle.
Pfohl, Stephen J.
  1977 "The 'discovery' of child abuse." Social Problems 24:310-23.
Riesman, David
  1950 The Lonely Crowd. New Haven: Yale University Press.
San Francisco Chronicle
  1970 "Capsule caused Halloween death." November 10:3.
Santino, Jack
  1983 "Halloween in America." Western Folklore 42:1-20.
Schoenfeld, A. Clay, Robert F. Meier and Robert J. Griffin
  1979 "Constructing a social problem." Social Problems 27:38-61.
Simpson, Jacqueline
  1983 "Urban legends in *The Pickwick Papers*." Journal of American Folklore 96:462-70.
Smelser, Neil J.
  1962 Theory of Collective Behavior. New York: Free Press.
Spector, Malcolm, and John I. Kitsuse
  1973 "Social problems." Social Problems 21:145-59.
  1977 Constructing Social Problems. Menlo Park, CA: Cummings.
Spiro, Peter
  1982 "Chaos by the capsule." New Republic 187 (December 6):10-1.
Stinchcombe, Arthur L., Rebecca Adams, Carol A. Heimer, Kim Lane Scheppele, Tom W. Smith and D. Garth Taylor
  1980 Crime and Punishment. San Francisco: Jossey-Bass.
Stone, Gregory P.
  1959 "Halloween and the mass child." American Quarterly 11:372-79.
Suttles, Gerald D.
  1972 The Social Construction of Communities. Chicago: University of Chicago Press.
Tierney, Kathleen J.
  1982 "The battered woman movement and the creation of the wife beating problem." Social Problems 29:207-20.
Time
  1982 "Copycats on the prowl." 120 (November 8):27.
Times (Beaverton, OR)
  1984 "Letters." October 25:36.
Troyer, Ronald J. and Gerald E. Markle
  1983 Cigarettes. New Brunswick, NJ: Rutgers University Press.
  1984 "Coffee drinking." Social Problems 31:403-16.
Trubo, Richard
  1974 "Holiday for sadists." PTA Magazine 69:28-9.
U.S. Congress: House of Representatives
  1982 Hearing on Tamper-Resistant Packaging for Over-the-Counter Drugs. Committee on Energy and Commerce, Subcommittee on Health and the Environment. 96th Congress, 2nd session. Washington: U.S. Government Printing Office.
U.S. Consumer Product Safety Commission
  1982 Annual Report. Washington: U.S. Government Printing Office.
Van Buren, Abigail
  1983 "Dear Abby." Fresno Bee (October 31):D2.
  1984 "Dear Abby." Fresno Bee (September 30):C4.

[11]

Fear and Loathing on Reality Television: An Analysis of "America's Most Wanted" and "Unsolved Mysteries"[*]

Gray Cavender, *Arizona State University*, and Lisa Bond-Maupin, *Southwest Missouri State University*

> From early newspapers to contemporary television drama, the media demonstrate a continuing fascination with crime. Two recent television programs, "America's Most Wanted" and "Unsolved Mysteries," claim to offer a different treatment of crime in that these programs dramatize "real" crimes and encourage the television audience to assist in locating fugitives. Content analysis of the programs reveals that depictions of crime are consistent with television crime drama, and that these dramatizations resemble urban legends in which crime symbolizes the uncertainties of modern life. The programs convey an unpredictable world filled with unsafe people and places. This sense of modern danger justifies the programs' solicitation of audience participation through surveillance.

Introduction

The media serve to stimulate our interest in crime. Newspapers, for example, detail the exploits of criminals, while television news and crime drama focus on crimes. Although most crime drama is fictional representation, programs like "The F.B.I." modify actual cases.

Recently, a new type of crime program has been presented to the public. "America's Most Wanted" (AMW) and "Unsolved Mysteries" (UM) present vignettes depicting actual crimes in which theories of crime are dramatized. These dramatizations feature actors, actual photographs or film footage, and interviews conducted with participants and the police. Viewers are urged to call the police or program representatives with information related to the crime, and police officers are on standby in the television studio to take these calls.

AMW and UM represent a hybrid programming format in that a news or public service format is superimposed on entertainment to produce a new television genre, reality programming. But, the line between fact and fiction is not so distinct in the media (Williams 1989, p. 5). Even the news represents a social construction of reality in which reporters transform occurrences into news events (Molotch and Lester 1974; Tuchman 1978). On television genres

Sociological Inquiry, Vol. 63, No. 3, August 1993
©1993 by the University of Texas Press, P.O. Box 7819, Austin, TX 78713

tend to blend together (Gitlin 1985, p. 6). However, such blending of fact and fiction represents a defining characteristic of reality programming inasmuch as these programs are intended to draw the audience into their reality through active participation.

Crime and Danger in the Media

Scholars analyze media crime depictions ranging from the amount of crime news to the demographics of crime drama. The findings of such studies suggest that newspaper coverage bears little relationship to official crime statistics (Davis 1952; Fishman 1978). Although some analysts are not concerned about the divergence of newspaper coverage from official statistics, because such statistics are, like the news, a social construction (Tuchman 1978; Ericson, Baranek, and Chan 1991, p. 54), still others (Graber 1980) argue that newspapers offer a misleading picture of crime and criminals. Newspapers disproportionately report violent crimes, and reporters tend to focus attention on sensational matters such as the capture of a criminal and high status offenders (Graber 1980; Garofalo 1981, pp. 323-325; Humphries 1981, pp. 195-196).

Crime news and fiction go hand-in-hand because a similar pattern emerges in television drama (Katz 1987). Dramatic criminal plots are featured —usually violence against individuals— and the chase is highlighted (Garofalo 1981, p. 327). Television criminals are predominately male and disproportionately white, over 30 years of age, and members of a profession (Comstock 1978, pp. 289-293; Pandiani 1978). Television crime is detached from the social context in which it is committed, and non-law-enforcement personnel often solve crimes and capture criminals (Humphries 1981; Lichter and Lichter 1983).

Some research addresses the effects of such depictions on the audience, but the scholarly debate continues unresolved as to whether television affects the public's perception of crime (Gerbner and Gross 1976; Hirsch 1980, 1981). Other researchers suggest that the "meaning" of media crime depictions should be addressed prior to evaluating the effects these depictions have on the public (Gitlin 1979).

The ideological and symbolic dimensions of crime are also present. Television crime drama presents mythic morality plays that privilege a social control orientation (Gitlin 1979, p. 257; Schattenberg 1981), while newspaper coverage reinforces the symbolism of the dominant order (Ericson et al. 1991). Still other researchers analyze the newsworthy effect of such stories (Ericson et al. 1991, pp. 140-148), suggesting that these stories are simple, easily dramatized and personalized, and depict the unexpected. Deviance and control stories meet these criteria. Jack Katz (1987, pp. 50-55) offers four additional criteria for newsworthiness of crime stories: (1) they exemplify human viciousness or audacity, (2) collective integrity is threatened, (3) people who violate moral boundaries are featured, and (4) high status criminals are involved.

Jack Katz's newsworthiness of crime stories criteria parallel the elements of urban legends. Urban legends circulate as true stories, referencing frightening strangers who prey upon unsuspecting victims (Best 1990). Urban legends, such as poisoned Halloween candy, symbolize the strains and unpredictability of modern life (Fine 1980, p. 237; Best 1990, p. 142). Newspaper crime stories produce motifs found in urban legends, expressing the frustrations of a world characterized by the fear of violence (Wachs 1988; Oring 1990).

Crime is an ideal idiom for expressing urban fear and a corresponding sense of danger. Sally Merry (1981, pp. 11-13), for example, identifies three aspects of danger that are linked to crime: a cognitive assessment of cues, harm that transcends the risk of crime, and danger, a cultural construct, learned as part of how the world functions. People who occupy ambiguous and interstitial statuses and roles, such as children, are likely victims (Merry 1981, p. 140). Criminals are beyond normal techniques of social control (Douglas 1966; Merry 1981, pp. 125, 163), and the fear of crime justifies increased control over those who are considered "dangerous" (Merry 1981, p. 220).

Television is especially suited for evoking fear. As a visual medium, television conveys situational cues that elicit fear, such as dark, isolated areas or menacing strangers (Merry, 1981; Stanko 1990; Warr 1990). Cinematographic techniques make these cues more realistic (Graber 1990; Kellner 1990). In the following section the image of crime, criminals, victims, police, and the world view presented by AMW and UM are analyzed. This analysis also includes images conveyed through cinematographic techniques and formats.

Method

A content analysis was conducted of AMW and UM programs that aired between January 25 and May 31, 1989. These programs were videotaped and a subsample of 16 episodes was randomly selected: nine half-hour-long AMW episodes and seven hour-long UM episodes. The 16 episodes contain 77 vignettes (48 AMW; 29 UM); the vignette serves as the unit of analysis. In the analysis, all percentages are calculated on these numbers of vignettes.

The protocol used for data collection was focused on three aspects of the programming: (1) *demographics*: types of crime and general information on the crime, criminals, and victims; (2) *characterizations*: specific depictions of crime, criminals, and victims, such as brutality, dangerousness, or a victim's vulnerability; (3) *world view*: relative safety of people and places, the terror and randomness of crime, and what the audience should do about crime.

Information about cinematographic techniques (for example, camera angles and soundtrack) was coded across all three categories. Both programs feature updates about fugitives depicted earlier who are sighted or captured. Such updates were coded with the vignettes in which they originally appeared.

Data and Discussion

There are three parts to the analysis. Part one compares AMW with UM with prior research on crime drama. Part two considers the parallels between AMW and UM's vignettes and urban legends. Part three focuses on the construction and the magnification of the dangers of the modern world depicted in these programs.

Television Crime Drama and Reality Programming

Television depictions differ significantly from official crime statistics. The analysis reveals that AMW and UM's depictions of "real life" crimes and criminals are consistent with crime drama representations.

Television crime is depicted as violent and usually directed against persons. AMW and UM offer a similar view of crime. As shown in Table 1, in 92 percent of AMW's vignettes ($n = 44$ of 48 vignettes), the crimes depicted also are violent and personal (murder, attempted murder, rape, kidnapping, armed robbery and child molestation). Sixty-two percent of UM's vignettes ($n = 18$) include violence against persons. For both programs, murder is depicted in 52 percent of the vignettes ($n = 40$).

Ninety-one percent of the vignettes ($n = 70$) depict male criminals. Four percent of the vignettes ($n = 3$) feature female criminals, and these are portrayed as accomplices. Criminals are 30 years or older in 56 percent of the vignettes ($n = 43$), and Caucasians are involved in 64 percent of all vignettes ($n = 44$). African-Americans ($n = 9$) and Hispanics ($n = 9$) are featured in 12 percent of the vignettes (see Table 2).

Contrary to television drama, criminals are frequently portrayed as professional criminals. Corporate and political criminals are absent from the vignettes. A motivation for crime is offered in over half of the vignettes ($n = 42$). Greed frequently prompts the crime, especially on UM ($n = 11$), while emotional motivations, such as jealousy, are prominent on AMW ($n = 6$). Some crimes are blamed on random violence or mistaken identity ($n = 9$).

AMW and UM provide a social history, re-enacting past key events in the life of the criminal, and describe their current lives. However, these caricatures tend to reinforce existing stereotypes about criminals.

Table 1
Number and Percentage of Vignettes that Depicted Offense Types by Program[a]

Program Vignettes

Offense	UM (N = 29) %	n	AMW (N = 48) %	n	Combined UM/AMW (N = 77) %	n
Murder	41	(12)	58	(28)	52	(40)
Theft/fraud/extortion	21	(6)	8	(4)	13	(10)
Escape	7	(2)	15	(7)	12	(9)
Bank robbery/armed robbery	10	(3)	10	(5)	10	(8)
Illegal arms/terrorism	0		4	(2)	3	(2)
Unexplained death/missing	14	(4)	2	(1)	7	(5)
Rape	3	(1)	6	(3)	5	(4)
Kidnapping	3	(1)	6	(3)	5	(4)
Child molestation	3	(1)	6	(3)	5	(4)
Attempted murder	0		4	(2)	3	(2)
Drug dealing	0		4	(2)	3	(2)
Other[b]	10	(3)	4	(2)	7	(5)

[a]Percentages are based on the total number of vignettes for each program. Note that a vignette may contain depictions of more than one offense type.
[b]The Other category includes bigamy and/or intimidation.

Table 2
Number and Percentage of Vignettes that Depicted Offender Characteristics by Program[a]

Characteristics	UM (N = 29) %	UM (N = 29) n	AMW (N = 48) %	AMW (N = 48) n	Combined UM/AMW (N = 77) %	Combined UM/AMW (N = 77) n
Gender						
Male	76	(22)	100	(48)	91	(70)
Female	3	(1)	4	(2)	4	(3)
Unknown/not depicted	21	(6)	0		8	(6)
Age						
20–29	21	(6)	31	(15)	27	(21)
30–39	17	(5)	21	(10)	20	(15)
40–49	21	(6)	31	(15)	27	(21)
50–59	14	(4)	6	(3)	9	(7)
Unknown/not depicted	28	(8)	10	(5)	17	(13)
Ethnicity						
Caucasian	66	(19)	63	(30)	64	(49)
African-American	3	(1)	17	(8)	12	(9)
Hispanic	7	(2)	15	(7)	12	(9)
Mixed ethnicity	3	(1)	0		1	(1)
Unknown/not depicted	21	(6)	6	(3)	12	(9)

[a] A vignette may contain depictions of male and female offenders or multiple offenders of the same gender, age, and ethnicity.

Citizens play a significant role on both programs. The program hosts credit viewers with captures, while the police are depicted as competent and accessible to the viewers. AMW and UM also provide more information about trial and sentencing than usually appears in crime drama.

AMW and UM as Urban Legends

Fear-evoking cues magnified by sophisticated cinematographic techniques enable AMW and UM to construct entertaining programs that fit the standard format of the television crime genre. The vignettes are symbolic morality plays about good and evil.

As in urban legends, the crime portrayed on AMW and UM symbolizes the dangers and complexities of modern life that threaten the social order. Brutal, violent crimes are featured (for example, UM 2-22-89; AMW 2-12-89), and graphic details are shown, including the number and location of a victim's wounds. For example, one victim is stabbed 30 times through the heart (AMW 2-12-89); another victim is shot "5 times and died of massive bleeding" (AMW 2-5-89).

Cinematographic techniques enhance the affective aspects of crime. In some vignettes, the film speed is reduced to slow motion as a criminal draws a gun and shoots the victim, capturing the muzzle flash (AMW 2-5-89, 2-12-89, 4-9-89). One vignette employs fear cues: the host, emerging from the night on a deserted road, references a common fear of driving on a lonely stretch of highway where one's cries for help would go unheeded (UM 4-12-89).

Described are dimensions of harm that go beyond the risk of victimization. Victims are "embarrassed and devastated" (UM 3-15-89), and their family and friends' lives are tragically disrupted (UM 1-25-89, 3-15-89, AMW 4-2-89). Dramatic irony intensifies the tragedy. Victims are murdered shortly after achieving an important goal (AMW 3-19-89) or on their birthday (UM 3-15-89). Victims do not merely lose property through theft, they lose "a precious family heirloom that was part of their heritage" (AMW 4-2-89). The narrative, the visual, and the soundtrack combine to communicate a sense of tragedy, e.g., the host notes that a slain policeman is buried with full honors. The vignette shows footage of his funeral as "Taps" is played in the background (AMW 2-5-89). Stories are simple and easily dramatized. Twenty AMW vignettes (42 percent) depict random, purposeless crimes often featured in urban legends, while nineteen UM vignettes (66 percent) offer such depictions.

Criminals. Like the villains of urban legends, criminals are dangerous people who are beyond social control. Thirty-seven AMW vignettes (77 percent) depict criminals in this manner. Nineteen UM vignettes (66 percent) offer such depictions.

Fugitives are characterized as dangerous (for example, AMW 2-5-89;

UM 4-12-89), and the bail bond imposed suggests that these criminals should be incarcerated (AMW 2-5-89). The camera often zooms in on a captured fugitive's handcuffs, providing a visual image of the physical restraints that are required to control these individuals (for example, AMW 2-12-89; UM 3-15-89).

Some criminals are traditional urban legend villains, such as drifters (AMW 3-26-89) and hitchhikers (UM 3-1-89). Other criminals are portrayed as satanists (AMW 4-16-89; UM 3-29-89). AMW and UM also feature criminals who are gang members (AMW 2-12-89) and drug dealers (AMW 2-5-89; 4-16-89).

AMW and UM feature frightening criminals who have ambiguous psychological capacity. One criminal is a "crazed killer, a psycho, a maniac" (UM 3-29-89), while others are characterized as "schizophrenic" (AMW 4-2-89) or "emotionally disturbed" (AMW 2-26-89). Both programs feature criminals who "showed no emotion" (for example, AMW 2-5-89; UM 3-29-89), or who demonstrate "a flamboyant disregard of authority" (AMW 4-12-89).

The programs define criminals through their actions, portraying criminality as a master status, noting such deviance is undifferentiated in that the criminal activity is generalized to other aspects of their lives. For example, one criminal "masqueraded as a construction worker but he was really an escaped murderer" (AMW 2-5-89). Another criminal who "appeared to be a model cop was in reality a child molester" (UM 3-1-89).

The program hosts provide physical descriptions of fugitives in derogatory terms, such as "a scraggly beard" (AMW 4-2-89), or "dirty blonde hair" (AMW 2-26-89). Other deviant behaviors unrelated to the crimes are mentioned, such as dabbling in voodoo (AMW 4-2-89). In one vignette, the host invites the audience to view the physical effects of depravity, using a time lapse technique on a series of photographs in which the criminal's physical appearance deteriorates (AMW 2-26-89).

Victims. The victims often occupy ambiguous and interstitial roles and statuses and, therefore, are vulnerable to harm. Victims are similar to those of urban legends. Twenty-four AMW (50 percent) and twenty UM vignettes (69 percent) depict such victims. Children are molested and kidnapped (UM 3-1-89, 1-25-89). In this regard, AMW's opening features a visual of an empty playground swing, accompanied by a voice-over of the word "kidnapped."

Women are frequent victims as well. Approximately one-half of the victims whose sex is noted are female, thereby reinforcing the fear of crime and violence that women experience.

AMW and UM offer information about victims designed to achieve viewer empathy. Victims are referred to by their given names, and friends share personal anecdotes. Crimes are re-enacted so as to promote identification with the victim; the camera takes the victim's perspective, reproducing a good/evil dichotomy, with the victim and the audience aligned against the criminal.

The programs focus on the victim's personal and professional worth. In contrast to the criminals, victims are "hard working" individuals (for example, UM 3-15-89; AMW 4-16-89). UM characterizes one victim as a "devoted wife and mother who was active in the community" (UM 3-29-89), and another as "the kind of girl you'd like to have for your daughter" (UM 3-15-89). One vignette featuring wild horses as victims establishes their worth in human terms: "They symbolize the freedom of the American West, and each animal has its own unique personality" (UM 1-25-89).

Modern Danger

Both programs create a sense of modern danger analogous to the fears that urban legends convey. This modern danger is characterized as a world in which no one, no matter how careful, is safe.

Just as urban legends are portrayed as true stories, AMW and UM act as media storytellers of "real life" and the terrible uncertainties of life. The reality program format enhances the sense of modern danger. As entertainment these hybrid programs combine fear cues and cinematographic techniques, and appeal to the conventions of news programming that bolster credibility of reality claims.

An Unsafe World. Good storytellers localize their tales in time and space. AMW and UM program hosts begin their stories with statements like, "27 years ago tonight" (AMW 2-5-89). Exact dates of crimes (UM 1-25-89) and phrases such as "20 days ago" (AMW 3-19-89) provide accessible temporal referents, contributing to reality claims.

Geographic settings are also important. Statements such as "it all started in this house on Chestnut Street" (AMW 2-19-89), or "a quiet blue collar suburb on the outskirts of Cleveland" (UM 5-31-89) produce an identifiable sense of place. Some locations, such as an unfamiliar area or dark alley, serve as fear cues.

Featured are crimes that occur in safe places, and program hosts draw special attention to such settings. One vignette, set in a conservative Louisiana community, represents, the host notes, an unlikely setting for a crime (UM 3-1-89). In another vignette, "dark forces swirled beneath a small town facade" (UM 2-22-89). Crimes often violate special places, such as the home. In one dramatization, the camera follows a schizophrenic killer as he observes the sleeping victims (AMW 4-23-89). Another vignette depicts a burglar sneaking through a house while the occupants host a dinner party. Later, a teenage girl showers and her unsuspecting mom works in a bedroom, while the burglar prowls through the house (AMW 4-2-89). When crime occurs in seemingly safe places, a sense of modern danger is enhanced.

Certain predictable people, such as menacing strangers, also serve as fear cues. However, the worst danger portrayed evolves from seemingly trustworthy persons. Likeable and normal people are portrayed as manipulative con artists or crazy (for example, UM 1-25-89; AMW 2-12-89, 4-9-89). In some instances, the unsuspecting criminal occupies a special role, such as a policeman who counsels abused children but who also molests these children (UM 3-1-89), or a sociopathic nurse who kidnaps a newborn baby at gunpoint (UM 1-25-89).

The most terrifying criminals hold a special status with respect to the victim. Examples include the husband who murders his wife while she begs him to spare her life (AMW 2-5-89). Other vignettes depict special criminals who hold an interstitial status, such as the "All American" kid who becomes a drug user and murders his parents (AMW 2-26-89). Such vignettes emphasize the thesis that no place is safe; no person is trustworthy.

Random Terror. One message is that the modern world is filled with danger. Random and terrifying danger lurks everywhere, awaiting the victim and, by implication, the viewer. Powerful, emotionally charged vignettes produce images that reinforce a sense of danger that is commonplace in modern society. Some of the vignettes emphasize the criminal. For example, as the host characterizes the criminal as dangerous, the frame freezes, leaving the criminal's intense stare directed at the audience (AMW 4-9-89). Program hosts urge the audience to remember these visually compelling images, and to be on the lookout for the fugitives.

Victims are also emphasized, many of whom are randomly chosen, innocent individuals who are "arbitrarily targeted" (UM 3-29-89) or murdered by mistake (AMW 4-16-89). On occasion a horror movie format is used in which the foolish character opens a door at the top of the stairs as the audience screams "No." People sense the impending danger and warn victims who rarely heed such warnings. Either victims do not appreciate the extent of the danger (AMW 2-12-89, 4-16-89), or they are engaged in common activities that escalate into sudden violence, such as the woman who became involved in a marital dispute and is murdered (UM 1-25-89).

Equally terrifying are the vignettes in which the victims realize their danger. The camera follows an obviously frightened woman leaving her house. Ominous music complements this fear as she nervously scans the street, searching for some threat. She is careful, but she still disappears (UM 1-25-89).

Other careful victims are murdered by maniacal killers (for example UM 3-29-89), or by satanic blood cults (AMW 4-16-89). Emphasizing victim terror, victims often describe their fear (UM 4-12-89). In other instances the host describes the fear, indicating how it feels for a family to be stalked by a prison escapee bent on revenge (UM 4-12-89).

Situational and fear cues heighten the sense of victim terror and audience frustration. Vignettes feature people who are isolated and alone when victimized (for example, UM 4-12-89). In other instances, people are nearby but do not render assistance to the victim. A woman whose baby has been kidnapped screams for help, but no motorist will stop (UM 1-25-89). Careful, normal, and hard-working people are victimized by base, depraved strangers. They are also victimized by their children, spouses, mates, and friends. In this area, AMW and UM programs extend beyond the content of urban legends, suggesting that modern danger is inescapable.

AMW and UM programs portray a world in which crime is so unpredictable and its consequences so devastating that public safety is at issue. Crime is a metaphor for a world gone berserk, for life out of control. The only recourse viewers have is to call the authorities or the program representative with information that will put criminals behind bars. Program updates attribute captures to viewer tips, and footage of captured fugitives supports these claims.

Modern danger legitimizes public surveillance. Forging a partnership between the police, the media, and the audience, these programs encourage wide dispersal of community social control.

Conclusion

Prior research has shown that television dramatizes stereotype depictions of crime and criminals. In the present study the authors conclude that reality programming presents similar images. Crimes are portrayed as violent and personal, and fugitives are portrayed as dangerous people.

However, the present study diverges from the more traditional media crime approach in that the focus is on program meaning. AMW and UM programs present images common to popular urban legends in that crime is used to symbolize the uncertainties of modern life, that criminals are evil, abnormal people, and victims are portrayed as being vulnerable. Such tales nurture the very fears that produce urban legends.

Using a combination of case selection, cinematographic techniques, and claims, these reality programs depict a sense of modern danger. AMW and UM programs present a world in which anyone can be cast into the role of a criminal or a victim. Such an image of reality is frightening because the victims are people with whom viewers can identify.

316   GRAY CAVENDER AND LISA BOND-MAUPIN

Reality programs nurture audience participation as one solution to the pervasiveness of crime, supporting the notion that viewers can be empowered in the fight against crime. Viewers are encouraged to watch for fugitives and report them either to the police or the program. Both programs claim that such surveillance leads to the capture of fugitives.

Reality program encouragement of surveillance supports the view that control is dispersing more widely into society. Images of dangerous fugitives who participate in a world characterized by violence and uncertainty justify surveillance and reporting to the police. This world view also supports the claim made by Gitlin (1979) and Schattenberg (1981) that crime drama endorses a control orientation.

In sum, AMW and UM's hybrid news and entertainment format continues the trend toward blurred television genres previously noted by media scholars. The influence of television is so great that it has become an important part of the viewer's reality. Participating in reality programs means the audience is a part of that reality, making that reality almost indistinguishable from any other aspects of life.

ENDNOTE

*The authors appreciate the comments of Nancy Jurik, Joel Best, Richard Ericson, and Erdwin Pfuhl.

REFERENCES

Best, Joel. 1990. *Threatened Children*. Chicago: University of Chicago Press.
Comstock, George. 1978. *Television and Human Behavior*. New York: Columbia University Press.
Davis, James. 1952. "Crime News in Colorado Newspapers," *American Journal of Sociology* 57: 325-330.
Douglas, Mary. 1966. *Purity and Danger: An Analysis of Concepts of Pollution and Taboo*. Hammondsworth: Penguin Books.
Ericson, Richard, Patricia Baranek, and Janet Chan. 1991. *Representing Order: Crime, Law and Justice in the News Media*. Toronto: University of Toronto Press.
Fine, Gary. 1980. "The Kentucky Fried Rat: Legends and Modern Society." *Journal of the Folklore Institute* 17:222-243.
Fishman, Mark. 1978. "Crime Waves As Ideology." *Social Problems* 25:531-543.
Garofalo, James. 1981. "Crime and the Mass Media: A Selective Review of Research." *Journal of Research in Crime and Delinquency* 18:319-349.
Gerbner, George, and Larry Gross. 1976. "Living With Television: The Violence Profile." *Journal of Communication* 26:173-199.
Gitlin, Todd. 1979. "Prime Time Ideology: The Hegemonic Process in Television Entertainment." *Social Problems* 26:251-266.
———. 1985. "Looking Through the Screen." Pp. 3-8 in *Watching Television*, edited by Todd Gitlin. New York: Pantheon Books.

Graber, Doris. 1980. *Crime News and the Public*. New York: Praeger.
———. 1990. "Seeing is Remembering: How Visuals Contribute to Learning from Television News." *Journal of Communication* 40:134-155.
Hirsch, Paul. 1980. "The 'Scary World' of the Nonviewer and Other Anomalies: A Reanalysis of Gerbner et al.'s Findings on Cultivation Analysis, Part 1." *Communications Research* 7: 403-456.
———. 1981. "The 'Scary World' of the Nonviewer and Other Anomalies: A Reanalysis of Gerbner et al.'s Findings on Cultivation Analysis, Part 2." *Communication Research* 8:3-37.
Humphries, Drew. 1981. "Serious Crime, News Coverage, and Ideology." *Crime and Delinquency* 27:191-205.
Katz, Jack. 1987. "What Makes Crime News?" *Media, Culture and Society* 9:47-75.
Kellner, Douglas. 1990. *Television and the Crisis of Democracy*. Boulder, CO: Westview Press.
Lichter, Linda and Robert Lichter. 1983. *Prime Time Crime*. Washington, DC: The Media Institute.
Merry, Sally. 1981. *Urban Danger: Life in a Neighborhood of Strangers*. Philadelphia: Temple University Press.
Molotch, Harvey, and Marilyn Lester. 1974. "News as Purposive Behavior: On the Strategic Use of Routine Events, Accidents, and Scandals." *American Sociological Review* 39:101-112.
Oring, Elliott. 1990. "Legend, Truth, and News." *Southern Folklore* 47:163-177.
Pandiani, J. 1978. "Crime Time TV: If All We Knew Is What We Saw. . . ." *Contemporary Crises* 2:437-458.
Schattenberg, Gus. 1981. "Social Control Functions of Mass Media Depictions of Crime." *Sociological Inquiry* 51:71-77.
Stanko, Elizabeth. 1990. *Everyday Violence: How Women and Men Experience Sexual and Physical Danger*. London: Pandora.
Tuchman, Gaye. 1978. *Making News: A Study in the Social Construction of Reality*. New York: Free Press.
Wachs, Eleanor. 1988. *Crime-Victim Stories: New York City's Urban Folklore*. Bloomington, IN: Indiana University Press.
Warr, Mark. 1990. "Dangerous Situations: Social Context and Fear of Victimization." *Social Forces* 68:891-907.
Williams, Raymond. 1989. *Raymond Williams on Television: Selected Writings*, edited by A. O'Connor. London: Routledge.

[12]

CLEVELAND AND THE PRESS:
Outrage and Anxiety in the Reporting of Child Sexual Abuse

Mica Nava

The phenomenon of child sexual abuse erupted on to the front pages of Britain's newspapers when it was discovered, in June 1987, that an unprecedented number of children in Cleveland, an area of high unemployment in the north-east of England, had been made subjects of place of safety orders and removed from their homes because it was suspected that they were victims of sexual abuse by adults. Over the following weeks the Cleveland story retained its status as important news and, indeed, continues to do so as I write and the official inquiry into the events there proceeds.

This article is not an attempt to establish 'the truth' of what happened in Cleveland, even if this were possible. What I want to do here is to explore the way the press tried to make sense of a phenomenon which had hitherto been kept a family secret, tabooed and disavowed, and which, as a consequence of media attention, grew over a period of weeks to occupy a position of prominence in public discourse and popular consciousness.

What conceptual apparatus – if any – did the press rely on in order to understand the issues on which it focused so much attention and anxiety? In what way – if any – did the shaping and selection of news contribute, not only to the way child sexual abuse was popularly understood, but also to the formulation and consolidation of a viewpoint which might be identified as belonging either to the left or to the right? To what extent were debates within feminism taken into account in this process?

In addition to addressing these questions, I want to look at the explosion of media preoccupation itself. Similar escalations of media concern have in the past been usefully illuminated by applying to them the notion of 'moral panic'.[1] These are likely to occur at particular moments of social crisis when people fear that traditional values and institutions are under attack. The media play a key part in sensationalizing the situation and, importantly – particularly in relation to the singling out of paediatrician Marietta Higgs in the Cleveland case – in identifying and legitimating the folk devils who become the targets for popular persecution. This process also includes the orchestration of 'expert' opinion which can contribute to increased demands for state intervention and the (re)formation of popular consent to a more conservative social order.

In certain important respects the Cleveland affair can be defined as a moral panic; and though it may not fit this definition in a predictable fashion, the way it does so is pertinent for feminists as well as for a study of the media. An investigation into how certain coded meanings were produced, and how Marietta Higgs was posed in opposition to Labour MP Stuart Bell, the other major figure in the controversy, can also offer an insight into the way the newspapers tried to establish for themselves a reasonably coherent position which would be consistent with their more general editorial policy. This was not an easy project, as we shall see. In fact, one of the most interesting things to emerge from an examination of the press coverage over this period is that despite the vilification of the tabloids – accusatory headlines and photos of Marietta Higgs dominated many front pages in late June and early July – a great deal of the reporting both in the popular press and in the qualities was characterized by confusion and contradiction.

This is not so surprising if one considers the deeply disturbing, opaque and unprecedented nature of the Cleveland events. Few other issues in recent years have provoked such acute dilemmas. The peculiarly complex combination of elements and circumstances in the Cleveland case has undermined previously reliable moral and conceptual schema, and it is not only the media that has been confused in its response. This has also been the case for feminists, for those involved professionally in the area and, not least, for the general public.

In order to formulate its stance in relation to Cleveland and make sense of the phenomenon of child sexual abuse, the press has had to evaluate the discourse and interventions of disparate medical, legal, social work, charity and psychoanalytical orthodoxies and practices. The 'experts' from these fields, upon whom the media rely in order to define and explain events, have themselves been deeply divided. Their conflicting interpretations have, in this emotionally charged instance, exacerbated the confusion of the press and made the task of 'orchestrating' and classifying expert opinion extremely difficult. In fact few other issues in recent times have done as much to reveal the way in which expert knowledge is politically inflected. To compound matters, the press has also had to take into account the views of politicians and of its readers. Politicians have not been a great deal of help. Tory and Labour MPs have not taken up consistent positions and new cross-party alliances have been formed (*The Times*, 29 June). Readers are not an easy constituency either: though they may be parents, they are also sons and daughters, and are as likely to identify with the survivors as with the abusers.

In many newspapers, the uncertainty that this lack of closure has produced has been manifest in the contradictory messages conveyed in different articles on the same page, and even within articles, as well as in editorials of different and sometimes consecutive days. The selection of objects of adulation and persecution – the targeting of goodies and baddies – has likewise not been straightforward. However, this attempt by newspapers to find and settle into interpretations with which they feel comfortable, this continual jostling of position, should not be read as evidence of infinite openness. It is important to recognize that the questions repeatedly posed, the solutions offered and the stories returned to, have all fallen within a narrow range. Moreover, they have been singularly neglectful of feminist argument.

Yet the paradox is that despite this, feminism has not been absent from the Cleveland affair. On the contrary, it has had an extraordinarily powerful symbolic presence in the person of Marietta Higgs. Whether this semi-conscious attribution by the press has been in the form of accolade or desecration, it has been there; and it has frequently taken the place of feminist critique. Certain clusters of meaning which have been evoked in references to her are evidence of this displacement. As the formation of a chain between Marietta Higgs and feminism begins to become apparent, we are reminded of the other more glaring association by which feminism, via Marietta Higgs, is linked to and even identified with the target of moral panic. In this way the spectre of feminism becomes folk devil.

How these chains of association and processes of displacement occur, and how, in conjunction with other associations connected with Stuart Bell, they might have affected the construction and appropriation by the newspapers of particular viewpoints on the Cleveland affair, I hope to uncover by looking in greater detail at some of the key moments and features of the narrative.

The narrative

By the final weeks of June 1987 the issue is firmly on the front page. The number of place of safety orders on children suspected of being victims of sexual abuse in the general area of Cleveland has risen to two hundred over the preceding few months, compared with thirty during the whole of the previous year. The orders appear to have been based only on physical diagnosis of sexual abuse (the reflex anal dilation test) made by two paediatricians at Middlesbrough General Hospital, Drs Marietta Higgs and Geoffrey Wyatt. It subsequently emerges, however, that many of the cases were referred by social workers and GPs. The abuse is assumed to have taken place in the home. The scale of the issue is brought to light when existing social service facilities are no longer able to cope with the number of children taken into care, and when parents of allegedly abused children demand second opinions and contact their local Labour MP, Stuart Bell.

By 24 June an 'independent panel of child-health specialists', which includes woman police surgeon Dr Raine Roberts, has been established to review the cases of suspected child abuse and concludes that there have been serious errors of diagnosis in seventeen cases; Roberts refers to 'the flimsiest of flimsy evidence'. This is the signal for a number of newspapers to begin to call in other 'experts' to evaluate the conflicting theories. What counts as evidence, social service policies and appeals procedures all begin to come under scrutiny, and there is a plethora of human interest stories, most of which focus on the anxieties of the parents whose children have been removed.

The disputed diagnoses also become the signal for Stuart Bell to begin to develop his public profile as the defender of misjudged parents. At the same time we witness an entrenchment of denials that incestuous child abuse has occurred. The response of the press in this instance must be contrasted with earlier reporting of phenomena like ChildLine, a help line for physically and sexually abused children, and the death of Kimberly Carlisle.[2] In these instances the press defended the interests of the children and called for more vigorous intervention by social workers. Now many of the popular newspapers, following the lead of Bell, who has claimed that *parents* have suffered many miscarriages of justice, turn around and call for the dismissal of Marietta Higgs and Geoffrey Wyatt on the grounds of their alleged incompetence.

However, it is soon clear that Wyatt is going to be a less significant personage in the evolving scenario than Higgs. It is her photograph that starts to act as a coded reference for the events of Cleveland, and her private and professional life that is examined in the daily press, not his. The Cleveland Social Services Department, with its policies of immediately removing the child from the family even where there is no evidence that the alleged abuse has been committed by the father,[3] also takes a back seat. It is Higgs who is attributed with the power and misguided dedication which then construct her as the causative agent in the crisis.

Over the following weeks Cleveland maintains an extremely high profile as newspapers respond to Bell's accusation in the House of Commons that Marietta Higgs and Sue Richardson, consultant social worker for Cleveland Social Services in charge of child abuse, have 'conspired and colluded' to exclude police surgeon Alistair Irvine from examining children suspected of having been abused. Media attention is bolstered yet again when Bell accuses Cleveland Social Services Department of exaggerating its child sexual abuse figures in order to increase its funding and 'empire build'. The story starts to diminish in importance, though does not disappear, once an official inquiry is conceded.

Denial and acknowledgement

Throughout this period many newspapers remain inconsistent in their reporting of the 'scandal' that they are themselves responsible for

The Daily Mirror *on the side of Stuart Bell*

promoting. What then are the contradictions which seem to have provoked such a crisis of irresolution?

Even for those not disposed to minimize the extent and the gravity of child sexual abuse, many of the Cleveland procedures have been deeply disturbing. Considerable anxiety has been expressed about the fact that, partly as a consequence of disputed – possibly exaggerated – estimates of the incidence of child sexual abuse, a number of children appear to have been arbitrarily subjected to a disagreeable type of clinical examination, the validity of which is contested. Social Services have responded to this disputed and apparently uncorroborated evidence of sexual abuse in quite inappropriate ways: children have been taken away, sometimes in the middle of the night, from their families, schools and communities. Parents appear to be refused access and have minimal rights of appeal. All this has caused suffering and it is not unreasonable to assume that the damage will be long term both for children and for parents.

Yet it is important to recognize that, although these worries have a rational and persuasive kernel, they constitute only a relatively modest part of a much broader position which is overwhelmingly characterized by denial and traditionalism. In this version, the seriousness, the extent, and sometimes even the existence of child sexual abuse are denied. The mythical 'traditional' family, and by implication the role of the father within this – the father as patriarch – is defended.

Thus, for example, in the *Daily Mirror* and in the *Sun* of 26 June it is defiantly reported that the children have suffered no other sexual abuse than that inflicted by the doctors who examined them. Michael Toner, in the *Sunday Express* of 28 June, asserts, without offering any evidence, that he simply does not 'believe in the avalanche of child abuse suggested by the Cleveland figures'. He also refers to 'fashionable' (i.e. not traditional) 'zeal'. A number of papers make comments of this order. Lesley Garner in her article in the *Daily Telegraph* of 1 July, entitled

Overboard on child abuse

The family unit can be vital to a child's welfare and should not be destroyed

From the Daily Telegraph

'Overboard on Child Abuse', prefaces an interview with Valerie Howarth, new director of ChildLine, by voicing 'the suspicion that we are encouraging, even inventing, a newly fashionable problem'. Awareness of child sexual abuse is being 'zealously encouraged', she says, and concludes by warning us that: 'Few people know what forces are unleashed once society begins to tamper with the mechanics of the family'. It must be noted, however, that Garner's succinct expression of denial and traditionalism is contradictorily placed at the beginning and end of a piece which, in the middle, gives serious attention to the views of Howarth.

Despite this kind of reporting, many newspapers do at the same time accept that children *are* sexually abused. This acknowledgement is what constitutes the core of the second, conflicting approach to the question. Thus although the press may express anxieties about aspects of the Cleveland Social Services response, it simultaneously gives a public platform to other professionals in the field whose arguments undermine the public denial of the seriousness of the problem. So from some newspapers it emerges that the rate of reported incidence of sexual abuse is growing all the time, particularly among children aged between three and five, and that abusers, who are overwhelmingly men and of whom a significant proportion are fathers and stepfathers, often intimidate children to such an extent that it becomes necessary to remove them to an environment where they will feel confident enough to reveal the details of their experience. In this view the family is not always a safe place, fathers (and sometimes mothers) can exploit the power they have over their children in astonishingly brutal ways. Survivors of incest and sexual abuse report harrowing stories of manipulation, threats of violence, long-term trauma and denial.

A number of newspapers express support for this general perspective. Among the most consistent is the now defunct *London Daily News*, which must be honoured for publishing early on one of the very few pieces clearly informed by feminism. Entitled 'The Sins of the Fathers', it argues that 'sexual abuse is the consequence of the way [boys] have learnt to "be men"' (Rutherford, 26.6.87). Other papers are both less sophisticated and less consistent. The *Sun*, for example, after running abusive headlines like 'SACK THE DOCS' (26.6.87), suddenly changes tack and acknowledges the existence of abuse in Cleveland in a front-page article entitled 'THANK GOD FOR DR HIGGS' (30.6.87) which is about a woman whose children were 'saved' by Marietta Higgs.

The London Daily News *was one of the few newspapers with a consistent position*

'Dr Higgs was marvellous. I'm very grateful,' the woman is reported as saying. The accompanying photograph shows Higgs with a wry smile. Inside, however, the *Sun* reverts to its old self with an article entitled 'DOC IN "HUSH-UP PLOT"' which continues: 'Woman doctor plots with social worker' (30.6.87).

The *Daily Mirror* also moves backwards and forwards from an abrasively anti-Higgs position which denies the occurrence of abuse (this is the dominant approach, see e.g. 26.6.87 and 30.6.87) to one which acknowledges its existence (28.6.87) and, echoing Esther Rantzen and Michele Elliott who are interviewed in the same issue, argues in its editorial that: 'Helpless children must not suffer simply because we cannot bear to face the facts.' The *Star*, surprisingly, given its reputation as one of the most scurrilous of all the tabloids, carries a rather progressive and comprehensive analysis (see Alix Palmer, 9.7.87 and 31.7.87). Palmer's position is that current child sexual abuse figures are probably an underestimate and that 'Cleveland is not alone'; she is critical of government cuts in social services and the impact of these on

Contradictory reporting in the Sun

social-worker morale; she acknowledges the violence of many abusing fathers yet is also anti-imprisonment, since this is likely to drive the problem underground, and argues for a programme 'in which abusers can take responsibility for their actions'.

The *Daily Mail* coverage of the Cleveland events has also been extremely interesting. The paper is often accused of producing the worst

The making of Marietta Higgs in the Daily Mail

of tabloid writing (and is referred to in this way during the course of the Cleveland events by several of the 'quality' papers, see e.g. the *Daily Telegraph*, 1.7.87 and the *Observer*, 28.6.87). During the crisis it ran a daily cover line announcing itself as the paper which 'revealed the scandal to the nation', and had regularly sensationalist headlines. Yet at the same time it often devoted space to the views of Higgs's supporters, and oscillated in the position it took up. Perhaps more than any other newspaper, it presented us with contradictory messages – with both approaches simultaneously. Thus the portrait of Marietta Higgs (Shears, 26.6.87) is sympathetic – it describes her devotion, expertise and integrity – even though in the title she is referred to as a 'crusader' and Adelaide, the city she trained in, as 'the abuse capital of the world' (Shears, 26.6.87). Roger Scott (13.7.87), in a thoughtful piece, though with predictably inflammatory headlines, acknowledges the problems of Cleveland and weighs up the issues surrounding child sexual abuse as carefully as journalists in the liberal or 'quality' Press. At the same time, however, there are many pieces which use the crudest conventions of gutter journalism like, for example, the lead article on 30 June which is headlined 'THE CONSPIRACY'.

The *Guardian* and the *Independent* are among the 'quality' papers which, particularly in the early days, acknowledge increases in child sexual abuse. 'We must not recoil from the implications', argues the *Guardian* (25.6.87) while the *Independent*, though quite critical of Dr Higgs, states in its editorial: 'Talk of balancing parents' and children's rights is completely mistaken in this context. Children are not their parents' personal property' (25.6.87). (This position will not be adhered to consistently, however, as I will demonstrate later.) A number of papers carry letters critical of their own traditionalist stance; see, for example, the letter page in *Today* (27.6.87) which is headed 'Why Criticise the Child Watchers?' The *News on Sunday*, a left paper which claims to have uncovered the Cleveland affair in the first place and has always taken the side of the parents, carries similar critical letters.

What we begin to see then as we open the newspapers each day through late June and early July is the emergence of two quite sharply differentiated sets of assumptions and emphases, even though these are often not yet clearly identified either with a party political position or with a newspaper's general viewpoint. It is an indication of the absence of a coherent sexual politics both on the left and on the right that this confusion over Cleveland occurred and persisted. So given this lack of a politically informed guidance, how did the public and the press make sense of the events and make up their minds about where to offer their moral support?

Higgs and Bell

Very early on in the crisis over the Cleveland events, Stuart Bell becomes identified as the central representative of the first position

The News on Sunday, *left-wing paper on the side of the parents*

outlined above, that of denial or reluctant acknowledgement, while Marietta Higgs is identified with the second. As the principal antagonists in this symbolic war of position, these two individuals will go on to become critical forces in the formation of national ideas about child sexual abuse.

Bell opens the battle with a salvo in defence of the beleaguered parents, and in doing so singles out and targets Higgs as his main opponent. It takes only a few days before Alistair Irvine, Cleveland police surgeon, recruits himself as Bell's second-in-command and further polarizes the situation. He contributes to the consolidation of Higgs as representative of a particular viewpoint when he publicly attacks her professional judgement and claims he has been prevented

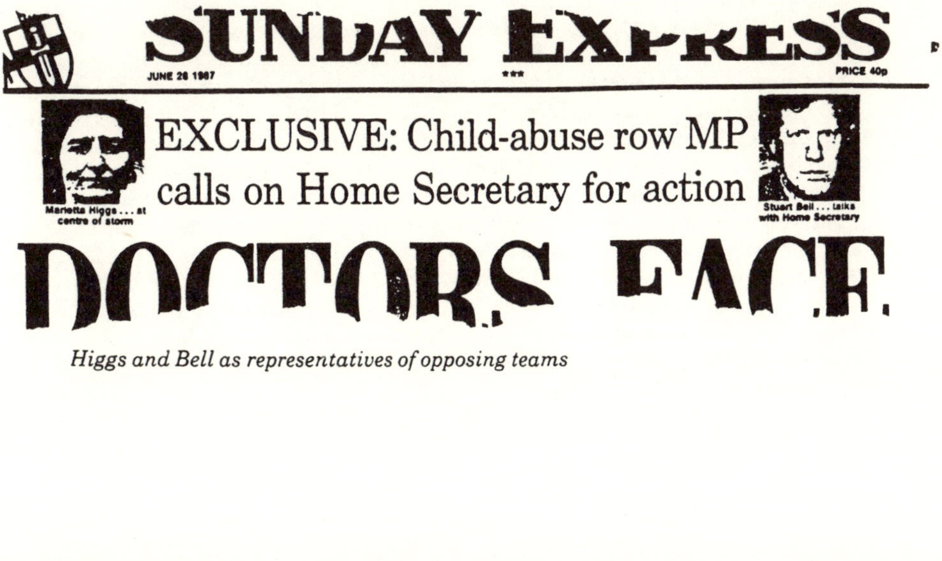

Higgs and Bell as representatives of opposing teams

The women accused in the Daily Mail

by her from examining suspected cases of child sexual abuse. Irvine is reported as saying, 'these doctors are seeing things that are not there... Dr Higgs' methods seem almost to be an obsession' (*Sunday Telegraph*, 28.6.87). The other main recruits to Bell's army are the Rev. Michael Wright, local priest and architect of parents' support groups, who writes a poignant article for the *Guardian* (29.6.87) entitled 'When Fear Stalks the Innocent', and local Tory MPs Richard Holt and Tim Devlin who join Bell in making political capital by calling vociferously for the suspension of Dr Higgs.

As the courts start to return children one by one to their parents (though they remain wards of court) because there is insufficient evidence of sexual abuse, and it becomes even more difficult to evaluate the situation, a number of figures step forward to declare their support for Marietta Higgs. The *Observer*, itself consistently sympathetic to her, reports on a statement of support from a group of twenty-five women doctors from Northumbria who provide a service to the police in cases of child sexual abuse and who claim that Dr Higgs has 'lifted the lid on the horrifying scale of sexual abuse from which we have averted our eyes for too long' (*Observer*, 28.6.87). However it is Sue Richardson, Middlesbrough consultant social worker in charge of child sexual abuse, who is appointed to the role of Marietta Higgs's chief second by Stuart Bell himself when he accuses both under parliamentary privilege of 'colluding and conspiring' to deny access to the police in sexual abuse cases (all papers report this on 30.6.87, the *Guardian* reports Sue Richardson's denial on 1.7.87).

Stuart Bell escalates the crisis yet again, and adds new recruits to Marietta Higgs's team, when he points the finger once more, this time at Dr Jane Wynne, Leeds University paediatrician responsible for developing the use of the diagnostic methods employed by Higgs and Wyatt. Bell objects to her presence on the panel of child sexual abuse professionals established to assess Middlesbrough Hospital practice, because, he argues, her presence might threaten its impartiality. Another recruit to Marietta's side, this time more of a volunteer than a victim of Bell's conscription methods, is Esther Rantzen. Well known as a TV personality and for her involvement in ChildLine, her voice is heard in a number of articles and interviews (see *Sunday Mirror*, 28.6.87 and the *Sunday Times* 5.7.87), as are those of Valerie Howarth, director of ChildLine (*Daily Telegraph*, 1.7.87 and the *Star* 9.7.87) and Michele Elliott, author of *Kidscape*. Rantzen focuses on the distress of the survivors, Howarth on policy and Elliott on educational projects with children. All three express general support for Higgs. In the House of Commons it is Labour MP Clare Short who is most outspoken in her defence. Marietta Higgs and Clare Short are together accused in an astonishingly sloppy article by Ferdinand Mount (*Daily Telegraph*, 3.7.87) of being 'panic-stirrers' who have *caused* the moral panic by 'ventilating the extraordinary claim' that 10 per cent of children in Britain are sexually abused. Although Cleveland Social Services spokespeople also publicly support Higgs, as do a substantial number of medical, psychiatric and social work professionals, these individuals are not personalized in the press in the way that the women are. And they rarely have their photographs printed.

Gradually, then, two opposing positions begin to emerge in the coverage of Cleveland, though neither fits neatly into existing political frameworks or is easy to evaluate. What we see instead is the formation of opposing teams of individuals whose public image we feel able to assess quite easily. Over this critical period the public images of these two teams become inextricably identified with two opposing positions on child sexual abuse. Indeed, it is the team personality, rather than the issues, which appears to influence the press, and therefore the public, in their response to the Cleveland affair.

If this is the case, we must examine the crucial components of these public images. What do the different people represent? How do these images operate to produce and convey particular meanings? The most striking feature of the teams as I have set them out above is that one is composed almost entirely of men and the other almost entirely of women. It is rare that professional women are singled out for public attention to this extent and in this fashion. The very clear division made between men and women in the Cleveland case points to a possible

War of position: the women and the men, from the Daily Mail

explanation of how the papers came to make sense, whether consciously or not, of what went on.

In addition to gender, each of the chief protagonists occupies other positions of symbolic significance. The meanings associated with these different positions need to be drawn out. Let us look first at Stuart Bell and his team. What does he stand for and support? What coded messages about him and his supporters are transmitted by the newspapers? How is his persona contrasted with that of Marietta Higgs? The first thing to note is that he is indigenous: a northerner, local, son of a Durham miner; salt of the earth, populist. The parents who he defends are 'his' people, he claims; his own five-year-old son, recently admitted to Middlesbrough Hospital after an accident, could have been one of the luckless children taken into care. He himself could have been one of the parents. For him and for his supporters, parents are an undifferentiated unit: fathers, almost always the perpetrators of abuse, are not distinguished from mothers; power relations are never made visible. Bell is a right-wing Labour MP: 'This is Middlesbrough not Russia', he is reported as saying in disbelief when he first heard of children being taken from their homes (*Daily Mail*, 15.7.87). Politically situated at the point where right-wing labourism merges into Thatcherite populism, he is against the growing influence of the left in local government and social services, and accuses his opponents of 'empire building'. I have already pointed out that his principal allies in the campaign to defend innocent parents (read fathers) are Tory MPs Richard Holt and Tim Devlin, the Rev. Michael Wright and police surgeon Dr Alistair Irvine. As Beatrix Campbell has said: 'These are the *traditional authorities*' (*New Statesman*, 31.7.87).

A number of quite different associations and prejudices are mobilized by the persona of Marietta Higgs. To start with, apart from being a woman, she is foreign and middle class – an outsider in Cleveland. We hear from the *Daily Mail* (27.6.87) that her German mother and Yugoslav father separated when she was two and that she was brought up by her mother and stepfather in a 'splendid' house in Australia. She is herself a working mother of five children and is unconventional in her domestic arrangements – her husband looks after the home and children. A number of commentators have hinted that these factors may have played a part in her diagnostic decisions (*Daily Mail*, 27.6.87 and *Daily Express*, 28.6.87). No allusions of this nature are ever made in order to explain the behaviour of Stuart Bell. Marietta Higgs is a modern career woman. She is personally neat, dignified, determined and professionally highly respected by colleagues for her dedication, integrity and clinical expertise. Many of the newspapers refer to this, yet it is almost as though these are coded references which simultaneously suggest that she is *too* conscientious and rather *too* clever – neither very English nor very feminine.

Worse than that, she is also identified with a group of younger 'committed' professional women and men in social services, with connotations here of the inner city, left radicalism and antipolice sentiment (see *Guardian* editorial, 1.7.87). Left intellectuals are also drawn into this network of associations when a couple of newspapers report that Sue Richardson is married to a lecturer in Humanities at Teeside Polytechnic. Oh horrors! Marietta Higgs's concern for the interests of children and her determination to uncover sexual abuse – described by *Today* (26.6.87) as her 'one-woman crusade' – construct her not only as anti-father, but possibly anti-men, possibly a feminist. This image produces another set of associations, and when these are in turn combined with her reputation as a conscientious worker, what emerges are numerous anxious references in newspapers across the political

The Independent *editorial*

spectrum to zeal: excessive zeal; fanaticism; obsession; fashionable zeal; fashionable prejudice, and so on. It is worth quoting the *Independent* editorial of 30 June at length in this respect:

> Social changes have made both sexual abuse, and the inclination to discover such abuse where it does not exist, more likely. Divorce, remarriage and the increasing acceptance of illegitimacy means that growing numbers of children live with a step-parent . . . forms of sexual activity which were, until recently, considered deviant have become commonplace. Lesbianism and homosexuality are now socially acceptable . . . Further, militant feminists are inclined to consider all men sexually aggressive and rapacious until proved innocent. The nuclear family, once the highest ideal, is now too often regarded as unnatural and unattractive . . . There is a danger that fashionable prejudice . . . [will] label parents guilty until proved innocent and break up families before rather than after abuse has been confirmed.

So here we have encapsulated the cluster of anxieties and associations triggered off by the persona and practice of Marietta Higgs. Modern fashionable ideas about sexual abuse are linked with unorthodox, dangerous ideas about sexual politics, with militant feminism, homosexuality and lesbianism, with the break up of the traditional family and with antifamily sentiment. Other newspapers make connexions with the left and with hostility to the police. The chain of meanings that is established here implies that ideas associated with Marietta Higgs should be treated with suspicion. In this conceptual manoeuvre the interests of the child, and her exploitation, are made invisible.

Conclusion?

I have tried to trace the way in which Marietta Higgs was transformed, through her media representations, into a symbol – a standard bearer – of feminism, and by association, of municipal socialism. It is important that we recognize this and understand the way in which newspapers have used her symbolic existence as a yardstick against which to work out their own positions. We must be aware of the way the Press has mapped out the field and controlled the parameters of the meanings that have been produced. If we are not, we run the risk of being pushed by the media construction of Marietta Higgs as the representative of feminism and anti-traditionalism into uncritically offering her our approval.

It is tempting to do this, because we have seen her become the target of a massive and violent seizure of misogyny. This public convulsion has been fuelled not so much by dislike as by fear: fear of the woman doctor, the professional woman, the woman with knowledge and public power. We have also witnessed an astonishing attempt by many of the newspapers, following Bell's lead, to displace the guilt for the sexual abuse of children from the perpetrators on to Marietta Higgs. Responsibility for causing the moral panic has similarly, by a remarkable sleight of hand, been removed from Stuart Bell and the press, and projected once again on to the unfortunate Marietta Higgs (Mount, 3.7.87).

Yet it is vital that we do not allow this powerful expression of misogyny to blind us to the problems in Higgs's diagnostic practice. Nor should Higgs's symbolic feminist presence be allowed to obscure the narrowness of the range of issues which were debated in the press. The marginalization of feminist critique is particularly disappointing given the body of feminist theoretical work on child sexual exploitation already in existence (and now augmented by this issue of *Feminist Review*). Few newspapers asked questions about power in the family or ideals of masculinity and femininity when they attempted to explain child sexual abuse. Similarly, although the press made token references to the 'rights' of children, there was very little discussion of what this might mean, nor of how the obedience and sexual ignorance of children might increase their vulnerability to sexual exploitation. With a few exceptions (for example, Weir in the *London Daily News*, 23.7.87) newspapers did not address the complex question of what Cleveland might represent in terms of the growing legitimation granted to the state to regulate and intervene in our domestic lives.[4]

Although it may be pleasing that feminism was so massively present in the reporting of the Cleveland affair in the symbolic form of Marietta Higgs, its vilification cannot give us much satisfaction. Although the issue of child sexual abuse emerged from its regime of silence and many papers engaged seriously with some of the progressive arguments, their continuous oscillation and the limited base of the debate do not amount to much of an achievement. As Roger Scott said in the *Daily Mail* (13.7.87): 'There is no black and white in this story. It is too complex . . . There are no winners. The children have lost the most.'

Notes

Mica Nava is a lecturer in the Department of Cultural Studies at North East London Polytechnic and a member of the *Feminist Review* editorial collective.

Many thanks to friends and family for their patience and support. Thanks also to Erica Carter, Peter Chalk, Catherine Hall, Angela McRobbie and the *Feminist Review* issue group for helpful comments.

1 See, for example, Cohen (1972), Hall *et al.* (1978) and Fitzpatrick and Milligan (1987).
2 Kimberly Carlisle was murdered by her stepfather and the inquiry into her death ended just before the Cleveland affair hit the headlines. This was one of the cases in which the Press criticized social workers for not being vigilant enough in their protection of children.
3 See the statement made by Cleveland Director of Social Services Michael Bishop and quoted in the Press on 26.6.87.
4 Although state intervention and the gathering of information about families is sometimes progressive and can benefit women, we cannot assume that this will always be the case.

References

CAMPBELL, Beatrix (1987) 'The Skeleton in the Family's Cupboard' *New Statesman*, 31.7.87.
COHEN, Stanley (1972) *Folk Devils and Moral Panics* London: MacGibbon & Kee.
FITZPATRICK, Michael and MILLIGAN, Don (1987) *The Truth about the Aids Panic*, London: Junius.
GARNER, Lesley (1987) 'Overboard on Child Abuse' *Daily Telegraph*, 1.7.87.
HALL, Stuart, CRITCHER, Chas, JEFFERSON, Tony, CLARKE, John and ROBERTS, Brian (1978) *Policing the Crisis: Mugging, the State, and Law and Order* London: Macmillan.
MOUNT, Ferdinand (1987) 'Children Need Justice Not Moral Panic' *Daily Telegraph*, 3.7.87.
PALMER, Alix (1987) '30,000 Children at Risk in Britain Today' *Star*, 31.7.87.
RANTZEN, Esther (1987) 'Listen to the Children's Cry' *Sunday Times*, 5.7.87.

RUTHERFORD, Jonathan (1987) 'The Sins of the Fathers' *London Daily News*, 26.6.87.
SCOTT, Roger (1987) 'How the Children Were Taken Away' *Daily Mail*, 13.7.87.
SHEARS, Richard (1987) 'The Making of Doctor Marietta Higgs, Crusader' *Daily Mail*, 26.6.87.
TONER, Michael (1987) 'Should a Father be Afraid to Kiss his Daughter Goodnight?' *Sunday Express*, 28.6.87.
WEIR, Stuart (1987) 'What if the State Kidnaps your Child?' *London Daily News*, 23.7.87.

Newspapers consulted

Guardian; Independent; The Times; Sunday Times; Observer; Daily Telegraph; Sunday Telegraph; Daily Express; Sunday Express; Daily Mail; Mail on Sunday; Daily Mirror; Sunday Mirror; Star; London Daily News; Evening Standard; Sun; News of the World; Today.

Chapter 6

Television and perceptions of crime: the British experience

Early British findings

Efforts to replicate Gerbner's findings among British samples in the late 1970s failed. Two studies, conducted by Piepe, Crouch and Emerson (1977) and by Wober (1978) tested relationships between levels of television viewing and personal fearfulness and interpersonal mistrust in the same manner as had been done previously by the Cultural Indicators research team at Philadelphia.

Piepe et al carried out 842 interviews in and around the Portsmouth area and related claimed amounts of television viewing to answers given to two wuestions: "These days a person doesn't know whom he can depend on", and "How often do you think that violent incidents happen around here?". For neither question did any substantial relationship emerge between claims of viewing and types of answers given.

The second survey, reported by Wober (1978), sampled over 1,000 adults over the age of 16 years throughout the United Kingdom. Again, respondents were posed two questions based on original items used by Gerbner and his colleagues, but worded in a slightly different way deemed to be more meaningful to British people. One of these items concerned the perception of how trustworthy people are and the other queried the perceived likelihood of being a victim of robbery. Together these items were combined to form a "security scale". Results indicated no systematic tendency for heavy viewers to have lower feelings-of-security scores than light viewers.

Several American writers subsequently challenged Wober's early findings on methodological grounds. Neville (1980) argued that Gerbner's Cultural Indicators items and the reworded items from Gerbner forming Wober's "Security Scale" measure different attitude dimensions. However, this argument is countered by the results of a third British study which employed both re-worded items and others from Gerbner's scales in their original form and found that all these items loaded together on the same factor-analytic dimension (Wober and Gunter, 1982). The latter study will be examined in greater detail a little further on.

Another challenge to early British findings from across the Atlantic, designed to explain away the differences in American and British cultivation effects, was put forward by Hawkins and Pingree (1980). They argued that heavy viewers in Britain, at least based on the evidence of Wober (1978), probably see fewer violence-containing programmes per week than do viewers who watch equivalent amounts of television in the United States. Wober estimated that heavy viewers in Britain at the time of his 1978 study saw on average about ten and a half one-hour-long violence-containing programmes a week. Hawkins and Pingree estimate, on the other hand, from data provided in Gerbner's 1978 Violence Profile for US network prime-time television, that similar viewers in their own country would on average be likely to see more than twice that number of violent programmes each week.

In fact, on these estimates, the British *heavy* viewer may see less television violence than many American *light* viewers whose two hours or so of daily viewing may yield approximately twelve hours per week of programmes containing violence.

There are two questionable inferences assumed in this criticism however which throw doubt on its validity. First, in their cultivation analysis research in the late 1970s, Gerbner et al assumed a linear relationship between amount of viewing and levels of social anxiety and interpersonal mistrust – an assumption which has since been challenged following re-analysis of the same data base (Hirsch, 1980). Many of the survey samples studied by Gerbner were divided up into light, medium and heavy viewers according to different criteria of viewing (see Gerbner et al, 1977, 1978). This is a point which we shall return to in more detail further on in this chapter. Thus, relative differences in levels of viewing of British and American television audiences should not preclude the occurrence of similar patterns of differences in levels of anxiety and mistrust between lighter and heavier viewers in both societies.

Secondly, there is an erroneous comparison on which Hawkins and Pingree's criticism of this early British research was based which relates to implications about relative levels of violence-viewing among British and American TV audiences. These writers claim that British viewers probably see less TV violence than many American viewers. However, this assumption is based on measures of the relative occurrence of violence obtained by Gerbner's content analyses of prime-time TV programming only, whilst measures of levels of viewing amongst the public are based on all programmes, both within and outside peak-viewing times. The occurrence of violence in non-prime-time programming may be much less than that observed during prime-time, although Gerbner and his associates have obtained no data on this. Hence, American viewing figures cannot provide accurate indications of how much violent content the average viewer normally sees over the course of a week's viewing. Wober's study, however, based its viewing figures, not on amounts of TV watching in hours per day estimated by respondents themselves, but on actual programmes watched (obtained from diaries covering one whole week's TV output on all networks) which in turn are classifiable separately as violent or non-violent. Therefore, a much closer match can be expected here between the amount of time respondents spent watching television and the quantity of violent content they were exposed to during this time.

How else then might the discrepancies in British and American findings in the late 1970s be explained? One possible explanation could be that the cultivation effects of television interpreted by Gerbner et al in their secondary analysis of national public opinion survey data are specific to American audiences. If much peak-time programming in the two countries is of a similar range of types, however, this specificity of effect may be a function of US society itself or perhaps of the way television fits into that society rather than just of the nature of what is shown on television.

Another factor could be that the Cultural Indicators studies (e.g. Gerbner and Gross, 1976; Gerbner et al, 1977, 1978) have not generally taken into account the real levels of violence in different localities which might jointly determine views of the reality of social threat *and* the amount of viewing done if people decided to stay indoors to escape what they perceive as a frightening world outside. For example, in their Canadian study Doob and MacDonald (1979) reported that while people who watch a lot of television are more likely to indicate fear of their environment, this relationship disappears when the actual incidence of crime in the neighbourhood is taken into account. Their results implied that television viewing and people's fear of being victims of violence or crime may not be directly causally related.

Television and personal threat in Britain: later evidence

Wober and Gunter (1982) explored the possibility that relationships observed by previous authors between amount and type of television viewing and social anxiety, mistrust and alienation might be explained in terms of characteristics other than demographic ones which relate to individuals' personalities. The findings of Doob and MacDonald (1979) indicated that fear of environmental crime was related more closely to actual levels of such crime than to television watching. It is possible also amongst this Toronto population that in addition to making them more fearful high local crime rates encourage individuals to stay indoors and watch television.

This introduces another problem of how exactly the television viewing – social anxiety relationship is to be interpreted. The findings of all the major studies are essentially correlational and hence they cannot be used to infer direct causation. Therefore, whilst television viewing may indeed cultivate social fearfulness, it is equally reasonable to explain this relationship in terms of a reverse hypothesis, that it is those individuals who are more anxious to begin with who watch more television.

There is evidence from experimental studies conducted in the mid-1970s which indicates that mood states can affect the tendency to watch, and also may influence the specific type of content a person prefers to watch, Boyanowsky, Newtson and Walster (1974). In a later experiment Boyanowsky (1977) replicated and expanded his initial demonstration of this effect.

If transient mood states such as those studied by Boyanowsky can produce short-term film preferences, Wober and Gunter (1982) argued that it is not unlikely nor unreasonable to assume that long-term viewing patterns may be influenced by permanent dispositions of individuals which relate not just to isolated environmental conditions or stimuli but to the prevailing social structure as a whole (see Srole, 1956; Merton, 1957). Rotter (1965) had developed an instrument designed to measure an enduring personality characteristic called *locus of control* which was supposedly shaped by the general and especially early experiences individuals had had with their social environment. What was more interesting about this measure was that the items used by Rotter were not dissimilar to those related to television viewing by Gerbner and his associates. The authors reasoned therefore that, rather than being a reaction simply to viewing large amounts of television drama as suggested by Gerbner *et al*, perception of social threat and danger may represent one aspect of a general system of beliefs associated with the underlying social reinforcement history of the individual. If this hypothesis is correct, then it was further reasoned that Rotter's measures of locus of control should correlate significantly with other measures of social anxiety and mistrust.

Whether or not it can be inferred that locus of control rather than television viewing underlies social anxiety depends on the demonstration of independent relationships of Rotter-type items and Gerbner-type items with viewing behaviour. A survey was therefore carried out amongst a sample of British viewers in London in which items (some reworded) from those used by Gerbner et al (1978, 1979) and others derived from

Rotter (1965) were used to test for variations in the degree of relatedness between amount of television viewing and perceptions of threat to personal security and of general mistrust and alienation.

Questionnaire-item responses were factor analysed and yielded four main factors which together accounted for 32 per cent of the common variance. Table 6.1 shows the factor loadings for each questionnaire item on these factors. Factor 1 was qualified by four items, including two Gerbner-type items on fear of victimization and thus was labelled *fear*.

Table 6.1. Factor loadings for opinion questionnaire items[a]

Factor name	Factors			
	1 Fear	2 Fate	3 Cynicism	4 Satisfaction
I am afraid to walk alone in my own neighbourhood at night (14)	0.79	0.15	0.11	-0.02
We live in a frightening world (15)	0.62	0.25	0.26	0.09
I worry about having my home burgled and property damaged (8)	0.42	0.21	0.20	-0.17
Most programmes are unsuitable for children (13)	0.39	0.18	0.33	-0.13
The pace of life is too much for me these days (3)	0.37	0.60	0.18	-0.08
Getting a good job depends mainly on being in the right place at the right time (11)	0.04	0.48	0.09	0.08
I feel that I have little influence over the things that happen to me (9)	0.27	0.46	0.21	-0.23
People's lives are controlled by accidental happenings (6)	0.07	0.45	0.12	0.04
Television news is the most reliable way to find out what is happening in the world (4)	0.14	0.41	-0.05	0.25
People are just out for what they can get these days (8)	0.14	0.07	0.66	-0.11
You've got to be pretty selfish these days (7)	0.14	0.07	0.66	-0.11
I am perfectly satisfied with my present standard of living (5)	0.05	-0.07	-0.01	0.58
Most people want to help you if you are in trouble (1)	0.00	0.09	-0.27	0.50
People are getting used to putting up with violence (2)	0.02	0.14	0.20	0.02
Family life is generally happier these days than it used to be (10)	0.02	-0.03	-0.08	0.13

[a]Varimax rotated factor matrix.
Note: Questionnaire item number given in parentheses.
Source: Wober and Gunter, 1982

Factor 2 was characterized by five items, including the three items from Rotter's locus of control scale and was termed *fate*. Factor 3 was defined by two items expressing feelings of selfishness or *cynicism* and factor 4 also consisted of two items which represented feelings of *satisfaction*.

Correlations were computed between these factors and viewing behaviour. These showed that amount of fiction viewing correlated significantly with the *fate* factor only, whilst amount of information viewing correlated significantly with all factors. At the same time correlations between factors themselves indicated that the Gerbner 'fear' factor and Rotter 'fate' factor were significantly correlated.

Viewing diaries which listed all programmes broadcast on the three major television channels during the week of the survey were used to measure amount of television viewing. Viewing was defined separately for two broad categories of programming – fiction and information. An initial series of correlations yielded a number of significant relationships between demographic variables (age and socio-economic class), and both opinions and television viewing. This left open the possibility that relationships between television viewing and social opinions were a function of third variables and had no independent association. Therefore, a series of partial correlations was computed to find out if the questionnaire factors had any residual relationship with viewing behaviours when the contribution of demographic variables was controlled. Analyses also looked at the effects of partialling out one factor on the strength of association between television viewing and the other factors. The results of these partial correlations are shown in Table 6.2.

Table 6.2. Partial correlations between social attitudes, demographic variables and TV viewing (n = 322)

Partial correlation between	Fear	Fate	Age	Class
Fate-fiction viewing	−0.23**	—	−0.25**	−0.22**
Fate-information viewing	−0.23**	—	−0.16*	−0.26**
Fear-fiction viewing	—	0.01	0.10	−0.08
Fear-information viewing	—	0.05	−0.06	−0.16*
Cynicism-fiction viewing	0.09	0.02	−0.11	−0.10
Cynicism-information viewing	0.10	0.04	−0.12	−0.14**
Satisfaction-fiction viewing	0.06	0.06	−0.11	0.05
Satisfaction-information viewing	−0.12	−0.12	0.06	−0.12
Age-fiction viewing	0.00	0.05	—	0.01
Age-information viewing	0.47**	0.45**	—	0.49**
Class-fiction viewing	0.14	0.10	0.16*	—
Class-information viewing	0.10	0.05	0.07	—

* $P < 0.01$
** $P < 0.001$
Source: Wober and Gunter, 1982

THE BRITISH EXPERIENCE

Wober and Gunter concluded that since the Rotter measure related significantly to the Gerbner factor while only the former was reliably associated with viewing behaviour in the presence of statistical controls for third variables, it could be that any relationships observed between fearfulness and television viewing may be little more than epiphenomena of deeper-seated personal dispositions or more general social conceptions, such as locus of control, which underlie both amount of viewing and the relatively superficial social perceptions tapped by fear of victimisation items.

As these findings are correlational, they can only be used to argue against the alleged source of distorted social perceptions, (that is, excessive television viewing) but not to establish another implied source of causation. This British evidence suggests, however, that whatever is measured by Gerbner's items is less robustly related to viewing behaviour than the factor measured by items derived from Rotter's scale (at least for viewers in Britain). Colloquially, it may not be television which makes viewers wary of the environment, but that people who are more fateful in their outlook on life generally stay in more to watch television and also express cautious attitudes.

The most recent British research has attempted to look in more detail at different levels of judgement about the prevalence of crime and of concerns about personal involvement, and how in each case they are related to viewing programmes with and without crime-related themes. Gunter and Wakshlag (1986) investigated the ways in which respondents' television viewing patterns (measured in terms of proportion of viewing time devoted to different categories of programming in addition to overall amount of viewing) were related to societal level and personal level judgements about crime in a variety of locations, urban and rural, both close to home and distant from it. We wanted to find out (a) whether societal level judgements were more closely related to television viewing than were personal level judgements; (b) whether perceptions of crime in some settings were especially closely related to television viewing; and (c) whether viewing of specific categories of programming, particularly those with crime-related content, predicted perceptions of crime better than did television viewing *per se*.

Television viewing diaries and attached questionnaires were sent to members of a London Panel maintained at the time of this research by the Independent Broadcasting Authority's Research Department for purpose of routine programme appreciation measurement. The diaries contained a complete list of all programmes broadcast on the four major television channels (BBC1, BBC2, ITV, Channel Four) in London during one week in February, 1985. Respondents assessed each programme seen on a six-point scale ranging from "extremely interesting and/or enjoyable" to "not at all interesting and/or enjoyable". Endorsements thus revealed not only appreciation levels, but also how many programmes had been seen, and of which kinds.

The questionnaire consisted of two parts. In the first part, respondents were asked about their personal experiences with crime and perceived competence to deal with an attack on themselves. More specifically, respondents were asked if they personally had ever been the victim of a violent crime, and if they knew anyone who had been. They were also asked to indicate along a five-point scale ranging from "strongly agree" to "strongly disagree" their extent of agreement with the statement "I could defend myself from an unarmed attacker". The latter item was presented with 11 items taken from or based upon Rubin and Peplau's (1976) Belief in a Just World scale. Some of these items were reworded in a more appropriate British idiom.

The second part of the questionnaire dealt with perceptions of the likelihood of crime and fears of personal victimisation, and was divided into three sections. In the first of these respondents were asked to estimate along a five-point scale (ranging from "not at all likely" [1] to "very likely" [5]) the probability that a person living in any of five locations would be assaulted in their lifetime (societal level judgements). The five locations given were London, Glasgow, Cotswolds, Los Angeles or on a farm in the United States. In the second section, estimates were requested from respondents concerning the likelihood that they might themselves fall victim to violent assault (personal level judgements) if they were to walk alone at night for a month around the area where they live, in a local park, through the streets of London's West End, through the streets of Glasgow, or through the streets of New York. They were also asked to say how likely they thought it was that they would become "the victim of some type of violent behaviour sometime in your lifetime" and that "you will have your home broken into during the next year".

In the final section, respondents were asked to say how concerned they would be for their personal safety (along a five-point scale ranging from "not at all concerned" [1] to "very concerned" [5]) if their car broke down at night in the English countryside, if they had to walk home alone late at night from a local pub, or if they found themselves having to walk through several streets in Los Angeles at night to reach their car.

A total of 448 usable diaries and attached questionnaires were returned giving a response rate of 47 percent. Data were then weighted to bring the sample in to line with population parameters.[1] With regard to television viewing behaviour, each respondent was given a score for the total number of programmes watched and the numbers watched for each of nine different categories of programmes: action-adventure, soap opera, British crime-drama, American crime-drama, films, light entertainment, sports, news and documentaries/general interest.

On the basis of a frequency distribution of the total number of programmes viewed during the survey week, respondents were divided into three categories by amount of viewing: light viewers (32 percent of the sample), medium viewers (34 percent) and heavy viewers (34 percent). Light viewers were those who watched fewer than 25 programmes during the week, which on the assumption of an average programme duration of half an hour, is equivalent to less than one and a half hours per day. Heavy viewers were those who watched more than 35 programmes a week (or more than three hours a day), and medium viewers were those who fell in between light and heavy viewing limits.

For each programme type, relative proportions of total viewing time devoted to each were computed by dividing the number of programmes seen in a category by the total number seen overall. This was done to obtain a more precise measure of how viewers shared out their total viewing time among different types of programmes. Frequency distributions were then computed on these viewing variables so that respondents could be divided into light, medium and heavy viewers within each programme category.

Experience with crime and competence to deal with it

Direct personal experience with violent crime was rare among this sample of London residents. Only seven percent of respondents said they had ever been the victim of a violent assault themselves. Indirect contact with violent assault through knowing someone else who had been a victim was more widespread; twenty-six percent said they knew a victim.

Further details are shown in Table 6.3, where a number of demographic differences in personal experience with violent crime can be discerned. Although men were only slightly more likely to say they had been victims themselves than were women, they were quite a lot more likely to know a victim. Age differences were apparent too. Younger people (aged under 35 years) were nearly twice as likely as older people to say they had been

[1]Demographic characteristics of the sample

	Total	Sex		Age			Class		
		Males	Females	16-34	35-54	55+	ABC1	C2	DE
n	448	218	230	183	139	126	311	130	106
%	100	49(48)	51(52)	41(36)	31(34)	28(28)	47(47)	29(26)	24(28)

Percentage figures in parentheses represent the known proportions for each demographic category in the London ITV region based on Broadcasters' Audience Research Board (BARB) Establishment Survey figures for 1985.

TELEVISION AND THE FEAR OF CRIME

victims of an assault. Indeed, nearly one in ten young people said they had had this experience.

Knowing a victim was equally likely across age-bands however. Directly experienced personal victimisation was more commonplace among working class (DE) respondents than among middle class (ABC1) respondents.

Respondents had mixed opinions about whether they could effectively defend themselves against an unarmed attacker. Responses were equally divided between those who judged that they could defend themselves (32 percent), those who thought they could not (34 percent) and those who were unsure either way (34 percent).

Once again, as Table 6.3 illustrates, there were marked differences of opinions among individuals associated most strongly with sex and age. Men were nearly three times as likely as women to have confidence in their ability to look after themselves, while younger and middle-aged respondents had greater confidence than did older respondents.

Table 6.3. Personal experience and competence to deal with violent assault upon oneself

	All %	Sex Male %	Female %	Age 16-34 %	35-54 %	55+ %	Class ABC1 %	C2 %	DE %
Have you ever been the victim of a violent crime?									
Yes	7	8	6	9	7	4	6	5	10
No	93	92	94	91	92	96	94	95	90
Has anyone you know ever been the victim of a violent crime									
Yes	26	31	21	24	33	25	28	22	25
No	73	69	79	76	67	75	72	78	75
I could defend myself from an unarmed attacker									
Agree	32	49	17	39	34	22	35	32	31
Disagree	34	19	47	26	29	48	32	35	35
Unsure	34	32	36	34	37	30	34	34	35

Perceived likelihood of victimisation: others

Respondents were asked to estimate the likelihood that a person living in each of five different locations would become a victim of a violent assault during their lifetime. Results indicated that greatest risk was perceived to exist for people living in urban locations. Such locations in the United States, however, held a great deal more danger than their equivalents in Britain. As Table 6.4 shows, the place seen as potentially the most dangerous to live in by Londoners was Los Angeles. Far fewer respondents perceived similar likelihood of a person being a victim of assault in Glasgow and central London. The locations perceived as safest of all were rural areas, both in Britain and the United States.

Women were more likely than men to perceive victimisation as a likely occurrence for others across four out of the five locations. There was also a marked class differential, particularly with respect to perceptions of risk in the West End of London. Working-class respondents were much more likely to perceive social danger for others.

Table 6.4. Perceived likelihood of victimisation for others during their lifetime*

	Sex		Age			Class		
All	Male	Female	16-34	35-54	55+	ABC1	C2	DE

Likelihood of being assaulted for a person living in:									
Los Angeles	77	72	81	77	76	77	74	78	81
Glasgow	49	44	55	46	47	56	48	48	54
London (West End)	43	38	46	46	32	49	36	41	56
Farm in USA	11	7	15	13	13	8	10	9	15
Cotswolds	3	3	3	3	4	2	1	2	7

* Percentages are of those who, on a five-point risk scale, scored likelihood of assault as either 4 or 5.

Perceived likelihood of victimisation: self

How much danger did respondents perceive in the world for themselves? Results once again showed that perceived likelihood of victimisation varied across different locations. The scenarios painted for respondents in this section of the questionnaire once again varied along one dimension in particular – their degree of proximity to where they lived. As Table 6.5 shows, perceived danger levels rose with increasing distance from home. Far and away the most dangerous place to walk alone at night, for this London sample, was New York. New York was perceived to hold real risks of personal assault for more than five times as many respondents as was their own neighbourhood. Few respondents perceived any real danger in their own neighbourhood.

TELEVISION AND THE FEAR OF CRIME

Table 6.5. Perceived likelihood of victimisation for self.*

	All %	Sex Male %	Female %	Age 16-34 %	35-54 %	55+ %	Class ABC1 %	C2 %	DE %
Likelihood of being assaulted oneself if walking after dark alone in:									
New York	83	70	87	85	81	84	84	81	87
Glasgow	53	45	59	46	55	57	49	58	52
London (West End)	41	33	53	47	38	44	33	50	57
Local Park	30	23	42	35	27	37	25	37	44
Own neighbourhood	15	10	19	12	11	20	12	13	21
Likelihood of being a victim in own lifetime	21	24	17	25	16	20	20	23	18
Likelihood of having home burgled in next year	23	23	27	20	22	36	22	26	30

* Percentages are those who, on a five-point risk scale, scored likelihood of assault or personal risk as either 4 or 5.

There were demographic differences in levels of perceived risk to personal safety. Across all locations, women more often perceived a strong likelihood of being violently assaulted than did men. The gap between the sexes was smallest with regard to perceived danger in the local neighbourhood, where it was reduced to nine percent. Age was not as consistently associated with differences in perceptions of danger to self across locations. The most marked difference emerged with respect to perceptions of risk in one's own locality, where older people more often thought they were likely to become victims than did younger or middle-aged people. Class was associated with risk perceptions for self, but only with respect to more proximal locations for respondents. Thus working class respondents were more likely than middle-class respondents to mention the possibility of danger to self from violence in central London, a local park and in their own neighbourhood. However, working class respondents did not think of themselves as likely to fall victim to any violence in their lifetime more often than middle class respondents.

Fear of victimisation

How afraid were respondents of being victims of violence? To what extent did concern for personal safety vary with the location in which one might find oneself? Three items were presented dealing with fear of victimisation. Results presented in Table 6.6 indicate that respondents said they would be most concerned for their personal safety if they found themselves walking alone after dark in the streets of Los Angeles. Fear of being assaulted was mentioned twice as often for Los Angeles as in either of two British locations. Respondents associated the least amount of fear with being stranded after dark in the English countryside.

Table 6.6. Fear of victimisation.*

	All %	Sex Male %	Sex Female %	Age 16-34 %	Age 35-54 %	Age 55+ %	Class ABC1 %	Class C2 %	Class DE %
Fearful of walking alone after dark in Los Angeles	87	61	81	67	67	84	69	69	81
Fearful of walking alone after dark from local pub	47	30	64	41	45	60	42	44	65
Fearful of being stranded in English countryside after dark	27	13	41	24	24	35	23	26	38

* Percentages of those who, on a five-point scale of concern for personal safety, scored either 4 or 5.

Demographic differences emerged associated with sex, age and class of respondents. Fear of personal victimisation was most often mentioned across all locations by women, the elderly and working-class respondents. Differences between the responses of men and women, the young and old, middle-class and working-class were quite substantial in every case.

Personal experience with violence and risk perceptions

To what extent do direct and indirect real life experiences with violence and belief in one's own ability to defend oneself against an assailant colour or mediate perceptions of social danger?

TELEVISION AND THE FEAR OF CRIME

As the results presented in Table 6.7 indicate, whether or not respondents had ever been victims of violence themselves or knew someone who had been, made little difference to their perceptions of the likelihood of others being victimised. Belief about one's competence to defend oneself, however, did make a difference. With respect to risk perceptions for people living in urban locations in particular, whether in Britain or the USA, respondents who felt incapable of defending themselves effectively were more likely to perceive danger.

Table 6.7. Personal experience and competence to deal with violence and perceptions of likelihood of assault for others.

	Whether been a victim		Whether know a victim		Competence to defend oneself	
	Yes %	No %	Yes %	No %	High %	Low %
Likelihood of being assaulted for a person living in:						
Los Angeles	75	77	81	77	63	76
Glasgow	53	50	55	48	40	54
London (West End)	44	42	44	42	38	50
Farm in USA	8	11	12	5	11	15
Cotswolds	2	3	4	3	4	4

One might expect personal experiences with violence to have a more substantial impact on perceived environmental risks to oneself than in relation to perceptions of risk for others. The results, however, as shown in Table 6.8, indicate otherwise. For most scenarios neither direct nor indirect experience with violence oneself differentiated risk perceptions relating to self. The one notable exception was for perceived chance of being assaulted in one's own neighbourhood. Respondents who had been victims of an assault before were more likely than those who had not to perceive danger near to home.

Once again, though, belief in one's own ability to handle trouble emerged as an important mediator of risk perceptions. Across all locations, local and distant, perceived likelihood of personal victimisation was greater among respondents who had little confidence in their ability to defend themselves.

Two more estimates of personal risk exhibited stronger associations with personal experiences with violence however. Victims of violence were three times as likely as others to say they thought they would be victims of criminal assault during their lifetime. Clearly, and not surprisingly, the experience of victims had coloured their outlook. Indirect contact with violence, through knowing a victim, proved less powerful as a discriminator of perceptions. And so too did belief in one's competence to defend oneself. Perceived likelihood of having one's home broken into was related in the opposite direction to the above perception to personal experience with violence. Victims were *less* likely to believe there was a good chance of being burgled during the next year. Perceived risk from burglary was predictably (given the above findings) greater among respondents lacking confidence in their ability to defend themselves.

Table 6.8. Personal experience and competence to deal with violence and perceptions of likelihood of assault for self

	Whether been a victim		Whether know a victim		Competence to defend oneself	
	Yes %	No %	Yes %	No %	High %	Low %
Likelihood of being assaulted oneself if walking after dark alone in:						
New York	85	85	88	84	73	85
Glasgow	49	53	58	51	40	61
London (West End)	49	42	38	45	36	53
Local Park	30	34	29	34	24	47
Own neighbourhood	24	14	12	16	5	26
Likelihood of being a victim in own lifetime	56	18	25	19	21	27
Likelihood of having home burgled in next year	17	26	26	24	21	33

Personal experience with violence and fear of victimisation

As Table 6.9 shows, respondents who had had previous experience of being victims of a violent assault were in general more concerned for their safety within each of the scenarios that had been painted for them. This factor made the most profound difference with respect to the most local of the three settings – the scenario in which respondents had to imagine themselves walking home alone late at night from a local pub.

TELEVISION AND THE FEAR OF CRIME

Indirect experience was a less powerful discriminator, although it did make some difference with respect to British scenarios. In contrast to direct experience, however, indirect experience with violence was associated with being less fearful.

The most powerfully related variable of all was belief in one's self defence competence. For judgements of concern for personal safety in settings at home and abroad, respondents who felt they could not effectively defend themselves against an unarmed attacker were more concerned about their chances of being assaulted.

Table 6.9. Personal experience and competence to deal with violence and fear of victimisation.

	Whether been a victim		Whether know a victim		Competence to defend oneself	
	Yes %	No %	Yes %	No %	High %	Low %
Fearful of walking alone after dark in Los Angeles	79	71	70	72	54	79
Fearful of walking alone after dark from local pub	60	46	41	50	31	73
Fearful of being stranded in English countryside after dark	33	26	20	30	18	46

Television viewing and perceptions and fear of victimisation

The results above indicate marked variations in some perceptions of victimisation associated with certain demographic characteristics of respondents, their direct and indirect experience of assault and perceived self-defence capability. In order to find out if television viewing or viewing of specific programme types were related to risk perceptions independently of these other variables, a series of multiple regression analyses was run in which ten television viewing variables, demographics, personal experience with violence (direct and indirect), belief in ability for self-defence, and belief in a just world, were related to each risk perception. Each regression procedure was executed with all independent variables entered equally.

Table 6.10 shows the results for perceptions of risk for others. As this

82

THE BRITISH EXPERIENCE

table shows, in the presence of multiple statistical controls for other variables, there was only one instance of a television viewing variable exhibiting a significant relationship with a victimisation-likelihood perception.

Viewing of television news was negatively related to perceived likelihood of victimisation for someone who lives in Los Angeles.

Heavier viewing of the news predicted the perception of less danger in Los Angeles for others. None of the serious drama or crime-related programme categories (e.g., action-adventure, US crime-drama, UK crime-drama) was significantly related to any perceptions of risk for others.

Table 6.10. Multiple regressions showing relationships between television viewing, personal experience with violence and demographics with perceived likelihood of victimisation for others

	_London		Los Angeles		Glasgow		Cotswolds		Farm in USA	
	Beta	t	Beta	t	Beta	t	Beta	t	Beta	t
Total TV viewing	.06	1.00	.02	.33	-01	-.25	.00	.07	.02	.26
Action adventure	.11	1.43	-07	-.87	.02	.31	-03	.43	-02	-.30
Soap operas	.05	.87	.10	1.69	.01	.25	.06	1.06	.03	.51
Sport	-0.44	-.77	-04	-.83	-05	-.91	-09	-1.73	-01	.14
Light entertainment	-04	-.78	-09	-1.53 *	.04	.73	-05	-.84	-10	-1.80
News	-04	-.64	-13	-2.05 *	-06	-.99	.00	.02	-03	-.45
Documentaries	-05	-.89	-02	-.35	-03	-.63	-04	-.82	-01	-.19
Films	-03	-.49	-05	.78	-10	-1.54	.02	.30	-01	-.20
US crime drama	-001	.10	.14	1.93	-00	.06	-01	.10	.13	1.82
UK crime drama	.02	.28	-08	-1.49	.04	.68	-03	-.60	-09	1.58 *
Sex	.09	1.68	.09	1.66	.07	1.38	-00	-.02	.11	2.09
Age	-00	-.01 **	.00	.05	.10	1.92	-06	-1.02	-05	-.88
Class	.14	2.84	.05	1.00	.07	1.28	.13	2.57	.06	1.22
Just world	-07	-1.44	-01	.16	.05	-1.09	-01	.27	.02	.41
Been a victim	-03	-.50	-04	-.79	-06	-1.12	-01	.27	.02	.41
Know a victim	-07	-1.25	-16	-3.09 **	-15	-2.16 **	-01	-.20	-12	-2.17 *
Defend oneself	.07	1.40	.06	1.04	.04	.80	.09	1.61	.06	1.13
Multiple R	.30		.31		.27		.23		.27	
Multiple R²	.09		.10		.07		.05		.07	
F	2.33		2.46		1.89		1.26		1.79	
df	17/399		17/392		17/398		17/399		17/390	
P	.002		.001		.02		ns		.03	

Levels of statistical significance: *** $P < 0.001$, ** $P < 0.01$, * $P < 0.05$

More significantly to these perceptions were whether respondents knew a victim of an assault. Respondents who knew a victim perceived greater danger for others who live in Los Angeles, Glasgow and rural USA.

Table 6.11 presents the results for similar analyses computed for perceptions of likely risk to self in different locations. Six significant relationships emerged between these perceptions and television viewing variables. Viewing of soap operas and of UK crime-drama predicted perceived risk in own neighbourhood. Heavier viewing of both programme types predicted the perception of greater danger to self in this setting. Total television viewing was significantly related to perception of potential danger in a local park and in London's West End at night. In both instances, heavier viewing predicted perception of greater risk. Finally, soap operas emerged as significant predictor of perceived personal danger if walking alone at night in the streets of New York and perceived likelihood of having one's home burgled in the next year. Heavier soap opera viewing predicted greater perceived danger in New York, but less perceived danger of being burgled.

Self-defence capability emerged most consistently as a significant predictor of perceived likelihood of self-victimisation across settings. Greater confidence is being able to defend oneself was associated with a reduction in perceived likelihood of being assaulted.

Table 6.12 presents the results for fear of victimisation. Heavier total television viewing was a significant predictor of level of concern in all three scenarios. Throughout, heavier television viewing predicted greater concern for personal safety. With regard to the scenario closest to home, (i.e., walking home alone at night from a local pub) concern for safety was also predicted by amount of viewing of action-adventure, US crime-drama and sport. Heavier viewing of each of these programme categories predicted greater concern for personal safety.

In summary, this survey among London residents which investigated their perceptions of crime at home and abroad, found that perceived likelihood of victimisation for others and for self, and concern about victimisation for self, varied with the situation, demographic characteristics of respondents, their direct experience with crime, and confidence in personal ability for self-defence in the face of an assault. Television viewing patterns, however, were relatively weak and inconsistent indicators of judgements about crime.

Unlike the findings of Tyler (1980, Tyler and Cook, 1984), no evidence emerged here that societal level judgements (e.g., perceived risks for others) were more strongly linked to media experiences than were personal level judgements about crime (e.g., perceived risk for self). If anything, television viewing variables were more often and more powerfully related to perceptions of risk for self. One note of consistency

Table 6.11. Multiple regressions showing relationships between television viewing, personal experience with violence and demographics with perceived likelihood of victimisation for self

Own area	Local park Beta	t	London west end Beta	t	New York Beta	t	Glasgow Beta	t	Victim lifetime Beta	t	Home burgled Beta	t	Own area Beta	t
Total TV viewing	.01	.19	.13	2.33*	.14	2.55**	.08	1.41	.06	1.08	.06	.95	.08	1.36
Action adventure	.05	.67	.04	.51	.02	.29	.01	.14	-.01	-.09	.08	1.07	.14	1.81
Soap operas	.12	2.10*	.06	1.16	.05	.82	.15	2.70**	.08	1.38	-.01	-.25	-.13	-2.21*
Sport	-.05	-.97	-.08	-1.68	-.10	-1.92	-.02	-.45	-.07	-1.38	-.05	-.86	-.08	-1.49
Light entertainment	-.11	-1.97	-.04	-.74	-.05	-.90	-.03	-.51	.04	.76	-.06	-.99	-.03	-.54
News	-.02	-.33	.04	.76	-.04	-.72	-.02	-.30	-.04	-.59	-.07	-1.19	-.01	-.20
Documentaries	-.07	-1.23	-.03	-.61	-.02	-.46	-.00	-.04	-.06	-1.15	-.04	-.77	-.03	-.49
Films	-.09	-1.41	-.07	-1.18	-.06	-.94	.06	.92	-.05	-.84	-.00	-.01	-.03	-.54
US crime	-.08	-1.19	-.01	-.10	-.00	-.04	-.00	.01	-.05	-.73	-.07	-1.03	-.08	-1.08
UK crime	.11	2.07*	.04	.83	.02	.30	-.04	-.75	.05	.96	.01	.23	.03	.62
Sex	.05	1.03	.20	3.89***	.10	1.90	.11	2.07*	.02	.31	-.07	-1.37	-.03	-.48
Age	.03	.55	-.00	.04	-.06	-1.13	-.08	-1.40	.07	1.28	-.05	-.99	.11	2.03*
Class	.10	2.08*	.13	2.69**	.22	4.37***	.04	.82	.04	.72	.00	.07	.07	1.41
Just world	-.06	-1.23	-.02	-.41	-.05	-1.04	.04	.76	-.09	-1.77	-.12	-2.48**	-.07	-1.37
Been a victim	-.02	-.41	-.04	-.82	.03	.63	-.01	-.28	.06	1.19	-.19	-3.59***	.00	.08
Know a victim	.04	.85	.01	.20	-.02	-.32	-.17	-3.19**	-.12	-2.23*	.00	.08	.04	.68
Defend oneself	.15	2.83**	.13	2.62**	-.09	1.65	.03	.53	.13	2.50*	.03	.54	.11	1.97*
Multiple R	.33		.41		.37		.30		.30		.29		.25	
Multiple R²	.11		.17		.14		.09		.09		.09		.06	
F	2.87		4.79		3.78		2.23		2.27		2.19		1.53	
df	17/399		17/399		17/399		17/392		17/396		17/399		17/397	
P	.0001		.0001		.0001		.004		.003		.004		.08	

Levels of statistical significance: *** p < 0.001, ** P < 0.01, * P < 0.05

TELEVISION AND THE FEAR OF CRIME

Table 6.12. Multiple regressions showing relationships between television viewing, personal experience with violence and demographics with fear of victimization.

	Concern if:					
	Stranded English countryside		At night in Los Angeles		Walk home at night from pub	
	Beta	t	Beta	t	Beta	t
Total TV viewing	.11	2.09*	.13	2.23*	.13	2.51**
Action adventure	.12	1.70	.00	.09	.14	4.02**
Soap operas	.05	.97	.10	1.74	.08	1.52
Sport	-06	-1.20	-09	-1.65	-15	-3.15**
Light entertainment	-01	.18	-06	-1.13	-03	-.57
News	.00	.07	-06	-.96	.04	-.73
Documentaries	-07	-1.51	-07	-1.28	-04	-.73
Films	-03	-.54	.02	.75	-06	-1.09
US crime drama	-11	-1.72	-02	-.35	16	2.45*
UK crime drama	.03	.58	.01	-15	.00	.03
Sex	.31	6.42***	.15	2.88**	.28	5.89***
Age	.03	.67	.08	1.46	.08	1.60
Class	.14	3.11**	.09	1.76	.15	2.23**
Just world	-02	-.37	-10	-2.02*	-00	-.04
Been a victim	-05	-.97	-06	-1.24	-09	-2.02*
Know a victim	.06	1.24	-03	-.51	.06	1.34
Defend oneself	.15	3.14**	.08	1.53	.12	2.50**
Multiple R	.51		.39		.54	
Multiple R²	.26		.15		.29	
F	8.35		3.90		9.22	
df	17/398		17/379		17/387	
P	.0001		.0001		.0001	

Levels of statistical significance: *** $P < 0.001$, ** $P < 0.01$, * $P < 0.05$

with Tyler, however, was the fact that personal experience with crime was an important predictor of personal level likelihood judgements and fear of crime.

At the personal level, victimisation perceptions varied with the situation. Respondents were less likely to perceive danger close to home than in more distant situations. Furthermore, in the case of one variable, self-defence capability, its significance as a predictor seemed to depend upon the situation about which judgements were being made. Thus, lacking confidence in one's ability to defend oneself predicted the

86

perception of greater danger to self and greater concern for safety, but only in British locations. There was no such obvious patterning to television viewing predictors of victimisation perceptions across different situations however.

Five television viewing variables emerged from the regression analyses as significantly related to perceptions of likelihood of self-victimisation and fear of victimisation. These were total amount of television viewing, soap opera viewing, sport, UK crime drama-viewing and US crime drama-viewing. The last three, however, were significantly related only to one perception in each case.

Perceived likelihood of self victimisation in one's own neighbourhood was greater among heavier than among lighter viewers of soap operas and UK crime-drama. Greater potential danger to self in a local park in London's West End at night was connected with heavier viewing of television in general. Heavier soap opera viewing meanwhile predicted greater perceived likelihood of personal attack at night in New York, but lower perceived likelihood of being burgled.

With regard to concern about being a victim of assault, however, there was some indication that television viewing was a better predictor in the context of situations closer to home. Greater fear of victimisation across all three situations was linked to heavier total television viewing. In the situation that was probably closest (geographically) to home for respondents in this survey, however, fear of victimisation when walking home alone late at night from a local pub was also predicted by heavier viewing of action-adventure, sport and US crime drama.

Researchers previously have noted the importance of content specificity in the relationship between television viewing and perceptions of crime (Weaver and Wakshlag, 1986). From this observation, one would expect crime perceptions to be predicted best of all by levels of exposure to programmes with crime-related content, such as action-adventure and crime drama. Evidence for this sort of linkage emerged sporadically in this study. Heavier UK crime drama viewing was associated with greater perceived likelihood of self-victimisation in one's own neighbourhood. Heavier viewing of action-adventure and US crime drama was linked with greater concern about personal safety if walking home from a local pub alone late at night.

In the context of personal-level likelihood-of-victimisation beliefs, the best programme category predictor was soap operas. Heavier viewing of soap operas predicted greater perceived danger in one's own area and in New York, but less chance of being burgled. These findings are not entirely inconsistent with the notion of content-specificity as a mediator of television's influence in social reality perceptions, however. It has been noted by several US researchers, for example, that crime had been a

TELEVISION AND THE FEAR OF CRIME

major theme in soap operas for a long time (Katzman, 1972; Cassata, Skill and Boadu, 1979) and that it is becoming a more prominent focus in these programmes (Sutherland and Siniawsky, 1982; Estep and Macdonald, 1985).

With respect to fear of crime, viewing of particular categories of programmes seemed to be less relevant than simply how much television is consumed overall. This may indicate that if television is the causal agent, it really does not matter which programmes individuals watch. Rather, it is general levels of exposure that are most significant. Alternatively, it could be that television is the affected agent, with viewing levels being influenced among other things by the fearfulness of individuals. Those who have greater anxieties about possible dangers to self in the social environment may be driven to spend more time indoors watching the box. Probably nearest to the truth though may be a notion of circularity in the relationship. Greater fear of potential danger in the social environment may encourage people to stay indoors, where they watch more television, and are exposed to programmes which tell them things which in turn reinforce their anxieties.

References

Boyanowsky, E.O. (1977) Film preferences under conditions of threat: Whetting the appetite for violence, information or excitement? *Communication Research, 4,* 33-145.

Boyanowsky, E.O., Newtson, D. and Walster, E. (1974) Film preferences following a murder. *Communication Research, 1,* 32-43.

Cassata, M.B., Skill, T.D. and Boadu, S.O. (1979) In sickness and in health. *Journal of Communication, 29,* 73-80.

Doob, A.N. and Macdonald, G.E. (1979) Television viewing and fear of victimisation: Is the relationship causal? *Journal of Personality and Social Psychology, 37,* 170-179.

Estep, R. and Macdonald, P.T. (1985) Crime in the afternoon: Murder and robbery on soap operas. *Journal of Broadcasting and Electronic Media, 29,* 323-331.

Gerbner, G. and Gross, L. (1976) Living with television: The violence profile. *Journal of Communication, 26,* 173-199.

Gerbner, G., Gross, L., Eleey., Jackson-Beeck, M., Jeffries-Fox, S. and Signorielli, N. (1977) Television violence profile no. 8: The highlights. *Journal of Communication, 27,* 171-180.

Gerbner, G., Gross, L., Jackson-Beeck, M., Jeffries-Fox, S. and Signorielli, N. (1978) Cultural indicators: Violence profile no. 9 *Journal of Communication 28,* 176-207.

Gerbner, G., Gross, L., Signorielli, N., Morgan, M. and Jackson-Beeck, M. (1979) The demonstration of power: Violence profile no. 10. *Journal of Communication, 29,* 177-196.

Gunter, B. and Wakshlag, J. (1986) *Television viewing and perceptions of crime among London residents.* Presented at the International Television Studies Conference, Institute of Education, London, July 10-13

Hawkins, R. and Pingree, S. (1980) Some progress in the cultivation effect. *Communication Research, 7,* 193-226.

Hirsch, P. (1980) The 'scary' world of the non-viewer and other anomalies: A reanalysis of Gerbner et al's findings on cultivation analysis: Part I. *Communication Research, 7,* 403-456.

Katzman, N. (1972) Television soap operas: What's been going on anyway? *Public Opinion Quarterly, 36,* 200-212.

Merton, R.K. (1957) Social theory and social structure. Glencoe, IL: Free Press.

Neville, T. (1980) *Television viewing and the expression interpersonal mistrust.* Unpublished doctoral dissertation, Princeton University.

Piepe, A., Crouch, J. and Emerson, M. (1977) Violence and television. *New Society, 41,* 536-538.

Rotter, J.B. (1965) General expectancies for internal versus external control of reinforcement. *Psychological Monographs, 80,* (1, Whole No. 609).

Srole, L. (1956) Social interpretation and certain corollaries. *American Sociological Review, 21,* 709-716.

Sutherland, J.C. and Siniawsky, S.J. (1982) The treatment and resolution of moral violation on soap operas. *Journal of Communication, 32,* 67-74.

Tyler, T.R. (1980) The impact of directly and indirectly experienced events: The origin of crime-related judgements and behaviours. *Journal of Personality and Social Psychology, 39,* 13-28.

Tyler, T.R. and Cook, F.L. (1984) The mass media and judgements of risk: Distinguishing impact on personal and societal level judgements. *Journal of Personality and Social Psychology, 47,* 693-708.

Weaver, J. and Wakshlag, J. (1986) Perceived vulnerability to crime, criminal victimisation experience, and television viewing. *Journal of Broadcasting and Electronic Media, 30,* 141-158.

Wober, M. (1978) Televised violence and paranoid perception: The view from Great Britain. *Public Opinion Quarterly, 42,* 315-321.

Wober, M. and Gunter, B. (1982) Television and personal threat: Fact or artifact? A British view. *British Journal of Social Psychology, 21,* 43-51.

4 Television, dramatization and the fear of crime

L'agression ne touche le corps qu'à travers les media, c'est dans ce sens que la médiatisation generalisée est à l'image d'une violence virale. Tous les faits d'agression et d'angoisse sont signifiés par avance, pris en charge par les discours et les récits des média.

H.-P. Jeudy, *La Peur et les média: essai sur la virulence*

Television and the 'scary world'

For many years a debate has continued (often ill-temperedly) about whether watching lots of television (and especially 'violent' television) provokes an increased level of fearfulness in at least some members of its audience. I have suggested (see Chapter 2 and following Giddens 1984) that, like other routine ways of spending time, watching television can in fact be seen as involved in maintaining security in the face of a range of anxieties. However, I have also suggested (Chapters 2 and 3), that the ways in which television might perform this task, and especially the extent to which its narratives of crime and law enforcement address a tension between anxiety and security, are problematic. In particular I have argued, that for at least a fraction of the audience television is felt to subvert not only the 'sense of place' (Meyrowitz 1985) but also, and more specifically, to violate a sense of propriety. In this respect the medium itself is a focus of anxiety, and is viewed in its felt relation to a range of social problems. Any such response tends to deploy interpretations of television content, and seeks to secure acceptance of those interpretations and not others. For these reasons it is impossible to accept an opposition between theories of the medium and its reception on the one hand (Meyrowitz 1985; Morley and Silverstone 1988) and theories of the ideological weight of television content on the other. Perspectives which stress the position of television in everyday life, and hence the active choices and uses made of it by a differentiated audience, will be incomplete unless they also attend to features of that which is chosen and used. Why do audiences prefer particular forms of television, and with what consequences? With what other dimensions of their social experience does television viewing intersect?

The question of the content of crime fiction on television is best construed in terms of the appeal it mounts to viewers in concrete social contexts. I shall argue here that one dimension of this appeal relates to viewers' prior beliefs about and anxieties concerning crime. This also gives rise to the conjecture that the representation of crime and law enforcement in television fiction also acts as a surrogate for other and more diffuse kinds of anxiety. One interesting feature of crime fiction, therefore, is the possibility of displacement (Knight 1980: 192; M. Williams 1982: 140). Crime fiction may permit ulterior uses of crime and disorder, in both arousing and placating social anxieties whose primary origin may or may not stem from criminal events as such. This may in turn influence the conduct and direction of political discourses about crime which, unlike the narrative itself, explicitly claim the force of truth. These include electoral law-and-order campaigns, as well as the activities of censorship lobbies and their associated beliefs about social trends.

The problem of 'content' and fear of crime

Disagreements about the significance of television, and in particular about the analysis of television content, in this area centre on three main issues, namely

1 the attribution of excessiveness or inappropriateness to the indices of fear elicited from viewers
2 the adequacy and pertinence of the measures of content which are proposed
3 the degree of determining influence which is claimed for characteristic kinds of television content over viewers' views of the world.

Most students of the depiction of crime and law enforcement on television have deployed quantitative techniques of content analysis (Gerbner et al 1969; Gerbner 1970; Dominick 1973; Gerbner and Gross 1976a; 1976b; Pandiani 1978; Krippendorf 1980). However, some observers, for example Gunter (1985), now argue that systematic content analysis necessarily tends to privilege its own readings of television content and hence to assume that viewers' orientations towards that content will more or less resemble one another. This objection has some force with respect to the kinds of content analysis which have hitherto been undertaken, especially by Gerbner and his collaborators. These tend to argue that crime fiction is troubling because of its variance from or distortion of reality, while acknowledging no special problem in recovering what that reality is like.

80   *Television and the drama of crime*

Such an approach seeks to isolate a determinate and measurable effect of viewing through multivariate statistical analysis. It also assumes a correspondence between measures of content, secured only by internal reliability between recorders of content scores, and viewers' responses. That is, it explicitly seeks to ground the objectivity of the analysis of content without particular regard to the variety and complexity of ordinary contexts of viewing.

Gunter's objection, however, is by no means insuperable in principle. His critique of content analysis accords poorly with his own repeated references to 'objective features of content'. Indeed, it is difficult to see, as Counihan for example shows (1975: 32), how it is possible to talk about the audience's preferences for particular kinds of programming without reference to at least an implicit theory of genre and meaning considered as inherent properties of texts.

There is no need, however, for the analysis of content to remain faithful to Lasswell's (1953) model (sender, message, receiver and channel) which relies on a literal enforcement of a 'conduit metaphor' of communication (Reddy 1979), and which was developed by Lasswell and others for the analysis of wartime propaganda (see Rowland and Watkins 1984: 16). Rather, the model of viewing which I have sketched in Chapter 2 stresses the importance of the sedimentation of genre over time, the role of scheduling in integrating generic forms within routines of domestic leisure, and the sense in which any genre opens on to other discursive areas which it may corroborate more or less closely. Equally, the way of interpreting television content which I shall propose (Chapter 5) seeks to be sensitive to stylistic questions as well as to taxonomies of events and episodes (see also Baggaley and Duck 1976: 31). There remains an obstinate coincidence between distributions of fear, correlative political attitudes, and patterns of viewing – a coincidence which it is the business of this analysis to make intelligible. However, as Christians and Carey (1981) observe, relevant issues do not turn simply on the enumeration of causal sequences but rather on the question 'what are the interpretations of meaning and value created in the media and what is their relation to the rest of life?' (1981: 347).

Traditions of research into fear and anxiety

Research into the fear of crime and its consequences, which sees fear as being in any important respect more than a simple product of the incidence of criminal events, is a comparatively recent emphasis in criminology. Most such research makes some reference to the role of mass media as one way of accounting for what are generally interpreted as discrepancies between comparatively low levels of risk and rather high reports of fear. Early considerations of the topic were conducted in the United States in the 1960s under the stimulus provided to survey research by the President's Commission on Law Enforcement and the Administration of Justice. The Commission funded attempts not only to estimate the scope of the 'dark figure' but also to achieve descriptive accounts of the impact of crime on the experience of particular localities (Lewis and Salem 1986: 4). Thus Biderman (1967) elaborated what he termed an 'Index of Anxiety'. Ennis (1967), meanwhile, introduced the now orthodox differentiation between fear (for self) and estimates of risk in general.

Attention to the fear of crime received a second profound stimulus from critiques advanced by radical observers (notably by Box 1971) of official statistics as an adequate basis for either research or policy conclusions. Radical criminologists argued forcefully that variations in official crime rates, especially where these appear to disclose dramatic surges or 'waves' in offending, are more often contingent upon variations in allocations of police resources and in practices of reporting and recording than upon changes in behaviour as such. Such work has been especially valuable in making manifest the dimension of differential *visibility* as between the commission of crimes in public and private space, and hence the disproportions in attention, anxiety and ease of enforcement which impinge upon the activities of socially marginal and disempowered groups, especially working-class youth (Pearson 1983). Considerable historiographical (Gatrell et al 1980) and ethnographic (Young 1971a) work has been devoted to demonstrating the chronic consequences of these disparities. This has focused, in particular, on the influence of mass media in equating the crimes of the powerless with crime as such (Young 1971b), in subsuming political dissent within general rubrics of deviation (Sumner 1982) and in constructing the ideological preconditions for policies of reaction and containment (S. Hall, 1980b).

Radical criminology's problematic of deviancy amplification envisaged a necessary concentration on the channels through which crime became and remained present to public attention and concerns. It thus produced a 'wave' of its own, of studies of the content and production of representations of crime, especially in the press. Fishman's statement of the theme is in some degree classic, if only for its concision:

> When we speak of a crime wave, we are talking about a kind of social awareness of crime, crime brought to public consciousness. It is something to be remarked upon at the corner grocery store, complained about in a community meeting, and denounced at the mayor's press conference. One cannot be mugged by a crime wave, but one can be scared. And one can put more police on the streets and enact new laws on the basis of fear. Crime waves may be 'things of the mind', but they have real consequences.
>
> (Fishman 1978: 531)

82 Television and the drama of crime

Notwithstanding its critical provenance, however, the awareness of these areas of difficulty (problems of criminal statistics, the oblique relationship between fear and incidence and the possible role of mass media as instigators of fear) has in some degree been recuperated by 'administrative' criminology (Young 1988). It is now more or less orthodox amongst survey researchers in both the USA (Garofalo 1980; Skogan and Maxfield 1981) and in Britain (Hough and Mayhew 1983; Maxfield 1984) to argue that neither fears for personal safety nor people's general assessments of crime-related problems can be uniformly or readily inferred either from actual experiences of victimization or objective indices of risk. Skogan and Maxfield summarize some empirical difficulties in this area:

> Fear is indeed a consequence of crime, but . . . most consequences of crime – including fear – are indirect. While victims of crime are more fearful as a result of their experiences, many more people have indirect contact with crime. The sources of this vicarious experience include the media, personal conversations with victims and others and observations of neighbourhood conditions. These convey a great deal of information about crime, and most urban dwellers cannot get through a day without being touched by it in one way or another.
>
> (Skogan and Maxfield 1981: 11)

Given these complexities most totalizing models of the nature and determinants of fear, most particularly perhaps those which have made the largest claims for the influence of mass media (Gerbner et al 1978) may seem crude and premature. Most researchers stress that a high level of fear, where fear is construed as a perception of threat to personal safety sufficiently large to influence whether one would go out alone after dark, is in general confined to larger urban areas. Overall levels of fear do not vary significantly between cities of similar size, but within urban areas fear is most intense in localities which suffer the highest rates of interpersonal violence and housebreaking (Maxfield, 1984: 38). To this extent fear and risk are indeed, unsurprisingly, closely coincident.

Meanwhile, it is true that anxiety – although not, according to some observers, risk (e.g. Hough and Mayhew 1983) – is compounded by gender and age. This finding leads some authorities to attribute excessiveness to the fears of women and elderly people. Other recent commentators (e.g. Maxfield 1984: 39), however, question the appropriateness of this attribution, arguing that physical vulnerability and the seriousness of the conseqences of victimization where it occurs, as well as more persistent (though not always criminal) forms of harassment and threat, should all be included in the calculus of the determinants of fear. Jones et al (1986: 75) claim that offences against women, especially sexual offences and domestic violence, remain under-reported even in (official) victim surveys. Equally, Maxfield argues (1984: 40) calculations should be broadened to include worry about the safety of others, such as children or elderly relatives. Each of these arguments undermines the claim that women's fear of crime is excessive or unrealistic. Hence, although as S. J. Smith (1986) indicates, a major focus in research on fear of crime has been its *independence* from victimization, with consequent readiness to attribute this disparity to the operation of mass media (see Fishman 1978), detailed examination of specific inner urban sites suggests that not only are fear and risk closely connected but also they are further compounded for relevant sub-populations by antagonistic or otherwise unsatisfactory contacts with police (Kinsey 1985; Jones et al 1986).

Recent contributors have therefore become reluctant to attribute any significant role to mass media in influencing the level of fear. Skogan and Maxfield (1981: ch. 8) examine this issue. Like all other observers they note the extreme concentration of both national and local media on crime, as well as the very high proportion of people who come into contact with media representations of crime on any one day (1981: 130). Yet they are unable to locate any independent influence of such representations on fear. There are a number of reservations to be noted however. The very consistency of this presence makes it unlikely that it will appear as a statistical *variance*. Similarly, it is questionable whether the multivariate techniques applied, which seek above all an *independent* 'effect', are appropriate to disclose the level at which media use is constitutive of daily routines. In general, the broader the scope of the survey, and the less concentrated its focus on realistic apprehensions of danger in inner urban locales, the more likely are attributions of excessive fear, stemming especially from media influences. This question of generality may account for some part of the disagreement between Hough and Mayhew (1983: 26) and Jones et al (1986: 81). Complications arise, however, and the bearing of the media on the constitution of public consciousness of crime is broached once again, where fears for personal safety and perceptions of risk in an immediate locality are differentiated from subjects' broader apprehensions of crime as a social problem and from perceptions of risk in other areas. It is at these levels that networks of communication retain a particular importance.

Crime, 'incivility' and the sense of place

S. J. Smith (1986) presents relevant issues lucidly by relating the spatial distribution of fear to other features of local social relations, in the context of the economic and political marginalization of an inner urban area. Smith concludes that if fear of crime is realistic in this setting it is because 'victimised populations and fearful populations (which anyway overlap) are structurally bound together by their shared location in social, economic and physical space' (1986: 117).

84 *Television and the drama of crime*

Equally, however, Smith (1986: 117) is concerned to show that whereas fear and risk do tend to coincide, they do not coincide uniformly; the sense of living in a dangerous place also has to do with awareness of economic and political marginality and of decline. These perceptions may crystallize in imputations of dangerousness across group (especially racial, but also age) boundaries, where the presence of incomers is experienced as an incursion upon previous familiarities and stability (S. J. Smith 1986: 111). In a similar way, Maxfield ventures (1984: 25; see also S. J. Smith 1986: 129) that fear may result from 'incivilities', where the behavioural improprieties of some groups, which may not be specifically criminal, are viewed by others as indices of social disorganization and of threat. In these senses diffuse anxieties result from social representations of the social and physical environment, whose sources are broader than the risk of victimization as such. Both Lewis (1980: 22) and Skogan and Maxfield (1981: 127) refer to these 'environmental' features as 'signs' of decay or trouble: yet neither goes any further in elucidating the nature of the *signification* in question.

One problem with the notion of 'incivility', therefore, is that it has been too narrowly conceived. In most usages it is a commonplace which is deployed either as a secondary way of censuring young people's use of public space, or else it is reduced to a simple set of 'cues' from the physical environment: the so-called 'broken window hypothesis' (Wilson and Kelling 1982). Each of these generates correlative policy strategies directed towards 'fear reduction' (Maxfield 1984; see also Bennett 1989), whether by increased surveillance of troublesome groups or by cosmetic improvements to the physical environment. Young's frustration with such measures (to which I alluded in Chapter 1) is that they constitute knowing manipulations of public perception, predicated on a presumed disparity between fear and risk (Young 1987; 1989).

Lewis and Salem (1986) propose a broader and more interesting notion of 'incivility'. For them the term incorporates a more general sense of disorder which in turn undermines any sense of well-being in the relation of specific publics to both their social and physical environments. In this respect 'incivility' also summarizes a problem in the relation of these publics to political authority since it derives from the failure to sustain adequate levels of public provision and participation, that is the preconditions for *civility* (Lewis and Salem 1986: 20; see also I. Taylor 1988). To this extent the incidence of crime and the fear of crime are not co-extensive but they share some of the same prior causes. These broader considerations also raise once again the question of the representations of crime in television and print, and the degree of attention which is paid to them in so far as these are informed not only by the fear of crime as such but also by the fear of disorder from which the former in part results (Lewis and Salem 1986: 22).

Communication and fear in everyday life

S. J. Smith (1986) shows that whether information circulating about crime is accurate or not, the fact of its circulation, the channels it follows and the motivations people have to attend to it remain important. The special significance of local news media, she argues, following Garofalo (1981), lies in the opportunity they provide for 'information seeking' consequent on the awareness of risk (S. J. Smith 1986: 117). The spatial distribution of events reported, as well as the specifically social proximity of the victims, both strongly influence the salience of reports of crime for any one individual (Skogan and Maxfield 1981: 74). This point of view is consistent with the more sophisticated outlook on risk-perception in general outlined by Douglas (1986; see also Chapter 1).

It is through such reports, and more particularly the networks of rumour and gossip for which, as forms of 'improvised news' (S. J. Smith 1986: 124), they provide the raw materials, that crime is constituted as an aspect of the social experience of a locality. Smith indicates a dual importance for rumour and gossip. At a manifest level rumour is a form of talk which mediates the transmission of crime-related information, on the basis of which strategies for the management of danger may be instituted. More obscurely, rumour is also consequential in defining and continually reproducing local social relations. Crime-related rumours flow most easily between socially and spatially proximate individuals. In so far as the sharing of a rumour is also a confirmation of this proximity rumours have multiple purposes and dimensions: they intrinsically exceed the information given. Members of particular networks agree on 'maps' (S. J. Smith 1986: 124) which designate both *sites* of danger and origins of danger in other sub-populations. Information about crime is thus integrated into local structures of affiliation and suspicion and the confirmation of their associated norms of propriety and censure. Such 'mapping' necessarily includes the potentiality for the overestimation of danger especially where demand for information exceeds its availability or where rumours refer to spatially or socially distant places or persons. It is in these terms that Smith understands the occurrence of 'fantastic rumour', where the ostensible topic of the rumour acts as a surrogate for more diffuse, discursively unavailable or socially unacceptable anxieties. In her own study of north-central Birmingham, Smith argues that the operation of fantastic rumour frequently results from mutual misperceptions across group boundaries, tending in this instance towards the exaggeration of race and crime issues (S. J. Smith 1986: 127).

Clearly Smith's analysis is consonant with the widespread finding that, even in high-crime areas where fear is arguably based on reasonable estimates of risk, subjects none the less tend to overestimate the dangers of other, further removed neighbourhoods and cities (Maxfield 1984: 28).

86 *Television and the drama of crime*

Even those observers who are most concerned to argue that fear of crime is realistically grounded in the inner cities (e.g. Kinsey 1985) acknowledge that those who live in areas with a lower incidence of interpersonal violence and robbery may none the less overestimate *both* overall dimensions of crime problems as they affect the whole society and, more particularly, the dangerousness of inner urban locales.

The apprehension of danger is, in part and for some people, closely consequent upon real risks. Yet to the extent that fear of crime is both more widely distributed than are risks and is bound up with other sources of social anxiety and stress it is also related to representations across social boundaries. In these respects fear is a function of *distance*. For these reasons the vocabulary and imagery in which these representations are encoded, the media through which they are disseminated and the political rhetorics and strategies within which they are subsumed remain important, notwithstanding the 'realist' challenge (Lea and Young 1984). Smith distinguishes between the levels at which fear impinges upon the experience of living in inner urban environments and at which it is co-ordinated in a national politics of law and order. To the extent that the latter is also 'mapped', as it were by a global rumour, it tends to ratify the surveillance of sites of agreed danger (Jones et al 1986: 62). Through the dynamics of distance and proximity inner urban residents (objectively exposed to the greatest risks) are doubly marginalized: subject, that is, not only to fearfulness but also to strategies of policing and investigation ulterior to their needs, stemming from the diffusion of anxiety throughout the social formation.

Given that media use and crime-related talk are diffuse and ramified it is premature to restrict the range of resources on which they are considered to draw. Just as information about crime in the news and elsewhere is differentially sought out, attended to and integrated into forms of talk and strategies for coping, so models of criminal process and more especially, paleo-symbolic systems of justification which are less clearly 'informational' may also receive attention and be put to use (Gouldner 1976). It is with regard to these two aspects of fear, the dynamics of distance and the modes of experience with which it coalesces, that the relevance of the narration of crime and law enforcement on television should be understood.

Television, crime and the 'cultivation hypothesis'

In view of the complexity of the distribution and determinations of fear, and of its embeddedness within locally sustained social relations, any attempt to attribute a significant degree of this variance to any one source or medium appears both grandiose and reductive. Nevertheless, two decades of research by Gerbner and his associates have addressed exactly this proposition, in the form of a hypothesis of the 'cultivation' by television of fear and a concomitant set of social beliefs.

As a general argument about the location of television in the cultures of the industrial societies, the 'cultivation hypothesis' asserts:

> We begin with the assumption that television is the central cultural arm of American society. It is an agency of the established order and as such serves primarily to extend and maintain rather than to alter, threaten or weaken conventional conceptions, beliefs and behaviors. Its chief function is to spread and stabilise social patterns, to cultivate not change but resistance to change. Television is a medium of the socialization of most people into standardized roles and behaviors. Its function is, in a word, enculturation.
> (Gerbner and Gross 1976a: 115)

Gerbner's 'violence profile' (Gerbner and Gross 1976a) applies this view to the representation of crime, law enforcement and violence on television. In Gerbner's terms the frequent reiteration of violent episodes 'cultivates' a misleading and exaggerated view of their incidence in the world. This distortion differentially affects those who watch most television. Gerbner's method, therefore, is annually to subject the whole of one week's prime-time broadcast television, available in one major American city, to an elaborate content analysis. This enumerates, among other things, violent incidents, the identities of their perpetrators and victims (demographic characteristics, relation to law enforcement agencies) as well as how often the use of violence is associated with a successful or happy outcome. On the basis of the index thus derived the researchers infer a set of 'television answers' to survey questions about the prevalence of violent crime, perceptions of personal vulnerability and the justifiability of policing strategies, especially the use of force and firearms. 'Heavy' viewers of television (those who watch four or more hours of television daily) are more likely, they suggest, to affirm the 'television answer' than they are to conform either to known facts of crime rates or to other sources of information discrepant with television (Gerbner et al 1978).

Carlson (1985) replicates Gerbner et al's investigations, and also expands on them. Following criticisms of their statistical manipulations (e.g. Doob and Macdonald 1979; Hughes 1980), Gerbner et al have introduced two refinements to the cultivation hypothesis, which they term 'resonance' and 'mainstreaming' (Gerbner et al 1980). By 'resonance' they understand an increased susceptibility to cultivation effects among those viewers whose social experience is most closely congruent with television's depiction of a 'mean' or 'scary' world, that is those who have most experience of victimization. That is, they claim, these viewers are subject to a 'double dose' of fear-inducing messages (Carlson 1985: 173). 'Main-

88 Television and the drama of crime

streaming' meanwhile refers to the claim that the messages of television entertainment are closely consonant with widespread and dominant world outlooks. In those whose views already fall within the cultural 'mainstream', therefore, cultivation processes are not visible as distinct and measurable 'effects'; rather they provide for the continual reconfirmation of an already given social identity. What *is* arguably visible is the 'mainstreaming' of those whose social position might place them outside the 'mainstream' but who are yet heavy viewers of television (Carlson, 1985: 8). Hence, it is argued, television tends to efface social difference, tugging all its viewers in the direction of a somewhat authoritarian consensus, underwritten by the uniformity of television content.

'Cultivation' and political socialization

Carlson (1985) emphasizes that the issue of the cultivation of a 'mean' or 'scary' perception of the world has a clear bearing on questions of political socialization (see also Gerbner et al 1984). Carlson finds little support for the notion of 'resonance'. In common with other investigators, notably Tyler (1980), he argues that first-hand experience of victimization *predominates over* rather than confirms mass mediated perspectives. On the other hand, Carlson (1985) argues that 'mainstreaming' is indeed strongly active. Briefly, Carlson claims to show that heavier viewers are comparatively ill-informed about legal processes and that they place a higher value than do those who view less on a starker version of a norm of compliance – that they are 'anti-heterodox' (see Weigel and Jessor 1973: 88; Corbett 1981: 330). He thus argues that they have a correlatively lower regard for civil liberties and that, in terms of Packer's two models of criminal justice, they therefore tend to favour 'crime control' at the expense of 'due process' (Packer 1969; Carlson 1985: 193). Heavy viewers believe that the world is a dangerous place. Yet they also entertain the contrary view that the police are effective in combating crime. Carlson further argues that there may be a 'spillover' from these kinds of orientations towards crime into more general and diffuse support for existing political arrangements and confirmation of the legitimacy of actually existing distributions of power (Carlson 1985: 191).

Carlson's argument is suggestive. In part its interest derives from its broadening of the scope of the 'cultivation' argument in the direction of the wider concerns of social theory with political socialization and social reproduction. It stipulates, that is to say, that the 'effects' of television, especially with reference to criminal justice, are interesting primarily in so far as they intersect with other dimensions of social being and political conduct. This being so, however, their visibility, *qua* effects of television, will be attenuated and conditional on these interactions. Nevertheless, given that Carlson's theory and method are wholly derived from

Gerbner, his argument is still vulnerable to the same series of conceptual and empirical objections which apply to the whole body of 'cultivation' research. These can now be briefly stated.

Theoretical criticisms of 'cultivation'
The authors of *Policing the Crisis* (S. Hall et al 1978) might well be gratified by Carlson's conclusions, although they never undertook empirical work at a comparable level of detail. Equally, however, Carlson does not develop his political sociology with their sophistication. Rather he allows his conceptions of authority and legitimation to rest on an undifferentiated structural-functionalist notion of social control, historically unspecific and evasive with regard to the weight accorded respectively to economic, political and ideological conditions.

To this extent Carlson's argument, like Gerbner's from which it derives, finally rests on certain very weakly defended propositions. For example, Carlson claims that

> To the extent that audiences share values that are system supportive, successful programs will be likely to be those that reflect viewpoints that contribute to the maintenance of the social and political order.
>
> (Carlson 1985: 2)

Carlson never specifies, except negatively with reference to passivity, what 'values that are system supportive' consist in, how strongly they need to be held nor whether they may coexist with other, potentially antagonistic, commitments. Evidently we are dealing here with what is more traditionally known as a theory of ideology, but it is not at all clear whether Carlson's conception of ideology is generic and neutral (i.e. that all belief is socially generated, all dominant social beliefs are inertial) or restrictive and critical (i.e. that ideology equals beliefs which underwrite sectional interests). In so far as all the important terms in his formulation (system, reflection, maintenance) go unexplained Carlson never emerges from his plausible circularity: like other functionalists, he merely presupposes the 'system persistence' (1985: 2) he purports to investigate. Under the guise of a bland and inoffensive suggestion a highly contentious, binding presumption of consensus is smuggled in: the claim that social order is 'maintained' is surely much stronger than the more contingent notions of transmission or reproduction across time and space. Carlson can thus offer no rejoinder to the objection that the mere survival of a given social system over time in no way presupposes the 'consolidation of consensus' within it, but rather only that its 'structural principles' remain recognizably similar (Giddens 1984: 180).

Similarly, cultivation research never adequately specifies either motivations to engage in television viewing, nor affiliations towards what is

90   *Television and the drama of crime*

viewed. Carlson rests his case as to why people watch television on a second thesis which also contrives to be both banal and presumptuous: 'If people choose the television programs they view, they are unlikely to choose those that will make them uncomfortable' (1985: 6). Again, the definition of viewing appears to be modest, established by plausible exclusion, but its covert purport is more ambitious, imposing an arbitrary restriction on the range of possible reasons for viewing and foreclosing the need to speak of them. The world is full of examples of people choosing to be made uncomfortable for reasons of pleasure, as anyone who has ever been pot-holing, let alone engaged in more recondite forms of masochism, knows (see Tuan 1979: 202 on the concept of 'eustress').

For all its wealth of empirical detail about alleged outcomes of viewing, the cultivation perspective is not at all enlightening about how viewing is constituted as a situated activity nor, consequently, about how differently it may be engaged in by viewers in diverse social locations

The text, the world and the viewer
Both these problems stem in large measure from the notions of 'reflection' and 'distortion' which underpin cultivation analysis and which provide the grounds upon which its criticism of the television medium is based (see Newcomb 1978). The causal force which is attributed to television in determining viewers' perceptions of the world is derived from a crudely 'reflectionist' notion of representation. Simply put, television 'reflects' dominant values for the very reason that it fails accurately to 'reflect' the real. Starting from this premise content analysis tends to take the form of an actuarial exercise in counting categories of events and their various combinations. The origin and salience of the categories themselves is not viewed as being especially problematic: neither, correlatively, are viewers' responses to them understood as being particularly contextually variable or complex. At the level of the text content analysis proceeds in virtual ignorance of issues of either narrative or discourse (Chatman 1978; Genette 1982), modes of narration (Browne 1982), or the stylistics of openness and closure (Eco 1979; J. Taylor 1980). Cultivation analysis presents itself as a theory of the colonization of the contemporary cultural field by television, yet it pays no attention to the particular features of the medium as a technology of inscription, storage and diffusion (Giddens 1987: 101).

Similarly, at the level of the audience, cultivation analysis is insensitive to the importance of the positioning of the viewer in leading to particular strategies of disambiguation (Pateman 1983). The principal difference between the content analytic notion of 'distortion' and that of 'systematic distortion' (S. Hall 1975) is that whereas the latter does infer a 'preferred reading' of any narrative it specifically also entertains the possibility of aberrant or oppositional readings. Pandiani (1978) offers a particularly clear instance of this problem within the cultivation perspective. Pandiani's interest in the place of crime within television entertainment lies in what would follow 'if all we knew was what we saw' (1978: 437). Since there are good grounds for supposing that what we see on television is not all we know of the social world and that, in any case, one thing we do know about television viewers is that they differentiate rather precisely between the two (Gunter and Wober, 1982; Gunter 1985) Pandiani's question holds little interest, even if it is presented as a counter-factual one.

Recent attempts to supplement and refine this kind of analysis have not altogether resolved these problems. For example Surette (1984) rightly notes that the simplicity and directness of prevalent attributions of effects of viewing can no longer be sustained. However, in the face of the challenge of delineating a more adequate 'model' of the place of televised crime in the lives of its viewers Surette continues to seek safety in a terminology which still does little more than nod in the direction of viewing as situated and reflexive activity:

> the path by which media influences its audience is not a direct or simple one, but rather it is a multi-stepped transactional process that is mediated through psychological and sociological variables.
> (Surette 1984: 324)

This clearly looks like a technical language, but it is still mainly a descriptive rather than a theoretical one: it does not guide us with respect to the level of generality at which it is appropriate to speak. It is revealing that even as he reminds us that contemporary media are complex and diverse Surette lapses into the use of the singular verb. This imprecision matters: how unitary, how systematic is the message system in fact?

The really vexed questions of media analysis lie beyond and beneath the largely descriptive statements which cultivation analysis has so far generated. The description of television content does not in and of itself illuminate the ways in which it is viewed. Why are television crime fictions pleasurable? What socially given needs do they answer? (See Baggaley and Duck 1976: 164.) Unless it attends to these questions content analysis tends to remain uninterestingly pedantic and to observe silence about the kinds of reality claims which television fiction lodges, the regimes of representation it deploys and the modes of participation in which viewers are invited to engage.

Substantive criticisms of 'cultivation'
Substantive objections to the empirical claims made by cultivation research about television viewing and the fear of crime are broadly of three kinds.

First, there is an argument that while the constellation of social beliefs identified as linking television viewing, the fear of crime and punitive

92 Television and the drama of crime

attitudes to criminal justice may indeed exist as a set of statistical correlates, the isolation of television viewing as the causal factor is spurious. As Wakshlag reminds us (Wakshlag et al 1983: 227; Weaver and Wakshlag 1984: 4), Gerbner's thesis relies on a causal claim about television's responsibility for this variance. If that claim cannot be sustained then this is sufficient to refute it in its present form. This is the argument advanced by Hirsch (1980; 1981) who indicates that apparent cultivation effects disappear when additional statistical controls are applied. Indeed Hirsch claims to show that non-viewers of television (whom Gerbner aggregates with light viewers) are more fearful than are either category of viewers (Hirsch 1980). Similarly, Hughes (1980) also reanalyses data used by Gerbner and his associates (Gerbner et al 1978). Hughes (1980: 293) argues that the strongest determinant of viewing is the amount of time available in which to view, which is in turn strongly related to prior socio-economic conditions, notably to age and gender. In Hughes's adjusted controls television viewing is much less strongly related to fear than are either gender or size of city of residence (1980: 296). Most interestingly Doob and Macdonald (1979) acknowledge that television viewing and fear of crime *are* correlated but argue that *both* are contingent on place of residence.

Second, one can argue that the kinds of correlations isolated by cultivation researchers may exist at some times and in some places but that they are much less general than Gerbner would wish to claim. Cultivation effects do not travel well. All attempts to replicate them in a British context (Gunter and Wober 1983; Gunter and Wakshlag 1986) have failed. That is, irrespective of whatever role television may play in some American instances, if it does something else somewhere else this undermines the force and generality of the underlying causal mechanism which is alleged.

The third and most important argument against Gerbner's strong version of a cultivation claim builds on the outcomes of the first two. As Hughes (1980) observes, given the inherent difficulties of content analysis it is by no means so obvious as Gerbner and Gross (1976b) seem to suggest what a 'television answer' would actually be in any given case. One can therefore argue that even if some version of a cultivation effect, more modestly conceived, does indeed exist, researchers have been premature in stipulating its likely strength and direction (Hughes 1980: 299). Drawing on the findings of Doob and Macdonald (1979), Wakshlag et al (1983: 229) argue that the present state of knowledge is less consonant with a basic cultivation hypothesis than with a thesis of selective preference for crime drama, predicated on prior anxieties. The finding by Boyanowski et al (1974) that under particularly intense conditions of perceived threat (immediately following the murder of a female student on a university campus) attendance at a violent film increased dramatically, in comparison with a light romance, seems to be suggestive of a similar conclusion. On these grounds Wakshlag et al (1983) suggest that, if it is indeed plausible that some kind of 'cultivation' results from the repeated viewing of somewhat similar narratives, there may nevertheless be equally good grounds for supposing that television cultivates security as fear and that this is in any case contingent on the motivations people have for using media in the ways they do, which may in turn be far more complex and variable than previously allowed.

The recognition, following Doob and Macdonald (1979), that both levels of fear and of television use may be contingent on place of residence, and by extension on the proximity of the experience of crime in a given locality, leaves open the possibility of a further relationship between the two. That is, it is at least conceivable that heightened perceptions of vulnerability dispose people towards a greater reliance on television. This may be for the simple reason that fearful people are more inclined to remain at home watching television (Gunter and Wakshlag 1986: 22), or it might also suggest that television is specifically helpful in *alleviating* anxiety (Weaver and Wakshlag 1984: 5).

Fear and viewing preferences

Research on the ways in which audiences selectively use and prefer particular kinds of television content thus makes at least two major alterations to the cultivation hypothesis.

The first is in the propositions such research introduces about television content. Zillman and Wakshlag (1987) points out that the vast majority of television crime drama emphasizes 'justice' in its outcomes. Hence, although crime drama programmes do include a high incidence of violent and transgressive action they are viewed in the expectation that order will be restored. Zillman (1980) posits that this dynamic holds a particular appeal for apprehensive individuals. This is both because the heightened experience of fear is met by a similarly greater pleasure at a happy outcome (Wakshlag et al 1983: 211) and because this encounter, which takes place under conditions of safety allows apprehensive viewers to experience a sense of the mastery of an initially 'scary' situation (Zillman and Wakshlag 1987: 13). On this view television crime drama permits a strategic manipulation of the viewers' sense of their relation to their environment in the direction of relief from anxiety (Wakshlag et al 1983: 229; Weaver and Wakshlag 1984: 26). In this sense attention to selective exposure to communication also suggests a renewed interest in content analysis, but in a form which emphasizes the organization and outcome of television narratives, as opposed to the mere enumeration of what they include. Given the predominant structure of television crime fictions, it is argued, instances which are simply conducive to the cultivation of fear will be rather rare.

94   *Television and the drama of crime*

Second, hypotheses of selective exposure construe the audience for television as being both more differentiated and more active than does the cultivation hypothesis in its original or strong version. For example, in experimental manipulations, Wakshlag et al (1983) suggest that apprehensive subjects incline markedly more than others towards crime drama which includes a 'just' resolution. The same subjects, moreover, are by no means drawn towards drama which includes violence in the absence of such a resolution. On these grounds the investigators conclude:

> The most compelling – and parsimonious – explanation for the present study's findings considers victimization and justice restoration in crime drama as a functional unit. . . . When suspenseful drama featuring victimization is known to contain a satisfying resolution, apprehensive individuals should anticipate pleasure and enjoyment and prefer such material. The initial distress that emerges from viewing the building of suspense in a program is clearly, then, conceived to be a critical part of eventual enjoyment.
>
> (Wakshlag et al 1983: 238)

Findings consistent with this thesis have now begun to proliferate. Thus, Wakshlag et al (1983) note heightened physiological indices of arousal as well as verbal expressions of involvement in crime drama among apprehensive viewers. Meanwhile, Weaver and Wakshlag (1984: 26) conclude that viewers who have been or who know victims of crime use television drama as part of a set of strategies for coping with and alleviating anxieties about the future. Moreover, and in contrast to the conclusions of Gerbner et al (1978) and Carlson (1985), it is easy to reconcile these findings with the predominant foci of research into the wider distributions of fear of crime (Skogan and Maxfield 1981) since they acknowledge that viewing is situated in relation to, and indeed perhaps encouraged by, the fear and incidence of crime in specific locales.

Similarly, the recognition of complexity in the use of crime on television also permits a more subtle treatment of the fears to which it relates. One reason why cultivation analysis has been unspecific at the levels of practice and experience is that it fails to distinguish dimensions *within* the general rubric of concern or fear about crime (Weaver and Wakshlag 1984: 24). Weaver and Wakshlag argue that it is possible to distinguish three component factors within perceptions of personal vulnerability which are related to the use of crime on television. These they summarize as concerns for personal safety in 'hypothetical' situations similar to those found in television crime drama, concern for the safety of the immediate residential environment and, third, the likelihood of becoming a victim at some future date (Weaver and Wakshlag 1984: 23). Like Tyler (1984), Weaver and Wakshlag argue that whatever then remains of a cultivation effect is operative at the level of abstract and global perceptions of crime – that is where these are not countermanded by personal experience (Weaver and Wakshlag 1984: 25) – and where television drama remains one of the resources on which viewers draw in actively constructing their view of the world.

In sum, the argument from 'selective exposure' is useful in that it reconsiders both the interpretation of television content and the interpretation of the audience. It acknowledges that viewers are not passive 'dopes', and that the uses viewers make of crime drama are contingent on their relation to social experience. Furthermore, this argument goes some way towards reconciling a serious interest in the nature and quality of television's narration of crime with the general concerns of research into the fear of crime. That is, it differentiates influences on the apprehension of the general and abstract from the experience of the personal and particular. Although the subsequent findings of Gunter and Wakshlag (1986: 21) are in some important ways at odds with those of Tyler (1984) they still seem to corroborate the overall thesis, including its emphasis on distance and proximity. In general, heavy viewing remains a statistical predictor of fear, although this is construed as an effect rather than a cause. Secondly, for a British population, crime drama in a British setting, that is one that is fictionally 'close', seems more closely related to personal fears than American counterparts are. Equally, however, British viewers consider New York and Los Angeles to be far more dangerous places than any British setting (Gunter and Wakshlag 1986: 11).

These conclusions are consistent with S. J. Smith's (1986: 124) interest in people's subjective 'maps' of their social environments. It may be that people's perceptions of spatially and socially distant places are stark and clear both because the available information about them is similarly simplified, and because these views are rather casually held. For a British viewer a lesser intellectual and emotional commitment is involved in expressing a view about the dangers of New York than about somewhere closer to home. Nevertheless, as Smith emphasizes, the views one holds about distant places are not, for that reason, of no consequence. It is perhaps in terms of such mapping that the known world is defined and differentiated from the alien, the foreign and the dangerous. Equally to the extent that crime is caught up in totalizing political rhetorics it is also intrinsically concerned with aspects of the world which are not directly known, and with the dangers that lurk in these penumbra. It has always been at the edges of maps that dragons and sea monsters live.

Some criticisms of 'selective exposure'

The return to Smith's argument, however, also highlights some important shortcomings of even the most sophisticated work on selective exposure

96 Television and the drama of crime

to television crime drama. In the first place, as Weaver and Wakshlag (1984: 24) insist (following Hawkins and Pingree 1982), if there is a significant relationship (of whatever kind) between fear of crime and television viewing, it is highly likely to be 'content specific'. In this regard the authors highlight the importance of just and unjust resolutions in narrative. Clearly, Gerbner's stratagem of aggregating violent incidents from various different genres of programming is mistaken, since we are interested not in violence 'as such' (whatever that might be: see Pringle 1972) but in its co-ordination within the economy of a particular genre of stories. One of our aims, then, must be to indicate the parameters of this genre, its norms and expectations. Yet work within the selective exposure problematic never does more than broach this issue: it does not provide the new and refined content analytic scheme on which, nevertheless, its propositions implicitly depend. For example, Zillman and Wakshlag build their entire argument about the importance of just and unjust resolutions on nothing more than an assertion that justice predominates (1987: 11).

Yet what justifies 'justice'? How is it known, recognized and established as just? How completely does the triumph of justice resolve the conflicts of the plot? These questions are scarcely raised, let alone properly addressed. The authors follow Zillman (1980: 160) in arguing that 'television drama distorts reality more toward security than toward danger'. They continue:

> It projects too just and perhaps too safe a world. . . . Such drama continually conveys the message that good forces (i.e. police, private investigators, vigilantes) are out there mopping up the scum of society. Their relentless good efforts make the streets safe again. This kind of message should be music to the ears of troubled citizens. They can relax and put their worries about crime and personal safety to rest.
> (Zillman and Wakshlag 1987: 11)

It is paradoxical, indeed frankly contradictory, to build an argument about the complexity of the viewer's response around such a crude and presumptive summary of programme content. Like Gerbner, Wakshlag and Zillman privilege their own reading of crime drama texts: but unlike Gerbner they provide no systematic justification for this reading, even if prima facie it seems more plausible. Since all their empirical investigations are based around these presumptions the investigators simply never say what *else* and what *more* than this viewers may be capable of finding in and retrieving from what they view. Television drama does not, in any simple sense 'convey a message that good forces . . . are out there'. It is not, strictly speaking, a report or 'conveyance' of anything. Rather it *constitutes* these forces as 'good': in the act of showing it also provides the properties of what is shown. Similarly, this perspective tends to throw out the baby of the political correlates of television viewing with the bathwater of the cultivation hypothesis. It is all very well for psychologists to construe television viewing in terms of 'belief in a just world' (Gunter and Wakshlag, 1986: 4), but to what notion of justice does this refer?

When Mills (1959: 1) simply says that 'Nowadays men feel that their lives are a series of traps' he begins to elaborate an idea about personal 'troubles' which acknowledges that they originate in more diffuse sources than their ostensible objects would seem to suggest. Weaver and Wakshlag's method cannot elicit the ways in which their subjects are 'troubled' by fears that they may know quite well have no empirical referent or basis. Equally, if television does console the fearful in the face of their real anxieties what are we to make of this form of distraction? What kind of *dependency* on television does it suggest? Weaver and Wakshlag beg these questions by merely positing that the alleviation of anxiety is 'beneficial' (1984: 6), whereas anxiety of course is 'maladaptive' (1984: 20). In open, but parallel, contradiction, Tyler (1984: 35) argues that public education campaigns around crime should seek to cultivate fear, because fear stimulates 'avoidance behaviours' and therefore prevents victimization. In either case the viewers are available for manipulation in their own best interests. Meanwhile, Weaver and Wakshlag (1984: 12) follow Zillman (1980) in thinking that because television 'distorts' reality in the direction of reassurance 'it trivializes crime and, with repeated exposure, diminishes the impact of previous experience and alleviates the victim's worries'. Is this 'trivialization' likewise a beneficial process? Weaver and Wakshlag themselves note that

> the volume of contradictory evidence accentuates the fact that critical questions concerning whether and how the latent messages of crime and violence are perceived by the television audience and how, if perceived, they are responded to, must be addressed before the proposed linkages can be adequately understood.
> (Weaver and Wakshlag 1984: 6)

Quite so: but both the theory and practice of the 'selective exposure' position suggest that the message, and its latent functions, are primary here, without providing any procedures for knowing them. In their eagerness to refute the cultivation hypothesis, advocates of a 'selective exposure' position have leapt too hastily to an opposite pole. Their inference that crime drama is 'beneficial' because reassuring is a simple inversion of Gerbner's views. It still takes insufficient account of the lived experience of fear-of-crime problems and is based on similarly reductive interpretations of texts.

Some conclusions

In this chapter I have mainly sought to evaluate, however briefly, two kinds of arguments which are current in research on television and the

98 Television and the drama of crime

fear of crime, namely that television either 'cultivates' undue fear or, conversely, provides (undue?) comfort to an already anxious audience. Neither of these positions seems to me wholly satisfactory, although the latter claim is clearly the less extravagant. 'Cultivation' has a rather mechanistic notion of viewing, slight understanding of story-telling and a simplified approach to some vexed criminological issues. 'Selective exposure' wins the argument easily, but gives away its gains by substituting another notion of narrative almost as inane as the first. One source of weakness for each, therefore, is their reliance on poorly defended interpretations of television content. In order to produce any more interesting or plausible hypothesis about viewers' responses to the depiction of crime and law enforcement on television it is first necessary to elaborate a more subtle and fertile view of the 'content' of those depictions. As a preliminary to future research of that kind, my argument must therefore take a step backwards – towards the message of television – and attempt to further elucidate its implicit categories of justice and resolution, and the regimes of representation within which they are deployed. The next chapter is devoted to a refinement of the available ways of inquiry into these matters.

References

Baggaley, J. and Duck, S. (1976) *Dynamics of Television,* Westmead: Saxon House.
Bennett, T.H. (1989) *Tackling Fear of Crime: A Review of Policy Options,* University of Cambridge, Institute of Criminology.
Biderman, A. (1967) *Report on a Pilot Study on Victimization and Attitudes towards Law Enforcement,* Washington, DC: US Government Printing Office.
Box, S. (1971) *Deviance, Reality and Society,* London: Holt, Rinehart & Winston.
Boyanowski, E., Newtson, D. and Walster, E. (1974) 'Film preference following murder', *Communication Research* 1: 32-4.
Browne, N. (1982) *The Rhetoric of Filmic Narration,* Ann Arbor, Mich.: UMI Research Press.
Carlson, J.M. (1985) *Prime-Time Law Enforcement: Crime Show Viewing and Attitudes Toward the Criminal Justice System,* New York: Praeger.
Chatman, S. (1978) *Story and Discourse: Narrative Structure in Fiction and Film,* Ithaca, NY: Cornell University Press.
Christians, C. and Carey, J.W. (1981) 'The logic and aims of qualitative research' in G.H. Stempel and B.H. Westley (eds) *Research Methods in Mass Communication,* Englewood Cliffs, NJ: Prentice-Hall.
Corbett, M. (1981) 'Public support for "Law and Order"', *Criminology* 19: 328-43.
Counihan, M. (1975) '"Reading Television": notes on the problem of media content', *Australian and New Zealand Journal of Sociology* 11: 31-6.
Doob, A. and Macdonald, G. (1979) 'Television viewing and the fear of victimization: is the relationship casual?', *Journal of Personality and Social Psychology* 37: 170-9.
Douglas, M. (1986) *Risk,* London: Routledge & Kegan Paul.
Eco, U. (1979) *The Role of the Reader,* London: Hutchinson.
Ennis, P.H. (1967) *Criminal Victimization in the United States,* Washington DC: US Government Printing Office.
Fishman, M. (1978) 'Crime waves as ideology', *Social Problems* 25: 531-43.
Garofalo, J. (1980) 'Victimization and the fear of crime' in E. Bittner and S. Messinger (eds) *Criminology Review Yearbook,* vol. 2, London: Sage.
Garofalo, J. (1981) 'Crime and the mass media: a selective review of research', *Journal of Research in Crime and Delinquency* 18: 319-50.
Gatrell, V., Lenman, B. and Parker, E. (eds) (1980) *Crime and the Law: the Social History of Crime in Europe since 1500,* London: Europa.
Genette, G. (1982) *Figures of Literary Discourse,* Oxford: Basil Blackwell.
Gerbner, G. and Gross, L. (1976a) 'Living with television: the violence profile', *Journal of Communication* 26 :173-199.
Gerbner, G. and Gross, L. (1976b) 'The scary world of TV's heavy viewer', *Psychology Today* April: 89-91.
Gerbner, G., Gross, L., Morgan, M., Signorielli, N. and Jackson-Beeck, M. (1978) 'Cultural indicators: violence profile no. 9', *Journal of Communication* 28: 176-207.
Gerbner, G., Gross, L., Morgan, M. and Signorielli, N. (1980) 'The mainstreaming of America: violence profile no. 11', *Journal of Communication* 30: 19-29.
Gerbner, G., Gross, L., Morgan, M. and Signorielli, N. (1984) 'Political correlates of television viewing', *Public Opinion Quarterly* 48: 283-300.
Giddens, A. (1984) *The Constitution of Society,* Cambridge: Polity Press.
Giddens, A. (1987) *Sociology and Modern Social Theory,* Cambridge: Polity Press.
Gouldner, A.W. (1976) *The Dialectic of Ideology and Technology,* London: Macmillan.
Gunter, B. (1985) *Dimensions of Television Violence,* Aldershot: Gower.
Gunter, B. and Wakshlag, J. (1986) 'Television viewing and perceptions of crime among London residents'. Paper presented to International Television Studies Conference, London, July.
Gunter, B. and Wober, J.M. (1982) 'Television and personal threat: fact or artifact?', *British Journal of Social Psychology* 21: 239-47.

Gunter, B. and Wober, M. (1983) 'Television viewing and public trust', *British Journal of Social Psychology* 29: 177-96.

Hall, S. (1975) 'Encoding and decoding in the television discourse'. Occasional Paper, Birmingham: Centre for Contemporary Cultural Studies.

Hall, S. (1980b) 'Drifting into a law and order society' (Cobden Trust Human Rights Day Lecture, 1979), London: Cobden Trust.

Hall, S., Clarke, J., Jefferson, T., Critcher, C. and Roberts, B. (1978) *Policing the Crisis: Mugging, Law and Order and the State,* London: Macmillan.

Hawkins, R. and Pingree, S. (1982) 'Television's influence on social reality' in D. Pearl, L. Bouthilet and J. Lazar (eds) *Television and Behavior,* vol. 2, Rockville, Md: National Institute of Mental Health.

Hirsch, P. (1980) 'The "scary world" of the non-viewer and other anomalies: a reanalysis of Gerbner *et al.'s* findings, part 1', *Communication Research* 7: 403-56.

Hirsch, P. (1981) 'On not learning from one's own mistakes: a reanalysis of Gerbner *et al.,* part 2', *Communication Research* 8: 3-37.

Hough, M. and Mayhew, P. (1983) *The British Crime Survey,* London: HMSO.

Hughes, M. (1980) 'The fruits of cultivation analysis: a re-examination of some effects of television watching', *Public Opinion Quarterly* 44: 287-302.

Jones, T., MacLean, B. and Young, J. (1986) *The Islington Crime Survey,* Aldershot: Gower.

Kinsey, R. (1985) *Merseyside Crime and Police Surveys: Final Report,* Liverpool: Merseyside County Council.

Lasswell, H. (1953) 'Why be quantitative?' in B. Berelson and M. Janowitz (eds) *Reader in Public Opinion and Communication,* Glencoe, Ill: Free Press.

Lea, J. and Young, J. (1984) *What is to be Done about Law and Order?,* Harmondsworth: Penguin.

Lewis, D. and Salem, G. (1986) *Fear of Crime,* New Brunswick, NJ: Transaction Inc.

Maxfield, M. (1984) *Fear of Crime in England and Wales,* London: HMSO.

Meyrowitz, J. (1985) *No Sense of Place,* Oxford: Oxford University Press.

Mills, C.W. (1959) *The Sociological Imagination,* Harmondsworth: Penguin.

Morley, D. and Silverstone, R. (1988) 'Domestic Communication'. Paper presented to the International Television Studies Conference, London, July.

Newcomb, H. (1978) 'Assessing the violence profiles of Gerbner and Gross. A humanistic critique and suggestion', *Communication Research* 5, 3: 264-82.

Packer, H.L. (1969) *The Limits of the Criminal Sanction,* Stanford, Calif: Stanford University Press.

Pandiani, J. (1978) 'Crime-time TV: if all we knew is what we saw . . .', *Contemporary Crises* 2: 437-58.

Pateman, T. (1983) 'How is understanding an advertisement possible?' in H. Davis and P. Walton (eds) *Language, Image, Media,* Oxford: Basil Blackwell.

Pearson, G. (1983) *Hooligan: A History of Respectable Fears,* London: Macmillan.

Pringle, A. (1972) 'Review of Glucksmann', *Violence on the Screen', Screen* 12, 3: 152-6.

Reddy, M. (1979) 'The conduit metaphor' in A. Ortony (ed.) *Metaphor and Thought,* Cambridge: Cambridge University Press.

Rowland, W. and Watkins, B. (1984) 'Introduction: beyond mass culture and normal science in television research' in W. Rowland and B. Watkins (eds) *Interpreting Television: Current Research Perspectives* (Sage Annual Reviews of Communication Research) vol. 12, London: Sage.

Skogan, W. and Maxfield, M. (1981) *Coping with Crime,* London: Sage.

Smith, S.J. (1986) *Crime, Space and Society,* Cambridge: Cambridge University Press.

Sumner, C.S. (ed.) (1982) *Crime, Justice and the Mass Media,* Cambridge: Institute of Criminology.
Surette, R. (1984) *Justice and the Media,* New York: Alfred Thomas.
Taylor, I. (1988) 'Left realism, the free market economy and the problem of social order'. Paper presented to the American Society of Criminology meetings, Chicago.
Taylor, T.J. (1980) *Linguistic Theory and Structural Stylistics,* Oxford: Pergamon.
Tuan, Yi-Fu (1979) *Landscapes of Fear,* Oxford: Basil Blackwell.
Tyler, T.R. (1980) 'The impact of directly and indirectly experienced events - the origin of crime-related judgements', *Journal of Personality and Social Psychology* 39: 13-28.
Tyler, T.R. (1984) 'Assessing the risk of criminal victimization: the integration of experience and socially transmitted information', *Journal of Social Issues* 40: 27-38.
Wakshlag, J., Bart, L., Dudley, J., McCutcheon, J. and Rolla, C. (1983) 'Viewer apprehension about victimization and crime drama programs', *Communication Research* 10: 195-217.
Weaver, J. and Wakshlag, J. (1984) 'Perceptions of personal vulnerability to crime, criminal victimization experience and television viewing'. Paper presented to Broadcast Education Association, Las Vegas, April.
Weigel, R. and Jessor, R. (1973) 'Television and adolescent conventionality', *Public Opinion Quarterly* 37: 76-90.
Wilson, J. Q. and Kelling, G. (1982) 'Broken windows', *Atlantic Monthly* March: 29-38.
Young, J. (1971a) 'The role of the police as amplifiers of deviancy, negotiators of reality and translators of fantasy' in S. Cohen (ed.) *Images of Deviance,* Harmondsworth: Penguin.
Young, J. (1971b) *The Drug-Takers,* London: MacGibbon & Kee.
Young, J. (1987) 'The tasks facing a realist criminology', Contemporary Crises 11 337-56.
Young, J. (1988) 'Radical criminology in Britain: the emergence of a competing paradigm', *British Journal of Criminology* 28: 159-83.
Zillman, D. (1980) 'Anatomy of suspense' in P. Tannenbaum (ed.) *Entertainment Functions of Television,* Hillsdale, NJ: Erlbaum.
Zillman, D. and Wakshlag, J. (1987) 'Fear of victimization and the appeal of crime drama' in D. Zillman and J. Bryant (eds) *Selective Exposure to Communication,* Hillsdale, NJ: Erlbaum.

Part IV
Political Spectacle and Fake

[15]

ELECTRONIC MEDIA AND STATE CONTROL:
The Case of Azscam

David L. Altheide*
Arizona State University

The significance of mass media formats for social control and public order is illustrated with materials from a "sting" operation conducted by the Phoenix Police Department and county control agents against elected state officials in Arizona in 1991. Videotaped materials of lawmakers accepting "bribes" to support a bill legalizing gambling were distributed to the various news media for public presentation before a single trial. The "programming" culminated in 7 (8 percent) members of the legislature resigning, and then being replaced by nonelected officials, without benefit of any court proceedings, with only one legislator opting for a trial. The implications for social control are discussed.

Something happening here, what it is ain't exactly clear.
Buffalo Springfield

Prologue

Originally cast as an antiwar song in the 1960s to celebrate a growing awareness of expanded social control, Buffalo Springfield's "For What It's Worth" is now incorporated into a news-music video urging viewers to watch for criminals! The following comments address how news media formats and communication logic are embraced by social control agents in a dance of domination.

INTRODUCTION

Social control, power and communication have been joined throughout history (cf. Innis 1951; McLuhan 1962). If the essence of power is the ability of one person to define the situation for others, then the capacity to communicate that definition becomes paramount. (For a different perspective on social control, see Gibbs [1982].)

Our purpose is twofold: First, to clarify how the communication order is implicated in the way Formal Agents of Social Control (FASC) representing state structures may shape, use, and be influenced by communication media and their attendant logics, particularly in regard to journalism. Second, to delineate some new ways in which formal social control

---

Direct all correspondence to: David L. Altheide, School of Justice Studies, Arizona State University, Tempe, AZ 85287.

The Sociological Quarterly, Volume 34, Number 1, pages 53-69.
Copyright © 1993 by JAI Press, Inc.
All rights of reproduction in any form reserved.
ISSN: 0038-0253.

work and news work are folded together. This inquiry is grounded in a case study of a 'sting' operation of the Arizona legislature, "Azscam," in which bribery transactions between a government stooge and a number of Arizona's legislators, including several (8 percent) who were subsequently indicted, were recorded on videotape that was strategically released to the news media prior to any trials. While the majority of those charged resigned their positions and/or accepted plea agreements, the defense efforts of those who opted for a hearing to put the evocative pretrial images in a different context, were stymied by the replaying of a barrage of 'guilty-looking' visuals for more than a year. Jury selection became a major problem. As one prospective juror stated, "I think you would have to be Ken or Barbie not to have some thoughts on it" (*The Arizona Republic*, Apr. 10 1992, B2).

Our topic of investigation concerns the social context, rationale, and the way these video images informed the entire "sting" operation, including how they were obtained, released by officials, used by news media, and their ultimate impact on the case. Materials for analysis include TV reports, articles from two newspapers, legal briefs, and interviews with several journalists who worked on the "story." Following an overview of some connections between power, communication, and information resources that had previously been controlled by police departments, we examine the changing face of journalism and information technology. This is followed by an analytical summary of one of the first video-stings, "Abscam" (1979–1980), in order to illustrate how FASC altered their use of the mass media for "Azscam" (1990–1991). Some of the consequences and implications for formal social control, journalism, and TV newswork are noted.

Communication Technology and Logic

Power and communication are not symmetrical (cf. Hall 1988). A central part of the communication process is the information technology, how it is organized and used, including the guiding logic or rationale for its operation. Innis (1951) suggested some general relationships in early attempts to chart the nature and implications of 'state control' or 'market control.' While state authorities are dominant news sources in any social/political context, there is a difference when the mass media are operating under state or market auspices. For example, when the technology and news organizations are controlled solely by the autocratic state, then messages (content) are likely to fully reflect their interests, that is, "propaganda" regardless of audience preferences. When, on the other hand, marketing logic, or what the audience approves of or "buys," informs message selection and production, then the whims and interests of the elites will be less definitive of content. In the context of journalism and news, messages will reflect those values and issues most likely to attract the largest and/or most lucrative audience. In the second instance, the underlying market principle of these media has been argued by Innis (1951) and others to actually promote more democratic state structures, because the audience members are an important factor in the success or failure of a newspaper or television news station. (We will not engage the argument here that the market and the state are two sides of the coin of domination [cf. Schiller 1989].)

The way in which 'interests' can be served through the use of information technology by journalists and formal agents of social control remains a significant issue. As work by Couch (1984) and others has shown, regimes throughout history and across cultures have grappled with the nature and consequences of controlling the technology (oral, print, or electronic), process and substance of communication. There remains the important question of how the dominant media are contextualized within a social order (Couch 1990, p.112):

> I advance the proposition that the relationship between the media and social structures are multilateral; that the consequences of a medium are different when it is contextualized by economic structures than when contextualized by state structures . . . [when the latter] it will reflect the interests of state officials.

It is this relationship between 'market or economic' logic and 'state or autocratic' logic that informs our inquiry into the changing role of the news media, and especially the electronic media in social order. We are particularly intrigued by the role of video imagery and its multifaceted uses by lay people, news people, and state workers, particularly Formal Agents of Social Control (FASC) explicitly charged with order maintenance, including the interpretation, surveillance, regulation, apprehension, and sanctioning of proscribed behavior (and intentions).

The following case study of a major "political sting" operation in Arizona provides a vantage point for investigating the changing face of communicated power, both as public discourse and social epistemology—"I saw it on TV." With an escalating number of interest group concerns, the domain of state control has expanded considerably, and the orientation and tactics of state power have also increased beyond the traditional domains of 'public life' to more proactive investigation and surveillance. As Marx (1988 p. 2 ff) notes:

> Social control has become more specialized and technical, and, in many ways, more penetrating and intrusive. In some ways, we are moving toward a Napoleonic view of the relationship between the individual and the state, where the individual is assumed to be guilty and must prove his or her innocence. That state's power to seek out violations, even without specific grounds for suspicion, has been enhanced. With this comes a cult and a culture of surveillance that goes beyond government to the private sector and the interaction of individuals.

The exponential growth of the 'surveillance' and undercover options across international, nation state, county and city jurisdictions has been widely documented (cf. Marx 1988). While much of this work has focused on the increased use of 'agents provocateurs,' our interest is in the way certain state tactics and orientations can be blended with prevailing mass communication routines and patterns. We now turn to some important changes in the nature of journalism.

FROM JOURNALISM TO POSTJOURNALISM

We choose to examine the nature, use and contextualization of information technologies as they apply to organized journalism in nonautocratic societies. We regard journalists as the important regulators (if not 'owners') of an information process about public concerns and issues. We are particularly interested in the expanded use of 'video' in everyday life as a context for the transformation of public discourse, including courts of law. The argument we are addressing can be simply stated: ***The Azscam case illustrates a major 'refolding' of social control and mass communication through a shared media logic*** that which has joined the market orientation of news agencies to the autocratic control of state agents. Stated differently, journalists and their sources now use common logics and procedures that are associated with visual formats. In order to complete the context for an event like "Azscam," it is helpful to set forth a conceptual summary of the relationships between journalism and especially the television format, market orientation (or commercialism), sources—especially FASC, and electronic technology, including TV visuals and formats.

The Television Format

The way in which certain elements of each are combined, taken for granted, and assumed by message producers and audience members has been delineated in previous work as *media logic*, or the process and perspective through which media present and transmit information. Part of this logic involves *format*, which entails how material is organized, the style in which it is presented, the focus or emphasis on particular characteristics, and the grammar of media communication. From this standpoint of media logic, format becomes a framework or a perspective that is used to present as well as interpret phenomena (Altheide 1985; Altheide and Snow 1991). An important feature of the TV format is the production and context of visuals.

The power of visuals is another key element in the changing relationship of state structures to communication and social control. News media, and especially TV newsworkers, entered the TV age with a radio and newspaper orientation. It would take nearly 30 years for a widespread and distinctive "television journalism" perspective to emerge (cf. Epstein 1973; Altheide 1976). One emergent approach for TV journalism was to use *visuals to tell time*; that is, since journalists wanted to maintain the audience, it was assumed that brief reports with plenty of entertainment value—visual drama, action, conflict, and emotion—would be the best formula; *movement on the screen was the key*. The realization that visuals matter more than dialogue and 'abstract meanings' became the guiding *format* for TV journalists: If the visuals could be about crime and death and mayhem and combat, so much the better, because this content had long been the staple of even newspaper news; the covenant of social control agencies and news organizations to protect order could be enhanced, and audiences would grow, if the action of crime, drama, emotion, conflict could be shown on the evening news. The working formula became: the more visual the action, the more time and attention the report would receive. Research has demonstrated that TV journalists preferred news sources that could provide enough advance warning and access to such events (Epstein 1973; Altheide 1976, 1985). To paraphrase a compelling line from the movie, "Field of Dreams," we can state that as far as TV news goes, "if they can film it, they will come."

The format of commercial TV news, then, is a kind of template or predictor for what an interesting news report will look like. Furthermore, those sources which provide the best stories compatible with TV news formats will be more likely to be selected for coverage. This realization by the dominant institutional news sources, which include a number of FASC, led to the development of stories that were selected/produced with TV formats in mind: The sources essentially adopted TV 'media logic' in preparing events for the news media to cover (cf. Ericson, Baranek, and Chan 1989). We have referred to this situation elsewhere as *postjournalism, in which journalists essentially are reporting on events that have been arranged for them and their criteria; while the journalist and their procedures* were always implicated in what they covered, we are in a new era when the sources and events of coverage are no longer distinguished from the journalists' own perspective; the sources now essentially construct their activities with media logic that was once the province of news workers; it is now part of public discourse, with the consequence that the object of journalism has disappeared (Altheide and Snow 1991). A pervasive marketing orientation further shaped the present context.

Information Technology and the Market Context

American journalists' work is primarily market oriented, while FASC work representing the autocratic state is not. However, journalists and FASC have more in common today than they used to. As specialists who focus on and are guided by information technology of the mass media, the work of contemporary journalists—and many of the sources they rely on for information—reflect this logic. As we note below, even though both have had an interest and orientation in 'preventing disorder,' (cf. Ericson et al. 1989), FASC were primarily a source for the journalists to use in presenting news reports about problems and issues. Historically, journalists controlled the information technology, access and the audience. FASC controlled the character and access to many events that were of interest to a market oriented journalism and thus became important news sources for journalists; readers (and later, listeners and viewers) were interested in crime news coverage. Thus, the perspective and interests overlapped, but they were not isomorphic. However, over time, journalists *taught* FASC the logic and perspective of information technology and news formats. This awareness enabled FASC to move beyond the 'separating hyphen" of the "journalist-source" relationship to *become the news*. A key mediating influence for their 'coming together' was the gradual realization among FASC that their services and demands were also subject to 'marketing' considerations; they realized that they had to compete for the support of publics whose perceptions of social order, problems and issues were increasingly mediated by entertaining programs, including TV news.

Entertainment and Social Control

The thrust of the journalists' efforts to maintain their respective audiences in our era may be summarized as "an entertainment orientation." From the audience member's perspective, entertainment implies a contrast with the mundane, providing spontaneous enjoyment and with potential for vicarious involvement (Altheide and Snow 1991, P. 16). Extraordinary crime, violence, conflict and destruction seem to qualify. It is partly for this reason that Park (1940), Hughes (1940), Chibnall (1977), Schudson (1978), Ericson et al (1987, 1989), and many others have noted that crime news, scandal, tragedy, and other human interest events and issues are the stuff of news. Numerous students of the history of news agree that crime news, and issues about social order and especially, 'disorder,' have not only been part of the history of journalism, but also that journalism is essentially part of the 'repairing' mechanism for breaches in the social order. As Ericson et al. note (1987, 1988):

> The defining characteristic of journalism is that it visualizes deviance and control as these relate to visions of social order and change. The journalistic search for procedural strays and signs of disorder is a means of charting the consensual boundaries of society and acknowledging order . . . News of deviance is a discourse of failure and, as such, is essential to imagining what might be better—the discourse of progress.

Equally important, is that entertaining news came to be viewed as very similar to 'crime news.' As noted, this history and mutual interest in order/disorder is partly responsible for the very close relationship between news organizations and news sources, especially FASC, for example, the police. The relevance and impact of this relationship on social order has informed mass communication research for several decades (cf. Surette 1992).

To briefly recap, a plethora of work on news organizations and news sources has documented the complex ties between contexts, commercialism, news routines, sources, and perspectives (cf. Epstein 1974; Altheide 1976, 1985; Tuchman 1978; Fishman 1980; Gitlin 1980; Snow 1983; Ericson et al. 1987, 1989). While there are a number of disagreements among news researchers on a host of complex issues, students of the media agree that the relationship between journalists and sources is a strategic locale for clarifying large questions about news bias, ideology, and hegemonic control. Much of this work documented the differences, and sometimes the similarities of the perspectives of journalists and news sources.

Even though journalists were interested in order maintenance, they were distinctive from their sources; they had a perspective, a market orientation, and clear organizational work routines and procedures for covering the news. Stated differently, the journalist had a craft orientation and a discourse consisting of 'news frames' for emphasizing *newsworthiness, relevance, and connectedness* which could be applied to any *item provided by a source*; journalists had an occupational *perspective* which included viewing the world of experience in terms of 'potential newsworthy items.'

Things were different for sources largely because their primary orientation was to the more self-serving view of their work and its points of interest to journalists. We already noted that the police, for example, had their discourse and frames for doing their work, and that their 'problems' were of interest to journalists because they dealt with examples—if not issues!—of social order. However, until relatively recently, formal control agencies were not primarily market oriented; they were state-mandated.

Changing economic conditions, assumptions, and some key political events contributed to an expanded media perspective by state agencies (cf. Altheide and Johnson 1980; Schlesinger 1991). The demands for more efficiency and accountability, were combined with historical events to increase public interest and questioning of the legitimacy of state authorities and services. The stature of the more authoritarian apparatus was called into question by some publics, and its legitimacy challenged regarding the nature and necessity of its services, for example, the Civil Rights movement of the 1960s, and the Vietnam War. Part of the deligitimation effort involved the news media, especially TV journalism and investigative reporting. Many state control authorities perceived that news revelations on topics ranging from the Gulf of Tonkin Resolution to the Pentagon Papers to several Presidential Commission reports on civil rights violations (cf. Marx 1988), including the events of Watergate, and a host of others, contributed to increasing public doubts about the efficacy, necessity, legitimacy, and standard operating procedures of state control agencies.

Such perceptions led numerous authorities to become more market oriented in the "selling" and promotion, if not the actual operations of their organizations. The slide toward a market orientation among FASC was proceeding at about the same time as TV news was becoming more sophisticated in its use of visuals and electronic signaling and editing.

From the 1970s on, it was clear that a media consciousness would inform national, state and local enforcement strategies (cf. Heinz, Jacob and Lineberry 1983). Widespread public relations changes were instituted at the federal, state and local levels. The state agencies, especially the police and the military, became more market oriented and embraced the media logic perspective of the journalists who reported on their activities. For example, police departments became more 'proactive' as they discovered public relations, 'positive' mass media coverage, and above all, a clearer sense that they had enemies—including the press—as well as more social service agencies, including competition for funds from local fire departments and probation offices which sought additional resources that had previously been controlled by police departments. As relationships between agencies and political interests became more *competitive*, the state agencies began to adopt more of a *market orientation* to promote their organization and activity as a necessary public service. This included paying more attention to the news media and expanding their efforts to influence news content in order to send the most advantageous messages to significant audiences.

The national change can be seen with war information. Disappointed with the news coverage of the Vietnam War—and seeking a scapegoat for the most massive bombardment in history to win a victory in Southeast Asia—the military strategy changed (cf. Braestrup 1978). The military's control of the press during the invasions of Grenada and Panama, in 1983 and 1989 respectively, illustrate the national response, which culminated in the 'hi-tech' and video Gulf War with Iraq in 1991. This TV war was heralded as a resounding success, largely because of the high-tech equipment, which included gun-sight visuals of 'smart bombs' decimating 'targets,' as well as 'Patriot' interceptor missiles knocking down 'Scuds.' The accolades of a high-tech success notwithstanding, it would be more than a year, in March, 1992, when a congressional investigation brought to light a report by the Department of Defense which showed that only a fraction of the Patriot missiles actually hit their mark, and that when a world-wide audience thought they were viewing Patriot hits on Cable News Network (CNN), they were being deceived. *They only looked like 'hits.'* The evocative impact of crime and war visuals from familiar television receivers in the personal and private space of viewers' homes is also part of the context for the changing market orientation of FASC and what eventually happened with Azscam. (Indeed, the first news of Azscam shared the front page of *The Arizona Republic* with speculations about the start of the 'ground war' in Desert Storm!)

From Abscam to Azscam

Mass media formats have been explicitly incorporated into the planning, execution and outcomes of formal social control (cf. Surette 1992). We are referring not only to the plethora of undercover, agent provocateur operations that have been delineated by Gary Marx (1988). Rather, our interest is on a new genre of such activities in which agents of control adjust their activities and discourse to fit news media formats in order to insure public interest. *On television, interest is predicted by entertainment values*. As we have stressed, getting public attention means gaining access to the news media, and especially television. This requires the sense of something 'extraordinary' and 'entertaining.' One example is "Gonzo Justice," whereby judges impose extraordinary sentences, for example, to wear a sign proclaiming "I'm a child molester," because they know that this is "newsworthy," and will be presented as an example of "doing good work" (Altheide 1992). Another example is the changing character of government "sting" operations in which an agent provocateur provides the opportunity and usually encouragement for someone to commit a crime before hidden video cameras capturing evocative visuals for broadcasting to millions of citizens. Azscam and its predecessor by a decade, Abscam, illustrate this convergence.

Our present focus is on the way video materials are obtained not only for use as "evidence" in a criminal trial, but more importantly, how an entire operation is organized around the collection of such materials in order to *display them publicly in entertainment formats so that the accused (implicated) will either withdraw or, in the case of criminal charges, plead guilty in order to avoid a trial*. While we cannot digress into a discussion about the legal problems associated with "stings," it is important to simply note that the "entrapment" feature of such operations continues to plague prosecutors. However, these problems, and in particular, entrapment as a defense are usually brought up during a trial. To avoid a trial, then, is to avoid the entrapment defense.

Azscam represents a new genre of mass mediated justice, but it emerged through a decade of experience with stings for crime stoppers and for audience members, as well. It began with Abscam ("Arab scam," but initially "Abdul scam"), the two-year F. B. I. "sting" which netted a dozen elected officials, including six Congressmen, a United States Senator, the mayor of Philadelphia, and several city council members.

The scenario was to entice these elected officials to accept money from a representative of an Arab Sheik who desired, among other things, a new immigration bill. All were captured with the aid of hidden video cameras as they discussed elements of bribery and conspiracy involving immigration legislation, gambling and real estate deals. For example, with hidden videotape cameras catching the action, Congressman Jenrette agreed to introduce such an immigration bill for an initial payment of $50,000, with the understanding that more would follow. The undercover and taping work ended in February 1980.

The videotaped materials in Abscam were collected and used primarily as legal evidence. The intent of this operation was to use the taped material as evidence in a court of law. News agencies first reported this operation and pending indictments on February 2, even though the initial indictments were not issued until May 22, with Congressman Jenrette's on June 14, 1980. *However, no actual evidence, that is, video or audio materials, were presented by the TV networks until October 14, when the Supreme Court gave approval to show videotapes that had been used as evidence in the first Abscam trial*. Within hours of this decision, all three networks led off their evening news programs with excerpts from the tapes. From the court's perspective, the key point was that one trial had already occurred. Referring to the "common law right to inspect and copy judicial records," the court found "a presumption in favor of public inspection and copying of any item entered into evidence at a public session of a trial" (*New York Times* October 18, 1980, A1). Notwithstanding the impact such coverage could have on other defendants who had not yet had their day in court, the fact that at least one trial had occurred was critical in the timing. Our point here is simply that *the video material was first used as evidence, and only later, following some four months and rather complex legal proceedings, were the tapes to be broadcast through TV news formats and other outlets*.

Replicating Abscam's success at visually capturing foul words from members of Congress, various states have used "stings" to trap burglars and other "street" criminals. There have been hundreds of such operations across the country (cf. Marx 1988). Indeed, most legislators across the country supported such methods as essential to "fight crime." But the nature of such operations, especially when they involve public officials, was a concern to a congressional oversight committee, whose review of Abscam pointed out major problems regarding public trust, civil liberties, and especially entrapment, stressing that the "tyranny of unchecked crime and the tyranny of unchecked governmental intrusion" be avoided (*New York Times* December 17, 1982, A29 ff). More recently, South Carolina and California have used "bribery" stings to fight corrupt legislators. Even though it is against the law to attempt to bribe public officials, these operations have been carried out by state police agencies which have expanded their usual reactive agendas to more proactive efforts with elected public officials. All of this is the context for Azscam.

Azscam or Arizona scam, joined the work of journalists and FASC through the TV news format as the criteria and perspective of the former essentially dominated the 'legal' perspective and format of the latter. This was accomplished by combining several features of Abscam, and rolled them into the context of a decade of reports about numerous police "sting" operations, usually of street criminals, drug dealers and the like. These reports served to help Arizona citizens (TV viewers and newspaper readers) become accustomed to such practices.

However, there were some rather important differences from Abscam (Table 1). For one thing, the operation, which ultimately changed 8 percent of the state legislature, and also influenced an ongoing election, was orchestrated by the Phoenix Police Department and the Maricopa County Attorney! Another difference is that while Abscam agents targeted specific individuals who had a history of "suspicious" activities, Azscam agents offered bags of money to numerous legislators in order to find out who could be tempted to support organized gambling legislation. Third, the liberal use of racketeering statutes or "RICO" legislation which permitted property forfeitures and seizures, gave the local authorities in excess of a million dollars to use at the discretion of the County Attorney! These funds bankrolled Azscam. Fourth, and a point to which we will return below, the videotaped materials and transcripts were warmly permitted to be published prior to any legal hearing. This was all part of Azscam.

Azscam was a "sting" operation designed to ferret out any legislators who would be susceptible to a bribe or "influence" money to get them to support legislation for organized

Table 1
A Comparison of ABSCAM and AZSCAM "Stings"

	ABSCAM	AZSCAM
Date Indictment(s)	May 22, 1980	February 5, 1991
Place	Washington, DC	Phoenix, AZ
Agency	F. B. I.	Maricopa County Attorney General. Phoenix Police Dept.
Targets	Specific US Congressmen and Senators referred by "middlemen"	Numerous members of Arizona legislature
Evidence	Video/audio recordings	Video/audio recordings
Charges	Bribes, re: immigrants, gambling, real estate	Bribes, re: gambling legislation
Number charged	12 people	20 people
Legal action	Trials	5 trials (7 people) (pending)
Outcomes	12 convicted 2 overturned (entrapment)	12 guilty pleas
Release of tapes to media	4 months, after 1 trial	1 day

gambling in Arizona. Unlike Abscam, in which the prime targets had been previously suspected, and in a few cases actually charged with inappropriate conduct, those persons involved in Azscam did not have a background of unethical or "near-criminal" activities. Indeed, several of the indicted legislators had been vocal supporters and sponsors of 'social gambling bills' for several years. Nevertheless, all indications are that numerous legislators were directly or indirectly approached, in a grab-bag fashion to see who would "bite."

The plan was to have the bag man, "Anthony Vincent" (a.k.a., Joseph Stedino) go from one legislator to another and offer money to anyone interested in working to support the legalization of organized gambling in Arizona. A 1987 Arizona law forbade gambling, but an amendment in 1988 and 1990 (Arizona Republic 4/13/91) did allow amusement and social gambling. Police Chief Ortega, the County Attorney, and the other FASC opposed even this form of gambling. Other law men would soon come on board the operation.

Seven members of the Arizona legislature, four lobbyists, and several others were indicted on a range of charges pertaining to the legalization of casino gambling in Arizona, on Feb. 5, 1991. The 18 month investigation was funded by drug forfeitures and seizures, and coordinated by the County Attorney's office and the Phoenix Police Department. Others would later be named in conjunction with a civil racketeering suit filed to recover the $1 million cost of operation Azscam. In one case, a Justice of the Peace of a Phoenix suburb was named because he agreed to fix a speeding ticket given to Joseph Stedino, a. k. a. "Vincent," the agent provocateur, a former Las Vegas TV personality, with a long police record. He was very good at his work.

At this writing there have been 20 people indicted. Of the seven who were legislators, (there was also one former legislator) six pleaded guilty to various charges ranging from bribery to accepting illegal campaign contributions. The amounts of money accepted from the "bag man," Vincent, ranged from some $660 to more than $60,000. All but one of the six received prison terms ranging from six months to five years, supplemented by fines ranging from $2,760 to $200,000, and the attendant probation sentences (18 months to seven years), with ample community service. It was devastating for all.

Members of the Arizona legislature became concerned during the "sting" that a "shady character" was attempting to spread influence in an untoward manner, and they notified the proper authorities. It is at least a class 4 felony in Arizona to offer a bribe to an elected official, with a presumptive sentence of 2 to 5 years in prison. Like most "sting" operations, the agents of social control elected to break some laws in order to capture any legislators who would accept money to work for the passage of organized gambling. Nevertheless, indications are that the process was working to prevent the "corruptible" from being "corrupted." During the operation several members of the legislature either mentioned "Vincent's" behavior to their colleagues, and on at least four occasions to law enforcement authorities.

While we remain uncertain exactly when some officials learned about the operation, there are indications that upon consulting with the County Attorney, they were "let in" on the operation, but did not tell the legislators this. This is important because had the police and other enforcement bodies taken their usual course of action when such suspicions were brought to their attention, "Vincent" would have been questioned, chased away, and the threat would have disappeared because the "corrupt legislator" would not, in fact, have been "corrupted." But that was not the plan; the plan was to tempt Arizona lawmakers into accepting bribes or "influence" funds, document it, and then indict them. Published news reports indicate that the first time the State Attorney General, Robert Corbin, learned about the "sting" was a result of a telephone call from legislator Jack Jewitt.

Jack Jewett, was approached by "Vincent," flashing large amounts of bills. Mr. Jewett described him as coming "off in my judgment as a real sleaze" (*Tempe Daily News* February 7, 1991, p. 3). Jewett told a reporter,

> It was obvious he wanted me to see it [money] . . . [this] confirmed my worst suspicion that something was wrong with the whole setup.

The next afternoon he returned to his home in Tucson and telephoned the Attorney General Corbin, who told him he would look into it, and that an investigator would contact him. What occurred next was quite remarkable. The investigator called Jewett later in the afternoon and he said,

> that I was not to talk to anyone about this incident, that they were going to investigate it. I complied with that request.

According to Attorney General Corbin, this was when he, the highest ranking law enforcement officer in Arizona, made some inquiries and learned about the operation. Yet, he stated that he could not inform Jane Hull, Speaker of the House, about the operation.

> By then I knew what was going on, but I couldn't talk about it. I just told her that we were aware of it and to sit tight. We were investigating it.

Thus, one of Arizona's most important elected representatives was misled by the Attorney General, who was receiving direction, apparently, from the County Attorney and the Chief of the Phoenix Police Department!

It is not irrelevant to our concerns that Jewett's account was published on the opposite page where a spokesperson for the American Civil Liberties Union, Mr. Louis Rhodes, protested the activity, opening his discussion with the assertion that "The job of the police should be to discourage crime, not create it." He concluded with, "The bottom line is only those who it appears were already engaged in criminal activity should have been targeted" (*Tempe Daily News* February 7, 1991, p. 2).

Public Disclosure and Media Logic

Arizona, like many states, has a public disclosure law which permits public access to a range of information collected by public officials, including FASC. Journalists routinely make such requests. The videotapes and transcripts of legislators and the government stooge would fall within the scope of this statute. Ultimately, of course, it is up to the FASC to grant the request. And, given the market orientation of most FASC, they were usually eager to cooperate in the release of information. One reason for not honoring a request would be if an investigation 'was continuing.' Journalists understand that this is a bit of a nonsequitur since virtually any investigation can be 'continuing.' As one TV journalist explained, "access delayed is access denied." They understand, in short, that ultimately it is up to the FASC official to release the information or not.

The newspaper and TV journalists interviewed agreed that the County Attorney's office was very helpful in getting very quick access to selected videotapes and transcripts. Several of the reporters interviewed could not recall such cooperation from FASC, especially when compared to a case several years prior involving drug charges against popular members of the Phoenix Suns basketball team, in which very little information was forthcoming. A reporter explained that in the Suns' case:

> What the prosecution did was to subpoena all reports under the cloak of the Grand Jury. They subpoenaed their own records 'as part of an ongoing investigation!' . . . When the agencies want to cover themselves or not be cooperative, they may invoke an 'ongoing investigation.' (Field Notes).

Azscam was treated much differently by Arizona FASC. Even though the prosecution claimed that more indictments would be forthcoming—and more were—the 'ongoing investigation' apparently did not apply to the video and audio materials that were released to the press. A motion to dismiss the charges against one defendant on the basis of pretrial publicity stated,

> Not only did the prosecution team do nothing to deter the dissemination of pretrial publicity, a helping hand was offered the media in obtaining any and all material in the prosecutor's possession, including, but not limited to, video and audio tape recordings which the prosecution knew would be used as evidence at the trial. The reporters were given *carte blanche* access to three long shelves of videotape and 39 notebooks of 400 pages each of transcripts. In the words of one reporter, evidence in the case was literally 'pushed on us.' While the Phoenix police chief was making almost daily comments, the evidence in the case was being made available to the media in wholesale lots, with the video provided by direct 'uplink' from police headquarters. The 'uplink' was necessary so the various television stations could review and edit those portions which they intended to show on that particular night's news. Copies of transcripts and other materials were prepared in advance for media distribution. . . (Motion to Dismiss—Pretrial Publicity July 30, 1991).

The indictments were made public on February 6, 1991, and the tapes and transcripts began to be published the next day. But they were not all turned over at once, so that widespread editorial discretion would be used. They were released serially to the news media, one segment at a time, one day at a time, of the "juiciest" transactions, taken out of context. Several selections were replayed dozens of times on local TV newscasts during the next 15 months. Interviews with some reporters suggest that this was intentionally done in order to promote the mass media presentations on local TV news in particular, and printing the transcripts in newspapers, in general. Typically, brief transcriptions in the newspapers would be accompanied by photos that were lifted from TV broadcasts and reproduced on the front page of the newspapers. For example, *The Arizona Republic* (February 7, 1991, A7) included the following transcript of a conversation between one of the people indicted, Raymond, and "Vincent," the bagman:

> Raymond told Vincent: 'I do deals.' Raymond said: 'I like the deals of the Legislature.' . . . Vincent told Raymond: 'If you can deliver 14 votes, and if you're gonna vote yes on my issue and help, there's nothing in the world I won't do to help you.' . . Raymond told Vincent that he controlled the majority of the votes in the

caucuses . . . Vincent asked Raymond what he could do for him and Raymond said: 'I have to raise about another $10,000. From a dollar to whatever you can help with, that's just fine.' . . . Vincent handed Raymond $10,000 in cash. Vincent said: 'When Tony does business, he does business.' Raymond told Vincent that his favorite line was: 'What's in it for me?"

The publication of the transcripts and video vignettes of shadowy figures exchanging greetings and packages continued for several days. The pre-trial propriety of this activity did receive some attention. On February 10, a law professor at Arizona State University, wrote in a "Perspective" piece that while it is certainly understandable and inevitable that the issue should be covered by the press,

What is not inevitable, and what seems to me to be extremely questionable, is the pretrial release by the prosecutor or police of masses of evidence in the form of hundreds of hours of video and audio tapes and transcripts. The evidence of guilt, I had thought, was supposed to be introduced at trial (*The Arizona Republic*, February 10, 1991, C1).

On February 12, 1991, Judge Ronald Reinstein, refused to impose a gag order on lawyers, police or witnesses, stating that the documents were public records available for media review under state law. He also stated that "sealing the documents was no longer an issue because media has had liberal access to them since last week" (*Tempe Daily News*, February 13, 1991, 1). (Paradoxically, Deputy County Attorney, James Keppel, told reporters on February 11 that "Judge Reinstein has urged us not to talk about the case, so I'm going to abide by his ruling" [*Tempe Daily News* February 12, 1991, 1]). The news sources had cleverly transformed the prosecutorial function into one of shaming, persecution, and overwhelming presumption of guilt.

By April 17 about nine weeks after the indictments all legislators except one (and one former legislator) had pled guilty, arranged plea bargains, and had resigned their posts. This was 8% of the legislature. Moreover, the "democratic process" was tainted by this operation since a number of the people who were indicted had used these funds to aid their own campaigns, and thus received an extra push over their opponents. Following the resignations, alternate representatives were appointed, not elected.

Arizona citizens had experienced another "soap opera," including an impeached governor, both U.S. Senators were implicated in the Savings and Loan debacle of anti-pornographer Charles Keating, and the failure of Arizona voters to approve a Martin Luther King holiday was about to cost them the 1993 Super Bowl, and substantial convention business. But this was different: the coverage and the lack of broader perspective on Azscam, painted a picture of inept and corrupt officials who could only be kept in line by undercover sting operations. Some of the opinion poll results were not comforting. They showed that immediately following the "sting," opinion was very negative about the legislators and elected officials, and quite supportive of police and law enforcement agencies.

There were other effects as well. The Chief of Police, Ruben Ortega, received some criticism for not checking with any of his superiors, such as the Mayor or the City Manager. Following some sparring over whether or not future operations should remain so secretive, the City Manager relented, but Ortega resigned anyway.

Then there is the agent provocateur, Mr. Stedino, who, like so many agents, was recruited because of his expertise in criminal affairs. He was a star, deserving of a four part series in local newspapers. True to our media condition and his background in television, he approached several people to write a book, to be made into a movie, but was temporarily derailed in this effort when other questions were raised about his conduct, and the role he would play as a witness if there would be legal proceedings. As the date for the first trial approached, Mr. Stedino was found guilty of perjury when he falsely testified that he had not had a 'social relationship' with a key FASC from the County Attorney's office. Mr. Stedino's attorney requested that if he should have to testify in court, that TV cameras be banned, since they were concerned that his life and reputation may be damaged via the coverage! This is no small irony considering how central TV was in his entire operation! Page proofs of his book appeared during the trial of one of the defendants, Carolyn Walker. Mr. Stedino noted that he was savaged in the media, and that although news coverage of the politicians in the 'sting' was cruel, he felt no remorse since it was "Tony Vincent that did it, not Joe Stedino" (*The Arizona Republic*, May 15, 1992). (To compound the irony, this same agent who engaged in widespread bribery attempts of elected officials, later stated several months later, when he was mistakenly arrested as a drug dealer by the Scottsdale police, "where was the probable cause to come through the door?" [*The Arizona Republic*, August 27, 1992, 1].)

Conclusion

Sting operations have apparently been accepted by elected officials, official control agencies, and a growing number of citizens. This work has accompanied the expanding effort by FASC to demonstrate their need and control of threats to social order. When this can be demonstrated through electronic communication formats that are evocative and resonant rather than discursive and more object oriented, journalism and FASC share a common language and perspective; what makes for good news also makes for good control, or rather the image of evil being checked through electronic symbolism. As Couch (1990, pp. 123–124) instructs,

> The biases of electronic broadcasting that favor evocative symbols infuse the head of state and citizen relationships with more emotionality than does print . . . Forceful acts and appearances have greater appeal in electronic broadcasting than do reflective assessments . . . It emphasizes character and depresses the significance of programs of action. Image, not policy, becomes the central concern of both candidates and citizens.

The agent provocateur of Abscam was normalized, celebrated, and presented in a TV special! But in that infamous investigation which publicly introduced videotapes as evidence in a court of law, and then as grist for the bump and grind of our popular culture, there remained the courtroom format where an individual accused of a crime could attempt a defense, including challenging the government's right to such intrusive acts. Another step was taken with Azscam.

Azscam marks a turning point in mass mediated justice, social control, and media logic. Despite the County Attorney's insistence in a newspaper article that his office was merely complying with the Arizona Public Records Law, there is every reason to doubt that such unprecedented cooperation with the news media accompanied the availability of video evidence. As the motion for dismissal of charges against one of the defendants stated,

> On a national level, no prosecutorial team has ever attempted wholesale distribution of trial evidence. Not in any of the more publicized serial killings, nor even in the Kennedy or Martin Luther King assassinations. In Arizona, the Don Bolles homicide [a journalist murdered in 1976] and the Phoenix Suns' drug scandal pale by comparison to the volume of raw evidence that spewed from the media day after day, week after week. (Motion to Dismiss—Pretrial Publicity July 30, 1991).

This was a prime case of "persecution without prosecution" as the journalists, the County Attorney, the agent provocateur and the citizens of Arizona were joined through dominant news formats. The legal formats were severely compromised, but few seemed to notice or care. We are not aware of a single piece by a journalist that has reflected on what this action means for the democratic process and social justice.

As one TV producer explained when he was asked if this piece of the story would be followed up, "while the public should be interested in this, they just don't give a shit" (Field notes).

The mass media, and especially TV, were integral features of the entire operation; the outcome was certainly consistent with any plan to entrap people, publicly expose them on videotape, and then get them to plea-bargain, and resign. The presumption seems to have been that the publicity effect would exact a toll, and it did. An effort to stifle pretrial publicity, but especially release of videotapes, was quashed before it began, as the prosecutors quickly dispensed these materials to get them on the air and in the hands of Arizona citizens. The subsequent appeal to stop what was then in full momentum was not supported, with the ruling that the information was already out. The mass media formats that promote dramatic action packed visuals were certainly consistent with the entire operation. It was regarded as "made for TV evidence," even if it may not have been perfect for "court room" evidence.

The implications for expanding social control by FASC abound. Historically, a key issue for control has concerned whether and to what extent the state and FASC would directly control the information technologies and their content. As video technology becomes more available, the visual will become more relevant in social life. Video on TV appears to be 'real,' and 'good enough,' largely because of the way audiences have been socialized to accept the typical TV narrative as self-contained. The key issue, of course, is one of context: just as 'hindsight' at the Gulf War videos of Patriot Missiles "missing-but-appearing-to-hit-targets" clarifies the importance of placing "even what we see" in a context of understanding, so too does the Azscam TV coverage; in the postmodern age when images (cf. Baudrillard 1983) are traded for "reality in context," FASC and others join in editing reality. When lay people are invited to contribute videotaped 'news reports' to TV stations, and when military strategists take the lead from the Desert Storm "infotainment" brigade and wrap 'war as action' into the evening news formats, we can rest assured, albeit not peacefully! that video reality, in the context of TV formats, has been mastered and is challenging other epistemologies of everyday life.

When 'seeing is believing' assumptions are integrated into the FASC arsenal of consensus and control, then we are likely to see even more state expansion into video-control.

The boundaries of this debate become more porous when good FASC is produced as good TV news, and when public discourse about complex issues involving government entrapment, the scope of state control efforts, and culpability are viewed through an electronic entertainment perspective. In such situations, the boundaries between 'freedom' and 'control' are dissipated through images and formats of control; charisma, programming and instant replays shadow reflection, ambiguity, and creativity.

> But the significance (danger) of electronic broadcasting may not stem solely from state control. The threat may also stem from the evocative biases of television (Couch 1990, p. 125).

Epilogue

Social order is a communicated order. As media logic is incorporated as a feature of everyday life of citizens and social institutions, the social worlds we experience will reflexively show this logic. The challenge for the student of social life is to understand how media logic can no longer be seen merely as content, or as an "independent" or "dependent" variable, but is a feature of discourse and meaning in our age. A recreated journalism and reflective observers must work hard to decode the "text without context" apparent in Azscam (Johnson and Altheide 1991). Only in this way can we gain a more adequate conceptual hold on "what's happening here."

NOTE

A draft of this paper was presented at the 50th Anniversary Meeting of the American Society of Criminology, November 20–23, 1991, San Francisco, CA. Note: Following a 6 month trial that ended in November, 1992, Carolyn Walker, the only former legislator who refused to plead guilty, was found innocent of 6 charges, including bribery, but was found guilty of 'conspiracy to commit bribery.' An appeal was expected.

ACKNOWLEDGMENTS

Many of the ideas expressed in this paper have benefitted from conversations and work with Robert P. Snow, Richard V. Ericson and John M. Johnson. Carl Couch's work, along with perceptive and persuasive suggestions, greatly improved an earlier draft. The general conceptual approach was further developed during a study of TV and conflict that was supported by the Graduate College's Distinguished Research Award from Arizona State University.

REFERENCES

Altheide, D.L. 1976. *Creating Reality: How TV News Distorts Events*. Beverly Hills, CA: Sage.
———. 1985. *Media Power*. Beverly Hills, CA: Sage.
———.1992. "Gonzo Justice." *Symbolic Interaction* 15: 69–86.
Altheide, D. and R.P. Snow. 1991. *Media Worlds in the Postjournalism Era*. Hawthorne, NY: Aldine de Gruyter.
Altheide, D. and J.M. Johnson. 1980. *Bureaucratic Propaganda*. Boston: Allyn & Bacon.
Baudrillard, J. 1983. *Simulations*. New York: Semiotext.

Braestrup, P. 1978. *Big Story: How the American Press and Television Reported and Interpreted the Crisis of Tet in 1968 in Vietnam and Washington.* Garden City, NY: Anchor.
Chibnall, S. 1977. *Law-and-Order News.* London: Tavistock.
Couch, C.J. 1984. *Constructing Civilizations.* Greenwich, CT: JAI.
———. 1990. "Mass Communications and State Structures." *The Social Science Journal* 27: 111–128.
Epstein, E.J. 1973. *News from Nowhere.* New York: Hastings.
Ericson, R.V., P.M. Baranek, and J.B.L. Chan. 1987. *Visualizing Deviance: A Study of News Organization.* Toronto: University of Toronto Press.
———. 1989. *Negotiating Control: A Study of News Sources.* Toronto: University of Toronto Press.
Fishman, M. 1980. *Manufacturing the News.* Austin, TX: University of Texas Press.
Gibbs, J. ed. 1982. *Social Control: Views from the Social Sciences.* Beverly Hills, CA: Sage.
Gitlin, T. 1980. *The Whole World is Watching.* Berkeley, CA: University of California Press.
Hall, P.M. 1988. "Asymmetry, Information Control, and Information Technology." Pp. 341–356 in *Communication and Social Structure*, edited by D. R. Maines and C. J. Couch Springfield, Ill: Charles C. Thomas.
Heinz, A., H. Jacob and R.L. Lineberry eds. 1983. *Crime in City Politics.* New York: Longman.
Hughes, H.M. 1940. *News and the Human Interest Story.* Chicago: University of Chicago Press.
Innis, H.A. 1951. *The Bias of Communication.* Toronto: University of Toronto Press.
Johnson, J.M., and D.L. Altheide. 1991. "Text Without Context and the Problem of Authority in Ethnographic Research. Pp. 53–58 *Studies in Symbolic interaction*, Vol. 12 edited by N. K. Denzin. Greenwich, CT: JAI.
McLuhan, M. 1962. *The Gutenberg Galaxy.* New York: New American Library.
Marx, G.T. 1988. *Undercover: Police Surveillance in America.* Berkeley, CA: University of California Press.
Park, R.E. 1940. "News as a Form of Knowledge." *American Journal of Sociology* 45: 669–686.
Schiller, H. 1989. *Culture, Inc.: The Corporate Takeover of Public Expression.* New York: Oxford University Press.
Schlesinger, P. 1978. *Putting 'Reality' Together.* Newbury Park, CA: Sage.
———. 1991. *Media, State and Nation: Political Violence and Collective Identity.* Newbury Park: Sage.
Schudson, M. 1978. *Discovering the News: A Social History of American Newspapers.* New York: Basic Books.
Snow, R.P. 1983. *Creating Media Culture.* Newbury Park, CA: Sage.
Surette, R. 1992. *Media, Crime and Criminal Justice: Images and Realities.* Pacific Grove, CA: Brooks/Cole.
Tuchman, G. 1978. *Making News: A Study in the Construction of Reality.* New York: Free Press.

[6]

The (almost) invisible candidate: a case study in news judgement as political censorship

JOSHUA MEYROWITZ

One of the most famous pictures in post-World War II Czechoslovakia was of Czech leader Klement Gottwald standing on a balcony in freezing weather and declaring the birth of the communist state to the crowds below. Next to him stood his close aide, Vladimir Clementis, who, fearing that his leader would take sick from the cold, lent him his hat. A few years later, however, Clementis, the hat-lender, was charged with treason and hanged. And the state propaganda apparatus quickly airbrushed the traitor out of history and out of all state photographs. The new version of the famous picture showed Klement Gottwald standing alone on the balcony. All that remained of his once-trusted aide was Clementis' hat atop Gottwald's head.[1]

It is difficult to imagine such a crude act of censorship taking place in a Western democracy, but airbrushing of a more sophisticated fashion is routinely practised. Consider, for example, the case of Larry Agran.

In September 1991, Agran was one of only two declared US presidential candidates at the Sioux City Democratic Party Unity Dinner. This was to be the first Democratic party event of the presidential campaign season and Agran, the other declared candidate (former Senator Paul Tsongas), and several potential candidates spoke there to an audience of 500 Democrats. A fleeting image appeared on Cable News Network of Agran being greeted by Paul Tsongas, Senator Tom Harkin, and Governor Bill Clinton. But when the same encounter appeared in an AP photo published by the lasting 'newspaper of record', *The New York Times*,[2] Agran was nowhere to be seen. Agran's metaphorical 'hat' in the photo is that the two figures on the left – Paul Tsongas and Tom Harkin – are clearly speaking to some unseen person beyond the right margin of the photograph.

94 Controlling broadcasting

Over the next weeks and months, as other well-known politicians declared their candidacies, the national press spent a considerable amount of time on them as well as speculating at length over whether two prominent non-candidates – the Rev. Jesse Jackson and New York Governor Mario Cuomo – would run. But the national media gave little or no attention to the Agran campaign. In the rare instances when his name did appear, he was described as a 'dark horse', a 'fringe candidate', or 'an obscure contender'. Agran was barred from most of the televised debates on the basis of criteria that shifted as he tried to meet them. When he *was* allowed to participate in forums with the so-called 'major' candidates, he was often left out of news reports of the events or was asked by press photographers to move aside. If he was scheduled to speak last, the press usually left before his talk, and was not there to hear or report on what he said or on the audience reaction. Agran would hold press conferences, and few if any journalists would attend, and still fewer news reports appeared. With paradoxical logic, Agran was told by news media executives that he had not earned the right to media exposure, because, among other things, he had not received enough media exposure.

My purpose in this chapter is to analyse the coverage and non-coverage of the Agran campaign for what it tells us about US presidential campaign coverage in general. After summarising Agran's campaign experiences and the results of some of my interviews with journalists, I will argue that there are at least three competing logics at work in the US for how presidential campaigns should be covered: national journalistic logic, local journalistic logic, and public logic. I will also give a brief sketch of some of the factors that I believe shape the journalistic logics. Finally, I will suggest that by marginalising Agran, the US press transformed his campaign into a form of social deviance and silenced him much more effectively than could have been accomplished by the crude acts of censorship used by totalitarian states.

THE AGRAN CAMPAIGN

Whether one approves or disapproves of the way that the US press handled Agran's campaign, it is not particularly surprising that he was treated the way he was. The press generally ignores more presidential campaigns than it agrees to cover. And Agran clearly did not have the background, experience, position, name recognition, wealth, and power the US press generally looks for in a 'major' candidate. Indeed, in a way, it is surprising that he received as much coverage as he did – a constant smattering, but never enough to enter public consciousness amid the flood of redundant coverage of the other candidates.

Nevertheless Larry Agran's presidential campaign provides an interesting case study to make some of the implicit patterns of coverage visible. Unlike virtually all the other so-called 'fringe candidates', he was not easy to dismiss out of hand. He was a member of one of the two major parties, he had an impressive twelve-year track record as an elected public official, he had some foreign policy experience (indeed, more than Bill Clinton), he was a Harvard Law School graduate and book author, he had the trappings of a serious campaign with a formal announcement speech and position papers, he had the campaign organisation necessary to do the arduous work of getting on most primary and caucus ballots (his failure in getting on the other ballots was usually related to the criterion of 'significant press coverage'), he had measurable showings in some early polls, he was sometimes included in forums with the 'major' candidates, where he often stood out for the strength of his ideas and presentation, he garnered endorsements from a few small newspapers, he outlasted most of the other candidates, he eventually qualified for federal matching funds, and he even received a few delegate votes at the Democratic convention.

Much of the mainstream national press, however, rejected Agran before a single vote was cast or any voter poll was taken. The national press placed him in the same category with any candidate who merely paid $1,000 to be put on the ballot only in New Hampshire and had little else in the way of background, experience, or a campaign.

To be fair to those making such news judgements, thirty-six candidates entered the Democratic primary in New Hampshire. Further, much of Agran's dark horse status derived from his unconventional credentials as a presidential contender. Although at this time he had devoted twenty years to public service, he had never held state-wide or national office. He served for a dozen years as an elected official in Irvine, California, America's largest master-planned city. Most national journalists I spoke with dismissed him, based on his having held only local office, just as they once would have dismissed anyone who was only a Congressmen, or was only a *former* Senator or Governor. As journalist Roger Mudd put it at the start of a rare TV interview with Agran: 'It does stretch credulity to think that a Jewish ex-mayor of a small, suburban California town can make it'.

Agran's supporters, however, pointed out that as Irvine's first directly-elected mayor, Agran initiated a whole series of progressive programmes that received national acclaim (childcare, elderly housing,

96 Controlling broadcasting

mass transportation, one of the nation's first kerbside recycling programmes, hazardous waste regulations, and many others). They noted that, as Executive Director of the Center for Innovative Diplomacy (a progressive foreign policy think-tank), Agran played a unique role as a 'global mayor', who pursued issues of international trade, arms reduction, and human rights, and earned his city a United Nations award for his pioneering legislation to eliminate ozone-depleting compounds – all from an unlikely base in deeply conservative Orange County, the county that had given Ronald Reagan and George Bush huge margins of victory. Agran's supporters pointed out that, regardless of anything else, since his campaign had done the work to get his name on about forty primary and caucus ballots, the voting public deserved to be told something about him in order to be able to make an informed choice in the voting booth. (No other major party candidate who was on that many primary ballots was being ignored by the press.) And they described him as the most articulate presidential contender with some of the clearest and most systemic plans for solving the country's problems, including the boldest and most specific blueprint for shifting cold war military spending to post-cold war domestic needs. Finally, they argued that the public's reaction to many of his appearances was so positive that his ideas deserved to be heard – and allowed to influence the platforms of the 'major' candidates – even if Agran himself had little chance of winning the nomination.

It is no surprise that Agran's supporters saw more in Agran than did most national journalists. What is surprising, however, is the extent to which they received encouragement from the coverage of the *local* New Hampshire press reporting on the first-in-the-nation primary as well as from at least two nationally-known columnists, Colman McCarthy and Sydney Schanberg. In New Hampshire, there were dozens of local newspaper articles, editorials, columns, and letters to the editor, which described Agran's exclusion and/or supported his right to be heard in national debates. Beyond New Hampshire, McCarthy and Schanberg both wrote columns challenging Agran's designation as a 'minor candidate' and endorsing his right to be heard and seen through debates and national news coverage.

Agran was also the highest-rated Democratic party candidate in some progressive publications, including the *Casco Bay Weekly* (20 February 1992) and *Nuclear Times* (Winter 1991–92), the latter calling him 'bright, earnest, and visionary' and saying he would 'bring the right values to the White House'. His campaign was followed closely on progressive computer networks, such as PeaceNet. Yet most national journalists apparently do not keep their ears to progressive grounds.

Agran's anomalous status as a candidate made his campaign a good lens through which to see aspects of campaign coverage that normally remain invisible. To make an analogy to academic tenure procedures, Agran was not simply like the great teacher who does no research and therefore is denied tenure by a ten-to-zero vote. He was like the great teacher who writes only one or two exceptional articles – articles that some argue are of higher quality than the typical book and/or dozen articles that will usually garner someone a permanent position – and then asks for early tenure. When such a person is denied tenure by an eight-to-two vote, the debates and justifications on both sides reveal quite a bit about the unwritten rules of the institution.

To his dismay, Agran found that for him one of the rules of the campaign was: 'To become visible, you must be disruptive'. When he was barred by the Chairman of the State Democratic Party from a televised Health Care Forum with presidential candidates in Nashua, New Hampshire, for example, he stood up in the audience and demanded to know by what criteria he was being excluded. Responding to a signal from a state party official, security police began to remove Agran from the hall, but the crowd's shouts of 'Freedom of speech!' and 'Let us vote!' embarrassed the men at the dais into inviting him to join them. This confrontation was Agran's first widely reported 'campaign event' – but little mention was made of his innovative proposals for health care reform.

To prevent this sort of public call for inclusion from happening again (the state party chair called it 'intimidation'), the state Democratic party moved its next debate to a high-security TV studio with no audience. Agran stood outside the studio, among a crowd of four hundred people who braved zero-degree temperatures to protest the exclusion of candidates from the debates. (Most of the protesters were supporters of New Alliance Party candidate Lenora Fulani, who ran as a Democrat in New Hampshire). As reported in the *local* press, the protest offered many dramatic moments, with the 'major' candidates forced to pass 'picket lines for democracy' as protestors shouted 'Scab! Scab! Scab!' Yet perhaps because there was no violence and the closed debate was not disrupted, the protest went unreported in *The New York Times*, *Washington Post*, and in all but Agran's home-county edition of the *Los Angeles Times*. (CNN Headline News made brief mention of a protest, without pictures, as a tag line about every fourth time it presented its well-illustrated report on the debate.)

98 Controlling broadcasting

The odd contrast between the local New Hampshire media and the national media on what was going on in the campaign was one of the things that drew my attention to this topic. Even though New Hampshire was flooded with national reporters, the local coverage of Agran had no impact on national coverage. When I asked an editor at a major link to the national media – the Associated Press in Concord, New Hampshire – about the lack of mention of these local articles, letters, and editorials, I was told bluntly: 'We don't report on editorials'. I was also told that the instructions about which candidates should receive 'blanket coverage' on the part of the local AP came from the national AP in Washington.

Agran and his staff believed that at some point local press attention would build into national exposure. But several reporters and editors at national newspapers and magazines whom I spoke with admitted that the longer one has not covered a candidate, the harder it becomes to do so. 'The obvious question in such situations', said Alvin Sanoff, a senior editor at *U.S. News and World Report*, 'is "Where have you been that you just discovered this person?" ' He also noted that 'it's always safer to stay with the pack and be wrong, than to risk going out on a limb and covering someone who then turns out to not be that important'.

When local press coverage and protests had no impact on his national media profile, Agran's campaign staff became convinced that his status as a 'fringe' candidate could be erased if he tied or passed one or more of the 'major' candidates in the polls. They were wrong.

When Agran made his first measurable showing in a University of New Hampshire/WMUR-TV (Channel 9) poll taken from 6 January to 11 January 1992, the AP story on the poll grouped Agran's score into a total score for 'minor candidates' without mentioning his name. (There was also no mention of the irony that a 'fringe candidate' who was receiving almost no national press coverage had tied 'major' candidate Virginia Governor Douglas Wilder, who had received a great deal of national press but little public enthusiasm, and who abandoned his campaign four days into the six-day polling period). When a 22 January poll, conducted by the American Research Group (ARG), showed Agran tied with former California Governor Jerry Brown and Iowa Senator Tom Harkin, the polling group's press release had three suggested headlines: 'Bush Rebounds in Republican Race', 'Democratic Debate Had Little Impact on Preference', and 'Agran Appears in Democratic Race'. But the Associated Press buried Agran's result in a single sentence two-thirds of the way through a story. When a follow-up ARG poll showed Agran doubling his support and moving ahead of Brown, the AP incorrectly referred to it as Agran's 'first measurable showing'. When the next ARG poll showed Agran still ahead of Brown, ABC's *World News Sunday* – perhaps to avoid the complexity of explaining the identity of a candidate they had not been covering – reported on the poll by simply skipping all mention of Agran, and moving directly from Harkin to Brown. Other news organisations solved the 'problem' by reporting only on the top three names.

ARG pollster Dick Bennett told me that had Agran's surprise strength in the polls been played up by news organisations it might well have led to a further rise in the polls. But instead, he said, 'the press completely ignored the story, and he began to sink'.

Agran's unusual appearance with four of the so-called 'major' candidates at the US Conference of Mayors in Washington DC led to the first significant mention of his campaign in *The New York Times*, which in effect declared him the winner of the debate. A 24 January article by Richard L. Berke, 'Mayors Unmoved by Major Candidates', began by saying that, after listening to the candidates, 'dozens of mayors ... seemed to agree on one thing: the single candidate who truly understands urban needs is Larry Agran'. Agran was mentioned in passing in several other newspaper reports on the conference. Yet none of the TV news reports I saw on the forum even mentioned Agran's presence. The AP release on the event also made no mention of Agran's participation. (A viewing of the C-SPAN video coverage of the forum confirms the positive reaction to Agran. It also reveals that at the pre-event 'photo-op' at least one photographer gestured for Agran to move to the end of the row of candidates, presumably so he could be cut from the picture. Agran refused to move, and none of the scores of shots taken by the bank of photographers is known by Agran's staff or the conference organisers to have appeared anywhere.)

Similarly, when Agran participated with the 'major' candidates in the Global Warming Leadership Forum in February, the audience, according to conference organiser Carole Florman 'was very enthusiastic about Larry Agran and less than enthusiastic about Bill Clinton and Bob Kerrey'. But the major national news organisations covering the event – ABC News, CBS News (through a local affiliate), and the AP – omitted all mention of Agran from their reports.

Most of the national journalists I spoke with at the *Los Angeles Times*, *Washington Post*, *Time*, *Newsweek*, *U.S. News and World Report*, *NBC News*, *Nightline*, *The Boston Globe*, and other places expressed little surprise over the press treatment that Agran received, and they offered similar explanations for it. Tom Rosenstiel, for example, who is based in Washington and writes on media and politics for the *Los Angeles Times*, suggests there are several reasons. For one thing, said Rosenstiel, political reporters tend to cover those candidates that their sources – the party professionals – tell them are the major candidates. Reporters ask them: 'What are you hearing? Who is lining up endorsements? Who is doing fundraisers for whom?' 'This year, especially', said Rosenstiel, 'the last thing the Democratic leaders want is to have attention paid to someone like Larry Agran, which would reinforce the impression that they are putting forward a "field of unknowns" '.

Journalists also look to each other to see who is being taken as a 'serious' candidate. Bill Wheatley of *NBC News*, which excluded Agran from its televised debate, told me that press coverage was 'certainly one of the factors'. He continued: 'A number of independent news organisations had made that judgement to exclude Agran. It's not a conspiracy. One needs to pay attention to one's colleagues' decisions'. Yet while Wheatley saw press decisions as 'independent', he admitted that 'journalistic consensus in part reflects consensus of party professionals who have some experience knowing who is electable'.

Similarly, Alvin Sanoff, Senior Editor at *U.S. News and World Report*, told me: 'Journalists all talk to the same people, the same readers of tea leaves. We have similar kinds of input from similar sources. It takes a leap of faith to say, "we're missing the story". . . . We all read and talk to each other. We speak to similar experts and gurus and poll takers. We're influenced by the same influences'.

Once Agran was excluded from 'the consensus', there seemed to be nothing that he could do to register with the national media. Press language even excluded evidence of 'minor' candidates' existence. CNN would report something such as: 'Four out of the five Democratic presidential candidates were in Manchester, New Hampshire today', as if there were no other candidates. Or a report would say: 'Bill Clinton spoke in Nashua, New Hampshire today. The other candidates were in other states' – while Agran was very much *in* New Hampshire and actively campaigning. National media would offer routine coverage of whatever the 'major' candidates were doing, such as Senator Bob Kerrey speaking uncomfortably to uncomfortable patrons at a local restaurant. But few journalists would attend Larry Agran's press conferences. To the best of my knowledge, Agran's name did not appear even once during the campaign in the pages of the major news magazines, *Time*, *Newsweek*, and *U.S. News and World Report*.

By the end of March 1992, Tom Harkin, Bob Kerrey, and Paul Tsongas had all joined Douglas Wilder in suspending their campaigns, but the narrowed Democratic field did not generate any increased attention to Agran. Indeed, the media's near silence with regard to Larry Agran set the stage for the criminalisation of his attempts to be included in campaign forums. Even when Agran garnered more voter signatures to be placed on the New York ballot than Jerry Brown, only Jerry Brown was allowed to participate in New York City debates with Bill Clinton. At the start of one debate on urban problems (Agran's specialty) at Lehman College in the Bronx, one of the five boroughs of New York City, Agran stood up and said 'I respectfully ask to be included in this forum'. For this crime, he was quickly tackled to the floor by plain-clothes police, dragged down a flight of stairs head-first, handcuffed, thrown into a police paddy-wagon until the debate was over, and then kept in custody at a Bronx jail for four hours on charges of disorderly conduct, trespassing, and resisting arrest. (Agran notes that his only crime was to speak, that he had a ticket to the event, and that he offered no resistance to the men who tackled him, who neither identified themselves nor told him he was under arrest.) Agran's New York campaign manager, who was merely sitting next to Agran was also arrested. The arrest received some coverage in New York, including a brief mention in *The New York Times*. Agran's home state paper, the *Los Angeles Times*, condemned the arrest in an editorial. But beyond that, there was largely silence. The *New York Post* (1 April 1992) covered it in a fashion, reporting: 'Two men were arrested inside the Lehman College auditorium when they started heckling the candidates, according to police'.

One criterion for coverage that journalists cited when I spoke to them early in the campaign was federal matching funds. (A candidate qualifies by collecting $5000 in twenty states, with maximum individual contributions of $250.) Agran, they told me, was unlikely to qualify. But when Agran, without any significant press coverage, did eventually qualify for federal matching funds in mid-May, there was virtually no press mention of this, and no change in the attention level he received.

As you might have guessed, Agran did not win his party's nomination. But he did receive a few delegate votes at the convention. They were listed on the TV screens as votes for 'Other'.

PRESS LOGIC VERSUS PUBLIC LOGIC

The media's handling of the Agran campaign reveals a gap between the public's and the press' view of campaigns. Although almost all the citizens I spoke with on this topic accepted that some candidates do

102 Controlling broadcasting

and should receive more coverage than others, many of them were also shocked to learn that a candidate articulating serious positions would be censored from reports of events that he participated in, especially when he was received very well by those at the event. In contrast, almost all the national journalists I spoke with were shocked that anyone would be shocked by this (and a few of them even started yelling at me for being so naive and stupid as to ask about such a thing).

In following the coverage and non-coverage of Agran's campaign and in interviewing journalists and in speaking to voters, I believe I discerned three distinct and competing logics for campaign coverage. Although the boundaries for these are not as neat as the following labels imply, I call them:

1   national journalistic logic;
2   local journalistic logic; and
3   public logic.

On some issues, two of these operated in tandem in contrast to the third. For example, both national and local journalists were very concerned with their limited resources and were eager to narrow the coverage down to a limited number of candidates as soon as possible, even as polls showed the public disenchanted with all the 'major' candidates and in search of alternatives.

In other cases, however, local and national journalistic logics were in competition with each other and with public logic. For example, when Agran participated in the Global Warming Leadership Forum in Tallahassee, Florida, the audience was much more enthusiastic about him than about a few of the 'major' candidates. The 'public logic' I encountered in speaking about this event with average citizens was that this fact should have been reported. The public had a 'let the best person win' philosophy and was hungry for 'good ideas' regardless of the source. Yet all the national news organisations covering the event omitted all mention of Agran's presence (and several journalists who did not cover it told me they would have omitted mentioning him had they covered it, regardless of his performance relative to the others). The national journalists saw all such events as symbolic of the national campaign, and regardless of what happened in that particular forum in that particular place, Agran was not viewed by them as a contender in the national arena. Their concern was not with ideas or with the public's reaction to ideas or with the winning of a local debate, but with 'who can win the presidency'.

Local journalistic logic seemed to fall between the other two: reporters described the event partly as a symbolic 'national' event, but also as one that happened 'in our town' in real space and time. (The logic seemed to be: 'Had you gone downtown to place X, this is what you would have seen'.) Local newspaper accounts therefore generally mentioned when Agran was at an event and summarised his views, but they usually focused primarily on the 'major' candidates. Much of the local excitement, after all, was over the local presence of nationally-recognised figures. Unlike the national media, however, the local media also had many stories that were just on Agran, based on the logic, 'He was *here*'.

The greatest contrasts were between national journalistic logic and public logic. Even when the two logics defined a problem in similar ways, the solutions were quite different. When, for example, *The New York Times* (2 February 1992) wrote that George Bush has no 'blueprints for the future' of the US, and that he has little competition among the major presidential contenders or in Congress, this reflected fairly accurately the scepticism of the public. But public logic dictated that one solution should be that the mainstream media look beyond the typical political spotlight for new ideas. National journalistic logic suggested otherwise. The national journalists I spoke with seemed to see this sad state of affairs as a reason to protect the 'insiders' even more. One journalist told me: 'One of the problems that people in DC see in the presidential primary season is that anyone can run. There's a body of thought among insiders, including the media, that this is not necessarily a good thing'. He pointed to former President Jimmy Carter as an example of someone who was too much of an outsider to know how to govern the country effectively. He noted that there is a 'divisiveness' that comes from candidates attacking and running against 'the institutions that run the country'. So while the public was clearly demanding change, national journalists seem closely aligned, perhaps more fiercely than ever, with the *status quo*. Within national journalistic logic, the public's anti-mainstream mood was even more of a reason not to give 'undue' coverage to 'fringe' candidates. (While the journalists I interviewed seemed very sensitive to the possibility that giving Agran coverage might unduly boost his campaign, they were hesitant to admit that not covering him might unduly hurt his campaign.)

When Governor Wilder dropped out early in the race, many ordinary citizens I spoke with felt that there was now 'an empty chair' for another candidate. But national journalists had the opposite reaction: 'We can't wait to winnow the race down even further', said Tom Rosenstiel of the

Los Angeles Times. He explained that it is difficult and expensive and confusing for the media to have to contend with a lot of candidates. 'Journalists don't sit around in newsrooms asking "Whom else should we cover?" The big question is "Whom can we *stop* covering?" ' Ultimately, Rosenstiel notes, 'if we think someone is not likely to win, then we do not think of them as someone to devote much time to'. Another journalist for a major newspaper echoed the desire to narrow the field as quickly as possible and noted that for his publication 'every extra candidate means another reporter and another $150 a day hotel bill'.

Similarly, rather than seeing Larry Agran's passing of Jerry Brown in some polls as a possible indication of the legitimacy of the Agran campaign, journalists I spoke with saw it as further proof of Brown's fringe status. 'It's just one marginal candidate passing another marginal candidate', said one reporter. (This was before Brown's surprise strength in a number of primary votes.)

Most of the voters I spoke with were hungry for a candidate with new ideas, and they saw a presidential campaign as fostering a national dialogue on key issues. But the national journalists I spoke with mostly saw the campaign as a horse race. According to Tom Rosenthiel: 'An election is not a matter of who is the smartest, the most articulate, or who has the best ideas. It's much more complicated than that. What it really comes down to is who can win the most votes'.

Similarly, Jonathan Alter, a senior editor at *Newsweek* described the 'fairly simple rules of the press pack: if we don't think that you have at least some chance of being elected, you just don't get any coverage. Perhaps it's not the way it should be, but that's the way it is.'

Regardless of which logic, if any, is correct, there is clearly a gap that needs to be addressed. The public does not seem to know or understand the national journalistic logic, and the national journalists do not seem to know, or perhaps simply do not care, that their own logic is at odds with the public's.

THE ORIGINS OF NATIONAL JOURNALISTIC LOGIC

In examining why the 1992 coverage/non-coverage followed the pattern that it did, I have been drawing partly on what journalists told me. But because many of their claims did not bear up under scrutiny (there was not a single criterion told to me that journalists would apply evenly to every candidate) I have also been relying on my own observations and interpretations, which have been informed by the excellent and rapidly growing literature on news practices.

Since the logic I encountered among national journalists was more at odds with public logic than was local journalistic logic, I have been focusing thus far primarily on the factors that interact to shape national journalistic logic. To keep this brief, I will merely outline some of the key variables I believe worked together to shape the logic used by the national media:

1 *Limited resources for gathering news within each organisation* (made worse in 1992 by a bad economy) and limited news space/time (made worse during this campaign by the decline in advertising revenues) led to a logical attempt to narrow the field of candidates.
2 National journalists' *reliance on 'official sources'* for definitions of what and who are 'news', for a general 'informed perspective', for 'objective reporting', and for feedback on their reporting, led the national media to define 'major' candidates in relation to what party officials believed – and wanted the press to report – rather than in relation to the potential response to candidates on the part of the public.
3 The significant *influence of centralised news organisations*, such as the Associated Press and the three major TV networks, and the *influence of the élite political press* (the *Washington Post, The New York Times,* and *Los Angeles Times*) allowed a relatively small number of decision-makers to shape the general patterns of coverage for over 200 million citizens.
4 National journalists' *herd instincts* led journalists to move into synchrony with each other in terms of who they were and were not covering, as well as the general style of coverage. Since this synchrony was not the result of an explicit conspiracy, it was viewed as the result of the independent judgement of many different journalists.
5 Journalists' *desire to hide the arbitrariness of news judgements* and the impact of such judgements on the outcome of campaigns led them to stick with their initial decisions not to give much coverage to Agran, regardless of what happened later. (To my mind, this also explains why journalists felt they had to cover no-party candidate Ross Perot as soon as he even hinted that he might enter the race. Since billionaire Perot had the money to buy direct access to the public through the media, *not* covering him would make the public aware of the media as 'censors'. In contrast, true third-party candidates, such as Lenora Fulani of the New Alliance Party and Libertarian André Marrou, were virtually ignored by the news media and were excluded from the nationally-televised debates.)
6 Journalists' *patronising attitudes about the public's intelligence and attention span* made them concerned about keeping the 'campaign story' and possible outcomes as simple as possible.
7 Journalists' *desire for 'prestige assignments'* led them to focus on 'the stars'.

106 Controlling broadcasting

(From the very beginning, the Clinton campaign was seen as the premiere assignment, which led to both more positive and more negative coverage of Clinton as the campaign proceeded.)

8 The *primacy of television in the campaign* lent weight to criteria that made sense to commercial TV network executives, such as keeping the debates short in order not to lose too much commercial time, and limiting the debates to celebrity candidates and celebrity journalists in order to maximise ratings (and flow through to subsequent commercial programmes).

9 *Non-campaign-season news conventions* limited the range of voices that were viewed as legitimate during the campaign. (The highly selective range of typical news narratives fostered the perception that only candidates who discussed domestic and foreign policy within those narrative frames were 'reasonable' and 'serious' and 'moderate' enough to be elected. One typical narrative within the US press with regard to foreign aid, for example, has involved the debate over 'how much the US should spend to promote democracy in other countries'. There has been little questioning of whether that is indeed what the money has been intended to do. Thus, Agran's plan to end all foreign *military* aid because it has typically gone to support dictators, and his suggestion to offer foreign '*people* aid', did not fit easily into a familiar mainstream press narrative and made him seem radical, non-serious, and 'fringy'.)

All these variables tended to foster a relatively closed system that was only slightly sensitive to high degrees of public dissatisfaction with so-called 'major' candidates.

CONCLUSION

The 1992 US presidential election stood out as one where opinion polls suggested an unprecedented level of voter dissatisfaction with politics-as-usual. Polls showed disenchantment with both parties and with all the so-called 'major' candidates. Voters expressed the wish that other candidates had entered the race. The press dutifully reported on these polls. But a truly responsive democratic press would go further. It would widen the spotlight beyond the centre-stage that is the subject of public discontent. The 1992 election was also the first to follow the revolutions in Eastern Europe that swept traditional leadership aside and brought to power those who had once inhabited the political margins, even jail cells. The US press generally applauded these changes and saw them as movements toward 'our way of life'. Yet there is little indication that the US press is willing to expand US democracy by widening its coverage, even now that the claimed threat that drove much US foreign policy and pervaded the image of the world presented by much US journalism has vanished.

I do not mean to suggest that there is a conscious conspiracy or that there are no exceptions to the general trends I describe. No conspiracy is necessary to reach general consistency of thought and action if journalists come to the situation with similar training, follow similar routines, interact with the same sources and with each other, and monitor each other's judgements. Through typical national press routines, incestuous and intersubjective judgements among a cluster of élite decision-makers (party officials, news executives, and debate organisers) take on the aura of objective reality.

In conclusion, I suggest that news judgements serve as a form of political censorship, but they comprise a system based on an internal logic that – unlike the clumsy deeds of Czech censors who manipulated a famous photo – makes journalistic practices seem reasonable and safe for democracy. Yet this case study points to the possibility that current national journalistic practice in the US is nevertheless at odds with public logic and with public good.

A presidential candidate who was shot or tortured by another country's secret police, would become a *cause célèbre*. But Agran, though physically unharmed, was much more effectively silenced. He was dubbed 'not newsworthy'. As a result, his sober quest for office was framed as an act of deviance, and his attempts to enter the arena of legitimacy were criminalised. With the non-reporting of a judge's ruling on the eve of the Democratic Convention in July to delay his trial, first until September and then twice more to later dates, Agran – though still under a threat of imprisonment for requesting inclusion in a debate – was pushed further and further into the black hole of non-news. There he and his plans for the country join many other throwaway candidates and many other throwaway ideas.

NOTES

1. This incident is recounted in Kundera (1980, p. 3). I thank John Shotter for making me aware of it.
2. *The New York Times*, whose motto is 'All the news that's fit to print', is generally considered to be the US's most comprehensive newspaper. Many US libraries keep a complete set of the newspaper on microfilm as an official record of daily events.

REFERENCES

Kundera, M. (1980), *The Book of Laughter and Forgetting* (trans. M.H. Heim), New York, Knopf.

3 The eagle and the sun: on panoptical systems and mass media in modern society[1]
Thomas Mathiesen

Panopticism

In 1975 Michel Foucault published his now widely acclaimed and controversial book *Surveiller et Punir* — on surveillance and punishment in modern society. The book appeared in English in 1977, under the title of *Discipline and Punish* (Foucault 1977/1979).

In this book, Foucault reintroduced the concept of 'panoptical' surveillance. The new disciplinary prisons which developed between 1750 and 1850 were 'panoptical': they were organized so that a few could supervise or survey a large number. Foucault discussed Jeremy Bentham's so-called 'panopticon' — a prison structure proposed by Bentham towards the end of the eighteenth century, which may have influenced the form of the new prisons. Bentham's 'panopticon' was (at least in one version) circular with a ring of cells on each floor, and with open barred doors towards the centre, so that all prisoners could be supervised simultaneously from a tower in the middle.

Prisons built during the nineteenth century bore the mark of the panopticon model, as indeed contemporary prisons also do, although concrete arrangements vary. A main point for Foucault, however, was the new kind of society which was implied by the transformation. 'In appearance', he said, panopticism 'is merely the solution of a technical problem, but, through it, a whole type of society emerges' (1977, p. 216). To Foucault, panopticism represented a fundamental movement or transformation *from the situation where the many see the few to the situation where the few see the many*.

He let the German prison reformer M.H. Julius describe the transformation. Antiquity had been a civilization of spectacle. 'To render accessible to a multitude of men the inspection of a small number of objects': this was the problem to which the architecture of temples, theatres and circuses responded. This was the age of public life, intensive feasts, sensual proximity. The modern age poses the opposite problem: 'To procure for a small number, or even for a single individual, the instantaneous view of a great multitude' (Julius 1831, in Foucault 1979, p. 216). Foucault formulated it this way: 'Our society is one not of spectacle, but of surveillance... We are much less Greeks than we believe. We are neither in the amphitheatre, nor on the stage, but in the panoptic machine, invested by its effects of power, which we bring to ourselves since we are part of its mechanism' (1979, p. 217).

'At the moment of its full blossoming', Foucault continued, the new society 'still assumes with the Emperor the old aspect of the power of spectacle'. The old monarch may be kept in the new state. But the tendency is that 'the pomp of sovereignty, the necessarily spectacular manifestations of power', gradually yield to 'the daily exercise of surveillance, in a panopticism in which the vigilance of intersecting gazes was soon to render useless both the eagle and the sun' (1979, p. 217). There is, in other words, a definite transformation.

On this background Foucault sketched how panopticism has been transported 'from the penal institution to the entire social body' (1979, p. 298). A carceral surveillance society has developed, in which the principle of panopticism gradually and imperceptibly has invaded large segments. And, as an observer of the development of modern control systems in Norway and other Western countries, I find the panoptical principle, where the few see the many, to be a pronounced aspect of various systems and parts of society. While Foucault's analysis raises a number of issues (such as that of the closer relationship among surveillance, effective control and actual discipline: see for example, Bottoms 1983), this particular development of the structure of surveillance is a striking feature of modern society.

Yet, even if it is a striking feature, the question remains: is it true, as Foucault emphasized, that our society has witnessed a development *from* a situation where the many see the few *to* a situation where the few see the many? Is it true, as he so vividly described, that 'the eagle and the sun', the symbols of unique power, have been rendered useless and superfluous?

The eagle and the sun
This crucial question, which is a question of our societal form, remains quite open. Even if society's surveillance policy has developed in the direction suggested above, it does not follow that a departure has taken place from the centralizing symbols of power, or from the corollary arrangements of spectacle where the many see the few vested with such symbols.

In fact, informal impressions suggest that such symbols and such arrangements have not really been discarded. Some countries still have their royal families, and some royal families still rely on the most extensive symbolism. The British royal family is a case in point. And if the country does not have a royal family, it usually has a president. The French president is not unfamiliar with pomp and circumstance. On given occasions the British royal family, as well as the French president, manage to gather large crowds. The streets may still be filled with enthusiasts.

The eagle and the sun 61

Now, it may be said that the British king or queen, and the French president, are not today's bearers of actual power. Those who own the means of production, broadly speaking the capitalist class, and those who develop and issue the general rules governing such ownership, broadly speaking the representatives of the state, come closer to power. And these bearers of power are no doubt more withdrawn than their predecessors. The owners of the means of production have moved to the outskirts of the cities, in order to live anonymously, and they prefer to undertake their transactions outside the public eye. To a considerable extent, the same is the case for the representatives of the state.

Nevertheless, even these bearers of power to some extent stand out, so that the many may see them, or at least see their substitutes. A walk through the streets of postwar Frankfurt reveals the colossal, towering dimensions of the bank palaces. Any demonstration against enlargement of the airport, or against atomic weapons, through the streets of Frankfurt will in this way be constantly reminded of an important seat of power. In Oslo things are smaller-sized, but the Oslo Credit Bank's building at Stortorvet, and Norwegian Hydro's building of glass and concrete in Bygdøy Allé, are enormous by Norwegian standards.

A walk through Oslo also convinces one of the outstanding and noticeable format of the Government Building — the state's material location. And still larger, and more central, are the state's buildings in other countries. To be sure, it is not always easy to determine whether it is in fact the state which is housed in these buildings. In an interesting article on the very topic of 'the state's buildings', the Norwegian architect Dag Myklebust has pointed out that in recent history state buildings have become much more anonymous and much more like other large edifices: 'There is nothing about the Government buildings which tells you that it is precisely that. The Prime Minister's office on the 15th floor might just as well have housed the managers of a saltpetre factory' (Myklebust 1984). But both types of buildings do in fact stand out *in bold relief*, and Myklebust has an interesting comment on the anonymity of modern state buildings that '[m]any will perhaps find it quite natural that the architectural expression of capitalism coincides with that of government power. As a matter of fact, lately the State's ownership in Hydro has increased' (1984, p. 12). Hydro is, in fact, a company engaged in saltpetre production.

This, however, is not the most important point. Still more important is the development, as a parallel to the panoptical process, of a unique and enormously extensive system enabling the many to see and contemplate the few, so that the tendency for the few to see and supervise the many is contextualized by a highly significant counterpart.

62 Transcarceration: Essays in the Sociology of Social Control

I am thinking of the development of the total system of the modern mass media. Corresponding to panopticism, imbued with certain basic parallels in structure, probably vested with certain reciprocal supplementary functions, and — during the past few years — merged with panopticism through a common technology, the system of modern mass media has been going through a most significant and accelerating development. The total time-span of this development — the past 150 years — coincides most remarkably with the period of modern growth of panopticism. Increasingly a few have been enabled to see the many, but also increasingly, the many have been enabled to see a few — to see the VIPs, the reporters, the stars, almost a new class in the public sphere.

A number of media and communications researchers have analysed the development in detail. The Americans Melvin DeFleur and Sandra Ball-Rokeach (1982) are among them. They have analysed the interesting and complex background and trends in the development of the modern newspapers, the film, radio and television. This is not the place to present this development in detail. Two conclusions to be drawn from their work may, however, be pointed out.

In the first place, the various mass media in the nineteenth and the twentieth centuries have followed each other and to some extent taken each other's place. The development of a new medium has, in some measure (and with variations) been followed by stagnation in older media.

But, in the second place, the media have by no means supplanted each other completely. To a considerable extent they accumulate and thus supplement each other. In fact several of them may actually interact and support each other rather than compete. For example, the popularity of the radio in the United States continued to increase after television, because the radio found new forms and new areas to cover. In Norway today, the modern tabloid newspapers increase their circulation as the modern television media develop.

In short, through the extraordinary development of the modern mass media, and as a highly significant parallel to the panoptical development, the many have also increasingly been enabled to see the few. It is surprising that students of panopticism have overlooked this for so long. Together with the development of panopticism, the organization of the spectacle has not been abandoned, the eagle and the sun have not been superfluous. In fact, the opposite is the case.

This may be made more concrete, in connection with the two main tendencies in media development summarized above: the tendency for the more modern media to partially supplant the older ones, and the tendency towards greater total exposure to media presentations.

In the first place, the foreground figures in the modern media have,

The eagle and the sun 63

in a very literal sense, become continually more visible. First came the newspapers without pictures. What the foreground figures had to say could be read, but only that. Then, after a while, the newspapers came with pictures, illustrating what the foreground figures had to say. Then came the film, which brought in a whole new area of real stars, whom people could now see, first without hearing them, but after a while also in sound. As a parallel the radio made it possible to hear still other special reporters, prominent men and women. And finally, in came television, after some time with large screens and wonderful colours, on which the foreground figures became more visible than ever, moving right into peoples' daily lives. At the same time, and in order to compete, the newspapers as well as the motion pictures changed. The newspapers changed in the direction of a continually greater emphasis on the cultivation of individual personalities, and in the direction of short articles, large pictures, and outstanding prominence of the individuals on whom they focused. The motion pictures changed towards large epics of various kinds — films about enormous catastrophes, future visions and star wars — spectacles in which the visible appearance of specific individuals is extremely pronounced.

Second, the greater visibility, in a literal as well as a symbolic sense, of foreground figures has at the same time been extended to a continually greater number of viewers. A continually larger number — and this development has been explosive — has been able to see the continually more visible few. In this way the visibility aspect and the quantity aspect merge into a common tendency contradicting the Foucaultian thesis that the many no longer see the few, the thesis that the spectacle has receded into the background and has had to give way.

So far, I have to some extent taken for granted that those who stand out and are seen are actually *few*. The point needs an elaboration. Of course, the newspapers are full of material from various sources. So are the motion picture, the radio and television. Nevertheless, the presentations are first of all characterized by material from, or about, the *relatively* few. This is probably especially the case in the most visual media such as television. Here specific news reporters, eminent media VIPs and interpreters are continually presenting themselves and are continually being seen. And, most significantly, the sources of the media are the societal elites. This fact has been corroborated in a number of media studies (for two Norwegian examples, see Olsen and Sætren 1980; Vaage 1985). Although the media present a tremendous amount of 'fluff' (or, to retain Foucault's language, 'feathers and rays'), the serious core information is *elite information*, presented within elite paradigms. Thus, although power is highly ramified and diversified in modern society, it is indeed people invested with power who are increasingly seen by the few.

64 *Transcarceration: Essays in the Sociology of Social Control*

Let us now look in more detail at some important *parallels in structure* between the panoptical surveillance systems and the modern mass media. By way of conclusion, I shall also briefly refer to some of the reciprocally supplementary functions of the two systems. Due to limitations of space, the analysis will be general — important variations, nuances and reservations are discussed elsewhere (Mathiesen 1984/85).

Parallels in structure
There are three parallels between the surveillance systems and the mass media which I wish to emphasize. Strictly speaking, the first one is not a parallel in structure, but rather a parallel in the history of the structures, but it is natural to discuss it here.

The 'archaic' form of the structures
In the first place, the panoptical surveillance structure and the media structure are archaic, or 'ancient', as means or potential means of power in society.

Clearly it was Foucault's view that the history of the panoptical control structure as a main model commenced in the late eighteenth and the early nineteenth centuries, though he also mentioned historical lines going further back (especially to the control structures created in plague-stricken towns: see Foucault 1979, pp. 195-200), and he did mention that the panoptical techniques taken 'one by one' have 'a long history behind them' (1979, p. 224). This historical understanding is expressed through the dramatic *break* which Foucault emphasized so strongly from the control policy of the mid-eighteenth century to that of the mid-nineteenth century, and the parallel transformation of discipline.

As far as I can comprehend, this historical understanding must be erroneous. It seems closer to the facts that a panoptical surveillance system, though strongly developed towards the end of the eighteenth century and especially in the nineteenth century, has ancient historical roots; that not only individual surveillance techniques, but *the very model* of the panoptical surveillance system, which in modern times has accelerated as a form, goes back to the beginning of the Christian era or before. In the Gospel of Luke (Luke 2:1) it is stated: 'And it came to pass in those days that there went out a decree from Caesar Augustus that all the world shall be taxed. And this taxing was first made when Cirenius was governor of Syria. And all went to be taxed, everyone into his own city.' In other words, the Roman State undertook such a large task as to tax, and thereby register, what was at that time 'all the world' in the archives of the state. The registration no doubt had several purposes in addition to that of taxation, and there is little reason to doubt that one of those purposes was surveillance of the large masses

The eagle and the sun 65

under Roman rule. Their surveillance was hardly always successful as a control measure — we need only remind ourselves that, during the first great registration, Herod failed in his search for at least one first-born male child. But this does not make the purpose of surveillance less important, and the intended consequences probably functioned to some extent. This was precisely the kind of surveillance which strongly emphasized that a few in centrally located positions were to see (at least important features of) the many. Probably all great state structures in history have had (at least the beginnings of) such systems. In our own historical past, two institutions have probably been particularly important: the *church* and the *military*. Especially the Catholic Church, with the confession, where the isolated individual confides his or her secrets to the unseen representative of the church who in turn observes the individual, has functioned as a setting in which the few have seen the many — undoubtedly with surveillance as part of the goal and function. The military has not only had a strict and disciplinary hierarchy, but also a hierarchy which has provided great possibilities for hidden surveillance from the upper echelons of the system. The church and the military may be seen as settings in which rather extensive construction and testing of panoptical surveillance have taken place — long before the eighteenth and nineteenth centuries.

There is probably less disagreement on the understanding that the structure of the modern media, with emphasis on maximum diffusion from a few leading figures of visual impressions, sound impressions, and other impressions, is also ancient in terms of basic form. Foucault emphasizes the ancient nature of this structure, though he does not relate it to the modern media — his point is that this *is* the old form. The older institutions of spectacle differ in several important respects from the modern ones. In the older context, people were gathered together; in the modern media context, the 'audience' has increasingly become delocalized so that people have become isolated from each other. In the older context, 'sender' and 'receiver' were in each other's proximity; in the modern media context, distance between the two has increased. Such differences, and especially the general fragmentation which is alluded to here, may have consequences for persuasion as well as protest. Yet, the similarity and continuity is also striking, and since the Roman State was mentioned above, we may refer to it again in the present context: the Colosseum, with the emperor present in extensive pomp and circumstance, provides a good example here. The church and the military also provide good examples — the Pope when he speaks from the Vatican at St Peter's, or the magnificent ceremonial entry of the military leader after his victory. We see, then, that the same concrete institutions have contained panoptical surveillance systems as well as mediation of the greatness of rulers. This overlap is important.

66 *Transcarceration: Essays in the Sociology of Social Control*

It is probably correct to say that the accelerating development of both models in the nineteenth and twentieth centuries involved their separation and specialization, in contrast to the archaic forms which more often coincided. It may be argued that towards the beginning of the twenty-first century the two models are perhaps merging once more, due to the common modern technology, so that the historical development may have followed a kind of U-shaped curve, from a state where the models were interwoven to a separation of them followed by renewed interweaving.

The main point here, however, is that the models of both systems go back far beyond the nineteenth century, and that they have historical roots in central social institutions. What has happened in the nineteenth and especially in the twentieth century, is that organizational and technological changes have advanced the use of both models by leaps and bounds. Organizationally, the perfecting of modern bureaucratic administrative systems and the transition to industrial production have probably been particularly important. The classical bureaucratic administrative system has formed the basis of a pyramidal structure emphasizing surveillance. The industrial factory has formed a similar base, not least through the foreman and other intermediary roles as modern supervisors. From a technological point of view, the development of media technology has of course been particularly important. The changes in organization and technology are in turn related to extensive and profound societal changes in our own time.

The fan-shaped form of the structures
Second, the panoptical control structure and the media structure have the fan-shaped form as a common property.

Going back once more to the nineteenth century prison, we see the fan-shaped form of the panoptical control system quite clearly. As is well known, the nineteenth century prison was constructed in a star form, as large wings converging in a centre from whence the wings could be supervised. But the fan-shaped form did not only characterize the nineteenth century prison, it characterized, and characterizes, the panoptical control structure in general — of course with modifications and variations. The panopticism of the church was star-shaped — people came (and are coming) to the centrally located church to listen and to confess, and from the church as a centre, surveillance could take place. In his analysis of the Spanish Inquisition, the Danish historian Gunnar Henningsen has given an insightful picture of the fan-shaped form of one of the most important panoptical church institutions in historical times:

As a spider it sat there on guard, watching so that catholicism was not exposed to harmful influences from abroad or from corrupted souls within the country itself. It had its own intelligence service, its own secret police, its own court, its own gaol (the 'secret prison'), its own penitentiary ('the penitence house'), its own doctor, but no executioner. He was borrowed from the town's secular authorities when he was needed. There were 18 similar tribunals distributed throughout the enormous Spanish Empire, and from each of them there were links to the super-spider in Madrid, *La Suprema*, called the Inquisition Council.

... If the inquisitors managed to agree, they governed the tribunal quite independently of Madrid, but if they could not agree, the tribunal was in constant correspondence with the Inquisition Council. (Henningsen 1981, p. 28, translated from the Danish by the present author)

We should note that this description of the Inquisition only pictures the 'internal' fan-shaped form of the organization, that is, the lines between the peripheral and central parts of the internal professional system. The main feature of the fan-shaped form, however, is that it stretches out to 'the clients', who also are related to the core system in a fan-shaped form. Such was the organization of church confession, the organization of the nineteenth century prison, of the Inquisition — and such is the organization of the most advanced surveillance systems in our own society.

As indicated already, the fan-shaped form is also a basic property of the media structure. The Norwegian historian and journalist Hans Fredrik Dahl has formulated the point as follows:

Many communication media — the telegraph, the telephone — create connections between one point and another. The characteristic of mass communication is the fan: transmission from one transmittor point to many receiver points at the same time. (Dahl 1973, pp. 18–19, translated from the Norwegian by the present author)

In the development of each medium, the leap from the point-to-point form to the fan-shaped form constitutes a set of well-defined historical processes. The use of the art of printing — to distribute periodicals, pamphlets and newspapers to many at the same time — was related to the special political conditions of eighteenth century England. The transition from wireless technology, used in point-to-point communication in shipping and the military, to 'broadcasting' or 'round-radio-telephony', was based on specific historical conditions during the years immediately following World War I. Technologically speaking, then, the modern mass media have their historical background in simpler point-to-point communication.

It should be mentioned that the dimensions of the fan show great variations among various mass media (Dahl 1973). State television and radio in Norway are today just about 'total' in the sense of distribution of sets — they reach almost the whole Norwegian population from one centre. The newspapers are considerably less 'total' if we look at the individual papers; for example, some are local newspapers addressing themselves to people within a specific geographical area. However, if we look at the newspapers in general, their fan is also close to 'total' — a large majority of people in the country read at least one newspaper. The same point can be made as well for the weekly magazines. In other words, the way the fan is characterized depends on the level of analysis.

The same holds, however, for the panoptical surveillance structure. Surveillance performed by the state is particularly important. Such surveillance may also be seen as divided into a number of different subsystems, with different — often consciously delimited — fans. But on a different level of analysis it may be said that very many people, if not all, are subject to one form of fan-shaped panoptical supervision or another — the prison, crime prevention systems in the community, the police, the various security agencies or companies, political surveillance, the taxation authorities, and so on.

People are not constantly under surveillance. Often surveillance is inactivated and only potentially present, but the same may of course be said of mediation through the modern media. A number of media studies suggest important variations in the use of different media throughout the population.

The one-way direction of the structures
Third, the panoptic surveillance structure and the media structure have a one-way direction in common as a basic property.

The one-way direction of panopticism is obvious, and is based on the fan-shaped form. We see it quite clearly in the nineteenth century prison — there the few in the centre one-sidedly supervise the many in the various wings; there is no reciprocal supervision. An exchange may take place, for example when the guard from a security company walks his round, but it is still the guard who is doing the supervising; at least he is supervising many different individuals on his round while those who see him do so individually. Important parts of police supervision, as well as political surveillance, take place with a minimum of exchange even on this individual level. Recent technological developments within the modern control structures probably enhance this tendency.

The one-way direction of the modern mass media is also very noticeable. Today the information, the message, the language symbols, or whatever the 'content of information' is called, goes from a central point to a number of other points. The newspapers, the film, the radio and television are cases in point. Today the tendency is greatly enhanced by the modern development of broadcasting and communication satellites. Powerful corporations control transmissions through them, they own the adjoining cable networks, and so on. A multiplication and diversification of transmission occurs, but the one-way direction is still fundamental on the national, international, and indeed the global level. As it is stated in the slogan of 'Sky Channel', a network which transmits soap operas, entertainment films and similar materials via satellite to a number of European countries, including Norway: 'Sky Channel REACHES OUT TO YOU!'

Yet, this parallel to panopticism must be looked at more closely. Mass communication technology is presently developing extremely fast; new techniques quickly make the technology of a few years ago obsolete. The growth of computer technology, minicomputer networks, cable television and communication satellites has led a number of communication analysts to predict the development of fundamentally new types of mass communication in the more or less near future (cf. DeFleur and Ball-Rokeach 1983, p.104; Parker 1973). One main emphasis has been a far more active participation by the receivers. Parker for example gives this presentation of the situation at an imagined breakfast table in the future:

> A fantasy trip into the future may give a feeling for such a communication medium. Sitting at the breakfast table, you might cause the latest headlines to appear on a small display screen simply by touching a key. These headlines might have been rewritten five minutes before. Pointing at a headline might get the story displayed. If it is a continuing story about, say, the Middle East or an election campaign, you might want to get either a report of the latest incident or background information or interpretation. For someone with a special interest — for example, in some legislation pending in Congress — it could be possible to retrieve the latest story whether or not it received a headline, or even appeared in the latest edition.
>
> With a slightly more expensive computer terminal, your news summary can be printed out for you while you are shaving or getting dressed. A wide variety of background information might be made available by an information utility, on demand by the receiver. Suppose you encounter a name of a person you would like to know more about: ask for a biographical sketch. Suppose you do not completely understand the economic reasoning behind an action by the International Monetary Fund: there might be available a short tutorial program on some aspect of international economics, or you may just seek a brief explanation of some technical term.... (Parker 1973, p. 622)

In this picture the old morning paper, on the doorstep, is quite out of date. If there is anything in such a picture, we should not be surprised that the old-fashioned newspapers of today wish to move into the new media.

To repeat, a main point is here the active participation of the

70 Transcarceration: Essays in the Sociology of Social Control

receivers. The one-way fan-shaped structure, through which standardized information is spread in a large circle, is apparently broken, and substituted by a two-way communication system in which the receiver gains access to specialized information, against the background of his own active input. According to this view, the break with the one-way fan, the active participation of the receivers, has two technical versions.

In the first place there is *the information utility*, of which we have already given a hypothetical example. Today we find this type of information utility, in which the receiver through active input may get the specialized information he or she wants, in the travel bureaus, in the banks, in the libraries, and so on. These are places where people themselves see how the information utility may be used, but it is also used in a number of other places, such as in the police, in the large oil companies, and in a number of other large economic organizations. The latter organizations received the information utilities first. The time-shared computer, which makes instant service to a large number of receivers possible, is the basic technological tool.

The second version is *two-way cable vision*, especially based on fibre-optic cable technology. The idea is that the one-way cable system of today will be modified so that the receivers may send as well as receive messages. When introduced on a large scale, this will presumably break the conventional monologue television form. We already find this beginning in television discussion programmes where the participants are brought into the discussion from several distant points. An attempt at a kind of 'electronic city council' has been established in Tulsa, Oklahoma, where 26 cable stations are connected so that people in each station may enter a dialogue with people operating from the other stations (DeFleur and Ball-Rokeach 1982, p. 107).

On this general basis, the future may be described in highly imaginative terms, as when the Norwegian lawyer and author Jon Bing describes a new type of novel: 'The computers make a new type of novel possible, the "interactive" or "reciprocal" novel. The author enters a dialogue with his computer, and carves out the action according to a proposal from the computer program through an advanced game.... The reader becomes the central person, and through the reader's choices the author discloses what consequences the choices have' (Dagbladet, 8 April 1983, translated by the present author; see also Bing 1984).

It is difficult to predict the future. Let us, however, assume that a certain, relatively high, level of interactive activity will be present in the mass media in the first part of the next century. The central question is whether such interactive activity in fact means that the media systems are met by terms set by the receivers.

It is my thesis that this will not be the case, other than in a very limited way. I have two arguments. First, there seems to be general empirical grounds for saying that information and communication systems in a society are first of all modelled and used in such a way that they maintain or support the power of groups which are already in power (cf. Innis 1950). I do not find good sociological reasons for maintaining that the future will be radically different in this way. Second, and more concretely, with the technological possibilities and sociological probabilities as we can foresee them today, the sender side will — even with a high degree of interactive activity — still define the criteria or frames of reference for the information which is to be stored, which is to be available, and which subsequently may be selected, combined and recombined. We can see it today: when the librarian helps us by providing a list of books which we need, the point of departure is databases built on criteria defined by others. The content is also defined by others. When the travel agency helps us to plan a vacation, the point of departure is defined by the possibilities of choice which the various airlines and companies have to offer. These possibilities are created on the basis of various considerations, especially considerations of profit. There is a reason to believe that the highly sophisticated future extensions of these systems, complex information utilities and multi-way cable television, will be based on similar definitions of criteria and terms.

From time to time the technological level of society is described as being characterized by 'inertia' (Østerberg 1971, p. 63). With the speed, changeability and pace of development of data technology, this description does not seem immediately appropriate: the technology may seem very elastic. In connection with the complex systems we are discussing here it may also seem as if the people who participate are the creators of terms or premises — just as the automobile driver may experience him- or herself as such a creator behind the wheel. And in a limited sense it is of course true that terms are established: the media participant acts so that specific new effects are introduced in the information utility, just as the driver drives in such a way that specific consequences are activated in the environment. But in a somewhat broader perspective this is not a question of creating terms or premises but of choosing among possibilities provided by terms set by others. In a somewhat broader perspective, then, the human actor in these contexts is *a chooser and not a creator*. The Norwegian sociologist Tom Johansen has formulated it as follows, and this formulation is relevant to the complex media future:

> When I have now demonstrated that the actions of daily life increasingly constitute choices among given alternatives, and that *the choice* as action is

becoming predominant, it is implied that action life is dislocated: Homo Creator yields to Homo Elector. It is a question of choice actions: not to manufacture things yourself or produce, but to select, to choose among the most handy utility articles, such is our time. (Johansen 1981, p. 112, translated from the Norwegian by the present author)

The choice among possibilities based on terms set by others, which will be the situation of the media participant, may also be formulated as a question of what Stein Bråten has called *model power* (Bråten 1983). Bråten distinguishes between participants who are strong in terms of models, that is, rich in conceptions and concepts within a given area, and participants who are weak in terms of models, that is, deficient in relevant conceptions. Bråten summarizes his theory of model power as follows:

1. For an actor A to control x, a model of x is presupposed, developed on A's terms (that is, as seen from A's standpoint).

2. For 2 actors, A and B, to enter a dialogue, it is presupposed that they have access to models of the issues to which they are referring, and of each other.

From the latter point follows, for an interaction situation between an A who is strong in models and a B who is weak in models, that:

3. The B who is weak in models will try to acquire the models of the A who is strong in models.

From 1 and 2 it follows that:

4. The more B 'succeeds' in acquiring A's models, which are developed on A's terms, *the more B comes under A's control.*

(Bråten 1983, p. 25, translated from the Norwegian by the present author)

Bråten points out that 'it is easy to find situations in which such mechanisms of model power are activated, regardless of how strong the will is for dialogue and communication: at the company board meeting which is based on a particular agenda, in the classroom situation which is based on issues specified in the curriculum, in the computer context with planning on the terms of experts. Insight may be offered, but not always self-insight as a precondition for autonomy and independence and for capacity to go beyond the current situation on one's own terms' (1983, pp. 25-6). Others have made the same point in a different terminology, as when media researchers have described the 'agenda function' of the media, and when phenomenologists raise the question of who 'defines the situation'. What Bråten's presentation particularly sensitizes us to, is how those 'weak in models' come under the control of those who are strong in models by in fact 'succeeding' in acquiring the models of the strong.

This analysis seems well suited for understanding the probable outcome of the interactive media of the future. In other words, the sender side in the future will still be strong in models, and will be defining the terms and the situation whereby the receiver side (precisely through this interactive participation) will acquire the models and come under the control of the senders. Perhaps the receiver side will, by its interactive participation, come even *more* under sender control than is the case in today's simpler media situation. When those who are weak in models enter actual and extensive interaction with those who are strong, the former are easily 'sucked up'. This is well known in the industrial context, the context of the school, and so on. It is 'co-optation' over again. There is reason to believe that co-optation will also take place in the media, even if the initial intention may be quite different.

In short, the term-setting from below will be *apparent*. As apparent, it will mask the fact that the one-way fan is maintained as far as the basic terms or premises go. It will make the one-way fan more diffuse and less visible, and hence all the more easily overlooked. The many will continue to see the few, and due to the interactive processes they will perhaps do so more extensively than before, but at the same time more often without knowing it.

Conclusions

Some threads may be tied together.

A number of analysts have emphasized the possible control function of the panoptical surveillance system. By 'control' is here simply meant actual behavioural influence in the direction of discipline. It has also been emphasized that as panopticism is decentralized, social control follows suit.

But a panoptical surveillance system, whether that of the Spanish Inquisition, the Catholic Church, the military machine or that of political surveillance of the modern state, presupposes a *context of beliefs* if it is to step up from mere surveillance to actual control. Although sanctions that are imposed may lead to control, these sanctions are usually invoked only in extreme cases. The very point of surveillance is essentially to avoid the expenses, efforts and illegitimacy of constant sanctioning. Yet in modern society surveillance is sufficiently imprecise and inefficient to require the frequent utilization of overt sanctions.

The Spanish Inquisition could rely on deep-seated and complex beliefs in the danger of witches and heretics. The Catholic Church could (and can) rely on deep-seated religious beliefs. And so on. Without the belief systems, the surveillance systems would, to a large

74 *Transcarceration: Essays in the Sociology of Social Control*

extent, have been ineffective. Witches and heretics would no longer have been given up to the authorities; people would no longer come to confession (the very seat of panoptical surveillance). The relationship between panoptical control and beliefs is complex. Suffice it here to say that it is dialectical. The present point is that without the belief system, the panoptical structure would crumble.

I contend that today *the modern mass media provide the most important belief context for the panoptical surveillance system*. The mass media are a functional equivalent to the medieval church in inculcating the necessary belief context of obedience and subservience. Curran has put the matter very succinctly:

> The mass media have now assumed the role of the Church, in a more secular age, of interpreting and making sense of the world to the mass public. Like their priestly predecessors, professional communicators amplify systems of representation that legitimise the social system. The priesthood told their congregations that the power structure was divinely sanctioned; their successors inform their audiences that the power structure is democratically sanctioned through the ballot box. Dissidents were frequently de-legitimised by churchmen as 'infidels' intent upon resisting God's will; dissidents in contemporary Britain are frequently stigmatised as 'extremists' who reject democracy ... The medieval Church taught that the only legitimate way of securing redress for injustice was to appeal to the oppressor's conscience and, failing that, to a higher secular authority; the modern mass media similarly sanction only constitutional and lawful procedures as legitimate methods of protest ... The medieval Church masked the sources of inequality by ascribing social injustice to the sin of the individual; the modern mass media tend, in more complex and sophisticated ways, to misdirect their audiences by the ways in which they define and explain structural inequalities ... By stressing the randomness of God's unseen hand, the medieval Church encouraged passive acceptance of a subordinate status in society; the randomness of fate is a recurrent theme in much modern media entertainment ... The Church none the less offered the chiliastic consolation of eternal salvation to 'the meek [who] shall inherit the earth'; the media similarly give prominence to show-business personalities and football stars who, as 'a powerless élite', afford easily identifiable symbols for vicarious fulfillment... (Curran 1982, pp. 227–228)

Though there are exceptions (Cohen 1971, 1972; Cohen and Young 1973; Hall *et al.* 1978), the study of panoptical surveillance systems, and of media systems, constitute two expanding but largely separate fields of research and inquiry. The Foucaultian thesis of a great historical development from the many who see the few to the few who see the many, from the eagle and the sun to panopticism, is perhaps a reflection of this bifurcation, and has at least promoted it. The bifurcation is unfortunate, first because it is historically incorrect: panopticism and its opposite number have significant reciprocally supplementary functions. Second, and more important, the greatly expanding mass media system provides the necessary belief context, the obedient, disciplined, subservient set of beliefs necessary for the surveillance systems to be functional. Concretely, surveillance in a broad sense, and certainly the policing of society, is given general legitimacy. The view that there are good grounds for combatting 'external and internal enemies of the state' is subtly inculcated. The belief that surveillance is in fact efficient, both as surveillance and as control, is disseminated, and this definition of the situation becomes real in its consequences. The belief that surveillance is *not* efficient, that we need *more* of it, is simultaneously disseminated, and this definition of the situation also becomes real in its consequence. Both definitions of the situation are important for panopticism to thrive.

If this analysis is correct, it also has consequences for political action. The political struggle against the development of modern surveillance systems must be strongly directed towards creating alternative communication networks for disseminating information about surveillance and political control in society. Space forbids detailed analysis of such alternative networks (for details see Mathiesen 1984/85), suffice it to say that communication must be as direct and as much characterized by dialogue as possible, in contrast to the indirect communication through a technology implying distance between 'sender' and 'receiver'. The latter technology stands a great chance of being co-opted by powerful forces and of becoming a one-way support of panopticism. A great deal of imagination must and may be put into the effort of creating such politically viable alternatives.

Lest panopticism is to continue to survive...

References

Bing, J., 'Mulighetenes skjerm. Om videospill og hjem-medatamaskiner', (The Screen of Possibilities. On Video Games and Home Computers), in Hilde Andresen (ed.), *Hva skjer foran skjermen*, Cappelen 1984

Bottoms, A.E., 'Neglected Features of Contemporary Penal Systems' in D. Garland and P. Young (eds), *The Power to Punish*, pp.166-202, Heinemann, London, Humanities Press, New York 1983

Bråten, S., *Dialogens vilkår i datasamfunnet* (The Conditions of Dialogue in Data Society), Universitetsforlaget, Oslo 1983

Cohen, S. (ed.), *Images of Deviance*, Penguin, Harmondsworth UK 1971

Cohen, S., *Folk Devils and Moral Panics: The Creation of the Mods and Rockers*, MacGibbon and Kee, London 1972

Cohen, S., and J. Young (eds), *The Manufacture of News: Deviance, Social Problems and the Mass Media*, London, Constable 1973

Curran, J., 'Communications, Power, and Social Order' in M. Gurevitch et. al. (eds), *Culture, Society and the Media*, Methuen, London 1982

Dahl, H.F., 'Når grensene krysses. Enintroduksjon til massekommunikasjonen', (When the Borders are Crossed. An Introduction to Mass Communication), in H.F. Dahl (ed.), *Massekommunikasjon*, Gyldendal 1973

Defleur, M., and S. Ball-Rokeach, *Theories of Mass Communication*, 4th edition, Longman, New York 1982

Foucault, M., *Discipline and Punish, The Birth of the Prison*, Pantheon, New York 1977

Hall, S.M., C. Critchley, A. Jefferson, S. Clarke, and B. Roberts, *Policing the Crisis: Mugging, the State, Law and Order*, Macmillan, London 1978

Henningsen, G., *Heksenes advokat - historiens største hekseproces* (The Witches' Advocate. History's Greatest Witch Hunt), Delta 1981

Innis, H.A., *Empire and Communication*, Oxford University Press, Oxford 1950

Johansen, T., 'Kulissenes regi' (The Staging of Human Action) in K. Andenæs, T. Johansen, and T. Mathiesen (eds), *Maktens ansikter*, Gylendal 1981

Mathiesen, T., *Seer - samfunnet* (The Viewer Society), The Norwegian Universities Press 1984, Korpen Publishers, Oslo 1985

Myklebust, D., 'Statens bygninger' (The State's Buildings), Samitiden, 1984

Olsen, J.P., and H. Sætren, 'Massemedier, eliter og menigmann' (Mass Media, Elites and Laymen) in J.P. Olsen (ed.), *Meninger om makt*, Universiteforlaget, Oslo 1980

Osterberg, D., *Makt og materiell* (Power and Material), Pax 1971

Parker, E.B., 'Technological Change and the Mass Media' in I. di Sola Pool and W. Schramm (eds), *Handbook of Communication*, Rand McNally, Chicago 1973

Vaage, O., *Krittik av Journalistikk Hovedrapport* (Critique of Journalism: Main Report), Norsk Journalisthogskole, Oslo 1985

Nicola A. Lisus and Richard V. Ericson

Misplacing memory: the effect of television format on Holocaust remembrance*

ABSTRACT

The Simon Wiesenthal Center's Beit Hashoah Museum of Tolerance in Los Angeles provides a case study of how museum designers use television formats to communicate and educate. A dramatic spectacle is created that shapes how visitors are to feel and think. This spectacle turns the museum into an emotions factory and functions as a 'format of control'. It exerts a 'creeping surrealism' upon the visitor that misplaces memory and history by degrees. The implications of being unable to transcend television formats in a post-Gutenberg-galaxy world are discussed.

INTRODUCTION

This paper provides an analysis of how television formats affect the experience of Holocaust remembrance. Research on the Simon Wiesenthal Center's newly built Beit Hashoah Museum of Tolerance in Los Angeles provides a case study of how television formats are employed in cultural contexts to communicate and educate (McLuhan 1964; Postman 1985; Meyrowitz 1985; Altheide and Snow 1991). Research included systematic observation at Beit Hashoah Museum of Tolerance and interviews with those involved in the design and administration of the museum. Other experts in Holocaust remembrance and museum design were also consulted.

In part one, entitled 'The Aesthetics of Emotion', the experience of visiting the Tolerance Center section of the Museum is described. Analysis reveals how museum designers have successfully harnessed the 'power of television' (Meyrowitz 1992) to evoke emotional sensibilities in visitors. Television formats are used to create a dramatic spectacle that shapes how visitors feel. The Museum uses television technology to function as an emotions factory, and thereby becomes a 'format of control' (Altheide 1985; Altheide and Snow 1991).

In part two, entitled 'Creeping Surrealism', the experience of visiting the Beit Hashoah section of the Museum is described. While inciting emotions, the dramatic power of spectacle employed in this section has a more subtle and profound effect upon the visitor's perceptions of reality. It urges upon the visitor a 'creeping surrealism' (Achenbach 1987) that displaces memory and history by degrees.

In part three it is concluded that we live in a post-Gutenberg-galaxy world from which there is no obvious escape. We are a generation weaned on the sensual forms and 'creeping surrealism' of television. Cultural, social and political change must be effected by communicating within television formats (Ericson 1991). The managers of the Museum are at least putting television power to good use. While the idea of offering gas chamber experience in the same way as pirate experience at Disney World repels, most people today would choose not to listen about gas chambers if the message was offered in any other format (Bauman 1993). Nevertheless, television formats offer only contained emotional experiences and limited theoretical explanations. The Museum managers operate with two highly problematic assumptions. First, there is the assumption that if emotions are played with through television experiences there will be a clear and direct translation into understanding of the phenomenon addressed for purposes of genocide prevention. Second, there is the assumption that prejudiced, intolerant people rather than obedient functionaries of modern bureaucratic machines are responsible for genocide in general and the Holocaust in particular. While these assumptions are limited and even dangerous, they may be the only ones communicable within television formats.

THE AESTHETICS OF EMOTION

Palm trees line the roads as we pass by the Beverly Hills Golf and Country Club, Century City, and Avenue of the Stars. Street banners lining the road and bus shelters announce arrival at the Museum. They read in striking colors of red, black and yellow: 'Hate Racism and Anti-semitism Have Finally Been Put in Their Place; Experience the New Museum of Tolerance'.

The intentions of the Museum are noble. As stated in its pamphlet, 'The Simon Wiesenthal Center's Museum of Tolerance is an exciting experiential museum that promotes understanding among all people'. The Museum attracted over 50,000 visitors in the three months following its opening on February 9, 1993. The opening was marked by a star-studded gala dinner at which Simon Wiesenthal and Arnold Schwarzenegger were among the honored guests. It was an event that marked the inevitable collusion of Hollywood and the Holocaust.

A docent arrives to lead us down a spiralling ramp to the entrance of

Misplacing memory 3

the exhibit. She explains that the Museum is 'different from any you've ever been in . . . Everything [there] you touch and listen to, and what it does is make you think'. Our docent anticipates our experience for us. Pointing toward a corridor that leads into the exhibitry she provides the interpretation of what we are to see. To rephrase McLuhan, the medium is the moral.

> This aisle here is going to have *big* photographs on each side and they keep changing . . . we call this 'A Celebration of America'. And why do we call it that? Because you are going to see all ethnicities, all ages, all occupations, all kinds of people. And then, as you walk through you're gonna see your shadow superimposed on that and that tells you that you are all part of this diversity that is America . . . and as such we must learn to live together with respect.

In providing a moral interpretation of the exhibitry for the viewer, the docent parallels the function of the journalist's voice-over in television. She 'points to' the meaning of visuals so as to effect closure on the possible readings of the exhibitry-as-text (Ericson *et al.* 1987).

Equipped with the moral of the Museum, we enter the exhibit. We rush through a hall of flashing pictures, catching glimpses of smiling faces – black, white, oriental, hispanic – as our docent is waiting for us at the end of the corridor. Beside her is a collage of television screens which provide images of our electronic 'host-provocateur'. Our docent introduces him as Mr. Big Mouth.

Mr. Big Mouth resembles a smarmy late night talk show host. His body is a constantly shifting collage of images: a woman's dress, an African's bare arm, a jester figure and so on. His voice imposingly 'ping pongs' across the room challenging our 'tacit biases while revealing his own' (Pitts 1993: 2).

> Hey there! You look like perceptive people! I mean, you've gotta be average or you wouldn't be in a museum in the first place, right? [Pause] Of course we all have our limits. And we should. There's no reason to accept the lousy way certain people drive, f'instance-not to mention how the you-know-whos do business. But I can tell you're not like them!

Mr. Big Mouth then points to neon-highlighted doors, one marked 'Unprejudiced', the other 'Prejudiced'. He purrs, 'You know which to choose. And remember, I like you.' The visitor is faced with a challenging choice. Our docent voices what the host has implied. 'OK, which door are you going to go in? Search into your own self and tell me which door you are going to go into.' But before the visitor is even allowed time to choose, and unaware that the unprejudiced door is locked, the docent pipes in: 'Well, I'm going to tell you, I wouldn't let you go in here anyhow . . .', pointing to the 'Unprejudiced' door. 'You know why? None of us is perfect.' What is initially presented as a choice turns out to be fixed.

Passing through the 'Prejudiced' door we enter the Museum of Tolerance. 'With its neon tubing, flashing colored signs and black matte ceilings, the main gallery of the Tolerance Center looks like a sophisticated video arcade' (Rugoff 1993: 36). The purpose of the Tolerance Center is to expose and challenge the tacit prejudices held within American culture. The Museum attempts to place the tacit prejudices on a larger continuum of hate that ends at Auschwitz. A ticker tape message flashes across the wall: 'Prejudice is prejudging someone before you really know them'.

Interactive media stations line the walls, enclosing us within what has been described as a 'sound and light show' (Miller 1990). It provides a re-enacted account of a dinner party. The camera zooms in on a white doctor talking to a friend, 'Guess who moved in next door?' The camera angle shifts to a second group. 'I mean right next door. Can you imagine?' exclaims a black business man. Again the camera shifts. 'These people, they live like animals', retorts a wealthy white woman. 'But I'm not racist . . .' '. . . prejudiced . . .' (Willwerth 1993: 55). The scene closes with these last words, breaking off into a harsh whisper that echoes repeatedly throughout the room, sending a shiver down one's spine.

Six media 'work stations' labelled 'Understanding the Riots' are the centerpiece of the exhibit. Punching in such categories as 'Video Timeline', 'Police Response' and 'Acts of Heroism' the viewer is provided with an analysis and chronicle of the 1992 L.A. riots. Many of the images on the video screens are familiar as they are network television news coverage of the events: an Asian woman crying, a truck driver being beaten, a minister protecting a beaten man, etc. Such clips are 'the preferred medium of history' (Rugoff 1993: 35).

We enter a small theater, where a ten minute film entitled 'It is called Genocide' is played upon a compilation of three television screens. Images of the horrors of the slaughter of Armenians by the Turks in 1915–17, the destruction of Latin American Indians by their own governments, and the murderous rampage of the Pol Pot regime, are displayed at Nintendo speed. A dead child lying in the water, heads on spear points, and a skull with jaw gaping open, flash simultaneously and combine in dazzling geometric patterns across the screens.

Entering a small walkway, enclosed on all sides with darkly cushioned gray walls called the 'Whisper Gallery', the visitor is assaulted with fiercely whispered insults piped in through speakers. 'What you gonna do about it, Jew!' 'Hey, Bitch . . .' 'Nigger . . .' 'Sexist Pig . . .' '. . . Kyke'. As we pass from one computer 'manipulative' to the next we are reminded of the presence of Mr. Big Mouth. His voice, emanating from hidden speakers in the gallery, asks provokingly, 'What do you need this for?'

Misplacing memory

Toward the end of the Tolerance Center, a cluster of 16 screens greets us. In similar style to twentieth-century genocide, this seven minute video entitled 'Ain't You Gotta Right?' chronicles the history of the black civil rights movement in America. Clips of Dr. Martin Luther King's 'I Have a Dream Speech', 'Glory, Glory Hallelujah', Rosa Parks and the Freedom Riders flash in designs across the screen. The result is a shifting collage of geometric patterns that dazzle the eyes and resoundly communicate the message, 'nobody shall overcome the tube' (Rugoff 1993: 35). Finally, we are met once again by our video host. Contained within a collection of video screens titled the 'Persuaders', he tells us we are on our own, its time to think for ourselves. He fades out and the monitors flash on neon messages 'Who's responsible? You are.'

The format of the Tolerance section is powerful. The visitor is bombarded with media simulation as stimulation. The primary audience that the Simon Wiesenthal Center wishes to engage is the MTV generation, those '. . . Nineties kids with mall-sized appetites and Nintendo spans who were remote-zapping in the cradle' (Hirshey 1993: 49). Defending the Museum's reliance upon television technology, Rabbi Hier, the founder of the Simon Wiesenthal Center and of the Museum, comments upon the degree to which television has saturated the life experiences of America's youth, particularly those who live in Los Angeles. He argues

> Where are your kids now? . . . They're at the computer, and after that they're going to watch television. That's the kids of America. This Museum wants to speak to that generation. We have to use the medium of the age (Tigend 1993: 3).

Increasingly, people look to television to define and explain the world in which they live. However, the format in which television frames the world offers only 'entertaining bits that follow each other in series as items of the same weight and size' (Fjellan 1992: 6). By placing the power of the remote in the viewer's hand, television technology provides the viewer with the right not to be bored. If a particular station does not entertain her, she may change the channel or turn the set off with less effort than a flick of the thumb. The result is a TV-dominated generation that augments its diminished attention span with each flickering effort to escape boredom.

To accommodate the 'free-flicker' generation, television produces competing bite-sized pieces that become shorter and more spectacular. For example the 6:00 p.m. news show, which takes us around the world in thirty minutes, feeds us a farrago of stories that range from a major flood in South East Asia to a terrorist attack in the Middle East to a story of the local baton twirler. All of this is narrated by an attractive broadcaster, who maintains the same pleasant countenance when reporting on the death toll in Asia as when reporting upon the color of the baton twirler's skirt.

In order to compete with the barrage of images and sensations provided by television, images, information and ideas in other cultural contexts have to contain a 'hook, a scary or amusing story' (Fjellan 1992: 10). That is, they have to appeal to the television-influenced 'feelings and impulses and imagery of the people' (Levitt and Shaffir 1993: 78). This mode of communication extends from advertising the best way to get rid of ring-around-the-collar to education about the Holocaust.

'Our society has been dramatized by the inclusion of constant dramatic representation as a daily habit and need' (Williams 1975: 10). As Postman argues, it is 'not that television is entertaining but that it has made entertainment itself the natural format for the representation of all experience' (Postman 1985: 87). Television demands symbols that engage emotions (Ericson *et al.* 1989: 247). Information becomes infotainment.

From the collection of prime time footage of the L.A. riots to the video walls of 'Ain't You Gotta Right?' and 'It is Called Genocide', the Museum of Tolerance engages the visual and sensual requirements of the infotainment format. These multimedia displays mimic the presentation of experiences that the visitor is accustomed to watching on television. As an official of the Simon Wiesenthal Center states, 'There is a design and a planned manipulation on the visitor . . . At all points [we are] cognizant of what you can do and cannot do with a monitor.'

The Museum's collection of prime-time footage of the L.A. riots – the central exhibitry piece of the Tolerance section – relates the story and analysis of the events through the lens and format of prime time television. The visitor is able to pull up those selfsame snippets of information that were played and replayed on television during and shortly after the events took place. The visitor is fed a profusion of images and stories of the highly complex event that was the L.A. riots with the same speed and flash as a news report played on prime time television.

The video walls on twentieth-century genocide and the black civil rights movement employ a similar format. The collage of images that collect and flash on and off in rapid succession perfectly suit the attention span of the 'free-flicker'. The images, accompanied by a music score in stereo sound, dutifully provide the stimulation and satisfaction the individual receives when, with the power of her remote, she travels through the collection of image, sensation and story channels contained within the television set. The images are flashy and powerful. The eye never rests as it moves from one screen to the next. The images that are exposed to us – the child lying dead in the water, the freedom riders, 'Glory! Glory! Hallelujah!' – they all exert a significant emotional impact upon the viewer.

Misplacing memory 7

In order to actualize this emotional impact, the Center recruited experts in the field of media effects. The producers of 'It is Called Genocide' also produce the MacNeal-Lehrer Newshour. They are perfectly aware of what the public expects from public discourse in the television age. As Robert MacNeal himself explained, the idea when creating a television piece

> is to keep everything brief, not to strain the attention of anyone but instead to provide constant stimulation through variety, novelty, action, and movement. You are required . . . to pay attention to no concept, no character, and no problem for more than a few seconds at a time. (As quoted in Postman 1985: 105)

While the Museum produces and packages lessons in tolerance within the dramatic formats of television, a certain tension has been created in the exhibit. This tension points to the power of the approach, and suggests that its designers may have 'transmodified' the emotive power of television. One official acknowledges this tension in pointing out that we exist in the era of the 'meta-medium . . . We all fit in one way or another, it's a question of how to tack that medium and how do you transmodify it, how do you transform it?'

On one level the designers of the Museum have mimicked presentation of information and ideas that the free-flicker generation has adapted to. All the displays within the Tolerance Center reflect the free-flicker format: short, sharp images and experiences that rely heavily on form and emotion and less on intellectual effect.

At the same time, a masterfully planned underlying dynamic exists within the walls of the Museum of Tolerance, which is extended in the second exhibit section. The 'power of the remote' is displaced from the viewer's hand to the hand of the Museum. Moreover the free flicker becomes a controlled flicker. Although the visitor is met with a barrage of visual, sensual and audio displays that occur in brief succession, mimicking the format of a remote control flicker, this format of images and sensations is pre-programmed and repetitively run in a planned sequence. While the visitor is provided with the sensation of being in a 'free-flicker' environment, the individual is not as free as she seems. Again she is subject to formats of control. Indeed, the phrase 'computer manipulatives' that our tour guide used to describe the exhibitry becomes an ambiguous term. Does it mean that the visitor manipulates the computers, or does it mean that the computers manipulate the visitor?

The ambiguity of the term 'computer manipulative' encapsulates the designed tension within the exhibitry. It reveals how the Museum has managed to tap into and mimic the emotive power of the television format but at the same time has managed to transmodify it. The Museum determines what images will be seen, and in what sequence, all the while making visitors feel that they are passing through a free-flow environment. Through the Museum, the Simon Wiesenthal Center has successfully modified the phrase, 'nobody shall overcome the tube' to 'he who has the remote has the power'. As expressed by the designers of the Museum, it is a 'masterpiece in design psychology' (James Gardener Studios Brochure). Through its design, the Museum has refined the notion of a 'captive audience' to mean a 'captivated audience'. The visitor is entertained into submission. The aesthetics of emotion become the aesthetics of control.

This tension between entertainment and control permeates all aspects of the exhibitry. Upon approaching the building, one is struck by the imposing presence of the structure. Despite the warm, pink granite from which the structure is built, the symmetrical windowless towers exert an imposing presence. Moreover, the building provides the physical expression of a control format, almost fortress-like, similar to many other buildings in Los Angeles (Davis 1990: 239–40).

The warm, sunlit, pastel atmosphere of the atrium of the Museum is undercut by the control format that the docents themselves orchestrate. The timed tours, accurate to the minute, the absence of amenities including even washrooms on the exhibit level, and the docent who makes sure we see and choose in the correct way, provide undiluted entertainment in its most controlling form.

The Museum exerts itself on the viewer, and then some. It satisfies the visitor's desire to be moved and affected and also determines what ought to move them. The Museum defines the 'free-flicker's' experience.

The Simon Wiesenthal Center has created an experiential exhibit where emotions and images, not objects, become the driving and powerful artifacts. It has created a dramatic event or spectacle within the Museum's walls that has become a model for education in tolerance. For example, there are plans to have the Los Angeles Police Department trainees visit it as part of their training, along with members of the military and the Beverly Hills Bar Association.

The Museum designers have succeeded in taking an already powerful medium and making it hegemonic. The Museum defines what intolerance looks like, what the black civil rights movement looked like, what twentieth-century genocide looks like and what being insulted feels like.

To suit the tastes of the MTV generation the Museum imposes a larger and dramatized version of life. How often do you go to a dinner party where everyone is racist and reciting racial slurs? When are you assaulted with a barrage of hateful whispers? When is genocide accompanied by music?

Within the Museum, and within North American society generally, however, it is irrelevant whether ideas and values are communicated in a manner that is more dramatic than life outside the spectacle. We have become accustomed to being constantly stimulated with a

Misplacing memory

barrage of simulations. Events and issues, and now history and memory, are communicated in stories that consist of dynamic images, supported by music in stereo sound. Even though these stories are more dramatic than our lives outside television, they become normal, the regular manner in which we communicate (Baudrillard 1983). We have become a generation of pleasure consumers who communicate and experience to the rhythm of the dramatic beat. In more hegemonic terms, 'it is not a matter of judgment but a statement of fact – we are a media dependent culture (Gumpert 1987: 7)'.

Possible causes of the L.A. riots are presented in a collection of bites from prime time television. The history of the civil rights movement in America is seven minutes long, as is our education on twentieth-century genocide. The Museum thereby reveals how 'the spectacle's domination has succeeded in raising a whole generation molded to its laws' (Debord 1988: 13). Moreover, it reflects a hegemonic force upon contemporary communication in that it 'goes beyond creating a conscious system of ideas and beliefs' toward 'the whole lived social process as practically organized by specific and dominant meanings and values . . . in effect, a saturation of the whole process of living' (Williams 1975: 9–10).

A microcosm of larger society, the Museum is a contained example of the manner in which the spectacle has saturated public discourse.

CREEPING SURREALISM

In the Beit Hashoah section of the Museum the control format radically intensifies. The multi-media *interactives* become multi-media *actives*, intentionally programming and directing the viewer *into* the dramatic event.

While the Museum of Tolerance bears the familiar format of television, it is not television. If going to the Museum was the same as watching television, people would not visit. The television experience is magnified in the Museum, making it hyper-television. The visitor not only watches images, she also interacts directly with the dramatic 'set'. In Beit Hashoah, this hyper-television experience intensifies. The visitor actually enters into the televised docudrama 'set' and *becomes* the format. She begins to feel at home in this staged environment because it seems so familiar and real. Inside the set, with its sound and light dioramas, reality is not only saturated by the spectacle, it is subsumed by it. Being subsumed by the spectacle is much like standing in the eye of the storm: the visitor is right in the middle of it, but not fully aware that she is.

In Beit Hashoah the visitor is brought back as a witness to the scene of the crime, to Germany in the 1930s. Our guides on this journey are three plaster figures: a researcher, a designer, and a historian. Their narrative – accompanied by spotlit sound and light dioramas, slide shows, and archival footage – directs us through the Nazi rise to power.

Chance for self-reflection is minimal to nil during our journey through Beit Hashoah. The highly formatted exhibitry propels us from scene to scene in an orderly manner, followed by the next group, so that there is not time to stand in contemplation. Our plaster hosts structure the journey. Just like our previous guides, the smarmy talk show host and docent, they ask the 'correct' questions and provide the 'correct' answers.

At one point on this dimly lit journey of simulations we eavesdrop on a simulated gathering of the Wannsee Conference, that infamous conference in 1941 where the Final Solution, the official plan to exterminate European Jewry, was set into motion. The voices of actors, in accented English, reading the minutes of the meeting, fall upon a simulated set of the Conference boardroom. We listen to the bureaucrats, politicians and intellectuals in the neutral language of bureaucracy finalize the fate of European Jewry as superimposed images of the *Einsatzgruppen* (mobile killing units) flash over the table.

Beyond the Wannsee Agreement the physical environment changes. The gray matted walls give way to simulated brick ruins, attempting to portray the visual image of tragedy and destruction. Set inside the synthetic bricks are screens which play archival footage of the *Einsatzgruppen*, and the brutality of the Eastern European collaborators. Invited by our hosts to 'come sit amongst the ruins' of a simulated Warsaw Ghetto, the screens flash images of persecution and killing, the Jewish resistance and the Warsaw uprising and its razing.

Pushed further along by the sound and light dioramas the environment changes again. The red carpet gives way to exposed stone. A map on the wall in black outlines the death camps. To our left is a recreated entrance to Auschwitz; a metal gate marked 'Arbeit Macht Frei'; an officers booth; and, two narrow passages, one marked 'Able bodied', the other marked 'Children and Others'. A sign off to the side states 'Millions Had to Pass Through Gates Like These'. Experiencing the helplessness felt by victims at the gates of Auschwitz, the visitor is expected to 'choose' which passageway to pass through.

An elderly lady in the group seems confused, as she faces the two passageways which light up beckoningly. She turns to the docent who is standing by the passageway and asks, 'Is this the only way out?' 'Yes', the docent replies. I am taken by this short exchange and hesitate, along with the elderly lady in front of me. Our hesitation was obviously too long as the lights flash out in the dark corridor. We are forced to feel our way along the dark passageway, having missed the timing of the lights.

The passageway opens up into an oblong room, the 'Hall of Testimony'. Done in rough stone with steel frames lining the sides, it defies exact definition, although it very much resembles a gas chamber. Eight synchronized screens line the walls offering visual narratives of the horrors of the Nazi regime. The stories, equally horrific and mesmerizing, draw us into the heart of Nazi Darkness (Rugoff 1993). When the testimony is over, we file out of the room past a neon sign that reads 'Hope Lives When People Remember'.

During the one-hour journey through Beit Hashoah there are no levers to pull, no buttons to push. The visitor becomes passive as she is led through the 'sets'. Again, she does not become part of an interactive, but rather the recipient of an active exhibitry.

Having completed our tour, a docent encourages us to make our own way to the 'Multi-Media Learning Center' and 'Artifacts Room' as a compliment to the central exhibitry on the lower floor. There we find a collection of interactive, multimedia computer systems that with the ease of a touch of the finger 'provide personalized research on tolerance, the Holocaust and World War II to various levels of users (Integrated Systems Pamphlet)'.

Reaching the final leg of the visit, we find ourselves inside the 'Artifacts Room'. Displayed behind glass are relics of the Nazi Regime which include uniforms of concentration camp victims, yellow Stars of David, a plate of medical instruments used by the doctors at Auschwitz and original correspondence between Anne Frank and a friend.

In Beit Hashoah the history of the Holocaust is presented in a docudrama format where the visitor is inducted as an extra within the production. The line between fact and fantasy, blurred in the Museum of Tolerance, dissolves in Beit Hashoah. As observed by a visiting official from Yad Vashem, Israel.

> You move along at a pace that's been preset. Whoever presses the button has started a chain reaction. And you are part of a chain reaction and they pull you through an ongoing movie set . . . [as if] you are an extra in a film.

The Simon Wiesenthal Center, aware of the limited attention spans of the Nintendo generation, has created a physical manipulation where the viewer receives her education in the form of a jolt. The designers of the exhibitry deal in quick, sharp shocks rather than contemplation

> The Museum's sole interest is in raising educational levels . . . The contemplation or the absorption of the experience would occur afterwards in which almost like a piece of film inside you, you could develop it later, but not develop it in segments.

Arnold Schwarzenneger – *the* cultural expert at riveting attention – put it aptly in the Museum's star-studded opening dinner

> The trick if you want to teach people is you have to first grab their attention, then teach them, then make sure it lasts. And this museum does all three of those things. (As quoted in Higgins 1993)

The intended resolve of the Museum's two main exhibits is to 'trade on emotions'. The visitor is to possess, as Edelman (1988: 9) would argue, 'a foggy knowledge of public affairs though often an intensely felt one'.

The central thrust of this 'argument from intellect' by Edelman and others is its opposition to the emphasis on emotion. Critics who adopt this viewpoint state that emotions alienate the individual from the event or issue being addressed, thus subduing the more analytical and reflexive inclinations of people. The public spectacle, as the argument goes, constructs an issue in black and white. It makes it easy to know who the bad guys are, what is right and what is wrong, what is morally virtuous and what is morally reprehensible. Moreover, the spectacle orders reality into comprehensible forms that, because of their purity, have strong effects upon the public (Ericson *et al.* 1991: chapter 4).

The political spectacle is considered a cultural opiate – it dulls the intellect but quickens the senses. As Neil Postman (1985: 11) argues, the pervasiveness of the television spectacle creates a 'public insensible to contradiction and narcotized by technology'. The emphasis upon emotion over intellect is of grave concern to critics of the power of spectacle. Indeed, the emotional clarity that the spectacle exerts over the viewer is considered a negative effect. These critics argue that the emotional force of the spectacle serves to separate the individual from that issue or event the spectacle represents. This separation is caused by those same shocking forms that engage and connect the individual when exposed to the spectacle. Because the forms are so fantastic, so unreal, so pure, they paradoxically mask the reality of the event or issue represented by the spectacle.

This 'argument from intellect' is too deterministic. It rests upon the faulty premise that emotion is not knowledge. More precisely, the argument is that emotionality, which often surfaces in the form of ethically motivated considerations, is the irrational counterpart of reason, and therefore a weak and unproductive mode of social education that ought to be overpowered by a more rational, intellectual approach. However, if one considers knowledge as the capacity to act (Stehr and Ericson 1992; Stehr 1992), then emotions become a key factor in the knowledge equation. Intellectual understanding becomes only one component of knowledge, the other part being feeling (Ericson *et al.* 1991). It is the dramatic event that moves people to action. It succeeds in connecting the personal to the political through sensual means. It jolts people out of emotional complacency by feeding them simplified, stylized images whose familiar forms strike a personal chord within the targeted group.

The dramatization and spectacularization of events and issues also satisfies peoples' taste for pure, shocking and sensual forms. It has the power to touch people intimately by engaging their emotions. Feelings should not be denigrated as their power is essential in counterbalancing the deadly potential of reason emancipated from emotion, of rationality from normative pressures (Bauman 1989: 108).

Indeed, it was the Nazi's reliance on emotionless reason that ensured their successful administration of the final solution. The logical 'intellect' of the modern nation state, transformed into huge rational bureaucracies, administered the final solution. In effect, it was rationality and cold intellect, separated from emotion, that created and administered

> an industry of death never before – or since – seen. An industry of continental size complete with railways, death camps, gas chambers and crematoria. An industry whose raw material was Jews and whose product was corpses. (Krauthammer 1993: 64)

The Simon Wiesenthal Center does attempt to achieve balance between cognitive and emotional understanding in the 'Multi-media Learning Center'. There a great deal of knowledge, including structural accounts of the reasons for the Holocaust, is held within computer banks. However, back on the central exhibitry floor, in the shadows of the debate over the values of emotional power versus the values of contemplative power, something else has been traded off unwittingly, namely memory and history.

This more subtle trade-off does not occur suddenly within Beit Hashoah. Rather it occurs over the two exhibits in a format that may best be described as 'creeping surrealism' (Achenbach 1987). This 'creeping surrealism' develops from the Museum of Tolerance and culminates in Beit Hashoah. The visitor's ability to define and maintain control over the experiences that are imposed upon her is incrementally lost. The real – or rather those things that define the real, namely memory and history – collapses, in degrees, into the fantastic, the fictional, the unreal.

This 'creeping surrealism' works by shifting the power of spectacle from a preponderant force to an all-encompassing one. The shift is achieved by reducing the dialogue that was evident between spectacle and spectator in the Museum of Tolerance. In the first half of the exhibit the visitor passes by the exhibitry, pulling levers, pressing buttons, playing an interactive role in the format of control. In a sense it is a 'negotiated control' between the spectacle and spectator (Ericson *et al.* 1989). In the second half of the exhibit, however, the visitor passes *into* the exhibitry. The relative distance and autonomy experienced by the visitor in the first part of the exhibit is eliminated in the simulated experience the visitor enters into in the second section of exhibitry.

The simulation, the induction of the viewer into the folds of the dramatic event, produces a profound effect well beyond a simple dramatization. The simulation creates an artificial format that orders the things it represents in accordance with its own rules of artifice. These rules of artifice are implemented so as to achieve the maximum effect upon the visitor – namely the ability to move, shock, rivet and maintain her attention.

A Museum official provided a compelling reason for turning to diorama-driven exhibitry over artifact-driven exhibitry. He observed that in the basement of the Simon Wiesenthal Center's Yeshiva building, next to the Museum, there is another museum. This 'Holocaust Museum' is still intact, but its primary function now seems to be a storage room. The exhibit includes a display of the Wannsee protocol, the document that outlined the Final Solution. When the Holocaust Museum was still in operation the protocol 'was on the wall and no one ever looked at it' (Cannon 1993). To overcome such inattentiveness to print media, the Wannsee protocol display in the new museum was designed with a theatrical stage set, actors' accented English, and video displays. As Umberto Eco (1986: 8) observes 'the diorama aims to establish itself as a substitute for reality, as something even more real. When it is flanked by a document . . . the little model is undoubtedly more real than the engraving.'

The creation of a simulated dioramic environment raises spectacle to its most profound level. The spectacle not only helps to shape experience and create what is real, it in effect creates the experience itself so that the spectacle *becomes* what is real. The difference between the signifier and the signified collapses in on itself. A real situation is created 'where signs of the real replace the real' (Baudrillard 1983: 7). The spectacle becomes our reality. It becomes what is normal and understood. In effect, this reliance upon simulation as a means of public discourse creates 'simulacra' – 'a real without origin or reality: a hyperreal' (Baudrillard 1983: 2). Dramatic forms that were once just signifiers of the signified (issues or events, or in the case of the Museum, memory and history) melt over the signified, reinventing a layer of reality in the shades of the dramatic and spectacular. 'Everything looks real, therefore it is real . . . even if, like Alice in Wonderland, it never existed . . . the real is flattened against the fake (Eco 1986: 10, 16).'

A poignant example of this designed confusion between the real and the fake is found in the two passageways that lead the visitor into the 'Hall of Testimony'. As a Museum official explains:

> Look, there's no sign anywhere that said 'Children and Others' . . . once again you want some kind of physical enactment to take place . . . How can you dramatically show that children and disabled . . . had no chance of survival whatsoever . . . that there is an immediate kind of separation out? So it's a dramatic re-representation of what took place.

Misplacing memory

The Museum recognizes the need to provide the visitor with the opportunity to experience the helplessness of the victims of the Holocaust, thereby providing a sense of authenticity. The strategy is to stage an event that will provide the visitor with this experience, thus injecting some artifice into the journey of simulation. In the result, however, the artifice becomes real. The visitor becomes oblivious to the knowledge of where reality ends and artifice begins.

The juxtaposition between the real and fake is physically enacted at the entrance of these two tunnels. Here we find ourselves at the gates to Auschwitz. A sign that states 'Millions Had to Pass Through Gates Like These' is placed ambiguously between the gates and tunnels. Fantasy and drama creep up upon the real. Thus, the dramatic effect these two tunnels impose upon the viewer is so real that there is no reason for the average visitor, generally uninformed about the Holocaust, not to believe that the entrances to the death chambers of Auschwitz really did have these signs mounted on them. The designers of the Museum have successfully manipulated history so as to make it comprehensible, clear and powerful to the unaware visitor.

This blurring of the real against the fake in the Tolerance Center, and the amalgamation of the two in the House of the Holocaust, reveals a larger cultural ethos of 'creeping surrealism' that exists in contemporary society. This ethos is best understood as a phenomenon whose dynamic encompasses its own extremes. In the less extreme forms of creeping surrealism people are able to tell the difference between the real and the fake. In the more extreme forms the difference between what is real and what is not becomes blurred. Moreover the unreal becomes the real. The central thread connecting all points is that the unreal is accepted as a part of ordinary public discourse.

Individuals are aware of the contradictions between the real and the fantastic. Within the closed environment of the Museum, visitors are aware that the bricks and stones of the two tunnels are fake, and that the cocktail party guests in the Museum of Tolerance are actors, just as they are aware that the bloody and dramatic shoot-outs so characteristic of Arnold Schwarzenegger movies are fake.

At the same time, at a more sublime level, the fake, through its saturation of public discourse, defines what is real. We know that the entrances to the chambers are fake but we are led to believe they are a recreation of something that really did exist in Auschwitz, just as we are surprised to see that someone being shot in real life is not at all like we see in the movies. However, 'none of it really matters, of course, because although Americans can still distinguish truth from fiction, they no longer think the distinction matters' (Achenbach 1987: 18). Thus, the confusion between reality and fantasy that occurs in different extremes along the median of creeping surrealism makes us both witting and unwitting collaborators within the drama of the simulated spectacle (Ericson *et al.* 1987: 339–41; Hartley 1992: 140–6).

A further illustration of the collaborative effort (whether witting or unwitting, we're not sure) to create an environment of creeping surrealism is evident in a Washington Post staff writer's description of the 'Hall of Testimony'. He states, 'The story of what happened in the real execution chambers and in the Warsaw Ghetto uprising is related in recordings by concentration camp survivors' (Cannon 1993). In actuality these are not voices of survivors. Rather it is the testimony of survivors read out by character actors. This reporter has been drawn into the technology of fakes. Clearly his reporting was inaccurate, but as Joel Achenbach would say, no one cares, the reporter and the reading audience included. It is not important whether it is fake. Drama supersedes truth, or more accurately, drama becomes truth.

An official explains the reason for using actors and actresses in those testimonies where survivors themselves could have been used.

> The problem is . . . these people don't speak well. If you try and get them to sit down and re-record it, English is not their first language . . . Originally what we tested was actors doing it in dialect and that just didn't work at all. So does it make sense to get a survivor who doesn't speak that well? That doesn't make sense so that's why we made the decision . . . to go to people who can really, in a proper way, render these stories.

Those people were Ed Azner (otherwise known as 'Lou Grant' in the Mary Tyler Moore Show) and Marianne Margolese who, according to the official is 'a very well known character actress, with a superb and sensitive voice'. The actor's and actress' voice is said to sound more real than the victims themselves. The dramatic becomes the yardstick for determining what's real. '[T]he American imagination demands the real thing and to attain it, must fabricate the absolute fake: where the boundaries between game and illusion are blurred . . . and falsehood is enjoyed in a situation of 'fullness', of *horror vacuii.*' (Eco 1986: 9)

Los Angeles is not only 'the city of quartz' (Davis 1990), it is also 'the city of illusions' (Young 1993: 308). As exemplified by the Beit Hashoah Museum of Tolerance, creeping surrealism is well underfoot. Here the unreal, the recreated and the voice-over form the yardstick by which we measure the real. Fantasy becomes the baseline for measuring truth. Drama overpowers reality. Characters of history become character actresses and voices from the past become voice-overs of the present.

In the language of the spectacle, this study offers a dramatic illustration of the role of spectacle in public discourse. The hegemonic force of the spectacle in contemporary culture imposes itself in degrees of creeping surrealism. The hegemonic process is acted out in accordance with the demands and expectations of the viewer, and the technology and planned artifice on the part of the spectacle designers.

The Museum reveals creeping surrealism's most powerful by-product, one that is hidden by its dramatic and emotive force, namely its ability to reduce memory and displace history. History and memory are displaced by the constant focus on the need to shock, motivate and move. The spectacle doesn't do history. It does effects. What then are the implications of collapsing memory and history into a spectacle where events and experiences are dramatized and clarified, mixed together and exaggerated? Possibly the most profound effect is that history is forgotten, not because it is willed but because it is misplaced by the spectacle of the present. Accordingly, events in history – even those events as horrendously monumental as the Holocaust that demand remembrance to prevent further occurrence – are also forgotten, or rather misplaced. As Jean Baudrillard (1987: 23) points out, 'forgetting the extermination is part of the extermination itself.'

The Beit Hashoah Museum of Tolerance relies upon television formats that place its operatives in ironic and contradictory circumstances. On the one hand, the Museum's operatives correctly perceive that they can only communicate to a wide audience if they use television technology to drive their emotion factory. On the other hand, in reducing the horror of the Holocaust to the same level as Hollywood, the pirate experience at Disney World, the baseball experience at Toronto's Skydome, or the McDonald's experience in no particular place, they end up trivializing both the Holocaust and their audience. It is indeed ironic that the Holocaust, fostered by the manipulation of emotive symbols and formats in the 1930s, is now to be prevented from happening again through the manipulation of emotive symbols and formats of television – formats which treat people as judgmental dopes and spoon-force-feed them on spectacles as truth (Altheide 1993).

While the facility is called the Beit Hashoah *Museum of Tolerance*, it is of course a strong expression of intolerance. Discourses and practices that exclude others – especially those that foster war, murder and other extreme forms of state terrorism – are not to be tolerated. At least television power is being put to good use in the Museum. Or is it?

Having employed television formats, Museum operatives must rely heavily on emotional understanding. As we addressed previously, emotional understanding is crucial in counterbalancing the deadly power of reason emancipated from emotion. As we had also pointed out, the Museum operatives had attempted to construct such a balance by including the Multi Media Learning Center as a cognitive supplement to the emotive totality of the Museum. However, this balance remains a tenuous one, as it exists within a larger cultural environment who's structure and logic continuously favor the emotive and fantastic over the average and banal.

18   *Nicola A. Lisus and Richard V. Ericson*

If the balance tips too far in the direction of simulation for emotional stimulation, it is not clear whether people will feel the need to translate their emotions into knowledge useful for the prevention of genocide. When, as a result of direct emotional experience, the person becomes part of the communication format, is it even possible to later desire a coherent picture and interpret it for practical action?

There is a second and equally profound problem with reliance upon television formats. At the same time that they privilege emotional understanding, television formats circumscribe explanatory understandings that can be communicated (Ericson *et al.* 1991). As a whole, the Museum exhibitry communicates a partial and faulty theory of the Holocaust: that prejudiced, intolerant people bear responsibility. This soporific view is not only limited but potentially dangerous, yet perhaps no alternative theory can be communicated effectively within the format requirements of television. The television format, whether applied to news (ibid.) or to the Museum-as-emotion factory, excludes information that fosters understanding of how society works. As such, it can only offer a *disarming* message (Bauman 1993). As Bauman (1989) has shown, the massive, co-ordinated, long-term operation of modern genocide requires that the main executors be good employees and good *pater familias*, regardless of whether they are prejudiced or intolerant. Are the Museum operatives unable to offer this more complex and truer explanation because of the compelling need to have television formats run their emotions factory?

(Date accepted: April 1994)

Nicola A. Lisus
Center of Criminology
University of Toronto
and
Richard V. Ericson
Green College
University of British Columbia

NOTE

*Preparation of this paper was funded by a research grant from the Social Sciences and Humanities Research Council of Canada, and by the Contributions Program of the Solicitor General of Canada to the Centre of Criminology, University of Toronto. We are grateful to David Altheide, Zygmunt Bauman and Geoffrey Hartman for their comments on an earlier version of this paper. Field research and interviews were undertaken by Nicola Lisus.

BIBLIOGRAPHY

Achenbach, J. 1987 'Reality to be Canceled?' *Miami Herald (Tropic Magazine)*, Dec. 13.

Altheide, D. 1985 *Media Power*, Beverly Hills: Sage.
Altheide, D. 1993 Personal communication.
Altheide, D. and Snow, R. 1991 *Media Worlds in the Postjournalism Era*, New York: Aldine de Gruyter.
Baudrillard, J. 1983 *Simulations*, New York: Semiotext.
Baudrillard, J. 1987 *The Evil Demon of Images*, Sydney: Power Institute Publications Number 3.
Bauman, Z. 1989 *Modernity and the Holocaust*, Ithaca, New York: Cornell University Press.
Bauman, Z. 1993 Personal Communication.
Cannon, L. 1993 'Confronting the Circle of Bigotry', *Washington Post Report*, Feb. 6.
Davis, M. 1990 *City of Quartz: Excavating the Future of Los Angeles*, London and New York: Verso.
Debord, G. 1988 *Comments on the Society of the Spectacle*, trans. Malcolm Imrie, London: Verso.
Eco, U. 1986 *Travels in Hyper Reality*, trans. William Weaver, Toronto: Harcourt Brace Jovanovich.
Edelman, M. 1988 *Constructing the Political Spectacle*, Chicago: University of Chicago Press.
Ericson, R. 1991 'Mass Media, Crime, Law and Justice: An Institutional Approach' *British Journal of Criminology* 31: 219–49.
Ericson, R., Baranek, P. and Chan, J. 1987 *Visualizing Deviance*, Toronto: University of Toronto Press; Milton Keynes: Open University Press.
Ericson, R., Baranek, P. and Chan, J. 1989 *Negotiating Control*, Toronto: University of Toronto Press. Milton Keynes: Open University Press.
Ericson, R., Baranek, P. and Chan, J. 1991 *Representing Order*, Toronto: University of Toronto Press; Milton Keynes: Open University Press.
Fjellan, S. 1992 *Vinyl Leaves*, Boulder, Colorado: Westview Press.
Gumpert, G. 1987 *Talking Tombstones and Other Tales of the Media Age*, New York: Oxford University Press.

Hartley, J. 1992 *The Politics of Pictures*, London: Routledge.
Hirshey, G. 1993 'Thirteensomething', *Gentlemen Quarterly*, February.
Higgins, B. 1993 'A Gala for a Museum to Remember', *Los Angeles Times* Feb. 9.
Integrated Systems Research Corporation 1993 *ISR MEDIA*, Brochure, Englewood Cliffs, New Jersey.
James Gardener Studios 1993 *3D Concepts*, Project Review, London.
Krauthammer, C. 1993 'Holocaust: Memory and Resolve', *Time*, May 3.
Levitt, C. and Shaffir, W. 1993 'The Swastika as Dramatic Symbol: A Case Study of Ethnic Violence in Canada' in R. Brym et al. (eds) *The Jews in Canada*, Toronto: Oxford University Press.
McLuhan, M. 1964 *Understanding Media*, New York: McGraw-Hill.
Meyrowitz, J. 1985 *No Sense of Place*, New York: Oxford University Press.
Meyrowitz, J. 1992 'The Power of Television', *The World and I*, June, 453–74.
Miller, J. 1990 *One, By One, By One*, New York: Simon & Schuster.
Pitts, L. 1993 'An Antidote to Hatred', *Miami Herald*, March 9.
Postman, N. 1985 *Amusing Ourselves to Death*, New York: Viking Penguin.
Rugoff, R. 1993 'Jump-Cut to Auschwitz', *LA Weekly*, Feb. 26.
Simon Wiesenthal Center 1993 *Beit Hashoah – Museum of Tolerance*, Los Angeles, California.
Stehr, N. 1992 *Practical Knowledge*, London: Sage.
Stehr, N. and Ericson, R. (eds) 1992 *The Culture and Power of Knowledge*, Berlin and New York: de Gruyter.
Tigend, T. 1993 'Spielberg "Blown Away" by Tolerance Museum', *Heritage Southwest Jewish Press*, March 5.
Williams, R. 1975 *Drama in a Dramatized Society*, Cambridge: Cambridge University Press.
Willwerth, J. 1993 'Museum of Hate' *Time*, Feb. 15.
Young, J. 1993 *The Texture of Memory*, New Haven: Yale University Press.

Part V
Business Commodification and Fetish

[19]

Constructing the Ownership of Social Problems: Fun and Profit in the Welfare State*

JOSEPH R. GUSFIELD, *University of California, San Diego*

Links between the emergence of social problems and the welfare state are examined, with particular attention to the place of the "troubled persons" professions, mass media and educational institutions, the place of the language of conflict and consensus in social problems activities, contested and uncontested definitions of problem conditions, how meanings and problems are transformed, and how mobilization activities contribute to these transformations. The paper ends with a plea to move the study of social problems closer to the study of how social movements and institutions affect and are affected by the interpretations, the language, and the symbols that constitute seeing a situation as a social problem in historical and institutional context.

The "Social Problems" Culture and the Welfare State

A cultural perspective toward social problems begins at the beginning; with the concept of our study itself, with "social problems," not as an abstract tool of scientific analysis but as a way of interpreting experience. It is not sociologists and their students alone who live in the shadow and sunlight of "social problems." As an object of attention, social problems are a part of modern societies. They have to be seen in an historical context and in a structural dimension interacting with cultural interpretations of experience.

The idea of "social problems" is unique to modern societies. I do not mean that modern societies generate conditions which are problem-laden and cry for reform and alleviation while primitive and pre-industrial ones do not. I do mean that modern societies, including the United States, display a culture of public problems. It is a part of how we think and how we interpret the world around us, that we perceive many conditions as not only deplorable but as capable of being relieved by and as requiring public action, most often by the state. The concept of "social problem" is a category of thought, a way of seeing certain conditions as providing a claim to change through public actions.

All human problems are not public ones. Unrequited love, disappointed friendships, frustrated ambitions, parent-child disputes, biological aging are among the most searing experiences of life, but they have not yet been construed as matters requiring public policy or even capable of being affected by public actions. Much that in primitive and non-industrial societies has been either resignedly accepted or coped with in the confines of the family is now construed as the responsibility of public institutions.

In his recent book, *Total Justice*, the legal historian Lawrence Friedman (1985) has described many new legal rights that have emerged in American justice in the past fifty years. These have created legal entitlements to government aid toward resolving grievances for which, in the past, the only response was "lump it." A small but instructive example makes the point: the special ramps and parking spaces to which physically handicapped people are now legally entitled in the United States. Add to these the vast proliferation of others: civil rights, women's rights, prisoner's rights, children's rights, gay rights, and an etcetra much too

---

* This paper is a revised version of the presidential address presented to the Society for the Study of Social Problems, Berkeley, California, August 1989. Correspondence to: Gusfield, Department of Sociology, University of California-San Diego, La Jolla, CA 92093.

lengthy to unpack. There is an inflationary trend that expands the areas described as "social problems," that spawns new movements for new rights and the recognition of new problems.

The concept of "social problems" is not something abstract and separate from social institutions. The late Ian Weinberg (1974) used the term "referral agencies" to describe the institutions and professions to which people turned to cope with public problems, a term I prefer to "social problems." To give a name to a problem is to recognize or suggest a structure developed to deal with it. Child abuse, juvenile delinquency, mental illness, alcoholism all have developed occupations and facilities that specialize in treatment, prevention and reform; for instance: shelters for runaway adolescents and battered women; alcohol and drug counsellors and recovery centers; community services for the aged; legal aid for the indigent; community mental health counselling, and centers for the homeless. There is even a national organization called the Society for the Study of Social Problems.

New professions and new rights are continuously emerging, almost in a symbiotic relationship. As sexual therapy becomes a recognized field requiring training, and medical insurance is extended to it, we may find that sexual satisfaction is becoming a social responsibility and a citizen's right. But I promised you an historical rose garden as well as a structural one. Both as a feature of contemporary culture and as a matter of social structure, the conceptualization of situations as "social problems" is embedded in the development of the welfare state. When I speak of "the welfare state" I have in mind the long-run drift in modern societies toward a greater commitment to use public facilities to directly enhance the welfare of citizens (Ehrenreich 1985). This disposition to turn private and familial problems into public ones is a characteristic of most modern societies. It reflects both a higher gross national product and a democratized politics that insures a floor to the grosser inequities of life and the free market (Briggs 1961; Heilbroner 1989). Underlying both of these is the optimism of a sense of progress according to which most of life's difficulties are inherently remediable. The concept of "social problems" does more than point to deplorable situations. It suggests a social responsibility for resolving the resolvable.

The "Troubled Persons" Professions: Profit in Social Problems

Here, I want to discuss two significant parts of social structure: the occupations that serve "social problems"—what I call the "troubled persons professions"; and the occupations and institutions that inform and entertain—the image-making industries, including schools as well as the mass media. They are significant parts of the process by which publics experience social problems, interpret and imbue them with meaning, and create and administer public policies.

Most of us who read this journal, as well as many others in this service economy, live *off* social problems as well as *for* them. There is no adequate census of the social problems profession. In my county of San Diego there are ninety-nine separate organizations and their personnel that owe their existence and livelihood to alcohol problems. This includes the staffs of treatment agencies, such as detoxification and recovery centers, special clinics, lobbying organizations, legally mandated classes for drinking-driver offenders and the staff of the County Alcohol Services Office, one arm of the Substance Abuse Programs. The aphorism about the American missionaries who went to Hawaii three generations ago is an overstatement but it captures some of the process. "They came to do good. They stayed and did well."

The development of professions dedicated to benevolence, the so-called "helping" professions, depend upon and accentuate the definition of problem populations as "sick," as objects of medical and quasi-medical attention. The "troubled persons" industries, as I like to call them, consist of the professions that bestow benevolence on people defined as in need. Such occupations include counsellors, social workers, clinical psychologists, foundation administrators, operators of asylum-like centers, alcohol rehabilitation specialists, researchers, and the many jobs where the task is to bring people who are seen as trouble to themselves or to others into the stream of "adjusted" citizens. Alvin Gouldner (1970:77) captured this when he wrote: "Increasingly, the Welfare State's strategy is to transform the sick, the deviant, and the unskilled into 'useless citizens,' and to return them to 'society' only after periods of hospitalization, treatment, counselling, training, or retraining."

The key term here is "treatment" ("rehabilitation" is analogous). An example is the disease concept of alcoholism. "Seeing" alcohol problems as primarily those of persons suffering from a condition akin to other diseases did two things. First, it weakened the onus of responsibility on the chronic drunk for his condition. In that sense it marshalled attitudes of commiseration and benevolence. The alcoholic was someone to be helped and not merely condemned. Second, it made it reasonable to develop a body of knowledge and a corps of people who could be trained in the skills and knowledge needed to help the alcoholics. (To a significant degree, it also provided employment for recovering alcoholics who now had capital in their past troubles.) The same logic exists in the development of juvenile delinquency and the rehabilitative orientation toward criminals.

If deviants and troubled people are to be "returned" to society, it requires a special group of workers trained to accomplish the task and to administer the institutions that accomplish it. If, however, the difficulties are understood to be those of moral diversity, of contested meanings, then the problem is a political issue and no system of training can provide help. If the condition is perceived as that of individual illness or deficiency, then there can be a social technology, a form of knowledge and skill, that can be effectively learned. That knowledge is the mandate for a profession's license to "own" their social problem. Insofar as it is accepted it constitutes the source of ownership of a problem.

To "own" a problem (Gusfield 1981) is to be obligated to claim recognition of a problem and to have information and ideas about it given a high degree of attention and credibility, to the exclusion of others. To "own" a social problem is to possess the authority to name that condition a "problem" and to suggest what might be done about it. It is the power to influence the marshalling of public facilities—laws, enforcement abilities, opinion, goods and services—to help resolve the problem. To disown a problem is to claim that one has no such responsibility. In the nineteenth and early twentieth centuries the Protestant churches were the dominant "owners" of the alcohol problem, a status that has since been lost to medical, governmental, and academic institutions.

Patricia Morgan (1980) has suggested that the definition of social problems as those of "troubled persons" is a form of depoliticizing problems. There is much merit in this view. The psychologizing or medicalizing of phenomena, as a way of seeing, draws attention away from the institutional or structural aspects. The slogan of the alcohol industry, "The fault is in the man and not in the bottle," suggests this disowning. An interpretation of a social problem as one of the individual's deficiencies and the emergence of professions based on such assumptions limits the perception of institutional features at work.

The Image-Making Industries: Social Problems as Fun

For many in this mass society, social problems are also an object of attention, a source of news interest and mass entertainment, a form of fun. Specific social problems are experienced directly by only a small segment of the population. Modern life is experienced both close-at-hand and far away. We know at first hand and face-to-face only a small portion of the stuff that makes up our perception of the "society." Verbal and visual images, the stuff of newspapers, magazines, books and education, of radio, movies, and television, make up the sources by which the larger world is mediated to us (Ericson, Baranek, and Chan 1987). They help to form our image of "society."

As part of this mass construction of reality, society is itself a spectacle, an object played before an audience. They may find it dull or exciting; informative or mysterious. It may be conveyed as a series of separate events or as a patterned sequence of activities. In this whirligig of acts, "social problems" constitute a constant and recurrent source of interest and, in popular culture, a basis for entertainment and even vicarious identification with evil. Crime, delinquency, drug addiction, child abuse, poverty, family violence, sexual deviance, prostitution, alcoholism make up a considerable part of news and popular drama. These provide much of the imagery with which social problems are perceived and acted upon. The criminal, the prostitute, the drug addict and the other objects of problems may be seen as deplorable, as troubled, as dangerous, but they are endlessly dramatic and interesting. Joel Best (1987) has shown how the problem of missing children was conveyed to the general public as the dramatic one of molested and mistreated children. His closer look found most of the cases to be those of children "kidnapped" by ex-husbands or ex-wives in disputes over custody, a much less interesting or lurid story.

In the content of much of popular culture we can find a great deal of the mythology of modern life (Cawelti 1976). The television presentation of the death of Candy Lightner's child in an auto accident dramatized the drinking-driving problem as a major cause of auto accidents. It portrayed the experience of auto accidents as a morality play; as a contest between villains and victims. It created an image opposite to that of the "troubled person," namely, the image of the "troublesome person"—the myth of the "killer-drunk," as a standard, mythologized "type" through which to see each event (Gusfield 1981).

Such modern myths serve to symbolize complex events, as ways to understand social problems in personal terms. As such they redirect attention from structural and institutional aspects and support a theory of social behavior, and the policies related to it, that sees social policy as geared to remake the person. They make the world a more interesting place, a place where bad people are responsible for evil (Stivers 1988). To build excitement and narrative around such subjects as safety belts, auto design, alcohol availability, and user friendly roads may be possible but seems to lack the possibilities of villainy that the drinking-driver drama contains.

Consensus and Conflict: The Public Status of Social Problems

The language and rhetoric of "social problems" is a language that assumes and points toward a basic consensus about the problematic character of the condition deplored, in the same fashion that a physician can assume that his/her patient wants to be cured. Child abuse, alcoholism, mental illness, prostitution, gender and racial discrimination, crime, drug addiction are just a few among many which are imbued with an aura of consensus. To challenge their status as social conditions requiring reform is unthinkable in the contemporary public arenas. The point is illustrated in one of my favorite comic strips, Miss Peach. The first-grade teacher has told her class that next week they will have a speaker on the topic of juvenile delinquency. "Oh, goody," says one of her young pupils, "Will he be for it or against it?"

Miss Peach's student made a profound utterance about most of the situations sociologists customarily study under the rubric of "social problem." They involve an assumed public consensus from which the behavior targeted for change or reform is perceived as outside the norm, as opposed to societally shared values. It is not publicly acceptable for anyone to be "for" mental illness, alcoholism, gender or racial discrimination, poverty, drinking-driving, air pollution, drug addiction, homelessness, or almost all the titles of chapters in the various texts in the field. To see a situation as a social problem is to set in motion a particular form of discourse and to channel policies in a particular direction.

Conventional language supports a psychologistic perspective. The concept of "substance abuse" locates the problem of alcohol in the abuser rather than the substance—its nature, availability and the conditions that make insobriety dangerous. "Mental illness" locates the phenomena in medical institutions and hospitals.

A point made by Murray Edelman (1977) in his analyses of the language of social problems is instructive. Aid to farmers, he pointed out, is called "parity," aid to business in the form of tax cuts is simply called aid to the general economy; aid to people at the poverty level is called "welfare" or "help." Differing language frames mean differing assessments and evaluations.

Edelman's discussion is pertinent. We use words like "welfare" and "helping" and "social problem" to emphasize the temporary and uncommitted nature of benevolence or control, rather than using the language of rights, which creates a different meaning. To use the language of "social problem" is to portray its subjects as "sick" or as "troublesome." We do not use a language of personal deficiencies to talk about economic concerns or to describe recession as the problem of sick businessmen, nor do we describe investment counsellors as "market therapists." The income of the client affects the language of the profession. Subsidies to the auto industry are not called "aid to dependent factories."

Nor is the consensus illustrated by Miss Peach something inherent in the objects attended to. It is a social construction in which an assumed consensus is not contested. It can be contrasted with issues such as abortion or gun control or vivisection where the existence of diversity, of conflict, is so evident that the claim to represent a consensus falls on its face. In these areas a claim to represent the "society" appears patently unacceptable.

Claims to use public resources for reform posit a "society" that is homogeneous, against which the problem situation can be contrasted. In this the nature of "social problems" has not changed much since 1943 when C. Wright Mills (1943) published his justly classic paper, "The Professional Ideology of Social Pathologists." In his critical examination of the field, Mills (1943:531-32) described the method of defining social problems by sociologists as "in terms of *deviation from norms*. The 'norms' so used are usually held to be the standards of the society."

Consider the following claims to benevolent action, 77 years apart. In each the speaker claims to be representing public interests and social standards. In Milwaukee, in 1912, the city council considered legislation restricting the use of premises connected with saloons for purposes of dance halls. Opponents of the ordinance, especially the labor unions, charged class legislation, since the dance halls were a major form of young working class recreation. A social worker replied to this, saying:

> This is not a fight against the Germans or the Poles. It is not a fight against the pleasures of the working class. All we want to do is lift the moral standards of the city. Give our working girls the liberty of a pure city, pure enjoyment, rather than this personal liberty the opposition speaks of (Harring 1983:185).

In 1989 the California State Supreme Court affirmed a lower court decision that prohibits staff members of mental hospitals from administering antipsychotic drugs against the wishes of patients committed for at least three-day to fourteen day periods. An attorney for one of the hospitals, in commenting on the case, objected to the decision, saying: "This decision may satisfy someone's notion of an abstract principle but the patients who supposedly would benefit are going to be denied effective treatment" (*Los Angeles Times* 1989).

The speakers assert a claim to be recognized among those who "own" a part of the problems of alcohol use and of mental disorder. In the process of presenting themselves the speakers do more than state a personal opinion. They make a claim to represent more than themselves, to speak for the interests of the public and the interests of those they are acting toward. Not what the "working girls" or the patients want, but what the speakers claim that they need. The speaker asserts that the condition of the dance halls is to be considered a problem even though others—the opposition—do not see it as such. The speaker represents herself to speak for a consensus—a "society," a "true public interest." The situation, as she presents it, is not one of divergent standards but of a consensual society and a deviant minority, a presumed normality and an abnormal condition. It is not a political issue between differing points-of-view and interests. It is a social problem and a united societal consensus affirms it.

Contested and Uncontested Meanings: Benevolence and Social Control

Writing about the state as parent, David Rothman (1981) has recently traced the history of "doing good" as an organized public endeavor. It was part of the legacy of the progressive movement—a legacy that lasted to the mid-1960s. The belief persisted that the problems of the dependent, the disadvantaged, the deviant, and the delinquent could be resolved through a top-down benevolence, "with the better off doing for the worse off" (Rothman 1981:xiii) and, importantly, with a minimum of alteration of the existing institutional structure.

In recent years the claims to benevolence as legitimating the authority of ownership have seemed to sociologists and others to be thin and unsubstantial. The critiques of the medicalization of social problems have stressed the social control aspects of welfare institutions, just as the critiques of poverty programs have stressed the political uses of welfare (Conrad and Schneider 1980; Szasz 1961; Goffman 1961; Piven and Cloward 1977). A stream of studies have documented the primacy of institutional self-preservation in the conduct of social problems organizations. In the very definition of situations as problems the social control elements emerge, whether or not the practitioners are aware of them. These studies have critiqued the claims of the "helping" professions to be helping "troubled persons" (Gusfield 1984).

The idea that there is a unity of concern or interest between those at the top who bestow their benevolence and those at the bottom who receive it is open to doubt. It cannot be maintained without the smirks and winks of skeptical critics. In the California case dealing with anti-psychotic drugs, the successful attorney for the mental patient, when interviewed by the press, said: "What this case essentially does is give the mentally ill the same rights as the mentally healthy. . . . Too often these drugs are used as a substitute for adequate staffing in the hospitals" (*Los Angeles Times* 1989).

The Transformation of Meanings and Problems

As a matter of rhetoric, a form of persuasion, the designation of a situation as a "social problem" involves the claim that a societal consensus exists. It has the effect of limiting or ignoring adversarial elements and turning the problem into a technical or legal one in which alternative frameworks are simply not thought about, not only in Miss Peach's class but in public arenas. The case of "child abuse" will make the point.

What Stephen Pfohl (1977) has called "the discovery of child abuse" occurred in the 1950s with the interpretation by radiologists that bruises and broken bones seen on X-rays of children could be interpreted as results of beatings by parents and guardians. When a prominent pediatrician reported these findings in an important medical journal, monitored regularly by the press, child abuse became a matter of public notice. The activities of the Children's Bureau and the mass media helped place it high on the public agenda (Nelson 1984). Between

1963 and 1967 every state passed some form of law requiring the reporting of child abuse incidents and providing for criminal charges.

"Child abuse" was defined as physical or sexual "abuse" by parents or guardians and consensus about it as a problem was close to complete. Systems of reporting, enforcement agencies, counselling for children and for abusing parents have developed a structure accommodated to the definition of the nature and deplorable character of "child abuse." The meaning of "child abuse" was clear. The problem was located within the family, as a matter of parental misbehavior.

In her study of child abuse and the making of a public agenda, the political scientist Barbara Nelson (1984) distinguished between "valence issues" and "position issues." She writes: "A valence issue such as child abuse elicits a single, strong, fairly uniform emotional response and does not have an adversarial quality. 'Position issues,' on the other hand, do not elicit a single response but instead engender alternative and sometimes highly conflictful responses" (Nelson 1984:27). This is similar to the distinction now being made in social movements literature between conflict movements and consensual movements (Lofland 1989; McCarthy 1988) or to that made by political scientists between consensus issues and conflict issues (Hayes 1981; Crenson 1971). Abortion is a conflict issue; pro-life and pro-choice are conflict movements and counter-movements. It was the absence of controversy, of adversaries, that made the child abuse legislation develop so rapidly, according to Nelson.

Yet Nelson's analysis of child abuse as a valence issue presumes that its character results from its content. Pfohl's description of the earlier child abuse movement of the late nineteenth century indicates the possibility that children might well be experienced as the subjects of a more politicized framework. The similar conception of "child neglect" in that period emphasized the homelessness and malnutrition of children of poverty and threw the onus on the social structure and public institutions which associated poverty with child neglect. This is a much more adversarial, more political definition of the "child abuse" problem. It touches on the institutional arrangements of social and political organization. It cannot be "handled" through reforming persons or law enforcement. There have been some efforts to counter the current emphasis on the problems of parental abuse of children with alternative conceptions or to emphasize the rights of parents against state intervention. However, these have not been mobilized to a point of converting the dominant definition of child abuse from an apolitical to a political one. It now is experienced through the concrete image of good people and bad people; villains and victims.

To be experienced as a "social problem" rather than a "political issue" is a significant step in the construction of phenomena in the public sphere. In his 1977 Presidential address for the Society for the Study of Social Problems, "The Politics of Speaking in the Name of Society," Bernard Beck (1978:357) pointed out that under the guise of a social problem many interests can be served: "working politicians have discovered the usefulness of conducting politics under the guise of treating social problems." Beck used the example of the deinstitutionalization of custodial organizations such as mental asylums. There, as in the case of the decriminalization of public drunkenness, action taken with an eye toward state budgets is justified as benevolence toward people with troubles. Politicians shun the conflicts that embitter and divide their electorates. They are happy when they can "turn over" issues to technicians or into legal decisions.

It is evident, just from the two cases described above—the 1912 dance hall and the 1989 mental patient decision—that the efforts to define situations as "social problems" are far from always successful. Some groups are capable of mobilizing to bring about change or to resist controlling definitions. The gay rights movement is perhaps the most salient example of how the ability to mobilize has enabled a subject group to transform its status. During this century, homosexuals have been thought of as sinful and as sick, objects of condemnation or of medical benevolence. What the gay rights movement did was to resist the public designation of deviance, of abnormality, by attacking the presumed norms and denying that homosexuality constituted a social problem. In the process the phenomenon of homosexuality lost its status as a "social problem" and became a matter of political and cultural conflict over the recognition of alternative sexual styles. What had been an uncontested meaning has been transformed into a political contest.

Again and again sociologists have pointed out how the conditions said to define the social problem are socially constructed, are only one of several possible "realities." The attempt to pose as the arbiters of standards is less and less taken for granted and more and more seen as an accompaniment to social control, to the quest for hegemony. Rothman (1981:87) writes, "As to any effort to define what constitutes normal sexual behavior—one has only to raise this point to recognize immediately how absurd any such attempt would be." The same is true of other areas that are becoming more adversarial, such as mental illness or juvenile delinquency as well as homosexuality. Perhaps George Bernard Shaw said it well when he wrote: "Do not do unto others what you would have others do unto you. Their tastes may be different."

The disposition to deny an adversarial quality to a social problem spills over into research as well. In the corpus of studies of alcohol I find very few that have studied the benefits of drinking and drunkenness. The standard study of the economic costs of alcohol makes little attempt to state the value of benefits of alcohol as well as its costs (Berry and Boland 1977; Weiner 1981:183-90). More importantly, there is no room for appreciation of the carnival point of view expressed by Omar Khayyam in the Rubaiyat:

> I often wonder what the vintner buys
> One-half so precious as the stuff he sells.

Mobilization for and the Transformation of Social Problems

I referred earlier to the gay rights movement as a striking example of how a mobilized social group has been able to bring about a change in the status of a social problem. The adversarial aspects of the alcohol problem are largely represented by the beer, whiskey, and wine industries. As a body, consumers are not well-mobilized. The National Rifle Association is a distinct and powerful exception. The alcohol question has emerged as either a matter of voluntary persuasion, as the alcoholism movement defined it, or, more recently, as a unilateral protection against "troublesome people" whose styles of leisure take on connotations of deviance and consequently need not be given much consideration.

I have been asserting the de-politicizing affects of professionalization and mass culture. Yet the situation is not as simple as a quick generalization might lead us to believe. Shifting interpretations of conditions are not at all inconsistent with some aspects of the professionalization process. The disease concept of alcoholism was both a shift in the character of the alcohol problem and a new interpretation of alcoholism. In the early 1970s this emphasis on "troubled persons" and medicalization underwent a transformation. The problems connected with alcohol were expanded and the drinker described as a "troublesome person."

This shift resulted both from the professions developed by the alcoholism movement and the appearance of new movements, such as Mothers Against Drunk Driving (MADD). The very existence of professionals and clients presents the facilities and occasions for mobilizing the clientele. The development of the National Institute on Alcohol Abuse and Alcoholism emerged out of the efforts of recovering alcoholics, organized in the National Council on Alcoholism, as well as the organization of alcohol treatment professionals. As champions of their clients they were able to mobilize them to achieve entitlements to treatment, to legislative protections, and to medical insurance. A similar process has been at work in the movements for the rights of mental patients and of prison inmates. Stigma becomes the basis of mobilization and entitlements in a manner we need to assess in understanding deviance in the modern society (Gusfield 1982). The entitlements associated with deviance suggest a power and a societal integration that clashes with conventional theory in sociology. In the welfare society deviance is a social status that obtains rights as well as obligations.

A clear instance of how these elements operated politically is evident in the raising of the minimum age of sale of alcohol to twenty-one. After the voting age was dropped to 18, most states lowered the minimum age of sale of alcohol to 18 or 19. Researchers concluded that the age group, 18 to 21, was a source of many deaths involving drinking-driving. The researchers also concluded that the 21-25 age group was even more "responsible" for such deaths, but no state even seriously considered extending the restriction to this fearfully more responsive group. Federal aid to highway construction was tied to state legislation raising the minimum age to twenty-one, and all 50 states passed such laws. The 18-21 group, the age group with lowest voting or political participation record, produced almost no opposition to the movement.

All of these movements are well within the meanings of an individualistic interpretation of social problems. They gloss over the possible role of institutional and structural features and, in this sense, depoliticize social problems. Yet any simple generalization should be resisted. The same movements and professions have played a key role in the emergence of what some are now calling "the new Temperance movement."

The more recent turn toward preventive policies that constitute considerations of industrial policy, of sales availability, of legal restrictions and liabilities, of automobile design, are products of the same movements that brought about the turn to criminalization. These do bring the problem into arenas of political conflict as they turn the alcohol problem away from medicalization and criminalization and towards a public health perspective (Beauchamp 1988). At the Surgeon-General's recent Workshop on Drunk Driving, advertisers and television networks, upset by the recommendation to restrict advertising, brought suit in an attempt to prevent the workshop from occurring.

In a way this paper, like most presidential addresses, is a sermon. The moral is not contained in any summative sentence but it is a plea to move the study of social problems closer to the study of how social movements and institutions affect and are affected by the interpretations, the language, and the symbols that constitute seeing a situation as a social problem. At the same time, we need to take care not to separate the study of meanings from the study of their historical and institutional settings.

As interpreters of social problems we earn our livings by other people's troubles. One person's poison is another's mead (not George Herbert or Margaret). What we can best contribute to assuage our guilt is to cast an ironical eye on the passing scene so as to make us all more aware of the possibilities and opportunities that the veils of cultural meanings and institutional arrangements hide from us. It is out of this humanistic self-awareness that societies may yet achieve some control over their own destinies.

References

Beauchamp, Daniel
    1988   The Health of the Republic. Philadelphia: Temple University Press.
Beck, Bernard
    1978   "The politics of speaking in the name of society." Social Problems 25:353-60.
Berry, Ralph and James Boland
    1977   The Economic Costs of Alcohol Abuse. New York: The Free Press.

440 GUSFIELD

Best, Joel
    1987   "Rhetoric in claims-making." Social Problems 34:101-21.
Briggs, Asa
    1961   "The welfare state in historical perspective." Archives of European Sociology 11:221-58.
Cawelti, John G.
    1976   Adventure, Mystery and Romance. Chicago: University of Chicago Press.
Conrad, Peter and Joseph W. Schneider
    1980   Deviance and Medicalization. St. Louis: C.V. Mosby.
Crenson, Matthew
    1971   The Un-Politics of Air Pollution. Baltimore: The Johns Hopkins University Press.
Edelman, Murray
    1977   Political Language. New York: Academic Press.
Ehrenreich, John H.
    1985   The Altruistic Imagination. Ithaca, N.Y.: Cornell University Press.
Ericson, Richard, Patricia Baranek, and Janet Chan
    1987   Visualizing Deviance. Toronto: University of Toronto Press.
Friedman, Lawrence
    1985.   Total Justice. New York: Russell Sage.
Goffman, Erving
    1961   Asylums. Garden City, N.Y.: Doubleday.
Gouldner, Alvin
    1970   The Coming Crisis of Western Sociology. New York: Basic Books.
Gusfield, Joseph R.
    1981   The Culture of Public Problems. Chicago: University of Chicago Press.
    1982   "Deviance in the welfare state." In Research in Social Problems and Public Policy, vol. 2, ed. Michael Lewis, 1-20. New York: JAI Press.
    1984   "On the side: practical action and social constructivism in social problems theory." In Studies in the Sociology of Social Problems, ed. Joseph W. Shneider and John I. Kitsuse, 31-51. Norwood, N.J.: Ablex.
Harring, Sidney
    1983   Policing a Class Society: The Experience of American Cities, 1865-1915. New Brunswick, N.J.: Rutgers University Press
Hayes, Michael
    1981   Lobbyists and Legislators. New Brunswick, N.J.: Rutgers University Press.
Heilbroner, Robert
    1989   "Reflections on capitalism." The New Yorker Magazine January 23:98-109.
Lofland, John
    1989   "Consensus movements: city twinning and derailed dissent in the American eighties." In Research in Social Movements, Conflict and Change, ed. Louis Kreisberg, 163-96. New York: JAI Press.
Los Angeles Times
    1989   "Mental patients allowed to refuse drugs. June 24.
McCarthy, John D.
    1988   "Exploring sources of rapid social movement growth." (Unpublished manuscript).
Mills, C. Wright
    1943   "The professional ideology of social pathologists." American Journal of Sociology 49:165-80. Reprinted in Power, Politics and People: The Collected Essays of C. Wright Mills, ed. Irving Horowitz, 525-52. New York: Ballantine Books, 1963.
Morgan, Patricia
    1980   "The state as mediator: alcohol problem management in the postwar world." Contemporary Drug Problems 9:107-36.
Nelson, Barbara
    1984   Making an Issue of Child Abuse. Chicago: University of Chicago Press.
Pfohl, Stephen
    1977   "The discovery of child abuse." Social Problems 24:310-23.
Piven, Frances Fox and Richard Cloward
    1977   Poor People's Movements. New York: Vintage Books.

Rothman, David
    1981   "The state as parent." In Doing Good, ed. Willard Gaylin, Ira Glasser, Steven Marcus, and David J. Rothman, 69-96. New York: Pantheon Books.

Stivers, Richard
    1988   "The concealed rhetoric of sociology: social problem as a symbol of evil." (Unpublished manuscript).

Szasz, Thomas
    1961   The Myth of Mental Illness. New York: Harper.

Weinberg, Ian
    1974   "Social problems that are no more." In Handbook of the Study of Social Problems, ed. Erwin Smigel, 637-72. Chicago: Rand McNally.

Weiner, Carolyn
    1981   The Politics of Alcoholism. New Brunswick, N.J.: Transaction Books.

2 Security and control in capitalist societies: the fetishism of security and the secret thereof
Steven Spitzer

> And you all know security is mortals' chiefest enemy.
> Hecate to the three witches in *Macbeth* (Shakespeare 1954: Act III, Scene 5, p. 59)

> *Security* is the supreme social concept of civil society, the concept of the *police*, the concept that the whole society exists only to guarantee to each of its members the preservation of his person, his rights, and his property ... Civil society does not raise itself above its egoism through the concept of security. Rather, security is the *guarantee* of the egoism.
> Karl Marx (1843) commenting on the French constitution of 1793 (1967, p. 236)

> In ... the religious world ... the productions of the human brain appear as independent beings endowed with life, and entering into relation both with one another and the human race. So it is in the world of commodities with the products of men's hands. This I call the Fetishism which attaches itself to the products of labour, so soon as they are produced as commodities, and which is therefore inseparable from the production of commodities.
> Karl Marx, *Capital*, Vol. 1, (1974, p. 77)

This chapter seeks to unravel some of the threads in the process through which security is transformed into a commodity and then bought and sold through a market system. A number of economic, political and ideological developments are explored in order to better understand the commodification of security and its fetishistic character in capitalist societies. But the commodification and fetishism of security are not taken as significant simply because they are associated with the rise of 'private justice' or institutions of 'private policing' in these societies — developments which are discussed elsewhere in this volume and which are clearly real and dramatic enough in their own right. Even more important, it is argued, are the links between these transformations and a broader and deeper set of changes in the ordering and disordering of modern life. Thus, while this analysis is very much concerned with the sources and consequences of the 'privatization' of policing and other control arrangements, this concern is rooted in a more general effort to critique and improve upon existing accounts of how modern systems of social control under capitalism have come into existence, how they operate, and what they might become in the years ahead.

44 Transcarceration: Essays in the Sociology of Social Control

The chapter begins by exploring the way in which security is a commodity, how security is related to the commodity system, and some of the definitional problems associated with the study of security markets. The utility of Marx's analysis of the fetishism of commodities is then explored as a framework for the study of security in capitalist societies. The framework is criticized in an effort to move beyond the conceptual and historical limitations of Marx's model, and to delineate a number of more productive directions in interpretation and research. To more effectively investigate these directions, a new perspective on security and social control is developed. Through this perspective it becomes possible to reassess the commodification of social control practices and products in capitalist societies, and to critique the existing range of state-centred theories of social control. Following a specific discussion of why 'commodity control' is both underestimated and misunderstood by many control theorists, a number of specific connections between security and modern capitalism are explored. These connections are investigated with special attention to the current mechanisms and strategies of 'private' control, and provide a framework for moving beyond forms of control which remain tied to either a decentralized and fragmented commerce in security on the one hand (the tyranny of the market), or a remote and interest-serving political apparatus (the tyranny of the state) on the other.

Security and the commodity system
The *Oxford English Dictionary* defines the condition of 'security' in terms of protection from danger; safety; and freedom from doubt, care, anxiety or apprehension. To be secure is to be assured, confident and safe. The central question that faces us is: how can this condition and the feelings that surround it be turned into a commodity that can be purchased in the market-place?

At first blush, the boundaries around security services and products appear to be clear. The security commodity is something that is produced and consumed to make people feel safe, free from doubt, care, anxiety or apprehension. Yet upon closer examination a problem appears: since efforts to achieve safety, freedom from danger, assurance and confidence are essential features of everyday life under capitalist (as well as many other kinds of social) arrangements, it is necessary to distinguish between those aspects of the 'security market' which have emerged to address directly the safety of persons and property, and those whose connection to security is less tangible and direct. While this distinction between direct and indirect security effects need not detain us for long, it is clear that the boundary between the two may be difficult to draw.

Security and control in capitalist societies 45

As we will see in the discussion below, the perceived dangerousness and uncertainty of social existence, and the many forms and forces of 'insecurity' and 'risk' are an important ingredient in many decisions to enter the market-place, irrespective of the commodity sought. The attractiveness and market value of a broad range of commodities is enhanced precisely because they promise a greater degree of safety and freedom from anxiety than their alternatives. Because safety (like love, happiness, prosperity, and fulfilment) is a social need which can be activated in a wide range of decisions to consume, virtually all commodities can be invested with the 'aura' of security — that is, presented, promoted, and ultimately consumed because of their ostensible ability to free the consumer from worry, trouble, and harm.

This interpenetration between specialized security products and services, and other products and services which are more attractive because they make us feel more secure, can be seen most vividly on the boundary between private goods and public miseries — a boundary which is relevant to the relationship between the 'privatization of profit' and the 'socialization of costs' (Birnbaum 1969; O'Connor 1973) in capitalist societies. Consumers buy private houses in 'good neighbourhoods' rather than suffer the ravages of public housing, use 'safe' private automobiles rather than 'risky' public transportation, enrol their children in 'wholesome' private rather than 'dangerous' public schools, and patronize expensive and highly trained (read trustworthy) medical specialists rather than rely upon either the overextended and primitive facilities of public clinics or the ministrations of lay healers.

Whatever the security value of commodities such as these, the decision to purchase them does not depend exclusively on their status as security products. This is also true of the security features of many products (for example, tamper-proof caps on over-the-counter drugs, anti-theft devices as standard equipment on automobiles, hotels with safes for valuables) which may enhance the attractiveness of the product without transforming it into a security device. In this sense, it is defensible to distinguish commodities which are purchased on the assumption that their primary function is to protect consumers from dangers to property and persons (for example, guard dogs, karate lessons, burglar alarms and 'risk' analyses) from those whose relationship to the reduction of anxiety and uncertainty is less direct. While we are more concerned with the former category in my subsequent analysis, it is also clear that specific markets in security arise in conjunction with, and are deeply embedded in, broader preoccupations with making micro- and macro-environments more secure. This pattern, tied as it is to a generalized paranoia and malaise in capitalist societies, means that security commodities can never be completely differentiated from commodities which are invested with

46 Transcarceration: Essays in the Sociology of Social Control

'security' attributes or generate 'security' effects. Indeed, it is this very confusion that lies, as we shall see, at the heart of the system of what we will call 'commodity control'.

Once we acknowledge the fact that the commodification of security is intimately related to our individual and collective feelings of insecurity, it is clear that any analysis of this process must investigate the subjectivity of the consumer and understand the forces shaping his or her 'security needs'. This is no less true for the corporation that undertakes an extensive programme of 'access control', 'loss prevention' and 'risk analysis' than for the individual who purchases an inexpensive security device. That these 'needs' may be redefined, expanded or contracted under many different conditions of social and political organization is obvious. What seems to be less obvious, at least to those who have studied security in capitalist societies, is that the study of security needs cannot be undertaken wholly from without. We must also be willing to enter the mist-enveloped regions of fear and desire (Ewen and Ewen 1982), and place emotion at the centre of the analysis.

Very few students of the security industry — 'critical', 'apologetic', or otherwise — have felt comfortable in analysing security in this way. It is far easier to remain in the realm of rational calculation, assuming that both the producers and the consumers of security services and devices are motivated by nothing more than that standard ingredient of bourgeois psychology — self-interest. And even though some critics have pointed out the ways in which security protects the interests of some at the expense of others (see Klare 1975; Shearing and Stenning 1981, 1983, 1985), these inquiries have, for the most part, remained wedded to the rationalistic discourse of 'rights' and 'interests', identifying the central dangers of the security industry as its encroachment on the civil liberties of the population. The problem with this approach is not only, as I will argue below, that it focuses too single-mindedly on the relationship between the controllers and the controlled, but also that it assumes that security can be understood without examining the hopes and fears of those who are willing, in ever increasing numbers, to purchase it in the market-place.[1]

The rise of structural explanations of the emergence and transformation of the security industry (see Shearing and Stenning 1985; Spitzer and Scull 1977, 1980) have not solved this problem. Rather, they have diverted attention from it by concentrating on the linkages between security activities and the patterning of political and economic life. And in so far as it is easier to impute rationality, if not omniscience, to corporate actors (both corporate producers and corporate consumers of the security commodity), those accounts which focus on the rationalization of security under corporate capitalism

(Shearing and Stenning 1981, 1983, 1985) also tend to ignore the subjective side of the security problem. The point here is not simply that this inattention leads to an assumption of rationality where there is really 'irrationality' or 'pseudo-rationality' at best, but that we must be much more sensitive to the relationship between the subjective dimensions of security and insecurity and the objective dimensions of social control.

A final point about the problems surrounding the analysis of security as a commodity: security is especially difficult to study in so far as it is primarily defined in negative terms. In other words, security is said to exist when something *does not* occur rather than when it does. Security in the more restricted sense in which it is used here exists when stores are not robbed, pedestrians are not molested, computer codes not broken, and executives and their family members are able to enjoy life free from threats, assassinations or kidnapping. In more general terms, we are secure when we can negotiate our daily existence without encountering the pitfalls and catastrophes which might conceivably befall us. Because security depends upon the *absence* of a certain range of foreseeable and unforeseeable events, conditions and activities, it is extremely difficult to specify what contributes or fails to contribute to security in any given case. Two contradictions are exposed through this realization. On the one hand, while security is presented as a sound, 'calculated', and 'rational' investment, it is an investment which is based on 'faith' — faith in the possibility, or (in the case of more sophisticated analyses) the probability, of achieving control over an unpredictable, risky and ultimately unknowable world. On the other hand, while the growth of capitalism depends, as Marx and Engels (1967, p.83) observed, on a 'constant revolutionizing of production, uninterrupted disturbance of all social relations, everlasting uncertainty and agitation', so that 'all that is solid melts into air' (see Berman 1982), the security market seems to have emerged as a profoundly conservative and defensive epicycle within this more general process. To be secure is to be safe, but to be safe is to be moribund — at least within the general logic of the capitalist system.

The first contradiction leads us in the direction of analysing security as a new form of 'magic' within a system that eschews the invisible and the unknowable. As we will see in the discussion below, because the full significance of this paradox remains poorly understood, there is a tendency to take the security complex too much on its own terms and, in consequence, fail to understand the inherent limits on the growth and effectiveness of security markets. The second contradiction forces us to confront, in a somewhat different way, the tensions between capitalist development and the security fetish. The security fetish may not only lead to restrictions on the forces which threaten to undermine

48   Transcarceration: Essays in the Sociology of Social Control

the capitalist order (this is the thrust of much of the Marxist critique of security: see Klare 1975; South 1984; Weiss 1978), it may also lead to restrictions on the development of capital itself. Security remains a conservative force which, like freedom, must — at least in bourgeois society (see Marx 1967; Neumann 1957, Ch. 6) — define itself in terms of freedom *from* some unwelcome intrusion, usurpation, or limitation. In this sense, it can become a fetter on, as well as condition for, capitalist growth. Security, as Gorz has indicated, always implies the preservation of 'an established order against whatever seems to threaten, disturb or endanger it from without or from within' (1984, p. 158). Viewed in this way, it is clear that security, even when it is being provided by and sold to capitalists, may paralyse as well as protect the forces of capitalist innovation. And if capitalism requires uncertainty for its development *as a system*, but individual actors and organizations need to reduce uncertainty to operate and profit, then security clearly stands in a complex and contradictory relationship to capitalist vitality and growth.

The security hieroglyph: Marx's method and beyond

In Section 4 of the first volume of *Capital*, Marx (1974) discusses 'The fetishism of commodities and the secret thereof'. He begins by suggesting that while commodities are actually nothing mysterious, within capitalist society they are changed into something transcendental and mystical. The essence of this transformation involves, according to Marx, the same kind of alienation that is found in the religious world (see the opening quote from *Capital* vol. I, p. 77).

The key for Marx is the separation of a commodity from its maker and its objectification — a process through which the social character of (wo)man's labour takes on what Lukacs (1971, pp. 83-222) has called a 'phantom objectivity' and confronts him/her as if it had a life of its own. Marx's purpose in attempting to decipher the hieroglyphic of the commodity is to reveal the secret behind the power that our social products seem to have over our lives — a power which both sanctifies the commodity and obscures the real relationship between the process of labour and its results. He is especially concerned with this second feature of the fetishism of commodities since he hopes to use this line of argument not only to demystify the capitalist system, but also to demonstrate the validity of his labour theory of value. Thus, for Marx, the essence of the commodity system resides in the fact that the commodities we worship are no more magical than the idols worshipped by primitive tribes; they are artifacts and images which are, in the final analysis, neither more nor less than the product of human minds and hands.

Security and control in capitalist societies 49

Applying this line of reasoning to the study of the security commodity it is clear that we have much to learn from Marx's insights. First, and perhaps most important, are the questions that Marx forces us to confront about the origins of security. Where does security come from? Who and what really makes us secure (both objectively and subjectively)? Why and how has security been separated from its true social context in human association and turned into something which seems to be beyond our control? These questions not only focus our attention on the contrasts between security under commodified and non-commodified conditions, they also lead us to ask further questions about the historical process through which those living under pre-capitalist social arrangements gradually lost touch with the real sources of security as a social process. Why is it that for most of human history and in many different social and cultural contexts, day-to-day security was provided through systems of self-help (Black 1980) — what Marx would call 'natural production units' — in which the participants were both the providers and the recipients of the security 'service'? How did the producers of security emerge as a specialized and distinctive class and why have the non-producers become so dependent on the goods and services they provide? Finally, what explains the emergence of security systems that are both alienated from those who really produce them *and* controlled through non-market forms of administration and allocation?

The last question in this interrogatory leads us to ponder why the reification and objectification of security takes place within the arena of the market-place rather than through the 'public' institutions of the state. This issue, of course, has been at the heart of those studies that have focused on the relationship between public and private policing (Hallcrest 1985; Scott and McPherson 1971; Shearing and Stenning 1981). A full understanding of the fetishism of security necessarily leads us into an analysis of the 'publicization' (cf. Spitzer 1975b, 1983a; Spitzer and Scull 1977; Unger 1976) as well as the 'privatization' (Spitzer and Scull 1980) of security, a path that would take us too far afield. At this juncture we may simply note that the commodification of security is not the only way in which the objective and subjective control of safety and protection have been wrested from, or relinquished by, those who need it; it is, however, a form of usurpation which is difficult, although not impossible, to imagine outside of a commodity system.[2]

Returning to the question of whether Marx's general approach to the fetishism of commodities can be fruitfully applied to the investigation of the peculiar commodity of security, it is apparent that there are many directions which we might want to pursue. Basic to all of these, however, is the examination of the 'dehumanized and dehumanizing function of the commodity relation' (Lukacs 1971, p. 92). Following the thrust of Marx's argument, the commodification of security means not only that security is alienated from our control and understanding, but also that the search for security through commodities — like the search for other forms of fulfillment within the commodity system — becomes a fundamentally 'alienating' experience in its own right. Instead of bringing us closer together and strengthening the bonds of community and society, the security commodity becomes a means of setting us apart. This is not only true in so far as we literally build walls around ourselves, but also in the sense that the search for market-based security makes the possibilities of genuine co-operation more remote. Paradoxically, the more we enter into relationships to obtain the security commodity, the more insecure we feel; the more we depend upon the commodity rather than each other to keep us safe and confident, the less safe and confident we feel; the more we divide the world into those who are able to enhance our security and those who threaten it, the less we are able to provide it for ourselves.

The 'quest for security'[3] through the market thus not only sets us apart from each other and leads us to see those beyond the commodity relationship as threats rather than resources, it may also directly contribute to a sense of insecurity as well. As Slater has observed, possessions may actually generate scarcity because 'the more emotion one invests in them the more chances for significant gratification are lost — the more committed to them one becomes the more deprived one feels, like a thirsty man drinking salt water' (1970, pp. 108–9). In the present context this means that one of the consequences of the commodification of security may be a growing inability to return to or re-invent a variety of non-commodified relationships within which 'true' security might be achieved. Or, as Gorz (1984) has argued, the striving for security, when it is removed from real human needs and possibilities, may become one of the most important barriers to both *feeling* and *being* secure — especially in a world where, as Orwell might have put it, 'war is peace'.

But however suggestive observations of this sort might be, a preoccupation with the alienated and alienating character of security may also lead us astray. If we become too obsessed with the relationship between commodities and their producers it is difficult to attend to other dimensions of the commodification process. Despite the tendency of many Marxists to treat the study of consumption as epiphenomenal, we might learn more about security in contemporary capitalist societies by exploring its relationship to the sphere of consumption than to the sphere of production.

Starting from the premise that both the capitalist system and its security 'needs' have been revolutionized in the years since Marx's breakthrough, and recognizing that the commodification of security has had as much to do with the changing forms of capitalist organization as with the unchanging characteristics of the commodity form,[4] we can begin to fashion a perspective that builds upon, but is not limited to, Marx's model of commodification.

As has already been pointed out, although security has become a commodity in modern capitalist societies, it is a peculiar one indeed since security is a derivative rather than a primary commodity form. Unlike the table which is transformed directly from wood in Marx's (1974, p.77) example in *Capital*, security is a commodity which is neither directly available to the senses nor defined exclusively in physical terms. At bottom, security remains a quality which is derived from rather than constituted within the physical commodity itself. This becomes obvious when we recognize that security 'uses' are in no sense the only uses to which 'security commodities' may be put: consider the gun that wounds its owner, the dog who licks the burglar, or the alarm that goes off for no apparent reason.

Moreover, there is a second step in the creation of the security commodity that is not present in the types of transformations with which Marx was concerned. Not only must the commodity be created physically (as in the manufacture of a fence from wood), but for security to assume a marketable form it must be created symbolically as well. This symbolic work defines the actual 'uses' to which security is put, since the relationship between the physical product and its uses (that is, its 'use value') is in no sense as straightforward or transparent as Marx's discussion would lead us to believe. And once we realize that use value is not simply a functionally specific, 'natural' and 'real' standard against which we can measure the objectified and 'artificial' character of 'exchange value', then it becomes increasingly difficult to claim that we have demystified the commodity form. If commodities such as security actually have fluctuating and variable 'use values' (see Baudrillard 1975), as well as fluctuating and variable 'exchange values', then a large part of the analysis of these commodities must move beyond the study of commodity production as a physical process. This is especially true to the extent that a commodity, such as security, is constituted primarily through a process of symbolic production — through the transformation of images and expectations as much as, if not more than, alterations of the material world.

From this perspective, security is one of those commodities which possesses a virtually limitless ability to absorb signifiers. Security attributes of various products and services are presented as an unqualified good in so far as they promise us freedom from fear, doubt, uncertainty, predation, and so forth. Like many other commodities, security takes on what Buxton (1983) has called 'enhanced use value'.

52 Transcarceration: Essays in the Sociology of Social Control

In contrast to the conception of 'use value' developed by Marx — a conception based on an assumption of direct functional use — enhanced use value does *not* inhere within the commodity itself; it is created, rather, through a loading of the commodity with special symbolic value. This value is not established in a vacuum or through the practical 'uses' to which the commodity is put; it is created, rather, through the organization of life around specific 'lifestyles' or modes of consumption. Clothing, music and food, as well as forms of transportation, housing, and recreation are not simply alternative means of consumption in capitalist (and perhaps many socialist) societies; they are symbolic arenas within which the meaning and significance of social objects and practices are defined. Viewed in this way, commodities clearly perform a number of important functions. Among these are the abilities to:

1. Identify consumers with specific values, customs and activities;
2. Differentiate and socially order consumers according to shifting assessments of social worth; and
3. Provide forms of transient bonding within what Boorstin (1973) has called 'consumption communities'.

Whether we choose to focus on the signalling, separating, or bonding functions of the modern commodity system, one thing is clear: any analysis of security as a commodity must involve a study of the social roots and consequences of the 'loading' that all commodities undergo in the 'culture of consumption' (Fox and Lears 1983).

The new commodity system is thus fetishistic in a double sense. Not only does the commodity take on meanings which are divorced from the process of production out of which it has been created, but those meanings are themselves socially organized and imputed through another kind of production — the production of claims, promises and representations by the modern industries of advertising and marketing (Ewen 1975; Ewen and Ewen 1982; Williams 1958). This second layer of production, a process of which Marx could have been only dimly aware, requires a fundamental rethinking of what it is that is actually being bought and sold in the operation of the commodity system. Rather than arguing that commodities can be meaningfully measured against, and defined in terms of, some utilitarian standard of 'needs' and 'uses', it is far more desirable to see the products of these two 'layers' of production as composed of 'bundles of attributes' (Leiss 1976). And it is within these attributes and their social construction that we find the secret of the security fetish. Even where the security industry justifies its social contribution in terms of specific technological devices and tangible security products, it is clear that the meaning of these products is based on the very 'bundles of attributes' of which Leiss speaks — attributes which become 'progressively more unstable, temporary collections of objective and imputed characteristics — that is, highly complex material-symbolic entities' (Leiss 1976, p. 89). Under these conditions the commodity becomes 'infinitely divisible and divorced from any cognitively stable context' (Agnew 1983, p. 71). It becomes, in other words, increasingly difficult to know what one has actually bought. In the case of security this problem is especially striking since, as has already been noted, the relationship between what makes us secure and insecure is always problematic.

It can be seen, therefore, that the process of commodification comes to be increasingly embedded in, and dependent upon, the social organization of consumption. And further, this process comes to reflect the more general transformations that have taken place in the movement of capitalism from a system based on accumulation and expansion of the means of production to one based upon disaccumulation (Sklare 1969) and the creation of a system of mass distribution and consumption (Ewen 1975; Lears 1981). While the complexities of this revolution *within* capitalism cannot be developed here, it is clear that it has profoundly altered the 'laws of motion' of the capitalist system and placed 'symbolic' commodities like security at the heart, rather than the periphery, of its organization.

The analysis of security is further complicated by the fact that much of the market in security commodities consists in the purchase and sale of services — activities which are defined as successful when they leave no visible alteration of the status quo, much less bring into being a physical product. The development of the 'service economy' (Singlemann 1978) and its increasing significance for the survival of capitalist arrangements were never fully appreciated by Marx, who viewed services primarily as the work of the 'unproductive classes' (Marx 1969, vol. I, pp. 401-7; 1973, pp. 468-9) and defined the market in services as extraneous to, and derivative from, capital accumulation. Treating the income derived from services as mere 'money' or 'revenue' rather than 'capital', Marx (1969, vol. I, p. 402) would have had a difficult time incorporating 'service industries', such as today's security corporations, within his analytical model. His materialism and 'productivist' orientation enabled Marx to penetrate the 'mist-enveloped' region of the physical commodity, yet it left him ill-equipped to investigate commodities whose 'use value' was realized through their non-material or extra-material effects. While it is possible to argue that services purchased by individuals, groups and organizations are ultimately justified in terms of, and become profitable through, their support for the system of material production, it is far more difficult — at least within the confines of an orthodox Marxist approach — to explain why these services have assumed such a central position in the expansion and transformation of modern capitalist

54 Transcarceration: Essays in the Sociology of Social Control

arrangements. For this reason, we must look beyond Marx's analysis of the commodity to grasp the full meaning and implications of the new 'trade in security'.

Taken together, the enhanced use value and service aspects of the security commodity lead us to a rethinking of the relationship between security and the capitalist system. This rethinking encourages us to explore the consumption side of the production-consumption link as well as the specific changes in the economic organization of capitalism that have taken place over the last seventy-five years. Perhaps the most visible symptom of these changes has been the rise of the 'culture of consumption'.

Described by a growing number of critical historians concerned with the significance of consumption within modern capitalist societies (Agnew 1983; Ewen and Ewen 1982; Fox and Lears 1983; Leiss 1976; Williams 1958), the culture of consumption has been traced to 'the maturation of the national market-place, including the establishment of national advertising; the emergence of a new stratum of professionals and managers, rooted in a web of complex new organizations (corporations, government, universities, professional associations, media, foundations, and others); and the rise of a new gospel of therapeutic release preached by a host of writers, publishers, ministers, social scientists, doctors, and the advertisers themselves' (Fox and Lears 1983, p. xi). The implications of these developments can be no more than sketched here, but their significance for our purposes is the way in which they have contributed to a hegemonic 'way of seeing' in contemporary capitalist societies.

This way of seeing is connected, on the one hand, with the rise of a social world where 'it increasingly *makes sense* that if solutions are to be had, they can be bought' (Ewen and Ewen 1982, p. 42), and, on the other hand, with the cultivation and shaping of polyvalent cultural symbols and their investment in the consuming act — an investment wherein the '*commodity* increasingly invades the realm of satisfaction' (Ewen and Ewen 1982, p. 262).

But this invasion is never launched in a vacuum; it is based, as one marketing specialist has observed, on striking the 'responsive chord' (Schwartz 1974, p. 65) in the consumer. Since all potential consumers have stored within them a 'lifetime of experiences', it is up to the advertising specialist to 'provide the stimuli to regenerate those experiences, bring them into the foreground, and associate them with the product' (Schwartz 1974, p. 65). The problem thus becomes one of tapping into a *self* which is the 'haunted repository of sensitivity, vulnerability, and emotion, or need and desire' (Ewen and Ewen 1982, p. 262). There are two directions in which this process has moved in contemporary capitalist societies:

1. Toward a stimulation and channelling of desires; and
2. Toward a stimulation and channelling of fears.

For the security commodity, and those who promote and sell it, it is the second of these processes which is decisive. To be more specific, the hegemony of the security commodity is complete when the ravages of insecurity (anxiety, doubt, uncertainty, and a whole range of concrete and generalized fears) are 'only a reminder to those who have not yet bought the right product' (Ewen and Ewen 1982, p. 74).

Towards a new conception of security and control
Over the last several years, a number of important contributions have been made to the analysis of social control (Black 1984a,b; Cohen 1985a; Cohen and Scull 1983; Davis and Anderson 1983; Garland and Young 1983). In contrast to the functionalist approach to theorizing about social control (cf. Janowitz 1975), each of these works has placed the state and public coercion at the centre of the drama surrounding the investigation of rules and rule-breaking. While this shift toward state-centred explanations has been valuable in many respects, it has also created a new problem: the tendency to overestimate the role of the state and underestimate the role of the market in interpreting how social control actually operates in capitalist societies. To the extent that advanced capitalist societies, with a few exceptions such as South Africa, are less likely to depend on the state and public institutions to achieve social control and more likely to resort to the market and 'private' mechanisms to effect the ordering of social life (Lindblom 1977), this tendency has distorted and truncated the analysis of social control. The consequences of this preoccupation with what might be described as an Orwellian/panoptic vision of state-centred control are significant — not only because this view misrepresents the dynamics of coercion in most Western societies, but also because it lessens our ability to work toward a better understanding of how politics and markets are related in the orchestration of coercive control across societies and over time. Such an understanding is indispensable in assessing the role of security in modern states.

Whether we begin with Weber's 'bureaucratization of the world' (Bendix 1960, pp. 421–2), Foucault's (1977) 'technologies of power', Bentham's (1843) 'panoptic vision', or Orwell's (1949) 'Big Brother', it is clear that much of modern theorizing about social control and the 'revisionist' history that has grown up along with it (Cohen 1985a, p. 13) seeks to develop a link between the purposes and 'functions' of social control on the one hand and the development of public bureaucracies on the other. While some explanations focus more on the institutions of public power themselves and others on those who gain access to them,

56 Transcarceration: Essays in the Sociology of Social Control

all are agreed that it is within the state's power to manipulate, dominate and constrain that we are to discover the secrets of social control in the modern age. Tracing the causes and effects of social control back to the operations of a reified 'state' and the elites who control it means that even in those instances when it appears that social control has become *less* repressive — through what Cohen (1985a, p. 31) calls the 'destructuring impulse' — it is still the state and its agenda of repression that are both the engine and beneficiary of social control. While there is little doubt that states have expanded their ability to regulate populations through the growth and legitimation of political institutions (Giddens 1985; Poggi 1978; Spitzer 1975a, 1983a) it is also true that the ways in which obedience is orchestrated in specific nation states will differ significantly over space and time (Spitzer 1983a). To the extent that the state-centred model overlooks the operation of informal and privatized systems of social control within 'totalitarian' societies (cf. Abel 1982a; Gross 1984), it is seriously flawed. But even more serious problems become apparent when we try to apply this model to understand how social control operates in 'weak states' (Hamilton and Sutton 1984; Skowronek 1982) — those Western capitalist societies in which 'free enterprise' has penetrated everyday life far more effectively and thoroughly than the state.

The paradox surrounding revisionist theories of social control is thus that they seek to link social control to political organization in those very societies in which the link is least developed, while ignoring the role played by economic organization in regulating social life. Focusing exclusively on political institutions, these theorists have failed to appreciate two important facts:

1. Capitalist societies are structurally different from non-capitalist societies in the sense that economic institutions are explicitly separated from political institutions; and
2. There is often a reciprocal relationship between political and economic control — political controls are most needed when economic controls break down, but most likely to prove counter-productive when economic institutions are operating smoothly (Wolfe 1977).

To clarify the relationship between economic and political organization under capitalism, it is important to remember that 'Capitalism is the first mode of production in history in which the means whereby surplus is pumped out of the direct producer is "purely" economic in form — the wage contract: the equal exchange between free agents which reproduces, hourly and daily, inequality and oppression. All other ... modes of exploitation operate through *extra-economic* sanctions — kin, customary, religious, legal or political'

(Anderson 1974, p.403). In other words, capitalism operates most effectively when social control is exercised *outside* of the economic system, while all other modes of production (including slavery, feudalism and arguably state-socialist command economies) depend upon an explicit and direct connection among economic, political and 'social' controls. What this means in practice is that we are most likely to see social regulation equated with political regulation in societies *without* 'official' markets in labour and other commodities. It also means that advanced capitalist societies, in contrast to the type of society envisioned by Orwell, must rely to a far greater extent on the social organization of need and gratification (an economic process) than the social organization of fear and terror (a political process).

To talk about the social organization of needs is to enter a terrain upon which very few social control theorists have been willing to tread. One reason for this is that most attempts to develop a critical perspective on social control (see Cohen and Scull 1983) have tried to break with the habit of examining the subjective states of the controlled. The motives, expectations and orientations of rule-breakers were a favourite topic of those (for example, Mead, Park and Burgess, Parsons, Ross) who equated the study of social control with the problem of internalizing social expectations. But in throwing out the 'bathwater' of older and one-sided 'socialization' models, we must be careful not to abandon the 'baby' that links social organization and social control — a link that is mediated as much by the consciousness, desires and goals of those who are to be controlled as the interests and agendas of the controllers.

To seriously consider the role played by needs in the organization of social control, attention must be focused on the ways in which fears and desires are channelled through social institutions. The market is one such institution, and an important one in the sense that it presents itself as an arena of free choice. When the market mediates human relationships it is the process of 'choice' rather than 'constraint' that governs associations. And in so far as people 'choose' the solutions to their problems and the methods of their own personal fulfilment, we need a model which goes beyond the concept of control as constraint. Control and constraint are often used synonymously; yet it is clear that in capitalist societies choice may be far more basic to the ordering of social life. From this perspective, any theory of social control must not only understand the ways in which control is exercised through what is prevented or punished, but also through what is allowed (D'Amico 1978, p.89). It is in this second sense that social control comes to be defined as 'the very mechanism which ties the individual to his society' — a mechanism which 'is anchored in the new needs which it has produced' (Marcuse 1964, p.9).

58 Transcarceration: Essays in the Sociology of Social Control

Shifting the study of social control from the context of constraint and deprivation to the context of choice and gratification requires a rethinking of the relationship among power, material conditions and subjective states. The central ingredients in the psychology of control under Fascism — material deprivation, identification with a powerful political leader and aggression toward internal and external enemies (Reich 1970) — are remote from the workings of modern capitalist systems. Most striking in this regard are the ways in which indulgence has replaced denial, and patterns of inclusion/exclusion are far more orientated toward 'consumption communities' and 'lifestyles' than races and nation states. While security and power may certainly be provided by identification with the state, it is the micro-environment of everyday consumption that most strongly addresses the anxieties of the masses. In this context, security becomes a personal and immediate concern, a problem which is much more likely to be solved by purchasing the right product or service than by either persecuting an objectionable minority or conquering the world.

In refining our view of security and control in modern capitalist states, it is important to remember that punishment and coercion have by no means ceased to perform a number of key political functions. The growth of private security has in no sense signalled the end of public coercion. What it has done, however, is to help establish a two-tiered and interdependent system of social control.[5] For those on the top tier, the market promises an escape (albeit largely illusionary) from the dangers, discomforts, and depredations of existence under capitalism; for the rest of society it is the state or 'community' that must be called upon to provide relief. Much like the other areas within which public and private sectors intertwine (that is, education, health care, transportation, and so on), each successive failure of the state provides yet another opportunity for the expansion of the market. In a society in which the collective responsibilities are taken seriously, the failure of public organizations and agencies to provide basic security would be the basis for a legitimacy crisis. But when individuals confront the social environment as consumers rather than citizens, the purchase of security represents a far more reliable and profitable choice. It is perhaps the ultimate irony that this choice, despite its short-run virtues, continues to undermine the possibilities for equality and community — two of the most important ingredients in any society which is to be both 'social' and 'secure'.

Endnotes

1. The growth of private security is documented in *The Hallcrest Report* (1985, p.112) which concludes that 'private protection resources (sic) significantly outnumber combined local, state and federal sworn law enforcement personnel and guards by a ratio of nearly 2 to 1'.
2. Early forms of 'thief-taking' and other varieties of 'putting-out' security served as precursors to the development of publicly organized and supported systems of policing. For a full account of this process in the areas of both policing and imprisonment see Spitzer and Scull (1977a/b).
3. A fascinating glimpse into the developing conception of the security commodity can be found in *Man's Quest for Security* (1966). In the foreword to that volume, based on a symposium sponsored by an insurance company, William Haber (pp. v-vi) observes that 'All of life — and business activity is no exception — is surrounded with a substantial degree of insecurity. Every institution in our society whose object is to provide protection against insecurity, whether to corporate institutions or families and individuals, against the vicissitudes of change, against the uncertainties of tomorrow, performs an indisposable function in society'.
4. The effort to discover the essence of capitalist institutions and legal arrangements within the commodity form has had a long and less than distinguished history. The limitations of this approach to the investigation of law are discussed in Redhead (1982) and Spitzer (1983b).
5. It is instructive here to consider the contrast between the portrait of state control presented by Orwell in *1984* and that which could readily be drawn from the study of control in contemporary capitalist societies. This is especially the case, in so far as a number of recent commentators on social control refer to elements of the Orwellian vision as a starting point for their understanding of the relationship between markets, states and the ordering of social life (cf. Cohen 1985a; Cohen and Scull 1983; Marx 1984). In Orwell's portrayal (1949) of state-directed political control — with all the attendant horrors of propaganda, identification, conditioning, and the systematic villification of internal and external enemies — the most assiduous application of these controls occurs in the case of party members —those who are fully participating in and shaping the movement of the system. The *proles*, on the other hand, are essentially left to rule themselves with occasional assistance from the bread, circuses and pornography dutifully produced by the Ministry of Truth. In contrast to this vision stands the fact that 'mass consumption' democracies have bifurcated their control systems in a very different way. Instead of coercing and intimidating the 'middle classes', these classes are bound to the social order through the symbols and rituals of acquisition, while the more direct political controls are focused on the 'proles', who in the contemporary context are far more likely to be managed through constraint than absorption. We must be careful, however, not to overstate the significance of coercion for the 'lower classes' who are tied to different, although no less powerful, forms of commodity identification.

References

Abel, R.L., 'The Contradictions of Informal Justice' in R.L. Abel (ed.), *The Politics of Informal Justice,* vol.1, pp.267-320, Academic Press, New York 1982a

Agnew, J-C., 'The Consuming Vision of Henry James' in R.W. Fox and T.J.J. Lears (eds), *The Culture of Consumption,* Pantheon, New York 1983

Anderson, P., *Lineages of the Absolutist State,* New Left Books, London 1974

Baudrillard, J., *The Mirror of Production,* Telos Press, St. Louis 1975

Bendix, R., *Max Weber: An Intellectual Portrait,* Doubleday, Garden City, NY, 1960

Bentham, J., *Works IV,* Bowring, London 1843

Berman, M., *All That is Solid Melts Into Air,* Simon and Schuster, New York 1982

Birnbaum, N., *The Crisis of Industrial Society*, Oxford University Press, New York 1969

Black, D.J., *The Manners and Customs of Police*, Academic Press, New York 1980

Black, D.J. (ed.), *Toward A General Theory of Social Control*, vol.I, Academic Press, New York 1984a

Boorstin, D.J., *The Americans: The Democratic Experience*, Random House, New York 1973

Cohen, S., *Visions of Social Control: Crime, Punishment and Classification*, Polity Press, Cambridge 1985a

Cohen, S., and A.T. Scull (eds), *Social Control and the State*, Martin Robertson, Oxford 1983

Davis, N.J., and B. Anderson, *Social Control: The Production of Deviance in the Modern State*, Irvington Publishers, New York 1983

Ewen, S., 'Advertising as a Way of Life', *Liberation*, 1975, January, pp.17-34

Ewen, S., and E. Ewen, *Channels of Desire*, McGraw-Hill, New York 1982

Foucault, M., *Discipline and Punish, The Birth of the Prison*, Pantheon, New York 1977

Fox, R.W., and T.J.J. Lears (eds), *The Culture of Consumption*, Panteheon Books, New York 1983

Garland, D., and P. Young, *The Power to Punish*, Heinemann, London 1983

Giddens, A., *The Nation-State and Violence*, University of California Press, Berkeley 1985

Gorz, A., 'Security: Against What? For What? With What?' , *Telos*, 1984, vol. 58, Winter, pp.158-167

Gross, J.T., 'Social Control under Totalitarianism' in D.J. Black (ed.), *Toward a General Theory of Social Control*, vol.2, Academic Press, New York 1984, pp.59-77

Hallcrest Systems, *The Hallcrest Report: Private Security and Police in America*, Chancellor Press, Portland, Oregon 1985

Hamilton, G.G., and J.R. Sutton, 'The Problem of Control in the Weak State: Domination in the US, 1880-1920', Unpublished paper, 1984

Janowitz, M., 'Sociological Theory and Social Control', *American Journal of Sociology*, 1975, vol.81, July, pp.82-108

Klare, M.T., 'Rent-a-Cop: The Boom in Private Police', *The Nation*, 1975, vol.221, pp.486-491

Lears, T.J.J., *No Place of Grace: Antimodernism and the Transformation of American Culture, 1880-1920*, Pantheon Books, New York 1981

Leiss, W., *The Limits to Satisfaction*, University of Toronto Press, Toronto 1976

Lindblom, C.E., *Politics and Markets*, Basic Books, New York 1977

Lukacs, G., *History and Class Consciousness*, MIT Press, Cambridge MA 1971

Marcuse, H., *One-Dimensional Man*, Beacon Press, Boston 1964

Marx, K., *Theories of Surplus-Value*, Pt. I, Progress Publishers, Moscow 1969

Marx, K., *Capital*, vol.I, Lawrence & Wishart 1974

Marx, K., and F. Engels, *The Communist Manifesto*, Penguin, Harmondsworth, England 1967

Neumann, F., *The Democratic and the Authoritarian State*, Free Press, New York 1957

O'Connor, J.R., *The Fiscal Crisis of the State*, St Martin's Press, New York 1973

Orwell, G., *1984*, Harcourt Brace, New York 1949

Park, R.E., and E.W. Burgess, *Introduction to the Science of Sociology,* The University of Chicago Press, Chicago 1969

Poggi, G., *The Development of the Modern State,* Hutchinson, London 1978

Reich, W., *The Mass Psychology of Fascism,* Farrar, Straus & Giroux, New York 1970

Schwartz, T., *The Responsive Chord,* Anchor, New York 1974

Scott, T.M. and M. McPherson, 'The Development of the Private Sector of the Criminal Justice System', *Law and Society Review,* 1971, vol. 6, no.2, pp.267-288

Shearing, C.D., and P.C. Stenning, 'Modern Private Security: Its Growth and Implications' in M. Tonry and N. Morris (eds), *Crime and Justice: An Annual Review of Research, vol.3,* University of Chicago Press, Chicago 1981, pp.193-245

Shearing, C.D., and P.C. Stenning, 'Private Security: Implications for Social Control', *Social Problems,* 1983, vol.30, no, 5, June, pp.493-506

Shearing, C.D., and P.C. Stenning, 'From the Panopticon to Disney World: The Development of Discipline' in A.N. Doob and E.L. Greenspan (eds), *Perspectives in Criminal Law - Essays in Honour of John Ll.J. Edwards,* Canada Law Book Company, Aurora, Canada 1985, pp.335-349

Singlemann, J., 'The Sectoral Transformation of the Labour Force in Seven Industrialised countries, 1920-1970', *American Journal of Sociology,* 1978, vol. 83, pp.1224-1234

Sklare, M.J., 'On the Proletarian Revolution and the End of Political-Economic Society', *Radical America,* 1969, vol.3, pp.1-41.

Skowronek, S., *Building a New American State*, Cambridge University Press, Cambridge 1982

South, N., 'Private Security, the Division of Policing Labour and the Commercial Compromise of the State' in S. Spitzer and A. Scull (eds), *Research in Law, Deviance and Social Control*, vol.6, JAI Press, Greenwich CT 1984, pp.171-198

Spitzer, S., 'Punishment and Social Organization: A Study of Durkheim's Theory of Penal Evolution', *Law and Society Review,* 1975a, vol.9, no.4, Summer, pp.613-637

Spitzer, S., 'Towards a Marxian Theory of Deviance', *Social Problems,* 1975b, vol.22, no.5, pp.638-651

Spitzer, S., 'The Rationalisation of Crime Control in Capitalist Society', in S. Cohen and A.T. Scull, *Social Control and the State,* Martin Robertson, Oxford 1983a, pp.312-333

Spitzer, S and A.T. Scull, 'Privatisation and Capitalist Development: The Case of Private Police', *Social Problems,* 1977, vol.25, no.1, pp.18-29

Spitzer, S., and A.T. Scull, 'Social Control in Historical Perspective: From Private to Public Responses to Crime' in D. Greenberg (ed.), *Corrections and Punishment,* Sage, Beverly Hills 1980

Unger, R.M., *Law in Modern Society,* The Free Press, New York 1976

Weiss, R., 'The Emergence and Transformation of Private Detective Industrial Policing in the United States, 1850-1940', *Crime and Social Justice,* 1978, vol.9, Spring-Summer, pp.35-48

Williams, R., 'Advertising: The Magic System' in R. Williams (ed.), *Culture and Society*, Oxford University Press, New York 1958, pp.170-212

Wolfe, A., *The Limits of Legitimacy*, Free Press, New York 1977

[21]

'Selling scandal': business and the media

Howard Tumber
DEPARTMENT OF SOCIAL SCIENCES, CITY UNIVERSITY, LONDON

In Britain, discussion about business and the media has been almost entirely located around questions of ownership and control. In particular, the work on political economy has attempted to theorize the history of modern communications as part of the capitalist economic system. It has demonstrated how large tracts of the cultural terrain have been taken over by big multinational conglomerates (Herman and Chomsky, 1988; Schiller, 1989; Golding and Murdock, 1991). This in turn has led to concern in the communications policy area over the increasing internationalization of media markets and the role of the transnational corporation in the information economy. Figures such as Murdoch, Maxwell and Berlusconi have become the villains of this new media landscape. Legislation at both the national and European level has been enacted in an attempt to curtail increasing concentration within the media industry and to control the abuse of power conferred by cross-media ownership.

A further issue in the political economy of the media has been the role of advertisers and sponsors in influencing commercial broadcasting and the press. This influence is set to increase in the new media map of Britain, with Channel 4 raising its own advertising finance, a possible fifth commercial terrestrial channel and the development of new satellite channels all having to compete for a slice of the limited advertising cake. Regarding the press, continuing concern has been expressed at the growth of advertising sponsorship which, in some instances, is deemed to distort the news values of the press and, besides influencing what topics are covered, affects the manner of the coverage (Curran, 1978: 240). In the United States the development of the marketing concept — treating the newspaper as a product to be sold and fashioned in response to marketing and competitive factors — has led to the temptation by managers to sacrifice news and pack in too much advertising. While producing short-term profits, this can alienate readers (Fink, 1990: 102).

It has been claimed that the political economic emphasis together with radical culturalist interpretations have been the main proponents of the argument that

> the power of politically and economically dominant groups in the society defines the parameters of the debate, ensures the privileged reproduction of their discourse, and by extension, largely determines the contours of the dominant ideology — of what is socially thinkable. (Schlesinger et al., 1991: 398)

Further, it has been argued that

> such work has paid inadequate attention to the communication process as a whole and that specifically it has neglected the conflictual processes that lie behind the moment of definition, both inside central institutions and within the media themselves. (Schlesinger et al., 1991: 398)

Golding and Murdock, two of the main British exponents of the political economy approach, have recently commented on Michael Schudson's 'misreading' of the political economy position. They take issue with Schudson's argument that political economy relates the outcome of the news process directly to the economic structure of news organizations, and that 'everything in between is a black box that need not be examined' (Golding and Murdock, 1991: 19). Many studies, though, have done precisely this, as Golding and Murdock acknowledge, but as they say 'it is only part of the story we need to tell' and they go on to argue for an examination of the production process and the activities of consumers (Golding and Murdock, 1991: 19).

Recent research has set out to demonstrate some of these complexities and to reveal some of the contents of the 'black box' by looking at: the role of journalists and government in time of war (Hallin, 1985; Morrison and Tumber, 1988); news source strategies and the limits of media centrism (Ericson et al., 1989; Schlesinger and Tumber, 1992); and government information policy and public relations (Golding, 1992; Tumber, 1992).

If a contested arena exists (albeit one uneven in the coverage of, for example, politics, crime, law, war), how far does business conform to this pattern? As Parsons states,

> Given that newspapers are so embedded in capitalism and the structures of power, it is inevitable that they also constitute a significant medium through which economic ideas and opinions are legitimated. They not only sell (to make a profit) the information which keeps the wheel of the economy turning but in so doing they also purvey and reinforce the values and ideas, language and culture, which underpin the existence of the market economy. (Parsons, 1989: 2)

However, even in the area of business and financial coverage, the mass media, whilst still having a central role in reproducing dominant ideology, do at times provide a more open terrain.

Business coverage and the public relations offensive

Some writers have suggested that business news is not often controversial, glamorous or dramatic and that financial matters are complicated and difficult to simplify (Baram, 1977; Berkman and Kitch, 1986). Further, it is suggested that reporters in general are less likely to investigate corporate press releases than they are government ones, because of the lack of access and lack of technical expertise to do so. The sources of information available to the business reporter have also been limited in that organized opposition to the corporation by environmental and consumer groups is a relatively recent phenomenon (Berkman and Kitch, 1986). In his study of news gathering in Australia, Tiffen found that the source structure of business reporting was mainly from within business itself but that, unlike the arenas of government and politics, leaking was much less frequent. One reason for this is that publicity via the news media could be harmful to companies pursuing their interests, but also the pressures toward disclosure are not as strong (Tiffen, 1989: 40).

Much of the literature (most of which has emanated from the USA) has been concerned with questions about the reasons for an increase in business and financial coverage (Hubbard, 1976; MacDougall, 1981; Gussow, 1984; Berkman and Kitch, 1986; Dreier, 1988), business content (Hynds, 1980; Dominick, 1984; Useem, 1984) and the question of anti-business bias (Hubbard, 1966, 1976; Rubin, 1977; Sethi, 1977; Simons and Califano, 1979; Theberge, 1981; Dreier, 1982, 1988; Peterson et al., 1982; Berkman and Kitch, 1986; Hoge, 1988).

One suggestion regarding the accusation of anti-business bias, put forward by Lichter and Rothman (1984, 1988) in their study of media elites, is that the socioeconomic, educational and cultural backgrounds of most of the leading reporters and editors for the influential media predispose them to liberal politics and cynicism about big business. This is refuted by others (Berkman and Kitch, 1986; Dreier, 1988) who suggest that high inflation, rising unemployment, the energy crisis and the general state of the economy from the late 1960s onwards may be a better explanation for the sharp drop in public confidence in big business.

It may also have been linked, as many writers have suggested, to a rise in investigative journalism in the post-Watergate era or, as large sections of business believe, to misrepresentation. Indeed, it has been argued that the most extensive attacks on business have come not from the news media but from books by environment and consumer champions such as Ralph Nader who put the Washington press corps to shame (Strentz, 1989: 121).

MacDougall has suggested that a corporate crime wave was another cause of the bad press business received in the 1970s. A survey by *Fortune* magazine stated that 117 of the largest corporations were convicted of federal offences or made out of court settlements (MacDougall, 1981: 2).

To counteract this perceived bias, big business, particularly the oil and energy companies that have been under scrutiny by government, environment and consumer groups, have adopted what has been termed an 'ideological offensive' (Dreier, 1988: 427). The most documented approach has been that of 'advocacy advertising', a method of championing particular positions on public policy. Most prominent has been the campaign of Mobil Oil 'which has broken the trail for many of its corporate brethren and is candid in its explanations of the importance of aggressively trying to influence public opinion' (Berkman and Kitch, 1986: 324). Writers such as MacDougall (1981) have stated that there is no question but that business advocacy has unbalanced debate over specific issues. Paradoxically, the accusations by companies such as Mobil, 'that television news overplays conflict, oversimplifies issues, encourages irresponsible behaviour by politicians, and shortchanges the public on basic information' (MacDougall, 1981: 46), are similar to ones levelled by more liberal and radical critics of the media. Discord between the media and business was nothing new but, as MacDougall states, 'it was not until the early 1970s that business accusations of ignorant, distorted, negative, biased coverage of business became commonplace' (MacDougall, 1981; 2). As Edward Bernays has noted, 'The rise of public interest groups and consumer advocates has required private interests to reassess their commitments to the communities in which they operate and to society at large' (Bernays, 1988: 17).

That an anti-business bias exists, though, is not accepted by all business executives. A study by Rippey (1981) found that local business persons generally had a favourable view of business coverage. However, during the 1970s, the business community in the United States became more vocal in its attacks on the media. In particular, Louis Banks, a former managing editor of *Fortune* magazine wrote an article entitled 'Memo to the Press: They Hate You Out There', in which he stated that

> No sensible student of the American scene expects business and the media 'to lie down together' but antagonism between the two has gotten out of hand and, in the opinion of this experienced journalist, it is the media that should take much of the blame and should now adjust to greater social responsibility. (Banks, 1978: 35)

During this period a number of conferences and seminars were held with business executives and leaders of press and television to discuss the relationship between the media and business. However, more recent comments from some corporate presidents have suggested that the public interest is best served by an adversarial relationship (Smith, 1988: 447), and, as Newman (1984: 241) notes, by 'appreciating that a well-informed press is in the long run more valuable than a good write up'. This is a view that has also been accepted by many of the institutional, voluntary and pressure groups involved in the criminal justice area (Schlesinger and Tumber, 1992).

Tedlow (1979: 186) bemoaned the dearth of scholarship in public relations and made a plea for more attention to be paid to the reasons for its growth and the nature of its impact. Since then, marketing and public relations have become part of our contemporary culture. What used to be the preserve of the commercial world has spread throughout the major institutions and social groups in our society. As Schlesinger and Tumber (1992: 196) point out

> the contemporary emphasis is on business practice as a model for public-sector organisation and on entrepreneurship as the way forward for all. In keeping with this shift, public-sector organisations have adapted their public relations to commercial models in order to provide themselves with a more acceptable image.

In his study of public relations twenty years ago, Kenneth Henry asked what role public relations plays in the service of bureaucratic and other institutional elites:

> Is 'managed news' actually effective in the formation of public opinion? Can national manipulation of events and personalities make a corporation loved, legitimate a war, elect a political candidate? Does public relations favor 'establishments' that can afford its services, to the detriment of other groups with smaller funds and possibly larger purpose? Does it tend to rigidify and perpetuate the present stratification of society, or does it also lend a stronger voice to protest groups and groups seeking social change in other ways? (Henry, 1972: 21)

Recent research on the activities of sources suggests that some of these questions are at last being addressed.

The public relations offensive launched by business in the 1970s has continued into the 1980s and 1990s. In Britain, companies, whilst having to refute criticisms over safety procedures and corporate responsibility in the face of a series of well-publicized disasters, such as the Zeebrugge ferry accident of 1987, have also had to respond to a number of well-publicized criminal cases and scandals, such as that which arose over the behaviour of Guinness in the takeover battle for Distillers and, very recently, the British Airways 'dirty tricks' campaign against Virgin Atlantic. In addition, government regulation has been a major factor in the growth of business and financial public relations. In the 1970s, the US government intervened directly in business affairs, particularly in the areas of health, safety and the environment. With government regulation requiring corporations to reveal more aspects of their operations, journalists have had a new source of information (Berkman and Kitch, 1986: 271). In Britain, changes in company law and accounting practice, as well as Stock Exchange regulations and the establishment of the Takeover Panel, have all contributed to the expansion in financial public relations (Newman, 1984: 240). Perhaps the most significant factor of all in the adoption of financial communications, according to Newman, has been the growth in dominance of the financial investor:

> As companies saw an increasing proportion of their equity concentrated in the hands of a small number of powerful investors, they recognised the need and opportunity for increased communications, set up investor relations programmes and adopted full-scale financial public relations. (Newman, 1984: 242)

The 1980s saw a huge increase in the amount of financial and business information available in Britain. As well as increased coverage in the national press, the specialist financial press expanded, with many new investment magazines, newsletters and tip sheets offering share recommendations to subscribers. The Conservative government's privatization programme was the main impetus for this increase and particularly for the emergence and growth of personal finance columns. Increased advertising and sponsorship from unit trust, insurance and other financial companies helped to sustain these personal finance columns, as it did in the 1970s (Curran, 1978; 240). As seven million people became shareholders and two-thirds of the population became home-owners, the tabloid press also jumped on the personal finance bandwagon. Advertisers began to increase the proportion of their advertising expenditure on the tabloid press. In 1987 the *Sun*, claiming that one in five of its twelve million readers had bought shares for the first time in 1986, relaunched the personal finance column which it had previously scrapped in 1981. The *Daily Mirror* started a weekly four-page money special in June 1987. It carried prices of sixty leading shares as well as City and personal finance news. The stock market crash in the autumn of 1987 did not immediately affect these activities, indeed many of these developments, particularly on television, occurred after the crash. However, the slowdown in economic activity and the move into recession dramatically affected advertising revenue and in the 1990s many of the stories in the personal finance columns have dealt with problems of debt and mortgage repossessions.

The economic climate of the 1980s ensured that business and finance became front-page news. But it was not all about the successes of 'people's capitalism'. White-collar crime, particularly major fraud, became big news and has continued to be so. The Guinness, County Natwest, BCCI and Maxwell stories featured on both front and City pages. The Guinness story fits in with the media's normal preoccupation with the lives of the rich and famous and, as Levi and Pithouse (1992: 239) point out, 'the extent of media obsession with some elite offenders does not involve depicting any harm done to the victims of those elite individuals'. However, there is a case for arguing that in some instances — BCCI, Barlow Clowes, the Maxwell pensioners — some space *was* given to the victims, their circumstances and the campaigns for compensation, although not as much as to the fraudster.

Other news about business that made the front pages during the 1980s and 1990s often featured sex and scandal. Tales featuring details of the lives of leading entrepreneurs became mixed up with stories concerning City takeover battles involving major companies. One example of this was the case, in 1987, of Sir Ralph Halpern, the chairman of the Burton Group, the High Street retail chain. This produced front-page headlines: 'Burton Boss Sex Scandal' followed by a huge page two and three feature titled 'My Five Times a Night With The £1m-A-Year Boss' (*News of the World*). 'I Was Burton Boss's Mistress' (the *People*); 'Topless Fiona and Burton top man rock City' (*Sunday Express*); 'Tycoon's Name Linked with Topless Model' (*Sunday Telegraph*), all appeared in the Sunday papers of 25 January. These stories arose at the time of the Department of Trade and Industry's investigation into Burton's 1985 takeover of Debenhams, another High Street retailer and a familiar name with the public. In addition, other news stories had recently appeared concerning Halpern's reported £1 million 1986 salary and the proposed performance-related scheme which was said to give him share options worth £8 million. Some papers reported that city 'jitters' were so strong that these scandals were having an effect on the Burton share price. 'That this story should be regarded as important in City circles says a great deal for the state of tension which exists in the Square Mile in the wake of the Guinness scandal' (*Sunday Express*, 25 January 1987). The *Sunday Telegraph* (25 January 1987) went so far as to comment on Halpern: 'His flamboyant style has come to sum up the new breed of entrepreneurs favoured by Mrs Thatcher'.

Many of these front-page stories are commensurate with the news values inherent in all press-reported scandal concerning leading figures in public life. But it is interesting to note how mixed up many of the items and features became in the companies' activities and in the ethics of business practice. The Guinness affair was a landmark in this respect in that it soured the flavour of 1980s people's capitalism. The increase in publicity given to business and finance coverage during the 1980s, particularly the space given over to the selling of the newly-privatized nationalized industries, meant that the public became much more familiar with business and City culture. When scandals broke, whether of a criminal or sexual nature, there was little doubt that they would feature prominently on the front pages of the press.

Scandal stories of this kind help to fulfil the audience-building strategies of the press. The fact that comment also centred on the working practices of business and the City, and not only on the personalities, must be taken into account when assessing strong or weak media effects. The press attacked the City and business practice and urged the government to enact regulation to control excesses. For example, on the same day that the Burton scandal broke, *Sunday Today* had a piece by its political editor headlined 'The Crooked Mile' which urged Thatcher to purge the City. The same day, the paper carried an editorial echoing this sentiment (25 January 1987: 10). Numerous articles in other papers featured similar comment.

Another interesting and recent scandal was the case of Ratners. Gerald Ratner, the former chairman and chief executive of Ratners, the High Street jewellery chain, declared at a lunch at the Institute of Directors (23 April 1991) that his business success was founded on selling people what they wanted: 'total crap'. Gerald Ratner told his audience that in his 1000 shops across Britain he sold gold earrings costing no more than a 99p Marks and Spencer prawn sandwich — 'but they probably won't last as long'. He also said that the shops sold things like 'a teapot for two quid' or an imitation open book to lay on your coffee table: 'The pages do not turn — but they have beautifully curled up corners and genuine antique dust. I know it is in the worst possible taste, but we sold a quarter of a million last year.' He went on to say that the shops also sold cut-glass sherry decanters complete with six glasses on a silver plated tray that your butler could serve you drinks on, and all for £4.95. 'People say how can you sell this for such a low price. I say because it is total crap' (*The Times* and *Guardian*, 23 April 1991). The next day the tabloid press went to town on the speech. The *Daily Mirror* ran the headline 'You 22-Carat Mugs' with a sub-heading underneath a picture of Gerald Ratner 'I sell #*I* says jewels king Ratner' (24 April 1991). The *Sun* (24 April 1991) ran with the headline 'ROTNERS' . . . boss admits "I'm selling total crap"'. The next day the *Sun* ran a feature on the 'House That Crap Built'. Alongside pictures of Ratner and his wife in the swimming pool of their £1.6 million mansion was a story and photograph of a bride weeping as she stared at her Ratners wedding ring (25 April 1991). Gerald Ratner's comments about his products were not new lines. According to press reports, he had used them several times before to financial journalists and City advisers. In fact the *Financial Times* in January 1988 had reported the 'total crap' gag (*Sunday Times*, 28 April 1991: Section 3 p. 1; *Independent*, 30 November 1991: 29). The difference this time was that the tabloid press got hold of the story, giving it the front-page treatment, and the quality press featured the story on its non-business pages. Since April 1991 Ratners' share price has slipped dramatically. From a high of nearly 200p the shares have dropped to 15p (price at 11 December 1992). In November 1992 Ratner quit as chairman and chief executive. As *The Times* (24 December 1992: 19) put it 'Hounded, as he felt, by the tabloid press and gutter journalists, he finally threw in the towel and resigned'.

It is difficult to determine the effect of the press treatment of Ratner following his comments to the Institute of Directors. Retail analysts to whom I spoke believed the recession and the bad publicity combined contributed to the problems for Ratners. The *Independent* (30 November 1991: 29) reported that Ratner's comments had not in themselves affected one particular City fund manager's assessment of the company, but that they 'had acted as a catalyst for our own doubts'. What media coverage may hasten is the demise of high profile entrepreneurs in companies attempting to reduce debt and fight declining sales. The requirement to present a less flamboyant and scandal-ridden image in the face of recession becomes paramount. Whilst business was booming, figures such as Gerald Ratner and Sir Ralph Halpern were kings of the High Street, epitomizing through publicity the success of their companies. In recessionary times, a lower profile is necessary and these entrepreneurs became surplus to requirements. In part, this is due to the manner in which the press has continued to refer to aspects of the original story. Indeed, the tabloids have included news stories that they might otherwise have ignored. For example, the *Sun* (3 December 1992: 21) featured a story headed 'Broke Firms Sue Ratners for £1m Bill'. The item concerned three suppliers who were owed money and had issued a writ: 'The suppliers believe they were treated like "crap" — the way Mr Ratner described his goods last year in a gaffe which sent shares crashing'. Even the business pages of the quality papers have found it hard to refrain from referring back to Ratner's comments. *The Times* (24 December 1992: 19), in a feature assessing the company's retail outlook over the Christmas period, spent the first three paragraphs reminding us of Ratner's famous speech. The problems of a company's image may haunt it for some time and this effect is particularly acute for those in direct contact with the public. In the past, companies have gone to considerable lengths to 'mend' their image when this was damaged by revelations of their activities by investigative journalists. More recently, they have also had to contend with the 'excesses' of the tabloids.

Other business stories reaching the front pages of the popular press recently have featured companies directly in contact with the public: excess profits of the privatized industries and directors' pay rises in particular. As MacDougall suggests of the USA:

> newspaper front pages tend to contain more negative stories (corporate over-

TABLE 1
Newspaper ratings of corporate comment, January–June 1992

Newspaper	Percentage Negative
People	89.7
Sunday Mirror	87.7
Daily Mirror	86.0
News of the World	84.6
Guardian	67.0
Sun	65.6
Sunday Times	59.7
Today	59.4
Daily Star	55.4
Independent	54.4
Daily Mail	54.0
Mail on Sunday	52.8
Daily Express	51.0
Independent on Sunday	49.3
Daily Telegraph	48.8
The Times	48.4
Financial Times	48.2
Sunday Express	43.4
Sunday Telegraph	35.6

Source: *The Presswatch Quarterly*,[1] April/June 1992.

charges, faulty products, monopolistic practices) than positive stories (corporations creating jobs, cooperating with the community, making technological innovations). But business and financial sections have the opposite orientation. Replete with corporate profits, executive promotion announcements, and other stories initiated by corporations, newspaper business sections generally more than offset the negative cast of page one. (MacDougall, 1981: 14)

To a large degree this picture was still the case in the late 1980s and early 1990s in Britain.

In an assessment of the general negative or positive stance of the national press towards UK companies during the first six months of 1992, *Presswatch* found that the tabloids were far more pessimistic than the qualities. The three Mirror group titles and the *News of the World* showed more than 80 percent of their coverage on the negative scale. These high scores were due to the high-profile, negative consumer-related stories focusing on BT (British Telecom) and British Gas. Not surprisingly given its left-of-centre political orientation, the *Guardian* had the highest negativity rating of all the daily quality papers whilst the *Financial Times* rated the lowest negative score.

However, the effect of the Guinness affair has meant that, at times, details of corporate wrong-doing have dominated the business pages. The *Observer* business section of 25 January 1987, the day that the Halpern scandal broke, featured five stories on its front page: 'DTI to act on Cazenove' concerning further investigations into aspects of the Guinness case; 'City link with offshore Guinness payments'; 'Banker on insider charges confirms American visit'; 'BA's standby price' about fears of lack of take-up by institutional investors in the airline's privatization; and 'DTI denies Burton probe'. In the recessionary 1990s, companies are fighting back against accusations of excessive profits and pay by enlisting the help of image experts to produce slick annual general meetings:

> catering for the press is, to some companies, as important as addressing shareholders. Wider share-ownership has meant that some of the major AGMs regularly make the evening news, giving boards an extra incentive to come up with a polished production. (*Observer*, 16 August 1992: 26)

During the 1980s consumer boom the biggest business stars of the media, skilled at public relations, included retailers such as Halpern of Burton, Davies of Next, Ratner of Ratners, Conran of Habitat, Mirman of Sock Shop and Branson of Virgin. While confidence was high and the economy growing, the press contained many complimentary stories, predominantly in the business and financial pages. But as the economy began to falter, and many companies struggled in the face of mounting debt, the front-page stories concentrated on the decline of some of these personalities as noted above. As Berkman and Kitch (1986: 274) point out:

> When business news is confined to the business pages, corporations maintain the upper hand. However, when big business becomes big news, moves to the front page, and becomes the lead story on network news, corporate news management techniques are severely weakened.

Television coverage

In Britain, the 1980s saw a dramatic change in the number of programmes devoted to business. Up to 1987, the BBC's *Money Programme*, which began in 1965, was the only regular business current affairs show. Three new programmes started in 1987: *The City Programme*, *The Business Programme* and *Business Daily*. Thames Television's Thursday night *City Programme* was a half-hour show scheduled after *News At Ten*. It was not widely networked across all regions and was supposedly designed for the City professional living in the London area and therefore potentially attractive to advertisers.

Business Daily and *The Business Programme* were Channel 4 commissioned programmes from Business Television, part of the Broadcast

Communications Group. *The Business Programme* went out on Sunday afternoon, an hour or two earlier than BBC 2's *Money Programme* following a similar format. According to Andrew Clayton, a former editor, it was angled rather more to a professional audience (*Broadcast*, 2 October 1987). Clayton moved on from *The Business Programme* to become editor of *Business Daily*, a news magazine programme which was commissioned for five half-hour shows a week all through the year. It was aimed at the business and financial community and, by comparison with *The Business Programme* was intended to be fast moving, very newsy and, according to Clayton, 'responding to the day's events without the longer, more considered films that the weekly programme carries' (*Broadcast*, 2 October 1987). All three programmes, which have now been dropped, were 'supportive' of the business and financial world. *Business Daily*, in particular, provided a regular platform for leading business figures to announce their companies' results. With an audience of under 200,000, the effect would be fairly marginal. However, there have been programmes adopting a more 'critical' stance. Channel 4 has commissioned a number of programmes which have investigated aspects of the business world. Fulcrum Productions has been one of the main independent production companies working in this area. Its first programme, 'The Curative Treatment' (1986) looked at the takeover boom. Other programmes included 'Empire' (1990), a profile of Rupert Murdoch; 'Change of Owner' (1987), which examined the track record of newly privatized industries; two investigations into insider trading and stock market manipulation — 'The Insiders' (1987) and 'At the Mercy of the Unscrupulous' (1989) — which revealed details of a Cabinet minister's controversial share dealings; 'When the Men With the Money Go Mad (1990), a critical examination of venture capital finance; 'Blood on the Screens' (1991) which charted the rise and fall of National Westminster Bank's merchant banking outfit, County Natwest, and the Blue Arrow scandal; and a series on the City of London, *Greed and Glory* (1992). Fulcrum also made a four-part series for the BBC, *Follow the Money* which enquired into the worlds of banking and accounting and investigated the extent of price-fixing in British industry. In addition to this kind of critical analysis, consumer-oriented shows such as *That's Life, Watchdog* and *The Cook Report* investigated corporate misdemeanours on behalf of the public.

Perhaps the most interesting cultural phenomenon of all the 1980s programmes was *The Stocks and Shares Show* which was billed at the time as an intelligent game show. Shares were offered to contestants each week and the best performing portfolio at the end of the series was the winner. The show began its short run at the beginning of 1988, three months after the stock market crash, and ended after one series.

Other developments during the 1980s were the financial updates and share checks which radio and television provided. Cable News Network has hourly financial updates and *Sky News* has a business report several times a day. In 1988, the European Business Channel, based in Switzerland, and transmitting on the Sky Channel satellite and cable systems throughout Switzerland, Germany and Austria started up. Broadcasting for an hour each weekday morning, the programmes, supported by advertising, were aimed at a pan-European audience, providing business news in a concise form. The first half-hour of the programme contained business and economics interviews and features in English followed by a second half-hour of the same material in German. The entire hour was then re-broadcast and a delayed repeat of the English programme went out over the British cable networks. The channel folded three years later.

Business Daily and the European Business Channel both suffered from the problem of appealing to a professionally 'interested' audience which obtains its financial information instantly via Reuters or Dow Jones. Reuters, one of the leading information suppliers in the world, offers numerous services providing a complete and continuous overview of market movements. Many of these services have become interactive, enabling money dealers first to access real-time information on currency and deposit rates, and then to use the network to complete the transactions (Chapman, 1991). In addition, the *Financial Times* and *Wall Street Journal* fill any remaining information gap. What function, then, do the television programmes serve? The audiences are relatively small and raising advertising revenue becomes increasingly difficult.

Coverage of business in fiction programmes tended to concentrate on the lives of the rich and famous as in *Dallas* and *Dynasty*, and in Britain on the not so rich and famous in the shape of *Minder*, *Budgie* and the family business dramas such as *The Brothers* and *Howard's Way*. These programmes, which Levi states 'could be construed as programmes about fraud', and which lacked concern for victims, were very popular. Perhaps even more symbolic of the 1980s economic climate was *Capital City*, the Thames Television drama of life in a London securities house. The production time-lag in television meant that the programme did not begin until 1990. Borrowing from American narrative styles used in *Hill Street Blues* and *L.A. Law*, the show centred upon a busy dealing room in order to unfold its multi-layered plot. There was no single, pivotal character as in the 1960s dramas about business such as *The Power Game*, *Mogul* and *The Troubleshooters*. Each episode tended to concentrate on the personal and professional problems of two or three of the characters and the 'City' plot was relatively simple. It had a regular audience of between 5 and 6 million.

Conclusion

The amount and type of business news in the mass media is linked to the state of the economy. As MacDougall (1981: 14) notes:

favourable news about business fell during the energy shortage and recession of 1973–75, rose during the economic upturn of 1976–78, then fell again in 1979 as the economy weakened, fuel prices soared, and the nuclear accident at Three Mile Island raised doubts about corporate competence and the future of nuclear power.

Stories appearing on the front and main news pages are exceptional and dramatic with an emphasis on crime, sex and scandal. The news values involved have not deviated from the old definitions of what is, or makes, news. What changed was that business became less remote and was processed through the news value criteria of the tabloid press. The majority of business coverage is supportive, complimentary and consonant with the media's role in reproducing dominant ideology. However, the media are not entirely closed to more critical comment. Recent work has suggested that a relatively open terrain of struggle may exist not accounted for by a one-dimensional view of what constitutes a dominant ideology (Ericson, 1991; Golding, 1992; Schlesinger and Tumber, 1992). In the case of business and financial coverage, 'opposition' may be limited to the different ways of managing capitalism. In times of severe economic crisis, an alternative discourse is more 'acceptable'. As Parsons notes about the 1970s, 'the financial press in both Britain and America played a leading role in challenging the prevailing economic wisdom by giving over space to the discussion of "supply-side" and "monetarist" ideas' (Parsons, 1989: 7).

In the 1990s, the deep and long recession in Britain has prompted fierce criticism in the Conservative press of government economic policy. This has included pleas, in some sections, for a return to intervention. Perhaps the most significant and symbolic feature of this was the decision of the *Financial Times* to endorse the Labour Party at the 1992 general election.

The rise of the consumer and environmental movements in the 1970s, adopting many of the public relations techniques of commerce, together with increasing government regulation and media investigation helped to force business to reassess its relationship with the public. The development of the corporate image became a phenomenon of the 1980s as business realized that it had to sell itself as well as its products.

We live in a promotional culture and the mass media have provided leading politicians with a way of publicizing themselves, as well as a way of making them newly vulnerable. As governments and institutions of the state 'are constantly faced with the risk of loss of legitimacy' and 'can have their institutional personal authority deconstructed by the mass media' (Ericson, 1991: 233), so the business world can face similar problems in the face of front-page scandals involving crime, sex, huge profits, chairmen and directors' salaries and environmental disasters.

How far these kinds of stories affect the public's perception of business over the long term is difficult to assess, as are the motives of the media. In a piece on news production, Schudson states that:

Daniel Hallin, borrowing from the work of Jürgen Habermas, has argued that the possibility for the media to offer dissenting views and to publicise scandalous news arises in part because they must attend as much to their own legitimation as to furthering the legitimation of the capitalist system as a whole. (Schudson, 1991: 147)

However, whilst dissenting views may possibly be offered as a result of the media's own legitimation needs, scandalous news is a direct consequence of the audience-building strategy of the media (although there may be some pompous editorial justification). Since the 1970s, business has been embraced within this realm.

Whilst government regulation of business may have a more direct bearing on people's lives, it may be the more scandalous stories which serve to undermine institutions in the public's mind. Scandal may be a more productive weapon for opening up an alternative and open terrain. The current pressure in Britain for increased regulation of the press may be an indication that sections of the government also believe this to be the case.

Note

1. *Presswatch Quarterly* is a commercial publication which monitors and evaluates national press coverage of UK companies. Press coverage is measured for negative and positive press comment and points are awarded according to a predefined scale related to newspaper circulations and readership profiles.

References

Banks, L. (1978) 'Memo to the Press; They Hate You Out There', *The Atlantic*, April: 35–42.
Baram, R. (1977) 'Newspapers: Their Coverage and Big Business', in B. Rubin (ed.), *Big Business and the Mass Media*. Lexington, MA: D.C. Heath & Co.
Berkman, R. and L.W. Kitch (1986) *Politics in the Media Age*. New York: McGraw-Hill.
Bernays, E.L. (1988) 'Social Responsibility of Business', pp. 17–29 in R.E. Hiebert (ed.), *Precision Public Relations*. New York: Longman.
Chapman, C. (1991) *How The Stock Markets Work*. London: Business Books.
Curran, J. (1978) 'Advertising and the Press', pp. 229–67 in J. Curran (ed.), *The British Press: a Manifesto*. London: Macmillan.
Dominick, J. (1984) 'Business Coverage in Network Newscasts', pp. 101-8 in D. Graber (ed.), *Media Power in Politics*. Washington, DC: Congressional Quarterly Press.
Dreier, P. (1982) 'Capitalists vs. the Media', *Media, Culture and Society* 4 (2): 111–32.

Dreier, P. (1988) 'The Corporate Complaint against the Media', pp. 425–43 in R.E. Hiebert and C. Reuss (eds), *Impact of the Mass Media*. New York: Longman.

Ericson, R. (1991) 'Mass Media, Crime, Law, and Justice: An Institutional Approach', *British Journal of Criminology*, 31 (3): 219–49.

Ericson, R. et al. (1989) *Negotiating Control: A Study of News Sources*. Milton Keynes: Open University Press.

Fink, C. (1990) *Inside the Media*. New York: Longman.

Golding, P. (1992) 'Communicating Capitalism: Resisting and Restructuring State Ideology — The Case of "Thatcherism"', *Media, Culture and Society*, 14 (4): 503–21.

Golding, P. and G. Murdock (1991) 'Culture, Communications, and Political Economy', pp. 15–32 in J. Curran and M. Gurevitch (eds), *Mass Media and Society*. London: Edward Arnold.

Gussow, D. (1984) *The New Business Journalism*. Santiago: Harcourt Brace Jovanovitch.

Hallin, D.C. (1985) *The 'Uncensored War': The Media and Vietnam*. Oxford: Oxford University Press.

Henry, K. (1972) *Defenders and Shapers of the Corporate Image*. New Haven, CT: College and University Press.

Herman, E.S. and N. Chomsky (1988) *Manufacturing Consent*. New York: Pantheon Books.

Hoge, J. (1988) 'Business and the Media: Stereotyping Each Other', pp. 422–5 in R.E. Hiebert and C. Reuss (eds), *Impact of the Mass Media*. New York: Longman.

Hubbard, J.T.W. (1976) 'Business News in the Post-Watergate Era', *Journalism Quarterly*, 53: 488–93.

Hynds, E. (1980) 'Business Coverage is Getting Better', *Journalism Quarterly*, 57: 297–304.

Levi, M. and A. Pithouse (1992) 'The Victims of Fraud', pp. 229–46 in D. Downes (ed.), *Unravelling Criminal Justice*. London: Macmillan.

Lichter, R. and S. Rothman (1988) 'Media and Business Elites', pp. 448–61 in R.E. Hiebert and C. Reuss (eds), *Impact of the Mass Media*. New York: Longman.

MacDougall, A.K. (1981) *Ninety Seconds to Tell it All, Big Business and the News Media*. Homewood, IL: Dow Jones Irwin.

Morrison, D. and H. Tumber (1988) *Journalists at War: The Dynamics of News Reporting during the Falklands Conflict*. London: Sage.

Newman, K. (1984) *Financial Marketing and Communications*. Eastbourne, East Sussex: Holt, Rinehart & Winston.

Parsons, W. (1989) *The Power of the Financial Press*. Aldershot, Hampshire: Edward Elgar.

Peterson, R.A. et al. (1982) 'Perceptions of Media Bias Toward Business', *Journalism Quarterly*, 59: 461–4.

Rippey, J. (1981) 'Perceptions by Selected Executives of Local Business Coverage', *Journalism Quarterly*, 58: 382–7.

Rothman, S. and R. Lichter (1984) 'Media and Business Elites: Two Classes in Conflict?' pp. 109–17 in D. Graber (ed.), *Media Power in Politics*. Washington, DC: Congressional Quarterly Press.

Rubin, B. (1977) *Big Business and the Mass Media*. Lexington, MA: D.C. Heath & Co.

Schiller, H. (1989) *Culture Inc: The Corporate Takeover of Public Expression*. New York, Oxford: Oxford University Press.

Schlesinger, P. and H. Tumber (1992) 'Crime and Criminal Justice in the Media', pp. 184–203 in D. Downes (ed.), *Unravelling Criminal Justice*. Basingstoke: Macmillan.

Schlesinger, P., H. Tumber and G. Murdock (1991) 'The Media Politics of Crime and Criminal Justice', *British Journal of Criminology*, 42 (3): 397–420.

Schudson, M. (1991) 'The Sociology of News Production Revisited', pp. 141–59 in J. Curran and M. Gurevitch (eds), *Mass Media and Society*. London: Edward Arnold.

Sethi, S.P. (1977) 'The Schism Between Business and American News Media', *Journalism Quarterly*, 54: 240–8.

Simons, H. and J. Califano (1979) *The Media and Business*. New York: Vintage Books.

Smith, W. (1988) 'Business and the Media: Sometimes Partners, Sometimes Adversaries', pp. 444–7 in R.E. Hiebert and C. Reuss (eds), *Impact of the Mass Media*. New York: Longman.

Strentz, H. (1989) *News Reporters and News Sources*. Ames, IA: Iowa State University Press.

Tedlow, R. (1979) *Keeping the Corporate Image: Public Relations and Business 1900–1950*. Greenwich, CT: JAI Press Inc.

Theberge, L.J. (ed.) (1981) *Crooks, Conmen and Clowns; Businessmen in TV Entertainment*. Washington, DC: The Media Institute.

Tiffen, R. (1989) *News and Power*. Sydney: Allen & Unwin.

Tumber, H. (1992) 'Marketing Politics: The Americanisation of Government Information Policy in the UK', paper presented to the Americanization of Culture Conference, University of Swansea.

Useem, M. (1984) *The Inner Circle: Large Corporations and the Rise of Business Political Activity in the US and UK*. New York: Oxford University Press.

Name Index

Abel, Richard L. 398
Accosta, Frank 144
Achenbach, Joel 352, 363, 366
Adler, Peter 81
Agnew, J-C. 395, 396
Agran, Larry 317–28 *passim*, 330, 331
Alter, Jonathan 328
Altheide, David L. xiii, xxii, xxiii, 3, 4, 11, 13, 17, 18, 39, 42, 83, 180–1, 299–315, 351, 367
Ammons, L. 58
Anderson, B. 397
Anderson, P. 399
Antunes, G. 135
Ashkins, C.D. 60
Auersperg, Alexander von 38
Axelrod, Kenneth 55
Aymar, B. 34
Azner, Ed 366

Babcock, Ginna M. 143
Bachman, Jerald G. 143, 145, 147, 151, 155, 156
Back, Kurt W. 210
Baggaley, J. 275, 286
Ball-Rokeach, Sandra 336, 343, 344
Banks, Louis 408
Baram, R. 407
Baranek, Patracia M. xi, xiii, xvi, xix, 3–31, 216, 302, 376
Barber, S. 34, 39
Barker, D. 43
Baron, R. xi
Barthes, R. 7
Bates, A. 8
Baudrillard, Jean 364, 367, 393
Bauman, Z. xxv, xxvi, 352, 363, 368
Beattie, J. xi
Beauchamp, Daniel 381
Beck, Bernard 379
Bell, Stuart 230–2 *passim*, 238–41 *passim*, 243
Bendix, R. 397
Bennett, Dick 323
Bennett, T.H. 279
Bentham, Jeremy 333, 397
Berke, Richard L. 323
Berkman, R. 407, 408, 410, 415

Berkowitz, L. xi
Bernays, Edward L. 408
Berry, Ralph 380
Best, Joel xx, 143, 203–14, 217
Biderman, A. 276
Bing, Jon 344
Birnbaum, N. 387
Black, D.J. 391
Bloomstein, Rex 100
Blumer, Herbert 156, 210
Blumler, J.G. 47
Blumrich 147, 148, 156
Boadu, S.O. 270
Bogart, L. 39
Boland, James 380
Bond-Maupin, Lisa xx, 215–27
Boorstin, D.J. 42, 136, 394
Bordua, D. 124
Bosk, Charles L. 98, 156
Bourdieu, P. xi
Box, S. 276
Boyanowsky, E.O. 252, 287
Braestrup, P. 305
Brannigan, A. 16
Branson, Richard 415
Bråten, Stein 346
Braungart, M. 131
Breton, T. 38
Briggs, Asa 374
Briggs, J. 78
Brissett, D. 84
Brock, B. 37
Brothers, Joyce 42
Brown, E.J. 164
Brown, Jerry 322, 323, 325, 328
Browne, N. 285
Brownmiller, Susan 124
Brunvand, Jan H. 207, 208, 209
Burgess, P. 399
Burnett, Carol 19
Burns, William D. 42
Burton, T. 36
Busfield, R.M. jr 41
Bush, George 84, 320
Buxton 393

Caesar Augustus 338

Califano, J. 407
Caplow, Theodore 212
Cardiff, D. 9
Carey, J. 47, 78, 275
Carlisle, Kimberley 232
Carlson, J.M. 282, 283, 284, 289
Carriere, K.D. xx, 17, 106, 107
Carroll, Peter N. 208
Carter, Jimmy 327
Cassata, M.B. 270
Cathcart, R. 43
Cavender, Gary xx, 215–27
Cawalte, J.G. 42
Cayley, D. 10
Chan, Janet B.L. xi, xiii, xvi, xix, 3–31, 216, 302, 376
Chapman, C. 417
Chatman, S. 285
Chibnall, S. 24, 61, 65, 120, 136, 303
Chomsky, N. 405
Christians, C. 275
Christie, Agatha xi
Christie, N. xi, xix, xxiii
Clarke, D. 24
Clattfelter, C. xxvi
Clayton, Andrew 416
Clemantis, Vladimir 317
Clinton, Bill 317, 319, 323, 325, 330
Cloward, Richard 378
Cohen, S. xi, xix, 348, 397, 398
Comstock, George 216
Condon, W.S. 84
Conrad, Peter 378
Conran, Terence 415
Converse, Philip E. 209
Cook, F.L. 266
Cook, P. xxvi
Corbett, M. 283
Corbin, Robert 309
Couch, Carl J. 91, 300, 301, 312
Counihan, M. 275
Crenson, Matthew 379
Crisell, A. xiii, xiv, 4, 6, 7, 8, 9, 10, 11, 12–13, 16, 17, 19, 21
Crouch, J. 249
Csikszentmihaly, M. 80, 89, 91
Cuomo, Mario 318
Curran, J. 348, 405, 410
Currie, E. 65

Dahl, Hans F. 341
D'Amico, R. 399
Danielian, Lucig H. 145, 153, 156
Davis, F. James 59, 109, 216

Davis, M. 358, 366
Davis, N.J. 397
DeBord, G. 359
DeFleur, Melvin 336, 343, 344
Dershowitz, A. 35
Deutschmann, P.J. 66
Devlin, Tim 240, 243
Devol, K.S. 44
Diamond, Edwin 144
Diamond, S.S. 175
Dominick, J.R. xi, 60, 274, 407
Doob, Anthony N. xvii, xviii, 161–78, 251, 282, 287, 288
Doret, D. 34
Dorfman, A. 78
Douglas, Mary 72, 217, 280
Draper, R. 19
Dreier, P. 407, 408
Drucker, Susan J. xiv, xv, 33–46
Duck, S. 275, 286
Dukakis, Richard 84
Dunne, D. 35, 36
Durkheim, Emile 50, 63, 64, 65, 67
Dussuyer, I. 19, 162
Dworkin, Ronald 16

Eco, U. 285, 364, 366
Edelman Murray xi, xxii, 362, 377
Edwards, Edwin 194
Ehrenreich, John H. 374
Elias, N. xi
Eliot, T.S. 17
Elliott, Michele 235, 241
Elliott, P. 18, 20, 21
Emerson, M. 249
Engels, Friedrich 389
Ennis, P.H. 276
Epstein, E.J. 10, 11, 17, 20, 21, 22, 302, 304
Ericson, Richard V. xi, xiii, xiv, xvi, xvii, xix, xx, xxii, xxiv, xxvii, 3–31, 98, 106, 107, 216, 302, 303, 304, 351–69, 376, 406, 418
Erickson, Kai 64, 65
Eron, L. 78
Erskine, Hazel 208
Estep, R. 270
Ewen, E. 388, 394, 396, 397
Ewen, S. 388, 394, 395, 396, 397

Featherstone, M. xxvi
Fine, Gary A. 207, 217
Fink, C. 406
Fishman, Mark xvii, 24, 48, 119–42, 156, 206, 216, 276, 278, 304

Fiske, J. 6, 7, 9, 10, 12, 16, 17, 78
Fjellan, S. 355, 356
Flanagan, T.J. 164
Florman, Carole 323
Foucault, M. 65, 333–4 *passim*, 337, 338, 397
Fox, R.W. 394, 396
Fulani, Lenora 321, 329

Galante, M.A. 42
Garland, D. xi, 397
Garner, Lesley 234
Garofalo, James 58, 60, 216, 277
Gatrell, V. 276
Geertz, Clifford 16
Genette, G. 285
Gerber, Jerg 143
Gerbner, George xxi, xxii, 216, 249, 250, 251, 254, 274, 276, 281, 282, 283, 284, 287, 289, 291, 292
Gibbs, J. 299
Giddens, Anthony xxv, 77, 78, 79, 80, 284, 285, 398
Gitlin, Todd 7, 17, 78, 216, 226, 304
Gleick, J. 78
Goetz, Bernard 193, 194
Goffman, Erving, 6, 8, 9, 11, 79, 378
Goldberg, Frank 145
Golding, P. 20, 405, 406, 418
Goldman, R. xxv, xxvii
Goldstein, M. 42
Goode, Erich 143, 155
Gordon, J.T. 162
Gordon, M. 120
Gorz, A. 390, 392
Gottwald, Klement 317
Gouldner, Alvin W. 281, 375
Graber, Doris A. xi, 57, 58, 60, 70, 109, 162, 216, 217
Grider, Sylvia 205, 207, 212
Gross, J.T. 398
Gross, Larry 216, 251, 274, 282, 287
Gumpert, G. 359
Gunter, Barrie xii, xxi, 249–76, 274, 275, 286, 287, 290
Gurevitch, M. 47
Gusfield, Joseph R. xxvi, xxvii, 373–83
Gussow, D. 407
Gutenberg, J. xxiv

Habermas, Jürgen 97, 419
Hagan, J. xiv
Hall, Edward 84, 87, 102
Hall, P.M. 300
Hall, S. xvi, 276, 284, 285

Hall, S.M. 348
Hallin, Daniel C. 406, 419
Halloran, Richard 151
Halpern, Sir Ralph 411, 413, 415
Hamill, R. 163
Hamilton, G.G. 398
Harkin, Tom 317, 322, 323, 324
Harris, Lou 79
Hartley, J. xxii, xxiv, 6, 10, 12, 15, 17, 366
Hatch, Jane M. 212
Hauptmann, Bruno 55, 56
Hawkins, R. 250, 291
Hay, D. xi
Hayes, Michael 379
Hearst, Patty 56
Heath, L. 162
Heilbroner, Robert 374
Heinz, A. 304
Henningsen, Gunnar 340–1
Henry, Kenneth 409
Herman, E.S. 405
Herod, King 339
Hier, Rabbi 355
Higgins, B. 361
Higgs, Marietta 230–2 *passim*, 235–46 *passim*
Hilgartner, Stephen 98, 156
Hirsch, Paul 216, 251, 287
Hirshey, G. 355
Hoge, J. 407
Holloran, J. xix
Holt, Richard 240, 243
Hoover, S. xxvi
Horiuchi, Gerald T. xx, 203–14
Hough, M. 164, 276, 278
Howarth, Valerie 234, 241
Hoyer, W. 131
Hubbard, J.T.W. 407
Hughes, E.C.
Hughes, H.M. 55, 62, 65, 70, 303
Hughes, M. 282, 287
Humphries, Drew 216
Hurley, P. 135
Huston, A.C. 40, 43
Hynds, E. 407

Imbert, Sir Peter 101
Innis, H.A. 299, 300, 345
Irvine, Alistair 239
Isaacs, Susan 204
Iyengar, Shanto xviii, 179–99

Jackson, Jesse 318
Jacob, Herbert 57, 59, 304
Jacobs, Norman 210

Janowitz, M. 397
Jensen, Erich L. 143
Jessor, R. 283
Jeudy, H-P. 273
Jewett, Jack 309
Johansen, Tom 345-6
Johnson, Donald M. 210
Johnson, John M. 145, 304, 314
Johnston, Lloyd D. 143, 145, 147, 149, 151, 155, 156
Jones, E.T. 58
Jones, T. 277, 278, 281
Julius, M.H. 33

Kahneman, D. 163
Katz, E. 47
Katz, Jack xv, 47-75, 216, 217
Katzman, N. 270
Keating, Charles 311
Keene, William B. 42
Kelling, G. 279
Kellner, Douglas 217
Kennedy, John F. 128, 313
Keppel, James 311
Kerckhoff, Alan C. 210
Kerr, Peter 144, 145, 151, 153, 156
Kerrey, Bob 323, 324
Khayyam, Omar 380
King, Don 194
Kingdon, John 99
Kinsey, R. 278, 281
Kitch, L.W. 407, 408, 410, 415
Kitsuse, John I. 154, 210
Klare, M.T. 388, 390
Knight, S. 274
Krauthammer, C. 363
Krippendorf, K. 274

Langer, J. 35, 36
Larsen, Otto N. 210
Lasswell, H. 275
Lea, J. 281
Lears, T.J.J. 394, 396
Leiss, W. 394, 396
Leonard, G. 84
Lertola, Joe 152
Lester, Marilyn 120, 132, 136, 215
Levi, M. 411
Levine, Harry G. 153
Levine, J. 90
Levitt, C. 356
Lewis, D. 276, 279
Lichter, Linda 216
Lichter, Robert 216, 407

Liebert, R. xi
Lindblom, C.E. 397
Lineberry, R.L. 304
Lisus, Nicola A. xxiv, 351-69
Lofland, John 210
Lukacs, G. 390, 392
Luther King, Martin 311, 313, 355
Lyman, S. 17

McCarthy, Coleman 320
McCarthy, John D. 379
McCombs, M.E. 78
MacDonald, G.E. 251, 270, 282, 287, 288
McDonnell, Patrick 79
MacDougall, A.K. 407, 408, 413-14, 417-18
McGarrell, E.F. 164
McLuhan, Marshall 83, 85, 299, 351, 353
MacNeal, Robert 357
McPherson, M. 391
McWhinnie, D. 8
Marcuse, Herbert 399
Margiotta, Joseph 55
Margolese, Marianne 366
Markle, Gerald E. 210
Marks, Sir Robert 107
Marrou, André 329
Martz, Larry 153, 156
Marx, G.T. 301, 304, 306
Marx, Karl 385, 386, 389, 390-7 *passim*
Mathiesen, Thomas xxv, 333-50
Maxfield, M. 277, 278, 279, 280, 289
Maxwell, Robert 405
Mayhew, P. 277, 278
Mead, George H. 80, 399
Medalia, Nahum Z. 210
Merriam, John E. 144, 145
Merry, Sally E. 209, 217
Merton, Robert K. 252
Meyer, J. 66
Meyer, Thomas J. 151
Meyrowitz, Joshua xiii, xx, xxiii, xxiv, xxv, 4, 9, 10, 13, 14, 18, 19, 21, 22, 27, 273, 317-31, 351
Midgley, M. 17
Mill, John Stuart 24, 25
Miller, J. 354
Miller, Mark 153, 156
Mills, C. Wright 292, 377
Mitchell-Banks, T. 163
Molotch, Harvey 120, 132, 136, 215
Monaco, J. 5, 9, 13, 16
Mondale, Walter 84
Morgan, Patricia 375
Morley, D. 273

Morris, N. 175
Morrison, D. 406
Mount, Frederick 241, 245
Moxon, D. 164
Mudd, Roger 319
Mulkay, M. 16
Murdoch, Rupert 101, 405, 416
Murdock, Graham xvi, 20, 95–118, 405, 406
Musto, David F. 144, 152
Myklebust, Dag 335

Nader, Ralph 408
Nava, Mica xxi, 229–47
Nelson, Barbara xvii, 378, 379
Neumann, F. 390
Neville, T. 249
Newman, K. 409, 410
Newtson, D. 252
Nisbett, R.E. 163
Nixon, Richard 56, 149

O'Bryan, Timothy 205
O'Connor, J.R. 387
Olins, Wolff 101
Olsen, J.P. 337
O'Malley, Patrick M. 143, 145, 147, 151, 155, 156
Orcutt, James D. xvii, 143–59
Ortega, Ruben 311
Orwell, George 392, 397
Østerberg, D. 345

Packer, H.L. 283
Palmer, Alix 235
Pandiani, J. 216, 274, 285, 286
Parenti, M. 78
Park, R.E. 61, 70, 303, 399
Parke, R. xi
Parker, E.B. 343
Parsons, Talcott 77, 399
Parsons, W. 406, 418
Pateman, T. 285
Paulu, B. 8
Pearson, G. xi, xix, xx, xxi, 276
Peat, F.D. 78
Peplau 256
Perot, Ross 329
Peterson, R.A. 407
Pfohl, Stephen J. 208, 210, 378, 379
Piepe, A. 249
Pietropaolo, D. 10
Pingree, S. 250, 291
Pithouse, A. 411
Pitts, L. 353

Piven, Frances F. 378
Platt Hunold, Janice 33
Poggi, G. 398
Pollan, M. 42
Ponting, Clive 104
Postman, Neil xii, xiv, xvi, 10, 12, 19, 27, 90, 351, 356, 357, 362
Primeau, R. 41
Prince, J. 37, 38
Pringle, A. 291
Putnam, Hilary 16, 17

Rantzen, Esther 235, 241
Ratner, Gerald 412, 413, 415
Reagan, Ronald 84, 185, 187, 320
Reddy, M. 26, 275
Reese, Stephen D. 145, 156
Reich, W. 400
Reinarman, Craig 153
Reinstein, Ronald 311
Reisman, David 212
Reiss, A. 124
Reynolds, Andrea 36
Rhodes, Louis 309
Richardson, Sue 232, 240
Rifkin, Jeremy 86, 91
Rippey, J. 408
Roberts, Julian V. xvii, xviii, 161–78
Roberts, Raine 232
Rosenstiel, Tom 323, 324, 327, 328
Roshco, B. 62, 119, 136
Roshier, Bob 25, 49, 58, 60, 109, 135
Rothman, David 378, 380
Rothman, S. 407
Rotter, J.B. 252, 253, 254, 255
Rowland, W. xii, 275
Royeton, Robert 204
Rubin, B. 256, 407
Rugoff, R. 354, 355, 361
Runciman, W.G. 15, 16
Russell, Cristine 151
Rutherford, Jonathan 234
Ryan, M. 35
Ryle, G. 16

Saetren, H. 337
Safire, William 151
Sagarin, E. 34
Salem, G. 276, 279
Sanoff, Alvin 322, 324
Santino, Jack 206, 212
Sciolino, Elaine 153
Schanberg, Sydney 320
Schattenburg, Gus xi, 216, 226

Schiller, H. xxvi, 19, 300, 405
Schlesinger, Philip xvi, xvii, xx, 14, 20, 24, 28, 95–118, 304, 406, 409, 418
Schneider, Joseph W. 378
Schoenfeld, A. Clay 210
Schudson, M. 136, 303, 418–19
Schwartz, T. 396
Schwarzenegger, Arnold xxiv, 352, 361, 365
Scott, M. 17
Scott, Roger 246
Scott, T.M. 391
Scull, A.T. 388, 391, 397, 399
Seaman, W. xxv
Seaton, J. 19, 24
Seligmann, Jean 154, 156
Sethi, S.P. 407
Shaffir, W. 356
Shakespeare, William 385
Shaw, D.L. 78
Shaw, George Bernard 380
Shearing, C.D. 388, 389, 391
Shears, Richard 238
Sheley, J.F. 60
Sherizen, S. 58, 70, 120, 135
Shibutani, T. xxii
Shoemaker, Pamela J. 144
Short, Clare 241
Sigal, L. 119, 136
Silverstone, R. 273
Silvey, R. 8
Simmel, Georg 77, 79
Simons, H. 407
Simpson, Jacqueline 209
Singer, B. xxvii
Singlemann, J. 395
Siniawsky, S.J. 270
Skill, T.D. 270
Sklare, M.J. 395
Skogan, W. 277, 278, 279, 280, 289
Skowronek, S. 398
Slater, P. 392
Smelser, Neil J. 210
Smith, A. xiv, 22, 23, 27
Smith, Richard M. 145, 147, 148, 154, 156
Smith, S.J. xxii, 278–80 *passim*, 290
Smith, W. 409
Snow, Robert P. xiii, xv, xvi, xxiii, 39, 42, 77–92, 302, 303, 304, 351
South, N. 390
Sparks, R. xi, xix, xx, xxii
Spector, Malcom 155, 210
Spencer 77
Spitzer, Stephen xxv, xxvi, xxvii, 385–403
Springfield, Buffalo 299

Srole, L. 252
Stanko, Elizabeth 217
Stedino, Joseph 308, 312
Stehr, N. 362
Stenning, P.C. 388, 389, 391
Stinchcombe, Arthur L. 59, 208
Stivers, Richard 376
Stone, Gregory P. 212
Strate, L. 42
Strentz, H. 408
Sudnow, D. 61, 124
Surette, R. 162, 286, 305
Sutherland, J.C. 270
Suttles, Gerald D. 209
Sutton, J.R. 398
Szasz, Thomas 378

Tannenbaum, P. xi
Taylor, I. 279
Tedlow, R. 409
Thatcher, Margaret 103, 189, 412
Theberge, L.J. 407
Thornton, Leslie-Jean 144
Tichi, C. xxi
Tierney, Katherine J. 210
Tiffen, R. 407
Tillman, R.H. 136
Tisdall, Sarah 104
Toner, Michael 233
Tonry, M. 175
Tosten, Kevin 205
Troyer, Ronald J. 210
Trubo, Richard 203, 204
Tsongas, Paul 317, 324
Tuan, Y-Fu 285
Tuchman, Gaye xvii, 22, 28, 62, 119, 136, 215, 216, 304
Tufte, Edward R. 152, 155, 156
Tumber, Howard xvi, xvii, xix, xx, xxvii, 95–118, 405–21
Turner, J. Blake xvii, 143–59
Tversky, A. 163
Twitchell, J.B. 78
Tyler, T.R. 266, 268, 283, 289, 290, 292
Tyler Moore, Mary 366

Unger, R.M. 391
Useem, M. 407

Vaage, O. 337
Van Buren, Abigail 203
Verdun-Jones, S. 163
von Bulow, Claus 34–8 *passim*, 40–4 *passim*
von Bulow, Cosima 35

von Bulow, Sunny 35, 36, 38
Voumvakis, S. xvii

Wagner-Pacifici, R. xix, 17
Wakshlag, J. xxi, 255, 269, 287, 288, 289, 290, 291, 292
Walker, Carolyn 312
Walker, L. 124
Walker, N. 164
Walster, E. 252
Walters, Barbara 35, 37
Wapner, Joseph A. 42
Watkins, B. 275
Weaver, J. 269, 287, 288, 289, 290, 292
Weber, Max 397
Weigel, R. 283
Weinberg, Ian 374
Weir, Stuart 245
Weiss, R. 390
Wheatley, Bill 324
Wheeler, G. 24
White, N.R. 163, 175
Whitehouse, Mary xi

Wiesenthal, Simon 352
Wilder, Douglas 322, 327, 328
Williams, Raymond xi, xix, 12, 65, 215, 324, 359, 394, 396
Williamson, Margaret H. 212, 274
Willwerth, J. 354
Wilson, J.Q. 279
Wilson, T.D. 163
Wober, M. 249, 250, 251, 252, 286, 287
Wolfe, A. 398
Wright, J.C. 43
Wright, Michael 243
Wright, Peter 104
Wright, Sam 55
Wright, W. 36
Wyatt, Geoffrey 231, 232, 241
Wynne, Jane 241

Young, J. 276, 277, 279, 281, 348, 366
Young, Lord 101
Young, P. 397

Zillman, D. xi, 288, 291, 292